THE CROSS-CHANNEL 1995 DRINKS GUIDE

TOM STEVENSON

Absolute Press

Absolute Press
14 Widcombe Crescent
Bath BA2 6AH

Cover and Book Design:
MONICA CHIA & SONIA ALEXIS
Maps: RAYMOND TURVEY
Resident representative responsible for research
and sample collection: Lyn Parry
Printed by Longdunn Press, Bristol

ISBN 0 948230 797

CONTENTS

INTRODUCTION

This second annual edition of The Cross-Channel Drinks Guide is to be published within just six months of the first! The reason for this is that we have decided to publish the Guide just prior to the Christmas spending spree each year. Bit of a grind for us, but two editions in such a short time has at least got across the message to the French-owned outlets, many of which were quite bemused by our initial approach – shop-by-shop, wine-by-wine guides being a totally alien concept in France. Now they have seen the end product, they understand what it is. And with readers coming into their shops brandishing the Guide, even the most reluctant French outlets have realised that their entry in it can affect their business.

Most important of all, they realise that the content of the entry is up to them, not us. If they submit lousy wines, they get a lousy review. If they submit excellent wines, they get an excellent review. There is no national prejudice, although most of them probably thought there would be. Now they have seen that, for two years running, the two runners-up to the Best Cross-Channel Drinks Outlet of the Year have indeed been French, and this year the two runners-up to the Best Cross-Channel Supermarket of the Year are also French. They could be owned by Martians for all we care.

A French group will one day win the Best Cross-Channel Supermarket of the Year award, of that we are sure, but we must admit that it is hard to imagine how any outlet could challenge The Grape Shop's claim to the Best Cross-Channel Drinks Outlet of the Year award, whether French, British *or* Martian. The range is so huge, it hardly makes commercial sense. Certainly we know of no other cross-Channel outlet that is contemplating expanding its range to anywhere near The Grape Shop's 800 wines. It is not, however, simply a matter of size; the quality, variety and value of the range is so exciting that we had no alternative but to create a special new 👍👍👍👍👍 'Superstar' category exclusively for The Grape Shop. We hope, however, that others will aspire to 👍👍👍👍👍 in the future.

Tom Stevenson
October 1994

THE FACTORY SHOP GUIDE FOR NORTHERN FRANCE

We have come across a super little book called *The Factory Shop Guide for Northern France*, for cross-Channel shoppers who want to buy more than drink. It is part of an established series of factory shop guides which, until recently, has concentrated on various areas of the UK. If you are not familiar with the term, a factory shop is where you can buy seconds and ends-of-lines direct from the manufacturer at greatly reduced prices. The authors of the new French edition, Gill Cutress and Rolf Stricker, have discovered no less than 234 factory shops in a small area of northern France, all within easy reach of Calais or Boulogne. You can pick up *Le Creuset* ovenware and *Cristal d'Arques* glassware for a song. Clothing ranges from *Levi's* and *Wrangler* for leisurewear, *Bally* for shoes, *Le Coq Sportif* and *Adidas* for sportswear. The choice for women includes *Weil of Paris* and *Paul Mausner* for fashion, and *Le Bourget*, *DD* and *Zanzi* for hosiery. There are factory shops for everything from lingerie to snail plates.

The Factory Shop Guide for Northern France gives detailed directions on how to find every shop, even down to a photograph of each one, so that you know what you are looking for! There is a special price-guide feature in the back of the book, so that you know in advance the sort of price you can expect to pay. This is the first publication of its kind for Northern France, it is essential for day-trippers and Francophiles alike, and such an ideal companion to *The Cross-Channel Drinks Guide*, we thought we should tell you about it. It is available from WH Smith and most good bookshops at £9.95, or direct from Gill Cutress, 1 Rosebery Mews, Rosebery Road, London SW2 4DQ (*tel*: 0181 678 0593) for £10.95 including p&p.

NO-LIMIT LIQUOR

The so-called "90-litre limit" you may have heard about is not a law, just a government guideline, officially called Minimum Indicative Limits, or MILs for short. Crossing from one member state of the EC to another is now no different than driving from Kent to Sussex. The UK Government has no more power to restrict the amount of wine, beer and spirits you fetch across the Channel than, for example, it has to restrict how much booze you may buy in Maidstone and take home to Brighton. The one, only and all-important difference is, of course, that you must not intend to resell it.

No matter how much booze you bring back for your personal use, there is no need – no facility even – to declare it. Customs & Excise can and do make spot-checks and although, on the one hand, this is a bit like being stopped in Tunbridge Wells and asked to explain the contents of your car, on the other hand, Customs & Excise are expected to prevent smuggling, not only of alcohol, but of hard drugs, explosives, weapons and other lethal or inhumane cargoes. If we expect them to perform this task, then spot-checks are a small price to pay. Besides, Customs & Excise do have the power to stop and search you in Tunbridge Wells or anywhere else for that matter.

If a Customs Officer does pick you out for a spot check and find that you have no more than the MILs (90 litres of wine, 10 litres of spirits, 20 litres of fortified wine and 100 litres of beer), then they will not and cannot detain you.

In theory, you could buy a million cases of booze in Calais and bring it back without incurring any UK duty, but if stopped by Customs, the more booze you have, the more convincing your story will have to be. The fact remains, nonetheless, that you do have the right to bring back as much booze as you like, but the onus is on you to prove that it is all for your personal use. How do you do that?

Personal use does not infer that you have to drink every drop yourself, rather it means that there is no intention to resell and thereby deny the Treasury the legitimate, if excessive, level of duty. You could give it away, providing that it is not a sham for selling or bartering, but you could give a present, say, of five cases of port from the birth-year of your godson to be laid down until he comes of age. Or it might be for your own cellar, a wedding reception, a party, stocking up for Christmas or New Year's Eve. Any of these things.

The hitch is, of course, that you cannot prove personal use unless you actually drink the stuff in front of the Customs Officer. But the law that gives him his powers is not designed to provide you with a hard time, but to make it easier for him to catch smugglers. Most Customs Officers are reasonable people, just like you and me, so tell them the truth – that it is for your own cellar, a party, a wedding or whatever. Furthermore, most Customs Officers do not want to complicate their lives. It is one thing, a feather in their cap, to nail a real villain, but to tie you up in their enquiries when you are just an innocent individual causes unnecessary paper work and will only attract the displeasure of their senior Officers should you complain to the Commissioners.

You would be very unlucky indeed if an Officer gets officious or awkward with you, but the law does put the onus of proof on you, so it is sensible to consider how that might be achieved. We therefore asked Customs & Excise what an honest person bringing back volumes in excess of the MILs for personal use could do to help satisfy an Officer that goods are genuinely for personal use and were told:

◆ *In advance of your journey be prepared to accept that you could be stopped by a Customs Officer and consider what evidence you could take with you to back up your claim of personal use.*

◆ *While not necessarily conclusive, if the drink is for a party or wedding reception, some proof of the date and venue would go a long way to satisfying an Officer.*

◆ *If it is for long-term consumption, the goods will have to be stored somewhere – where?*

And here are a few tips of our own:

◆ It is unlawful for one person to bring back goods on behalf of another, even if they are for that other person's personal use. This means that so-called "buying groups" are illegal, which might come as a surprise to people who have collectively hired a lorry to bring back purchases made on a co-operative basis. If caught, you will be required to pay the full UK duty, so do not join any such groups unless, that is, every member intends to accompany the vehicle for the entire journey.

◆ If you originally intended the goods to be for your personal use, but later change your mind, it is not an offence providing you notify HM Customs & Excise prior to any such sale and pay the appropriate amount of duty on demand.

◆ The law states that you must open, unpack and re-pack your bags, but Customs Officers will offer to do this for you.

◆   If Customs Officers unload your car or pull the vehicle to pieces, they must return everything to the way they found it.

◆   If a Customs Officer damages anything belonging to you, they must tell you how to claim compensation. They try to settle all claims within a month, but straightforward ones seldom take longer than 10 days. If your claim takes longer to settle than one month, Customs & Excise must explain in writing the reason for the delay.

◆   If you think that you have been treated unfairly, first ask to speak to a Senior Customs Officer. If you are still not satisfied, write to your Head of Customs (the Collector), who should be in the telephone directory. He must reply to you within 10 days. If you remain unhappy, you can write to your MP or refer your complaint to the Ombudsman. For more detailed information about complaints procedures, you can obtain a copy of *Complaints against Customs & Excise* from your local Customs office.

THE CROSS-CHANNEL DRINK AWARDS

From this year's series of blind tastings, we re-tasted fresh bottles of all potential award-winning wines to decide the following top awards.

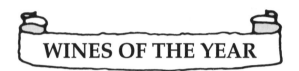

WINES OF THE YEAR

Red Wines of the Year

BEST-CHEAPEST RED WINE OF THE YEAR
Jean de Plessac NV Vin de Pays de l'Hérault
(Match, 4.95FF or 60p)

BEST-VALUE RED WINE OF THE YEAR
Domaine de Pons 1991 Côtes du Ventoux
(Centre Leclerc, 13.95FF or £1.72)

BEST-QUALITY RED WINE OF THE YEAR:
Penfolds Cabernet Sauvignon Bin 707 1990 South Australia
(The Beer & Wine Company, Calais & Cherbourg, 101.25FF or £12.50; The Grape Shop, Boulogne, 45FF or £5.56)

BEST-QUALITY ABC RED WINE OF THE YEAR
Awarded to the best "Anything But Cabernet" wine we tasted
Crozes-Hermitage 1991 Bernard Chave
(The Grape Shop, Boulogne, 45FF or £5.56)

White Wines of the Year

BEST-CHEAPEST WHITE WINE OF THE YEAR
Chilean White Wine NV Tesco
(Tesco, Eurotunnel-Calais, 14.90FF or £1.84)

BEST-VALUE WHITE WINE OF THE YEAR
Danie de Wet 1993 Chardonnay
(Sainsbury's, 32.48FF or £4.01)

BEST-QUALITY WHITE WINE OF THE YEAR
Beaune Chaume Gaufriot 1991 Domaine Henri Clerc
(The Grape Shop, Boulogne, 92FF or £11.36)

BEST-QUALITY ABC WHITE WINE OF THE YEAR
Awarded to the best "Anything But Chardonnay" wine we tasted
Le Viognier du Domaine de Gourgazaud 1993 Vin de Pays d'Oc
(Milles Vignes, Boulogne, 47FF or £5.80)

Rosé Wines of the Year

BEST-CHEAPEST ROSÉ WINE OF THE YEAR
Cinsault Rosé 1993 JP Chenet
(Champion, 11.80FF or £1.46)

BEST-VALUE ROSÉ WINE OF THE YEAR
Domaine de Montmarin 1993 Cépage Cabernet Sauvignon
(The Grape Shop, Boulogne, 18FF or £2.22)

BEST-QUALITY ROSÉ WINE OF THE YEAR
Reuilly 1993 Chassiot
(Le Tastevin, St-Malo, 43FF or £5.31)

Sparkling Wines of the Year

BEST-CHEAPEST SPARKLING WINE OF THE YEAR
Seppelt NV Great Western Brut
(The Grape Shop, Boulogne, 24FF or £2.62)

BEST-VALUE SPARKLING WINE OF THE YEAR
Champagne Serge Mathieu NV Prestige
(The Grape Shop, Boulogne, 98FF or £12.10)

BEST-QUALITY SPARKLING WINE OF THE YEAR
Champagne Vilmart Grand Cellier Rubis
(The Grape Shop, Boulogne, 147FF or £18.15)

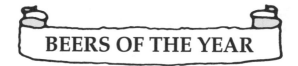

BEERS OF THE YEAR

Light Beers of the Year

BEST-CHEAPEST LIGHT BEER OF THE YEAR
Mosel Bier, Amos (Metz)
(The Beer & Wine Company, Calais & Cherbourg, 1.38FF or 17p per
25cl bottle)

BEST-VALUE LIGHT BEER OF THE YEAR
Grolsch Premium lager
(Beer Lovers Cash & Carry, Calais, 4.37FF or 54p per 50cl can;
The Beer & Wine Company, Calais & Cherbourg, 3.71FF or 46p
per 50cl can)

 BEST-QUALITY LIGHT BEER OF THE YEAR
Budweiser Budvar, Budweiser Budbräu
(EastEnders, Calais, 3.58FF or 44p per 33cl bottle; The Beer &
Wine Company, Calais & Cherbourg, 4.72FF or 58p per 33cl
bottle)

Dark Beers of the Year

 BEST-CHEAPEST DARK BEER OF THE YEAR
Draught Guinness
(Beer Lovers Cash & Carry, Calais, 6.06FF or 75p per 50cl can)

 BEST-VALUE DARK BEER OF THE YEAR
Draught Guinness
(Beer Lovers Cash & Carry, Calais, 6.06FF or 75p per 50cl can)

 BEST-QUALITY DARK BEER OF THE YEAR
Draught Guinness
(Beer Lovers Cash & Carry, Calais, 6.06FF or 75p per 50cl can)

Speciality Beers of the Year

 BEST-CHEAPEST SPECIALITY BEER OF THE YEAR
L'Écume des Jours, Bière Sur Lie
(EastEnders, Calais, 8.50FF (£1.05) per litre bottle)

 BEST-VALUE SPECIALITY BEER OF THE YEAR
L'Écume des Jours, Bière Sur Lie
(EastEnders, Calais, 8.50FF (£1.05) per litre bottle)

 BEST-QUALITY SPECIALITY BEER OF THE YEAR
L'Écume des Jours, Bière Sur Lie
(EastEnders, Calais, 8.50FF (£1.05) per litre bottle)

Cross-Channel Shopping Guide

Our prediction in the first edition of rapid movement in the choice of cross-Channel wines was right on the mark, as virtually every British outlet has expanded its range, and The Grape Shop is leading the way with no less than 800 different wines! Some British outlets are also branching out: The Calais Wine & Beer Company, for example, has muscled in on the Cherbourg market, and the irrepressible Dave West has popped-up in no less than three different locations throughout Calais. Sainsbury's opened up just after the first edition was published, but Tesco will not open its Cité Europe branch until March 1995, although we managed to twist a few arms at Tesco to give our readers a sneak preview of some wines it can expect to find.

The Good Lobster Guide

We were severely chastised for our sweeping condemnation of the French hypermarkets in the first edition by a reader who pointed out that they at least sold fresh lobster whereas the British supermarkets did not. We are sorry if any other readers mistook our *Guide* for that other famous cross-Channel publication, *The Good Lobster Guide*, but we do try to make it reasonably clear that we concern ourselves only with booze. We have never suggested that readers avoid French hypermarkets *per se*. You should shop in them for whatever you like, but just be a bit wary when it comes to wine.

After the tastings for the second edition, we remain concerned about buying wine from French supermarket and hypermarket groups. This is not simply a frog-bashing exercise. France makes most of the best wines in the world, and various French-owned outlets perform very well in the *Guide*. It is just that French-owned supermarkets have a totally different philosophy than British-owned ones when it comes to wine, buying purely on price. Not that it is all their fault, as the bulk of French hypermarket shoppers seem equally oblivious to what's in the bottle, as long as the price is right. There is, therefore, little reason why they should bother to change – except, that is, in the Channel ports, where the more discerning British shoppers will not be fobbed-off with inferior goods.

Looking for good French supermarkets

To tell the truth, we do not think it is particularly clever to universally condemn the range, quality, value and imagination (or lack of it) of the wines that French supermarkets sell. We would much rather find something exciting to recommend, but the French do not help themselves by not helping us, we can only go by our own experience, and the results of that can be gleaned from each group's entry in the following chapters.

We know full well that some French supermarkets must be better than others. It stands to reason. We are also sure that there must be some wines to recommend in all the French chains. If our random purchases have unearthed some good buys, there must be many more, but the only way we can make a truly fair appraisal of the French supermarket groups is if they submit a good selection of their wines, so that we may taste them blind against wines of a similar category and price from all the other cross-Channel outlets. This is something the British groups have long been used to, hence we have received submissions from Tesco, although its Cité Europe outlet is not due to open until March 1995.

To be fair, the concept of a shop-by-shop, shelf-by-shelf wine guide is totally alien to the French, who do not have such publications. Last year, it was hard to explain what *The Cross-Channel Drinks Guide* was about, as it did not even exist, but it was equally difficult to explain this to the independent outlets in France, as it was to the supermarket groups, yet we managed to secure the co-operation of a large number of independent French outlets for the first edition. The French supermarket groups could not be bothered. Indeed, few of them could even be bothered to reply to our correspondence, despite each group receiving at least three of our letters or faxes.

We tried even harder to obtain their co-operation this year, sending copies of the first edition of the *Guide* to both the chairman and managing director of every supermarket group, asking them if they wanted a more enthusiastic appraisal in the next edition, and whether they knew that their senior management had not had the courtesy to reply to our correspondence. It seems that the boardroom in these companies are as unco-operative and as discourteous as their senior management, as only three of the 30 directors in the 15 firms contacted replied! Is this merely contempt for the British cross-Channel shoppers, or is it because they genuinely fear putting their wines to the ultimate blind-tasting test against those of their competitors? Of those who did reply, all three promised full co-operation but, as it turned out, only one, Cedico (owned by Tesco), fulfilled its promise.

At least one French group was keen to let us and other British journalists taste their best wines over 70FF at their own premises, but we declined. Most cross-Channel bargains are under 34FF, thus concentrating on a supermarket's top of the range wines tells us nothing about the bulk of wines their customers buy. Furthermore, tasting them in isolation would have been unfair to all the other retail outlets, whose wines must compete with others of a similar style and price under blind conditions. After we explained this, it took the supermarket in question six weeks to agree – again – to submit samples, but by this time we had completed our tastings. We will try again next year, but in the meantime, we strongly advise readers to be wary of any publication that suddenly starts raving about French supermarket groups, especially if much of the praise is being heaped on ines of 70FF and more.

Wines en Vrac

Buying wines in bulk, usually by filling up a 10-litre *cubitainer* for bottling-off at home, is very popular with a growing number of Brits who travel abroad, but while there are some good value wines offered for sale in this way, there are some basic hazards that should be recognised before jumping into the habit feet first. In the first place, *vins en vrac* are notorious for their variability, not the least because one delivery of the 'same' wine can be totally different from another, but there is also the uncertain time lag between when the shop receives the wine and when the customer takes it away. What state of oxidation is the wine in? It might taste even better with the oxidation underway than it does when fresh, so it is not necessarily something that can be identified, and even if it could, the critical question is how much free sulphur there is in the wine? Because even a fresh *vin en vrac* needs the preservative property of sulphur. Maybe there is not enough, and the oxidative process is so far advanced that it is too late to add an effective dose yourself? And when you have your container filled with wine, its oxidation will increase, as it will once again, when you open it to fill your bottles back home. Maybe the supplier or the retailer has been over cautious and there is too much sulphur anyway? If this is the case, then at least you have a chance of detecting it when you taste the wine. These are, therefore, some of the reasons we do not include any of these wines in the *Guide*. We have nothing against *en vrac* in principle, it is just that anything we might taste is highly unlikely to be the 'same' as the wine you would encounter just a few weeks later, and how it tastes when you eventually drink it is dependent on too many factors of transport, storage and bottling.

Fuming about sulphur!

If you are so anti-SO^2 that our advice here is an anathema to you, then you should also avoid any prepared food because $SO2$ is in virtually everything we eat (look out for E220 and its sulphuric derivatives E221 through to E227). Every quality-conscious winemaker tries to use as little sulphur as possible, of course, but the amounts found in wine are small compared to, say, reconstituted orange juice, yet no one complains of getting a headache from fruit juice.

For those who have never purchased wine in this way, the usual procedure is to bring your own receptacle (any size), which is filled on the spot, although most *en vrac* specialists will also stock their own 5-litre or 10-litre containers for any customer who may call on a whim. We suggest you buy some Campden tablets (proprietary form of sulphur in easy to use tablet form) from a chemist or home brew shop in the UK, and simply pop them in at the wine shop. Without running an analysis, it would be impossible to determine precisely how much sulphur you should add, but for every 10 litres of wine a good safety measure would be 2 tablets for a full-bodied red or a sweet wine, 1 tablet for a crisp, dry white wine, and 1.5 tablets for a rosé, medium sweet or light red wine. Make sure that your container is full to the brim before you secure the cap, unless you actually want to encourage the oxidation process. And before filling the container, you should of course sterilise it with a solution of sodium metabisulphite (2 Campden tablets dissolved in 0.5 litre of warm water, then cooled down with one litre of cold water). Bottles and corks should be similarly sterilised.

Readers experienced in buying *en vrac* will sterilise containers, bottles and corks, and add sulphur to the wines purchased as a matter of course, although there will always be somebody who will dismiss such precautions as unnecessary. Such people have invariably become so accustomed to oxidised wines over the years that they probably genuinely believe their home-bottled wines are how all wines should be, but unless you like your red and white table wines to smell and taste of sherry or vinegar, we strongly advise that you take no notice of them.

RECOMMENDED WINES & BEERS: In the words of a long-forgotten advertisement, it is the wines and beers the *Guide* rejects that make *The Cross-Channel Drinks Guide* the best. All the wines and beers recommended in this book are, at the very least, good buys for their quality or value. We do not include any that are merely decent, drinkable, but moderate in quality, which is why we rejected more than half of the 850-odd wines and beers tasted under blind conditions for this edition. A lot of those rejected were drinkable, but being merely drinkable is not a sufficient qualification for recommendation in this publication, even if it is for others. We taste wines according to their category of style and price, and only those distinctly above the norm deserve our recommendation, thus even the lowliest wine or beer in the book should give you satisfaction relative to other wines or beers of similar style and price. The cream of the wines in this book are graded by bronze, silver and gold medals. Of all the wines tasted, just 14% were awarded bronze medals, 10% silver medals, and only 7% got gold.

PRICES: In all but two instances, the retail outlets covered by this edition priced their wines for us in French Francs, which is why we lead with that currency, immediately followed by brackets showing the price in British pounds at an exchange rate of 8.10FF to the £UK. This is a good rule of thumb exchange rate, but *do not take this conversion as absolute*: the exact price will depend on the rate of exchange in force at the time of purchase and, as every traveller knows, this can change for the better or worse. It was, for example, 8.10FF to the pound at the time of tasting, but down to 7.96FF as I write this and no one knows how much it will be worth by the time you read this book. *We strongly advise you check out any in-store conversions, as they might not be accurate and the difference could affect your decision to buy.*

VERDICT? This summarises our opinion of the outlet in question in the following categories:

👍👍👍👍👍 Superstar status

👍👍👍👍 Formerly the highest recommendation in the *Guide*

👍👍👍 Visit strongly recommended

👍👍 Visit recommended

👍 Could be worth a visit SUBJECT TO QUALIFICATION in the text

❓ Verdict ON HOLD pending more information

👎 Not worth a visit

The Best Drink Outlets of the Year

With the exception of the specialist nomination (Best Beer, and Best Spirit), only outlets with a minimum of 👍👍👍 can qualify for the following awards and commended outlets.

BEST CROSS-CHANNEL OUTLET OF THE YEAR
The Grape Shop, Boulogne 👍👍👍👍👍
Runners up: Bar à Vins, Calais 👍👍👍👍
The Calais Wine & Beer Company, Calais 👍👍👍👍
La Maison du Vin, Cherbourg 👍👍👍👍

BEST CROSS-CHANNEL SUPERMARKET OF THE YEAR
Sainsbury's 👍👍👍👍
Runners up: Cedico 👍👍👍
Monoprix 👍👍👍
Tesco* 👍👍👍

NOTE *The runner up designation for Tesco* is awarded on the proviso that this store opens as scheduled, and its drink selection consists of at least those recommended.*

BEST CROSS-CHANNEL BEER OUTLET
NOT AWARDED

We were interested in two categories of beer. The first category (and most important to our readers) is cheap beer – really dirt-cheap stuff – but all we demand is something clean and drinkable, and if it has a hint of character, then it becomes medal-worthy. We received a lot of beers in this category, and if we were told once that they would all be the same, we were told a thousand times, but it was not true. There is a great variance in quality and character of these beers, with some that are really quite good in terms of value, whereas others were tasteless. Tasteless, however, became an enviable quality, as a number were really disgusting (one reeked of dog's breath, and another was milky-white and still fermenting in the bottle). The other category we were interested in was, of course, quality or specialist beers. Although we awarded medals to a few individual beers, no outlet either showed us a sufficiently large and interesting range of medal-winning beers. Or, for that matter, provided us with a sufficiently large and interesting list.

Runners up: The Calais Wine & Beer Company 👍👍👍👍
EastEnders 👍👍👍
Beer Lovers 👍👍

Best Cross-Channel Drinks Outlets

BEST DRINKS OUTLET IN BOULOGNE
The Grape Shop 👍👍👍👍👍

Runners up: Mille Vignes 👍👍👍
The Wine Society 👍👍👍

BEST DRINKS OUTLET IN CAEN (JOINT)
Caves Entrepôts 👍👍👍
& Vins sur Vingt 👍👍👍
Runners up: None

BEST DRINKS OUTLET IN CALAIS
Bar à Vins 👍👍👍👍
Runners up: The Calais Wine & Beer Company 👍👍👍👍
EastEnders 👍👍👍
Sainsbury's 👍👍👍👍

BEST DRINKS OUTLET IN CHERBOURG
La Maison du Vin 👍👍👍👍
Runners up: Inter Caves 👍👍👍
The Wine & Beer Company* 👍👍👍👍

NOTE *The runner up designation for The Wine & Beer Company* is awarded on the proviso that this store opens as scheduled, and its drink selection consists of at least those recommended.*

BEST DRINKS OUTLET IN DIEPPE
L.C. Vins 👍👍👍
Runners up: None

BEST DRINKS OUTLET IN DUNKERQUE
Tastevins de Flandre 👍👍👍
Runners up: None

BEST DRINKS OUTLET IN LE HAVRE
Chais de la Transat 👍👍👍
Runners up: None

BEST DRINKS OUTLET IN OOSTENDE
Wijnhuis Douchy 👍👍👍
Runners up: None

BEST DRINKS OUTLET IN ROSCOFF
Les Caves de Roscoff 👍👍👍👍
Runners up: None

BEST DRINKS OUTLET IN ST-MALO
Le Tastevin 👍👍👍
Runners up: Inter Caves 👍👍👍
Cave des Jacobins 👍👍👍

BOULOGNE

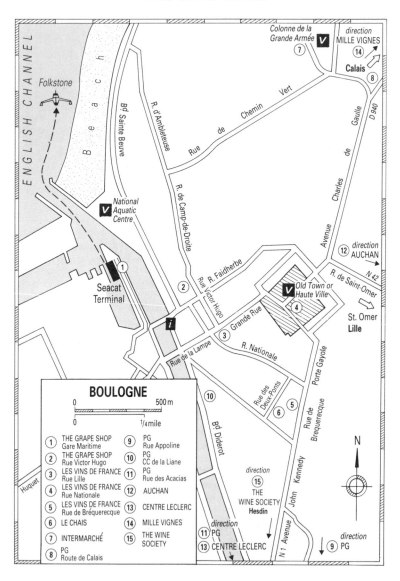

BOULOGNE

0   500 m

0   ¼ mile

1. THE GRAPE SHOP
Gare Maritime
2. THE GRAPE SHOP
Rue Victor Hugo
3. LES VINS DE FRANCE
Rue Lille
4. LES VINS DE FRANCE
Rue Nationale
5. LES VINS DE FRANCE
Rue de Bréquerecque
6. LE CHAIS
7. INTERMARCHÉ
8. PG
Route de Calais
9. PG
Rue Appoline
10. PG
CC de la Liane
11. PG
Rue des Acacias
12. AUCHAN
13. CENTRE LECLERC
14. MILLE VIGNES
15. THE WINE
SOCIETY

Calais might be the place where most cross-Channel shoppers go, but Boulogne is home to **The Grape Shop**, winner of *The Cross-Channel Drinks Outlet of the Year* award for the second year running. Heaven only knows why a million ferries, hovercraft and Seacats plough the Channel between Dover and Calais, while just a few kilometres down the coast the far more picturesque port of Boulogne has become a virtual backwater, attracting just six crossings at the height of the season. Calais might be slightly more convenient for getting to Paris, Reims or wherever, but Boulogne is just 20 minutes away from Calais by direct autoroute link, so convenience cannot be the main reason. Furthermore, those British tourists who use this route actually go to Boulogne, rather than through it. Why then has it been ignored by the ferry companies? Should they find they have an over-capacity of resources when the Channel Tunnel opens, they could do worse than divert some of their ferries to this route and actively promote the advantages Boulogne has over Calais.

Did you know?

• Boulogne was already flourishing as an international port at the time that Julius Caesar arrived with no less than 800 boats to conquer Britain, when we were running around in skins.

• According to local legend, in 636AD a statue of the Virgin Mary was washed up on the beach, making Boulogne a famous pilgrimage site.

• Boulogne was also Napoléon's staging post for the invasion of England in 1803, when he amassed some 900 ships and 2000 flat-bottomed troop-carriers here, but later aborted the attempt.

Boulogne Factfile

• **HOW TO GET THERE:** Hoverspeed's Seacat service operates out of Folkestone, with a 55-minute crossing time (see pages 340-355 for details of service and prices)

• **LOCATION AND DISTANCES:** Situated 34km (21 miles) south of Calais; Boulogne is 115km (71 miles) from Lille, 150km (93 miles) from Dieppe, 243km (151 miles) from Le Havre, 312km (195 miles) from Caen, 400km (250 miles) from Cherbourg, 480km (300 miles) from St-Malo, 659km (412 miles) from Roscoff and 245km (152 miles) from Paris.

• **POPULATION:** 50,000

• **TOURIST INFORMATION OFFICE:** Boulevard de la Poste, 62200 Boulogne-sur-Mer, *tel:* (21) 31.68.38. Open Mon-Sat 9am-8pm, Sun 10am-7pm. Oct-May Mon-Sat 9am-7pm, Sun 1pm-5pm.

• **WHERE TO STAY:** During the peak season, it is always best to book your hotel in advance, but if you are caught out, try the Tourist Information Centre, which offers a free accommodation service, keeping track of all the vacancies left in the town. The best place to stay: *Hôtel Cléry* (Hesdin-l'Abbé, *tel:* (21) 83.19.83), which is a charming château some 9km (6 miles) outside of Boulogne itself, where a double room can range from just 300FF (bit cramped) to 540FF (impressive). Some cheap but clean stays include: *Hôtel de la Mirador* (2-4 rue de la Lampe, *tel:* (21) 31.38.08) where a double en-suite with TV will cost 120-220FF per room.

• RESTAURANTS: The best place to eat in town is the one-star Michelin restaurant *La Matelote* (80 boulevard Ste-Beuve), after which *La Liégeoise* (10 rue Monsigny) offers a cuisine that is almost as fine, but at slightly less expensive prices, but compared to both of these establishments, the excellent cooking at the *L'Huîtrière* (11 place de Lorraine) seems to be real budget haute cuisine, although we are still not talking cheap lunch for the kids here. Just outside Boulogne, there is another one-star Michelin restaurant called *Hostellerie de la Rivière* at Pont-de-Briques (17 rue Gare), which is just 5km (8 miles) south of Boulogne on the D940 and does a splendid salmon baked in cabbage leaves. However, the last time we ventured out of town, we preferred *Le Relais de la Brocante*, which is housed in a former school, former church and former hôtel de ville all rolled into one. It is found at Wimille (2 rue de Ledinghem), which is also 5km from Boulogne. Best-cheapest eats: *An Bascaille-la* (place de Godefroy) for 69FF fixed-price menus on a sunny terrace. Where to find most restaurants, including some of the cheaper places to eat: overlooking the water, on or around boulevard Gambetta.

• BEST BAR OR PUB IN TOWN: We found two and one maybe. M. & Mme Le Grand, the owners of *Le Royale* (rue Thiers), are almost overwhelming in their friendliness, while their establishment is everything we expect from a chic, French café-bar. Martin Brown, the debauched owner of The Grape Shop, considers *Le Pullman* (rue Victor Hugo) to be the best bar in Boulogne, describing it as having 'a friendly atmosphere, charming landlady, pool table and lots of young totty'. Talking of The Grape Shop, our maybe bar is *The Vole Hole* (rue de Lille), which is owned by its former manager, Roger Young. It is only a maybe because it had not opened at the time of writing, and when it does (*circa* early October), will probably qualify as the smallest bar in the world. There is hardly room to stand, let alone stock the range of beers and wines (from The Grape Shop, of course), but if you want to have a drink, why not ask Roger why his bar is called *The Vole Hole*, and what connection it has with a pile of prehistoric vole remains that were unearthed in Essex.

• MARKET DAYS: All day Wednesday and Saturday morning (place Dalton)

• WORTH A VISIT: Gourmets regularly pilgrimage to Boulogne just to shop at Philippe Olivier's world famous cheese shop in rue Thiers. It's a great opportunity to taste some of those fancy French cheeses you often wondered about but were afraid to buy. The fabulous £16 million *National Aquatic Centre* (*Nausicaa*), which overlooks both the beach and harbour, attracted a million visitors within 16 months of opening. It would be foolish to visit Boulogne and not take in this lavish, new attraction, which makes Calais' Aquarium Museum seem very seedy indeed. The Old Town or *Haute Ville* miraculously escaped damage despite the 487 Allied bombing raids that Boulogne endured in the Second World War. Surrounded by its massive 13th century ramparts, the *Haute Ville* makes a peaceful retreat from the madding crowd of the more commercial parts of Boulogne. Just off the RN1 in the direction of Calais, you will come across the *Colonne de la Grande Armée*, a 160ft column erected to commemorate the gathering of Napoléon's invading army.

• FESTIVALS: *Fête de Poisson* (last weekend in September) attracts 20,000 seafood lovers to Boulogne each year.

⑫ AUCHAN

RN42
62200 St-Martin Boulogne
Boulogne-sur-Mer
Tel: (21) 92.06.00

Selling area: 12,750m^2 (compare this with the size of other stores featured in the area, to gauge their relative size and you will have a rough idea of how big the range of wines, beers, spirits and other goods will be).

Opening hours? Mon-Fri 8.30am-10pm, Sat 8am-10pm, closed Sun

Foire aux Vins: October

Comment: Auchan outlets are usually amongst the biggest, brightest and most welcoming of the French hypermarket chains, but Boulogne's Auchan is immense. It is obviously popular with British tourists too, as nearly every Brit we saw in this store was going crazy at the sight of such a supersized hypermarket. It is not surprising, then, that the Boulogne branch of Auchan accepts British currency. We had even less response from Auchan's directors this year than we did with its wine buyer last time, as neither the chairman (Gérard Mulliez) nor its managing director (Michel Pecqueraux) even acknowledged our correspondence.

The wines: The wines are displayed from the floor right up to the ceiling – well almost to the ceiling. There are many more reds than whites, with the greatest emphasis placed predictably enough on Bordeaux (approximately 40-50 different wines), after which Burgundy and Languedoc-Roussillon offer the most choice (about 20 wines each), although white Burgundies fare less well (just six), and the choice of Loire in any colour is abysmal. There are about 10 different Alsace, but the only white wines stocked in any serious way are Champagne and other sparklers. We purchased six wines (the cheapest red and cheapest white, plus four wines that a knowledgeable consumer might consider interesting or good value), but only one qualified for recommendation in this *Guide*, and two of those that failed the test we would not touch with a barge pole, even if Auchan gave them away. A hit-rate of just one in six is bad enough: we hate to think how the average consumer, who has to rely on pot-luck, would fare.

For explanation of products, check the A-Z Guide to Wines, Beers & Spirits, and the Glossary at the rear of the book.

WHITE WINES
Alsace Riesling 1992 Pierre Dumoulin-Storch
25.90FF (£3.20) Dry white wine lifted by a slight spritz.
Verdict? 👎

(6) **LE CHAIS**
Bréquerecque Village,
49 rue des Deux Ponts
62200 Boulogne-sur-Mer
Tel: (21) 31.65.42
English spoken? Not really
Opening hours? 9am-12noon & 2.30pm-7pm seven days a week (but lunch break overran when we called)
Parking? Yes (private car park)
Shopping trolleys? Yes
Do they offer to help carry the goods to the car? Yes
Methods of payment? Sterling, French Francs, Visa, Mastercard
Any wines for tasting in store? Yes
Comment: Part of a small chain of two wine warehouses called Le Chais (the other being in Calais) and three town shops called Les Vins de France, all of which are located in Boulogne. The Boulogne branch has the largest range of the two Le Chais outlets and the three Les Vins de France shops have a more upmarket presentation, but smaller range with slightly more expensive prices. Le Chais is a nicely presented wine warehouse, which will sell wines by the bottle, but is more geared up for sales by the case. Coaches are welcome by prior appointment. In the first edition, we reported that this group planned to open a big warehouse in April 1994 at a service station, just outside Calais on the autoroute towards Dunkerque, but this did not happen, although we are assured it is more a matter of postponement than cancellation.
The wines: No samples were submitted last year, but we did receive a comprehensive price list, and were impressed by many of the wines (Alsace from Klipfel, Rhône from Paul Jaboulet, Burgundy from Jadot and Mommessin, and a very good selection of Bordeaux). This time, however, we received no list, but Le Chais did submit samples, although the disappointing news is that only two passed the test. Those wines that did not qualify were all drinkable, but two recommendations and no medal-winning wines is hardly justification for

Medals are awarded relative to price, thus a silver medal 30FF wine will be superior to a silver medal 20FF wine, and possibly inferior to a bronze 40FF wine.

the 👍 👍 we awarded Le Chais on the strength of its list alone last time. We do not think this firm is doing itself any favours by submitting wines that do not reflect the depth, quality and value of its list, albeit last year's, but even if we had an up-to-date one, we could not rely on it to boost this outlet's ranking twice running. We must let the wines we taste do the talking, but we qualify this by saying this is a good, serious warehouse-style operation that certainly offers more worthwhile wines than the two below, and probably deserves a better result than our verdict suggests. And if it still lists half the beers it did last time, it would probably have romped home as the Best Cross-Channel Beer Outlet of the Year for the second time in a row.

RED WINES
Côtes-du-Rhône 1993 Marquis de Richevigne 19.80FF (£2.44) Not special, but a good basic red Rhône sold at an unpretentious price.

WHITE WINES
Château Bel-Air 1992 Bergerac Sec 17.50FF (£2.16) Fresh suck-a-stone style Sauvignon, with a definite touch of pétillance.
Verdict? 👍

🏵 BEST CROSS - CHANNEL OUTLET OF THE YEAR
★ BEST DRINKS OUTLET IN BOULOGNE

• 30 GOLD MEDALS
• 21 SILVER MEDALS
• 14 BRONZE MEDALS

(1) THE GRAPE SHOP
Gare Maritime
62200 Boulogne-sur-Mer
Tel: (21) 30.16.17

AND

(2) THE GRAPE SHOP
85-87 rue Victor Hugo
62200 Boulogne-sur-Mer
Tel: (21) 33.92.31
English spoken? Yes
Opening hours? Mon-Fri 10am-7.30pm (rue Victor Hugo), 8.30am-9pm seven days a week (Gare Maritime)
Parking? Ample
Shopping trolleys? No
Do they offer to help carry the goods to the car? Yes
Methods of payment? Sterling, French Francs, Traveller's cheques, Eurocheques, Visa, Mastercard
Any wines for tasting in store? Yes
Additional information:
* No-quibble money-back guarantee if dissatisfied

(The wine does not have to be off, simply not to your satisfaction, and you do not have to lug it back to Boulogne, as you can return it to The Grape Shop in Northcote Road, London SW11.)

* Cheaper than UK prices guarantee (*As we pointed out in the first edition, most cross-Channel bargains are in the under 34FF category, and the more expensive the wine, the less likely that you will save any money at all, with some wines, usually* cru classé *Bordeaux, costing up to a staggering £50 a bottle more across the Channel than they do in the UK. Well, you need not worry about losing money on the wines that you buy from The Grape Shop, as it guarantees that no matter the price category, all its wines are at least £1.50 cheaper than you can purchase them in the UK. Should you discover a wine that is not, and you can produce a list to prove this, then The Grape Shop will reduce accordingly. The only proviso is that the list is a regular one and up-to-date – it can be from any retailer, be it Oddbins, WineRack, Lay & Wheeler or whoever– and the price indicated is not a special offer.)*

Comment: Although the original outlet is still in use, and will remain so for the time being, shoppers will find it much more rewarding to visit The Grape Shop's new Hoverspeed premises at the Gare Maritime, where the Seacat docks. The traffic is being re-routed to pass the front of the new shop, so there should be no problem finding it. What can we say about The Grape Shop that winning our Best Cross-Channel Outlets of the Year two years running does not already say? Last year it boasted by far the largest range on the entire Channel coast, with no less than 400 different wines, yet this year The Grape Shop has a phenomenal 800 wines in stock. Last year's manager, the rotund Roger Young, has been replaced by the far more shapely Katrina Thom, the Japanese night club hostess with a degree in Economics and Middle Eastern Politics, and is ably assisted by another brainy bimbo, Shazza Essex Girl.

The wines: With 100 Burgundies, 80 Bordeaux, and 105 Australian wines, The Grape Shop not only offers a larger range of better value from traditional areas than any of the French competition, but has as an outstanding range of wines from Australia, the UK's flavour of the month. And with 34 Italian wines, mostly selected from Winecellars' star-studded list, we can no longer complain that there is no decent Italian wines across the briny, although there is a way to go before it is properly balanced in styles, weight and price. The Grape Shop's weakest areas are Alsace (17 wines) and New Zealand (18 wines). Although these are better than can be found in most cross-Channel outlets, they do lack imagination, and a quick look at what WineRack is offering from these areas will illustrate what we mean. This is perhaps rather churlish, considering how outstanding The Grape Shop is in virtually all other respects. There can be no denying owner Martin Brown's determination to retain his cross-Channel crown, submitting no less than 119 wines this year. However, numbers alone cannot guarantee a win, for although the more wines submitted probably means that a greater number will survive our tastings and receive a recommendation by the *Guide*, there is also the percentage success-rate to take into consideration. In purely numerical terms, submitting 119 wines gave The Grape Shop an obvious advantage, but in percentage terms it is much harder to achieve a decent success rate with so many wines than it is with, say, just the three or six wines (as some French retailers submitted), as it is relatively easy to select a small number of exceptional wines. Yet no less than 70% of the 119 wines submitted by The Grape Shop passed our blind tastings, notching up an incredible 30 Gold, 20 Silver, and 14 Bronze medals. If that is not enough, The Grape Shop also won the Best-Quality White Wine of the Year, Best-Value Rosé of the Year, Best-Cheapest Sparkling Wine of the Year, Best-Quality Sparkling Wine of the Year, Best-Quality Red Wine of the Year, and Best-Quality ABC (Anything But Cabernet) Red Wine of the Year. With such a chestful of honours, there can be no doubt that The Grape Shop is the Best Cross-Channel Outlet of the Year.

RED WINES

Vin de Pays du Var NV L.V.B. 12FF (£1.48) Medium-bodied red with soft, agreeable, peppery fruit.

SILVER MEDAL

Domaine le Noble 1992 Cabernet Sauvignon 18FF (£2.22) Smooth oaky bouquet, lovely silky fruit. This elegant wine with its long, lush flavour was so obviously well made that we were not in the least bit surprised to discover it to be a Hugh Ryman wine when the covers came off the wines.

BRONZE MEDAL

Domaine de Terre Megere 1993 Merlot 21FF (£2.59) Rich, thick and soupy, with a grassy edge to the fruit, yet we quite liked this wine at the price.

Le Colombey NV Bordeaux 22FF (£2.72) Round and fruity.

La Vieille Ferme 1992 Côtes du Ventoux 23FF (£2.84) Tough and tannic red that will turn into a rich and serious wine if left in bottle for 2-3 years.

GOLD MEDAL | *Domaine Saint François 1992 Côtes-du-Roussillon* 23FF (£2.84) An elegant, medium-to-full bodied red with lots of lovely, silky, blackcurrant fruit. Ideal for both sipping and partnering food, and truly deserves a Gold medal at this price.

Château Tour des Gendres 1992 Bergerac 24FF (£2.96) Good basic Bordeaux with a decent structure, this wine shows best with food.

Château La Grave Singalier 1992 Bordeaux Supérieur 24FF (£2.96) Honest Bordeaux with just enough fruit to match its tannic structure.

Salice Salentino Riserva 1989 Candido 27FF (£3.33) Sweet, sappy fruit with a firm, alcoholic finish.

GOLD MEDAL | *Domaine de Terre Megere 1992 Les Dolomies* 28FF (£3.46) The delicious Bordeaux-like blackcurrant fruit flavours in this Coteaux du Languedoc are quite extraordinary. You would have to shell out at least double this price to find anything comparable from Bordeaux itself.

Madiran 1991 Domaine Sergent 28FF (£3.46) Good typicity: chewy fruit with a sturdy flavour, character and structure that will improve for several years in bottle.

GOLD MEDAL | *Côtes-du-Rhône 1991 E. Guigal* 30FF (£3.70) Lovely balance, all components already in perfect harmony, succulent fruit, and at the best cross-Channel price (20-30% cheaper than in other outlets).

BRONZE MEDAL | *Salisbury Estate 1992 Cabernet Shiraz* 30FF (£3.70) Plenty of fruit, but totally dominated coffee-toffee oak.

GOLD MEDAL | *Grant Burge Oakland 1991 Shiraz Cabernet* 31FF (£3.83) We can forgive the Australian tendency to over-oak their wines when they are as rich and as classy as this, with its luscious, long, warm, spicy-fruit flavour.

SILVER MEDAL | *Parallèle 1993 Paul Jaboulet* 33FF (£4.07) Needs to be cellared. You just will not believe how cheap this powerful wine was if you buy it now, and keep it 6-9 years.

Château Lescalle 1991 Bordeaux Supérieur 35FF (£4.32) A decent basic Bordeaux that needs food to show at its best.

SILVER MEDAL

Château Grossombre 1990 Bordeaux 35FF (£4.32)
A very good Bordeaux that is nicely concentrated,
and will continue to improve over the next 12-18
months. This wine deserves its Silver for both its
potential and value.

*Touraine 'Première Vendange' 1993 Henry
Marionnet* 36FF (£4.44) According to the back
label this is a pure Gamay wine, but it has a
distinctly un-gamaylike grassy character. As
'pure' in EC terminology means a minimum of
85%, we suspect it must contain 15% Cabernet
Franc.

Buzet 1990 Domaine du Pech 36FF (£4.44) Good,
honest fruit. Not special, but well focused.

Vacqueyras 1990 Delas Frères 39FF (£4.81) Nice
silky fruit on the palate, but there is a barely
perceptible blurring of characteristics on the nose,
which might be the start of a problem, or could
simply be going from one stage of development to
another. We like the wine, but we're not sure.

SILVER MEDAL

Chénas 1991 Domaine des Duc 42FF (£5.19) Real
depth of succulent, silky Gamay fruit. Who said
that Beaujolais could never be a serious wine?

SILVER MEDAL

Château de Belcier 1990 Côtes de Castillon 43FF
(£5.31) Classic, well-structured, flavour-packed
Côtes-de-Castillon that needs another two or three
years in bottle to outlive the dominance of its
barrique-ageing.

SILVER MEDAL

Parrina 1990 Riserva, Franca Spinola 44FF (£5.43)
A rich, dark and oaky Chianti, with lots of depth,
and some sweetness on the finish.

GOLD MEDAL
BEST-QUALITY ABC
(Anything But Cabernet)
RED WINE OF THE YEAR

Crozes-Hermitage 1991 Bernard Chave 45FF
(£5.56) Not THE Chave, but this wine stands out
above the rest as if it were. A beautifully crafted,
flavour-packed wine, full of soft, silky, sensuous
Syrah fruit. Great finesse.

GOLD MEDAL

Coudoulet de Beaucastel 1992 Côtes-du-Rhône
45FF (£5.56) Gorgeous depth of flavour, lovely
rich fruit, with spicy freshness. Capable of
developing much finesse and complexity over the
next 2-3 years, but an absolute delight to drink
now, with or without food.

SILVER MEDAL

Brouilly 1993 Domaine des Coteaux de Vuril 46FF
(£5.68) The soft, ripe fruit in this wine glides down
the back of the throat, after which sweet,
perfumed Gamay aromas rise up to remind you
what you have just consumed, and if that does not
make you take another, which makes you take
another, and another, then you will never drink an
entire bottle of Beaujolais in your life!

GOLD MEDAL	*Bourgogne 1991 Domaine Lorenzon* 46FF (£5.68) Fine Pinot Noir aromas, elegant fruit, supple tannins, and gentle oak make this classic Burgundy, despite its generic appellation.
GOLD MEDAL	*Moulin-à-Vent 1991 Clos des Maréchaux* 46FF (£5.68) If you like oak on your Beaujolais, then this wine is certainly for you, but even purists should thoroughly enjoy it, as this *cru* Beaujolais also manages to retain the lightness, elegance and purity of its Gamay fruit.
BRONZE MEDAL	*Bourgogne Hautes Côtes de Beaune 1991 Domaine Henri Naudin-Ferrand* 48FF (£5.93) An oaky Burgundy with a good concentration of fruit, this wine is capable of improving further in bottle, but beware the bottle variation, as two of our three samples were maderised.
BRONZE MEDAL	*Château Panigon 1990 Cru Bourgeois, Médoc* 48FF (£5.93) A well-structured, full-bodied red with plenty of fruit and more than a hint of blackcurrants.
	Sancerre 1993 Domaine Croix Saint Ursin 48FF (£5.93) This would be a good value red wine, if £2.00 cheaper, and not meant to be a pure Pinot Noir.
GOLD MEDAL	*Bourgogne 1992 Thierry Violot-Guillemard* 49FF (£6.05) A really classy wine for the basic Bourgogne appellation, this wine has a noticeably oaky nose, but it is definitely oaky-Pinot, with lots of fine Pinot fruit on the palate, and excellent acidity. A joy to drink on its own.
GOLD MEDAL	*Dolcetto d'Alba 1993 Pianromualdo, Mascarello* 49FF (£6.05) Dark, inky-rich, hot-blooded Italian wine with sumptuous youthful fruit.
SILVER MEDAL	*Rocca Rubia 1990 Carignano del Sulcis Riserva* 52FF (£6.42) A big wine with sweet fruit, this tastes as if it has been made to hit judges between the eyes at competitions. It will develop into a more complex wine, of course, but it is just a pity that a red wine of this class should be so sweet. Unless, that is, you have a sweet tooth.
	Château Barrabaque 1989 Canon-Fronsac Cuvée Prestige 54FF (£6.67) Elegantly structured fruit with light menthol undertones.
	Sancerre, La Croix au Garde 1993 Domaine Henry Pellé 54FF (£6.67) Although this cannot hack it with Burgundies of the same price, it is very good for Sancerre, so if you are rich enough to be able to be able to afford the philosophy that enables you to drink wines for their own sake, regardless of value, then buy this.
GOLD MEDAL	*Gigondas 1990 Guigal* 65FF (£7.74) If you like

Guigal's Côtes-du-Rhône 1991, then you will love this lovely big rich, oaky wine, which just gets better and better in the bottle.

SILVER MEDAL   *Isole e Olena 1991 Chianti Classico* 59FF (£7.28) This big-bodied Chianti is so obviously a classy wine, but it is still tight and it would be infanticide to drink it within 3-4 years. Keep it that long, however, and you will be rewarded with a wine so much easier to drink, yet far more complex, with multi-layered fruit and flavour.

GOLD MEDAL   *Barolo 1990 Cantine Ascheri Giacomo* 62FF (£7.65) A beautifully balanced wine of great finesse and complexity. Lovely harmonious fruit. Class.

SILVER MEDAL   *Mercurey 1991 Château de Chamilly* 67FF (£8.27) An elegant Pinot Noir, long and luscious, with a good depth of fruit, and likely to be even better in another two or three years.

GOLD MEDAL   *Château Rahoul 1989 Graves* 68FF (£8.40) The classic, supple-tannin structure and lovely rich fruit make this a wine that will age gracefully.

GOLD MEDAL   *Côte de Nuits-Villages 1991 Domaine Henri Naudin-Ferrand* 69FF (£8.52) Very oaky for Burgundy, but has lots of fruit, good concentration and is unmistakably Pinot Noir.

SILVER MEDAL   *Mercurey 1er Cru, Les Champs Martin 1990 Domaine Lorenzon* 74FF (£9.14) Although a bit tight and tannic now, this is a powerful wine that will become something special to drink in 5-6 years from now.

BRONZE MEDAL   *Château Dalem 1986 Fronsac* 75FF (£9.26) Rich, mature and really quite oaky.

GOLD MEDAL   *Mercurey 1990 Château de Chamilly* 80FF (£9.88) Elegant yet well structured, with apricot fruit on the finish, and good for drinking with food, but will be immeasurably better in another three years.

GOLD MEDAL   *Beaune Clos du Roi 1990 Chanson* 93.95FF (£11.60) Elegant, sweet-ripe Pinot fruit, but its supple tannin structure will enable this wine to improve for at least another three years.

GOLD MEDAL
BEST-QUALITY RED WINE OF THE YEAR   *Gevrey-Chambertin 1991 Michel Magnien* 98FF (£12.10) Young but serious Burgundy. Too easy to drink now, but lay it down for 18 months, then try a bottle every three months until you're suddenly mesmerised by a stunning Burgundy, and that will be when it is really ready for drinking.

GOLD MEDAL   *Penfolds Cabernet Sauvignon Bin 707 1990 South Australia* 114FF (£14.07) Too many blind tastings end up making the biggest wines the best, but this is one case when the biggest wine truly is the best! Not a cheap wine, nor the cheapest cross-Channel we could find (The Wine & Beer Company in Calais and Cherbourg sell it for 101.25FF or £12.50), but it is almost a pound cheaper than Oddbins sell it for in the UK. There is no disguising the quality of this dark star; you could put it in a blind tasting of Bordeaux 1st Growths and its huge, intense, complex flavours would punch their way through. If, however, you want to drink it at its peak, then you'll have to wait until at least 2004.

WHITE WINES

Domaine de Papolle 1993 Vin de Pays des Côtes de Gascogne, Peter Hawkins 14FF (£1.73) Compared to Domaine de Barroque, its lesser-quality sister-wine, Papolle has a more perfumed character, which shows through on the palate and enhances the aftertaste. This certainly gives Papolle the edge, but neither it nor Barroque have the special quality that marked their 1992 vintage. Taste the 1992 and 1993 Papolle together and you will see the remarkable similarity of their perfumed character, but the fruit in 1993 does not have the same depth. This might be due to the different grape varieties used, as the 1992 was based on 60% Ugni Blanc, whereas the 1993 was based on 60% Colombard. Furthermore, there were vinification difficulties in 1993, with the end of the fermentation dragging on far longer and more slowly than desirable, and this may be the cause of its amylic-peardrop aroma, which may make it very fresh, but is more expressive of technology than either grape or soil. At the time of writing this edition of the *Guide*, the 1992 was still drinkable, but had lost the spark of vitality that helped it to run away with both 'Best White Wine of the Year' and 'White Wine Snip of the Year' awards in the first edition (the only wine to pick up two 'Wine of the Year' awards, by the way). We should remember, however, that this wine is just a modest *vin de pays* and that the wines of this area are better-suited to distillation (into Armagnac) than to drinking for their own sake. Yet that was what made the 1992 so special. Indeed, it was special, as 1992 was a deliberate move away from the more commercial style of previous vintages. The irony is that it did not sell so well, which is why Peter Hawkins went back to a more commercial style in 1993, and irony upon irony, this has sold like hot-cakes on the back of the rave review in the first edition of the *Guide*! If Hawkins just wants turnover, then he should continue to make the more commercial style, but in doing so, he will make a wine that is no different than every other Vin de Pays des Côtes de Gascogne. No better or worse: just invisible.

If, however, he wants to make a name for himself, and for Domaine de Papolle, then he must at least devote a portion of his harvest to pursuing the more expressive style adopted in 1992 and, hopefully, improving on it year after year.

SILVER MEDAL *Chardonnay 1992 Vin de Pays de Côtes Catalanes* 15FF (£1.85) Quite fat and full-bodied for the price, with sweet, fresh Chardonnay fruit. Well-made, and excellent value.

BRONZE MEDAL *Domaine de Maubet 1993 Vin de Pays Côtes de Gascogne* 18FF (£2.22) A nice dry white with lots of tasty gooseberry fruit flavour.

Domaine du Pigeonnier 1993 Bergerac Sec 19FF (£2.35) Clean tasting with fresh, well-structured fruit: best with food.

BRONZE MEDAL *Domaine de Rombeau 1993 Côtes de Roussillon* 19FF (£2.35) Soft and fruity, yet has enough structure to partner food.

Servus 1993 Burgenland Dry White Wine 21FF (£2.59) A dry white with a slight pepperiness to its fruit, the Servus has filled out since its launch a year ago. Although worthy of recommendation in the *Guide*, we do wonder why no retailer has bothered to look out some of the vastly more superior, potential medal-winning wines from this country. Austrian wines lose out in the UK because their relatively high production and shipment costs make them too costly for all but the out-and-out enthusiast, but what is cross-Channel shopping for, if not to provide a more level playing field?

SILVER MEDAL *Château Tour des Gendres 1993 Bergerac Blanc Sec* 24FF (£2.96) Elegant dry white wine with lots of refreshing, lemon-pie fruit. Although more than twice the price of the cheapest white Bordeaux or Bordeaux style we encountered, 18FF was the cheapest we found that we could recommend, and this is such exceptional value that it deserved the best-cheapest tag more than any of the other wines.

Salisbury Estate 1993 Sauvignon Blanc 25FF (£3.09) Tastes sweet in the company of other Sauvignon Blancs, this wine's tropical/opal fruit flavour is not how Europeans perceive this variety, nor is it anything like the super-successful

Kiwi concept, but it is an enjoyable New World white in its own right.

GOLD MEDAL *Château de Briacé 1993 Muscadet de Sèvre-et-Maine* 26FF (£3.21) The finest Muscadet we encountered in terms of typicity, this wine has extremely fresh aromatic qualities, lovely fruit and a truly elegant style. Just shows that Muscadet can produce the goods, but there are 100 bottles of dross for every one of this quality.

SILVER MEDAL *Domaine Le Noble 1993 Chardonnay* 28FF (£3.46) Rich and quite classy for a *vin de pays*, this Hugh Ryman wine has been made for early and easy drinking, yet should improve over the next 12 months.

Salisbury Estate 1993 Chardonnay 28FF (£3.46) The extraordinary ripe flavours in this wine are a bit OTT for us, and they are heading for the canned asparagus character we also do not like, but some do, and if that is you, then this is very well made for its style, and well worth the price.

GOLD MEDAL *Côtes-du-Rhône 1993 E. Guigal* 33FF (£4.07) So easy to zap past this in a blind tasting without realising its true quality, but if you sit down and eat a meal with it, you can appreciate its complexity and finesse.

BRONZE MEDAL *Mâcon-Fuissé 1993 Le Moulin du Pont* 36FF (£4.44) Fresh, young lemony fruit. Refreshing and tasty.

SILVER MEDAL *Domaine des Dorices, Cuvée Grande Garde 1987 Muscadet de Sèvre et Maine sur lie* 38FF (£4.69) Not to everyone's taste, but a bargain for lovers of old Muscadet, this seven-year-old wine is rich and toasty, with some complexity and a peachy aftertaste.

BRONZE MEDAL *Bourgogne Aligoté 1992 Gérard Mouton* 39FF (£4.81) This oaky Aligoté has a smoky aftertaste and is about as good as Burgundy's minor grape gets.

BRONZE MEDAL *Bourgogne Blanc 1991 Domaine Henri Clerc* 39FF (£4.81) Easy to flit past this one in a blind tasting, but there was something there that made us go back to it a couple of times. It is not an obvious wine, but we think that it will mature gracefully if given another 2-3 years in bottle.

GOLD MEDAL *Grant Burge Old Vine Semillon 1993 Barossa Valley* 40FF (£4.94) A near-perfect integration of oak and fruit provides an absolutely delightful cocktail of lemony-vanilla flavours. Quite superb.

Chablis 1992 Domaine de Vauroux 42FF (£5.19) A crisp, clean and correct Chablis that should fatten out a bit over the next year or so.

Riesling 1993 André Thomas 43FF (£5.31) A wine that needs time, but should pay dividends over the next 2-3 years.

Sancerre 1993 Domaine Croix Saint Ursin 43FF (£5.31) A fine, bottle-mature Sauvignon that you will love or hate, but cannot ignore.

SILVER MEDAL | *Riesling, Coteau du Haut-Koenigsbourg 1992 Claude Bléger* 44FF (£5.43) Firm yet fleshy dry Riesling with lots of character and aftertaste of peach-stones. Will age well.

SILVER MEDAL | *Coudoulet de Beaucastel 1992 Côte-du-Rhône* 46FF (£5.68) A Burgundy-style Rhône that will go wonderfully toasty if kept a year or two.

SILVER MEDAL | *Bourgogne 1992 Domaine de la Galopière* 46FF (£5.68) Toasty aromas on the nose with lemon-pie fruit on the palate, this is a rich wine with just the right amount of mouthwatering acidity to drink on its own.

SILVER MEDAL | *Menetou-Salon Morogues 1993 Domaine Henry Pellé* 46FF (£5.68) Fine, elegant, classy Sauvignon Blanc best suited to accompany food. Serious stuff.

GOLD MEDAL | *Château Haut Bertinerie, Blanc Sec 1992 Première Côtes de Blaye* 46FF (£5.68) The class of this wine, with its beautifully integrated fruit and oak, made it stand out, head and shoulders above the rest, in our tasting of dry white Bordeaux.

BRONZE MEDAL | *Bourgogne Chardonnay 1992 Mestre-Michelot* 49FF (£6.05) Fat, round and oaky.

GOLD MEDAL | *Gewurztraminer, Coteau du Haut-Koenigsbourg 1992 Claude Bléger* 52FF (£6.42) This wine has gentle, elegant fruit and already possesses quite a lot of spice, but will develop more in bottle. Try with smoked haddock.

GOLD MEDAL | *Pouilly-Fumé 1993 Châtelain* 54FF (£6.67) If only all Loire Sauvignons had such beautiful, light, elegant, and ripe fruit.

GOLD MEDAL | *Pouilly-Fuissé 1992 Le Moulin du Pont* 54FF (£6.67) A rich and beautifully balanced little wine, lovely to sip on its own, yet ideal with food, but it is a wine that deserves consideration, and should not be gulped down unthinkingly.

GOLD MEDAL | *Ladoix Côte de Beaune 1992 Domaine de la Galopière* 62FF (£7.65) An elegant, rich and oaky wine that has the fruit to match and will improve steadily for the next year or two, when it deserves to be partnered with food.

GOLD MEDAL
BEST-QUALITY WHITE WINE OF THE YEAR | *Beaune Chaume Gaufriot 1991 Domaine Henri Clerc* 92FF (£11.36) Classic Burgundy! Simply the best Chardonnay we tasted, even if it was the most expensive. It demolished almost everything else submitted, although Danie de Wet's

Chardonnay (Sainsbury's £4.01) gave it quite a run for its money.

ROSÉ WINES

Domaine de Montmarin 1993 Cépage Cabernet Sauvignon 18FF (£2.22) Has the flavour, depth and length of a good red Bordeaux, but without the tannin, which makes it soft and easy to drink: a rosé of real quality and character.

Château Tour des Gendres 1992 Bergerac Rosé 24FF (£2.96) An unusual combination of a spritzy wine with bottle-mature fruit.

SPARKLING WINES

Seppelt NV Great Western Brut 24FF (£2.62) Although up 2FF in price from last year, Seppelt Great Western still represents one of the best cross-Channel bargains of the year compared to its UK price of £4.99 (Oddbins). Not a classy wine, perhaps, but it is not meant to be anything other than a tropically-fruity fizz that is easy to glug down.

Clos de l'Abbaye NV Saumur Brut 37FF (£4.57) Not a bad drop of fizz if you like the taste of peppery Cabernet Franc. Goes well with food.

Louis de Grenelle NV Rouge Mousseux 46FF (£5.68) If you like sparkling red wines, then you will certainly find this is one of the more serious examples of the style, with crisp, clean Cabernet Franc fruit and a genuinely dry finish, but is it really worth £5.68 at UK prices, let alone cross-Channel?

Crémant d'Alsace NV Claude Bleger 48FF (£5.93) Crisp, clean fizz with fresh, tangy fruit.

Bouvet Tresor 97FF (£11.98) This wine proves that the Loire can produce sparkling wines of the quality of good Champagne, although its new oak influence puts it more in the New World in terms of style. If this wine happened to be a couple of pounds cheaper, it would be Gold Medal material, although it is certainly cheaper here than it is in the UK (£15.99, Selfridges).

Champagne Serge Mathieu NV Prestige 98FF (£12.10) This superb wine proves that a dedicated producer in the Aube can match the quality of a dedicated producer in the best grands crus of the famous districts of the Marne. A very rich Champagne with lots of lovely ripe acidity, it is succulent and fruity, has an exquisite balance, and great finesse.

BRONZE MEDAL

Champagne Guy Larmandier NV Brut Premier Cru 102FF (£12.59) Has richness and plenty of flavour. *Champagne Georges Gardet 1983 Brut* 145FF (£17.90) A mature Champagne with a vanilla-rich complexity that really comes out with food, yet there was considerable bottle variation, making it impossible to award the Silver Medal this wine would deserve if you could count on every bottle being in perfect condition. Of the three samples we tasted, one bottle stank of rotten cabbage and another simply lacked vitality, and prior to our tasting, we had already experienced a marked variation in various bottles of this wine in the UK, suggesting a problem with storage or transport. Most unfortunate.

GOLD MEDAL

Champagne Henri Goutorbe 1986 Special Club Brut 147FF (£18.15) Forget the skittle-shaped bottle, this is a Champagne of real class, with multi-dimensional richness of delicious, creamy-fruit and the potential to improve further in bottle over the next 2-5 years. A narrow miss for the Best-Quality Sparkling Wine of the Year award.

GOLD MEDAL
BEST-QUALITY SPARKLING WINE OF THE YEAR

Champagne Vilmart Grand Cellier Rubis 147FF (£18.15) The epitome of finesse. If a *Grande Marque* released a special *cuvée* rosé of this quality, you would be lucky to find it at double the price of this wine.

Verdict? 👍👍👍👍👍

RUNNER UP FOR BEST CROSS-CHANNEL SUPERMARKET OF THE YEAR
• 1 GOLD MEDAL
• 3 SILVER MEDALS
• 5 BRONZE MEDALS

◯ **CEDICO**
CC rue Georges Besse
62520 Le Touquet-Paris Plage
Tel: (21) 94.20.04
Opening hours? Mon-Sat 9am-12noon & 2.30pm-7pm, closed Sun
Special directions: To reach Le Touquet-Paris Plage, go south from Boulogne on the D940.
Foire aux Vins: Two each year – [1] Easter, [2] Sept/Oct
Comment: Small but bright and welcoming, Cedico stores have more of a local supermarket image. Cedico belongs to the Catteau group, which was taken over by Tesco in 1993, and includes the Hyper Cedico and Cedimarche chains.
The wines: This chain's performance should be a salutary lesson to other French supermarket and hypermarket groups because although Cedico does not stock a particularly large range, and we spied nothing outstanding on its shelves, when allowed to do the talking, Cedico's wines collected

eight medals, earning the chain runner-up position for the Best Cross-Channel Supermarket of the year. And it is not as if Cedico has had to resort to showing us its top of the range; most of Cedico's wines are in the 20-50FF bracket, and that is exactly what they submitted. The point other French chains should take note of is that although 16 of the 30 wines submitted by Cedico's buyer, Bruno Meens, did not survive our tastings, we still found plenty worth recommending. Presumably other supermarket groups could do just as well, if only they bothered.

RED WINES

Côtes du Lubéron 1992 L'Aiguebrun 14.50FF (£1.79) A cheap red Rhône with decent tasty fruit.

SILVER MEDAL *Château Cadouin Segur 1992 Bordeaux* 17.80FF (£2.20) Violety nose, elegant silky fruit. Very good value.

Château Picon 1992 Bordeaux Supérieur 22.50FF (£2.78) Good basic Bordeaux, with clean, nicely structured fruit for the price.

Château Roumaguet 1992 Bordeaux 23.90FF (£2.95) Another good basic Bordeaux in a light Merlot style, this wine has less body than the Picon, but a touch more elegance.

BRONZE MEDAL *Chinon 1992 Domaine du Verger Peintier* 24.85FF (£3.07) It is not common to find a soft and easy to drink red Loire, and when they are as cheap as this, you should snap them up, as future vintages are seldom as attractive.

BRONZE MEDAL *Château Labory 1989 Fronsac* 27.60FF (£3.41) Plenty of blackcurranty fruit backed up by a good tannin structure. Still has tight-packed flavours that need more time in bottle. Keep 2-3 years.

BRONZE MEDAL *Château Caronne Ste-Gemme 1987 Haut Médoc* 35.50FF (£4.38) Mature claret English-style. Allow to breathe two hours prior to drinking.

Saumur-Champigny 1990 Domaine des Hauts de Sanziers 38.90FF (£4.80) Attractive blackcurrant fruit on the nose, but closed on the palate, requiring a further 1-2 years in bottle to open up.

SILVER MEDAL *Château La Rose Perruchon 1989 Lussac-St-Émilion* 41.65FF (£5.14) Well concentrated wine with multi-layered fruit that stood up to the even higher scoring Château Seguin 1991 Cuvée Prestige, which came immediately before this wine in the blind tasting.

SILVER MEDAL *Château La Tour Carnet 1992 Haut-Médoc* 49.90FF (£6.16) Young toasty fruit on the nose, plenty of flavour and length on the palate. A wine of some

class that still has room to improve and develop in
bottle.

WHITE WINES
*Domaine de Barroque 1993 Vin de Pays des Côtes
de Gascogne, Peter Gascogne* 13.95FF (£1.72) Nice
but not special (unlike the 1992 vintage, which
was a little bit special), this is simply a light-
bodied, dry white wine with fresh peardrop fruit.
Riesling Réserve 1993 Dopff 30FF (£3.70) Full,
fresh and sprightly.

BRONZE MEDAL   *Pouilly Fumé 1990 Domaine de Maltaverne*
42.95FF (£5.30) This is a fine quality Sauvignon
Blanc with noticeable bottle-age. Not everyone's
cup of tea, and certainly not ours, but for those
who enjoy this style of wine, it fully deserves its
bronze medal.
La Touchère 1993 Chablis 45FF (£5.56) Not easy to
drink on its own, this wine certainly has a touch of
genuine Chablis 'steel' and makes a good food
wine.

GOLD MEDAL   *Sancerre 1993 Domaine des Vieux Pruniers* 48.50FF
(£5.99) A delightful Sauvignon with elegant fruit.
Classic dry Sancerre, genuinely dry yet eminently
drinkable.

ROSÉ WINES
BRONZE MEDAL   *Domaine les Cabassiers NV Côtes de Provence*
17.90FF (£2.21) It is not easy to achieve a rosé of
this quality in the dry heat of Provence. Real fruit,
good body and well-suited to food.
Verdict? 👍 👍 👍

• 1 BRONZE MEDAL   ⑦ **INTERMARCHÉ**
Avenue Percier et Fontaine
62200 Boulogne-sur-Mer
Tel: (21) 80.28.28
Selling area: 1,700m² (compare this with the size
of other stores featured in the area, to gauge their
relative size and you will have a rough idea of
how big the range of wines, beers, spirits and
other goods will be).
Opening hours? Mon-Thurs 9am-12.15pm & 2pm-
7.15pm, Fri 9am-12.15pm & 2pm-7.30pm, Sat 9am-
7.15pm
Comment: The branches in Caen and Le Havre are
slightly larger than this one, but most Intermarché
on the Channel coast are relatively small, and
although they can be quite large further inland,
this chain is more of the superheat ilk than
hypermarket. It is also relatively down-market,

with a mostly dull and uninteresting range of wines, often dominated by a display of 3-litre wine containers. There are around a dozen different Champagnes, and the fine wines are usually displayed separately (we saw Ducru Beaucaillou 1989 at 85FF, and Pavillon Rouge 1990 at 105FF). We had no success with chairman Marcel Robin, who steadfastly refused to answer our correspondence. It was the same story as last year, with M. Le Goff, Intermarché's drinks buyer. **The wines:** We purchased six wines along the same lines as those we bought at Auchan, and when it came to the crunch, Intermarché fared much better, with half of the wines warranting our recognition, and one even picking up a Bronze medal. And two of those that did not qualify were perfectly drinkable, even if not special enough to qualify for the *Guide*. If only the management of this firm had enough faith in its products to submit a substantial range of its inexpensive wines, they might do well, if this random sampling is anything to go by.

RED WINES
Beaujolais NV Cuvée Joannès 12FF (£1.48) Although not medal potential, you could have knocked us down with a feather when this wine, the second-cheapest Gamay submitted, turned out not only to be drinkable, but expressive of its variety, rather than maceration carbonique.
Côtes-du-Rhône 1993 Réserve Lescarrat 13FF (£1.60) This soft and fruity wine has a touch more elegance than the other red Rhônes in its price category.

WHITE WINES

BRONZE MEDAL

Reuilly 1993 Cave PD 22.90FF (£2.83) This fresh and assertive Sauvignon is not a wine for wimps. **Verdict?** 👍

• 2 SILVER MEDALS

⑬ CENTRE LECLERC
Boulevard Industriel de la Liane
62230 Outreau
Boulogne-sur-Mer
Tel: (21) 80.83.71
Selling area: 3,200m² (compare this with the size of other stores featured in the area, to gauge their relative size and you will have a rough idea of how big the range of wines, beers, spirits and other goods will be).
Opening hours? Mon-Thurs 9am-10pm, Fri 9am-

10.30pm, Sat 8.30am-10.30pm, closed Sun
Comment: Last year we went through Gallec,
which owns Leclerc, Groupe de Travail Liquides,
which supplies Leclerc, and Leclerc's chief buyer,
but all to no avail, so this time we went straight to
the top, and we were pleased to receive Michel-
Edouard Leclerc's assurance that his chain would
extend the *Guide* full co-operation in supplying
whatever samples and information we wanted. He
delegated the matter to Jean Maurice, who runs
Leclerc Scapertois, which supplies all the stores in
the Pas-de-Calais and Normandy. Unfortunately
M. Maurice had other ideas, inviting us instead to
spend the day at Scapertois, where we could taste
their best wines over 70FF. We would be wined
and dined, and afterwards we would be given
some *cru classé* Bordeaux to take away. Apparently
he has tried this wheeze on other British
journalists with a certain amount of success, but
we are not in this job to fill the car boot with cases
of château-bottled claret, so we declined,
immediately and in no uncertain terms. We again
explained that most cross-Channel bargains are
under 34FF, as indeed are most of Centre Leclerc's
sales, thus concentrating on its top of the range
wines tells us nothing about the bulk of wines
most Leclerc customers buy. Besides which,
tasting them in isolation would have been unfair
to the other retail outlets, whose wines must
compete with others of a similar style and price
under blind conditions. After more
correspondence with M. Leclerc, we received a
letter from the head of Sobadis, a subsidiary of
Leclerc's, which handles the distribution of its
products in Normandy. Referring to our last
correspondence with Michel-Edouard Leclerc, he
offered us exactly what we wanted, even a choice
of branches from which we could collect our
samples from. Unfortunately our last
correspondence with M. Leclerc had been over six
weeks earlier, and our tastings had come and
gone. Still, if Centre Leclerc keeps to its word, and
submits samples without delay or hesitation for
the next edition, all the hassle we have endured
this year will at least be worthwhile.
The wines: Most branches are basic warehouse-
type operations, and very utilitarian. In the bigger
stores, the range can include as many as 250
different lines, with a good selection of fine wines,
albeit almost entirely from Bordeaux. Centre
Leclerc seems to be quite good on Beaujolais, with

most *cru villages* covered, and the one we tried from Juliénas certainly fared well, earning a silver medal no less. With four wines out of six random purchases qualifying for recommendation in the *Guide*, including two silver medals, one of which grabbed a Wine of the Year award, it makes us look forward to greater co-operation next year, to see how the range as a whole performs.

RED WINES

SILVER MEDAL
BEST-VALUE RED
WINE OF THE YEAR

Domaine de Pons 1991 Côtes du Ventoux 13.95FF (£1.72) We had to taste almost 30 red Rhônes up to 27FF before we found a wine to equal this. An elegant wine with a good depth of silky-plummy fruit, and nicely structured supple tannins.

Carayon-la-Rose 1986 Cuvée Exceptionnelle, Bordeaux Supérieur 18.95FF (£2.34) This is not bad as a basic Bordeaux, but unless you see the vintage on the label, you would hardly think that you are tasting an eight-year-old claret.

SILVER MEDAL

Juliénas 1992 les Vouillants Chedeville 26.50FF (£3.27) Bags of flavour. A real wine, and a true *cru* Beaujolais (we rejected most of the *cru* Beaujolais because they lacked the significant increase in quality and intensity of varietal flavour they should possess).

Château Roches Guitard 1989 Montagne-St-Émilion 30.85FF (£3.81) A good Bordeaux with sweet fruity aromas that follow through onto the palate.

Verdict? 👍

RUNNER UP FOR
BEST DRINKS OUTLET
IN BOULOGNE
• 2 GOLD MEDALS
• 1 SILVER MEDAL
• 3 BRONZE MEDALS

⑭ **MILLE VIGNES**
42 rue de la Gare
62126 Wimille
Pas-de-Calais
Tel: (21) 32.60.13
English spoken? Yes
Opening hours? Wed-Sun 10am-6.30pm, Mon-Tues by arrangement
Parking? Yes (private parking next to shop)
Shopping trolleys? No
Do they offer to help carry the goods to the car? Yes
Methods of payment? Sterling, French Francs, Eurocheques, Mastercard, Access, Visa
Any wines for tasting in store? Yes
Special directions: Take the D940 from Boulogne to Wimereux – in Wimereux turn into rue Carnot – at the end of rue Carnot turn right under the railway viaduct – after a quarter of a mile you will

be in Wimille, and will find Mille Vignes on your left, just before the level crossing.

Comment: Anglo-French-owned business managed by ex-Oddbins employee Simon Hill, Mille Vignes is housed in a former candle factory, just six minutes from Boulogne. Apart from wine, Mille Vignes sells real cider from Pierre Huet (and we agree with the comment in the list that it's 'a league apart from the super-strength muck in England'), superb vintaged Cassis from Trenel, and Calvados. In the corner by the old wax boiler, there is even a selection of walking sticks and carving knives for sale.

The wines: The range is small, but as Simon Hill tried to tell us, and we now know, well selected. There is nothing here for the 10FF a bottle shopper, but if Mille Vignes wishes to attract the more discerning British wine drinker, there will have to be some New World input on its list, which is 100% French (except for Château Pajzos, Tokaji Dry Furmint, from Hungary). If Hill does not realise this, then he learnt nothing from his experience at Oddbins, but he is switched on in most other respects, so we imagine it is more a matter of getting the message across to the owners.

RED WINES

BRONZE MEDAL | *Syrah 1993 Antonin Rodet* 23FF (£2.84) The quality of this Syrah actually does live up to the promise of the presentation of its obviously expensive, ludicrously oversized bottle. Keep 18 months before opening.

SILVER MEDAL | *Domaine de Parenchère 1993 Cuvée des Faugères* 24FF (£2.96) This sappy, almost soupy Bordeaux, with its blackcurrant fruit, is the second wine of Château de Parenchère, and makes for nice current drinking.

Château de Camarsac 1990 Bordeaux 29FF (£3.58) A tasty claret with the sweetness of ripe fruit, this is from the Lucien Lurton stable in the Entre-Deux-Mers.

BRONZE MEDAL | *Château Etang des Colombes 1991 'Bicentenaire' Vieilles Vignes* 33FF (£4.07) A typical Rhône-style blend of Grenache, Carignan, Mourvedre and Syrah, aged 10 months in oak, this needs to be served with food at the moment, but will develop into a much better, more flexible wine, if kept another two years or so.

BRONZE MEDAL | *Bourgogne Pinot Noir de Vieilles Vignes 1990 André Montessuy* 38.50FF (£4.75) Another wine that needs time, this will be a classy little Pinot for its price and appellation in 2-3 years. André Montessuy is a *sous marque* of Antonin Rodet.

WHITE WINES

GOLD MEDAL *Clos de Beauregard 1992 Leroux Frères* 27.70FF (£3.42) Another peachy-Muscadet (the other being Domaine du Vieux Chai 1993 from La Maison du Vin in Cherbourg), only this one is fatter, with hints of vanilla and botrytis, making it even more atypical. The Gold Medal therefore carries a warning, as no regular Muscadet drinker would even recognise this as Muscadet, let alone enjoy it. Most wine lovers with a broader palate (and that can include those who like to search for the Holy Grail of Muscadet) will, however, recognise for its true if idiosyncratic quality, and thus agree that Clos de Beauregard 1992 more than deserves a Gold purely and simply as a white wine, wherever it happens to come from.

GOLD MEDAL
BEST-QUALITY ABC
(Anything But Cabernet)
WHITE WINE OF THE YEAR

Le Viognier du Domaine de Gourgazaud 1993 Vin de Pays d'Oc 47FF (£5.80) Don't think of this as being expensive for a *vin de pays*, but as a half-price alternative for Condrieu. Indeed, this beautifully ripe and elegant wine with its luscious, fleshy peachlike fruit shows greater typicity and quality than most Condrieu. Huge progress has been made in white Rhône wines over the last five years, but some of the most expensive products have been some of the most misguided. We had white Rhônes up to 92FF or £11.36, but not only was this Viognier immeasurably the best, none of the more expensive wines even warranted an inclusion in the *Guide*.
Verdict? 👍 👍 👍

• 1 BRONZE MEDAL

⑧ **PG**
Route de Calais
62200 St-Martin Boulogne
Boulogne-sur-Mer
Tel: (21) 83.72.72
Selling area: 1,700m^2

AND

⑨ **PG**
Rue Appoline
62200 St-Martin Boulogne
Boulogne-sur-Mer
Tel: (21) 90.02.55
Selling area: 1,800m^2

AND

⑩ **PG**
CC de la Liane
62200 Boulogne-sur-Mer
Tel: (21) 30.43.67
Selling area: 1,800m²

AND

⑪ **PG**
Rue des Acacias
62200 Boulogne-sur-Mer
Tel: (21) 80.49.24
Selling area: 1,500m² (compare this and the size of the PG branches above with size of other stores featured in the area, to gauge their relative size and you will have a rough idea of how big the range of wines, beers, spirits and other goods will be).
Opening hours? Mon-Thurs & Sat 9am-12noon & 2pm-7.30pm, Fri 9am-8pm, closed Sun
Comment: Our initial reaction last year was to hang out the flags, because although these are fairly small outlets, PG is a local chain of real character, with some really interesting wines, the better ones of which are stored lying down in bins. Furthermore, after the usual hassle of chasing from one contact to another, we latched on to Xavier Diers, the buying director, who was friendly, helpful and agreed to send us any samples we wanted. Only, of course, he did not, so we pulled in the flags and gave PG a cautious verdict. This year we did not get so much as a reply from PG, let alone promises, so at least they kept their word this time!
The wines: With this year's lack of response, we decided to check more stores before buying our random samples (two cheapest, plus four interesting looking wines), and we were less impressed with the range than we were last time, although for the small supermarket it is, PG is not bad, and at least has a moderate choice in the 15-20FF bracket. Gone, however, are the excellent Blanck wines from Alsace, only to be replaced with Freyermuth, which churns out huge quantities at cheap prices. And we saw no Mommessin quality wines from Burgundy. The fine wine section lying down in bins was still there, but the wines displayed were noticeably lacking in the 'fine' department, and the prices were relatively high. As for our tastings, just two of the six wines purchased passed the test, although one of those did earn a bronze medal.

BRONZE MEDAL | *Château du Paraza 1991 Minervois* 9.90FF (£1.22) Soft and tasty, with creamy fruit and good length for a cheap red, and enough of a tannin structure to partner food.

Château Grand Champs 1988 Bordeaux 15.90FF (£1.96) Six-year-old Bordeaux for under £2.00 a bottle cannot be bad, but there is an assertive character that gives the mature fruit in this wine a certain youthful edge, and this does not quite ring true. It is, however, definitely worth recommending at this price.
Verdict? ⚐

SHOPI

Opening hours? Mon-Sat 8.30am-7.30pm, closed Sun

Comment: Although none of the Shopi, which belong to the Promodes group (*see* Champion entries for details), qualify for the 1000m² limit we have set on supermarkets to be included in the *Guide*, there seem to be so many in the Calais-Boulogne area that readers are bound to come across these brightly lit outlets, and might want some guidance, whether or not they are pinpointed on our maps.

The wines: Basically a boring range of wines that can be found elsewhere at cheaper prices. Of the six wines purchased, just one qualified.

ROSÉ WINES

Grenache Gris NV Vin de Pays d'Oc 11.90FF (£1.47) Fresh, clean and easy to drink, and a nice bit of alliteration too.
Verdict? ⚑

③ **LES VINS DE FRANCE**
11 rue Nationale
62200 Boulogne-sur-Mer
Tel: (21) 30.51.00

AND

④ **LES VINS DE FRANCE**
4 rue Lille
62200 Boulogne-sur-Mer
Tel: (21) 80.55.96

AND

⑤ **LES VINS DE FRANCE**
28 rue de Bréquerecque
62200 Boulogne-sur-Mer
Tel: (21) 80.55.96

Comment: These three shops are owned by Le Chais, but have a smaller range of the same products at slightly higher prices, and open on Sunday mornings, whereas Le Chais does not. *See* Le Chais entry above for more details, commentary and recommended wines.

Verdict? 👍

RUNNER UP FOR
BEST DRINKS OUTLET
IN BOULOGNE
• 1 GOLD MEDAL
• 3 SILVER MEDALS
• 2 BRONZE MEDALS

⑮ THE WINE SOCIETY, FRANCE

1 rue de la Paroisse
62140 Hesdin
Tel: (21) 86.52.07

English spoken? Yes

Opening hours? Mon-Sat 8am-12.30pm & 1.45pm-6pm, closed Sun

Parking? Ample parking in the Place d'Armes, in the centre of Hesdin, except for Thursday morning (market day)

Shopping trolleys? No

Do they offer to help carry the goods to the car? Yes

Methods of payment? Until 9 May 1994, only French Francs in cash was accepted, but the methods of payment now include Bankers Draft or Cheques (French Franc accounts only), Visa, Mastercard

Any wines for tasting in store? Yes

Special directions: From Boulogne, take the RN1 and then the RN39 to Hesdin (approximately 30 minutes).

Additional information:

* This cross-Channel outlet is available to members of The IEC Wine Society only. If you would like to join, lifetime membership costs £20. Apply to The IEC Wine Society, Gunnels Wood Road, Stevenage, Hertfordshire, SG1 2BG, tel: 0438 741177.

* Members travelling by Hoverspeed (either via hovercraft to Calais, or by Seacat to Boulogne) can benefit from special rates. For more details, telephone the Society's number above, and ask for Membership Services.

* Members wishing to stop over locally can benefit from special rates agreed with *Les Trois Fontaines* (rue d'Abbeville, tel: (21) 86.81.65), where a double en-suite with TV would normally cost 380FF without breakfast – the norm in France – but to anyone who identifies themselves as members, it will cost just 300FF *including* breakfast.

* Members may pre-order wines for collection on a specified date by telephoning the order office at

Stevenage (minimum of three days notice). This facilitates the swiftest possible service. Otherwise you can take your time to purchase wines on the spot.

* All purchases available by the case only. No splits.

Comment: There is no need to hype The Wine Society to its members, who total 64,000 and are only too well aware of the depth, consistency and quality of The Wine Society's 800-strong wine and spirit list. Since the Society opened its cross-Channel shop in Hesdin, more than 1,500 members have used the facility, forcing the Society to move to the above new premises, also in Hesdin.

The wines: Of the full range of 800 wines and spirits available in the UK, the Society stocks 100 of its most popular lines at Hesdin. The only pity is that we did not taste more of these wines, as it was the only cross-Channel outlet to achieve a 100% hit-rate with all the wines submitted receiving at least a recommendation in this *Guide*. If there had been two or three more gold medal wines, the Society would certainly have warranted 👍 👍 👍 👍. And if we extrapolate the Society's performance across its entire range of 100 wines, it would probably have rated at least 👍 👍 👍 👍. The Society did not get more golds, and we cannot extrapolate, of course, but we can say that 👍 👍 👍 is a cautious rating, and that any reader who does not belong to The IEC Wine Society should at least enquire about the benefits of membership.

RED WINES

SILVER MEDAL

Cent'Are, Rosso 1989 Duca di Castelmonte 32.50FF (£4.01) Very smooth, very Italian, with a lovely creamy-oak finish.

BRONZE MEDAL

Château de la Grave 1991 Côtes de Bourg, Grand Vin de Bordeaux 34.17FF (£4.22) Rich, tasty, and well-structured for drinking both with food and on its own.

GOLD MEDAL

Crozes-Hermitage, Wine Society 1990 UVF, Tain l'Hermitage 42.08FF (£5.20) A little bit of new oak gives the warm, spicy Syrah fruit in this wine a fashionable elegance seldom seen in Crozes-Hermitage. This wine lucked-out, falling between the Best-Value and the Best-Quality Rhône-style. It could so easily have picked-up both awards, yet failed to collect either.

SILVER MEDAL

Château Beaumont 1989 Haut-Médoc, Cru

Bourgeois 56.67FF (£7.00) An elegantly structured, mature claret, with fine plummy fruit and some mellow complexity.

WHITE WINES
Marqués de Alella, Classico 1993 Alella, Parxet
31.67FF (£3.91) A dry white with simple, easy to drink fruit in a spritzy style.

SILVER MEDAL

The Society's Gewurztraminer 1990 Hugel, Alsace
57.50FF (£7.10) More like a Vendange Tardive than a basic Gewurztraminer, with lots of richness and a definite sweetness to the fruit, but it is really quite fat for Hugel, whose wines when rich tend to lean more towards elegance than fatness. We think this wine is already at its best, but it will continue at this level for a few years yet. Reading back over that, you might think that we do not like it, but we do, which is why it gets a Silver Medal.
The Society's Celebration White Burgundy 1985 Seigneurie de Posanges, Côte d'Or 83.33FF (£10.29) An oily-textured, mature Burgundy that needs food to bring out the fruit. A good buy for lovers of Golden Oldies.

SPARKLING WINES

BRONZE MEDAL

Conde de Caralt NV Cava Brut 38.30FF (£4.73) Conde de Caralt is one of the better Cavas, and this particular *cuvée* is as good as it gets.
Verdict? 👍 👍 👍

CAEN

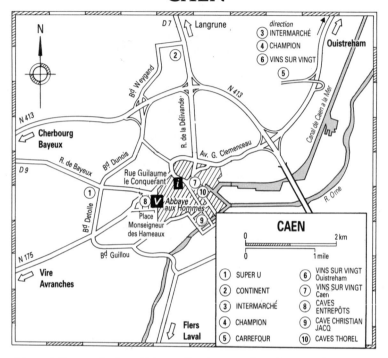

You might wonder how Brittany Ferries can advertise a service to Caen, when it is, after all, 14km (9 miles) inland. Although ferries could reach Caen by canal, which is used for the export of steel and import of coke, they do not. The ferries do not dock at Caen, but at Ouistreham, which hardly anyone in the UK has heard of. As Caen is a university town and the capital of Calvados, UK citizens are more likely to have heard about it than little old Ouistreham, so we can at least understand Brittany's economy with the truth.

Caen was totally destroyed in 1944, but has been completely restored, and is well worth visiting, but do not think you have to go there as soon as you disembark, as Ouistreham itself has a charm, and should be explored. Why not stop for a coffee, a drink at a bar or something to eat? You really ought to take a drive along the old coastal road because this is where D-Day happened. The all too familiar names of Sword, Juno, Gold and Omaha loom into view when driving along the D514, making an eerie but fitting reminder of the British, American and Canadian forces who also risked and lost their lives on these beaches.

Apart from *Vins sur Vingt*, we found no specialist wine shops of either a serious or good value nature and would greatly appreciate any readers reports that might expand our coverage of Caen in this respect. If, however, you want to find a big hypermarket for a spending spree on non-drink products, then we suggest Carrefour, which is bright and cheerful, rather than Continent, which is not.

Did you know?

• Caen was the seat of William the Conqueror.
• The two golden lions on the standard flying above the castle ruins are the origin of our British heraldic lions.
• Caen has an unusually high proportion of young inhabitants, with over 45% of its population under 25 years of age.

Caen/Ouistreham Factfile

• HOW TO GET THERE: Brittany Ferries operate out of Portsmouth, with a 6-hour crossing-time (*see* pages 340-355 for details of service and prices).

• LOCATION AND DISTANCES: Ouistreham is 14km (9 miles) north of Caen, which is situated almost halfway between Cherbourg (119km or 74 miles) and Rouen (124km or 78 miles), 107km (67 miles) southwest of Le Havre, 312km (195 miles) from Boulogne, 344km (215 miles) from Calais, 107km (67 miles) from Le Havre, 118km (74 miles) from Cherbourg, 163km (102 miles) from St-Malo, 170km (106 miles), from Dieppe 344km (215 miles) from Roscoff and 222km (139 miles) from Paris.

• POPULATION: 200,000 (Ouistrehem 5,700)

• TOURIST INFORMATION OFFICE: Place St-Pierre, 14000 Caen, *Tel:* (31) 86.27.65. Mon-Sat 9am-7pm, Sun 10am-12.30pm & 3pm-6pm; Oct-May Mon 10am-12noon & 2pm-7pm, Tues-Sat 9am-12noon & 2pm-7pm, Sun 10am-12.30pm.

• WHERE TO STAY: During the peak season, it is always best to book your hotel in advance, but if you are caught out, try the Tourist Information Centre, which offers a free accommodation service, keeping track of all the vacancies left in the town. The best place to stay: *Relais des Gourmets* (15 rue de Geôle, *tel:* (31) 86.06.01) is anattractive, well-run establishment with a range of double rooms from 265-840FF (£33-104). Some cheap but clean stays include: *Hôtel St-Jean* (20 rue des Martyrs, *tel:* (31) 86.23.35) for a quiet setting and modern doubles with shower for 180FF; *Hôtel du Parc* (44 rue Jules Guesde, 14460 Colombelles, *tel:* (31) 72.40.18) offers smart, modern double rooms en-suite with TV for 170-250FF, just a dog's leg trek from Ouistreham towards Caen.

• RESTAURANTS: The best place to eat in Ouistreham is *La Normandie* (71 avenue Michel Cabieu), a simple but elegant restaurant where chef Christian Maudouit enjoys local renown. In Caen the two-star Michelin restaurant *La Bourride* (15-17 rue du Vaugueux) is a pretty little inn with low ceilings and big beams, where Michel Bruneau, the most famous chef in Lower Normandy, has earned a great reputation for his highly personal expression of Norman cuisine. The next best restaurant is *Daniel Tuboeuf* (8 rue Buquet), which serves exquisite food, after which try *Le Dauphin* (29 rue Gémare) for its seafood, although it also operates as a 22-bedroom hotel. At *La Petite Auberge* (17 rue des Equipes-d'Urgence) you can even get budget cuisine minceur (haut-cuisine on a diet) for fixed-menu price of 58FF. Best-cheapest eats: *Au Petit Chef* (40 rue de l'Oratoire), crêpes from 10FF and omelettes from 20FF. Where to find most restaurants, including some of the cheaper places to eat: quartier Vaugueux near the château, and between the churches of St-Pierre and St-Jean.

• BEST BAR OR PUB IN TOWN: *Welcome Pub's Club* (22 rue de Falaise) is run by M. Olivier, who is the only Master Brewer in the region, and looks more like a Squadron Leader in the RAF than the owner of a French bar. He stocks a wide selection of distinctive beers, opening from 5pm 'til late'.

• MARKET DAYS: Friday morning (place St-Saveur) and Sunday morning (place Courtonne)

• WORTH A VISIT: For the historically-minded, there are two places that simply must be visited. The first is the *Abbaye aux Hommes*, which houses the tomb of William the Conqueror, an extraordinary exhibition of Caen under German occupation and a most moving audio-visual account of the D-Day landings. The second requires a short trip west to Bayeux where, of course, the famous tapestry is located. Oh and don't forget Sword, Juno, Gold and Omaha ...

• 1 SILVER MEDAL
• 2 BRONZE MEDALS

⑤ CARREFOUR

CC St-Clair
14200 Hérouville St-Clair
Tel: (31) 94.81.00

Selling area: 8,200m² (compare this with the size of other stores featured in the area, to gauge their relative size and you will have a rough idea of how big the range of wines, beers, spirits and other goods will be).

Opening hours? Mon-Sat 8.30am-10pm, closed Sun

Comment: Every attempt to solicit a civil response from Carrefour was ignored last time, and the chairman, M. René Brillet, was equally elusive this year.

The wines: We were not very impressed with the overall selection of wines for such a large store, and the prices were generally higher than other hypermarkets. Pommard at 30FF was an exception, and to be fair we were pleasantly surprised to find that Carrefour actually had an English wine, Car Taylor Hastings, in stock! There were even some decent Spanish wines from Torres, and we struck lucky with our random purchases, with three out of six not simply qualifying for recommendation in the *Guide*, but picking up a medal each along the way. So there you have it: although Carrefour's wine range looks uninteresting on the shelf, when randomly purchased samples are put to the test, they do well enough to earn 👍 👍. It could be, of course, that we were just lucky this year, as last time none of Carrefour's wines survived, but it does make us curious how a large selection of this store's biggest-selling lines might fare against those of its competitors under strictly blind conditions. Hopefully M. Brillet will have the courtesy to reply to our correspondence next year.

RED WINES

SILVER MEDAL   *Côtes de Bourg 1992 DFF, Carrefour* 17.90FF (£2.21) A touch of oak lifts this above other Bordeaux at this price.

BRONZE MEDAL   *Pommard 1992 Caves de l'Echanson* 30FF (£3.70) This wine is still tight and obviously needs a little more time to loosen up, but it is good Pinot, and amazingly cheap for Pommard (it was on offer at this price, so we're not sure what it might be by the time the book comes out).

WHITE WINES

BRONZE MEDAL   *Domaine Bellevue 1993 Touraine* 16FF (£1.98) The best-cheapest Sauvignon Blanc we tasted, this has good, clean varietal character and is a joy to drink. **Verdict?** 👍 👍

⑨ CAVE CHRISTIAN JACQ

21 rue des Jacobins
14000 Caen
Tel: (31) 23.84.02
English spoken? No
Opening hours? Mon 2.30pm-7.30pm, Tues-Sat 9.30am-12.30pm & 2.30pm-7.30pm, closed Sun
Parking? Metered parking in nearby streets (not easy)
Shopping trolleys? No
Do they offer to help carry the goods to the car? Yes
Methods of payment? French Francs, Traveller's cheques, Eurocheques, Visa, Mastercard, Access, American Express, Diners Card
Any wines for tasting in store? Yes, on demand
Comment: We spotted this lovely little specialist shop as we were driving around Caen. A gorgeous shop run by the very affable Christian Jacq, who stocks a fabulous range of 600 wines, from 25/30FF to the sky's the limit.
The wines: Although prices are not very

competitive, the choice here is wonderful. For example, there are no less than six different St-Nicolas-de-Bourgueil, five Madirans, four Cahors, several vintages of each Bordeaux château (going back to the 1970s in many cases), 40 Champagnes. The all too often neglected Alsace range is packed with goodies from such greats as Trimbach, Hugel and Schlumberger, plus heaps more. We even noticed a range of Madeira, which is nothing short of a miracle for the French, who have historically purchased only the cheapest Madeira, and think it is fit for nothing else but cooking with. After all this, we are only sorry that Christian Jacq's wines did not fare better. Perhaps he should have submitted some of those St-Nicolas-de-Bourgueil, Madirans and Cahors? In theory, this is a potential 🍾 🍾 🍾 🍾 outlet, but Christian Jacq was lucky to get 🍾 on the basis of our tastings.

RED WINES
Bonnnege Brouilly 1993 Cru de Beaujolais 38FF (£4.69) Soft and easy to drink.
Verdict? 🍾

★ BEST DRINKS OUTLET IN CAEN (JOINT)
• 1 GOLD MEDAL
• 4 BRONZE MEDALS

⑧ CAVES ENTREPÔTS
6 place Monseigneur des Hameaux
14000 Caen
Tel: (31) 38.26.80
English spoken? Yes
Opening hours? Mon-Fri 9.30am-12.30pm & 3pm-7.30pm, Sat 9.30am-7.30pm, Sun 10.30am-1pm
Parking? Plenty of parking in the square (Place Monseigneur des Hameaux)
Shopping trolleys? No
Do they offer to help carry the goods to the car? Yes
Methods of payment? Sterling, French Francs, Traveller's cheques, Eurocheques, Visa, Access, Mastercard
Any wines for tasting in store? Yes
Comment: This outlet is part of the Inter Caves group (*see also* branches in Calais, Cherbourg and St-Malo), which consists of approximately 90 shops spread throughout France, plus a few additional outlets in Germany.
The wines: We were promised a list, but did not receive one, and our representative reported a dozen Champagnes from smaller, lesser known producers, which sound interesting, but the only one submitted was Champagne De Saval, which does not exist as such, but is made by another

producer (Baron Albert, we think), and although drinkable was not special. Hopefully we can taste some real small producer Champagnes next time, but submitting a larger number of better selected wines this year has paid off, giving the Inter Caves group a far more impressive entry in this year's *Guide* than it got in the first edition.

RED WINES

BRONZE MEDAL   *Domaine le Pian 1992 Vin de Pays du Gard* 19FF (£2.35) Soft, silky blackcurrant fruit.

Chatellenie de Lastours NV Corbières 29FF (£3.58) Rich and robust, with a herbal-oak undertone.

GOLD MEDAL   *Château de Pech Redon 1991 La Clape* 29.50FF (£3.64) Absolutely delightful fruit underpinned by bubble-gum oak, which creates a sort of raspberry ripple flavour. Although it might not sound like it, this is an elegant, classy wine.

Massana 1991 Côtes du Roussillon 29.90FF (£3.69) Could be Rioja if we did not know better.

BRONZE MEDAL   *Bourgogne Pinot Noir 1992 Philippe de Marange* 35.70FF (£4.41) An elegant Burgundy for the price, with ripe-cherry Pinot Noir fruit.

BRONZE MEDAL   *Domaine Duseigneur 1991 Lirac* 39.50FF (£4.88) An elegant, fruity Rhône, but we have come across two versions of apparently the same wine: one with a neck-label that has the word 'Lirac' either side of the vintage, and the other with a neck-label that has 'Cru' one side of the vintage and 'Race' the other, and the latter of these seems to have a more smoky-toasty finish.

Juliénas 1992 Domaine de la Bottière 44FF (£5.43) Has some potential for development over the next year or two.

Saumur-Champigny 1992 Domaine du Val Brun 45FF (£5.56) This may lack charm on the nose, but it has good fruit underneath, and should develop more attractive bottle-aromas over the next 18 months or so.

Domaine des Lucques 1990 Graves 47FF (£5.80) Probably a lot better 18 months ago, but still makes a decent glass of Bordeaux, even if prematurely mellow.

WHITE WINES

Baron de Peyrac, Sauvignon 1993 Bordeaux Blanc 17.90FF (£2.21) Although this wine's fresh aroma shows good typicity, it is too soft to be classic Sauvignon, although this very softness is what makes it so easy to drink.

BRONZE MEDAL

Clos du Zahnacker 1988 Vin d'Alsace 60FF (£7.41)
One of the very few classic blends of Alsace, this
wine was probably easier to drink two years ago,
and will undoubtedly find greater harmony in two
years from now, but is currently in a stage of
development where the Riesling is battling with
the Gewurztraminer.

ROSÉ WINES
*Château la Croix de l'Hosanne 1993 Bordeaux
Clairet* 22.90FF (£2.83) Highly perfumed, off-dry
rosé with plenty of fruit.
Verdict? 👍👍👍

⑩ **CAVES THOREL**
32 rue Neuve St-Jean
14000 Caen
Tel: (31) 86.07.46
English spoken? Yes
Opening hours? Mon-Fri 7am-10pm
seven days a week
Parking? On the street (with some difficulty)
Shopping trolleys? No
Do they offer to help carry the goods to the car?
Yes
Methods of payment? Sterling, French Francs,
Belgian Francs, Traveller's cheques, Eurocheques,
Visa, Access
Any wines for tasting in store? 'Soon to be'
Comment: Small, upmarket, fine-wine shop with a
bar attached. The bar has stone arches, adding to
the nice, inviting ambience of the place.
The wines: The range is small, with very few
inexpensive wines, although there were a number
in the middle-price bracket.
Verdict? 👍

• 2 BRONZE MEDALS

④ **CHAMPION**
Route de Caen
14150 Ouistreham
Tel: (31) 96.88.89
Selling area: 1,400m² (compare this with the size
of other stores featured in the area, to gauge their
relative size and you will have a rough idea of
how big the range of wines, beers, spirits and
other goods will be).
Opening hours? Mon-Sat 8.30am-10pm, closed
Sun
Comment: Part of the Promodes group, which
owns Continent, Shopi and various other smaller

outlets. We made contact last year with no less than six top people at Promodes and its various offshoots, but to no avail, so this year we wrote to the managing director of Promodes, M. Pierre Merle, but he could not be bothered to reply either.

The wines: The range consists of primarily Bordeaux and the Southwest, a smattering of decent Burgundy (eg., Labouré Roi Pommard 1989 at 69.70FF), and a few interesting looking, domaine-bottled *cru* Beaujolais. There is a good selection of *petit châteaux*, especially from St-Émilion and its satellites, (top flight vintages 1989 and 1990). Champion also has a comparatively large selection of spirits for a French supermarket group. For one week in June, this store was selling the cheapest beer we could find anywhere, Brandenberg Bier Blonde at 19.95FF for 24 x 25cl bottles (beware: we occasionally see beers at seemingly cheaper prices, only to discover the pack contains 20, rather than 24, bottles – so check the number of contents before purchase).

Although we found the inexpensive white wines to be generally very boring, there is a good range of reds between 15-30FF (mainly Cahors, Côtes-du-Ventoux, and Côtes-de-Duras). Our biggest criticism of Champion is that all the bottles were standing upright, including the fine wines, yet of the six random purchases, four qualified for recommendation, which is good by French supermarket standards. Furthermore two of these picked up medals, and one was the best-cheapest wine of its style we found on the entire cross-Channel market. The two wines that did not warrant a recommendation were perfectly drinkable, even if they were not good enough for inclusion in this publication. On the basis of this performance, it is hard to see what M. Merle has to hide.

RED WINES

BRONZE MEDAL

Château Bois Clair 1993 Bordeaux 11.90FF (£1.47) Light but honest, easy-drinking basic Bordeaux.
Bourgogne Hautes Côtes de Beaune 1990 Labouré Roi 31.90FF (£3.94) Sweet Pinot fruit on the nose, firm structure and still unwinding, but a medium-term developer, not a long-term one. Good with food.
Château Saint-Lô 1989 Saint-Émilion 34FF (£4.20) Good fruit on a firm structure of ripe tannins.

ROSÉ WINES

BRONZE MEDAL
BEST-CHEAPEST ROSÉ
WINE OF THE YEAR

Cinsault Rosé 1993 J.P Chenet 11.80FF (£1.46)
Looks more like a brandy bottle than a wine
bottle, but who cares at this price, especially when
it's full of fruit with such good acidity. This is a
real wine at a make believe price (and for one
week in June, it was even cheaper, on offer at
9.95FF!).
Verdict? 👍👍

• 1 SILVER MEDAL
• 1 BRONZE MEDAL

② CONTINENT

Boulevard Mal Juin
14000 Caen
Tel: (31) 44.31.34
Selling area: 7,950m^2 (compare this with the size
of other stores featured in the area, to gauge their
relative size and you will have a rough idea of
how big the range of wines, beers, spirits and
other goods will be).
Opening hours? Mon-Sat 8.30am-10pm, closed
Sun
Comment: Part of the Promodes group, which
owns Continent, Shopi and various other smaller
outlets. We made contact last year with no less
than six top people at Promodes and its various
offshoots, but to no avail, so this year we wrote to
the managing director of Promodes, M. Pierre
Merle, but he could not be bothered to reply
either.
The wines: There is quite a big range in the larger
Continent stores such as this, but not a
particularly wonderful selection in the price
category most cross-Channel shoppers are
interested in (15-30FF), although we did strike
lucky with two of the six wines we purchased at
random. The Bordeaux selection is eclectic and
spotty, with some good *cru classé*, but prices are
not competitive, although they do have some on
offer (eg., Ducru-Beaucaillou 1991 at 86FF, and
Fieuzal at 72FF).

RED WINES

BRONZE MEDAL

Les Mélusines 1993 St-Nicolas-de-Bourgueil 27FF
(£3.33) A tasty wine indeed, and with an authentic
grassy Loire Cabernet edge that does not detract
from its drinkability.

WHITE WINES

SILVER MEDAL

**Jean Marie Strubbler Gewurztraminer 1993 Vin
d'Alsace** 22.90FF (£2.83) Good value
Gewurztraminer, with assertive, spicy fruit. The

acidity is somewhat high for this grape, giving the wine a finer balance than most.
Verdict? ⚑

• 1 BRONZE MEDAL

③ **INTERMARCHÉ**
69 avenue du Capitaine Guynemer
14000 Caen
Tel: (31) 84.48.76
Selling area: 2,300m² (compare this with the size of other stores featured in the area, to gauge their relative size and you will have a rough idea of how big the range of wines, beers, spirits and other goods will be).
Opening hours? Mon-Thurs 9am-12.15pm & 2pm-7.15, Fri 9am-12.15pm & 2pm-7.30pm, Sat 9am-7.15pm
Comment: Most Intermarché on the Channel coast are relatively small, and although they can be quite large further inland, this chain is more of the supermarket ilk than hypermarket. It is also relatively down-market, with a mostly dull and uninteresting range of wines, often dominated by a display of 3-litre wine containers. There are around a dozen different Champagnes, and the fine wines are usually displayed separately (we saw Ducru Beaucaillou 1989 at 85FF, and Pavillon Rouge 1990 at 105FF). We had no success with chairman Marcel Robin, who steadfastly refused to answer our correspondence. It was the same story as last year, with M. Le Goff, Intermarché's drinks buyer.
The wines: We purchased six wines along the same lines as those we bought at Auchan, and when it came to the crunch, Intermarché fared much better, with half of the wines warranting our recommendation, and one even picking up a Bronze medal. And two of those that did not qualify were perfectly drinkable, even if not special enough to qualify for the *Guide*. If only the management of this firm had enough faith in its products to submit a substantial range of its inexpensive wines, they might do well, if this random sampling is anything to go by.

RED WINES
Beaujolais NV Cuvée Joannès 12FF (£1.48)
Although not medal potential, you could have knocked us down with a feather when this wine, the second-cheapest Gamay submitted, turned out not only to be drinkable, but expressive of its variety, rather than *macération carbonique*.

Côtes-du-Rhône 1993 Réserve Lescarrat 13FF (£1.60) This soft and fruity wine has a touch more elegance than the other red Rhônes in its price category.

WHITE WINES

BRONZE MEDAL *Reuilly 1993 Cave PD* 22.90FF (£2.83) This fresh and assertive Sauvignon is not a wine for wimps. **Verdict?** 👍

• 1 BRONZE MEDAL

(1) SUPER U
185 route de Bayeux
14000 Caen
Tel: (31) 74.61.23
Selling area: 1,700m² (compare this with the size of other stores featured in the area, to gauge their relative size and you will have a rough idea of how big the range of wines, beers, spirits and other goods will be).
Opening hours? Mon-Sat 8.30am-10pm, closed Sun
Comment: Part of Système U, which also includes Unico and Hyper U, but all our letters and faxes to this group have been ignored.
The wines: Although Super U is quite a small supermarket, the wine selection is well presented on wooden shelves, looks interesting, with different wines than the normal supermarket choice, and all reasonably priced. The wines are mainly *petit vins*, but each region is represented. There is a fine wine section, and a good selection of half-bottles. No one expects much of Super U wines, yet our report this year is far more promising than what we had to say in the first edition, with four of the six randomly purchased wines qualifying for recommendation, and one even picking up a medal.

RED WINES
Vins de Pays des Pyrénées-Orientales NV CVVR 8.60FF (£1.06) A nice touch of tannin makes this wine, the third-cheapest red we came across, more suited to food than most of the very cheapest reds you will find.

BRONZE MEDAL *Le Pretoire des Ondines 1992 Bourgogne Pinot Noir* 23.20FF (£2.86) The cheapest Pinot Noir we tasted, and yet it has a purity of fruit and the true elegance of Pinot Noir. A light-bodied wine, maybe, and certainly not a great quality Pinot, but at this price category, it's a little gem.

WHITE WINES
Fringant 1992 Muscadet de Sèvre et Maine sur Lie
19.80FF (£2.44) A good dry white with some
fatness on the finish.

ROSÉ WINES
Domaine du Sémaphore NV Gris de Gris 11.80FF
(£1.46) Light, easy, clean fruit.
Verdict? 👍

★ *BEST DRINKS OUTLET
IN CAEN (JOINT)*
• 1 GOLD MEDAL
• 4 BRONZE MEDALS

(6) **VINS SUR VINGT**
17 rue Mer
14150 Ouistreham
Tel: (31) 96.54.16

AND

(7) **VINS SUR VINGT**
43 rue Neuve St-Jean
14000 Caen
Tel: (31) 85.69.83
English spoken? No
Opening hours? Mon-Sat 9.30am-12.15pm &
2.30pm-7.15pm, closed Sun
Parking? On street (quite difficult for the Caen
shop)
Shopping trolleys? No
Do they offer to help carry the goods to the car?
Yes
Methods of payment? French Francs,
Eurocheques, Visa, Mastercard, Access
Any wines for tasting in store? No
Comment: We discovered the Ouistreham shop
last year, but found it shut. This year it was open,
and we discovered another Vins sur Vingt in
Caen. Both are owned by M. Esnault Gilles, both
are equally attractive little shops, and both have
the same range of wines (and a few spirits), well
presented on shelves, with the better wines lying
down. The Ouistreham branch receives more Brits
because it is on the way to the ferry.
The wines: This upmarket wine shop has a very
good selection of claret and Sauternes, including
an impressive range of magnums, although the
prices are mostly more expensive than can be
found in the UK. There are some good
Burgundies, and a number of interesting little
numbers, such as Château Grillet 1990, which
costs 390FF a bottle. Although there are some
medium-priced products, Vins sur Vingt is really
a haven for the fine wine buff. Because of this, we
were not expecting the few, relatively inexpensive

wines submitted to perform particularly well in our blind tasting. We were, however, delighted to discover all but one of these not only warranted our recommendation, but picked up a medal. M. Esnault Gilles obviously selects his wines with great skill and knowledge.

RED WINES

BRONZE MEDAL

Château de la Limagère 1989 Bordeaux Supérieur 25FF (£3.09) After coming through a patch of 20 or so mostly boring or dodgy Bordeaux wines in this price category, we were delighted to find this had some real flavour and length, with a nice touch of tannin in the structure.

BRONZE MEDAL

Sablet 1991 Domaine de Boissan 30FF (£3.70) A tasty, tannic wine that will go well with stews and hot-pots in the winter months.

WHITE WINES

BRONZE MEDAL

Muscadet de Sèvre et Maine sur lie 1992 Domaine du Maillon 21FF (£2.59) Although this wine has some bottle-mature aromas, it is quite refreshing on the palate, with some zip and zing, and good tasty fruit.

GOLD MEDAL

Vouvray 1990 Maison Darragon 34FF (£4.20) One of the very few Vouvray to be labelled Sec, yet it is most definitely medium in sweetness and its beautifully clean, luscious fruit makes it easily the best we tasted.

BRONZE MEDAL

Château Simon 1991 Graves Supérieure 38FF (£4.69) Attractive botrytis nose, rich fruit on the palate and quite complex. Indubitably a good quality wine, but lacks the finesse to warrant anything higher than a Bronze at this price.
Verdict? 👍👍👍

CALAIS

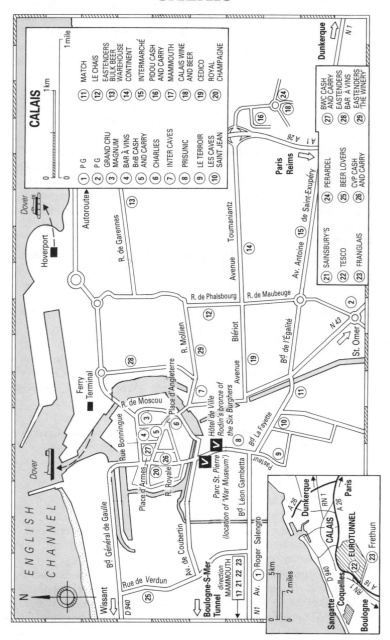

CALAIS

1. P G
2. P G
3. GRAND CRU MAGNUM
4. BAR À VINS
5. BnB CASH AND CARRY
6. CHARLIES
7. INTER CAVES
8. PRISUNIC
9. LE TERROIR
10. LES CAVES SAINT JEAN
11. MATCH
12. LE CHAIS
13. EASTENDERS BULK BEER WAREHOUSE
14. CONTINENT
15. INTERMARCHÉ
16. PIDOU CASH AND CARRY
17. MAMMOUTH
18. CALAIS WINE AND BEER
19. CEDICO
20. ROYAL CHAMPAGNE
21. SAINSBURY'S
22. TESCO
23. FRANGLAIS
24. PERARDEL
25. BEER LOVERS
26. CVP CASH AND CARRY
27. BWC CASH AND CARRY
28. EASTENDERS BAR À VINS
29. EASTENDERS 'THE WINERY'

The nearest of all the Channel ports, Calais receives up to 70 ferries, hovercraft and Seacats a day at the height of the season, whereas the second-busiest cross-Channel port, Cherbourg, receives a modest 14 ferries a day. With more than 11 million British travellers visiting Calais every year, tourism has certainly proved to be a nice little capitalist earner for its Communist controlled town council. Over two million trippers spent an estimated half billion pounds in the run-up to the first Christmas since the duty-free barriers came down, and it will be even more hectic this year, so we urge you to use the *Guide* to plan out your shopping route. You will save a lot of time and heartache.

Until just a few years ago, Calais was infamous for beaches littered with half-blitzed bunkers and great concrete wedges that were erected to prevent allies from landing, but most of these relics have now been erased. Quite why it took 50 years to clear up the mess is a puzzle, but almost every aspect of Calais' post-war record has been a mystery. Its industrially blighted coastline is an architectural and environmental nightmare, even without Rommel's assault course. With one sight of this and the autoroute beckoning, it is no wonder that most travellers using Calais have never seen the town. On the one hand, it is good that you can roll off the ferry and be on your journey without even a glimpse of the town, reaching Champagne or Paris within two hours of hitting French soil. On the other, if you do make your way through the drab outskirts of Calais, you will discover a quaint Old Town surrounded by water on all sides, which really has some charm. However, should you decide to do this be sure to keep your eyes peeled for the very first turning right (signposted Centre Ville) because if you get caught up with the rest of the traffic, you will be on the autoroute and miles from Calais before you even realise what has happened. If you are going into Calais for a hypermarket, you will find the Mammouth in a far brighter, more pleasant Centre Commercial than the one where Continent is located.

Did you know?

• Calais belonged to the English for 210 years.
• Calais belonged to the Spanish between 1596 and 1598.
• Calais was once a hive of pirate activity, from where the infamous Pedrogue plundered British merchant shipping, causing Edward III to describe Calais as 'that nest of pirates'.
• The most important work of art in Calais also reflects the English conflict. Rodin's famous 19th century bronze outside the Hôtel de Ville depicts the *Six Burghers* who, during the Hundred Years War, were forced to surrender to Edward III wearing nothing but their

shirts. The English king demanded that six of the town's most respected burghers bring him the keys to the castle and beg his mercy, but they had to be barefoot and clad only in nightshirts, with a noose around their necks. Rodin clearly shows the wretched look of their fear and humiliation, before they were spared upon the direct intervention by Philippine, Edward's French wife, who was bearing his child at the time.

• The first regular cross-Channel ferry to operate between Great Britain and the Continent began in 1821, when the steam boat Rob Roy went into service between Dover and Calais.

• The Channel Tunnel was first conceived by a French engineer almost 200 years ago, and Napoléon took considerable interest in the project, but it was shelved when war with England resumed.

• After running up gambling debts and quarrelling with the Prince Regent, the English dandy, George 'Beau' Brummel, fled to Calais, where he lived out the rest of his days in self-exile, broke and, for the last three years, an imbecile in a pauper's lunatic asylum.

Calais Factfile

• HOW TO GET THERE: P&O (75 minutes), Stena Sealink (90 minutes) and Hoverspeed (35 minutes) all operate out of Dover (*see* pages 340-355 for details of service and prices).

• LOCATION AND DISTANCES: Situated 34km (21 miles) north of Boulogne, Calais is 40km (25 miles) from Dunkerque, 60km (37 miles) from the Belgium border and 92km (57 miles) from Oostende, 176km (110 miles) from Dieppe, 283km (177 miles) from Le Havre, 344km (215 miles) from Caen, 464km (290 miles) from Cherbourg, 510km (319 miles) from St-Malo, 691km (432 miles) from Roscoff, 272km (169 miles) from Reims and 292km (181 miles) from Paris.

• POPULATION: 80,000

• TOURIST INFORMATION OFFICE: 12 boulevard Georges Clémenceau, 62100 Calais, tel: (21) 96.62.40. Open Mon-Sat 9am-1pm & 2pm-7pm.

• WHERE TO STAY: During the peak season, it is always best to book your hotel in advance, but if you are caught out, try the Tourist Information Centre, which offers a free accommodation service, keeping track of all the vacancies left in the town. The best place to stay: *Holiday Inn Garden Court* (boulevard des Alliés, tel: (21) 34.69.69) might not be the most Gallic establishment in Calais, but it does have by far the best appointed rooms in town, a double en-suite ranging from 420-500FF (£52-62). Some cheap but clean stays include: *Hôtel Liberté* (boulevard Jacquard, tel: (21) 96.10.10) where a small but modern double with private bath and TV will cost 155FF; *Hôtel le Littoral* (71 rue Aristide Briand, tel: (21) 34.47.28) where a large double with shower costs 150FF; *Cottage Hôtel* (rue de Tunis, tel: (21) 96.06.06) surrounded by columns and lit-up at night, this looks more like a wedding cake than a hotel, but has very clean and modern double rooms en-suite with TV for 255FF.

• RESTAURANTS: Most critics will say that the best places to eat in town are *La Channel* (3 boulevard Résistance) and *Au Côte d'Argent* (1 Digue Gaston Berthe, overlooking Calais beach), but, good though they are, we think *George V* (36 rue Royale) is at least its equivalent, and *La Diligence* (7 rue Edmond Roche) even better. We have just found *Le Pacific* (40 rue du Duc de Guise), which was recommended to us by the owner of *Le Terroir* (see the entry on this wine shop below), no doubt because he supplies some of the wines, but turned out to deserve a mention. Not only is the wine list at *Le Pacific* good, but the owner also has a good private cellar on the premises, from which he might be persuaded to sell you something, if you express an interest. The menus start at 80FF and although the food is good, it is not special, but where in Calais can you find a cuisine that is special? There are numerous cheap eating houses in the town, including some decent cheap pizzerias and if you are one of those Out To Flunch Fanatics, you can always try the ludicrously cheap Flunch at the Continent hypermarket. *Taverne Kronenbourg* (46 rue Royale) is a really lively venue with a good 75FF fixed-price menu and friendly service. At *Videotel* (RN1, 62231 Coquelles) you can choose from a fairly interesting menu or eat and drink yourself silly at the Buffet, which for 75FF lets you eat as much as you like and drinks are included in the price. Best-cheapest eats: *Court Paille* (on the roundabout at the junction between the A26 and RN43) for a three course fixed-price menu at 59FF including wine or beer. Where to find most restaurants, including some of the cheaper places to eat: rue Royale and boulevard Jacquard.

• MARKET DAYS: All day Thursday and Saturday morning (place de Crève-Coeur)

• WORTH A VISIT: Some of the medieval defences that withstood the siege in 1346 and 1347 of Edward III (Calais was, of course, under English sovereignty for more than 200 years) have also miraculously survived the far more extensive bombardment inflicted by Allied bombers in the Second World War, warranting a walk around the perimeter of the old quarter. The War Museum has a fascinating collection of wartime artifacts in a building that housed the German Navy's centre of communications for Northern France during the Second World War, the museum is located in Parc St-Pierre on the opposite side of boulevard Jacquard to the *Hôtel de Ville* and Rodin's bronze of the *Six Burghers*. Halfway to Boulogne along the N1 you will come across the Eurotunnel Information Centre, which might not sound very exciting, but does provide a fascinating overview of one of the world's greatest engineering feats, including an audio-visual extravaganza that consists of not less than 46 projectors, 14 synchron-ised films and a laser gun. There is also a café, gift shop and a viewing tower from which you have an unparalleled view of the massive Eurotunnel complex, which in addition to the terminal itself, has a vast shopping complex called Cité Europe.

RUNNER UP FOR
BEST CROSS-CHANNEL
OUTLET OF THE YEAR
★ *BEST DRINKS OUTLET*
IN CALAIS

④ **BAR À VINS**
52 place d'Armes
62100 Calais
Tel: (21) 96.98.31
English spoken? Yes
Opening hours? 9am-8pm daily, closed Wed

- 5 GOLD MEDALS
- 6 SILVER MEDALS
- 6 BRONZE MEDALS

Parking? Yes (plenty of space in the place d'Armes)

Shopping trolleys? Yes

Do they offer to help carry the goods to the car? Yes

Methods of payment? Sterling, Irish Punts, French Francs, Traveller's cheques, Eurocheques, Visa, Access, Mastercard, American Express, Diners Card

Any wines for tasting in store? Yes

Comment: Luc Gille's favourite story for his English customers concerns the great *débarquement* commemorations of June 1994. He was sitting in a deck-chair on Calais beach waiting for the first ships to appear on the horizon. He'd been there thirty minutes and had not seen a single ship, then one moment there was nothing, the next an armada. With thousands of ships on the horizon, Luc's friend, who was occupying the deck-chair next to him, turned and said in a matter-of-fact tone, 'They surely all can't be cross-Channel shoppers.' For newcomers to the *Guide*, you should know that we have nothing but praise and warm affection for this little venture, run by Luc Gille, who was born in Provence and sells wine because he loves it. A sweet little shop that also operates as a bar and café, hence the name Bar à Vins, you can taste or even drink the wines before buying them or you can just stop off for a cup of coffee. He delivers his samples personally, in his vintage van with dinky Bar à Vins signs either side. Twice he has done this, and twice we have hoped that Luc's wines would fare well, but the tastings are blind, the bottles coded, and we have no idea how any retailer has done until everything is keyed into the computer, and we print up the results. But twice a smile has grown on our faces as we look at these results.

The wines: The Bar à Vins is not for the 10FF a bottle brigade. The range of wines is very classic in the French sense, so do not expect anything from beyond the nation's borders, let alone from the New World.

RED WINES

GOLD MEDAL

Domaine de St-Julien-les-Vignes 1992 Cuvée du Château 28FF (£3.46) Although the fruit is attractively sweet and succulent, with intriguing aromas of herbal scrub, there is an undeveloped inky texture, but this merely indicates the wine will be even better in a year or two. Look out for

Cuvée du Château on the label, as the cheaper, basic Domaine de St-Julien-les-Vignes has an almost identical label, but is nowhere near the quality of this wine. There is nothing wrong with the basic Domaine de St-Julien-les-Vignes: it is perfectly drinkable, but it does not come up to the standards set by this *Guide*, whereas the Cuvée de Château is easily a gold medal winner, and it is only 3FF more expensive!

SILVER MEDAL | *Domaine des Chaberts 1991 Coteaux Varois Cuvée Spéciale* 30FF (£3.70) Full-bodied well structured with a good depth of youthful fruit, this wine should improve for another two or three years at least.

Côtes-du-Rhône, La Vieillo Jasso 1992 Château de Husson 34FF (£4.20) A light-bodied Rhône with a peppery nose and a sweet finish.

BRONZE MEDAL | *Domaine Barreau-La-Grave 1990 Premières Côtes de Blaye* 42FF (£5.19) Elegantly structured with attractive fruit and some style.

BRONZE MEDAL | *Bourgogne Côte Chalonnaise 1989 Michel Champion* 56FF (£6.91) Sweet, ripe and nicely mature fruit.

GOLD MEDAL | *Auxey-Duresses Côte de Beaune 1990 Bernard Fèvre* 70FF (£8.64) Obviously very good quality, but it is quite concentrated, and needs time. If you are going to pay this money for a good Burgundy, you should be prepared to lay it down for a few years.

SILVER MEDAL | *Châteauneuf-du-Pape 1990 Château de Husson* 82FF (£10.12) Soft and easy to drink on the one hand, yet rich, with quite intense, spicy fruit on the other. It is the ripeness of the tannins that is responsible, providing a substantial yet very supple structure to support the fruit. Drink now or in five years.

GOLD MEDAL | *Pommard 1992 Bernard Fèvre* 118FF (£14.57) Pommard as it should be. Still very young and will mature gracefully into an elegantly rich and sensuous Burgundy, but the fruit is already supple and delicious. Bernard Fèvre is an excellent grower, and normally very reliable, but we were very concerned by the unpleasant esters dominating the nose and a disagreeable sourness on the palate of all three samples we received of his Saint-Romain 1992 (white). We normally do not bother to condemn a wine in the *Guide*, as we prefer to fill the space available with as many positive recommendations as possible, but as we have gone overboard about Fèvre's Pommard, readers may feel inclined to buy other Fèvre wines, and we want to make sure that you avoid the Saint-Romain 1992, although you should stand an above average chance of success if you take pot-luck with any other Fèvre wine.

WHITE WINES

SILVER MEDAL   *Muscadet de Sèvre et Maine, Sur Lie 1993 Cuvée des Lions, Serge Saupin* 32FF (£3.95) This wine would give a young Mâcon a run for its money.

BRONZE MEDAL   *Mâcon-Villages 1990 Claudius Rongier* 36FF (£4.44) This mature Burgundy has lots of ripe fruit, and is big and fat for Mâcon.

BRONZE MEDAL   *Tokay Pinot Gris, Réserve du Domaine, Vin d'Alsace 1992 G. Metz* 46FF (£5.68) The fresh banana undertone in this wine will eventually transform into the spicy character that Alsace Pinot Gris is famous for, although its acidity balance suggests more of a medium-term developer than a long-term one.

BRONZE MEDAL   *Vouvray 1992 Domaine La Saboterie* 49FF (£6.05) The Chenin fruit in this wine has good, varietal, greengage character. Clean as a whistle and medium-dry.

GOLD MEDAL   *Vouvray, Moelleux 1990 Domaine La Saboterie* 49FF (£6.05) Not as sweet as one expects from a moelleux, but this is very good quality, with oodles of beautifully clean, medium-sweet, tangy-rich Chenin fruit.

GOLD MEDAL   *Grand Cru Muenchberg Riesling 1992 Gérard Metz* 56FF (£6.91) The youthful almondy-fruit in this wine demonstrates its potential as a classic Riesling, if cellared for at least 2-3 years.

Petit Chablis 1992 Daniel Gounot 64FF (£7.90) A good, lightly balanced, oaky-fruity wine.

ROSÉ WINES

Domaine de St Julien les Vignes 1993 Cuvée du Château 28FF (£3.46) Better than most Provence rosé.

BRONZE MEDAL   *Domaine des Chaberts 1993 Coteaux Varois Cuvée Spéciale* 30FF (£3.70) Soft, easy to drink, with refreshing fruit.

Château de Villepreux 1993 Bordeaux Rosé 39FF (£4.81) Very fresh aromas, exceptionally clean, crisp fruit, with a touch of spritz. Good food wine.

SILVER MEDAL   *Pinot Noir, Vin d'Alsace 1992 G. Metz* 48FF (£5.93) The strawberry fruit in this wine is typical of good Alsace Pinot Noir, but its style is betwixt and between rosé and red.

SPARKLING WINES

SILVER MEDAL
Champagne François Heucq NV Brut Réserve 95FF
(£11.73) A touch sweet for a *brut*, but has plenty of
ripe, biscuity-mature fruit.

SILVER MEDAL
*Champagne A. Lancelot-Pienne NV Brut, Blanc de
Blancs* 125FF (£15.43) A rich and satisfying
Champagne with very creamy fruit.
Verdict? 👍👍👍👍

• 2 GOLD MEDALS

㉕ **BEER LOVERS**
Avenue de Verdun
62100 Calais
Tel: (21) 97.72.00
English spoken? Yes
Opening hours? 24 hours a day, seven days a
week
Parking? Yes
Shopping trolleys? Yes
Do they offer to help carry the goods to the car?
Yes
Methods of payment? Sterling, Irish Punt, French
Francs, Belgian Francs, Traveller's cheques,
Eurocheques, Visa, Mastercard, Access
Any wines for tasting in store? Yes (but not
Champagne)
Comment: A recently opened (January 1994) cash
& carry in what looks like an old supermarket site,
Beer Lovers is packed high with pallets of beer
and cheap wine, all of which the British eagerly
buy, and apparently come back for more.
The wines: Although Beer Lovers picked up a
couple of golds, they were both for beers. Only
one wine passed our test. The owner, Gérard
Heddebaux, told us 'We sell over 60,000 bottles of
Liebfraumilch, and 50,000 bottles of Lambrusco
every week ... they might not be to our taste, but
they are very appealing to most English
customers'. No Liebfraumilch or Lambrusco we
tasted this year warranted a mention in the *Guide*,
and Beer Lovers were neither the cheapest, nor the
best of those we encountered. Most Liebfraumilch
and Lambrusco drinkers are unpretentious people
who simply want a fresh and fruity wine, with a
flowery aroma and a grapy taste, but we found
none that stood out in these respects. Most
Liebfraumilch and Lambrusco drinkers will
probably find the Beer Lovers wines acceptable,
but our job is to look for the exception, not the
rule. As far as we are concerned, there is such a
thing as a gold medal Liebfraumilch, and when
we find it, then every Liebfraumilch drinker will

be able to judge the difference for themselves. We hope that Beer Lovers shows us such a wine for the next edition, although I am sure our opinion does not worry M. Heddebaux, who sells over 3 million bottles of Liebfraumilch each year anyway.

RED WINES
50ème Anniversaire 1944-1994 NV Bordeaux 15.40FF (£1.90) An assertive wine with good grassy Cabernet fruit, this is a decent food wine for the price.

BEERS
Beck's, Bräueri Beck 4.22FF (52p) per 33cl bottle, sold in 101.25FF (£12.50) Light and crisp, this is better than the Mosel Bier (The Calais Wine and Beer Company), but only just, and it's three times the price – hence no Bronze. God only knows why it is so popular. It is, however, much cheaper here than it is at Sainsbury's cross-Channel outlet, where it costs less than 71p for a 27.5cl bottle!

GOLD MEDAL
BEST-VALUE LIGHT BEER OF THE YEAR

Grolsch Premium Lager 4.37FF (54p) per 50cl can, sold in 24s at 104.90FF (£12.95) This fine, delicate, flowery-hopped brew was by far the best-value lager style beer we tasted: ten times the quality of Beck's and nothing like the price, although Grolsch is even cheaper at The Wine & Beer Company (Calais and Cherbourg), where it costs just 46p for a 50cl can.

GOLD MEDAL
BEST-CHEAPEST DARK BEER OF THE YEAR
BEST-VALUE DARK BEER OF THE YEAR
BEST-QUALITY DARK BEER OF THE YEAR

Draught Guinness 6.06FF (75p) per 50cl can, sold in 24s at 145.39FF (£17.95) The finest draught stout available. Guinness invented the 'widget' to generate a head not with CO_2, which makes its bottled Guinness so fizzy, but with nitrogen, the gas that is responsible for the dense, creamy head of its famous Draught Guinness, when drawn straight from the barrel. To achieve this in a can was a technological breakthrough. The difference between Guinness and Murphy's is that although both are creamy and mellow, Guinness has a touch more toasted-roasted, true stout bitterness, which gives it the cleaner finish and, in our opinion, the edge over Murphy's, hence its Best-Quality award. We still love Murphy's, and if you prefer your stout to have more mellowness, then Murphy's will be the Best-Quality. When comparing prices, remember that this is a full half-litre (if that's not Irish), whereas the Murphy's is 44cl.
Dragon Stout, Desnoes & Geddes (Kingston,

Jamaica) 5.75FF (71p) per 28.4cl bottle, sold in 24s at 137.30FF (£16.95) This gets a mention as a curiosity. We even opened up a second bottle to see if it should taste like it did, but it was exactly the same. At least it gets marks for consistency! We could not possibly drink this intensely sweet, mint-coffee and molasses brew, but maybe there is somebody out there with a cast-iron stomach who could?
Verdict?

• 1 GOLD MEDAL
• 2 SILVER MEDALS

(5) BnB CASH & CARRY

22 rue Madrid
62100 Calais
Tel: (21) 34.41.78
English spoken? A little
Opening hours? 9am-8pm seven days a week
Parking? Only on street
Shopping trolleys? No
Do they offer to help carry the goods to the car? Yes
Methods of payment? Sterling, Irish Punts, French Francs, Eurocheques, Visa, Access, Mastercard
Any wines for tasting in store? Yes
Comment: BnB stands for Bernard and Beatrice (Cornille), the two owners of this operation, which is located down a side street, but quite easy to find. An upmarket shop it is not: you are even invited to write your own graffiti on one of the walls!
The wines: The range starts from cheap and, frankly, not so nice, carrying through to more expensive wines. Most of the finer wines are Bordeaux. The more expensive wines from Burgundy and other French regions do not look very exciting, but BnB does have a few interesting or odd little lines, such as Tokaji 4 Puttonyos. The Cornilles also sell a small selection of Belgian beers (not tasted), along with fancy beer glasses to drink them from.

RED WINES

Bin 39 NV Cuvée du Patron, Vin Rouge 11FF (£1.36) If the French want to sell this sort of wine to the Brits, they should take a leaf out of Piat d'Or's book and describe it on the label as 'soft and fruity' not 'medium dry red'. Brits are notorious for talking dry, drinking sweet, which is why Brits made and marketed Piat d'Or, the sweetest dry red wine in the world. Now it's the world's largest-selling red wine. Bin 39 and others like it should take note.

GOLD MEDAL *Merlot 1991 Domaine de la Caumette* 36FF (£4.44) Big and rich, but not fat, this wine has oodles of ripe Merlot fruit, well supported by oak and supple tannins. A very classy *vin de pays.*

SILVER MEDAL *Château Suau 1989 Premières Côtes de Bordeaux* 38.50FF (£4.75) A classy little Bordeaux with excellent depth of fruit and a fine, supple tannin structure, making it an ideal accompaniment to a good Sunday roast.

WHITE WINES
Chablis 1993 Jean Bouchard 45FF (£5.56) Quite fat for a Chablis, yet has the correct acidity, and a good depth of well structured flavour.

FORTIFIED WINES
SILVER MEDAL *Muscat de Rivesaltes NV Arnaud de Villeneuve* 49FF (£6.05) Beautifully well-made with delicious, elegant, musky aromas and rich, succulent, satisfying fruit. Lovely balance.
Verdict? 👍👍

㉗ **BWC CASH & CARRY**
62 place d'Armes
62100 Calais
Tel: (21) 34.72.00
English spoken? Yes
Opening hours? 10am-8pm seven days a week
Parking? Yes (place d'Armes)
Shopping trolleys? No
Do they offer to help carry the goods to the car? Yes
Methods of payment? Sterling, French Francs, Traveller's cheques, Eurocheques, Visa, Mastercard, Access, American Express
Any wines for tasting in store? Yes
Comment: This small shop opposite the Bar à Vins in the place d'Armes is crammed with beers and wines. Owned by a small Chinaman called Mr Chung, BWC had been opened just two months when we called, but was heaving with English customers frantically trying to buy whatever they could lay their hands on.
The wines: The bulk of the range is cheap, mostly *vins de table* and nondescript beers, although we noted the odd interesting wine. Only one of the three wines we tasted passed the test, but we obviously need to taste a larger selection to come

to any realistic conclusion.

RED WINES
Montagne St-Émilion NV Grand Vin de Bordeaux
24FF (£2.96) Light and very soft, yet fills the
mouth with flavour.
Verdict? ♟

(18) THE CALAIS WINE & BEER COMPANY
Rue de Judée
Zone Marcel Doret
62100 Calais
Tel: (21) 97.63.00
English spoken? Yes
Opening hours? 7am-10pm seven days a week
Parking? Yes (private car park)
Shopping trolleys? Yes
Do they offer to help carry the goods to the car?
Yes
Methods of payment? Sterling, French Francs,
Traveller's cheques, Eurocheques, Visa, Access
Any wines for tasting in store? Yes
Additional services:
* Orders can be placed through the London shop
(0181 875 1900) so that the goods will be packed
and ready for your collection
Comment: This British-owned operation probably
has the best location in Calais, as far as attracting
British ferry travellers is concerned. Most
travellers heading for the ferry will notice this
warehouse-type operation, even if they have never
heard of it. The Calais Wine & Beer Company is
owned by Marco Attard, who started off selling
wine from a leased London lock-up, and sleeping
in the empty boxes at night. Now he owns four
outlets in two countries, a proper bed and a real
bedroom. On 1 November 1994 he is due to open
up a second cross-Channel branch in Cherbourg.
The wines: We found the range fairly
comprehensive in the first edition, and it has
improved since then, hence its extra 🍷, although
Portugal still gets such a meagre coverage that it
may as well not exist. The Spanish section has
been greatly enhanced, mostly with the help of
Torres wines, but there are one or two other
interesting additions. A good selection of
inexpensive fizz nicely complements a handful of
decent Champagnes. Australia, New Zealand,
Chile, South Africa, California and Eastern Europe
are all well served in relation to the overall size of

the range. We would like to see a better choice from Alsace, and a couple of serious German wines, but would anyone buy them?

RED WINES
Château Laval 1993 Costières de Nîmes 15.31FF (£1.89) Soft, easy-drinking red.
Rioja Vega 1992 Bodegas Muerza 19.28FF (£2.38) This light, peppery red could come from anywhere, but at this price you cannot expect much more from Rioja.
Sliven Cabernet Sauvignon 1987 Reserve 20.17FF (£2.49) Not a bad drop of wine, but when it comes to Bulgarian Cabernet Sauvignon, the Sliven 1987 is not as rich or as satisfying as the Lovico 1988.

BRONZE MEDAL | *Denham Estate 1993 Shiraz Cabernet Sauvignon* 26.65FF (£3.29) There is jamminess that should not be present in an Australian wine of this cross-Channel price, but the menthol-vanilla undertones to the fruit provides the overriding interest in this wine.

SILVER MEDAL | *Cooks Endeavour Collection 1992 Cabernet Sauvignon - Pinot Noir* 28.27FF (£3.49) Despite its higher proportion of Cabernet grapes, this wine seemed to be dominated by Pinot Noir when tasting against Cabernet or Bordeaux-type blends, yet sticks out like a sore thumb amongst Pinot wines, making this a very ripe, easy to drink hybrid.

Denham Estate 1993 Cabernet Sauvignon 30.70FF (£3.79) Rather grassy and astringent for Oz Cabernet, but quite a good wine nonetheless.

BRONZE MEDAL | *Santa Rita Reserva 1990 Cabernet Sauvignon* 32.32FF (£3.99) Rather inky and soupy, but there is no denying the fruit and satisfying flavour in this wine.

SILVER MEDAL | *Côte de Beaune Villages 1989 Dominique Laurent* 48.28FF (£5.96) Mature plummy Pinot fruit. Nice now, but will be even better in 2-3 years.

Villa Antinori Chianti Classico 1989 Riserva 48.92FF (£6.04) Soft and easy to drink, with plenty of fruit.

SILVER MEDAL | *Château Musar 1987 Gaston Hochar* 53.38FF (£6.59) Succulent, perfumed fruit: ideal to sip on its own.

BRONZE MEDAL | *Torres Gran Coronas 1988 Reserva* 56.62FF (£6.99) At an intermediate point in its development, this vintage of Torres Gran Coronas has lost its youthful flush of life and will develop into a serious, complex wine in 2-3 years.

SILVER MEDAL | *Château de Lescours 1987 Saint-Émilion Grand*

Cru 56.62FF (£6.99) The fruit-gum aroma and flavour of this wine is more like Burgundy than Bordeaux, but this is no criticism of the wine as a wine *per se*, as we certainly enjoyed it very much.

SILVER MEDAL *Amiral de Beychevelle 1990 Saint-Julien* 89.02FF (£10.99) An elegant wine that will continue to improve over the next 2-3 years.

GOLD MEDAL
BEST-QUALITY RED
WINE OF THE YEAR
Penfolds Cabernet Sauvignon Bin 707 1990 South Australia 101.25FF (£12.50) Too many blind tastings end up making the biggest wines the best, but this is one case when the biggest wine truly is the best! Not a cheap wine, but this is the best price we could find, and it is £2.49 cheaper than Oddbins sell it for in the UK. There is no disguising the quality of this dark star; you could put it in a blind tasting of Bordeaux 1st Growths and its huge, intense, complex flavours would punch their way through. If, however, you want to drink it at its peak, then you'll have to wait until at least 2004.

WHITE WINES
Santa Rita 120 1993 Riesling 24.22FF (£2.99) Fresh, petrolly Riesling nose and totally dry fruit. A bit big for a Riesling by European standards, but has a good structure to accompany food.
Denham Estate 1993 Semillon Chardonnay 26.65FF (£3.29) Standard Semillon that has been lifted by, rather than beefed-up with, a decent dollop of ubiquitous Chardonnay. Best drunk within the next nine months.
Torres Gran Vina Sol 1992 Chardonnay 29.57FF (£3.65) Nice, fresh and tasty dry white wine, but very little Chardonnay character.
Principe de Viana 1992 Chardonnay 31.19FF (£3.85) Quite a nice, tasty wine with not as much wood influence as there is on the Principe de Viana tinto.

SILVER MEDAL *Orvieto Classico, Campogrande 1993 Abboccato, Antinori* 31.51FF (£3.89) Gosh! If only all Italian wines were as well-made as this. Crystal-clear and refreshingly clean, with mouthwatering medium-sweet fruit. A joy to drink.

GOLD MEDAL *Seaview 1993 Chardonnay* 32.32FF (£3.99) Really luscious! Bags of oak, but even a purist would have to admit that there is more than enough succulent fruit to take it.

SILVER MEDAL *Cooks Discovery Collection 1992 Chardonnay* 32.32FF (£3.99) Lots of oak, but very rich and weighty, with lemony acidity and a touch of ripe peach on the finish. Good food wine, especially

with smoked fish or meat.
Cooks Discovery Collection 1993 Sauvignon Blanc
32.32FF (£3.99) Good, but not great, New Zealand
Sauvignon in typical ripe gooseberry style.
Château des Herbeux 1989 Bourgogne Chardonnay
40.42FF (£4.99) An oily-textured, oaky wine that is
now at its best.

SPARKLING WINES

BRONZE MEDAL

Seppelt NV Premier Cuvée Brut 40.42FF (£4.99)
Very rich, fresh, creamy-lemony fruit. A lively and
satisfying sparkling wine.
*Champagne Rolland d'Orfeuil NV Brut Extra
Quality* 64.72FF (£7.99) Decent fizz with sweet,
clean and creamy fruit.

BRONZE MEDAL

Champagne Jacquesson & Fils NV Perfection, Brut
96.79FF (£11.95) Fine quality for a second label
Champagne. Has some complexity.

BEERS

BRONZE MEDAL
*BEST-CHEAPEST LIGHT
BEER OF THE YEAR*

Mosel Bier, Amos (Metz) 1.38FF (17p) per 25cl
bottle, sold in 24s at 32.56FF (£4.02) Not too gassy,
with a good smooth flavour, this is the best cheap
beer we could find. Although 2p more expensive
than the very cheapest cross-Channel beers, would
you rather buy 24 drinkable bottles at 11p each or
24 undrinkable bottles at 9p each? And believe us
when we say that some of the cheap 25cl beers we
tasted were undrinkable (some were still
fermenting inside the bottle, were milky in colour,
and sour to taste).

GOLD MEDAL
*BEST-QUALITY LIGHT
BEER OF THE YEAR*

Budweiser Budvar, Budweiser Budbräu 4.72FF
(58p) per 33cl bottle, sold in 24s at 113.32FF
(£13.99) In terms of pure quality, Budweiser
Budvar (look out for 'Budvar', which indicates
that it is the genuine article, which should not be
confused with the bland-tasting Budweiser
brewed in the USA, or under licence in the UK)
was unbeatable.

GOLD MEDAL
*BEST-VALUE LIGHT
BEER OF THE YEAR*

Grolsch Premium Lager 3.71FF (46p) per 50cl can,
sold in 24s at 88.94FF (£10.98) This fine, delicate,
flowery-hopped brew was by far the best-value
lager style beer we tasted: ten times the quality
of Beck's for almost a third of the price that you
would have to pay for Beck's at Sainsbury's.
Verdict? 👍👍👍👍

⑩ **LES CAVES SAINT JEAN**
4 place Crèvecoeur
62100 Calais
Tel: (21) 36.09.50
English spoken? A little

Opening hours? Tues-Sat 9.30am-12.15pm & 3pm-7pm, closed Sun & Mon

Parking? Yes (lots of space in the place Crèvecoeur)

Shopping trolleys? No

Do they offer to help carry the goods to the car? Yes

Methods of payment? Sterling, Irish Punts, French Francs, Traveller's cheques, Eurocheques, Visa, Access, Mastercard, American Express, Diners Card

Any wines for tasting in store? Yes, but not so much in the try-before-you-buy ilk, more as promotional event that is held most Saturdays, when a producer will often be there to present his own wines.

Comment: Annick Castille is the friendly owner of this small shop, which, she claims, has a range of 400 different wines, although where most of these are we could not deduce.

The wines: The range in the shop looks small to us, and not too inspiring at that. Maybe she has access to many more, much better wines somewhere else, but even if she does, it begs the question why they are not on display and those that are, are! We received a beautifully hand-written list last year, but it did not indicate who the producers are, and was thus totally useless. We did not even get a list this year, but we did receive samples, albeit only three, and two of those failed the test. We like you Ms. Castille and would love to give you a glowing report, so why not help us to help you by supplying a list indicating the domaine or producer for every wine, and a more representative selection to taste next time?

RED WINES
Château Frontenac 1990 Bordeaux 27.20FF (£3.36)
Young, fruity style.
Verdict? ♟

RUNNER UP FOR BEST CROSS-CHANNEL SUPERMARKET OF THE YEAR

⑲ **CEDICO**
Rue Delaroche
62100 Calais
Tel: (21) 96.75.17
Selling area: 1,500m²

AND

CEDICO

• 1 GOLD MEDAL

- 3 SILVER MEDALS
- 5 BRONZE MEDALS

34 rue Bauduin
62340 Guines
Tel: (21) 82.63.00
Selling area: 1,200m^2

AND

CEDICO
Avenue des Alliés
62370 Audruicq
Tel: (21) 35.31.64
Selling area: 1,800m^2 (compare this with the size of other stores featured in the area, to gauge their relative size and you will have a rough idea of how big the range of wines, beers, spirits and other goods will be).
Opening hours? Mon-Sat 9am-12noon & 2.30pm-7pm, closed Sun
Foire aux Vins: Two each year – [1] Easter, [2] Sept/Oct
Comment: Small but bright and welcoming, Cedico stores have more of a local supermarket image. Cedico belongs to the Catteau group, which was taken over by Tesco in 1993, and includes the Hyper Cedico and Cedimarche chains.
The wines: This chain's performance should be a salutary lesson to other French supermarket and hypermarket groups because although Cedico does not stock a particularly large range, and we spied nothing outstanding on its shelves, when allowed to do the talking, Cedico's wines collected eight medals, earning the chain runner-up position for the Best Cross-Channel Supermarket of the year. And it is not as if Cedico has had to resort to showing us its top of the range; most of Cedico's wines are in the 20 – 50FF bracket, and that is exactly what they submitted. The point other French chains should take note of is that although 16 of the 30 wines submitted by Cedico's buyer, Bruno Meens, did not survive our tastings, we still found plenty worth recommending. Presumably other supermarket groups could do just as well, if only they bothered.

RED WINES

SILVER MEDAL

Côtes du Lubéron 1992 L'Aiguebrun 14.50FF
(£1.79) A cheap red Rhône with decent tasty fruit.
Château Cadouin Segur 1992 Bordeaux 17.80FF
(£2.20) Violety nose, elegant silky fruit. Very good value.
Château Picon 1992 Bordeaux Supérieur 22.50FF

(£2.78) Good basic Bordeaux, with clean, nicely structured fruit for the price.

Château Roumaguet 1992 Bordeaux 23.90FF (£2.95) Another good basic Bordeaux in a light Merlot style, this wine has less body than the Picon, but a touch more elegance.

BRONZE MEDAL   *Chinon 1992 Domaine du Verger Peintier* 24.85FF (£3.07) It is not common to find a soft and easy to drink red Loire, and when they are as cheap as this, you should snap them up, as future vintages are seldom as attractive.

BRONZE MEDAL   *Château Labory 1989 Fronsac* 27.60FF (£3.41) Plenty of blackcurranty fruit backed up by a good tannin structure. Still has tight-packed flavours that need more time in bottle. Keep 2-3 years.

BRONZE MEDAL   *Château Caronne Ste-Gemme 1987 Haut Médoc* 35.50FF (£4.38) Mature claret English-style. Allow to breathe two hours prior to drinking.

Saumur-Champigny 1990 Domaine des Hauts de Sanziers 38.90FF (£4.80) Attractive blackcurrant fruit on the nose, but closed on the palate, requiring a further 1-2 years in bottle to open up.

SILVER MEDAL   *Château La Rose Perruchon 1989 Lussac-St-Émilion* 41.65FF (£5.14) Well concentrated wine with multi-layered fruit that stood up to the even higher scoring Château Seguin 1991 Cuvée Prestige, which came immediately before this wine in the blind tasting.

SILVER MEDAL   *Château La Tour Carnet 1992 Haut-Médoc* 49.90FF (£6.16) Young toasty fruit on the nose, plenty of flavour and length on the palate. A wine of some class that still has room to improve and develop in bottle.

WHITE WINES

Domaine de Barroque 1993 Vin de Pays des Côtes de Gascogne, Peter Gascogne 13.95FF (£1.72) Nice but not special (unlike the 1992 vintage, which was a little bit special), this is simply a light-bodied, dry white wine with fresh peardrop fruit.

Riesling Réserve 1993 Dopff 30FF (£3.70) Full, fresh and sprightly.

BRONZE MEDAL   *Pouilly Fumé 1990 Domaine de Maltaverne* 42.95FF (£5.30) This is a fine quality Sauvignon Blanc with noticeable bottle-age. Not everyone's cup of tea, and certainly not ours, but for those who enjoy this style of wine, it fully deserves its bronze medal.

La Touchère 1993 Chablis 45FF (£5.56) Not easy to drink on its own, this wine certainly has a touch of genuine Chablis 'steel' and makes a good food wine.

GOLD MEDAL

Sancerre 1993 Domaine des Vieux Pruniers 48.50FF (£5.99) A delightful Sauvignon with elegant fruit. Classic dry Sancerre, genuinely dry yet eminently drinkable.

ROSÉ WINES

BRONZE MEDAL

Domaine les Cabassiers NV Côtes de Provence 17.90FF (£2.21) It is not easy to achieve a rosé of this quality in the dry heat of Provence. Real fruit, good body and well suited to food.
Verdict? 👍 👍 👍

⑫ LE CHAIS
40 rue de Phalsbourg
Centre Frader
62100 Calais
Tel: (21) 97.88.56
English spoken? Not really
Opening hours? 9am-12noon & 2pm-7pm seven days a week
Parking? Yes
Shopping trolleys? Yes
Do they offer to help carry the goods to the car? Yes
Methods of payment? Sterling, French Francs, Visa, Mastercard
Any wines for tasting in store? Yes
Comment: Part of a small chain of two wine warehouses called Le Chais, the other being in Boulogne, where the company also runs three town shops called Les Vins de France. Le Chais is a nicely presented wine warehouse, not far from the town centre, and has the advantage of plenty of parking space. This outlet will sell wines by the bottle, but is more geared up for sales by the case. Coaches are welcome by prior appointment. In the first edition, we reported that this group planned to open a big warehouse in April 1994 at a service station, just outside Calais on the autoroute towards Dunkerque, but this did not happen, although we are assured it is more a matter of postponement than cancellation.
The wines: No samples were submitted last year, but we did receive a comprehensive price list, and were impressed by many of the wines (Alsace from Klipfel, Rhône from Paul Jaboulet, Burgundy from Jadot and Mommessin, and a very good selection of Bordeaux). This time, however, we received no list, but Le Chais did submit samples.

The disappointing news is that only two passed the test. Those that did not qualify were all drinkable, but two recommendations and no medal-winning wines is hardly justification for the 👍👍 we awarded on the strength of its list alone. We do not think that Le Chais is doing itself any favours by submitting wines that do not truly reflect the depth, quality and value of its list, albeit last year's, but even if we had an up-to-date one, we could not rely on it to boost this outlet's ranking twice running. We must let the wines we taste do the talking, but we qualify this by saying this is a good, serious warehouse operation that certainly offers more worthwhile wines than the two below, and probably deserves a better result than our verdict suggests.

RED WINES
Côtes-du-Rhône 1993 Marquis de Richevigne
19.80FF (£2.44) Not special, but a good basic red Rhône sold at an unpretentious price.

WHITE WINES
Château Bel-Air 1992 Bergerac Sec 17.50FF (£2.16) Fresh suck-a-stone style Sauvignon, with a definite touch of pétillance.
Verdict? 😕

⑥ CHARLIES
14 rue Cronstadt
62100 Calais
Tel: (21) 97.96.49
English spoken? Yes
Opening hours? Sun-Fri 8am-8pm, closed Sat (a mighty odd day of the week to close!)
Parking? Only on street (easy enough)
Shopping trolleys? Yes
Do they offer to help carry the goods to the car? Yes
Methods of payment? Sterling, French Francs, Traveller's cheques, Eurocheques, Visa, Access, Mastercard, American Express, Diners Card, British cheques (with card)
Any wines for tasting in store? A few
Additional services:
* Toilet facilities available in the store
* Foot passengers given a lift to the ferry
Comment: Another British outlet, Charlies is owned by Alan Thompson, Kevin McDermott and Stephen Dolan. Thompson spent 15 years in the

licensed trade and fronts up the business in Calais, while his partners attend to their own companies, in completely different trades, in the UK. The reason it is called Charlies is because it was Champagne Charlies before the CIVC put pressure on the firm, on the grounds that it was a registered trademark. The truth, however, is that the trademark is Champagne Charlie, in the singular, not Champagne Charlies, and its owner the Champagne house Charles Heidsieck stopped using it several years ago, much to the chagrin of those of us at the *Guide* who loved the wine, and thought the name most appropriate. Furthermore, it strikes us as odd that the British-owned Champagne Charlies is forced to drop the word Champagne from the title of its business, yet the authorities have not said a word to the French-owned Royal Champagne in the same town.

The wines: Charlies is a large, warehouse-type operation with British staff who make UK customers feel at home. There have been some improvements since our first visit, most notably the shelving that has been erected around the store to display the wines. We are told that the range of Champagnes is due to be enlarged, but when and by how much is as yet uncertain.

RED WINES
Château Haut-Sarie 1992 Bordeaux 13FF (£1.60) Light and sappy with a wisp of smokiness in the fruit.
Cahors 1990 Carte Noir 22FF (£2.72) Some silky-violet fruit with a slight hint of mint.

WHITE WINES
Domaine de Barroque 1993 Vin de Pays des Côtes de Gascogne, Peter Hawkins 13.75FF (£1.70) Nice but not special (unlike the 1992 vintage, which was), this is simply a light-bodied, dry white wine with fresh peardrop fruit.
Domaine de Papolle 1993 Vin de Pays des Côtes de Gascogne, Peter Hawkins 13.75FF (£1.70) Compared to Domaine de Barroque, its lesser-quality sister-wine, Papolle has a more perfumed character, which shows through on the palate and enhances the aftertaste. This gives Papolle the edge, but neither it nor Barroque have the special quality that marked their 1992 vintage. Taste the 1992 and 1993 Papolle together and you will see the remarkable similarity of their perfumed character, but the fruit in 1993 does not have the

same depth. This might be due to the different grape varieties used, as the 1992 was based on 60% Ugni Blanc, whereas the 1993 was based on 60% Colombard. Furthermore, there were vinification difficulties in 1993, with the end of the fermentation dragging on far longer and more slowly than desirable, and this may be the cause of its amylic-peardrop aroma, which may make it very fresh, but is more expressive of technology than either grape or soil. At the time of writing this edition of the *Guide*, the 1992 was still drinkable, but had lost the spark of vitality that helped it to run away with both 'Best White Wine of the Year' and 'White Wine Snip of the Year' awards in the first edition (the only wine to pick up two 'Wine of the Year' awards, by the way). We should remember, however, that this wine is just a modest *vin de pays* and that the wines of this area are better-suited to distillation (into Armagnac) than to drinking for their own sake. Yet that was what made the 1992 so special. Indeed, it was special, as 1992 was a deliberate move away from the more commercial style of previous vintages. The irony is that it did not sell so well, which is why Peter Hawkins went back to a more commercial style in 1993, and irony upon irony, this has sold like hot-cakes on the back of the rave review in the first edition of the *Guide*! If Hawkins just wants turnover, then he should continue to make the more commercial style, but in doing so, he will make a wine that is no different than every other Vin de Pays des Côtes de Gascogne. No better or worse: just invisible. If, however, he wants to make a name for himself, and for Domaine de Papolle, then he must at least devote a portion of his harvest to pursuing the more expressive style adopted in 1992 and, hopefully, improving on it year after year. **Verdict?** 🥄

• 1 SILVER MEDAL

• 1 BRONZE MEDAL

(14) **CONTINENT**
ZUP du Beau Marais
Avenue Georges Guyneme
62100 Calais
Tel: (21) 97.99.75
Selling area: 6,450m² (compare this with the size other stores featured in the area, to gauge their relative size and you will have a rough idea of how big the range of wines, beers, spirits and other goods will be).
Opening hours? Mon-Sat 8.30am-10pm, closed

Sun

Comment: Part of the Promodes group, which owns Continent, Shopi and various other smaller outlets. We made contact last year with no less than six top people at Promodes and its various offshoots, but to no avail, so this year we wrote to the managing director of Promodes, M. Pierre Merle, but he could not be bothered to reply either.

The wines: There is quite a big range in the larger Continent stores such as this, but not a particularly wonderful selection in the price category most cross-Channel shoppers are interested in (15-30FF), although we did strike lucky with two of the six wines we purchased at random. The Bordeaux selection is eclectic and spotty, with some good *cru classé*, but prices are not competitive, although they do have some on offer (eg., Ducru-Beaucaillou 1991 at 86FF, and Fieuzal at 72FF).

RED WINES

BRONZE MEDAL

Les Mélusines 1993 St-Nicolas-de-Bourgueil 27FF (£3.33) A tasty wine indeed, and with an authentic grassy Loire Cabernet edge that does not detract from its drinkability.

WHITE WINES

SILVER MEDAL

Jean Marie Strubbler Gewurztraminer 1993 Vin d'Alsace 22.90FF (£2.83) This is good value Gewurztraminer, with assertive, spicy fruit. The acidity is somewhat high for this grape, giving the wine a finer balance than most.

Verdict? ☝

26 CVP CASH & CARRY

Cellier Caves des Vieux Papes Cash & Carry
21 rue Tom Souville
62100 Calais
Tel: (21) 34.30.10
English spoken? Yes
Opening hours? Mon-Sat 10am-7pm
Parking? Yes (private car park)
Shopping trolleys? Yes
Do they offer to help carry the goods to the car? Yes
Methods of payment? Sterling, Irish Punt, French Francs, Belgian Francs, Traveller's cheques, Visa, Mastercard, Access

Any wines for tasting in store? Yes
Comment: This small warehouse-type operation had only been open two weeks when we found it. **The wines:** Moderately large range, strongest on Loire, and not bad on Bordeaux, Burgundy and Beaujolais, but nothing seemed to stand out from a spot check point of view, and with only two wines submitted it would be impossible to make any realistic judgement. The wines seem to be middle of the road in both quality and price, but it is an extremely new outlet, and maybe the selection will improve with time.

WHITE WINES
Muscadet de Sèvre et Maine sur lie 1993 Carte d'Or, Sauvion 22.50FF (£2.78) A wine of fine aroma and delicate flavour: do not over-chill and serve with a light-flavoured dish for best effect.
Verdict? ♟

㉙ **EASTENDERS 'THE WINERY'**
110-112 rue Mollien
62100 Calais
Tel: (21) 34.00.81
Opening hours? 8am-8pm seven days a week
Parking? Yes (private car park)

㉘ **EASTENDERS BAR À VINS**
Rue du Quai de la Loire
62100 Calais
Tel: (21) 34.53.33
Opening hours? 8am-8pm seven days a week
Parking? Yes (in the road)

⑬ **EASTENDERS BULK BEER WAREHOUSE**
Beer & Wine Cash & Carry
Rue Garennes
Zone Industriale des Dunes
62100 Calais
Tel: (21) 34.53.33
English spoken? Yes (for all three outlets)
Opening hours? Continuously from 8am Sun to 8pm Sat every week
Parking? Yes (private car park)
Shopping trolleys? Yes ('The Winery' only)
Do they offer to help carry the goods to the car? Yes
Methods of payment? Sterling, French Francs, Traveller's cheques, Eurocheques, Visa, Access,

Mastercard. Note that the Bulk Beer Warehouse accepts only cash or cheques, and that there is a surcharge of £3 per cheque and 2% on all credit card transactions.

Any wines for tasting in store? A policy of 'try before you buy' on most wines at 'The Winery'.

Comment: Dave West now has three different outlets. His original warehouse in the rue Garennes frightened off some of our readers, who claimed to have seen a number of Neanderthals roaming the place. Some readers who summoned up the courage to get out of their vehicles and ask whether they actually sold from there were met with a 'Maybe, maybe not' response (and we know that for a fact, our representative having received exactly the same treatment!). For a while, this led to most wine purchases being conducted at what West calls his Bar à Vins, a former doss house called the Transit Hôtel in the rue du Quai de la Loire, just round the corner from rue Garennes. When we last saw it, there were only EastEnders Cash & Carry signs, with no evidence of a *bar à vins* as such. Just a shop crammed with boxes of wine, presided over by Dave West and two massive Alsatians, and we're not sure who was in charge of whom. When he gets a manager, it will no doubt be converted into a pucker *bar à vins*, where you can relax with a glass of wine or a cup of coffee. When he does, hopefully he will find someone who can operate the Espresso machine (we were offered a cup of coffee and, seeing the machine, accepted, only to be given mugs of Nescafé!). Anyone wanting to buy wine should avoid both these premises, and head straight for 'The Winery' where you should get the greatest selection of products to taste and buy. Dave West does not mind being called a cowboy, Cockney or otherwise, and claims 'I might be a rogue, but I try to be a likeable one, and compared to some of the villains in this town, I'm probably the most honest person in Calais'.

The wines: Dave West has seriously expanded and improved his range since last year, and if he had picked up another couple of golds and had a few less duff wines (50% did not pass our test), he would certainly have got 👍 👍 👍 👍 and would have been one of the runners up for Best Cross-Channel Outlet of the Year. We have not seen the stock with our own eyes, but West claims to stock every Champagne that Perardel does, only at cheaper prices.

RED WINES

Château les Plantes 1992 Grand Vin de Bordeaux 14FF (£1.73) Not bad as a red wine *per se*, but hardly stands out as a Bordeaux, let alone Graves. Still, at this price, who cares?

Château la Clede 1991 Bordeaux Supérieur 17FF (£2.10) Good basic Bordeaux character, well worth £2.10.

BRONZE MEDAL *Château Pargade 1989 Bordeaux* 18FF (£2.22) Very soft and easy to drink.

BRONZE MEDAL *Château Lagarde 1988 Bordeaux Supérieur* 18FF (£2.22) We can imagine the blackcurrant fruit in this wine was once fresh, bright and bouncy, but although it now quite mature, and should be drunk up, rather than kept, it is still well worth a bronze at this price.

Seigneurie de Donneuve 1992 Fitou 19.50FF (£2.41) The elegant, plummy fruit in this red wine makes it easy to sip on its own.

Château Tour de Peyraney 1992 Bordeaux 20FF (£2.47) Basic Bordeaux, but with a better structure than most. Good food wine. Should improve a little in bottle.

Fitou 1991 Mont Tauch 23FF (£2.84) Good on its own and with food, this wine has plenty of soft fruit on a supple tannin structure.

Côtes du Ventoux NV Paul Jaboulet 23FF (£2.84) Tough and tannic now, but should turn into a rich and rewarding wine, if kept three years or more.

Côtes du Ventoux 1993 Paul Jaboulet 24FF (£2.96) Another tough and tannic red that will pay dividends if laid down for three years or so.

BRONZE MEDAL *Sable View 1990 Cabernet Sauvignon* 25FF (£3.09) Lots of lovely, mellow, blackcurranty fruit.

Mâcon 1991 E. Brocard 25FF (£3.09) No hint of Gamay, let alone anything Burgundian, but as a red wine plain and simple, this is quite tasty, and has enough sappy tannins to provide the structure to accompany food.

BRONZE MEDAL *San Vicente Cabernet Sauvignon 1990 Maule Valley* 25FF (£3.09) Soft, almost sweet, blackcurrant fruit.

BRONZE MEDAL *Château les Graves 1989 Médoc* 26FF (£3.21) This wine has intense flavours that are tight, concentrated and closed-in, making it a good inexpensive Bordeaux to lay down.

SILVER MEDAL *Côtes-du-Rhône NV Paul Jaboulet* 27FF (£3.33) This is serious stuff for what is, frankly, a ridiculously cheap price. Rich and powerful, you should be able to glimpse the potential of this wine if you drink it with a good Sunday roast, but you would be best advised to cellar it for 5-7 years.

BRONZE MEDAL *Château de Lardiley 1991 Marthe Lataste* 28FF (£3.46) Quite an oaky wine for its weight of fruit, but it makes a more than satisfying, current drinking wine for oako'philes.

SILVER MEDAL *Parallèle 1993 Paul Jaboulet* 29FF (£3.58) Needs to be cellared. You just will not believe how cheap this powerful wine was if you buy it now, and keep it 6-9 years.

Château la Croix de Pez 1989 St-Estèphe 31FF (£3.83) Thick, deep, rich and rustic.

BRONZE MEDAL *Château Vieux Veyrac 1990 St-Émilion* 32FF (£3.95) It is the chocolate-cherry character of the fruit that makes this an interesting St-Émilion for the price.

SILVER MEDAL *Vacqueyras 1993 Paul Jaboulet* 38FF (£4.69) You would hardly credit that this elegant Rhône, with its eminently drinkable silky-violety fruit is from the 1993 vintage, but it does have good structure, and a firm dry finish, and will continue to improve for 2-3 years.

SILVER MEDAL *Crozes Hermitage 'Les Jalets' 1992 Paul Jaboulet* 39FF (£4.81) There's no denying the finesse of Syrah fruit on the nose of this wine, but it needs a couple of years to soften the fruit on the palate.

SILVER MEDAL *Châteauneuf du Pape NV Paul Jaboulet* 59FF (£7.28) Even though the alcohol is noticeable on the finish (rare error for Jaboulet), there is so much else about this big, rich, spicy wine we like that it still got a high score.

SILVER MEDAL *Châteauneuf-du-Pape 'La Grappe des Papes' 1990 Paul Jaboulet* 63FF (£7.78) More harmonious than Jaboulet's non-vintage Châteauneuf-du-Pape, it is softer, with a more supple, mellow finish, but will still continue to improve for several years.

WHITE WINES

BRONZE MEDAL *Dry Creek Estate 1993 Semillon Chardonnay* 16FF (£1.98) Typical Oz-style oaky white, give or take a grape variety or two, with quite a bit of fruit to back up the oak, and an easy-to-drink, off-dry finish.

Château Les Plantes 1992 Graves 18FF (£2.22) The cheapest drinkable dry white Bordeaux: clean, fresh and soft with ripe fruit. Will go with food, but drinks well enough on its own.

Sable View 1993 Chardonnay 25FF (£3.09) One of those rare wines where the description on the back label actually fits the wine inside the bottle, this South African Chardonnay does indeed have 'citrussy fruit with a hint of oak'.

SPARKLING WINES

Lovely Bubbly NV EastEnders 7.50FF (93p) We tasted medium-sweet sparkling wines up to 17FF, but as in the first edition, EastEnder's Lovely Bubbly proved to be the best. We won't wax lyrical about this wine, it is dirt-cheap and has a jokey label, but it is clean, fresh and easy to drink, which is a darn sight more than most medium-sweet sparkling wines bearing famous Loire names and sold at significantly higher prices. If you have been happy with a medium-sweet bubbly that costs more, we suggest you at least try this unpretentious wine, which is the best we have been able to find in the Channel ports so far.

BEST BLUE WINE OF THE YEAR

Croisiere Curaçao Brut NV Société Rémoise des Vins 12FF (£1.48) What is blue, orange and fizzy? Well Croisiere Curaçao Brut, of course. Only it is turquoise rather than blue, and is not *brut* as the label indicates, but rather sweet. It does, however, taste of Curaçao oranges. This unique product must be recommended for its class, which should enable it to fit unobtrusively between the Greek liqueurs and the Mateus Rosé lampshade, on the corner bar in the lounge of Mr & Mrs Nouveau Riche.

SILVER MEDAL

Croisiere Peche Brut NV Société Rémoise des Vins 12FF (£1.48) Even for people who do not like flavoured sparkling wines (amongst whom you can include us), the beautiful aroma and sumptuous peachy flavour of this particular product should be hard to resist. We are not sure if we would actually drink it, but we know plenty of people who would. If you like flavoured sparkling wines, you will love this and at just £1.48 it's a snip.

BRONZE MEDAL

Croisiere Framboise Brut NV Société Rémoise des Vins 12FF (£1.48) Pure raspberry aroma, lots of sweet, fizzy raspberry fruit, and only 6% of alcohol, this is not serious stuff, but lots of people will enjoy it.

BRONZE MEDAL

Champagne De Lieucourt NV Brut 51FF (£6.30) The soft, sweetly-ripe fruit aromas melt into a nice, satisfying, creamy-sweet flavour on the palate. Made by the technically adept firm of Duval-Leroy, this was the cheapest Champagne we tasted, and although by no means a fine-quality Champagne, it at least managed to get a bronze medal at this price level, whereas other far more expensive Champagnes did not even merit inclusion in the *Guide*.

BEERS

Wappenbräu Premium Pils, Nach Deutschen Reinheitsgebot 1.17FF (14p) per 25cl bottle, sold in 24s at 28FF (£3.46) Light, dry and not too fizzy, this beer just scrapes in for recommendation because of its very low price.

Noordheim Bière Blonde de Luxe 1.17FF (14p) per 25cl bottle, sold in 24s at 28FF (£3.46) There is nothing deluxe about this very light and rather neutral flavoured beer, but the aftertaste is clean and vaguely beery, which gives it an advantage over most 25cl cheap beers.

E.S.P. Pils Bière Blonde de Luxe 1.20FF (15p) per 25cl twist-cap bottle, sold in 24s at 29FF (£3.58) Another so-called deluxe beer that is merely a bog-standard brew, but at least it is drinkable and has an attractive flowery-hop aroma.

GOLD MEDAL
BEST-QUALITY LIGHT BEER OF THE YEAR

Budweiser Budvar, Budweiser Budbräu 3.58FF (44p) per 33cl bottle, sold in 24s at 86FF (£10.62) In terms of pure quality, Budweiser Budvar (look out for 'Budvar', which indicates that it is the genuine article, which should not to be confused with the bland tasting Budweiser brewed in the USA, or under licence in the UK) was unbeatable. But for Grolsch, Budweiser Budvar would have been the best-value brew too, as this is very sharp pricing indeed (it's 58p for a 33cl bottle at The Wine & Beer Company (Calais and Cherbourg), and 99p or more in the UK).

GOLD MEDAL

Murphy's Draught 5.42FF (67p) per 44cl can, sold in 24s at 130FF (£16.05) Dark, mellow and creamy, with a mild smoky aftertaste, this is the smoothest draught stout in a can on the market.

Beck's, Bräueri Beck 3.83FF (47p) per 33cl bottle, sold in 24s at 92FF (£11.36) Light and crisp, this is better than the Mosel Bier (Calais Wine and Beer), but only just, and it's almost four times the price – hence no Bronze. This price is, however, the cheapest you will find Beck's (it costs 52p for a 33cl bottle at Beer Lovers, and no less than 71p for a smaller-sized 27.5cl bottle at Sainsbury's!), so if Beck's your beer, EastEnders is where to buy it.

GOLD MEDAL
BEST-CHEAPEST SPECIALITY BEER OF THE YEAR
BEST-VALUE SPECIALITY BEER OF THE YEAR
BEST-QUALITY SPECIALITY BEER OF THE YEAR

L'Écume des Jours, Bière Sur Lie 8.50FF (£1.05) per litre bottle. Even if the value of this beer did not surprise us, the quality and character did, coming from Brasserie Steinbeer, a brewery better known for churning out cheapie 25cl stuff under a multitude of labels. As its 'sur lie' designation infers, this beer has been refermented in the bottle, which gives it a yeasty-fruity plumpness, and explains the small amount of sediment. It is, however, very easy to pour without clouding-up. This beer, which is sealed with a Champagne-type cork, is best served chilled, but not iced. It really is quite good, with a touch of sweetness, and the sort of taste we could imagine that lager had a century ago.

Verdict? 👍 👍 👍

- 1 GOLD MEDAL
- 1 SILVER MEDAL
- 1 BRONZE MEDAL

23 FRANGLAIS

CD 215 Fréthun
62185 Fréthun
Tel: (21) 85.29.39
English spoken? Yes
Opening hours? Mon-Fri 8.30am-7.30pm, Sat 7.30am-6.30pm, Sun 9am-6pm
Parking? Yes (private car park)
Shopping trolleys? Yes
Do they offer to help carry the goods to the car? Yes
Methods of payment? Sterling, French Francs, Traveller's cheques, Eurocheques, Visa, Mastercard, Access
Any wines for tasting in store? Yes
Special directions: Turn left when exiting Calais ferry terminal. This leads directly to the A26 Paris-Reims autoroute. Take the A16 turn-off signposted Boulogne. Continue along the A16 autoroute until you reach Sortie 11 (Exit 11) signposted to Gare TGV. Leave autoroute, turn left over the bridge, and you will find Franglais 500 yards on the right. Total journey time from ferry terminal 10 minutes approximately.
Additional information:
* Membership of 'Friends of Franglais' entitles you to further discounts and special offers. For more information phone/fax 0206 272868.
Comment: This large, bright and very clean warehouse-type operation is owned by two French-Canadians and one Englishman.
It is strategically situated en route to the Channel Tunnel, and has a specific tasting area, which is staffed and has a large number of wines available for tasting. We like this – it is so much less intimidating than those outlets that offer 'taste before you buy' yet have no easily discernible facility, or even have the odd open bottle on the counter to reassure potential customers. Almost everything about Franglais is neat and logical,

from the bottles displayed on shelves with cases underneath, and bulk stock on pallets in an adjacent store. At the back of the warehouse there is even a range of toiletries, biscuits, flan dishes, and Le Creuset cookery ware. The explanation for these other goods did not amuse Lyn Parry, our representative, who was told that they are 'for the ladies'. Apparently, while hubby is busy buying the wines, the missus can keep herself amused by browsing through the toiletries ... Perhaps the one English partner forgot to tell his co-owners that more than 60% of all the wines sold in the UK are purchased by women, and that a selection of girlie-mags to keep the men amused might be more appropriate!

The wines: The manager of this outlet also buys the wines, and was formerly a wine buyer for Centre Leclerc, which probably explains why the range consists of about 80% *négociant* wines, and represents no more than you would expect to find in a French supermarket. Nevertheless, of the seven wines submitted, four passed the test, and three of these picked up medals, which suggests that the manager had at least bothered to think about the wines he selected for us. But if he knows the few that are outstanding, it also suggests that he knows most are not, and if he could apply the same amount of discrimination he showed us to his entire selection of Franglais wines, this could be one of the best cross-Channel outlets around.

RED WINES

Fortant Rubis 1993 Vin de Pays d'Oc 12.40FF (£1.53) Soft, supple red with a good fill of fruit.

BRONZE MEDAL *Domaine Dougnac 1992 Minervois* 15.30FF (£1.89) Full, sturdy red with sappy-plummy fruit.

WHITE WINES

GOLD MEDAL *Domaine Maury 1992 Vin de Pays d'Oc* 21.95FF (£2.71) Real Chardonnay flavour and structure. This is a very classy wine for the price. If we had not tasted the Beaune Chaume Gaufriot 1991 Domaine Henri Clerc (The Grape Shop, Boulogne), the Danie de Wet 1993 Chardonnay (Sainsbury's, Calais) would have been the Best-Quality Chardonnay, and this would have been the Best-Value.

SILVER MEDAL *Domaine de la Roche 1993 Muscadet de Sèvre et Maine sur Lie* 28.85FF (£3.56) Concentrated and well structured, this is a serious dry white wine that demands food.

Verdict? 👍 👍 👍

• 1 GOLD MEDAL
• 1 BRONZE MEDAL

③ GRAND CRU MAGNUM

24 rue du Commandant Bonningue
62100 Calais
Tel: (21) 34.58.71
English spoken? A little
Opening hours? Mon 2pm-7.30pm, Tues-Sat
8.30am-12noon & 2pm-7.30pm, closed Sun
Parking? Only on street
Shopping trolleys? No
Do they offer to help carry the goods to the car?
Yes
Methods of payment? Sterling, Irish Punts,
French Francs, Traveller's cheques, Eurocheques,
Visa, Access, Mastercard, American Express
Any wines for tasting in store? Not confirmed.
Comment: This former high street shop has
moved from 1 rue Royale into more spacious, less
upmarket premises, and now operates along the
lines of a wine warehouse. Grand Cru Magnum no
longer has any connection with its former owner,
SODICRU (a Bordeaux *négociant*), but belongs to
M. Miot, who has always managed this outlet.
The wines: M. Miot still specialises in Bordeaux,
and carries a few high class Rhônes from Guigal,
but we did not receive a list, and it is impossible to
justify a more generous verdict on the basis of just
the four wines submitted, even if three of them
qualified, and two of these earned medals.

RED WINES

GOLD MEDAL

Domaine les Grand' Terres 1992 Côtes du Ventoux
19FF (£2.35) A nice bouquet of perfumed fruit.
Côtes-du-Rhône 1991 E. Guigal 40FF (£4.94)
Lovely balance, all components already in perfect
harmony, succulent fruit.

WHITE WINES

BRONZE MEDAL

Vin de pays du Vaucluse NV Cellier St-Siffrein
13FF (£1.60) Gentle, ripe fruit and not quite dry,
but that does make it all the more commercial.
Verdict? 👍👍

• 1 GOLD MEDAL
• 4 BRONZE MEDALS

⑦ INTER CAVES

Le Géant du Vin
26 rue Mollien
62100 Calais
Tel: (21) 96.63.82
English spoken? Yes
Opening hours? Tues-Sat 9.30am-12.15pm &
2.30pm-7.30pm, Sun 10am-12.30pm, closed Mon

Parking? Only on street
Shopping trolleys? No
Do they offer to help carry the goods to the car?
Yes
Methods of payment? Sterling, French Francs,
Traveller's cheques, Eurocheques, Visa, Access,
Mastercard
Any wines for tasting in store? Yes, minimum of
20 different wines, mostly restricted to the La
Fontaine wine-boxes, but includes various bottled
wines
Comment: Part of the Inter Caves group (*see also*
branches in Caen, Cherbourg and St-Malo), which
consists of approximately 90 shops spread
throughout France, plus a few additional outlets
in Germany. The whole Inter Caves group is very
professionally run, and any branch is well worth a
visit, but of all the Inter Caves along the Channel
coast, the Calais outlet is our favourite. Although
the Caen branch was awarded joint best outlet in
that port, they all offer roughly the same range,
and have particularly helpful and knowledgeable
staff, although the staff at Calais are perhaps a
touch happier.
The wines: We were promised a list, but did not
receive one, and our representative reported a
dozen Champagnes from smaller, lesser known
producers, which sound interesting, but the only
one submitted was Champagne De Saval, which
does not exist as such, but is made by another
producer (Baron Albert, we think), and although
drinkable was not special. Hopefully we can taste
some real small producer Champagnes next time,
but submitting a larger number of better selected
wines this year has paid off, giving the Inter Caves
group a far more impressive entry in this year's
Guide than it got in the first edition.

RED WINES

BRONZE MEDAL

Domaine le Pian 1992 Vin de Pays du Gard 19FF
(£2.35) Soft, silky blackcurrant fruit.
Chatellenie de Lastours NV Corbières 29FF (£3.58)
Rich and robust, with a herbal-oak undertone.

GOLD MEDAL

Château de Pech Redon 1991 La Clape 29.50FF
(£3.64) Absolutely delightful fruit underpinned by
bubble-gum oak, which creates a sort of raspberry
ripple flavour. Although it might not sound like it,
this is an elegant, classy wine.
Massana 1991 Côtes du Roussillon 29.90FF (£3.69)
Could be Rioja if we did not know better.

BRONZE MEDAL | *Bourgogne Pinot Noir 1992 Philippe de Marange* 35.70FF (£4.41) An elegant Burgundy for the price, with ripe-cherry Pinot Noir fruit.

BRONZE MEDAL | *Domaine Duseigneur 1991 Lirac* 39.50FF (£4.88) An elegant, fruity Rhône, but we have come across two versions of apparently the same wine: one with a neck-label that has the word 'Lirac' either side of the vintage, and the other with a neck-label that has 'Cru' one side of the vintage and 'Race' the other, and the latter of these seems to have a more smoky-toasty finish.

Juliénas 1992 Domaine de la Bottière 44FF (£5.43) Has some potential for development over the next year or two.

Saumur-Champigny 1992 Domaine du Val Brun 45FF (£5.56) This may lack charm on the nose, but it has good fruit underneath, and should develop more attractive bottle-aromas over the next 18 months or so.

Domaine des Lucques 1990 Graves 47FF (£5.80) Probably a lot better 18 months ago, but still makes a decent glass of Bordeaux, even if prematurely mellow.

WHITE WINES

Baron de Peyrac, Sauvignon 1993 Bordeaux Blanc 17.90FF (£2.21) Although this wine's fresh aroma shows good typicity, it is too soft to be classic Sauvignon, although this very softness is what makes it so easy to drink.

BRONZE MEDAL | *Clos du Zahnacker 1988 Vin d'Alsace* 60FF (£7.41) One of the very few classic blends of Alsace, this wine was probably easier to drink two years ago, and will undoubtedly find greater harmony in two years from now, but is currently in a stage of development where the Riesling is battling with the Gewurztraminer.

ROSÉ WINES

Château la Croix de l'Hosanne 1993 Bordeaux Clairet 22.90FF (£2.83) Highly perfumed, off-dry rosé with plenty of fruit.

Verdict? 👍 👍 👍

• 1 BRONZE MEDAL

⑮ **INTERMARCHÉ**
56 avenue Antoine de St-Exupéry
62100 Calais
Tel: (21) 34.42.44
Selling area: 1,700m² (compare this with the size of other stores featured in the area, to gauge their

relative size and you will have a rough idea of
how big the range of wines, beers, spirits and
other goods will be).

Opening hours? Mon-Thurs 9am-12.15pm & 2pm-
7.15pm, Fri 9am-12.15pm & 2pm-7.30pm, Sat 9am-
7.15pm

Comment: Most Intermarché on the Channel coast
are relatively small, and although they can be
quite large further inland, this chain is more of the
supermarket ilk than hypermarket. It is also
relatively down-market, with a mostly dull and
uninteresting range of wines, often dominated by
a display of 3-litre wine containers. There are
around a dozen different Champagnes, and the
fine wines are usually displayed separately (we
saw Ducru Beaucaillou 1989 at 85FF, and Pavillon
Rouge 1990 at 105FF). We had no success with
chairman Marcel Robin, who steadfastly refused
to answer our correspondence. It was the same
story as last year, with M. Le Goff, Intermarché's
drinks buyer.

The wines: We purchased six wines along the
same lines as those we bought at Auchan, and
when it came to the crunch, Intermarché fared
much better, with half of the wines warranting our
recommendation, and one even picking up a
Bronze medal. And two of those that did not
qualify were perfectly drinkable, even if not
special enough to qualify for the *Guide*. If only the
management of this firm had enough faith in its
products to submit a substantial range of its
inexpensive wines, they might do well, if this
random sampling is anything to go by.

RED WINES

Beaujolais NV Cuvée Joannès 12FF (£1.48)
Although not medal potential, you could have
knocked us down with a feather when this wine,
the second-cheapest Gamay submitted, turned out
not only to be drinkable, but expressive of its
variety, rather than *macération carbonique*.

Côtes-du-Rhône 1993 Réserve Lescarrat 13FF
(£1.60) This soft and fruity wine has a touch more
elegance than the other red Rhônes in its price
category.

WHITE WINES

BRONZE MEDAL

Reuilly 1993 Cave PD 22.90FF (£2.83) This fresh
and assertive Sauvignon is not a wine for wimps.
Verdict? 🥄

⑰ MAMMOUTH

CC Calais Ouest
Fort Nieulay
Route de Boulogne (RN1)
62100 Calais
Tel: (21) 34.04.44

Selling area: 6,800m² (compare this with the size of other stores featured in the area, to gauge their relative size and you will have a rough idea of how big the range of wines, beers, spirits and other goods will be).

Opening hours? Mon-Sat 9am-9pm (some outlets open Sun)

Comment: Last year we were authorised by Mammouth's buyer Jean-Claude Alti to approach the manager of this branch, M. Walter, who we were assured would be particularly helpful, since his experience at Calais meant that he knew the English market well. M. Walter, however, did not want to know. This year we approached Christian Toulouse, the chairman of Mammouth's parent company, Paridoc, but he did not even bother to reply. This apathy is a pity because Mammouth outlets are usually amongst the largest, brightest and most welcoming of all the French hypermarket chains, and obviously a favourite with British customers.

The wines: When we visited this branch it was packed out with trippers from the UK, all eagerly stuffing their trolleys with cheap wines and beers, while the tills at Sainsbury's next door were ominously quiet. They cannot have bothered to compare the wines, as anyone who read Robert Joseph's column in *The Sunday Telegraph* last April will be able to verify. Joseph set up a table between Mammouth and Sainsbury's, took a Beaujolais, Rhône and Bordeaux from each store, wrapped them in foil, and asked passers by to say which ones they preferred. Sainsbury's wines won easily. Even M. Walter and his regional boss, M. Le Bail, reckoned that the Mammouth products lacked fruit and freshness by comparison. How embarrassing. We have to agree, as only one of the six wines randomly purchased from Mammouth survived the test, and although we saw a number of *cru classé* clarets (Haut-Brion 1990 at 220FF, Branaire-Ducru 1991 at 75FF), they were all standing upright!

RED WINES
Bourgogne NV Passetoutgrains 15FF (£1.85)

Decent Gamay with a bit of extra backbone.
Verdict? 👎

• 1 BRONZE MEDAL

⑪ MATCH
206 Boulevard Lafayette
62100 Calais
Tel: (21) 97.32.59
Selling area: 1,700m² (compare this with the size
of other stores featured in the area, to gauge their
relative size and you will have a rough idea of
how big the range of wines, beers, spirits and
other goods will be).
Opening hours? Mon-Sat 9am-7.30pm, Sun 9am-
1pm
Comment: The senior management at Match
ignored our correspondence last year, so we wrote
to the chairman, Jean Paul Giraud, who
maintained the company's couldn't care less
attitude. The stores themselves are, however, far
more welcoming: they are pleasant, attractive
shops where someone has obviously made an
effort with the decor to produce a more convivial
atmosphere than most French-owned
supermarkets.
The wines: Match has a moderately large range,
which is mostly Bordeaux and the Southwest, but
also includes the odd Rioja, Errazuriz Panquehue
from Chile, a Chianti, a Tunisian wine, and a
number of half bottles. Although only two of the
six wines purchased here survived our tasting,
one of those was a medal-winner, while the other
picked up a Wine of the Year award. Match also
offers a good range of beers, including a number
of specialist brews from Belgium.

RED WINES

BEST-CHEAPEST RED
WINE OF THE YEAR

Jean de Plessac NV Vin de Pays de l'Hérault
4.95FF (61p) Soft and very fruity, this is the
cheapest wine we came across, yet we would
drink it, and that is more than we could say for
most of the more expensive wines submitted!
Remember, however, that this is a non-vintage
blend. We hope that it's the same one when you
buy it, but Match could be on a different blend.
Supermarkets do not go in for 'taste before you
buy', so purchase just one bottle first, try it, and if
you like it, grab as much as you can. Even if the
blend has changed and is now undrinkable, at
4.95FF a bottle, you won't have lost much.

BRONZE MEDAL

Château Chapelle la Rose 1990 Lussac-St-Émilion
31.60FF (£3.90) A ripe, stylish, classy little number

at this price.
Verdict? 🥄🥄

(1) **PG**
1 Avenue Roger-Salengro
62100 Calais
Tel: (21) 34.17.34
Selling area: 1,400m²

AND

(2) **PG**
Route St-Omer
62100 Calais
Tel: (21) 34.65.98
Selling area: 1,600m² (compare this with the size of other stores featured in the area, to gauge their relative size and you will have a rough idea of how big the range of wines, beers, spirits and other goods will be).
Opening hours? Mon-Thurs & Sat 9am-12noon & 2pm-7.30pm, Fri 9am-8pm, closed Sun
Comment: Our initial reaction last year was to hang out the flags, because although these are fairly small outlets, PG is a local chain of real character, with some really interesting wines, the better ones of which are stored lying down in bins. Furthermore, after the usual hassle of chasing from one contact to another, we latched on to Xavier Diers, the buying director, who was friendly, helpful and agreed to send us any samples we wanted. Only, of course, he did not, so we pulled in the flags and gave PG a cautious verdict. This year we did not get so much as a reply from PG, let alone promises, so at least they kept their word this time!
The wines: With this year's lack of response, we decided to check more stores before buying our random samples (two cheapest, plus four interesting looking wines), and we were less impressed with the range than we were last time, although for the small supermarket it is, PG is not bad, and at least has a moderate choice in the 15-20FF bracket. Gone, however, are the excellent Blanck wines from Alsace, only to be replaced with Freyermuth, which churns out huge quantities at cheap prices. And we saw no Mommessin quality wines from Burgundy. The fine wine section lying down in bins was still there, but the wines displayed were noticeably lacking in the 'fine' department, and the prices were relatively high. As for our tastings, just two

of the six wines purchased passed the test, although one of those did earn a bronze medal.

RED WINES

BRONZE MEDAL *Château du Paraza 1991 Minervois* 9.90FF (£1.22) Soft and tasty, with creamy fruit and good length for a cheap red, and enough of a tannin structure to partner food.

Château Grand Champs 1988 Bordeaux 15.90FF (£1.96) Six-year-old Bordeaux for under £2.00 a bottle cannot be bad, but there is an assertive character that gives the mature fruit in this wine a certain youthful edge, and this does not quite ring true. It is, however, definitely worth recommending at this price.

Verdict? ⚅

- 1 SILVER MEDAL
- 1 BRONZE MEDAL

(24) PERARDEL

Rue Marcel Doret
62100 Calais
Tel: (21) 97.21.22
English spoken? Yes
Opening hours? 8am-8pm seven days a week
Parking? Yes (private car park)
Shopping trolleys? Yes
Do they offer to help carry the goods to the car? Yes
Methods of payment? Sterling, French Francs, Belgian Francs, Eurocheques, Visa, Mastercard, Access
Any wines for tasting in store? Yes
Additional information:
* Special offers on the Perardel's excellent hotel, *Aux Armes de Champagne*, at L'Epine.
Comment: Since opening up in Avenue St-Exupéry early 1994, this warehouse operation has moved to its current premises, just across the road from The Calais Wine & Beer Company, and a far more eye-catching location for anyone heading for the ferry terminal. Very friendly staff.
The wines: Jean-Paul Perardel claims to stock 500 wines from more than 100 different producers, but we did not receive a list, and were not going to count them. It certainly looks like a very large range. Strong on *cru classé* Bordeaux, including some interesting older vintages. Particularly strong on mid-price Burgundies, with some good *négociants* (Leroy, Drouhin, Faively, Thevenot) and some not so good, but typically French in being devoid of growers, even though the Perardels have a shop in Beaune. Alsace includes Sparr and

Becker. Moderate Loire selection. With a vast range extending from Liebfraumilch and 3-litre boxes, through all price levels, to Romanée Conti and First Growth clarets, this is probably the best French-owned wine warehouse on the Channel coast, but just seven wines were submitted, and only three of these passed the test, hence our cautious verdict.

RED WINES

Beaujolais Perardel 1993 Cave Beaujolais du Beau Vallon 22FF (£2.72) Fresh, light, supple Gamay.

SILVER MEDAL *Bourgogne Pinot Noir 1989 Louis-Violland* 29FF (£3.58) Fatness in a Pinot Noir can be its downfall, yet this wine has some fat, and still shows pure, nicely perfumed fruit.

WHITE WINES

BRONZE MEDAL *Bourgogne 1992 Chardonnay, Cuvée Ste-Jehanne de Chantal* 39FF (£4.81) A rich, round, dry white wine that needs food to show at its best.
Verdict? 👍👍

⑯ PIDOU CASH & CARRY
190 rue Marcel Dassault
62100 Calais
Tel: (21) 96.78.10
English spoken? Not revealed
Opening hours? 8am-8pm seven days a week
Parking? Yes (private car park, especially easy for large vehicles)
Shopping trolleys? Yes
Do they offer to help carry the goods to the car? Doubtful
Methods of payment? Sterling, French Francs and 10 other currencies accepted, Traveller's cheques, Eurocheques, Visa, Mastercard, Access
Any wines for tasting in store? No
Additional information:
* Toilet facilities available in the store
* Coffee machine
Comment: A large, impersonal warehouse with mountains of beer, Pidou is the sort of operation that welcomes coaches with open arms, and loves to sell case loads of Mateus, Liebfraumilch, and Lambrusco. Owner M. Pille was unhelpful for our first edition, did not answer our correspondence this year, and was absent when we called.
The wines: Basically there is a lot to chose from here, but nothing as far as we could tell of any

particular interest, whatever the price category. It has to be admitted that there are lots of beers to choose from, including a range of bumper 5-litre 'tinnies', but Pidou does not sell the cheapest beer in town (the cheapest when we were there was 25cl Blondebrau, 28.95FF for 24), nor are the finer beers competitively priced (eg., Grolsch at 109.95FF compared to 88.94FF at The Calais Wine & Beer Company just around the corner). We gave Pidou the benefit of doubt last time, but with no wines or beers submitted, and none of those purchased passing the test, we simply cannot recommend this outlet.

Verdict? 👎

- 2 SILVER MEDALS
- 1 BRONZE MEDAL

⑧ PRISUNIC
17 boulevard Jacquard
62100 Calais
Tel: (21) 34.58.05
Selling area: 1,950m² (compare this with the size of other stores featured in the area, to gauge their relative size and you will have a rough idea of how big the range of wines, beers, spirits and other goods will be).

Opening hours? Mon-Sat 8.30am-7.30pm, closed Sun

Comment: Prisunic is primarily geared up for sales of shoes, clothes, jewellery and household goods, its food and wine section tucked away at the back of the store. Last year we managed to get the Dieppe branch to answer our questionnaire, but received no price list, let alone samples from Prisunic head office, which did not bother to respond to our correspondence. This year we wrote to Gilles Denisty, who is chairman of the group, but he turned out to be just as unresponsive.

The wines: It is a pity that Prisunic shows no interest in communicating with British consumers because, although its range is small, it does contain some interesting second wines from good to great Bordeaux vintages (Moulin de Duhart 1989, Fiefs de Lagrange 1986, L'Ermitage Chasse-Spleen 1989), and five of our randomly purchased samples survived our gruelling blind tasting, with no less than three picking up a medal. If we had the same sort of result from a larger selection of wines, Prisunic could have upset some of the big French chains in the chase for the Best Cross-Channel Supermarket of the Year.

RED WINES

Bergerac NV Chatelier 12.50FF (£1.54) Good basic Bordeaux-style with just enough tannin to partner food.

BRONZE MEDAL *Côtes du Ventoux 1992 la Cuvée des Toques* 18.50FF (£2.28) Ripe and tasty fruit.

SILVER MEDAL *Commanderie de la Bargemone 1990 Coteaux d'Aix en Provence* 24.45FF (£3.02) This full-bodied red is a bit thick and soupy in style, which would normally put us off, but we twice increased our marks on re-tasting it, which pleased us when we found out what it is, as we have been following Commanderie de la Bargemone since the 1981 vintage, and we know that it does improve.

SILVER MEDAL *Château Guillon 1990 Graves* 26.60FF (£3.28) An intensely flavoured wine currently in the process of mellowing out, making it be more accessible, and as its aroma turns toasty, so the fruit will take on more plummy complexity. Exceptional value.

WHITE WINES

Riesling Vin d'Alsace NV Laugel 25.50FF (£3.15) A dry white with fresh, very pure, apple-blossom fruit.

Verdict? 👍👍

• 1 BRONZE MEDAL

⑳ ROYAL CHAMPAGNE

9 rue André Gerschell
62100 Calais
Tel: (21) 96.51.62
English spoken? None
Opening hours? Tues-Sat 10am-12.30pm & 3pm-7.30pm & Sun 10am-1pm, closed Mon
Parking? Only on street
Shopping trolleys? No
Do they offer to help carry the goods to the car? Yes
Methods of payment? French Francs, Visa, Access, Mastercard,
Any wines for tasting in store? Only if buying large quantities.
Comment: This small shop is owned by Annick Ehrlich, who specialises in grower Champagne and takes pride in her cool storage at the back, with everything lying down properly and only dummies on show in the shop.
The wines: Last year Ms Erlich did not submit any samples, but did send us her list, which we assumed did not actually constitute her entire range, as it was so small, and consisted of just a

few grower Champagnes. We have since ascertained, however, that this is her whole range. This year Ms Erlich submitted three Champagnes, but only qualified for recommendation in the *Guide*. One, however, was corked (and according to Sod's Law, we had no back-up, Ms Erlich having sent us just one sample of each wine), so this performance may be misleading. We are always interested in good grower Champagnes, so the others on her list still interest us. We trust that next year she might send us her entire range, as it is not that big, and more than one sample of each, not just as back-up, but in the hope that some of the wines are good enough to progress through to the tasting for potential award-winners. This is a small operation and with every wine on the list a relatively high cost product, Ms Erlich may not be able to afford to do this, but she should at least try to persude her suppliers, who are few in number, that it would be worth their while as much as hers.

BRONZE MEDAL

Champagne Prin Père et Fils NV Chavot Courcourt 95FF (£11.73) Good strength and concentration, this Champagne will age well. **Verdict?** ⅌

★ *BEST CROSS-CHANNEL SUPERMARKET OF THE YEAR*
• 4 GOLD MEDALS
• 2 SILVER MEDALS
• 5 BRONZE MEDALS

㉑ SAINSBURY'S
CC Calais Ouest
Fort Nieulay
Route de Boulogne (RN1)
62100 Calais
Tel: (21) 34.04.44
Opening hours? Mon-Sat 9am-8pm
Special directions: Situated in the Mammouth shopping complex itself.
Comment: You have to walk past Mammouth in order to shop at Sainsbury's, and not that many Brits were doing this on the occasions we visited this outlet, when Mammouth was full of UK shoppers on a frenzied spending spree, while the Sainsbury's tills were ominously quiet. We have no objection to anyone shopping at Mammouth, particularly for non-drinks products, but all its wines tasted for two editions of this *Guide* were grossly inferior to those of Sainsbury's and, indeed, several other French supermarket groups. Even M. Walter, the manager of the Calais branch of Mammouth, and M. Le Bail, his regional director, prefer Sainsbury's wines to their own, according to Robert Joseph of *The Sunday Telegraph* (*see* earlier Mammouth entry). Not everything

about this Sainsbury's outlet is right, but if you want to take home the best value, most enjoyable cheap wines, then we suggest you buy your booze at Sainsbury's before shopping at Mammouth for other products. The aspects of Sainsbury's that are not to our liking include the outlet itself, which is not very exciting, with little effort put into fitments or displays. It's all rather bare and unfriendly, with just two tills at the check-out, and not the friendliest of French staff. Let's have somebody with a big, beaming smile, some charisma, and a loud English voice to attract the day trippers with.

The wines: Although the wines are impressive by French supermarket standards, the range is limited compared to that offered by the larger Sainsbury's stores in the UK. Although a lot of space is rightly donated to Liebfraumilch, gin, Teachers and beer, because these are the biggest sellers, *every* Sainsbury's line should be available, and it would not take much imagination or space to display one bottle of each, with a stock level proportionate to demand stored elsewhere. Liebfraumilch and beer are obviously the big sellers, but if Sainsbury's concentrates too much on these lines, it will reduce its appeal to a category of shoppers who – especially in Calais – are driven to find any product as long as it is at the cheapest price. The problem is that Sainsbury's is not the cheapest. Sainsbury's Liebfraumilch (not submitted to our tastings) is 9.90FF because it is selected on a value for money basis, but the cross-Channel shopper can find Liebfraumilch for as little as 8.50FF in Calais. Sainsbury's has nothing to compete with 25cl beers, which average 28FF for 24, and we have come across offers below 20FF. Grolsch at Sainsbury's costs 149FF for 24, yet 88.94FF at The Calais Wine & Beer Company, while Beck's costs 138FF for 24x27.5cl bottles (two packs of 12), yet only 92FF at EastEnders for 24 larger 33cl bottles! Obviously we are pleased that a British supermarket has won the Best Cross-Channel Supermarket of the Year award, but some of the French groups will be trying much harder next year, and Sainsbury's is not only going to have to solve these pricing anomalies (either by competing or by accepting they are an embarrassment, and dropping them), but it will also have to provide a complete range of wines if it hopes to attract the more discerning shoppers.

RED WINES

BRONZE MEDAL — *Lovico Suhindol Reserve Cabernet Sauvignon 1988 Bulgarian Red Wine* 14.90FF (£1.84) per litre bottle. Rich, rustic red with plenty of mature Cabernet fruit dominated by lots of less than subtle oak. But for the equivalent of £1.38 a bottle, who cares about subtlety?

Sainsbury's Valpolicella Classico NV Casa Vinicola Cav. Pietro Sartori 14.90FF (£1.84) Not special, but surprisingly satisfying for a cheap Valpolicella.

SILVER MEDAL — *Chais Baumière 1992 Merlot* 23.49FF (£2.90) Rich and tasty, this is a real gluggy wine at a bargain of a price.

SILVER MEDAL — *Sainsbury's Beaujolais Villages 1992 Les Roches Grillées* 26.49FF (£3.27) If you want to know what the real flavour of Gamay tastes like, then this is a good wine to start with.

GOLD MEDAL — *Penfolds 1990 Coonawarra Cabernet Sauvignon* 56.54FF (£6.98) Big, dark, intensely flavoured wine, with a long, tannic flavour, and overtones of caramel-oak. This is the Red Wine of the Year at *WINE* magazine's International Wine Challenge, only it costs £1 less across the Channel.

GOLD MEDAL — *Devil's Lair 1991 Cabernet Sauvignon* 68.93FF (£8.51) We loved this and were not a little bit intrigued by the label either. The wine looks like another huge, dark, inky, New World Cabernet, and indeed it is, but it tastes rather finer and more elegant than its structure suggests. This fruit is nice and tangy, making the wine easy to drink now, but it is only just beginning to develop its true complexity, and will pay great dividends if you can manage to keep your hands off it for 4-6 years.

GOLD MEDAL — *Château Maucaillou 1989 Moulis* 89.91FF (£11.10) Delicious, and delicately rich, with exquisitely integrated fruit and oak. An elegant bourgeoise growth of *cru classé* finesse, this wine is beautiful to drink now, but will continue to improve and when it does start to age, it will age very gracefully.

WHITE WINES

BRONZE MEDAL — *Sainsbury's Muscadet de Sèvre et Maine NV V.N.* 14.90FF (£1.84) Clean and crisp with very fresh fruit, just like all Muscadet should be like.

BRONZE MEDAL — *Moldova Chardonnay 1992 Hincesti* 14.90FF (£1.84) This fresh, designer-wine could just as easily be Australian as Moldavan (albeit made by an Englishman with Australian assistants), but then, who knows what a Moldavan Chardonnay should taste like anyway?

Rueda 1992 Hermanos Lurton 23.49FF (£2.90) A soft, fruity dry white in the Sauvignon style, but is it worth a cross-Channel £2.90?

BRONZE MEDAL

Chais Baumière 1991 Chardonnay 23.49FF (£2.90) A full and tasty wine that was at its peak in the summer of 1994, and retailers should be on to the next vintage of this wine long before now.

GOLD MEDAL
BEST-VALUE WHITE WINE OF THE YEAR

Danie de Wet 1993 Chardonnay 32.48FF (£4.01) The best Chardonnay we tasted bar just one – just – and that was the most expensive submitted. How Danie de Wet, who is a mountain of a man, can produce such a delicate and exquisite wine as this is beyond our comprehension. This is a textbook example of how to cram so much flavour, depth and length into a wine and still maintain the lightest of touches in its balance. Not only did this Chardonnay trash wines twice its price, we genuinely consider it to be superior to most Burgundies we regularly encounter at four times its price. Not every Burgundy at four times the price, of course, but better than most, which is no small compliment. Stunning!

SPARKLING WINES

Sainsbury's Champagne Extra Dry NV Duval-Leroy 79.87FF (£9.86) Firm, capable of improving in bottle.

BEERS

BRONZE MEDAL

Sainsbury's Czech Pilsener 3.32FF (41p) per 25cl bottle, sold in 10s at 33.50FF (£4.14) Rather rich for a true Czech Pilsener, and does not have the floweriness, but has a good, slightly bitter, hopped finish.

Beck's, Bräueri Beck 5.75FF (71p) per 27.5cl bottle, sold in 12s at 69FF (£8.52) Light and crisp, this is better than the Mosel Bier (Calais Wine and Beer), but only just, and it's almost four times the price. This price is, however, over 60% more expensive than you can buy Beck's at Beer Lovers, where it costs just 101.25FF or £12.50 for 24, rather than 12, larger 33cl bottles.
Verdict? 👍 👍 👍 👍

SHOPI

Opening hours? Mon-Sat 8.30am-7.30pm, closed Sun
Comment: Although none of the Shopi, which belong to the Promodes group (*see* Champion

entries for details), qualify for the 1000m^2 limit we have set on supermarkets to be included in the *Guide*, there seem to be so many in the Calais-Boulogne area that readers are bound to come across these brightly lit outlets, and might want some guidance, whether or not they are pinpointed on our maps.

The wines: Basically a boring range of wines that can be found elsewhere at cheaper prices. Of the six wines purchased, just one qualified.

ROSÉ WINES
Grenache Gris NV Vin de Pays d'Oc 11.90FF (£1.47) Fresh, clean and easy to drink, and a nice bit of alliteration too.
Verdict? 🖐

• 2 BRONZE MEDALS

(9) **LE TERROIR**
29 rue Fontinettes
62100 Calais
Tel: (21) 36.34.66
English spoken? Just a little
Opening hours? Mon-Sat 9am-7.30pm, Sun 9.30am-1pm
Parking? On the street
Shopping trolleys? No
Do they offer to help carry the goods to the car? Yes
Methods of payment? Sterling, French Francs, Eurocheques, Visa, Mastercard, Access
Any wines for tasting in store? Yes
Comment: Le Terroir has been in operation for 12 years, which makes it the oldest *cave* in Calais, according to its owner M. Morvan. Morvan is a very friendly man, and his shop is a must for all wine enthusiasts, with everything neatly displayed in bins or on shelves.
The wines: We did not receive a list, so we cannot give specific examples other than those tasted, but Le Terroir does have a large range of some 300 products. This starts at 20FF, and include 60 different whiskies and 40 Champagnes, but no beers. His fine wines include a collection of vintages going back to 1929, but that sort of thing is much cheaper back home, although he is always on the look for old vintages, so if you have any to dispose of, it might pay you to sell them here, rather than the UK (certainly it would do you no harm to write to M. Morvan, but do not forget to mention the level of the wines). Six of the 10 wines submitted passed the test.

RED WINES

Château Nuit des Dames 1991 Côtes-du-Rhône
20FF (£2.47) An unusual wine, quite pale in colour and with aromas hinting more of Pinot sweetness than any Rhône character.

BRONZE MEDAL *la Sélection du Terroir 1991 Haut-Médoc* 35FF (£4.32) This oaky Bordeaux tastes like it has been pepped-up with a good dollop of Rioja, although we are not suggesting that it has, of course.

Calais Vieille Étape 1993 la Sélection du Terroir 35FF (£4.32) Creamy-fruit aromas on both nose and palate.

WHITE WINES

Abbaye Saint-Laurent 1992 Muscadet sur Lie 21FF (£2.59) A delicately flavoured wine that shows best when partnered with equally delicately flavoured food.

Château Roque-Peyre 1993 Montravel 21.85FF (£2.70) Soft and easy to drink.

BRONZE MEDAL *Riesling Klur Stoecklé 1992 Vin d'Alsace* 27.55FF (£3.40) An elegant dry Riesling wine that will improve dramatically over the next 12 months.
Verdict? 👍👍

RUNNER UP FOR
BEST CROSS-CHANNEL
SUPERMARKET OF
THE YEAR
• 4 SILVER MEDALS
• 14 BRONZE MEDALS

(22) TESCO

Cité Europe
62231 Coquelles
Tel: N/A
Opening hours? 9am-7.30pm seven days a week
Selling area: 2,500m² (compare this with the size of other stores featured in the area, to gauge their relative size and you will have a rough idea of how big the range of wines, beers, spirits and other goods will be).
Additional information:
* The runner up designation for Tesco is awarded on the proviso that this store opens as scheduled, and its drink selection consists of at least a good proportion of those recommended.
Comment: When Sainsbury's opened in the Mammouth complex in April, there was much speculation about Tesco's cross-Channel outlet, but it was not due to open until March 1995. It is an interesting fact that when Tesco committed itself to opening in March 1995, Eurotunnel was publicly promising that its Le Shuttle service, once scheduled to commence in 1993, wouldn't start in March 1994, but later postponed it to April ... then May ... probably August ... not before September. Now it seems that March 1995 might be more

realistic. It makes you wonder whether Tesco knew something we didn't. I mean, why plan to open up one year after everything is up and running? Surely Tesco did not want to miss out on the first year's income, which would include a bonus from the curiosity factor? The big difference between Tesco and Sainsbury's is that Tesco will be selling a wide range of products, not just wines, beers, and spirits. It will be interesting to see just what other products Tesco will sell, as there are three factors working against UK chains selling non-drinks products in France: firstly there is no discernible saving in duty, secondly UK supermarket chains traditionally have higher profit margins, and this is compounded by the third factor, social insurance, which effectively increases the cost of wages by 56.63% (37.3% employer's contribution, 19.3% employee's contribution, only they traditionally expect their rate of pay to 'cover' this). We wish Tesco good luck, but think it will be very difficult, especially in its Cité Europe location, if last year's prediction that Le Shuttle is a flop comes true.

The wines: To be a runner up to the Best Cross-Channel Supermarket of the year is an impressive achievement. Not just because this outlet is not even open, but also because we had to twist some arms to get any wines at all, and those sent were not necessarily the best wines to submit (most of those were either vintages of lines not yet available). Tesco had not chosen its range when we made our approach, and its buyers explained that the range would not be finalised until the new year, when many more new purchases could be considered. We therefore told Tesco to send us the safe (but necessarily the most exciting) lines: the wines they could rely on as being part of the basic range, and of vintages and *cuvées* that will either still be the same in March 1995, or have a track record of not deviating much from shipment to shipment. The range submitted was very basic and limited, which explains the absence of any Gold medals, but 3 Silver and, especially, 13 Bronze is a tremendous achievement for what is, unless Tesco has told us porkies, merely a rudimentary selection.

RED WINES
Rosso del Salento NV Marchese del Casa 14.90FF (£1.84) Good basic light-bodied red with more fruit than most cheap Italian wines and none of

the bitterness that is supposed to typify the red wines of this country.

Australian Shiraz/Cabernet Sauvignon NV South Eastern Australia Dry Red Wine 14.90FF (£1.84) Not special, but this Shiraz dominated wine is decent enough, and merits recommendation at this cheap price.

Chilean Red Wine NV Tesco 14.90FF (£1.84) Good honest red that will not improve much in bottle, but should last a good 18 months without losing fruit or drying up.

Claret NV Yvon Mau, Bordeaux 14.90FF (£1.84) An elegant, light, luncheon-style claret. Very little tannin.

Marques de Chivé NV Tempranillo, Vicente Gandia 14.90FF (£1.84) The oaky character of this wine has been marred by – it appears to us – too much emphasis on aeration during racking, which speeds up the maturity of a wine, but sucks the freshness out of the fruit and coats the finish with a touch of toffee. On the palate, the fruit is initially raspberry, but turns to coconut, and quickly picks up this toffee character.

BRONZE MEDAL   *Bulgarian Cabernet Sauvignon Reserve 1988 Suhindol, Domaine Boyar* 19.52FF (£2.41) Theoretically the same as the litre bottle sold by Sainsbury's, but unless our imagination is getting the better of us, this has a more peachy aftertaste.

BRONZE MEDAL   *Australian Red Wine NV Shiraz/Cabernet Sauvignon, South Eastern Australia* 19.52FF (£2.41) Although slightly jammy, the richness of blackcurrant fruit in this wine warrants recommendation at this price, and it has just enough edge to accompany food, which is rare for a cheap, gluggy Australian red.

Mexican Cabernet Sauvignon 1990 Baja California, L. A. Cetto 23.49FF (£2.90) Sweet fruit with a very soft finish.

Chianti Classico 1992 Ampelos 23.49FF (£2.90) Nice amount of sweet fruit on the finish.

BRONZE MEDAL   *New Zealand Cabernet Sauvignon/Merlot 1991 Gisborne* 23.49FF (£2.90) Lightly rich, slightly spicy fruit totally dominated by oak.

BRONZE MEDAL   *Chilean Cabernet Sauvignon NV Maipo* 23.49FF (£2.90) There is some grassy assertiveness that typifies old-style Kiwi Cabernet more than it does Chilean, which, old or new, should be riper and more chocolatey. Still, typicity to one side, this is not a bad wine.

SILVER MEDAL   *Domaine de Lanestousse, Madiran 1989 D. de Robillard* 31.51FF (£3.89) With its inky nose and dark, inky fruit, this wine gives the impression that it was once as pure as fresh-picked blackcurrants. It is, however, merely in a transitionary stage and will develop into an excellent, long-lived red wine of real character and complexity, if given several more years in bottle.

WHITE WINES

BRONZE MEDAL
Dorgan NV Vin de Pays de l'Aude 12.88FF (£1.59) Fresh dry white wine with a touch of pétillance.
Marques de Chivé NV Vino de Crianza 14.90FF (£1.84) Bags of vanilla and coconut on the nose, but not much fruit underneath, although completely clean tasting. Should be ideal for lovers of white Rioja on a budget.
English Table Wine NV High Weald Winery 14.90FF (£1.84) Assertive Sauvignon-style. Good value.

BRONZE MEDAL
Australian White Wine NV Rhine Riesling, South Eastern Australia 14.90FF (£1.84) Rather full-bodied for the European concept of a Riesling wine, but it does have some varietal character, and for the cheapest Riesling in the tasting, this off-dry wine had more than enough tangy, green-apple fruit.

BRONZE MEDAL
Muscadet de Sèvre et Maine NV Celliers du Prieuré 14.90FF (£1.84) Softer than most Muscadet, yet has the correct crispness, making this the best-cheapest Muscadet we found.

SILVER MEDAL
BEST-CHEAPEST WHITE WINE OF THE YEAR
Chilean White Wine NV Tesco 14.90FF (£1.84) Fat and tasty, with a bit of oomph, good acidity and a grassy character that makes you think more of New Zealand than Chile.

BRONZE MEDAL
South African White NV Stellenbosch 14.90FF (£1.84) Although from a completely different continent, this wine tastes quite similar to the Chilean White (which itself hints of New Zealand!), only somewhat softer in style.

BRONZE MEDAL
Australian Colombard/Chardonnay NV South Eastern Australia Dry White Wine 19.52FF (£2.41) Hardly any evidence of Chardonnay's part in the blend, but there is lots of fresh, spritzy fruit and a long, crisp, off-dry finish that makes it ideal for an afternoon tipple or barbecue wine.

BRONZE MEDAL
New Zealand Dry White Wine NV Tesco 20.17FF (£2.49) Very easy to drink, the fruit just slips down the throat, although the Chilean White has the edge, not just as a good value dry white wine, but for its Kiwi typicity!
Domaine St Pierre Chardonnay 1993 Les Domaines, Vin de Pays d'Oc 23.49FF (£2.90) Fresh,

light, but not lacking, with lots of gentle, tropical fruit flavour.

BRONZE MEDAL *Australian Chardonnay NV South Eastern Australia Dry White Wine* 23.49FF (£2.90) Ripe New World fruit, plenty of body, and a long flavour.

SILVER MEDAL *Robertson Chardonnay 1994 Johann de Wet* 23.49FF (£2.90) This delicious Chardonnay reminded us of sherbert lemons, but what is so amazing is that any wine could be so easy to drink just months after the harvest, before the 1994 grapes in the northern hemisphere had even started to ripen! This wine deserves its Silver Medal not just for its technological genius, but for being such good value for money.

BRONZE MEDAL *Domaine de la Source Muscat 1992 Les Domaines, Vin de Pays de l'Hérault* 27.86FF (£3.44) Delightfully fresh, clean and flowery Muscat made in a true dry style that is easy to drink. Lovely floral after-aromas. Try this with fresh asparagus.

SILVER MEDAL *New Zealand Chardonnay NV Gisborne* 29.97FF (£3.70) Bags of vanilla on the nose and palate of this wine, with perhaps too much oak influence for the purists, but the fruit is also very rich, and there is plenty of ripe acidity, so it wont go flabby.

ROSÉ WINES
California White Zinfandel NV August Sebastiani 23.49FF (£2.90) This smells more like a grassy Sauvignon Blanc than Zinfandel, but this character is due to early harvesting, which seems incongruous in a sweet-tasting wine.

SPARKLING WINES
BRONZE MEDAL *Asti Spumante NV Perlino* 30.21FF (£3.73) Fresh and fragrant with sweet, grapy fruit and a fine mousse, this was by far the best sweet sparkling wine, but it is merely good-average Asti, not special.

BRONZE MEDAL *Australian Sparkling Wine, Brut NV Seppelt* 31.51FF (£3.89) A fizzy, lime-and-lavender-tasting concoction that relies more on richness than finesse, but has a satisfying effect nonetheless. Better on its own than with food.

Champagne Tesco NV Premier Cru Brut 89.91FF (£11.10) A gentle Champagne with sweet-ripe fruit.

Verdict? 🍷🍷🍷

CHERBOURG

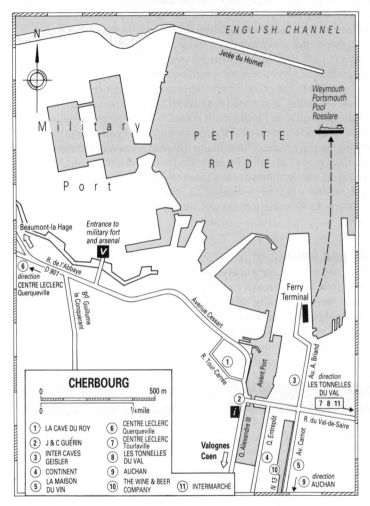

ENGLISH CHANNEL

Jetée du Homet

Weymouth
Portsmouth
Pool
Rosslare

Military

P E T I T E

R A D E

Port

Beaumont-la-Hage

Entrance to
military fort
and arsenal

R. de l'Abbaye
D 901

⑥ direction
CENTRE LECLERC
Querqueville

Bd Guillume
le Conquerant

Avenue Cessart

Ferry
Terminal

R. Tour-Carrée

①

Avant Port

③ direction
LES TONNELLES
DU VAL

Au. A. Briand

7 8 11

CHERBOURG

0 — 500 m
0 — ¼ mile

① LA CAVE DU ROY	⑥ CENTRE LECLERC Querqueville	
② J & C GUÉRIN	⑦ CENTRE LECLERC Tourlaville	
③ INTER CAVES GEISLER	⑧ LES TONNELLES DU VAL	
④ CONTINENT	⑨ AUCHAN	
⑤ LA MAISON DU VIN	⑩ THE WINE & BEER COMPANY	⑪ INTERMARCHÉ

**Valognes
Caen** ⬇

②
ℹ

R. du Val-de-Saire

Q. Alexandre III

Q. Entrepôt

N 13

④

⑩

Av. Carnot

⑤

⑨ direction
AUCHAN

There is no direct autoroute link to the ferry terminal, as there is at
Calais, but it is easy to drive out of Cherbourg without seeing the
heart of the town. If you want to see something of Cherbourg, keep a
sharp eye out for the *Centre Ville* signs. Cars are banned from parts of
the town centre, but there are three large car parks, each adequately
signposted, within the immediate vicinity. The nearest parking to the
place du Général de Gaulle, which houses the market three days a
week and constitutes the best focal point for shopping in Cherbourg,

is just over the swing-bridge Pont Tournant. Once over, turn first right down the quai de Caligny and first left into the car park. On the other side of the car park you will find the rue du Commerce, rue de Château and rue des Portes pedestrian shopping area, although for this convenience you must pay a small parking fee. If you begrudge paying to park the car, then turn left over the bridge into the quai Alexandre III and you will see a sign pointing to free parking spaces on your right in the place Divette (approach from either rue Vastel or avenue Delaville). If you visit the nearest hypermarket, which is Continent in quai de l'Entrepôt, it is best to leave the car there, walk up the quayside and go over the bridge on foot, if you want to wander around the town itself. The walking distance is not much different than from place Delaville. To get to Continent, take the second major turning on the right into avenue François Millet and first right again. If you want the best hypermarket, Continent is rather drab, while Auchan in La Glacerie is more welcoming and the bigger of the two stores.

Did you know?

• The port of Cherbourg was originally built as a naval base and fought over by the French and English during the 11th century. The English were eventually driven out by King Charles VII, but returned in 1758 when they mounted a surprise attack and pillaged the town.
• Napoléon intended to make Cherbourg the naval stepping stone to his empire in Egypt, but an inscription on his statue in the quai de Caligny is the only product of that intention.

Cherbourg Factfile

HOW TO GET THERE: Brittany Ferries operate out of Poole, with a 4 hour 30 minute crossing-time; P&O operates out of Portsmouth, with a 4 hour 45 minute (day), up to a 9 hour 45 minute (night) crossing-time; Stena Sealink operates out of Southampton, with a 4-5 hour crossing-time. From the Republic of Ireland, Irish Ferries operate out of Cork, with an 18 hour 30 minute crossing-time (see pages 340-355 for details of service and prices).

LOCATION AND DISTANCES: Situated on the northern coast of the Cotentin peninsular, a hop and a skip from Alderney, 119km (74 miles) northwest of Caen, 400km (250 miles) from Boulogne, 464km (290 miles) from Calais, 286km (179 miles) from Dieppe, 227km (142 miles) from Le Havre, 118km (74 miles) from Caen, 187km (117 miles) from St-Malo, 366km (229 miles) from Roscoff and 341km (213 miles) from Paris.

POPULATION: 30,000

TOURIST INFORMATION OFFICE: 2 quai Alexandre III, 50100 Cherbourg, *tel:* (33) 43.52.02. Open Mon-Sat 9am-12noon & 2pm-6pm, closed Sun.

WHERE TO STAY: During the peak season, it is always best to book your hotel in advance, but if you are caught out, try the Tourist Information Centre, which offers a free accommodation service, keeping track of all the vacancies left in the town. The best place to stay: *Hôtel Le Mercure* (Gare Maritime, *tel:* (33) 44.01.11) for a splendid breakfast overlooking the harbour, with doubles en-suite from 380-520FF or £47-64. Some cheap but clean stays include: *Hôtel Divette* (15 rue Louis XVI, *tel:* (33) 43.21.04) offers large, traditionally furnished doubles with shower for 150FF; *Hôtel le Curie* (12 rue Pierre-Curie, 50130 Octeville) smart doubles en-suite with TV for 220FF, located in the outskirts of Cherbourg.

RESTAURANTS: The Michelin guide recommends the *Gandgousier* (21 rue de l'Abbaye) and *L'Ancre Dorée* (27 rue de l'Abbaye), but we think the *Café de Paris* (40 quai de Caligny) is equally as good, and it is certainly the best place to eat seafood overlooking the harbour. If you are in a bit of a hurry, *Le Flore* (Place du Général de Gaulle) offers an express fixed-price three-course menu of the day for just 39.50FF, children's menu 18FF and a reasonably priced à la carte menu. *Le Biniou* (34 rue Victor Grignard) is a decent, cheap crêperie.
Best-cheapest eats: Monsieur Pain runs a cheap and lively place called *Le Faitout* (25 rue Tour Carré), which serves good, wholesome food, while those who like Tex-Mex should try *Duke's Diner* (5 rue Christine). Where to find most restaurants, including some of the cheaper places to eat: the area enclosed by the quai de Caligny, rue Tour Carrée and place de la République.

MARKET DAYS: Tuesday, Thursday and Saturday (place du Général de Gaulle)

WORTH A VISIT: You could try visiting the military port and its arsenal, which is open only to French citizens with identity cards. This is in clear violation of the treaty, for while no European citizen has the right to visit any member state's military bases on the grounds of security, no member state has the right to discriminate between citizens of the European Union when it opens the door of such a facility to the public: either every European citizen has the right of entry or no one has. So why not make a European nuisance of yourself?

(9) AUCHAN
RN13
50470 La Glacerie
Tel: (33) 44.43.44
Selling area: 8,000m^2 (compare this with the size of other stores featured in the area, to gauge their relative size and you will have a rough idea of how big the range of wines, beers, spirits and other goods will be).
Opening hours? Mon-Fri 8.30am-10pm, Sat 8am-10pm, closed Sun
Foire aux Vins: October
Comment: These outlets are usually amongst the biggest, brightest and most welcoming of the French hypermarket chains, and the one near

Cherbourg is very large indeed, although only two-thirds the size of the one in Boulogne. Auchan is very popular with the British, who are apt to go spend-crazy in any supersized hypermarket. We had even less response from Auchan's directors this year than we did with its wine buyer last time, as neither the chairman (Gérard Mulliez) nor its managing director (Michel Pecqueraux) even acknowledged our correspondence.

The wines: The wines are displayed from the floor right up to the ceiling – well almost to the ceiling. There are many more reds than whites, with the greatest emphasis placed predictably enough on Bordeaux (approximately 40-50 different wines), after which Burgundy and Languedoc-Roussillon offer the most choice (about 20 wines each), although white Burgundies fare less well (just six), and the choice of Loire in any colour is abysmal. There are about 10 different Alsace, but the only white wines stocked in any serious way are Champagne and other sparklers. We purchased six wines (the cheapest red and cheapest white, plus four wines that a knowledgeable consumer might consider interesting or good value), but only one qualified for recommendation in this *Guide*, and two of those that failed the test we would not touch with a barge pole, even if Auchan gave them away. A hit-rate of just one in six is bad enough: we hate to think how the average consumer, who has to rely on pot-luck, would fare.

WHITE WINES
Alsace Riesling 1992 Pierre Dumoulin-Storch
25.90FF (£3.20) Dry white wine lifted by a slight spritz.
Verdict? 🖒

① **LA CAVE DU ROY**
47 rue Tour Carrée
50100 Cherbourg
Tel: (33) 53.05.21
English spoken? Not revealed
Opening hours? Tues-Sat 9am-12.30pm & 2.30pm-7.30pm, Sun 9am-12.30pm, closed Mon
Parking? On street (difficult)
Shopping trolleys? No
Do they offer to help carry the goods to the car? Yes
Methods of payment? Sterling, French Francs, Traveller's cheques, Eurocheques, Visa, Access,

Mastercard, American Express, Diners Card
Any wines for tasting in store? No
Comment: We liked this little shop, which is in the old part of town and well worth the detour. It is owned and run by M. & Mme Fesnien, a young couple who both seem keen, knowledgeable and friendly. The wines are stored and presented well, with beautiful cellars below. A fine range of AOC cheeses is also offered.
The wines: Last year just three wines were submitted, which was not enough to get a grip on the range, especially as only one passed the test. This year we hoped to taste more widely, but M. Fresnien did not submit any. No list was forthcoming either. Obviously we cannot assess La Cave du Roy this year, but the Fresniens remain as friendly as ever, we still love their wonderful little shop, and there is nothing to stop readers from rooting around for themselves.
Verdict? ?

• 2 SILVER MEDALS

⑥ CENTRE LECLERC
5 rue des Clairs
50460 Querueville
Tel: (33) 03.55.43
Selling area: 4,300m^2

AND

⑦ CENTRE LECLERC
Rue des Metiers
50110 Tourlaville
Tel: (33) 22.20.80
Selling area: 2,850m^2 (compare this with the size of other stores featured in the area, to gauge their relative size and you will have a rough idea of how big the range of wines, beers, spirits and other goods will be).
Opening hours? Mon-Thurs 9am-10pm, Fri 9am-10.30pm, Sat 8.30am-10.30pm, closed Sun
Comment: Last year we went through Gallec, which owns Leclerc, Groupe de Travail Liquides, which supplies Leclerc, and Leclerc's chief buyer, but all to no avail, so this time we went straight to the top, and we were pleased to receive Michel-Edouard Leclerc's assurance that his chain would extend the *Guide* full co-operation in supplying whatever samples and information we wanted. He delegated the matter to Jean Maurice, who runs Leclerc Scapertois, which supplies all the stores in the Pas-de-Calais and Normandy. Unfortunately M. Maurice had other ideas, inviting us instead to

spend the day at Scapertois, where we could taste their best wines over 70FF. We would be wined and dined, and afterwards we would be given some *cru classé* Bordeaux to take away. Apparently he has tried this wheeze on other British journalists with a certain amount of success, but we are not in this job to fill the car-boot with cases of château-bottled claret, so we declined, immediately and in no uncertain terms. We again explained that most cross-Channel bargains are under 34FF, as indeed are most of Centre Leclerc's sales, thus concentrating on its top of the range wines tells us nothing about the bulk of wines most Leclerc customers buy. Besides which, tasting them in isolation would have been unfair to the other retail outlets, whose wines must compete with others of a similar style and price under blind conditions. After more correspondence with M. Leclerc, we received a letter from the head of Sobadis, a subsidiary of Leclerc's, which handles the distribution of its products in Normandy. Referring to our last correspondence with Michel-Edouard Leclerc, he offered us exactly what we wanted, even a choice of branches from which we could collect our samples. Unfortunately our last correspondence with M. Leclerc had been over six weeks earlier, and our tastings had come and gone. Still, if Centre Leclerc keeps to its word, and submits samples without delay or hesitation for the next edition, all the hassle we have endured this year will at least be worthwhile.

The wines: Most branches are basic warehouse-type operations, and very utilitarian. In the bigger stores, the range can include as many as 250 different lines, with a good selection of fine wines, albeit almost entirely from Bordeaux. Centre Leclerc seems to be quite good on Beaujolais, with most *cru villages* covered, and the one we tried from Juliénas certainly fared well, earning a silver medal no less. With four wines out of six random purchases qualifying for recommendation in the *Guide*, including two silver medals, one of which grabbed a Wine of the Year award, it makes us look forward to greater co-operation next year, to see how the range as a whole performs.

RED WINES

SILVER MEDAL
BEST-VALUE RED
WINE OF THE YEAR

Domaine de Pons 1991 Côtes du Ventoux 13.95FF (£1.72) We had to taste almost 30 red Rhônes up to 27FF before we found a wine to equal this. An elegant wine with a good depth of silky-plummy

fruit, and nicely structured supple tannins.
*Carayon-la-Rose 1986 Cuvée Exceptionnelle,
Bordeaux Supérieur* 18.95FF (£2.34) This is not bad
as a basic Bordeaux, but unless you see the vintage
on the label, you would hardly think that you are
tasting an eight-year-old claret.

SILVER MEDAL
Juliénas 1992 les Vouillants Chedeville 26.50FF
(£3.27) Bags of flavour. A real wine, and a true *cru*
Beaujolais (we rejected most of the *cru* Beaujolais
because they lacked the significant increase in
quality and intensity of varietal flavour they
should possess).
*Château Roches Guitard 1989 Montagne-St-
Émilion* 30.85FF (£3.81) A good Bordeaux with
sweet fruity aromas that follow through onto the
palate.
Verdict? 👍

• 1 SILVER MEDAL
• 1 BRONZE MEDAL

④ **CONTINENT**
CC quai de l'Entrepôt
50100 Cherbourg
Tel: (33) 43.14.11
Selling area: 6,200m² (compare this with the size
of other stores featured in the area, to gauge their
relative size and you will have a rough idea of
how big the range of wines, beers, spirits and
other goods will be).
Opening hours? Mon-Sat 8.30am-10pm, closed
Sun
Comment: Part of the Promodes group, which
owns Continent, Shopi and various other smaller
outlets. We made contact last year with no less
than six top people at Promodes and its various
offshoots, but to no avail, so this year we wrote to
the managing director of Promodes, M. Pierre
Merle, but he could not be bothered to reply
either.
The wines: There is quite a big range in the larger
Continent stores such as this, but not a
particularly wonderful selection in the price
category most cross-Channel shoppers are
interested in (15-30FF), although we did strike
lucky with two of the six wines we purchased at
random. The Bordeaux selection is eclectic and
spotty, with some good *cru classé*, but prices are
not competitive, although they do have some on
offer (eg., Ducru-Beaucaillou 1991 at 86FF, and
Fieuzal at 72FF).

RED WINES

BRONZE MEDAL
Les Mélusines 1993 St-Nicolas-de-Bourgueil 27FF
(£3.33) A tasty wine indeed, and with an authentic

grassy Loire Cabernet edge that does not detract from its drinkability.

WHITE WINES

SILVER MEDAL

Jean Marie Strubbler Gewurztraminer 1993 Vin d'Alsace 22.90FF (£2.83) Good value Gewurztraminer, with assertive, spicy fruit. The acidity is somewhat high for this grape, giving the wine a finer balance than most.
Verdict? ☹

M. GOSSLIN
Rue de Verrûe
50550 St-Vaast-la-Hogue
Tel: (33) 54.40.06
Comment: We are indebted to reader Major Sandys-Renton of Thirsk in North Yorkshire for this late addition, which we will certainly check out next year. St-Vaast-la-Hogue is a pretty little fishing port just a few kilometres east of Cherbourg. It has a large marina, which many British sailors use, particularly for the Saturday market. According to the Major, 'Gosslin is known as the "Harrods of Normandy" ... a high class grocery with a very upmarket wine selection, all bottles stored horizontally'. He also quite rightly told us off for not mentioning Pommeau. Sorry Major! Pommeau is a sweet concoction of apple juice and Calvados, which was made at home and consumed locally, but since 1991 there has been an official appellation called Pommeau de Normandie, which restricts production to 31 specified varieties of apple growing in the Calvados area, and controls how it should be made. We are not sure whether the home-made stuff can still be sold, but knowing the French, even if it officially cannot, unofficially it still will be. Apparently M. Gosslin sells Pommeau, but we are not sure which type.
Verdict? ☹

② J&C GUÉRIN
56 quai Caligny
50100 Cherbourg
Tel: (33) 43.02.01
English spoken? No
Opening hours? Mon-Sat 8.45am-12noon & 2pm-7.15pm, closed Sun
Parking? Some parking across the road, but not easy

Comment: Having received no reply to our correspondence last year, we called on this outlet only to find it closed, despite the fact that it was nearly 2.30pm. This year we were a bit more lucky, the shop was at least open. Our representative, however, received a frosty reception from a very stony-faced lady who we assume must be Mme Guérin, although she would not confirm this. She just kept repeating that she was not interested, and that she was not going to bother her husband with our presence. Who are we to complain, having done exactly the same thing to doorstep salesmen ourselves? We later found out from locals that – allegedly – this had once been a thriving business, delivering duty-free goods to customers on the ferries, but now that the owners no longer have this business, they wish to retire, only are prevented from selling up by some complicated French administrative reasons.
Verdict? ?

RUNNER UP FOR
BEST DRINKS OUTLET
IN CHERBOURG
• 1 GOLD MEDAL
• 4 BRONZE MEDALS

③ **INTER CAVES (Geisler)**
27 bis rue Aristide Briand
50100 Cherbourg
Tel: (33) 44.48.03
English spoken? Yes
Opening hours? Mon 3pm-7.30pm, Tues-Sat 9.30am-12.30pm & 3.00pm-7.30pm & Sun 10am-12.30pm
Parking? Only on street
Shopping trolleys? No
Do they offer to help carry the goods to the car? Yes
Methods of payment? Sterling, French Francs, Traveller's cheques, Eurocheques, Visa, Mastercard
Any wines for tasting in store? Yes
Comment: This outlet is part of the Inter Caves group (*see also* branches in Caen, Calais, and St-Malo), which consists of approximately 90 shops spread throughout France, plus a few additional outlets in Germany. This shop is conveniently situated for the ferry, but there is not as much room as the manager would like, hence his range is smaller than most other branches of Inter Caves, although this is less of a hindrance to the locals, as he can always order other wines in.
The wines: We were promised a list, but did not receive one, and our representative reported a dozen Champagnes from smaller, lesser known producers, which sounded interesting, but the

only one submitted was Champagne De Saval, which does not exist as such, but is made by another producer (Baron Albert, we think), and although drinkable was not special. Hopefully we can taste some real small producer Champagnes next time, but submitting a larger number of better selected wines this year has paid off, giving the Inter Caves group a far more impressive entry in this year's *Guide* than it got in the first edition.

RED WINES

BRONZE MEDAL
Domaine le Pian 1992 Vin de Pays du Gard 19FF (£2.35) Soft, silky blackcurrant fruit.

Chatellenie de Lastours NV Corbières 29FF (£3.58) Rich and robust, with a herbal-oak undertone.

GOLD MEDAL
Château de Pech Redon 1991 La Clape 29.50FF (£3.64) Absolutely delightful fruit underpinned by bubble-gum oak, which creates a sort of raspberry ripple flavour. Although it might not sound like it, this is an elegant, classy wine.

Massana 1991 Côtes du Roussillon 29.90FF (£3.69) Could be Rioja if we did not know better.

BRONZE MEDAL
Bourgogne Pinot Noir 1992 Philippe de Marange 35.70FF (£4.41) An elegant Burgundy for the price, with ripe-cherry Pinot Noir fruit.

BRONZE MEDAL
Domaine Duseigneur 1991 Lirac 39.50FF (£4.88) An elegant, fruity Rhône, but we have come across two versions of apparently the same wine: one with a neck-label that has the word 'Lirac' either side of the vintage, and the other with a neck-label that has 'Cru' one side of the vintage and 'Race' the other, and the latter of these seems to have a more smoky-toasty finish.

Juliénas 1992 Domaine de la Bottière 44FF (£5.43) Has some potential for development over the next year or two.

Saumur-Champigny 1992 Domaine du Val Brun 45FF (£5.56) This may lack charm on the nose, but it has good fruit underneath, and should develop more attractive bottle-aromas over the next 18 months or so.

Domaine des Lucques 1990 Graves 47FF (£5.80) Probably a lot better 18 months ago, but still makes a decent glass of Bordeaux, even if prematurely mellow.

WHITE WINES

Baron de Peyrac, Sauvignon 1993 Bordeaux Blanc 17.90FF (£2.21) Although this wine's fresh aroma shows good typicity, it is too soft to be classic

Sauvignon, although this very softness is what makes it so easy to drink.

BRONZE MEDAL | *Clos du Zahnacker 1988 Vin d'Alsace* 60FF (£7.41) One of the very few classic blends of Alsace, this wine was probably easier to drink two years ago, and will undoubtedly find greater harmony in two years from now, but is currently in a stage of development where the Riesling is battling with the Gewurztraminer.

ROSÉ WINES
Château la Croix de l'Hosanne 1993 Bordeaux Clairet 22.90FF (£2.83) Highly perfumed, off-dry rosé with plenty of fruit.
Verdict? 👍👍👍

• 1 BRONZE MEDAL

⑩ **INTERMARCHÉ**
Rue du Grand Pré
50110 Tourlaville
Tel: (33) 43.54.20
Selling area: 1,200m² (compare this with the size of other stores featured in the area, to gauge their relative size and you will have a rough idea of how big the range of wines, beers, spirits and other goods will be).
Opening hours? Mon-Thurs 9am-12.15pm & 2pm-7.15, Fri 9am-12.15pm & 2pm-7.30pm, Sat 9am-7.15pm
Comment: Most Intermarché on the Channel coast are relatively small, and although they can be quite large further inland, this chain is more of the supermarket ilk than hypermarket. It is also relatively down-market, with a mostly dull and uninteresting range of wines, often dominated by a display of 3-litre wine containers. There are around a dozen different Champagnes, and the fine wines are usually displayed separately (we saw Ducru Beaucaillou 1989 at 85FF, and Pavillon Rouge 1990 at 105FF). We had no success with chairman Marcel Robin, who steadfastly refused to answer our correspondence. It was the same story as last year, with M. Le Goff, Intermarché's drinks buyer.
The wines: We purchased six wines along the same lines as those we bought at Auchan, and when it came to the crunch, Intermarché fared much better, with half of the wines warranting our recommendation, and one even picking up a Bronze medal. And two of those that did not qualify were perfectly drinkable, even if not special enough to qualify for the *Guide*. If only the

management of this firm had enough faith in its products to submit a substantial range of its inexpensive wines, they might do well, if this random sampling is anything to go by.

RED WINES
Beaujolais NV Cuvée Joannès 12FF (£1.48) Although not medal potential, you could have knocked us down with a feather when this wine, the second-cheapest Gamay submitted, turned out not only to be drinkable, but expressive of its variety, rather than *macération carbonique*.
Côtes-du-Rhône 1993 Réserve Lescarrat 13FF (£1.60) This soft and fruity wine has a touch more elegance than the other red Rhônes in its price category.

WHITE WINES

BRONZE MEDAL

Reuilly 1993 Cave PD 22.90FF (£2.83) This fresh and assertive Sauvignon is not a wine for wimps. **Verdict?** 👍

RUNNER UP FOR
BEST CROSS-CHANNEL
OUTLET OF THE YEAR
★ *BEST DRINKS OUTLET*
IN CHERBOURG
• 5 GOLD MEDALS
• 10 SILVER MEDALS
• 8 BRONZE MEDALS

⑤ LA MAISON DU VIN
71 avenue Carnot
50100 Cherbourg
Tel: (33) 43.39.79
English spoken? Yes
Opening hours? 10am-7pm seven days a week
Parking? Yes (large private car park)
Shopping trolleys? Yes
Do they offer to help carry the goods to the car? Yes
Methods of payment? Sterling, Irish Punts, French Francs, Traveller's cheques, Eurocheques, Visa, Access, Mastercard
Any wines for tasting in store? Yes
Additional information:
* Orders can be placed through the UK shop (01929 480352) so that the goods will be packed and ready for your collection.
Comment: This British-owned outlet, with friendly, welcoming staff and medal-winning range of wines is the place in Cherbourg to do your cross-Channel shopping.
The wines: Richard Harvey MW started off this shop in June 1993 with a small selection of 50 wines, but by the time our first edition had been published, the range was up to 100, and now it is about 130. It won't get much larger, probably 150 wines max, but the skill of selection is such that there is not much chaff, with no less than eight out of every 10 wines submitted passing our test.

RED WINES

Club d'Or NV Donatien Bahuaud 12FF (£1.48) We are not lovers of Beaujolais Nouveau, but if you are, why not buy this wine, which is the same style and at least as good, but pretends to be nothing other than a *vin de table*.

BRONZE MEDAL

Domaine de la Ferrandière 1992 Cabernet Sauvignon 16FF (£1.98) The leafy-blackcurrant fruit gives this wine some interest, and makes it stand out in its price category, although it is best appreciated with food.

BRONZE MEDAL

Château Richard 1992 Bergerac, Sélection les Vieux Charmes 25FF (£3.09) Very soft and silky fruit, good length and an interesting mix of aromas on the aftertaste.

Côtes-du-Rhône 1992 Domaine Duseigneur 26FF (£3.21) A serious red Rhône with plenty of flavour and good structure. The finish is firm, but not harsh, making the wine an ideal accompaniment to food.

SILVER MEDAL

Domaine de Ribonnet 1990 Dénomination Comté Tolosan 32FF (£3.95) This wine has quite a special taste and style, with a menthol finesse and a nice, dry woody finish.

BRONZE MEDAL

Touraine, Gamay 1993 Domaine de la Charmoise 32FF (£3.95) This is a simple wine in the most positive sense of the term, its uncomplicated Gamay fruit making it such a joy to drink.

BRONZE MEDAL

Beaujolais Villages 1993 Joël Rochette 33FF (£4.07) Plenty of flavour and a good structure for accompanying food, bot rare characteristics as far as most Gamay wines are concerned.

SILVER MEDAL

Château Lamartine 1990 Cahors 34FF (£4.20) Serious Cahors: big structure with solid fruit that needs time to mellow.

SILVER MEDAL

Château Rozier 1990 Bordeaux - Côtes de Francs 34FF (£4.20) The quality of rich, toasty fruit in this wine stood out.

GOLD MEDAL

Côtes-du-Rhône 1991 E. Guigal 35FF (£4.94) Lovely balance, all components already in perfect harmony, succulent fruit.

BRONZE MEDAL

Domaine Duseigneur 1991 Lirac 39.50FF (£4.88) An elegant, fruity Rhône, but we have come across two versions of apparently the same wine: one with a neck-label that has the word 'Lirac' either side of the vintage, and the other with a neck-label that has 'Cru' one side of the vintage and 'Race' the other, and the latter of these seems to have a more smoky-toasty finish.

SILVER MEDAL

Brouilly Pisse-Vieille, Cru du Beaujolais 1993 Joël Rochette 45FF (£5.56) Soft, ripe, elegant fruit. And yes, Pisse-Vieille does mean what you think it means, but the story why is too long to explain here.

WHITE WINES

Blanc de Blancs, Dry NV Donatien Bahuaud 12FF (£1.48) Clean tasting, has fruit and is well made, all of which is very welcome at this price level. The label even looks quite stylish: what more could you ask?

SILVER MEDAL   *Riesling Select 1992 Josef Friederich* 17FF (£2.10) Refreshing Riesling with delicious tangy, lemon & lime fruit and a crisp, medium-ish finish. Astonishingly good. Anyone who likes inexpensive German wine, or medium-dry or medium-sweet Loire wines should compare this to their favourite regular tipple.

Château Bauduc 1993 Bordeaux Sec 24FF (£2.96) Crisp, Sauvignon-style dry white.

SILVER MEDAL   *Domaine de la Ferrandière 1993 Chardonnay* 25FF (£3.09) A rich and satisfying wine with just the right structure to suit both food and drinking on its own.

GOLD MEDAL   *Château Richard Cuvée Spéciale 1992 Bergerac Sec* 25FF (£3.09) With more than a hint of botrytis on the nose and rich, oily, off-dry, botrytis-affected fruit on the palate, this might not be what most people looking for a typical dry white Bordeaux want, but it has quality and is a bit special.

GOLD MEDAL   *Domaine du Vieux Chai 1993 Muscadet de Sèvre et Maine Sur Lie* 26FF (£3.21) One of the three highest-scoring Muscadets, its peachy aroma and soft, ripe fruit is, however, completely atypical for the appellation, although it makes for a charming wine in its own right.

GOLD MEDAL   *James Herrick Chardonnay 1993 Vin de Pays d'Oc* 32FF (£3.81) This is the same price as the 1992 vintage was in the first edition. We reckoned the 1992 to be one of the best cross-Channel bargains around, and the 1993 is even better but, like the 1992, will probably get a bit overblown in the bottle, therefore we recommend that you drink this at its most terrifically fresh, and start queuing for the 1994!

GOLD MEDAL   *Côtes-du-Rhône 1992 E. Guigal* 35FF (£4.07) Has developed exceptional finesse for what is a rather nondescript year.

SILVER MEDAL   *Domaine de l'Aigle 1992 Chardonnay* 35FF (£4.32) Fine lemony fruit neatly underpinned with elegant oak. A charming wine for the price.

SILVER MEDAL   *Touraine, Sauvignon 1993 Domaine de la*

Charmoise 35FF (£4.32) Fresh, clean 'suck-a-stone' style Sauvignon of some finesse.

BRONZE MEDAL *Nicolas Zusslin 1992 Gewurztraminer* 39FF (£4.81) A big, meaty Gewurztraminer, with nicely pungent spice and good acidity.

SILVER MEDAL *Sirius 1990 Sichel* 39FF (£4.81) Serious quality, oaked white Bordeaux is full of plump fruit, and just shows what a négociant can do with a blend, if the determination is there.

Chablis 1993 Jean-Paul Droin 49FF (£6.05) Clinically clean and correct.

ROSÉ WINES

Château Bauduc 1992 Bordeaux Clairet 24FF (£2.96) Quite dark in colour and more red wine in character than rosé.

SPARKLING WINES

BRONZE MEDAL
BEST-VALUE SPARKLING WINE OF THE YEAR
Seppelt NV Great Western Brut 29FF (£3.58) This still represents one of the best cross-Channel bargains of the year compared to its UK price of £4.99 (Oddbins). Not a classy wine, perhaps, but it is not meant to be anything other than a tropically-fruity fizz that is easy to glug down.

BRONZE MEDAL *Champagne Alexandre Bonnet NV Brut Cuvée Prestige* 85FF (£10.49) An attractive combination of richness and fine acidity gives this wine the ideal balance for current drinking.

SILVER MEDAL *Champagne Alfred Gratien NV Réserve Brut* 125FF (£15.43) Classic Champagne of real depth, body and flavour, this *cuvée* is well-matured yet fresh, and ready to drink now, but will improve for several years to come.

Verdict? 🥄🥄🥄🥄

⑧ LES TONNELLES DU VAL

102 rue Médéric
50110 Tourlaville
Tel: (33) 22.44.40
English spoken? No
Opening hours? Mon-Sat 9am-12noon & 2pm-7pm, closed Sun
Parking? Yes (private car park)
Shopping trolleys? No
Do they offer to help carry the goods to the car? Yes
Methods of payment? French Francs, Traveller's cheques, Eurocheques, Visa, Access, Mastercard, American Express, Diners Card
Any wines for tasting in store? Yes
Comment: Although this small but spacious

warehouse is out of town, it is easy to find and well worth the detour for its friendly atmosphere and the ability to browse in peace.

The wines: As we said last year, owner Corinne Abikhalil is very keen and helpful, and the wines are well presented, but only one of the nine wines submitted passed our test, so the very best we can assess this outlet at is a question mark. We would love to upgrade Les Tonnelles du Val, but we could already be accused of an over-generous verdict. If we did not think that there might be something worth discovering here, and a relaxed atmosphere in which to look for it, we would have been justified in giving this outlet the thumbs down on the basis of our tasting. We are, however, rather taken with the place. We just hope that this performance is an anomaly, and that next year the wines will be better selected.

RED WINES
Côtes de Bourg 1990 Château Haut-Lansac 35FF (£4.32) Mature Merlot fruit that is already peaking, and should be drunk, not kept.
Verdict? ❓

RUNNER UP FOR
BEST DRINKS OUTLET
IN CHERBOURG
• 4 GOLD MEDALS
• 7 SILVER MEDALS
• 6 BRONZE MEDALS

⑪ THE WINE & BEER COMPANY
London - Calais - Cherbourg
CC quais de l'Entrepôt
50100 Cherbourg
Tel: Not available at the time of writing
English spoken? Yes
Opening hours? 7am-10pm seven days a week
Parking? Yes (private car park)
Shopping trolleys? Yes
Do they offer to help carry the goods to the car? Yes
Methods of payment? Sterling, French Francs, Traveller's cheques, Eurocheques, Visa, Access
Any wines for tasting in store? Yes
Additional services:
* Orders can be placed through the London shop (0181 875 1900) so that the goods will be packed and ready for your collection
Comment: This British-owned operation probably has the best location in Calais, as far as attracting British ferry travellers is concerned. Most travellers heading for the ferry will notice this warehouse-type operation, even if they have never heard of it. The Calais Wine & Beer Company is owned by Marco Attard, who started off selling

wine from a leased London lock-up, and sleeping in the empty boxes at night. Now he owns four outlets in two countries, a proper bed and a real bedroom. On 1 November 1994 he is due to open up a second cross-Channel branch in Cherbourg. **The wines:** We found the range fairly comprehensive in the first edition, and it has improved since then, hence its extra thumb-up, although Portugal still gets such a meagre coverage that it may as well not exist. The Spanish section has been greatly enhanced, mostly with the help of Torres wines, but there are one or two other interesting additions. A good selection of inexpensive fizz nicely compliments a handful of decent Champagnes. Australia, New Zealand, Chile, South Africa, California and Eastern Europe are all well served in relation to the overall size of the range. We would like to see a better choice from Alsace, and a couple of serious German wines, but would anyone buy them?

RED WINES

Château Laval 1993 Costières de Nîmes 15.31FF (£1.89) Soft, easy-drinking red.

Rioja Vega 1992 Bodegas Muerza 19.28FF (£2.38) This light, peppery red could come from anywhere, but at this price you cannot expect much more from Rioja.

Sliven Cabernet Sauvignon 1987 Reserve 20.17FF (£2.49) Not a bad drop of wine, but when it comes to Bulgarian Cabernet Sauvignon, the Sliven 1987 is not as rich or as satisfying as the Lovico 1988.

BRONZE MEDAL *Denham Estate 1993 Shiraz Cabernet Sauvignon* 26.65FF (£3.29) There is jamminess that should not be present in an Australian wine of this cross-Channel price, but the menthol-vanilla undertones to the fruit provides the overriding interest in this wine.

SILVER MEDAL *Cooks Endeavour Collection 1992 Cabernet Sauvignon - Pinot Noir* 28.27FF (£3.49) Despite its higher proportion of Cabernet grapes, this wine seemed to be dominated by Pinot Noir when tasting against Cabernet or Bordeaux-type blends, yet sticks out like a sore thumb amongst Pinot wines, making this a very ripe, easy to drink hybrid.

Denham Estate 1993 Cabernet Sauvignon 30.70FF (£3.79) Rather grassy and astringent for Oz Cabernet, but quite a good wine nonetheless.

BRONZE MEDAL *Santa Rita Reserva 1990 Cabernet Sauvignon* 32.32FF (£3.99) Rather inky and soupy, but there is no denying the fruit and satisfying flavour in this wine.

SILVER MEDAL *Côte de Beaune Villages 1989 Dominique Laurent* 48.28FF (£5.96) Mature plummy Pinot fruit. Nice now, but will be even better in 2-3 years.

Villa Antinori Chianti Classico 1989 Riserva 48.92FF (£6.04) Soft and easy to drink, with plenty of fruit.

SILVER MEDAL *Château Musar 1987 Gaston Hochar* 53.38FF (£6.59) Succulent, perfumed fruit: ideal to sip on its own.

BRONZE MEDAL *Torres Gran Coronas 1988 Reserva* 56.62FF (£6.99) At an intermediate point in its development, this vintage of Torres Gran Coronas has lost its youthful flush of life and will develop into a serious, complex wine in 2-3 years.

SILVER MEDAL *Château de Lescours 1987 Saint-Émilion Grand Cru* 56.62FF (£6.99) The fruit-gum aroma and flavour of this wine is more like Burgundy than Bordeaux, but this is no criticism of the wine as a wine *per se*, as we certainly enjoyed it very much.

SILVER MEDAL *Amiral de Beychevelle 1990 Saint-Julien* 89.02FF (£10.99) An elegant wine that will continue to improve over the next 2-3 years.

GOLD MEDAL
BEST-QUALITY RED WINE OF THE YEAR *Penfolds Cabernet Sauvignon Bin 707 1990 South Australia* 101.25FF (£12.50) Too many blind tastings end up making the biggest wines the best, but this is one case when the biggest wine truly is the best! Not a cheap wine, but this is the best price we could find, and it is £2.49 cheaper than Oddbins sell it for in the UK. There is no disguising the quality of this dark star; you could put it in a blind tasting of Bordeaux 1st Growths and its huge, intense, complex flavours would punch their way through. If, however, you want to drink it at its peak, then you'll have to wait until at least 2004.

WHITE WINES

Santa Rita 120 1993 Riesling 24.22FF (£2.99) Fresh, petrolly Riesling nose and totally dry fruit. A bit big for a Riesling by European standards, but has a good structure to accompany food.

Denham Estate 1993 Semillon Chardonnay 26.65FF (£3.29) Standard Semillon that has been lifted by, rather than beefed-up with, a decent dollop of ubiquitous Chardonnay. Best drunk within the next nine months.

Torres Gran Vina Sol 1992 Chardonnay 29.57FF (£3.65) Nice, fresh and tasty dry white wine, but very little Chardonnay character.

Principe de Viana 1992 Chardonnay 31.19FF
(£3.85) Quite a nice, tasty wine with not as much
wood influence as there is on the Principe de
Viana tinto.

SILVER MEDAL | *Orvieto Classico, Campogrande 1993 Abboccato,
Antinori* 31.51FF (£3.89) Gosh! If only all Italian
wines were as well made as this. Crystal-clear and
refreshingly clean, with mouthwatering medium-
sweet fruit. A joy to drink.

GOLD MEDAL | *Seaview 1993 Chardonnay* 32.32FF (£3.99) Really
lusciously! Bags of oak, but even a purist would
have to admit that there is more than enough
succulent fruit to take it.

SILVER MEDAL | **Cooks Discovery Collection 1992 Chardonnay**
32.32FF (£3.99) Lots of oak, but very rich and
weighty, with lemony acidity and a touch of ripe
peach on the finish. Good food wine, especially
with smoked fish or meat.

Cooks Discovery Collection 1993 Sauvignon Blanc
32.32FF (£3.99) Good, but not great, New Zealand
Sauvignon in typical ripe gooseberry style.

Château des Herbeux 1989 Bourgogne Chardonnay
40.42FF (£4.99) An oily-textured, oaky wine that is
now at its best.

SPARKLING WINES

BRONZE MEDAL | *Seppelt NV Premier Cuvée Brut* 40.42FF (£4.99)
Very rich, fresh, creamy-lemony fruit. A lively and
satisfying sparkling wine.

*Champagne Rolland d'Orfeuil NV Brut Extra
Quality* 64.72FF (£7.99) Decent fizz with sweet,
clean and creamy fruit.

BRONZE MEDAL | *Champagne Jacquesson & Fils NV Perfection, Brut*
96.79FF (£11.95) Fine quality for a second label
Champagne. Has some complexity.

BEERS

BRONZE MEDAL
*BEST-CHEAPEST LIGHT
BEER OF THE YEAR* | *Mosel Bier, Amos (Metz)* 1.38FF (17p) per 25cl
bottle, sold in 24s at 32.56FF (£4.02) Not too gassy,
with a good smooth flavour, this is the best cheap
beer we could found. Although 2p more expensive
than the very cheapest cross-Channel beers, would
you rather buy 24 drinkable bottles at 11p each or
24 undrinkable bottles at 9p each? And believe us
when we say that some of the cheap 25cl beers we
tasted were undrinkable (some were still
fermenting inside the bottle, were milky in colour,
and sour to taste).

GOLD MEDAL
*BEST-QUALITY LIGHT
BEER OF THE YEAR* | *Budweiser Budvar, Budweiser Budbräu* 4.72FF
(58p) per 33cl bottle, sold in 24s at 113.32FF
(£13.99) In terms of pure quality, Budweiser

Budvar (look out for 'Budvar', which indicates that it is the genuine article, which should not to be confused with the bland tasting Budweiser brewed in the USA, or under licence in the UK) was unbeatable.

GOLD MEDAL
BEST-VALUE LIGHT
BEER OF THE YEAR

Grolsch Premium Lager 3.71FF (46p) per 50cl can, sold in 24s at 88.94FF (£10.98) This fine, delicate, flowery-hopped brew was by far the best-value lager style beer we tasted: ten times the quality of Beck's for almost a third of the price that you would have to pay for Beck's at Sainsbury's.
Verdict? 👍👍👍👍

DIEPPE

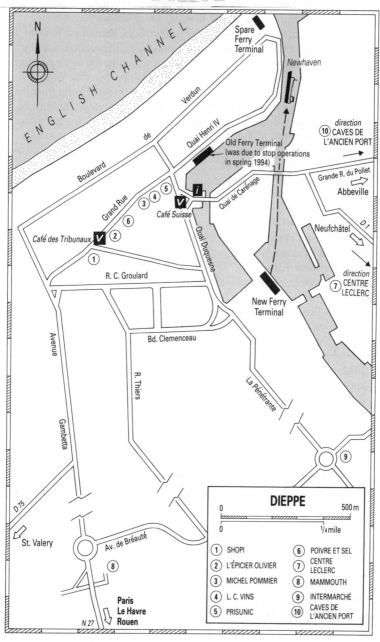

N

ENGLISH CHANNEL

Spare Ferry Terminal

Newhaven

Verdun

de

Quai Henri IV

Boulevard

Old Ferry Terminal
(was due to stop operations
in spring 1994)

direction
⑩ CAVES DE
L'ANCIEN PORT

Grand Rue

⑤

③ ④

V

i

Café Suisse

Quai de Carénage

Grande R. du Pollet

Abbeville

D 1

⑥

Café des Tribunaux **V** ②

Neufchâtel

①

Quai Duquesne

direction
⑦ CENTRE
LECLERC

R. C. Groulard

New Ferry
Terminal

Avenue

Bd. Clemenceau

R. Thiers

La Pénétrante

Gambetta

⑨

D 75

St. Valery

Av. de Bréauté

⑧

**Paris
Le Havre
Rouen**

N 27

DIEPPE

| 0 | | 500 m |

| 0 | | ¹/₄ mile |

① SHOPI	⑥ POIVRE ET SEL
② L'ÉPICIER OLIVIER	⑦ CENTRE LECLERC
③ MICHEL POMMIER	⑧ MAMMOUTH
④ L. C. VINS	⑨ INTERMARCHÉ
⑤ PRISUNIC	⑩ CAVES DE L'ANCIEN PORT

Often called the Brighton of France, Dieppe is the oldest seaside resort in France, the Duchesse du Barry having started things in 1806 when she encouraged her aristocratic friends to take a dip in its chilly, choppy waters. Dieppe is by far the prettiest of Channel ports, with its quaint harbour full of colourful boats unloading their catch, although for some time now they have not been allowed into the inner harbour because of the ferries docking there. This was due to a change in spring 1994, when Stena Sealink was supposed to start using the new east harbour ferry facilities, but nothing had happened at the time of writing. When it does, it should be a great relief to both the ferry line and its passengers, as the loading and unloading of cars in the old terminal was a nightmare of clutter and confusion. It should also prove a boon to the centre of Dieppe, the character of which will once again be embellished by the throng of small fishing boats and pleasure craft.

Did you know?

• It was from Dieppe in 1524 that Giovanni da Verrazano, the famous Italian navigator who was in the employ of the French, set sail to discover New York.

• Lord Salisbury enjoyed Dieppe so much that he laid a cable across the Channel to his holiday home, so that he could be in direct contact with the Foreign Office. He went back to this port year after year until an over-zealous customs officer charged him duty on a consignment of Scotch, after which he never returned.

• Dieppe is also known for the disastrous allied raid on 19 August 1942, when over 1000 allied soldiers, mostly Canadian, died on its shores. The raiding party had run into a German convoy and although British gunboats sank the two enemy escorts, the landing craft were hopelessly scattered during the action. Most managed to limp home, but, unaware of the overall situation, seven landing craft pressed on. With less than a third of its designated force and the Germans alerted by the mid-Channel skirmish, the horrific outcome was inevitable.

Dieppe Factfile

HOW TO GET THERE: Stena Sealink operates out of Newhaven, with a 4 hour crossing time (*see* pages 340-355 for details of service and prices).

LOCATION AND DISTANCES: Situated 150km (93 miles) southwest of Boulogne, 105km (66 miles) northeast of Le Havre, Dieppe is 176km (110 miles) from Calais, 166km (104 miles) from Caen, 286km (179 miles) from Cherbourg, 333km (208 miles) from St-Malo, 514km (321 miles) from Roscoff and 170km (106 miles) from Paris. POPULATION: 35,700

TOURIST INFORMATION OFFICE: Pont Jehan Ango, quai du Carenage, 76200 Dieppe, tel: (35) 84.11.77. Open 9am-12.30pm & 1.30pm-7pm seven days a week; Sept-April Mon-Sat 9am-12noon & 2pm-6pm.

WHERE TO STAY: During the peak season, it is always best to book your hotel in advance, but if you are caught out, try the Tourist Information Centre, which offers a free accommodation service, keeping track of all the vacancies left in the town. The best place to stay: Auberge Clos Normand (22 Henri IV, Martin-Église 76200, tel: (38) 82.71.01) is just 6km (4 miles) out of town, along the D1 towards Arques, and well worth the drive, because you will not find anywhere of this quality and character in Dieppe itself. Double rooms start at under 300FF (£37), but it is best to go for the more expensive ones, as they only go up to 450FF (£56) and you would have to pay almost twice that for similar accommodation anywhere else in France. Some cheap but clean stays include: Hôtel de la Jetée (5 rue de l'Asile, tel: (35) 84.89.98) Large doubles from 125-260FF; the Select Hôtel (place de la Barre, tel: (35) 84.14.66) is run by ex-Brighton couple Stuart & Chieko Gale, who offer a double en-suite room for 185-240FF.

RESTAURANTS: The best places to eat in town are La Mélie (2 grande rue Pollet) and Le Saint-Jacques (12 rue de l'Oranger), but just 3.5km (2 miles) south of Dieppe La Boucherie at St-Aubin-sur-Scie (route de Rouen) is even better. Three other very fine restaurants in town are Armorique (17 quai Henri IV) and Marmite Dieppoise (8 rue St-Jean) and Le Panoramic ((1 boulevard de Verdun). The Café des Tourelles (rue du Cdt Fayolle) is where the locals go, if only to eat M. Larsonneur's fabulous tarte normande. If you want an authentic English Breakfast cooked by Brits, try the Select Hôtel (see above), where the full Monty costs 65FF, and is available to non-residents as well as residents. Cheap meals abound in many pizzerias and an increasing number of good Chinese restaurants offer value for money in middle price bracket. Best-cheapest eats: Restaurant de Rouen (3 rue du Fauberg du Barre) 52FF fixed-price menu, lunch only. Where to find most restaurants, including some of the cheaper places to eat: quai Duquesne

BEST BAR OR PUB IN TOWN: Cambridge Arms Pub (2 rue de l'Épée) for a good range of beers, whiskies and cocktails. Here's a tip: pick up a booklet from the Tourist Information Office called A Taste of Dieppe, in which you will find this pub's advertisement with a coupon offering a free second beer.

MARKET DAYS: Tuesday and Thursday morning and all day Saturday (place Nationale and grande rue)

WORTH A VISIT: Paradoxically, although Dieppe is the prettiest of Channel ports, there is not much to see! If it is site-seeing you want, then Dieppe is merely the means, being the shortest route to Paris, just an hour's drive from the historic city of Rouen and at the eastern extremity of the so-called Alabaster Coast, a 60 mile stretch of the most magnificent cliff-top views in France, but if you just want to plant your feet down and watch the world go by, there is no better place to go than the Café des Tribunaux or the Café Suisse. The Tribunaux is Dieppe's oldest café and the favourite watering hole of British artists and writers at the turn of the century. It was the images of this town's waterfront that earned Jack the Ripper's alleged alter ego Walter Sickert the title 'the Canaletto of Dieppe' and it was at the Tribunaux that he told Gaugin to give up art and return to being a stockbroker. The Café Suisse is mentioned in Simmonet's Dieppe novel L'Homme de Londres and it was at the Suisse that Oscar Wilde spent most of his time while in exile, either meeting friends or writing. It is said that Wilde wrote *The Ballad of Reading Gaol* at this café, although he would not recognise it today, nor would he expect to be served a pizza!

⑩ CAVES DE L'ANCIEN PORT

56 rue de l'Ancien Port
Etran
Martin Église
76200 Dieppe
Tel: (35) 84.28.71
English spoken? Not revealed
Opening hours? Tues-Sat 9.15-12noon & 2pm-7pm, closed Sat & Sun
Parking? Yes (easy)
Shopping trolleys? No
Do they offer to help carry the goods to the car? Yes
Methods of payment? Sterling, French Francs, Traveller's cheques, Visa, Access, Mastercard, American Express
Any wines for tasting in store? Yes
Comment: This warehouse-type operation is owned by Michel Pommier (*see* Michel Pommier below), and is situated in an industrial area not far from the ferry, with good parking, which makes it handy for travellers, but it was closed when we visited. We asked M. Pommier about this outlet, and he simply said that the range was similar, but smaller.
Verdict? ☿

• 2 SILVER MEDALS

⑦ CENTRE LECLERC

Hameau d'Etran
Martin Église
Tel: (35) 82.56.95
Selling area: 3,000m² (compare this with the size of other stores featured in the area, to gauge their relative size and you will have a rough idea of how big the range of wines, beers, spirits and other goods will be).
Opening hours? Mon-Thurs 9am-10pm, Fri 9am-10.30pm, Sat 8.30am-10.30pm, closed Sun
Comment: Last year we went through Gallec, which owns Leclerc, Groupe de Travail Liquides, which supplies Leclerc, and Leclerc's chief buyer, but all to no avail, so this time we went straight to the top, and we were pleased to receive Michel-Edouard Leclerc's assurance that his chain would

extend the *Guide* full co-operation in supplying whatever samples and information we wanted. He delegated the matter to Jean Maurice, who runs Leclerc Scapertois, which supplies all the stores in the pas-de-Calais and Normandy. Unfortunately M. Maurice had other ideas, inviting us instead to spend the day at Scapertois, where we could taste their best wines over 70FF. We would be wined and dined, and afterwards we would be given some *cru classé* Bordeaux to take away. Apparently he has tried this wheeze on other British journalists with a certain amount of success, but we are not in this job to fill the car-boot with cases of château-bottled claret, so we declined, immediately and in no uncertain terms. We again explained that most cross-Channel bargains are under 34FF, as indeed are most of Centre Leclerc's sales, thus concentrating on its top of the range wines tells us nothing about the bulk of wines most Leclerc customers buy. Besides which, tasting them in isolation would have been unfair to the other retail outlets, whose wines must compete with others of a similar style and price under blind conditions. After more correspondence with M. Leclerc, we received a letter from the head of Sobadis, a subsidiary of Leclerc's, which handles the distribution of its products in Normandy. Referring to our last correspondence with Michel-Edouard Leclerc, he offered us exactly what we wanted, even a choice of branches from which we could collect our samples. Unfortunately our last correspondence with M. Leclerc had been over six weeks earlier, and our tastings had come and gone. Still, if Centre Leclerc keeps to its word, and submits samples without delay or hesitation for the next edition, all the hassle we have endured this year will at least be worthwhile.

The wines: Most branches are basic warehouse-type operations, and very utilitarian. In the bigger stores, the range can include as many as 250 different lines, with a good selection of fine wines, albeit almost entirely from Bordeaux. Centre Leclerc seems to be quite good on Beaujolais, with most *cru villages* covered, and the one we tried from Juliénas certainly fared well, earning a silver medal no less. With four wines out of six random purchases qualifying for recommendation in the *Guide*, including two silver medals, one of which grabbed a Wine of the Year award, it makes us look forward to greater co-operation next year, to see how the range as a whole performs.

RED WINES

Domaine de Pons 1991 Côtes du Ventoux 13.95FF (£1.72) We had to taste almost 30 red Rhônes up to 27FF before we found a wine to equal this. An elegant wine with a good depth of silky-plummy fruit, and nicely structured supple tannins.

Carayon-la-Rose 1986 Cuvée Exceptionnelle, Bordeaux Supérieur 18.95FF (£2.34) This is not bad as a basic Bordeaux, but unless you see the vintage on the label, you would hardly think that you are tasting an eight-year-old claret.

Juliénas 1992 les Vouillants Chedeville 26.50FF (£3.27) Bags of flavour. A real wine, and a true *cru* Beaujolais (we rejected most of the *cru* Beaujolais because they lacked the significant increase in quality and intensity of varietal flavour they should possess).

Château Roches Guitard 1989 Montagne-St-Émilion 30.85FF (£3.81) A good Bordeaux with sweet fruity aromas that follow through onto the palate.

Verdict? 👍

② L'ÉPICIER OLIVIER

16 rue St. Jacques
76200 Dieppe
Tel: (35) 84.22.55

English spoken? Partly (M. Olivier's son speaks English, but he is not always around)

Opening hours? Tues-Sat 7.30am-12.30pm & 2pm-5.30pm, Sun 8am-12.30pm, closed Mon

Parking? Yes (in the road in front of shop or around the Church St-Jacques, 200 yards away)

Shopping trolleys? No

Do they offer to help carry the goods to the car? Yes

Methods of payment? Sterling, Irish Punts, French Francs, Traveller's cheques, Eurocheques, Visa, Mastercard

Any wines for tasting in store? For large quantities

Additional information:
* Free delivery to the ferry of any order of two cases or more.

Comment: This is a large, upmarket shop with a wonderful selection of herbs, pâtés, and more than 100 cheeses (all French, of course). Six different coffees are roasted on the premises. M. Olivier is renowned as a bit of a character, so it did not phase our representatives that he 'kind of glared' at them upon presenting themselves, and within a few minutes he was practically telling them his life story.

The wines: M. Olivier has a comprehensive list of fine wines, as can be expected from such a classy épicerie. Although half the range is from Nicolas, M. Olivier selects and buys the other half himself. He even lists a Swiss Fendant (73.50FF) and the Blue Pyrenees Estate 1986 Cabernet-based red wine from Australia (albeit for 135FF), but the biggest emphasis is on Bordeaux, of course, and there are most of the major *grande marque* Champagnes, and some excellent Alsace from Beyer. Producers under the Burgundy, Rhône and Loire sections are mostly listed anonymously as '*Propriétaire*', which makes it easy for M. Olivier to chop and change his selections without having to reprint the list, but makes it impossible to make any judgement over and above the wines we tasted. Look out, also, for his *cru* ciders (Cidre du Pays de Caux, Cidre du Cotentin, Cidre du Pays d'Auge at 16-18FF).

RED WINES

SILVER MEDAL

Château de Cointes 1992 Côtes de la Malepère 18FF (£2.22) Quite a serious wine for the price, with a good structure for accompanying food, yet elegant, violety fruit that is easy to drink on its own.

WHITE WINES

SILVER MEDAL

Jurançon Sec 1993 Grain Sauvage 32FF (£3.95) Good dry white wine with ripe grapefruit flavour, and some individual character.

ROSÉ WINES

Château Bellevue la Forêt 1993 Côtes de Frontonnais 32.50FF (£4.01) Young, fresh and very fruity.

Verdict? 🖐 🖐

• 1 BRONZE MEDAL

⑨ INTERMARCHÉ
Avenue de Bréauté
Rouxmesnil-Boutteilles
Tel: (28) 25.28.45

Selling area: 2,000m² (compare this with the size of other stores featured in the area, to gauge their relative size and you will have a rough idea of how big the range of wines, beers, spirits and other goods will be).

Opening hours? Mon-Thurs 9am-7.15pm, Fri 9am-8pm, Sat 9am-7pm

Comment: Most Intermarché on the Channel coast are relatively small, and although they can be quite large further inland, this chain is more of the supermarket ilk than hypermarket. It is also relatively down-market, with a mostly dull and uninteresting range of wines, often dominated by a display of 3-litre wine containers. There are around a dozen different Champagnes, and the fine wines are usually displayed separately (we saw Ducru Beaucaillou 1989 at 85FF, and Pavillon Rouge 1990 at 105FF). We had no success with chairman Marcel Robin, who steadfastly refused to answer our correspondence. It was the same story as last year, with M. Le Goff, Intermarché's drinks buyer.

The wines: We purchased six wines along the same lines as those we bought at Auchan, and when it came to the crunch, Intermarché fared much better, with half of the wines warranting our recommendation, and one even picking up a Bronze medal. And two of those that did not qualify were perfectly drinkable, even if not special enough to qualify for the *Guide*. If only the management of this firm had enough faith in its products to submit a substantial range of its inexpensive wines, they might do well, if this random sampling is anything to go by.

RED WINES

Beaujolais NV Cuvée Joannès 12FF (£1.48) Although not medal potential, you could have knocked us down with a feather when this wine, the second-cheapest Gamay submitted, turned out not only to be drinkable, but expressive of its variety, rather than maceration carbonique.

Côtes-du-Rhône 1993 Réserve Lescarrat 13FF (£1.60) This soft and fruity wine has a touch more elegance than the other red Rhônes in its price category.

WHITE WINES

BRONZE MEDAL

Reuilly 1993 Cave PD 22.90FF (£2.83) This fresh and assertive Sauvignon is not a wine for wimps. **Verdict?** 👍

★ *BEST DRINKS OUTLET IN DIEPPE*
• 1 GOLD MEDAL
• 1 BRONZE MEDAL

④ **L.C. VINS**
1 grande rue
76200 Dieppe
Tel: (35) 84.32.41
English spoken? Not revealed
Opening hours? Mon-Sat 9am-12.15pm & 2pm-

7.15pm, Sun 9am-12.15pm
Parking? Only on street
Shopping trolleys? No
Do they offer to help carry the goods to the car?
Yes
Methods of payment? French Francs, Traveller's
cheques, Eurocheques, Visa, Access, Mastercard,
American Express
Any wines for tasting in store? Only by prior
appointment
Comment: L.C. stands for Luc Carpentier, owner
of L.C. Vins, a small but serious outlet, with air-
conditioning both in the shop and in the cellars.
M. Carpentier also owns *Le Clos Ste-Cathérine*, a
restaurant and wine bar at 22-24 rue l'Épée, where
you can taste his wines, or drink them by the glass
or bottle, before you purchase anything by the
case.
The wines: He stocks some 200 wines and about
50 spirits. There are not many wines under 75FF,
but of those listed, there were a fair few we had
not come across before, so we were interested to
see how they fared in our blind tastings. We were,
therefore, pleased to discover that all but one of
the 10 wines submitted passed the test. M. Olivier
is serious about his wines, really enjoys helping
customers to choose, and even though he does
not have many moderately priced wines, he is
obviously adept at selecting the ones he does
have.

RED WINES
*Domaine de la Combe 1993 Vin de Pays des
Coteaux de Foncaude* 13.75FF (£1.70) A light-
bodied red with soft, ripe fruity flavour and a
gentle touch of tannin to hold everything together.
Domaine Maurel 1993 Cabernet 16FF (£1.98)
Young, leafy-Cabernet fruit. Needs another year in
bottle.
Domaine de Rolland 1991 Fitou 29FF (£3.58)
Sappy, plummy fruit hanging on supple tannin
structure. Good for immediate consumption.
Château Ballan-Larquette 1990 Bordeaux 33FF
(£4.07) Basic Bordeaux – a soft and easy style.
Beaujolais-Villages 1992 Georges Rollet 34FF
(£4.20) Good amount of true Gamay fruit.
BRONZE MEDAL *Clos Rougeard 1990 Saumur-Champigny* 69FF
(£8.52) Oak-fiends will love this, but under blind
conditions it is difficult to discern either its Loire
origins or the Cabernet Franc's varietal
characteristics, let alone any expression of its

Saumur *terroir*, but it does have plenty of fruit and drinks well.

GOLD MEDAL

Château les Ormes Sorbet 1989 Médoc 79FF (£9.75) Serious stuff! Very elegant, with succulent fruit and beautifully integrated oak. Not cheap, but has great finesse.

WHITE WINES
Domaine la Tuilière Ravoire 1993 Vin de Pays de Vaucluse 18FF (£2.22) A tasty, well-made dry white that should go well with food.
Verdict? 👍👍👍

⑧ MAMMOUTH
CC du Val Druel
76200 Dieppe
Tel: (35) 82.65.50
Selling area: 5,650m^2 (compare this with the size of other stores featured in the area, to gauge their relative size and you will have a rough idea of how big the range of wines, beers, spirits and other goods will be).
Opening hours? Mon-Sat 9am-9pm (some outlets open Sun)
Comment: Last year we were authorised by Mammouth's buyer Jean-Claude Alti to approach the manager of this branch, M. Walter, who we were assured would be particularly helpful, since his experience at Calais meant that he knew the English market well. M. Walter, however, did not want to know. This year we approached Christian Toulouse, the chairman of Mammouth's parent company, Paridoc, but he did not even bother to reply. This apathy is a pity because Mammouth outlets are usually amongst the largest, brightest and most welcoming of all the French hypermarket chains, and obviously a favourite with British customers.
The wines: Only one of the six wines randomly purchased from Mammouth survived the test.

RED WINES
Bourgogne NV Passetoutgrains 15FF (£1.85) Decent Gamay with a bit of extra backbone.
Verdict? 👎

• 1 BRONZE MEDAL

⑥ POIVRE ET SEL
101 grande rue
76200 Dieppe
Tel: (35) 82.08.76
English spoken? Yes

Opening hours? Tues-Sun 10am-7.30pm, Mon
2.30pm-7.30pm
Parking?
Shopping trolleys? No
Do they offer to help carry the goods to the car?
Yes
Methods of payment? Sterling, French Francs,
Traveller's cheques, Eurocheques, Visa,
Mastercard
Any wines for tasting in store? Yes
Comment: M. & Mme Nasset, who own this shop,
were very welcoming when we visited them,
apologising for not replying to our
correspondence last year, but they had not heard
about the *Guide* and thought that we must be 'a
bad joke'! This year they communicated with us,
and were happy to submit wines. If you think you
have seen M. Nasset before, it could have been on
the Dieppe stand at the Brighton Fair, where he
sells Normandy cider every year. Poivre et Sel also
specialises in speciality foods from the Southwest
of France, which look truly delicious, and gourmet
food in tins, which the Nassets say are very
popular with the English.
The wines: The range is very moderate, with
wines in the medium price bracket, mostly 25-
50FF, yet they appear to be expensive for what
they are. There are some fine wines, a few *cru
classé* Bordeaux, of course, and Alsace from
Schlumberger. They also kept some Champagne
chilled in a small fridge, which is unusual for a
French wine shop, but useful if you want
something off the shelf to go with your picnic.
After taking us seriously this year, we were
disappointed to find that only one of six wines
submitted survived our blind tasting. Hopefully
the wines will be better selected next year. In the
meantime, why not browse around the gourmet
food section?

WHITE WINES

BRONZE MEDAL
*Colombelle Plaimont 1993 Vin de Pays des Côtes
de Gascogne* 23FF (£2.84) Softer fruit than most
Côtes-de-Gascogne dry whites.
Verdict? ?

(3) **MICHEL POMMIER**
22 place Nationale
76200 Dieppe
Tel: (35) 84.14.62
English spoken? No

Opening hours? Mon-Sat 8.30am-12.15pm & 2pm-7.15pm, Sun 10am-12.30pm

Parking? Only on street (or try around the Church St-Jacques)

Shopping trolleys? No

Do they offer to help carry the goods to the car? Yes

Methods of payment? Sterling, French Francs, Traveller's cheques, Visa, Access, Mastercard, American Express

Any wines for tasting in store? Yes

Comment: As our representative reported, you just have to follow your nose to find this shop, the smell of its freshly ground coffee being so wonderful. In addition to coffee, Michel Pommier sells tea and wine. He has an excellent list of spirits, and also owns a wine warehouse out of town called Caves de l'Ancien Port. Two shops down the road in place Nationale, we noticed another cellar where he appears to be selling wines *en vrac*, which might be worth checking out.

The wines: As we said last year, this shop stocks some very fine wines indeed, but most of these are more expensive than can be commonly found in the UK. This year M. Pommier explained that he also has some 25 medium-priced wines, and submitted three such products to reflect this range, but although two of them were perfectly drinkable, none stood out in our blind tasting. This is, therefore, another outlet we hope will select better wines next year. Regrettably we cannot recommend any wines, but we strongly recommend you visit the shop, as the aromas are literally intoxicating, and you should at least buy some coffee.

Verdict? ☿

• 2 SILVER MEDALS
• 1 BRONZE MEDAL

⑤ **PRISUNIC**

5 arcades de la Bourse
76200 Dieppe
Tel: (35) 82.51.60

Selling area: 1,000m² (compare this with the size of other stores featured in the area, to gauge their relative size and you will have a rough idea of how big the range of wines, beers, spirits and other goods will be).

Opening hours? Mon-Sat 8.30am-7.30pm, closed Sun

Comment: Prisunic is primarily geared up for sales of shoes, clothes, jewellery and household goods, its food and wine section tucked away at the back of the store. Last year we managed to get the Dieppe branch to answer our questionnaire, but received no price list, let alone samples from Prisunic head office, which did not bother to respond to our correspondence. This year we wrote to Gilles Denisty, who is chairman of the group, but he turned out to be just as unresponsive.

The wines: It is a pity that Prisunic shows no interest in communicating with British consumers because, although its range is small, five of our randomly purchased samples survived our gruelling blind tasting, and no less than three of these picked up a medal. If we had the same sort of result from a larger selection of wines, Prisunic could have upset some of the big French chains in the chase for the Best Cross-Channel Supermarket of the Year.

RED WINES

Bergerac NV Chatelier 12.50FF (£1.54) Good basic Bordeaux-style with just enough tannin to partner food.

BRONZE MEDAL   *Côtes du Ventoux 1992 la Cuvée des Toques* 18.50FF (£2.28) Ripe and tasty fruit.

SILVER MEDAL   *Commanderie de la Bargemone 1990 Coteaux d'Aix en Provence* 24.45FF (£3.02) This full-bodied red is a bit thick and soupy in style, which would normally put us off, but we twice increased our marks on re-tasting it, which pleased us when we found out what it is, as we have been following Commanderie de la Bargemone since the 1981 vintage, and we know that it does improve.

SILVER MEDAL   *Château Guillon 1990 Graves* 26.60FF (£3.28) An intensely flavoured wine currently in the process of mellowing out, making it more accessible, and as its aroma turns toasty, so the fruit will take on more plummy complexity. Exceptional value.

WHITE WINES

Riesling Vin d'Alsace NV Laugel 25.50FF (£3.15) A dry white with fresh, very pure, apple-blossom fruit.

Verdict? 👍👍

(1) **SHOPI**
59 rue de la Barre
76200 Dieppe
Tel: (35) 84.04.09
Selling area: 1,000m² (compare this with the size

of other stores featured in the area, to gauge their relative size and you will have a rough idea of how big the range of wines, beers, spirits and other goods will be).

Opening hours? Mon-Sat 8.30am-7.30pm, closed Sun

Comment: Although none of the Shopi, which belong to the Promodes group (*see* Champion entries for details), qualify for the 1000m^2 limit we have set on supermarkets to be included in the *Guide*, there seem to be so many in the Calais-Boulogne area that readers are bound to come across these brightly lit outlets, and might want some guidance, whether or not they are pinpointed on our maps.

The wines: Basically a boring range of wines that can be found elsewhere at cheaper prices. Of the six wines purchased, just one qualified.

ROSÉ WINES
Grenache Gris NV Vin de Pays d'Oc 11.90FF (£1.47) Fresh, clean and easy to drink, and a nice bit of alliteration too.
Verdict? 👎

DUNKERQUE

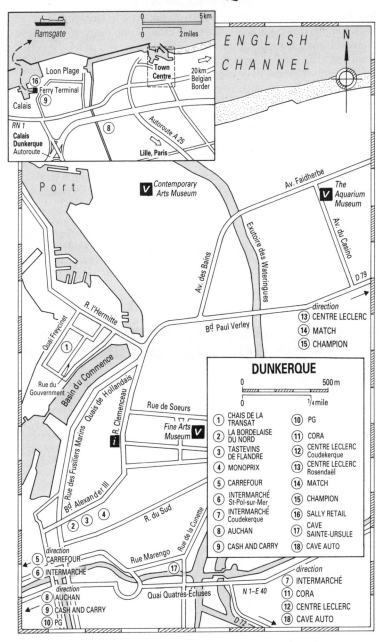

DUNKERQUE

0 — 500 m

0 — 1/4 mile

1. CHAIS DE LA TRANSAT
2. LA BORDELAISE DU NORD
3. TASTEVINS DE FLANDRE
4. MONOPRIX
5. CARREFOUR
6. INTERMARCHÉ St-Pol-sur-Mer
7. INTERMARCHÉ Coudekerque
8. AUCHAN
9. CASH AND CARRY
10. PG
11. CORA
12. CENTRE LECLERC Coudekerque
13. CENTRE LECLERC Rosendaël
14. MATCH
15. CHAMPION
16. SALLY RETAIL
17. CAVE SAINTE-URSULE
18. CAVE AUTO

The only ferry company operating between the UK and Dunkerque is the Sally Line, which sails from Ramsgate and, although this is the third largest port in France, the ferries do not dock in Dunkerque itself, but just down the coast, at a place called Loon Plage. If you take the road from the ferry harbour at Loon Place, you will quickly reach a junction with the RN1, where you may either turn left into the town of Dunkerque or cross over and follow the signs for the Calais-Dunkerque autoroute. Although the autoroute is a pointless detour for anyone going into Dunkerque itself, it is the best route away from the coast to anywhere you might be heading for in either France or Belgium.

Coming from the Sally Line harbour, the first wine outlet you encounter will be **Cash & Carry**, the closest commercial centre is at Grande-Synthe, on the western outskirts of Dunkerque, where you can find the **Auchan** hypermarket, after which you are in Dunkerque proper.

The Dunkerque Carnival is famous and the largest of its kind in northern France, with thousands of people attending from all over the country. It is, in fact, four carnivals rather than one, each held on a different day in various parts of the town: in the Old Town itself on the Sunday before Shrove Tuesday, in Rosendaël on Shrove Tuesday, Malo-les-Bains on the Sunday after Shrove Tuesday and Petite-Synthe on the third Sunday.

Dunkerque Factfile

HOW TO GET THERE: The Sally Line operates out of Ramsgate, with a 2 hour 30 minute crossing-time (*see* pages 340-355 for details of service and prices).

LOCATION AND DISTANCES: Situated almost halfway between Calais (40km or 25 miles) and Oostende (44km or 27 miles), Dunkerque is just 20km (12 miles) from the Belgian border, 77km (48 miles) northwest of Lille and 274km (170 miles) from Paris.

POPULATION: 75,000

TOURIST INFORMATION OFFICE: Belfry of Dunkerque, rue de l'Amiral Ronarc'h, 59140 Dunkerque, *tel:* (28) 26.27.28 or (28) 66.79.21. Open Mon 2pm-6.30pm, Tues-Fri 9am-12.30pm & 1.30pm-6.30pm, Sat 9am-6.30pm.

WHERE TO STAY: During the peak season, it is always best to book your hotel in advance, but if you are caught out, try the Tourist Information Centre, which offers a free accommodation service, keeping track of all the vacancies left in the town. The best place to stay: *La Meunerie* (174 rue des Pierres, *tel:* 28.26.14.30) is just a few miles outside town, and best known for its restaurant (*see* below), but offers by far the best rooms, from 450FF. Some cheap but clean stays include: *Hôtel de Tigre* (8 rue Clémenceau, *tel:* 28.66.75.17) a decent double room with shower and TV will cost 200FF; *La Fasthotellerie* (rue de la Porte de Lille, ZAC du Courghain, 59760 Grande-Synthe, *tel:* 28.21.90.20) offers basic but clean doubles with bath and TV for just 150FF.

RESTAURANTS: The best place to eat in town is the *Richelieu* (the station buffet) and the *Soubise* (49 route Bergues), but *Le Métropole* (28 rue Thiers) is very good, especially if serving its sublime gratin of salmon and asparagus. *L'Islandais* is well frequented by locals for the freshness of its fish and its home-made foie gras. Not in Dunkerque itself, but the very best place in the vicinity is *La Meunerie* (174 rue des Pierres), a one-star Michelin restaurant at Tétegham, just 6km (4 miles) southeast of the town. Just a few kilometres inland, you can enjoy farmhouse cooking at the *Auberge de la Becque* (rue de l'Est, 59380 Warhem). The gourmets among our readers will already know that no Channel port has more Michelin starred restaurants within a short drive of its town centre than Dunkerque, although most of them are just across the border in Belgium. Best-cheapest eats: *The Pavois* (175 digue de Mer) is always crowded, and for good reason, as its seafood dishes are incredible cheap. Where to find most restaurants, including some of the cheaper places to eat: along the seafront, east of the port.

MARKET DAYS: All day Wednesday and Saturday (place du Général de Gaulle)

WORTH A VISIT: *The Contemporary Art Museum* is a spectacular building situated in the Jardin de Sculptures, the first floor of which houses the main collection in eight rooms, while the mezzanine is reserved for temporary exhibitions. *The Fine Arts Museum* is situated in the Old Town, near the theatre and contains hundreds of paintings from the 16th to the 20th century. It is famous for its naval gallery and a basement display of the 1939-45 period of Dunkerque's history. *The Aquarium Museum* is situated in Parc Malo, near the beach, where you can see 21 aquariums of rare and exotic fish.

(8) AUCHAN

Route Nationale 40
59760 Grande Synthe
Dunkerque
Tel: (28) 27.99.99
Selling area: 10,400m² (compare this with the size of other stores featured in the area, to gauge their relative size and you will have a rough idea of how big the range of wines, beers, spirits and other goods will be).
Opening hours? Mon-Fri 8.30am-10pm, Sat 8am-10pm, closed Sun
Foire aux Vins: October
Comment: These outlets are usually amongst the biggest, brightest and most welcoming of the French hypermarket chains, and this one is very large indeed, although not quite as immense as the one in Boulogne. Auchan is very popular with British, who are apt to go spend-crazy at any supersized hypermarket. We had even less response from Auchan's directors this year than we did with its wine buyer last time, as neither the chairman (Gérard Mulliez) nor its managing

director (Michel Pecqueraux) even acknowledged our correspondence.

The wines: The wines are displayed from the floor right up to the ceiling – well almost to the ceiling. There are many more reds than whites, with the greatest emphasis placed predictably enough on Bordeaux (approximately 40-50 different wines), after which Burgundy and Languedoc-Roussillon offer the most choice (about 20 wines each), although white Burgundies fare less well (just six), and the choice of Loire in any colour is abysmal. There are about 10 different Alsace, but the only white wines stocked in any serious way are Champagne and other sparklers. We purchased six wines (the cheapest red and cheapest white, plus four wines that a knowledgeable consumer might consider interesting or good value), but only one qualified for recommendation in this *Guide*, and two of those that failed the test we would not touch with a barge pole, even if Auchan gave them away. A hit-rate of just one in six is bad enough: we hate to think how the average consumer, who has to rely on pot-luck, would fare.

WHITE WINES
Alsace Riesling 1992 Pierre Dumoulin-Storch
25.90FF (£3.20) Dry white wine lifted by a slight spritz.
Verdict?

② LA BORDELAISE DU NORD
21 rue Lion d'Or
(off boulevard Alexandre III)
59140 Dunkerque
Tel: (28) 66.00.41
English spoken? Yes
Opening hours? Monday 2pm-7pm, Tues-Sat 10am-7pm, closed Sun
Parking? Yes (parking metres)
Shopping trolleys? No
Do they offer to help carry the goods to the car? Yes
Methods of payment? Sterling, Irish Punts, French Francs, Traveller's cheques, Eurocheques, Visa, Access, Mastercard, American Express
Any wines for tasting in store? No (except for Beaujolais Nouveau in November!)
Comment: This posh establishment is run by Yves Cuisinier, who has an utterly upmarket range and

a shop with an atmosphere that is best suited to those who willingly spend masses of money on classic wines.

The wines: As per last year, we received no samples from this outlet, but as our representative said, at least the owner was polite about it. As he explained, he cannot very well give us samples of first growth clarets. Nor would we want them, M. Cuisinier. As much as we would enjoy the tasting, we would never be able to recommend them because they are infinitely cheaper in the UK. We would love to know just what his cheapest wines cost, but he sent no list. If you want to pay through the nose for Pétrus or Romanée Conti, this is the place for you, but if you are after a bargain, you will feel rather hot and sticky under the collar.

Verdict? ♆

• 1 SILVER MEDAL

• 2 BRONZE MEDALS

⑤ CARREFOUR

CC St-Pol Jardin
ZAC des Jardins
59430 St-Pol-sur-Mer
Dunkerque
Tel: (28) 64.79.11

Selling area: 6,100m² (compare this with the size of other stores featured in the area, to gauge their relative size and you will have a rough idea of how big the range of wines, beers, spirits and other goods will be).

Opening hours? Mon-Sat 8.30am-10pm, closed Sun

Comment: Every attempt to solicit a civil response from Carrefour was ignored last time, and the chairman, M. René Brillet, was equally elusive this year.

The wines: We were not very impressed with the overall selection of wines for such a large store, and the prices were generally higher than other hypermarkets. Pommard at 30FF was an exception, and to be fair we were pleasantly surprised to find that Carrefour actually had an English wine, Car Taylor Hastings, in stock! There were even some decent Spanish wines from Torres, and we struck lucky with our random purchases, with three out of six not simply qualifying for recommendation in the *Guide*, but picking up a medal each along the way. So there you have it: although Carrefour's wine range looks uninteresting on the shelf, when randomly purchased samples are put to the test, they do well enough to earn 👍 👍. It could be, of course, that we were just lucky this year, as last time none of Carrefour's wines survived, but it does make us curious how a large selection of this store's biggest-selling lines might fare against those of its competitors under strictly blind conditions. Hopefully M. Brillet will have the courtesy to reply to our correspondence next year.

RED WINES

SILVER MEDAL

Côtes de Bourg 1992 DFF, Carrefour 17.90FF (£2.21) A touch of oak lifts this above other Bordeaux at this price.

BRONZE MEDAL

Pommard 1992 Caves de l'Echanson 30FF (£3.70) This wine is still tight and obviously needs a little more time to loosen up, but it is good Pinot, and amazingly cheap for Pommard (it was on offer at this price, so we're not sure what it might be by the time the book comes out).

WHITE WINES

BRONZE MEDAL

Domaine Bellevue 1993 Touraine 16FF (£1.98) The best-cheapest Sauvignon Blanc we tasted, this has good, clean varietal character and is a joy to drink. **Verdict?** 👍 👍

• 1 BRONZE MEDAL

⑨ **CASH & CARRY**
Près du Terminal Sally Line
Loon Plage
59140 Dunkerque
Tel: (28) 27.35.70
English spoken? Not revealed
Opening hours? Mon-Fri 8am-12midnight, Sat & Sun 11.30am-7.30pm
Parking? Yes (private car park)
Shopping trolleys? Yes
Help with carry goods to the car? Yes
Methods of payment? Sterling, French Francs, Traveller's cheques, Visa, Mastercard, American Express
Any wines for tasting in store? Possibly in the future
Comment: We do wish this had a more exciting name. No, strike that, we just wish this had a name ... any name ... how about Loonies? This is a large, fairly basic, warehouse-type operation, conveniently situated on the way to the ferry.
The wines: Although only two wines of the six submitted qualified for recommendation, one did

get a bronze medal and all but one of the four rejected were perfectly drinkable. This is a vast improvement over last year, when none of the wines tasted survived the test, and probably reflects the fact that the range has been expanded since then. Ever the optimists, we look forward to a further improvement in performance next year. The beers are piled high on pallets, and seem very popular with the passing lorry drivers.

SPARKLING WINES

BRONZE MEDAL *François D'Orbay NV Blanc de Blanc* 23FF (£2.84) This was the cheapest drinkable dry sparkling wine we found. Although it did not seriously challenge Seppelt Great Western (24FF, The Grape Shop) for the Best-Cheapest Sparkling Wine of the Year award, this really is quite good, especially for a basic French fizz of no fixed abode, and it is immeasurably better than most Loire sparklers.

BEERS

La Strasbourgeoise Bière d'Alsace 1.20FF (15p) per 25cl bottle, sold in 24s at 28.90FF (£3.57) More fruity than beery, with a hint of sweetness on the finish, this just scrapes through on price for those who do not like their beers too dry.
Verdict? ♉

⑱ CAVE AUTO
38 rue de Bergue
59210 Coudekerque Branche
Tel: (28) 24.28.24
English spoken? No
Opening hours? Tues-Sat 9am-12noon & 2.30pm-7pm, closed Sun & Mon
Parking? Yes (in the warehouse)
Shopping trolleys? No
Do they offer to help carry the goods to the car? Yes
Methods of payment? French Francs, Access, Visa, Mastercard
Any wines for tasting in store? No
Comment: As the name implies, this is supposed to be a drive-in wine store, rather like the Aussie bottle-store concept, but with the facility to taste (although the *salle de dégustation* was closed when we visited). The company is Société G.B.L, which is owned by a M. Laplace. The person we spoke to began shaking his head before we could introduce ourselves. He seemed a bit aggressive, had a touch

of Mediterranean temperament, impolitely used the *'tutoyer'* form of address, and generally did not give the impression that British custom would be welcome.

The wines: No samples or list. We saw Taittinger at 100FF, some Mommessin Burgundies, and some *cru classé*, but this outlet does not have much in the really fine wine division (thankfully, as it would not be any cheaper than back home anyway) and does not seem to be competing at the very bottom end of the market either. In fact, it is a pity that M. Laplace did not want to submit anything because the wines between 25 and 50FF looked very interesting. Some Belgian beer, plus a few others.

Verdict? ⸮

⑰ CAVE SAINTE-URSULE

45 bis rue Marengo
59140 Dunkerque
Tel: (28) 21.17.03
English spoken? A little
Opening hours? Tues-Sat 9.15am-12.15pm & 2.30pm-7.30pm, closed Sun & Mon
Parking? On the street
Shopping trolleys? No
Do they offer to help carry the goods to the car? Yes
Methods of payment? French Francs, Access, Visa, Mastercard
Any wines for tasting in store? Yes (for *en vrac* only)

Comment: This bright new shop is owned by M. Marquette, and has been open barely more than a year. It is large and airy, and just a few minutes from the centre of town.

The wines: Cave Sainte-Ursule appears to be the only shop in Dunkerque that sells *en vrac* (although we are open to correction on that). It stocks just wines, no beers. A moderate selection, including 12 Bordeaux, 12 Loire, 8 Alsace (all from J-L Dirringer), just six Champagnes, and only two Rhône. We cannot give an assessment of these wines because the owner was very wary about submitting wines to any British publication. M. Marquette told us that someone had already approached him, saying that they were doing a guide, and demanding a sample of every single one of his wines. We do not know who this person was, but hopefully the sight of our second edition should convince M. Marquette that this is a pucker publication, and one he could benefit from if his wines stand up to the challenge of our blind tastings.

Verdict? ？

• 2 SILVER MEDALS

⑬ **CENTRE LECLERC**
2 rue des Forts
59240 Rosendaël
Dunkerque
Tel: (28) 60.06.84.
Selling area: 1,700m²

AND

⑫ **CENTRE LECLERC**
89 avenue Jean-Baptiste Lebas
59210 Coudekerque Branche
Dunkerque
Tel: (28) 64.68.50
Selling area: 2,000m² (compare this with the size of other stores featured in the area, to gauge their relative size and you will have a rough idea of how big the range of wines, beers, spirits and other goods will be).
Opening hours? Mon-Thurs 9am-10pm, Fri 9am-10.30pm, Sat 8.30am-10.30pm, closed Sun
Comment: Last year we went through Gallec, which owns Leclerc, Groupe de Travail Liquides, which supplies Leclerc, and Leclerc's chief buyer, but all to no avail, so this time we went straight to the top, and we were pleased to receive Michel-Edouard Leclerc's assurance that his chain would extend the *Guide* full co-operation in supplying whatever samples and information we wanted. He delegated the matter to Jean Maurice, who runs Leclerc Scapertois, which supplies all the stores in the Pas-de-Calais and Normandy. Unfortunately M. Maurice had other ideas, inviting us instead to spend the day at Scapertois, where we could taste their best wines over 70FF. We would be wined and dined, and afterwards we would be given some *cru classé* Bordeaux to take away. Apparently he has tried this wheeze on other British journalists with a certain amount of success, but we are not in this job to fill the car boot with cases of château-bottled claret, so we declined, immediately and in no uncertain terms. We again explained that most cross-Channel bargains are under 34FF, as indeed are most of Centre Leclerc's sales, thus concentrating on its top of the range wines tells us nothing about the bulk of wines most Leclerc customers buy. Besides which,

tasting them in isolation would have been unfair to the other retail outlets, whose wines must compete with others of a similar style and price under blind conditions. After more correspondence with M. Leclerc, we received a letter from the head of Sobadis, a subsidiary of Leclerc's, which handles the distribution of its products in Normandy. Referring to our last correspondence with Michel-Edouard Leclerc, he offered us exactly what we wanted, even a choice of branches from which we could collect our samples from. Unfortunately our last correspondence with M. Leclerc had been over six weeks earlier, and our tastings had come and gone. Still, if Centre Leclerc keeps to its word, and submits samples without delay or hesitation for the next edition, all the hassle we have endured this year will at least be worthwhile.

The wines: Most branches are basic warehouse-type operations, and very utilitarian. In the bigger stores, the range can include as many as 250 different lines, with a good selection of fine wines, albeit almost entirely from Bordeaux. Centre Leclerc seems to be quite good on Beaujolais, with most *cru villages* covered, and the one we tried from Juliénas certainly fared well, earning a silver medal no less. With four wines out of six random purchases qualifying for recommendation in the *Guide,* including two silver medals, one of which grabbed a Wine of the Year award, it makes us look forward to greater co-operation next year, to see how the range as a whole performs.

RED WINES

SILVER MEDAL
BEST -VALUE RED
WINE OF THE YEAR

Domaine de Pons 1991 Côtes du Ventoux 13.95FF (£1.72) We had to taste almost 30 red Rhônes up to 27FF before we found a wine to equal this. An elegant wine with a good depth of silky-plummy fruit, and nicely structured supple tannins.

Carayon-la-Rose 1986 Cuvée Exceptionnelle, Bordeaux Supérieur 18.95FF (£2.34) This is not bad as a basic Bordeaux, but unless you see the vintage on the label, you would hardly think that you are tasting an eight-year-old claret.

SILVER MEDAL

Juliénas 1992 les Vouillants Chedeville 26.50FF (£3.27) Bags of flavour. A real wine, and a true *cru* Beaujolais (we rejected most of the *cru* Beaujolais because they lacked the significant increase in quality and intensity of varietal flavour they should possess).

Château Roches Guitard 1989 Montagne-St Émilion 30.85FF (£3.81) A good Bordeaux with sweet fruity aromas that follow through onto the palate.

Verdict? 👍

★ *BEST DRINKS OUTLET IN DUNKERQUE*
• 2 GOLD MEDALS
• 3 SILVER MEDALS
• 1 BRONZE MEDAL

① CHAIS DE LA TRANSAT

25 rue Gouvernement
Quartier Citadelle
59140 Dunkerque
Tel: (28) 63.78.25
English spoken? Yes
Opening hours? Tues-Sat 9.30am-12.30pm & 2pm-7pm, closed Sun & Mon
Parking? Yes
Shopping trolleys? Yes
Do they offer to help carry the goods to the car? Yes
Methods of payment? French Francs, Traveller's cheques, Eurocheques, Visa
Any wines for tasting in store? Yes
Comment: In addition to Dunkerque, Chais de la Transat wine warehouses can be found at Le Havre, Rouen and Paris. This small group is all that remains of the old Compagnie Générale Transatlantique, which was known simply as Transat and ran the famous French Line, which for 120 years operated such famous liners as the 'Normandie', 'Libertie' and – the last, greatest and finest of all – the 'France'. After the 'France' made her final voyage in 1974, the firm opened its cellars in Le Havre to sell off the stocks and, recognising that Transat had represented the pinnacle of French gastronomy for over a century, the public descended like vultures eager to plunder its bargains. Such was the response that a trading company was quickly set up and, to satisfy demand, new warehouses were opened in Dunkerque, Rouen and Paris. Chais de la Transat warehouses are well-run and offer a good range of wines and spirits, but no beers.

The wines: Although single bottles are not strictly ruled out, they are not exactly encouraged either, most wines being sold in cases of 3, 6 or 12. Nostalgic own-labels abound and various offers and promotions are made each month. The range is particularly strong on Bordeaux, with what appears to be some good names on the list and concentrating on the better vintages, although it is not always the right name for the right vintage, so be choosy and taste before you buy whenever possible. Chais de la Transat intend introducing a range of beers by the end of 1994 – especially for the Brits!

RED WINES

Vieux Domaine de Meneau 1992 Premières Côtes de Blaye 24FF (£2.96) From the nose through the palate to the finish, this is unusually peppery for Bordeaux, but quite a tasty wine nevertheless.

SILVER MEDAL ***Château Monbadon 1990 Côtes de Castillon*** 29FF (£3.58) Firm, rich and tasty with a good tannin structure. Perfect food wine, yet excellent to drink on its own.

SILVER MEDAL ***Château Hautes Graves de By 1990 Médoc Cru Bourgeois*** at 34FF (£4.20) has very good depth of colour for such an elegant wine, with lots of silky fruit and just the right sort of firm finish to tell you this is real Bordeaux.

GOLD MEDAL ***Côtes-du-Rhône 1990 E. Guigal*** 35FF (£4.07) This is even bigger and more luscious than when we tasted it from various outlets last year. A succulent wine of wonderful spicy aromas and rich, raisiny-plummy fruit.

WHITE WINES

GOLD MEDAL ***Côtes-du-Rhône 1992 E. Guigal*** 35FF (£4.07) Has developed exceptional finesse for what is a rather nondescript year.

BRONZE MEDAL ***Numero 1 1992 Dourthe*** 39FF (£4.81) There is plenty of real fruit in this soft, ripe and gentle dry white wine, which also has an elegantly perfumed aftertaste.

SPARKLING WINES

SILVER MEDAL ***Champagne Palmer NV Brut*** 98FF (£12.10) Quality co-operative Champagne from the co-op the houses respect the most.

Verdict? 👍 👍 👍

• 2 BRONZE MEDALS

⑮ CHAMPION
CC Le Meridien
Boulevard de l'Europe
59240 Malo-les-Bains
Dunkerque
Tel: (28) 69.44.99
Selling area: 1,750m² (compare this with the size of other stores featured in the area, to gauge their relative size and you will have a rough idea of how big the range of wines, beers, spirits and other goods will be).
Opening hours? Mon-Sat 8.30am-10pm, closed Sun

Comment: Part of the Promodes group, which owns Continent, Shopi and various other smaller outlets. We made contact last year with no less than six top people at Promodes and its various offshoots, but to no avail, so this year we wrote to the managing director of Promodes, M. Pierre Merle, but he could not be bothered to reply either.

The wines: The range consists of primarily Bordeaux and the Southwest, a smattering of decent Burgundy (eg., Labouré Roi Pommard 1989 at 69.70FF), and a few interesting looking, domaine-bottled *cru* Beaujolais. There is a good selection of petit châteaux, especially from St-Émilion and its satellites, (top flight vintages 1989 and 1990). Champion also has a comparatively large selection of spirits for a French supermarket group. For one week in June, this store was selling the cheapest beer we could find anywhere, Brandenberg Bier Blonde at 19.95FF for 24 x 25cl bottles (beware: we occasionally see beers at seemingly cheaper prices, only to discover the pack contains 20, rather than 24, bottles – so check the number of contents before purchase). Although we found the inexpensive white wines to be generally very boring, there is a good range of reds between 15-30FF (mainly Cahors, Côtes-du-Ventoux, and Côtes-de-Duras. Our biggest criticism of Champion is that all the bottles were standing upright, including the fine wines, yet of the six random purchases, four qualified for recommendation, which is good by French supermarket standards. Furthermore two of these picked up medals, and one was the best-cheapest wine of its style we found on the entire cross-Channel market. The two wines that did not warrant a recommendation were perfectly drinkable, even if they were not good enough for inclusion in this publication. On the basis of this performance, it is hard to see what M. Merle has to hide.

RED WINES

Château Bois Clair 1993 Bordeaux 11.90FF (£1.47) Light but honest, easy-drinking basic Bordeaux.

BRONZE MEDAL | *Bourgogne Hautes Côtes de Beaune 1990 Labouré Roi* 31.90FF (£3.94) Sweet Pinot fruit on the nose, firm structure and still unwinding, but a medium-term developer, not a long-term one. Good with food.

Château Saint-Lô 1989 Saint-Émilion 34FF (£4.20)
Good fruit on a firm structure of ripe tannins.

ROSÉ WINES

Cinsault Rosé 1993 J.P Chenet 11.80FF (£1.46)
Looks more like a brandy bottle than a wine
bottle, but who cares at this price, especially
when it's full of fruit with such good acidity.
This is a real wine at a make-believe price (and for
one week in June, it was even cheaper, on offer
at 9.95FF!).
Verdict? 👍👍

⑪ CORA

Rue Jacquard
59210 Coudekerque Branche
Dunkerque
Tel: (28) 64.55.00
Selling area: 8,000m² (compare this with the size
of other stores featured in the area, to gauge their
relative size and you will have a rough idea of
how big the range of wines, beers, spirits and
other goods will be).
Opening hours? Mon-Sat 8.30am-10pm, closed
Sun
Comment: Cora is a larger, more upmarket,
hypermarket comparable to Auchan and
Mammouth, with a wine section that is neatly and
attractively displayed on shelves, with each region
clearly delineated. Although our letters and faxes
to Cora were ignored last year, they were not this
time. We contacted M. Gérard Bouriez, the
chairman of Cora, who instructed Jean-Marc
Dubois, the manager of this branch, to furnish us
with whatever information and samples we
required. That's the good news. The bad news is
that although M. Dubois put himself at our
disposal in writing, but when it came to exploiting
this offer we came up against the impenetrable
barrier of his secretary, who was exceedingly
unhelpful, and if our representatives had not had
copies of our correspondence to hand, she would
have continued to plead ignorance, even though
she must have typed the letters herself! These
French groups seem to make a concerted effort to
frustrate our aims, but we simply purchased half-
a-dozen wines at random, as we did the year
before, and we will continue to chip away until we
can achieve mutual respect and, hopefully, some
genuine co-operation.

The wines: The range consists mainly of Bordeaux, with offers on various *cru classé* (there was even a notice explaining that if you want Latour, Pétrus etc., these could be ordered at the reception area!). The range starts at sub-7FF wines such as Vin de Pays du Var, which was on offer at 25.90FF for a 3-litre demijohn (which itself would cost more than that from a home-brew shop in the UK!), and there are one or two wines from other countries (Italy, Germany, Tunisia, Morocco and Spain). Although none of the wines we purchased passed our blind tasting this year, we believe that a good selection of Cora's main range could do well in a blind tasting.

• 1 BRONZE MEDAL

⑦ **INTERMARCHÉ**
109 rue de Furnes
59210 Coudekerque Branche
Dunkerque
Tel: (28) 63.35.40
Selling area: 1,200m²

AND

⑥ **INTERMARCHÉ**
Rue Boussekey
59430 St-Pol-sur-Mer
Dunkerque
Tel: (28) 25.28.45
Selling area: 1,200m² (compare this with the size of other stores featured in the area, to gauge their relative size and you will have a rough idea of how big the range of wines, beers, spirits and other goods will be).
Opening hours? Mon-Thurs 9am-12.15pm & 2pm-7.15pm, Fri 9am-12.15pm & 2pm-7.30pm, Sat 9am-7.15pm
Comment: Most Intermarché on the Channel coast are relatively small, and although they can be quite large further inland, this chain is more of the supermarket ilk than hypermarket. It is also relatively down-market, with a mostly dull and uninteresting range of wines, often dominated by a display of 3-litre wine containers. There are around a dozen different Champagnes, and the fine wines are usually displayed separately (we saw Ducru Beaucaillou 1989 at 85FF, and Pavillon Rouge 1990 at 105FF). We had no success with chairman Marcel Robin, who steadfastly refused to answer our correspondence. It was the same story as last year, with M. Le Goff, Intermarché's drinks buyer.

The wines: We purchased six wines along the same lines as those we bought at Auchan, and when it came to the crunch, Intermarché fared much better, with half of the wines warranting our recommendation, and one even picking up a Bronze medal. And two of those that did not qualify were perfectly drinkable, even if not special enough to qualify for the *Guide*. If only the management of this firm had enough faith in its products to submit a substantial range of its inexpensive wines, they might do well, if this random sampling is anything to go by.

RED WINES
Beaujolais NV Cuvée Joannès 12FF (£1.48) Although not medal potential, you could have knocked us down with a feather when this wine, the second-cheapest Gamay submitted, turned out not only to be drinkable, but expressive of its variety, rather than *macération carbonique*.
Côtes-du-Rhône 1993 Réserve Lescarrat 13FF (£1.60) This soft and fruity wine has a touch more elegance than the other red Rhônes in its price category.

WHITE WINES
BRONZE MEDAL
Reuilly 1993 Cave PD 22.90FF (£2.83) This fresh and assertive Sauvignon is not a wine for wimps.
Verdict? 👍

• 1 BRONZE MEDAL

⑭ MATCH
Avenue de Rosendaël
59240 Rosendaël
Dunkerque
Tel: (28) 66.07.49
Selling area: 1,800m^2 (compare this with the size of other stores featured in the area, to gauge their relative size and you will have a rough idea of how big the range of wines, beers, spirits and other goods will be).
Opening hours? Mon-Sat 9am-7.30pm, Sun 9am-1pm
Comment: The senior management at Match ignored our correspondence last year, so we wrote to the chairman, Jean Paul Giraud, who maintained the company's couldn't-care-less attitude. The stores themselves are, however, far more welcoming: they are pleasant, attractive shops where someone has obviously made an effort with the decor to produce a more convivial atmosphere than most French-owned supermarkets.

The wines: Match has a moderately large range, which is mostly Bordeaux and the Southwest, but also includes the odd Rioja, Errazuriz Panquehue from Chile, a Chianti, a Tunisian wine, and a number of half bottles. Although only two of the six wines purchased here survived our tasting, one of those was a medal-winner, while the other picked up a Wine of the Year award. Match also offers a good range of beers, including a number of specialist brews from Belgian.

RED WINES

BEST-CHEAPEST RED
WINE OF THE YEAR

Jean de Plessac NV Vin de Pays de l'Hérault
4.95FF (61p) Soft and very fruity, this is the cheapest wine we came across, yet we would drink it, and that is more than we could say for most of the more expensive wines submitted! Remember, however, that this is a non-vintage blend. We hope that it's the same one when you buy it, but Match could be on a different blend. Supermarkets do not go in for 'taste before you buy', so purchase just one bottle first, try it, and if you like it, grab as much as you can. Even if the blend has changed and is now undrinkable, at 4.95FF a bottle, you won't have lost much.

BRONZE MEDAL

Château Chapelle la Rose 1990 Lussac-St-Émilion
31.60FF (£3.90) A ripe, stylish, classy little number at this price.
Verdict? 👍👍

RUNNER UP FOR
BEST CROSS-CHANNEL
SUPERMARKET OF
THE YEAR
RUNNER UP TO
BEST DRINKS OUTLET
IN DUNKERQUE
• 1 GOLD MEDAL
• 2 BRONZE MEDALS

④ **MONOPRIX**
9 place de la République
59140 Dunkerque
Tel: (28) 59.01.11
Selling area: 1,100m² (compare this with the size of other stores featured in the area, to gauge their relative size and you will have a rough idea of how big the range of wines, beers, spirits and other goods will be).
Opening hours? Mon-Sat 8.30am-8pm, Sun closed
Comment: These stores concentrate on clothes, toys and toiletries, and are not dissimilar to the Woolworths concept, only with food and wine.
The wines: Monoprix have only a small range of beers, but we were surprised by its selection of wines, which is equal to or better than that of some of the larger chains. At just 1,100m² the Dunkerque store barely qualifies as a supermarket worth the attention of the *Guide*, yet in addition to its range of French wines, it has wines from Yugoslavia, Algeria, China, Argentina, California

(St-Supery, Glen Ellen), South Africa (Zonnenbloem), Portugal, Spain, Germany (including a Pinot Noir from Baden), and Italy. Okay, so there are just one or two wines from each of these countries, but at least it is an effort, and it puts the xenophobic hypermarkets to shame.

RED WINES

BRONZE MEDAL | *Mas de Lunès 1992 Domaines Jeanjean* 11.80FF (£1.46) Good full-bodied red that is well-perfumed and has more than a hint of blackcurrant to its fruit.

GOLD MEDAL | *Les Tournons 1991 Crozes-Hermitage* 28.85FF (£3.56) Almost unbelievable that you can buy such a classic Syrah at this price, but the elegant, smoky, summer-fruit aromas are 100% authentic, and mirrored beautifully on the palate.

BRONZE MEDAL | *Château Les Pradines 1990 St-Estèphe* 36.50FF (£4.51) Firm and well structured, with plenty of depth. Good partner to well-flavoured dishes.
Verdict? 👍 👍 👍

• 1 BRONZE MEDAL

⑩ PG
ZAC Route de Gravelines
59279 Loon Plage
Dunkerque
Tel: N/A
Selling area: 1,200m² (compare this with the size of other stores featured in the area, to gauge their relative size and you will have a rough idea of how big the range of wines, beers, spirits and other goods will be).
Opening hours? Mon-Thurs & Sat 9am-12noon & 2pm-7.30pm, Fri 9am-8pm, closed Sun
Comment: Our initial reaction last year was to hang out the flags, because although these are fairly small outlets, PG is a local chain of real character, with some really interesting wines, the better ones of which are stored lying down in bins. Furthermore, after the usual hassle of chasing from one contact to another, we latched on to Xavier Diers, the buying director, who was friendly, helpful and agreed to send us any samples we wanted. Only, of course, he did not, so we pulled in the flags and gave PG a cautious verdict. This year we did not get so much as a reply from PG, let alone promises, so at least they kept their word this time!
The wines: With this year's lack of response, we decided to check more stores before buying our random samples (two cheapest, plus four

interesting looking wines), and we were less impressed with the range than we were last time, although for the small supermarket it is, PG is not bad, and at least has a moderate choice in the 15-20FF bracket. Gone, however, are the excellent Blanck wines from Alsace, only to be replaced with Freyermuth, which churns out huge quantities at cheap prices. And we saw no Mommessin-quality wines from Burgundy. The fine wine section lying down in bins was still there, but the wines displayed were noticeably lacking in the 'fine' department, and the prices were relatively high. As for our tastings, just two of the six wines purchased passed the test, although one of those did earn a bronze medal.

RED WINES

BRONZE MEDAL

Château du Paraza 1991 Minervois 9.90FF (£1.22) Soft and tasty, with creamy fruit and good length for a cheap red, and enough of a tannin structure to partner food.

Château Grand Champs 1988 Bordeaux 15.90FF (£1.96) Six-year-old Bordeaux for under £2.00 a bottle cannot be bad, but there is an assertive character that gives the mature fruit in this wine a certain youthful edge, and this does not quite ring true. It is, however, definitely worth recommending at this price.

Verdict? ?

⑯ SALLY RETAIL

Sally Terminal
59279 Loon Plage
Dunkerque
Tel: (28) 27.35.44
English spoken? Yes
Opening hours? 8am-8.30pm seven days a week
Parking? Yes (at terminal)
Shopping trolleys? Yes
Do they offer to help carry the goods to the car? Yes
Methods of payment? Sterling, French Francs, British cheques (with card), Traveller's cheques, Eurocheques, Visa, Mastercard, Access
Any wines for tasting in store? 'Maybe' (bit restricted for space)
Comment: This shop, which belongs to the Sally ferry company, is actually in the terminal itself. Although it is quite small, it is certainly an improvement on its previous premises, a mobile hut in the car park. Sally Retail has been open

since mid-1993, and is geared up purely for British tourists.

The wines: There are about 150-200 lines between £1 and £3.50. The British manager, Tim Martin, buys in the wines from wherever he can find the cheapest prices, and does not pretend the shop is for the connoisseur. The beers are mostly French and English, with some German, but only a couple from Belgium (due to price, no doubt). This is not a very exciting outlet as far as wines go, although it is possible, if unlikely, to buy a good-value wine on price alone, so who knows how some of the selections might fare in a blind tasting? We don't. We were promised a list and samples, but nothing turned up, and when we chased the manager, who was most helpful and friendly during our visit, he sent us a ferry brochure for the Ramsgate to Dunkerque and Oostende service!

Verdict? ℟

★ *BEST DRINKS OUTLET IN DUNKERQUE*

③ **LES TASTEVINS DE FLANDRE**
2 rue Dampierre
59140 Dunkerque
Tel: (28) 21.00.99
English spoken? A little
Opening hours? Tues-Sat 9.30am-12noon & 2.30pm-7pm, closed Sun & Mon
Parking? Yes (parking metres)
Shopping trolleys? No
Do they offer to help carry the goods to the car? Yes
Methods of payment? Sterling, French Francs, Eurocheques, Visa
Any wines for tasting in store? From time to time.
Comment: Located on the corner of rue Lion d'Or, this wine shop is a few doors down from the stratopherically upmarket La Bordelaise du Nord, but far more hospitable. Tastevins de Flandre is a tasteful, well-designed shop, with a comprehensive range of interesting wines, which are sensibly arranged. Its owner, Bernard Messiaen, is a professor of history, professor of geography and a doctor of sciences, but most importantly for us, he obviously loves wine, which is why he runs this friendly little shop, rather than sitting in an ivory tower at some university.

The wines: The range specialises in small growers, yet also encompasses classic Bordeaux *cru classé* châteaux going back to 1964, plus a superb range of wooden gift boxes, offering enough choice for both the élitist and the bargain-hunter. What are we going to do with M. Messiaen? None of the wines tasted passed the test, yet we still gave him 👍👍👍 because there were many wines on this list that would have excelled. This time he has done a bit better with two wines of the six he submitted qualifying for recommendation, yet we could pick far more wines from his list that would not only pass the test, but should be medal-winners. It seems a bit potty to give him the same rating again, yet it would hardly be fair to downgrade Les Tastevins de Flandre when he has improved his performance, and it is not misleading readers, who will find a lot to interest them here, and should in any case taste before buying. We'll give M. Messiaen one more year to submit wines that truly reflect the strength of his list, and if we cannot award him 👍👍👍 on the merit of our tastings, we will have to relegate his outlet to ⁇ until he does. We cannot be fairer than that.

RED WINES
Château La Cousterelle 1989 Cahors 40FF (£4.94) Very fruity, but appears to be peaking, so best drunk up, not laid down.
Château Les Videaux 1989 Premières Côtes de Blaye 42FF (£5.19) A decent medium-to-full bodied Bordeaux, drinking well now, but will still improve.
Verdict? 👍👍👍

LE HAVRE

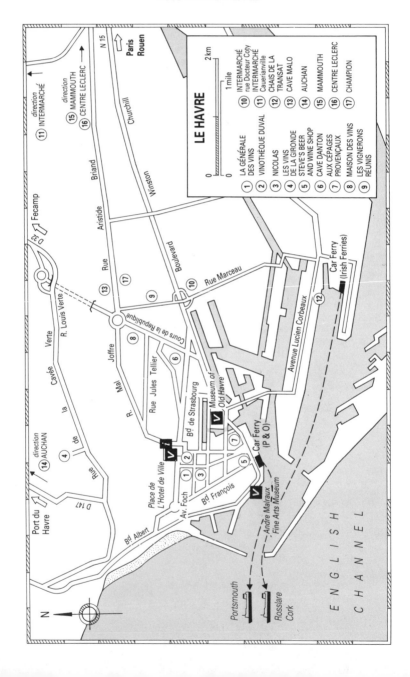

LE HAVRE

1. LA GÉNÉRALE DES VINS
2. VINOTHÈQUE DUVAL
3. NICOLAS
4. LES VINS DE LA GIRONDE
5. STEVE'S BEER AND WINE SHOP
6. CAVE DANTON
7. AUX CÉPAGES PROVENÇAUX
8. MAISON DES VINS
9. LES VIGNERONS RÉUNIS
10. INTERMARCHÉ rue Docteur Coty
11. INTERMARCHÉ Cauerianville
12. CHAIS DE LA TRANSAT
13. CAVE MALO
14. AUCHAN
15. MAMMOUTH
16. CENTRE LECLERC
17. CHAMPION

Le Havre is the second-largest commercial port in France and the country's first and worst concrete jungle. Having been flattened by allied bombers in 1944, Le Havre was reconstructed by Auguste Perret, the foremost exponent of reinforced concrete structures, who made an even greater mess of this once-picturesque 16th century port than the combined efforts of the USAF and RAF.

Did you know?

• Although Le Havre has the reputation of being a great port, it was just a fishing village until 1517, when François I ordered the construction of a harbour, which he called Havre-de-Grâce or 'Heaven of Grace', hence its name today.

• Le Havre was enlarged and fortified under Cardinal Richelieu and Louis XIV, and further improved under Louis XVI in the late-18th century and by Napoléon III in the mid-19th century. Yet, despite this 400-year history of construction, the only building of note that remains is the Notre Dame cathedral and quite how that survived the carpet-bombing of the port facilities surrounding it on three sides has always been something of a miracle.

Le Havre Factfile

HOW TO GET THERE: P&O operates out of Portsmouth, with a 5 hour 45 minute (day), 7-9 hour (night) crossing-time. In the Republic of Ireland, Irish Ferries operate out of Cork and Rosslare, both with a 21 hour 30 minute crossing-time (*see* pages 340-355 for details of service and prices).

LOCATION AND DISTANCES: Situated at the mouth of the Seine estuary on the right bank, opposite Deauville, 105km (66 miles) southwest of Dieppe and 107km (67 miles) northeast of Caen, Le Havre is 243km (151 miles) from Boulogne, 283km (177 miles) from Calais, 227km (142 miles) from Cherbourg, 274km (171 miles) from St-Malo, 454km (284 miles) from Roscoff and 203km (127 miles) from Paris.

POPULATION: 200,000

TOURIST INFORMATION OFFICE: place de l'Hôtel-de-Ville, 76600 Le Havre, *tel:* (35) 21.22.88. Open Mon-Fri 8.45am-12.15pm & 1.30pm-7pm (1.30pm-6.30pm Oct-March), closed Sun.

WHERE TO STAY: During the peak season, it is always best to book your hotel in advance, but if you are caught out, try the Tourist Information Centre, which offers a free accommodation service, keeping track of all the vacancies left in the town. The best place to stay: the *Bordeaux* (147 rue Louis-Brindeau, *Tel:* (35) 22.69.44) is the preferred accommodation in town, with doubles from 300-550FF (£37-68), although if you are looking for a combination of class, comfort and individual character, you need to get as far away from Le Havre as possible. Some cheap but clean stays include: *Hôtel Jeanne d'Arc* (91 rue Emile-Zola, *Tel:* (35) 41.26.83) a friendly, family-run establishment where a double with shower will cost 135FF; or the *Hôtel Séjour Fleuri* (71 rue Emile-Zola, *Tel:* (35) 41.33.81) where a small double with shower will cost 145FF.

RESTAURANTS: Le Havre is an excellent place to dine, the best place in town being *La Chaumette* (17 rue Racine), but you have to pay for the privilege. Next come two superb restaurants, *Le Montagne* (50-52 quai Michel-Féré), where Bruno Barboux creates culinary delights of great finesse and *Les Trois Mâts* (Chaussée d'Angoulême), which is very friendly, has a wonderful view of the ports, serves exquisite food and boasts an impressive wine list. Both are significantly less expensive than La Chaumette, although not by any means cheap, after which *L'Interdit* (18 boulevard Albert-1er, formerly *La Manche*), *La Marine Marchande* (27 boulevard de l'Amiral Mouchez), *Le Monaco* (16 rue de Paris) and *La Petit Auberge* (32 rue de Ste-Adresse) all offer excellent cuisine. Cheaper dining can be found at *Le Tilbury* (39 rue Jean de la Fontaine) and Le P'tit Comptoir (corner of rue de la Fontaine and avenue Faidherbe). where an excellent three-course fixed price lunch can be enjoyed for just 56-58FF. Two taverns, *La Taverne Basque* (73 avenue Foch) and *Taverne de Maâtre Kanter* (22 rue Georges-Braque) must also be recommended for those who prefer to dine later in the evening. Vinothèque Duval (*see* outlet entry below) owns *Le Vin en Bouche* (2 rue Jean Borda), a new bistro that offers 15 different wines by the glass. Best-cheapest eats: Restaurant *la Salamandre* (33 rue Jean de la Fontaine) where you can fill up on tasty *crêpes* from just 8FF; and for the young and lively set, the second floor of the *Maison des Jeunes et de la Culture* (2 avenue Foch), where you can eat well for 30FF. Where to find most restaurants, including some of the cheaper places to eat: down the side streets between the quai Lamblardie and the rue de Paris.

BEST BAR OR PUB IN TOWN: *La Coeur des Miracles* (rue Guillemard) for its friendly atmosphere, owner and barmaid.

MARKET DAYS: Tuesday, Thursday and Saturday (cours de la République)

WORTH A VISIT: The *place-de-l'Hôtel-de-Ville* is one of the largest squares in Europe and an ideal place to start for any first time visitor, who may choose to wander down the rue de Paris, with its grand concourse of shops or, perhaps, to stroll down the leaf-shaded *avenue Foch*, which leads to the Porte Océane and the beach. If you want to see how charming Le Havre was before Auguste Perret, then go to the *André Malraux Fine Arts Museum* opposite the P&O terminal and the *Museum of Old Havre* at 1 rue Jérôme-Bellarmato. The Fine Arts Museum has many works of Raoul Dufy, who ironically studied at the same École des Beaux-Arts in Paris as Perret, but thankfully was influenced by the bright colours of Fauvism, rather than the dull conformity of concrete; Dufy's vivid washes of Le Havre at the turn of the century are as expressive as you will find. For stark reality, however, there is nothing more alarming than the photographs of Le Havre before and after the allied bombings at the Museum of Old Havre.

⑭ AUCHAN
CC du Mont-Gaillard
76620 Le Havre
Tel: (35) 54.71.71
Selling area: 10,500m^2 (compare this with the size of other stores featured in the area, to gauge their

relative size and you will have a rough idea of how big the range of wines, beers, spirits and other goods will be).

Opening hours? Mon-Fri 8.30am-10pm, Sat 8am-10pm, closed Sun

Foire aux Vins: October

Comment: These outlets are usually amongst the biggest, brightest and most welcoming of the French hypermarket chains, and this one is very large indeed, although not quite as immense as the one in Boulogne. Auchan is very popular with British, who are apt to go spend-crazy at any supersized hypermarket. We had even less response from Auchan's directors this year than we did with its wine buyer last time, as neither the chairman (Gérard Mulliez) nor its managing director (Michel Pecqueraux) even acknowledged our correspondence.

The wines: The wines are displayed from the floor right up to the ceiling - well almost to the ceiling. There are many more reds than whites, with the greatest emphasis placed predictably enough on Bordeaux (approximately 40-50 different wines), after which Burgundy and Languedoc-Roussillon offer the most choice (about 20 wines each), although white Burgundies fare less well (just six), and the choice of Loire in any colour is abysmal. There are about 10 different Alsace, but the only white wines stocked in any serious way are Champagne and other sparklers. We purchased six wines (the cheapest red and cheapest white, plus four wines that a knowledgeable consumer might consider interesting or good value), but only one qualified for recommendation in this *Guide*, and two of those that failed the test we would not touch with a barge pole, even if Auchan gave them away. A hit-rate of just one in six is bad enough: we hate to think how the average consumer, who has to rely on pot-luck, would fare.

WHITE WINES
Alsace Riesling 1992 Pierre Dumoulin-Storch
25.90FF (£3.20) Dry white wine lifted by a slight spritz.
Verdict? 👎

• 1 BRONZE MEDAL

(7) **AUX CÉPAGES PROVENÇAUX**
15 quai Notre Dame
76600 Le Havre
Tel: (35) 22.59.20

English spoken? Not revealed
Opening hours? Tues-Sat 10am-12.30pm &
2.15pm-7pm, closed Sun & Mon
Parking? Only on street
Shopping trolleys? No
Do they offer to help carry the goods to the car?
Yes
Methods of payment? French Francs in cash only!
Any wines for tasting in store? All *vins en vrac*
Comment: This looks quite a fun outlet, but
primarily Aux Cépages Provençaux specialises in
vins en vrac, although it also sells wonderful
olives, olive oil, tapenades and honey – all from
Provence, of course.
The wines: Mme Poupel visits Provence every
three weeks, bringing back each wine in the large
plastic containers that sit in the back of her shop,
where it is nice and cool. But there is no use of
sulphur, the only precaution against oxidation is a
floating cap, which hopefully keeps the air out,
but certainly does nothing to retard the oxidation
process that may already have set in. We do not
taste *vins en vrac* (*see* Wines *en vrac* at the
beginning of the Cross-Channel Shopping Guide
section), and only three bottled wines were
submitted. Not much to go on, but two passed the
test and one of these picked up a medal.

RED WINES

BRONZE MEDAL

Bordeaux 1992 Producteurs des Hauts de Gironde
16FF (£1.98) The smoky-violety character of the
fruit made this stand out from other Bordeaux
wines of this price.
Côtes de Provence 1991 Le Brame 37FF (£4.57)
Medium-to-full bodied with elegant, spicy fruit,
this wine shows good Provençal typicity.
Verdict? 👍

(6) CAVE DANTON
74 rue Casimir Delavigne
76600 Le Havre
Tel: (35) 41.27.37
English spoken? No
Opening hours? Tues-Sat 9.30am-12.30pm &
2.30pm-7.15pm, closed Sun & Mon
Parking? Yes (on street, quite easy)
Shopping trolleys? No
Do they offer to help carry the goods to the car?
Yes

Methods of payment? French Francs, Traveller's cheques, Eurocheques, Visa, Mastercard, Access
Any wines for tasting in store? Yes (but *en vrac* only)
Comment: No beers or spirits, owner M. Falaise buys only small parcels of wine to promote as special offers, and once they are sold, he buys another. The range is mainly cheapo stuff and *en vrac*. This is a bit of a lucky-dip shop: you might hit lucky with a bargain, but it would not be around the next time you called.
Verdict? 👎

③ **CAVE MALO**
293 rue Aristide Briand
76600 Le Havre
Tel: 35 41 27 37
English spoken? No
Opening hours? Tues-Sat 8.30am-12.30pm & 3pm-7.15pm, Sun 9am-12noon, closed Mon
Parking? On street, but with difficulty
Shopping trolleys? No
Do they offer to help carry the goods to the car? Yes
Methods of payment? French Francs, Visa, Mastercard, Access
Any wines for tasting in store? No
Comment: For a wine shop on a main street in a major Channel port frequented by British travellers, Mme Pierron seemed strangely uninterested in our publication, only just managing to remain polite! A pity, as Cave Malo looks as if it has an interesting range in the medium price 20-50FF bracket, plus fine Alsace from Schlumberger, brilliant Burgundies from the talented Edmond Cornu, and good *négociant* stuff too (Mommessin).
Verdict? 👎

• 2 SILVER MEDALS

⑯ **CENTRE LECLERC**
Route Oudalle
76700 Gonfreville
Le Havre
Tel: (35) 49.02.22
Selling area: 2,000m² (compare this with the size of other stores featured in the area, to gauge their relative size and you will have a rough idea of how big the range of wines, beers, spirits and other goods will be).
Opening hours? Mon-Thurs 9am-10pm, Fri 9am-

10.30pm, Sat 8.30am-10.30pm, closed Sun

Comment: Last year we went through Gallec, which owns Leclerc, Groupe de Travail Liquides, which supplies Leclerc, and Leclerc's chief buyer, but all to no avail, so this time we went straight to the top, and we were pleased to receive Michel-Edouard Leclerc's assurance that his chain would extend the *Guide* full co-operation in supplying whatever samples and information we wanted. He delegated the matter to Jean Maurice, who runs Leclerc Scapertois, which supplies all the stores in the Pas-de-Calais and Normandy. Unfortunately M. Maurice had other ideas, inviting us instead to spend the day at Scapertois, where we could taste their best wines over 70FF. We would be wined and dined, and afterwards we would be given some *cru classé* Bordeaux to take away. Apparently he has tried this wheeze on other British journalists with a certain amount of success, but we are not in this job to fill the car boot with cases of château-bottled claret, so we declined, immediately and in no uncertain terms. We again explained that most cross-Channel bargains are under 34FF, as indeed are most of Centre Leclerc's sales, thus concentrating on its top of the range wines tells us nothing about the bulk of wines most Leclerc customers buy. Besides which, tasting them in isolation would have been unfair to the other retail outlets, whose wines must compete with others of a similar style and price under blind conditions. After more correspondence with M. Leclerc, we received a letter from the head of Sobadis, a subsidiary of Leclerc's, which handles the distribution of its products in Normandy. Referring to our last correspondence with Michel-Edouard Leclerc, he offered us exactly what we wanted, even a choice of branches from which we could collect our samples from. Unfortunately our last correspondence with M. Leclerc had been over six weeks earlier, and our tastings had come and gone. Still, if Centre Leclerc keeps to its word, and submits samples without delay or hesitation for the next edition, all the hassle we have endured this year will at least be worthwhile.

The wines: Most branches are basic warehouse-type operations, and very utilitarian. In the bigger stores, the range can include as many as 250 different lines, with a good selection of fine wines, albeit almost entirely from Bordeaux. Centre Leclerc seems to be quite good on Beaujolais, with most *cru villages* covered, and the one we tried from Juliénas certainly fared well, earning a silver medal no less. With four wines out of six random purchases qualifying for recommendation in the *Guide*, including two silver medals, one of which grabbed a Wine of the Year award, it makes us look forward to greater co-operation next year, to see how the range as a whole performs.

RED WINES

SILVER MEDAL
BEST-VALUE RED
WINE OF THE YEAR

Domaine de Pons 1991 Côtes du Ventoux 13.95FF (£1.72) We had to taste almost 30 red Rhônes up to 27FF before we found a wine to equal this. An elegant wine with a good depth of silky-plummy fruit, and nicely structured supple tannins.

Carayon-la-Rose 1986 Cuvée Exceptionnelle, Bordeaux Supérieur 18.95FF (£2.34) This is not bad as a basic Bordeaux, but unless you see the vintage on the label, you would hardly think that you are tasting an eight-year-old claret.

SILVER MEDAL

Juliénas 1992 les Vouillants Chedeville 26.50FF (£3.27) Bags of flavour. A real wine, and a true *cru* Beaujolais (we rejected most of the *cru* Beaujolais because they lacked the significant increase in quality and intensity of varietal flavour they should possess).

Château Roches Guitard 1989 Montagne-St-Émilion 30.85FF (£3.81) A good Bordeaux with sweet fruity aromas that follow through onto the palate.

Verdict? 👍

★ *BEST DRINKS OUTLET*
IN LE HAVRE
• 2 GOLD MEDALS
• 3 SILVER MEDAL
• 1 BRONZE MEDAL

⑫ **CHAIS DE LA TRANSAT**
Avenue Lucien Corbeaux
76600 Le Havre
Tel: (35) 53.66.65
English spoken? Yes
Opening hours? Tues-Sat 9.30am-12.30pm & 2pm-7pm, closed Sun & Mon
Parking? Yes
Shopping trolleys? Yes
Do they offer to help carry the goods to the car? Yes
Methods of payment? French Francs, Traveller's cheques, Eurocheques, Visa
Any wines for tasting in store? Yes
Comment: In addition to Le Havre, Chais de la Transat wine warehouses can be found at Dunkerque, Rouen and Paris. This small group is all that remains of the old Compagnie Générale Transatlantique, which was known simply as

Transat and ran the famous French Line, which for 120 years operated such famous liners as the 'Normandie', 'Libertie' and – the last, greatest and finest of all – the 'France'. After the 'France' made her final voyage in 1974, the firm opened its cellars in Le Havre to sell off the stocks and, recognising that Transat had represented the pinnacle of French gastronomy for over a century, the public descended like vultures eager to plunder its bargains. Such was the response that a trading company was quickly set up and, to satisfy demand, new warehouses were opened in Dunkerque, Rouen and Paris. Chais de la Transat warehouses are well-run and offer a good range of wines and spirits, but no beers.

The wines: Although single bottles are not strictly ruled out, they are not exactly encouraged either, most wines being sold in cases of 3, 6 or 12. Nostalgic own-labels abound and various offers and promotions are made each month. The range is particularly strong on Bordeaux, with what appears to be some good names on the list and concentrating on the better vintages, although it is not always the right name for the right vintage, so be choosy and taste before you buy whenever possible. Chais de la Transat intend introducing a range of beers by the end of 1994 - especially for the Brits!

RED WINES

Vieux Domaine de Meneau 1992 Premières Côtes de Blaye 24FF (£2.96) From the nose through the palate to the finish, this is unusually peppery for Bordeaux, but quite a tasty wine nevertheless.

SILVER MEDAL *Château Monbadon 1990 Côtes de Castillon* 29FF (£3.58) Firm, rich and tasty with a good tannin structure. Perfect food wine, yet excellent to drink on its own.

SILVER MEDAL *Château Hautes Graves de By 1990 Médoc Cru Bourgeois* at 34FF (£4.20) has very good depth of colour for such an elegant wine, with lots of silky fruit and just the right sort of firm finish to tell you this is real Bordeaux.

GOLD MEDAL *Côtes-du-Rhône* 1990 E. Guigal 35FF (£4.07) This is even bigger and more luscious than when we tasted it from various outlets last year. A succulent wine of wonderful spicy aromas and rich, raisiny-plummy fruit.

WHITE WINES

GOLD MEDAL *Côtes-du-Rhône 1992 E. Guigal* 35FF (£4.07) Has

developed exceptional finesse for what is a rather nondescript year.

BRONZE MEDAL *Numero 1 1992 Dourthe* 39FF (£4.81) There is plenty of real fruit in this soft, ripe and gentle dry white wine, which also has an elegantly perfumed aftertaste.

SPARKLING WINES

SILVER MEDAL *Champagne Palmer NV Brut* 98FF (£12.10) Quality co-operative Champagne from the co-op the houses respect the most.

Verdict? 👍👍👍

• 2 BRONZE MEDALS

⑰ CHAMPION

260 rue Aristide Briand
76600 Le Havre
Tel: N/A

Selling area: 1,750m^2 (compare this with the size of other stores featured in the area, to gauge their relative size and you will have a rough idea of how big the range of wines, beers, spirits and other goods will be).

Opening hours? Mon-Sat 8.30am-10pm, closed Sun

Comment: Part of the Promodes group, which owns Continent, Shopi and various other smaller outlets. We made contact last year with no less than six top people at Promodes and its various offshoots, but to no avail, so this year we wrote to the managing director of Promodes, M. Pierre Merle, but he could not be bothered to reply either.

The wines: The range consists of primarily Bordeaux and the Southwest, a smattering of decent Burgundy (eg., Labouré Roi Pommard 1989 at 69.70FF), and a few interesting-looking, domaine-bottled *cru* Beaujolais. There is a good selection of petit châteaux, especially from St-Émilion and its satellites, (top flight vintages 1989 and 1990). Champion also has a comparatively large selection of spirits for a French supermarket group. For one week in June, this store was selling the cheapest beer we could find anywhere, Brandenberg Bier Blonde at 19.95FF for 24 x 25cl bottles (beware: we occasionally see beers at seemingly cheaper prices, only to discover the pack contains 20 rather than 24 bottles – so check the number of contents before purchase).

Although we found the inexpensive white wines to be generally very boring, there is a good range of reds between 15-30FF (mainly Cahors, Côtes-du-Ventoux, and Côtes-de-Duras. Our biggest criticism of Champion is that all the bottles were standing upright, including the fine wines, yet of the six random purchases, four qualified for recommendation, which is good by French supermarket standards. Furthermore two of these picked up medals, and one was the best-cheapest wine of its style we found on the entire cross-Channel market. The two wines that did not warrant a recommendation were perfectly drinkable, even if they were not good enough for inclusion in this publication. On the basis of this performance, it is hard to see what M. Merle has to hide.

RED WINES
Château Bois Clair 1993 Bordeaux 11.90FF (£1.47) Light but honest, easy-drinking basic Bordeaux.

BRONZE MEDAL

Bourgogne Hautes Côtes de Beaune 1990 Labouré Roi 31.90FF (£3.94) Sweet Pinot fruit on the nose, firm structure and still unwinding, but a medium-term developer, not a long-term one. Good with food.

Château Saint-Lô 1989 Saint-Émilion 34FF (£4.20) Good fruit on a firm structure of ripe tannins.

ROSÉ WINES

BRONZE MEDAL
BEST-CHEAPEST ROSÉ WINE OF THE YEAR

Cinsault Rosé 1993 J.P Chenet 11.80FF (£1.46) Looks more like a brandy bottle than a wine bottle, but who cares at this price, especially when it's full of fruit with such good acidity. This is a real wine at a make believe price (and for one week in June, it was even cheaper, on offer at 9.95FF!).
Verdict? 🖒 🖒

① LA GÉNÉRALE DES VINS
79 rue Victor Hugo
76600 Le Havre
Tel: (35) 22.90.90
English spoken? Not revealed
Opening hours? Mon 2pm-7pm, Tues-Sat 9am-12noon & 2pm-7pm, closed Sun
Parking? Yes (private car park)
Shopping trolleys? Yes
Do they offer to help carry the goods to the car? Yes
Methods of payment? French Francs, Visa, Mastercard
Any wines for tasting in store? No

Comment: This bright, spacious operation is located just off the main street, with its own car park, a godsend in Le Havre, which is prone to pedestrian-only areas.

The wines: This outlet has a comprehensive list of fine French wines, at least half of which is Bordeaux, but these wines are of more interest to local enthusiasts, than British ones, who can purchase most of these wines far cheaper in the UK. Although prices start at just under 20FF, quite how good these medium-priced wines are is difficult to discern, as both this year and last only three wines have been submitted. This is obviously too little to assess an entire range with, but it should be relatively easy to select just three that will do well, yet only one wine passed the test last year, and none did this time. Le Générale des Vins is therefore lucky to retain its questionmark status, and only does so on the basis of its list. Despite this lacklustre performance, we enjoyed browsing around the wines in this shop, and we are sure that you will too, but unless the wines submitted next time fare much better, I am afraid that it will be the thumbs-down for Le Générale des Vins.

Verdict? ?

• 1 BRONZE MEDAL

⑩ **INTERMARCHÉ**
8 rue Docteur Coty
76600 Le Havre
Tel: (35) 14.44.11
Selling area: 3,000m2

AND

⑪ **INTERMARCHÉ**
34 avenue 8 Mai 1945
Cauerianville
76000 Le Havre
Tel: (35) 49.53.57
Selling area: 2,000m^2 (compare this with the size of other stores featured in the area, to gauge their relative size and you will have a rough idea of how big the range of wines, beers, spirits and other goods will be).

Opening hours? Mon-Thurs 9am-12.15pm & 2pm-7.15pm, Fri 9am-12.15pm & 2pm-7.30pm, Sat 9am-7.15pm

Comment: Most Intermarché on the Channel coast are relatively small, and although they can be quite large further inland, this chain is more of the supermarket ilk than hypermarket. It is also relatively down-market, with a mostly dull and uninteresting range of wines, often dominated by a display of 3-litre wine containers. There are around a dozen different Champagnes, and the fine wines are usually displayed separately (we saw Ducru Beaucaillou 1989 at 85FF, and Pavillon Rouge 1990 at 105FF). We had no success with chairman Marcel Robin, who steadfastly refused to answer our correspondence. It was the same story as last year, with M. Le Goff, Intermarché's drinks buyer.

The wines: We purchased six wines along the same lines as those we bought at Auchan, and when it came to the crunch, Intermarché fared much better, with half of the wines warranting our recommendation, and one even picking up a Bronze medal. And two of those that did not qualify were perfectly drinkable, even if not special enough to qualify for the *Guide*. If only the management of this firm had enough faith in its products to submit a substantial range of its inexpensive wines, they might do well, if this random sampling is anything to go by.

RED WINES

Beaujolais NV Cuvée Joannès 12FF (£1.48) Although not medal potential, you could have knocked us down with a feather when this wine, the second-cheapest Gamay submitted, turned out not only to be drinkable, but expressive of its variety, rather than *macération carbonique*.

Côtes-du-Rhône 1993 Réserve Lescarrat 13FF (£1.60) This soft and fruity wine has a touch more elegance than the other red Rhônes in its price category.

WHITE WINES

BRONZE MEDAL

Reuilly 1993 Cave PD 22.90FF (£2.83) This fresh and assertive Sauvignon is not a wine for wimps. **Verdict?** 👍

⑧ **LA MAISON DES VINS**
59-61 rue Jules Tellier
76600 Le Havre
Tel: (35) 25.39.73
English spoken? Yes
Opening hours? Tues-Sat 8.30am-12.30pm & 2.30pm-7.30pm, Sun 9am-12.30pm, closed Mon
Parking? Only on street

• 1 SILVER MEDAL
• 1 BRONZE MEDAL

Shopping trolleys? No

Do they offer to help carry the goods to the car? Yes

Methods of payment? Sterling, French Francs, Visa, Mastercard

Any wines for tasting in store? From 'eventually' last time to 'occasionally' this year

Comment: This traditional French wine merchant is owned by Hubert le François, who is very friendly and chatty. He has good, cool, dark cellars beneath his shop, where he stores wines in bins, and he even keeps his *en vrac* wines here, although the bottling machine is in a room at the back of his store.

The wines: A typical upmarket French wine list, dominated by a large number of very good Bordeaux, mostly red and including some fine old vintages, but as the reader is aware by now there is little value for money in that particular category of wine for British shoppers, who can find an even greater selection in the UK, where the prices are generally much cheaper. He does, however, have a range of over 200 wines, which includes cheaper, medium priced products. Although M. François submitted just three wines, two of these were medal winners, and when we can establish if this sort of performance is the norm across his range, La Maison des Vins could be looking at least at another thumbs-up in our rating.

RED WINES

BRONZE MEDAL

Château Moulin de Gassiot 1989 Bordeaux 26FF (£3.21) Intense flavours, still tight, will mellow and improve with further age in bottle.

SILVER MEDAL

Saint Véran 1991 Domaine des Maillettes 52.50FF (£6.48) You could easily zap past this wine, as on one level it is just as fresh and as clean as any decent St-Véran should be, but take a few glasses and you begin to see that it has a level of richness normally reserved for the very best Pouilly-Fuissé.
Verdict? 👍👍

⑮ MAMMOUTH

CC la Lezarde
76290 Montivilliers
Le Havre
Tel: (35) 30.11.11
Selling area: 9,400m² (compare this with the size of other stores featured in the area, to gauge their relative size and you will have a rough idea of

how big the range of wines, beers, spirits and other goods will be).

Opening hours? Mon-Sat 9am-9pm (some outlets open Sun)

Comment: Last year we were authorised by Mammouth's buyer Jean-Claude Alti to approach the manager of this branch, M. Walter, who we were assured would be particularly helpful, since his experience at Calais meant that he knew the English market well. M. Walter, however, did not want to know. This year we approached Christian Toulouse, the chairman of Mammouth's parent company, Paridoc, but he did not even bother to reply. This apathy is a pity because Mammouth outlets are usually amongst the largest, brightest and most welcoming of all the French hypermarket chains, and obviously a favourite with British customers.

The wines: When we visited the Calais branch it was packed out with trippers from the UK, all eagerly stuffing their trolleys with cheap wines and beers, while the tills at Sainsbury's next door were ominously quiet. They cannot have bothered to compare the wines, as anyone who read Robert Joseph's column in *The Sunday Telegraph* last April will be able to verify. Joseph set up a table between Mammouth and Sainsbury's, took a Beaujolais, Rhône and Bordeaux from each store, wrapped them in foil, and asked passers-by to say which ones they preferred. Sainsbury's wines won easily. Even M. Walter and his regional boss, M. Le Bail, reckoned that the Mammouth products lacked fruit and freshness by comparison. How embarrassing. We have to agree, as only one of the six wines randomly purchased from Mammouth survived the test, and although we saw a number of *cru classé* clarets (Haut-Brion 1990 at 220FF, Branaire-Ducru 1991 at 75FF), they were all standing upright!

RED WINES
Bourgogne NV Passetoutgrains 15FF (£1.85)
Decent Gamay with a bit of extra backbone.
Verdict? 🖐

• 2 SILVER MEDALS
• 2 BRONZE MEDALS

③ **NICOLAS**
Les Halles Centrales
Rue Bernadin de St-Pierre
76600 Le Havre
Tel: (35) 42.24.63

English spoken? A little
Opening hours? Mon 2.30pm-7.30pm, Tues-Fri 8.30am-12.30pm & 2.30pm-7.30pm, Sat 8.30am-7.30pm (non-stop), closed Sun
Parking? Private parking for the
Shopping trolleys? Yes
Do they offer to help carry the goods to the car? Yes
Methods of payment? French Francs, Visa, Access, Mastercard, American Express
Any wines for tasting in store? Once a month!
Comment: One of the oldest retail chains in the country and a wine merchant in Paris since 1822, Nicolas is a sort of French cross between Berry Bros & Rudd and Victoria Wine. Since the chain was purchased by the Castel group in 1988, Nicolas has been revitalised and is now expanding its operations. This particular branch is run by a very efficient and friendly manager, and situated within an indoor market, surrounded by shops with lots of other tempting products – patisserie, charcuterie, coffee .... making Les Halles Centrales well worth a visit for shopping in general, not just wine.
The wines: Nicolas stocks an interesting range of medium priced wines, plus excellent Alsace from Muré, a large range of Champagnes, and a splattering of 'foreign' wines, ranging from Torres and Marques de Cacérès from Spain, through Hardy's Cabernet-Shiraz from Australia, to Opus One, would you believe, from California (well, it is half French isn't it?).

RED WINES

BRONZE MEDAL *Bordeaux 1990 Réserve de la Maison Nicolas* 34FF (£4.20) This tasty own-label claret is 6FF more than last year, but it is still a pleasure to drink.

SILVER MEDAL *Clos la Coutale 1990 Cahors* 39.50FF (£4.88) The first impression is soft and very silky, with lots of elegant fruit, but there is also plenty of acidity and a fine tannin structure, which suggests that the wine will continue to develop in bottle for several years to come.

BRONZE MEDAL *Réserve de la Maison Nicolas 1991 Bourgogne* 45FF (£5.56) Firm and meaty, yet still retains the purity of Pinot Noir. Promises to be quite tasty, but needs a year or two in bottle.

Domaine Baron de Rothschild 1990 Cuvée Spéciale 48FF (£5.93) Well structured wine with plenty of flavour, but lacks finesse at this price level, and would have scored much higher if £2.00 cheaper.

SILVER MEDAL

WHITE WINES
Jurançon Sec 1993 Grain Sauvage 32FF (£3.95)
Good dry white wine with ripe grapefruit flavour,
and some individual character.

ROSÉ WINES
*Château Bellevue la Forêt 1993 Côtes de
Frontonnais* 32.50FF (£4.01) Young, fresh and very
fruity.
Verdict? 👍👍

⑤ STEVE'S BEER & WINE SHOP

21 rue Paris
76600 Le Havre
Tel: (35) 42.11.78
English spoken? Yes
Opening hours? 6am-10pm seven days a week
Parking? Only on street
Shopping trolleys? Yes
Do they offer to help carry the goods to the car?
Yes
Methods of payment? Sterling, Irish Punts,
French Francs, Traveller's cheques, Eurocheques,
Visa, Mastercard
Any wines for tasting in store? Yes
Comment: Etienne Comont alias 'Steve' was not at
all pleased with us for spoiling his little ruse last
year. When we asked where this Steve guy was,
"Oui, je suis Steve" he replied. He then went on to
give us a lot of hype about how they are
'contacting some *petit producteurs* ... to discover
wines giving new sensations' and how they had to
consult a university-trained oenologist 'with two
years hands-on experience making rosé' in order
to choose the wines of great quality. Yet when we
asked what his best wine was, he told us Mouton-
Cadet! Steve might not be English, but he can
certainly express himself in our language, telling
our mild-mannered representative that he didn't
"give a toss about the f*****g guide"!
The wines: It doesn't matter that Steve's Beer and
Wine Shop is not exactly what it seems. We would
be rather amused at the Steve turning out to be
Etienne if he had actually something interesting to
sell. But he does not. He gave our representative a
Chinon at 68FF to taste, to demonstrate how well
chosen his wines are, and it was dreadful. Then he
gave her a taste of a Champagne, which sells for
120FF, and this was okay, but not special. If he
submitted wines for a future edition and they did

well, we would not shrink from recommending this outlet, however many expletives Steve throws at us, but for the moment, we can find absolutely no reason to shop here.
Verdict? 👎

• 1 BRONZE MEDAL

⑨ LES VIGNERONS RÉUNIS
71-73 rue Jean-Jacques Rousseau
76600 Le Havre
Tel: (35) 42.64.36
English spoken? A little
Opening hours? Mon-Sat 8am-12noon & 2pm-7pm, closed Sun
Parking? Only on street
Shopping trolleys? No
Do they offer to help carry the goods to the car? Yes
Methods of payment? French Francs, Visa, Mastercard
Any wines for tasting in store? Yes
Comment: We met both owners this year, Messrs. Fanonnel and Beziat, and thought they looked quite jolly and professional, in their clean blue pinnies.
The wines: No beers here, but as in all Normandy drink outlets, plenty of cider. They have Wantz from Alsace, which is not top stuff, but does have some interesting wines such as Klevener de Heiligenstein. Délas from the Rhône, which again is not special, but can be very good value. Generally, however, the range at this outlet centres on medium-priced wines of the Southwest. Just three wines were submitted.

BRONZE MEDAL

RED WINES
Buzet 1993 Le Lys 32FF (£3.95) An exuberant wine, with delightfully young and fresh fruit.

ROSÉ WINES
Buzet 1992 Le Lys 32FF (£3.95) Gentle fruit, some elegance.
Verdict? 👍👍

② VINOTHÈQUE DUVAL
23 rue Robert de la Villehervé
76600 Le Havre
Tel: (35) 41.31.72
English spoken? A little
Opening hours? Mon-Fri 9.15am-12.15pm & 3pm-7.30pm, Sat 9am-12.15pm & 2.30pm-7.30pm, closed Sun

Parking? Only on street (opposite side of road)

Shopping trolleys? No

Do they offer to help carry the goods to the car? Yes

Methods of payment? French Francs, Traveller's cheques, Eurocheques, Visa, Access, Mastercard

Any wines for tasting in store? Sometimes on request

Comment: Vinothèque Duval is very near the centre and you cannot miss the giant Bordeaux bottle standing outside, although parking can be a bit tricky at times, as this is a pedestrian area. The shop is nice and appealing and its owner Thierry Duval, who used to be a sommelier and specialises in advising customers how to match wine with food, is bright, efficient and business-like. In addition to wines and spirits, he sells the usual accessories, such as cork-screws, and some very nice decanters, plus foie gras, confit, and other food from the Southwest.

The wines: This outlet has a reasonable range of medium-priced wines. It did quite well with a couple of wines in last year's tasting, but none of the three submitted this time passed the test, so it holds on to a single thumbs-up on the strength of his range, which has not altered in any substantial way. We do not know what went wrong with his selections this year, but hope that he shows us a greater number of better selected wines next year, so that our tasting results can accurately reflect the strength of his range.

Verdict? 👍

④ LES VINS DE LA GIRONDE

43 rue Sadi Carnot

76620 Le Havre

Tel: (35) 46.01.66

English spoken? No

Opening hours? Mon-Sat 8.30am-12.30pm & 4pm-7pm

Parking? Yes (on street)

Shopping trolleys? No

Do they offer to help carry the goods to the car? Yes

Methods of payment? French Francs, Visa, Mastercard, Access

Any wines for tasting in store? Yes (but only *en vrac*)

Comment: Owned by M. Duboc, this is a small, old-fashioned *caviste* in the town's oldest cellars or, at any rate, the oldest surviving cellars. Don't be put off by the empty bottles on the shelf – at least they prove he regularly tastes his stock! The wines *en vrac* are kept in real wooden barrels (if you get a chance, take a look at them in the cellar), and he will bottle some off for you as well. If you are having a party, and warn him in advance, he can let you have the wine in a small barrel, which you must return (we assume there will be a deposit). Most of M. Duboc's customers are French, although they occasionally bring along their British chums. We received a list, but no wines.

Verdict? ?

OOSTENDE

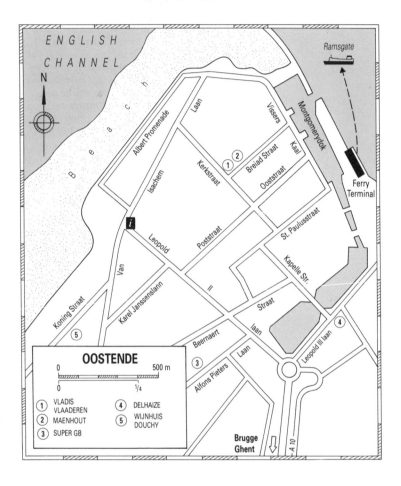

Oostende, or Ostend as we normally spell it, is Belgium's largest seaside resort, and the most important commercial port in the country. Sustaining this position will be difficult, as foreign trade – be it goods or tourism – is Oostende's lifeblood, and this has been under increasing threat from the closer French ports, and more recently Zeebrugge's very modern port facilities, and with the Channel Tunnel looming. Oostende's older harbour is, however, more quaint, and this town also benefits from five bathing beaches, each well equipped with showers, cabins, and, that great British favourite, the deck-chair.

Generally it is cheaper to buy gin and Belgian beer in Belgium, and wine in France.

Did you know?

• In 1601, the archduchess Isabella Clara Eugenia, who ruled the Spanish Netherlands, laid siege to Oostende, the last Dutch stronghold in Belgium. She vowed not to change her shirt until the town fell, which it did, but not until three years later. Whether this was due more to the constant onslaught of Spanish forces or Isabella's shirt, has been lost in the mists of time.

• Oyster beds have been farmed in Oostende since 1733.

• Oostende was a major U-boat base in the First World War, until the British sank the blockship HMS Vindictive, sealing the port in 1918.

• The so-called 'Ostend Manifesto' was written by three American diplomats who, in 1854, were ordered by William L. Marcy, the US Secretary of State, to meet in Ostend, after the Spanish had refused his attempt to buy the island of Cuba. In the 'Ostend Manifesto', the three diplomats brazenly recommended the seizure of Cuba by force, in order to expand US slave territory, but this advice was rejected, and when the document was leaked to the Republican press, it was branded as pandering to Southern opinion.

• Oostende was flooded in 1953, when the Oostende-Knokke dyke broke.

Oostende Factfile

HOW TO GET THERE: The Oostende Line, operates in partnership with the Sally Line from Ramsgate, with a 4 hour (ferry), 105 minute (jetfoil) crossing-time (*see* pages 340-355 for details of service and prices).

LOCATION AND DISTANCES: Situated roughly halfway between Calais (92km or 57 miles) and Antwerp (97km or 61 miles), Oostende is just 24km (15 miles) from the French border, 44km (27 miles) from Dunkerque.

POPULATION: 68,400

TOURIST INFORMATION OFFICE: Monacoplein 2, *Tel:* (059) 70.11.99. Open May-Sept 9am-7pm seven days a week, Oct-April 9am-6pm seven days a week.

WHERE TO STAY: During the peak season, it is always best to book your hotel in advance, but if you are caught out, try the Tourist Information Centre, which offers a free accommodation service, keeping track of all the vacancies left in the town. The best place to stay: *Hotel Ter Kade* (Visserskaai 49, *Tel:* (059) 50.09.15) is a typical seafront, high-rise tourist establishment, but its rooms are spacious and at 3100-3500BF (£66-75) for a double en-suite with TV, seaview and all facilities, well worth the money. Some cheap but clean stays include: *Andromeda* (Albert-I-Promenade

60, *Tel:* (059) 80.66.11) and *Thermae Palace* (Koningin Astridiaan, *Tel:* (059) 80.66.44), both of which offer doubles en-suite for 1000-2000BF (£21-42).

RESTAURANTS: The *Marina* (Albert 1 Promenade 2) offers good Italian cuisine for 760BF (£16) for a three-course lunch. Best-cheapest eats: *Haddock's* (Kemmelbergstraat 25) for a relaxed, bistro-type atmosphere. Where to find most restaurants, including some of the cheaper places to eat: Visserkai, overlooking the harbour.

BEST BAR OR PUB IN TOWN: *Den Artiest* (Kapucijenstraat 13) for good beer and real music, or do we mean real beer and good music?

MARKET DAYS: From 8am to 1pm on Monday, Thursday and Saturday (Thursday is the main market day), in three squares: Wapenplein, Mijnplein & Groentemarkt.

WORTH A VISIT: On the Wapenplein, in the centre of old Oostende, is the *Feestpalais*, the first floor of which is a local museum, featuring the history of Oostende as a fishing town (since the 9th century) and as resort (since the British discovered it in the 'Belle Epoque'; while the second floor houses a museum of fine art (particularly good for James Ensor, Constant Permeke and other Belgian artists). If you want to learn more about Ensor, his home is just north of the *Feestpalais*, at Vlaanderenstrat 27, and is now a museum open to the public.

• 2 BRONZE MEDALS

④ DELHAIZE
Leopold III Laan 7
8400 Oostende
Tel: (059) 80.39.11
English spoken? Not revealed (but the local manager has good written English)
Opening hours? Mon-Thur & Sat 9am-8pm, Fri 9am-9pm, and (during holiday periods) Sun 9am-1pm
Parking? Yes (private car park, plus numerous smaller parking areas surrounding the shop)
Shopping trolleys? Yes
Do they offer to help carry the goods to the car? No
Methods of payment? Sterling, Belgian Francs, Traveller's cheques, Eurocheques
Any wines for tasting in store? No
Comment: In Belgium, Delhaize is a well-known, quality-conscious supermarket group that uses its wine range as the unique selling point that differentiates it from other supermarket chains. Delhaize has 107 shops in Belgian, which between them sell 30 million bottles of wine, which is almost 12% of the total wine sold in the country. The firm also owns over 1,000 stores in the USA, with 45 in Dallas alone, but while that's another story, it does illustrate its open-minded approach,

which is in stark contrast to the blinkered mentality of French supermarket groups.

The wines: The range at Delhaize concentrates on, but is not confined to, France, taking in wines (both good and not so good) from California, Chile, Germany, Italy, Spain and Portugal. Even Switzerland is featured and there are no less than six wines from Luxembourg. This looks like a very interesting shop, with some obvious bargains (working on an exchange rate of some 50 Belgian francs to the pound), on top of which there is a 10% discount for purchases of 24 bottles or more. There are fine Alsace wines from Schlumberger, but do not overlook the good value ones from the Ingersheim co-operative. There is obviously a number of good wines, particularly from Bordeaux and Southwestern France. The Rhône and Burgundy are difficult to assess because there is no indication who the producers are for most of the wines listed. As may be expected, there is a fair share of boring, commercial branded wines and it is easy to spot the odd bottle of dross, but there's a whole load of stuff that requires tasting in order to sort the chaff from the wheat. Unfortunately, Delhaize again declined to submit samples, so we had to resort to purchasing six at random, and two of these passed the test with flying colours. We think that this supermarket is probably worth 👍 👍 👍, but until it submits a decent selection from its range, we will not be able to confirm this.

RED WINES

BRONZE MEDAL

Château Impériale 1992 Bordeaux 18.15FF (£2.24) An elegant, inexpensive Bordeaux with a nice balance between freshness and roundness of fruit.

BRONZE MEDAL

Domaine de la Grand'Ribe 1993 Côtes-du-Rhône 20.35FF (£2.51) Gentle fruit with a nice touch of pepperiness and an attractive supple finish.
Verdict? 👍

② MAENHOUT

1 & 2 Groentemarkt
8400 Oostende
Tel: N/A
English spoken? No (not even French!)
Opening hours? Mon-Sat 9am-1pm & 2pm-7pm, Sun 9am-12.30pm
Parking? Yes (on street)

Shopping trolleys? Yes
Do they offer to help carry the goods to the car?
No
Methods of payment? French Francs, Belgian
Francs
Any wines for tasting in store? No
Comment: A small, newly fitted supermarket with
an average range of wines, mostly French and
mainly Bordeaux, but other countries represented
include Germany, Portugal, Spain and Bulgaria
(Welschriesling). Not very interesting, except for a
good range of ports, sherries and beers. Prices not
cheap. No wines tasted.

WHITE WINES
Muscadet de Sèvre et Maine 1992 André Poirier
21.30FF (£2.63) This wine scores well for its initial
fruit, but drops a point or two for its short finish.
Verdict? ?

③ **SUPER GB**
Alfons Pieterslaan
8400 Oostende
Tel: (059) 80.43.37
English spoken? Yes
Opening hours? Mon-Fri 9am-8pm, Sat 9am-9pm,
closed Sun
Parking? On street (with great difficulty)
Shopping trolleys? Yes
Do they offer to help carry the goods to the car?
No
Methods of payment? Sterling, French Francs,
Irish Punt, Belgian Franc (cash only)
Any wines for tasting in store? No
Comment: A supermarket on a main street in
Oostende, Super GB (those were the days) takes
only cash. The wines are mostly from France, but
with a better emphasis on whites than is the norm
in French supermarkets. Wines from other
countries were present, including Bulgaria, Chile
(Santa Rita), Australia (Jacob's Creek), Spain,
Portugal, Italy, Germany and Greece, although
there was about only one wine from each.
Verdict? ?

★ *BEST DRINKS OUTLET*
IN OOSTENDE
• 1 GOLD MEDAL
• 1 SILVER MEDAL
• 2 BRONZE MEDALS

⑤ **WIJNHUIS DOUCHY**
56 Koningstraat
8400 Oostende
Tel: (059) 70.97.23
English spoken? Not revealed
Opening hours? Mon-Tues & Thus-Sat 9.30am-
7.30pm, closed Sun

Parking? Yes (in street)
Shopping trolleys? No
Do they offer to help carry the goods to the car?
Yes
Methods of payment? Belgian Francs,
Eurocheques, Visa
Any wines for tasting in store? Yes (dedicated
tasting area in back of shop)
Comment: This outlet is easy enough to find, with
its giant bottle outside the shop entrance, and M.
Douchy is friendly, helpful and eager to please,
which probably explains his regular British
custom. Wijnhuis Douchy is a well presented
shop, with wooden floors. Wines are stored in
stoneware bins.
The wines: This outlet has a very comprehensive
range, which is mostly French and mainly
Bordeaux, but there is also a good range of ports,
sherries and spirits. Seven of the 10 wines
submitted passed the test, and even the three
rejected were all perfectly drinkable, although not
special enough for the *Guide*.

RED WINES

Rocbère Vieux 1991 Corbières 135BF (21.87FF or
£2.70) Soft and almost too easy to drink – not for
food, or for keeping, so drink it up!

SILVER MEDAL | *Château de Seguin 1990 Bordeaux Supérieur* 295BF
47.79FF (£5.90) A lovely combination of oak, fruit
and supple tannins.

GOLD MEDAL | *Château de Seguin, Cuvée Prestige 1991 Bordeaux
Supérieur* 415BF (67.23FF or £8.30) An elegantly
oaky wine of some finesse, and a marvellous
richness of succulent fruit. Distinctly better than
the basic Château Seguin 1990, as good as that
wine is. Just a pity that we did not get to taste the
1990 Cuvée Prestige.

WHITE WINES

Château Couronneau 1993 Bordeaux Blanc Sec
145BF (23.49FF or £2.90) Dominated by its 65%
content of Sauvignon Blanc, which gives the wine
a freshness that stands out amongst most blended
Bordeaux at this price.

BRONZE MEDAL | *Sauvignon de Seguin 1993 Sauvignon de Bordeaux*
230BF (37.26FF or £4.60) Soft, ripe and fruity, this
makes a change from the more assertive style of
the Loire Sauvignon, yet still provides all the snap
and freshness expected from the Sauvignon grape
variety.

BRONZE MEDAL

SPARKLING WINES

Champagne Ruffin & Fils NV Chardonnay 430BF (69.66FF or £8.60) per half bottle. A sweet, creamy Champagne with elegant, apple blossom aromas, from Etoges, south of the Côte des Blancs. Good quality, hence its bronze medal, but ridiculously overpriced.
Verdict? 👍👍👍

① VLADIS VLAADEREN
3 Groentemarkt
Tel: 059 70 81 39
English spoken? Yes
Opening hours? Mon-Sat 9.30am-12.30pm & 2pm-7pm, closed Tues (and Sun out of season)
Parking? Yes (on street)
Shopping trolleys? No
Do they offer to help carry the goods to the car? Yes
Methods of payment? Sterling, Irish Punt, French Francs, Belgian Francs (cash only)
Any wines for tasting in store? No
Comment: The owner of this fairly large wine shop was on a buying trip in France when we paid a visit, but we met his assistant who remembered seeing our correspondence, and duly pulled it out of a pile, although nothing had been done about it. If you are interested in collecting miniatures, this is the place for you, as it has no less than one thousand on sale! Huge selection of spirits too. As for the wines, apart from the fine wine selection, most of which is Bordeaux and sold at non-advantageous prices as far as Brits are concerned, there are a number of promotional lines that could be worth buying. However, with no samples submitted, we are unable to say whether they are.
Verdict? ❓

ROSCOFF

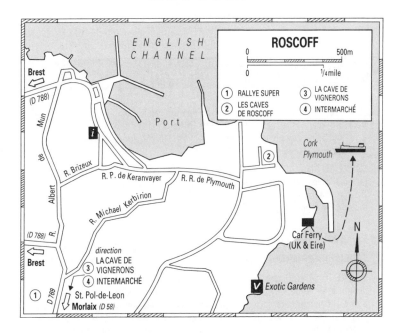

Roscoff is a small but popular seaside town with lovely old cottages, an attractive harbour surrounded by cafés and bars and its own form of seawater spa. Roscoff was once the most noteworthy port of entry for France, but its importance dwindled, and the port would now be abandoned but for the local farmers. This is one of the great market garden centres of France, but with the home market depressed in the late 1960s, the farmers were so desperate that they set up their own ferry service to sell their produce in the UK. In 1973 the locals dredged a deep-water harbour, set up a ferry service and from this local enterprise grew the massive company of Brittany Ferries. It is only because of this local-born enterprise that Roscoff became one of the favourite destinations of British travellers, despite its tiny size and being so far off the beaten track.

Did you know?
• Roscoff became the refuge of Bonnie Prince Charlie after his fearful defeat at Culloden.
• The warm influence of the Gulf Stream is such that in 1889 Dr Bagot chose Roscoff as the location for Roch Kroum, the world's first

thalassotherapy (seawater therapy) centre, and it is as popular now as it has ever been.

• Several of the surrounding islands can be reached on foot at low tide.

Roscoff Factfile

HOW TO GET THERE: Brittany Ferries operate from Plymouth, with a 6 hour crossing-time. In the Republic of Ireland, Brittany Ferries operate from Cork, with a 13 hour 30 minute crossing-time (*see* pages 340-355 for details of service and prices)

LOCATION AND DISTANCES: Situated on the northwestern tip of Brittany, 659km (412 miles) from Boulogne, 691km (432 miles) from Calais, 514km (321 miles) from Dieppe, 454km (284 miles) from Le Havre, 344km (215 miles) from Caen, 366km (229 miles) from Cherbourg, 189km (118 miles) from St-Malo and 564km (352 miles) from Paris.

POPULATION: 3,800

TOURIST INFORMATION OFFICE: 46 rue Gambetta, 29211 Roscoff, *Tel:* (98) 69.70.70

WHERE TO STAY: During the peak season, it is always best to book your hotel in advance, but if you are caught out, try the Tourist Information Centre, which offers a free accommodation service, keeping track of all the vacancies left in the town. The best place to stay: *Le Yachtsman* (boulevard Ste-Barbe, *Tel:* (98) 69.70.78) is a charming château hotel overlooking the sea, with doubles en-suite from 350-580FF (£43-72). Some cheap but clean stays include: The charming *Hôtel d'Angleterre* (28 rue Albert de Mun, *Tel:* (98) 69.70.42) offers doubles with WC at 148FF, and doubles en-suite at 257FF.

RESTAURANTS: Not being a large choice of restaurants, most critics recommend *Le Temps de Vivre* (place Lacaze-Duthiers), which rates a couple of spoons and forks in the Michelin guide, but we think you should try *Le Yachtsman*, not only the best place to stay in Roscoff (*see* above), but has a fine restaurant with a gifted cuisine, which is particularly renowned for the combination of flavours found in its seafood. *Le Gulf Stream* (rue Marquis de Kergariou) is not quite as good, but has a better wine list. In general, an abundance of fresh vegetables and locally-caught lobster are the specialities of the area. Best-cheapest eats: try either *Le Goeland* (9 rue Albert de Mun) or *La Poste* (12 rue Gambetta), both crêperies. Where to find most restaurants, including some of the cheaper places to eat: try walking up rue Gambetta and rue Amiral Réveillère into the place de l'Église, then out of the place de l'Église down rue Albert de Mun.

BEST BAR OR PUB IN TOWN: The *Albatross* in the Hôtel Bellevue (boulevard Ste-Barbe) is more plush than most French bars, and has a warm, welcoming atmosphere and friendly service. English spoken.

MARKET DAYS: The nearest is at St-Pol-de-Léon on Thursday morning

WORTH A VISIT: Roscoff is small and quaint. It is a place to relax in, idling away time at one of the harbour-side bars and cafés and also makes a useful base for seeing other parts of Brittany, but there are no great sights as such in Roscoff itself. Beer enthusiasts might like to visit *La Brasserie des Deux Rivières* (1 place de la Madeleine) in neighbouring Morlaix, where for just 10FF you can have a guided tour of the brewery before sampling the products (tours are Mon-Wed, 10.30am, 2pm & 3.30pm).

③ LA CAVE DE VIGNERONS

Croissant de Kerçompez
29250 St-Pol-de-Léon
Tel: (98) 29.04.24
English spoken? No
Opening hours? Tues-Sat 9am-12noon & 2pm-7pm, closed Sun & Mon
Parking? Yes
Shopping trolleys? No
Do they offer to help carry the goods to the car? No
Methods of payment? French Francs only
Any wines for tasting in store? Yes
Comment: This sweet little cave on the road leading to St-Pol-de-Léon was busy with locals filling up with *vins en vrac* when we called. M. Combes, the owner, bottles off the Château de Beck, Costières de Nîmes himself. This is the only wine he sells in the bottle (23FF for the red, 20FF for the white and rosé), otherwise only *en vrac* at 8FF per litre.
Verdict? ✗

★ *BEST DRINKS OUTLET IN ROSCOFF*
• 5 GOLD MEDALS
• 1 SILVER MEDAL
• 3 BRONZE MEDALS

② LES CAVES DE ROSCOFF

Port de Bloscon
29680 Roscoff
Tel: 98) 61.24.10
English spoken? Yes
Opening hours? 10am-8pm seven days a week (until 10.30pm prior to sailings)
Parking? Yes (private car park)
Shopping trolleys? Yes
Do they offer to help carry the goods to the car? Yes
Methods of payment? Sterling, French Francs, Traveller's cheques, Eurocheques, Visa, Access, Mastercard, American Express, Diners Card
Any wines for tasting in store? Yes
Comment: Les Caves de Roscoff is a British-owned warehouse-type operation, which was opened in March 1993 by Tim Hanbury and Andrew Bruce (who buys the wines), and is

conveniently sited just 150m from the ferry terminal. When we visited this outlet we found a friendly atmosphere and helpful, English-speaking French staff.

The wines: Last year we were relatively disappointed with this outlet due to its rather limited range and the poor performance of one or two wines. Only relatively disappointed though, as its 👍👍 rating did place it in the top 20% of the outlets we reviewed. In any case, the range has now expanded from just 54 wines to well over 100. This time around we were, thank goodness, spared Jean-Claude Bougrier's 1992 Anjou Blanc and the wines submitted were far better selected, as the clutch of gongs and its new rating indicate. The range still lacks any choice from the New World, and there are too many instances where no producer is listed. These traits, more French than British, make the list look lacklustre, and do nothing to attract newcomers to this outlet, but as anyone who has visited knows, there is a good choice in the less expensive and medium-priced range to browse through.

RED WINES

Chianti NV Minini 20FF (£2.47) Light but mouthfilling fruit. Good typicity.

Château Les Grandchamps 1993 Bordeaux 23FF (£2.84) Perfumed aroma, soft and easy to quaff.

Domaine Sarda-Malet 1993 Côtes du Roussillon 25FF (£3.09) Fresh, light and fruity red.

BRONZE MEDAL   *Château Haut Saint Martin 1990 Bordeaux Supérieur* 27FF (£3.33) An elegant Bordeaux with perfumed fruit and just enough tannin to help it partner food.

BRONZE MEDAL   *Domaine de Sours 1991 Bordeaux* 34FF (£4.20) A soft and easy-drinking red wine with a touch of almost Provençal herbal-brush bringing some complexity to the finish.

GOLD MEDAL   *Côtes-du-Rhône 1991 E. Guigal* 36FF (£4.44) Lovely balance, all components already in perfect harmony, succulent fruit.

GOLD MEDAL   *Gigondas 1990 Guigal* 65FF (£7.74) If you like the Côtes-du-Rhône, then you will love this lovely big rich, oaky wine, which just gets better and better in the bottle.

SILVER MEDAL   *Châteauneuf-du-Pape 1981 Grangette des Grés* 69FF (£8.52) Although the first bottle was corked, the second was an oaky-rich delight of a wine, with heaps of ripe, spicy-mature fruit and a splendid amount of fine, life-preserving, acidity. One of the most expensive wines in the *Guide*, but a bargain for 13-year-old Châteauneuf-du-Pape.

WHITE WINES
Chardonnay 1993 Antonin Rodet 25FF (£3.09) This *vin de pays* is good Chardonnay, but not as good as Antonin Rodet's Syrah in the same oversized-bottle range (Mille Vignes, Boulogne, 23FF). Its clean, sweet aroma and delicate Chardonnay fruit does not have quite the right structure or balance of acidity to be special, but shows a potential that might come right in the next couple of vintages, making this more a wine to watch than drink.

BRONZE MEDAL | *Virginie 1993 Chardonnay* 26FF (£3.21) The delicious, creamy-ripe, tropical fruit in this wine has a better acidity balance than the Antonin Rodet Chardonnay. We get the impression that Rodet is aiming for a finer quality than Virginie, but until and if it achieves that, this is the wine to drink.

GOLD MEDAL | *Côtes-du-Rhône 1993 E. Guigal* 36FF (£4.44) So easy to zap past this in a blind tasting without realising its true quality, but if you sit down and eat a meal with it, you can appreciate its complexity and finesse.

SPARKLING WINES
GOLD MEDAL | *Champagne Ruinart NV Brut* 123FF (£15.19) One of the most underrated *grande marque* Champagnes on the market. Although this house's top Champagne, Dom Ruinart, is one of the greatest prestige *cuvées* available, its reputation tends to overshadow Ruinart's standard non-vintage *brut*, which is a pity, as it is consistent, always easy to drink and yet capable of maturing gracefully in the bottle for a good five years or more.

BEERS
GOLD MEDAL
BEST-VALUE LIGHT
BEER OF THE YEAR

Grolsch Premium Lager 5.38FF (66p) per 50cl can, sold in 24s at 129FF (£12.95) This fine, delicate, flowery-hopped brew was by far the best-value lager-style beer we tasted: ten times the quality of Beck's and nothing like the price (as much as 71p for a small 27.5cl bottle at Sainsbury's), although Grolsch is just 54p for a 50cl can at Beer Lovers Cash & Carry (Calais), and even cheaper at The Wine & Beer Company (Calais and Cherbourg), where it costs a mere 46p. **Verdict?** 🍺🍺🍺🍺

• 1 BRONZE MEDAL

④ INTERMARCHÉ

ZAC des Carmes
29250 St-Pol-de-Léon
Tel: (98) 69.22.89
Opening hours? Mon-Thurs 9am-12.15pm & 2pm-7.15pm, Fri 9am-12.15pm & 2pm-7.30pm, Sat 9am-7.15pm

Comment: Most Intermarché on the Channel coast are relatively small, and although they can be quite large further inland, this chain is more of the supermarket ilk than hypermarket. It is also relatively down-market, with a mostly dull and uninteresting range of wines, often dominated by a display of 3-litre wine containers. There are around a dozen different Champagnes, and the fine wines are usually displayed separately (we saw Ducru Beaucaillou 1989 at 85FF, and Pavillon Rouge 1990 at 105FF). We had no success with chairman Marcel Robin, who steadfastly refused to answer our correspondence. It was the same story as last year, with M. Le Goff, Intermarché's drinks buyer.

The wines: We purchased six wines along the same lines as those we bought at Auchan, and when it came to the crunch, Intermarché fared much better, with half of the wines warranting our recommendation, and one even picking up a Bronze medal. And two of those that did not qualify were perfectly drinkable, even if not special enough to qualify for the *Guide*. If only the management of this firm had enough faith in its products to submit a substantial range of its inexpensive wines, they might do well, if this random sampling is anything to go by.

RED WINES

Beaujolais NV Cuvée Joannès 12FF (£1.48) Although not medal potential, you could have knocked us down with a feather when this wine, the second-cheapest Gamay submitted, turned out not only to be drinkable, but expressive of its variety, rather than *macération carbonique*.

Côtes-du-Rhône 1993 Réserve Lescarrat 13FF (£1.60) This soft and fruity wine has a touch more elegance than the other red Rhônes in its price category.

WHITE WINES

BRONZE MEDAL

Reuilly 1993 Cave PD 22.90FF (£2.83) This fresh and assertive Sauvignon is not a wine for wimps.
Verdict? 👍

• 1 BRONZE MEDAL

① RALLYE SUPER

RN Kerguennic
29211 Roscoff
Tel: (99) 69.79.79
Selling area: 1,200m² (compare this with the size of other stores featured in the area, to gauge their relative size and you will have a rough idea of how big the range of wines, beers, spirits and other goods will be).
Opening hours? Mon-Sat 8.30am-7.30pm, closed Sun
Comment: Rallye Super is partly owned by Casino, which does not have any stores of its own in the Channel ports. Both Casino and Rallye failed to reply to our various communications last year, and neither Antoine nor Yves Guichard, the joint managing directors of Casino, responded this time.
The wines: Three of the six wines we purchased at random survived the test, which is at least three more than last time.

RED WINES

Corbières NV Les Chais du Pré la Reine 7.95FF (98p) Soft and peppery.
Château des Vignerons 1992 Côtes de Castillon 18.95FF (£2.34) Basic Bordeaux with more length of flavour than most.

BRONZE MEDAL

Château Haut-Brignon 1990 Premières Côtes de Bordeaux 22.80FF (£2.81) Silky, plummy, violety fruit with a nice touch of tannin.
Verdict? 👎

ST-MALO

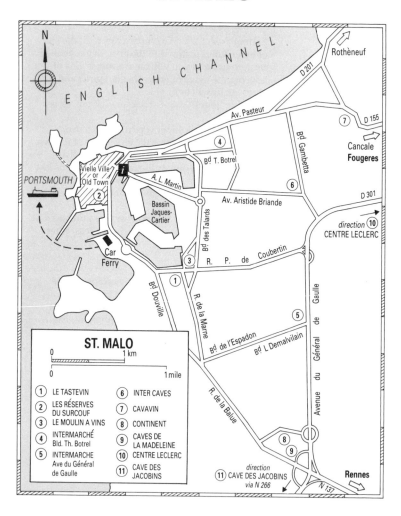

ST. MALO

0 — 1 km

0 — 1 mile

1. LE TASTEVIN
2. LES RÉSERVES DU SURCOUF
3. LE MOULIN A VINS
4. INTERMARCHÉ Bld. Th. Botrel
5. INTERMARCHE Ave du Général de Gaulle
6. INTER CAVES
7. CAVAVIN
8. CONTINENT
9. CAVES DE LA MADELEINE
10. CENTRE LECLERC
11. CAVE DES JACOBINS

The Old Town of St-Malo is, without doubt, the most appealing of all the Channel ports, yet nearly all of what appears to be Old Town and much of the ancient ramparts are merely a brilliant reconstruction. On 30 July 1944 General Patton wrote in his diary 'We are in the biggest battle I have ever fought and it is going fine except at one town [St-Malo] ... I am going there in a minute to kick someone's ass', but the Germans, who believed the allied invasion could not succeed without the Brittany ports, were intent on defending St-Malo to the last man. To overcome such resistance, eighty per cent of the Old Town had to be obliterated in order to wheedle out the battle-hardened SS units, consequently St-Malo did not fall to Patton's 3rd Army until 16 August, despite his ass-kicking. It says something about the pride of the locals who survived the horrors of such a bombardment that they were determined to replicate the Old Town stone by stone, rather than accept the modern concrete block concept that dominated architecture in the early 1950s, as Le Havre and other towns of former beauty did. If you intend to stop in St-Malo for a few hours, it is best to keep to the Old Town, unless you need to go to a specific shop elsewhere because there is nothing much to see or enjoy beyond the ramparts, although with just one ferry a day, even in the height of the season, you will not run into any lager-louts, which has to be a big bonus.

Did you know?

• St-Malo was originally called Alet, but derived its current name from a Welsh monk called Maclow (although he definitely sounds Scottish to us), who became the Bishop of Alet some time in the 6th century.
• St-Malo is sometimes referred to as the 'City of Great Men' because the list of those born in this port includes Jacques Cartier, Robert Surcouf, Maupertuis, Lamenais, Châteaubriand and many others.
• St-Malo has sent out ships of exploration to the most far-flung and exotic corners of the world since the 12th century.
• St-Malo used to offer a safe haven to pirates and privateers, protecting them from the English, French and Normans.

St-Malo Factfile

HOW TO GET THERE: Brittany Ferries operate out of Poole, with an 8 hour crossing-time; P&O operates out of Portsmouth, with a 5 hour 45 minute (day), 7-9 hour (night) crossing-time. In the Republic of Ireland, Brittany Ferries operate out of Cork, with an 18 hour 30 minute crossing-time (*see* pages 340-355 for details of service and prices).

LOCATION AND DISTANCES: Situated on the Rance estuary opposite Dinard, St-Malo is on the so-called Emerald Coast and almost equidistant between Cherbourg (187km or 117 miles) to the north and Nantes (178km or 111 miles) to the south, 480km (300 miles) from Boulogne, 510km (319 miles) from Calais, 333km (208 miles) from Dieppe, 274km (171 miles) from Le Havre, 163km (102 miles) from Caen, 189km (118 miles) from Roscoff and 419km (262 miles) from Paris.

POPULATION: 47,000

TOURIST INFORMATION OFFICE: Esplanade St-Vincent, 35400 St-Malo, *Tel:* (99) 56.64.48. Open Mon-Sat 9am-8pm, Sun 10am-6pm. Sept-June Mon-Sat 9am-12noon & 2pm-7pm, Sat 10am-12noon & 2pm-5pm.

WHERE TO STAY: During the peak season, it is always best to book your hotel in advance. The best place to stay: *Grand Hôtel des Thermes* (100 boulevard Hébert, *Tel:* (99) 40.75.75) is the one with the most stars, but we prefer *La Korrigane* (39 rue de la Pomellec, *Tel:* (99) 81.65.85) in the suburb of St-Servan, for its luxurious double rooms en-suite decorated with antiques from 450-700FF (£56-86). Some cheap but clean stays include: *Hôtel le Neptune* (21 rue de l'Industrie, *Tel:* (99) 56.82.15) for doubles with shower at 180-200FF; *Les Chiens du Guet* (4 place de Guet, *Tel:* (99) 40.46.77), which is adjacent to the old ramparts and offers doubles with shower at 180-240FF.

RESTAURANTS: The best place to eat in town always used to be *A la Duchesse Anne* (5-7 place Guy de la Chambre), but it is not what it used to be and three restaurants have now risen well above its declining standards: *Le Franklin* (4 chaussée du Sillon) on the front just outside the Old Town and formerly operating under the name Robert Abraham, this place probably has the edge over the other two, although *Le Chalut* (8 rue de la Corne du Cerf) in the Old Town and *La Métairie de Beauregard* (Bourg St-Etienne, Blanche Roche) have both improved out of all recognition of their former modest selves, despite the latter being some 2km (1.25 miles) south of town. The *Cap Horn* (100 boulevard Hébert), just one street back from the front and *Manoir de la Grassinais* (12 rue de la Grassinais) 2km (1.25 miles) south of the town are the next best restaurants and we are always impressed by the tremendous value offered by *St-Placide* (6 place Poncel) and *Delaunay* (6 rue Ste-Barbe). When choosing what dishes to order, it is worth remembering two things. First that St-Malo possesses the only cod-fishing fleet in Brittany and, unlike Britain, where cod is cheap and thus a common staple of our diet, the French regard its brilliant white tasty flesh as something of a speciality. Second that the writer and statesman Châteaubriand was born in St-Malo and it was, of course, the great man's chef Montmireil who invented the dish that was subsequently named after his master. There is no guarantee that either cod or châteaubriand will be on the menu, but you should try these dishes whenever they are. Best-cheapest eats: *Le Petit Malouin* (6 rue de la Vieille Boucherie), where three-*crêpes* fixed-price menus start at just 38FF. Where to find most restaurants, including some of the cheaper places to eat: down the myriad of small side streets in the Old Town.

BEST BAR OR PUB IN TOWN: *Cunningham's Bar* (2 rue des Hauts Sablons) is the preferred watering hole for Marc Robineau of Le Tastevin. Or try the bar at the *Hôtel de l'Univers* (place Châteaubriand) for its wide range of specialist beers.

MARKET DAYS: Tuesday and Friday (Old Town)

WORTH A VISIT: There are various museums and galleries, but the one place that demands a visit is the ancient ramparts and it is worth paying for an escorted tour. Two organisations provide English-speaking tour guides: Émeraude Guides on (99) 82.34.54 and Le Comptoir de Baviere (99) 82.60.02. The small town Dinard on the opposite side of the estuary is well worth a visit for its quaint fairytale cottages, fine seafront houses and pretty beaches, the combination of which made it such a popular haunt of the English at the turn of the century. Use the tidal-power damn to cross over the estuary. In the first two weeks of June, a *Foire aux Vins* is held by growers of Anjou and Coteaux du Layon (check the Tourist Information Office for details).

⑦ **CAVAVIN**
34 rue Gustave Flaubert
35400 St-Malo
Tel: (99) 40.89.16
English spoken? Not revealed
Opening hours? 9.30am-12.30pm & 3pm-7.30pm seven days a week in July and August, closed Monday rest of the year
Parking? Only on street
Shopping trolleys? No
Do they offer to help carry the goods to the car? Yes
Methods of payment? French Francs, Traveller's cheques, Eurocheques, Visa, Access, Mastercard, American Express, Diners Card
Any wines for tasting in store? Yes
Comment: This small shop is nicely presented, but off the tourist's beaten track, although there appear to be some good wines, which could make it worth a visit if you are in the area. The owner was absent when we made our visit last year, but his assistant was very helpful. This year we found the owner in, and promptly wished we hadn't! If he is equally as aggressive and rude to British customers as he is to us, we advise you steer well clear.
Verdict? 👎

RUNNER UP TO
BEST DRINKS OUTLET
IN ST-MALO

⑪ **CAVE DES JACOBINS**
3 rue Ste-Claire
22100 Dinan
Tel: (96) 39.03.82
Comment: We can thank Stuart Heather of Southampton for this late entry in the *Guide*. Although it was too late to include Cave des Jacobins in our tastings, its 400-strong list of wines ranging from 12.50FF to 850FF certainly warrants strong recommendation. As per most French lists, it is dominated by expensive *cru classé* from Bordeaux, but it also contains some medium-priced wines that we recognise as Gold-medal winners from other outlets. The list also contains the best selection of Burgundy we have so far found in any Channel port. There are some 80

lines in half bottles. Mr Heather tells us that he has also found bin ends, various promotions, and good *vins de pays* in addition to the wines listed. Purely on the strength of this outlet's list, we are inclined to agree with Mr Heather's opinion that it is a gold mine, thus our high provisional ranking below. The owner speaks English.

Verdict? 👍👍👍

⑨ **LES CAVES DE LA MADELEINE**
ZAC la Madeleine
Rue de la Saulaire
35400 St-Malo
Tel: (99) 81.69.48
English spoken? No
Opening hours? Tues-Sat 10.15am-12noon & 3pm-7pm, closed Sun & Mon
Parking? Yes (private car park)
Shopping trolleys? Yes
Do they offer to help carry the goods to the car? Yes
Methods of payment? French Francs, Traveller's cheques, Eurocheques, Visa, Access, Mastercard, American Express
Any wines for tasting in store? From time to time
Comment: Located on an industrial estate close to the Continent hypermarket, this is a very friendly place with helpful, extremely jolly French staff.
The wines: Les Caves de la Madelaine is due to be extended, and the new area used for *vins en vrac*, and other cheaper wines, although the current range will also be maintained. We would like to taste a bigger, better selection of wines from this outlet, but only one of the four wines submitted passed the test, hence its rating below. Also stocks some interesting vintage Armagnacs from Pierre Cournet (1972, 1976, 1978 & 1979).

ROSÉ WINES
Les Fabrices NV Vin de Pays d'Oc Galland Frères
10.50FF (£1.30) Positive colour and a light, fresh, fruity flavour. The best-cheapest rosé we tasted.
Verdict? 🏆

• 2 SILVER MEDALS

⑩ **CENTRE LECLERC**
55 boulevard des Deportes
La Croix Desilles
35400 St-Malo
Tel: (99) 81.70.39
Selling area: 3,250m² (compare this with the size

of other stores featured in the area, to gauge their relative size and you will have a rough idea of how big the range of wines, beers, spirits and other goods will be).

Opening hours? Mon-Thurs 9am-10pm, Fri 9am-10.30pm, Sat 8.30am-10.30pm, closed Sun

Comment: Last year we went through Gallec, which owns Leclerc, Groupe de Travail Liquides, which supplies Leclerc, and Leclerc's chief buyer, but all to no avail, so this time we went straight to the top, and we were pleased to receive Michel-Edouard Leclerc's assurance that his chain would extend the *Guide* full co-operation in supplying whatever samples and information we wanted. He delegated the matter to Jean Maurice, who runs Leclerc Scapertois, which supplies all the stores in the Pas-de-Calais and Normandy. Unfortunately M. Maurice had other ideas, inviting us instead to spend the day at Scapertois, where we could taste their best wines over 70FF. We would be wined and dined, and afterwards we would be given some *cru classé* Bordeaux to take away. Apparently he has tried this wheeze on other British journalists with a certain amount of success, but we are not in this job to fill the car boot with cases of château-bottled claret, so we declined, immediately and in no uncertain terms. We again explained that most cross-Channel bargains are under 34FF, as indeed are most of Centre Leclerc's sales, thus concentrating on its top of the range wines tells us nothing about the bulk of wines most Leclerc customers buy. Besides which, tasting them in isolation would have been unfair to the other retail outlets, whose wines must compete with others of a similar style and price under blind conditions. After more correspondence with M. Leclerc, we received a letter from the head of Sobadis, a subsidiary of Leclerc's, which handles the distribution of its products in Normandy. Referring to our last correspondence with Michel-Edouard Leclerc, he offered us exactly what we wanted, even a choice of branches from which we could collect our samples from. Unfortunately our last correspondence with M. Leclerc had been over six weeks earlier, and our tastings had come and gone. Still, if Centre Leclerc keeps to its word, and submits samples without delay or hesitation for the next edition, all the hassle we have endured this year will at least be worthwhile.

The wines: Most branches are basic warehouse-type operations, and very utilitarian. In the bigger stores, the range can include as many as 250 different lines, with a good selection of fine wines, albeit almost entirely from Bordeaux. Centre Leclerc seems to be quite good on Beaujolais, with most *cru villages* covered, and the one we tried from Juliénas certainly fared well, earning a silver medal no less. With four wines out of six random purchases qualifying for recommendation in the *Guide*, including two silver medals, one of which grabbed a Wine of the Year award, it makes us look forward to greater co-operation next year, to see how the range as a whole performs.

RED WINES

SILVER MEDAL
BEST-VALUE RED
WINE OF THE YEAR

Domaine de Pons 1991 Côtes du Ventoux 13.95FF (£1.72) We had to taste almost 30 red Rhônes up to 27FF before we found a wine to equal this. An elegant wine with a good depth of silky-plummy fruit, and nicely structured supple tannins.

Carayon-la-Rose 1986 Cuvée Exceptionnelle, Bordeaux Supérieur 18.95FF (£2.34) This is not bad as a basic Bordeaux, but unless you see the vintage on the label, you would hardly think that you are tasting an eight-year-old claret.

SILVER MEDAL

Juliénas 1992 les Vouillants Chedeville 26.50FF (£3.27) Bags of flavour. A real wine, and a true *cru* Beaujolais (we rejected most of the *cru* Beaujolais because they lacked the significant increase in quality and intensity of varietal flavour they should possess).

Château Roches Guitard 1989 Montagne-St-Émilion 30.85FF (£3.81) A good Bordeaux with sweet fruity aromas that follow through onto the palate.

Verdict?

• 1 SILVER MEDAL
• 1 BRONZE MEDAL

⑧ CONTINENT

CC La Madeleine
35400 St-Malo
Tel: (99) 82.33.50

Selling area: 7,300m² (compare this with the size of other stores featured in the area, to gauge their relative size and you will have a rough idea of how big the range of wines, beers, spirits and other goods will be).

Opening hours? Mon-Sat 8.30am-10pm, closed Sun

Comment: Part of the Promodes group, which owns Continent, Shopi and various other smaller outlets. We made contact last year with no less than six top people at Promodes and its various offshoots, but to no avail, so this year we wrote to the managing director of Promodes, M. Pierre Merle, but he could not be bothered to reply either.

The wines: There is quite a big range in the larger Continent stores such as this, but not a particularly wonderful selection in the price category most cross-Channel shoppers are interested in (15-30FF), although we did strike lucky with two of the six wines we purchased at random. The Bordeaux selection is eclectic and spotty, with some good *cru classé*, but prices are not competitive, although they do have some on offer (eg., Ducru-Beaucaillou 1991 at 86FF, and Fieuzal at 72FF).

RED WINES

BRONZE MEDAL

Les Mélusines 1993 St-Nicolas-de-Bourgueil 27FF (£3.33) A tasty wine indeed, and with an authentic grassy Loire Cabernet edge that does not detract from its drinkability.

WHITE WINES

SILVER MEDAL

Jean Marie Strubbler Gewurztraminer 1993 Vin d'Alsace 22.90FF (£2.83) Good-value Gewurztraminer, with assertive, spicy fruit. The acidity is somewhat high for this grape, giving the wine a finer balance than most.
Verdict? ♟

RUNNER UP TO
BEST DRINKS OUTLET
IN ST-MALO
• 1 GOLD MEDAL
• 4 BRONZE MEDALS

⑥ **INTER CAVES**
107 avenue Aristide Briand
35400 St-Malo
Tel: (99) 40.85.81
English spoken? Yes
Opening hours? Mon-Fri 10am-12.30pm & 3.00pm-7.30pm, Sat 9.30am-12.30pm & 3pm-7.30pm, Sun 9am-12noon
Parking? Yes (private car park)
Shopping trolleys? No
Do they offer to help carry the goods to the car? Yes
Methods of payment? French Francs, Traveller's cheques, Eurocheques, Visa, Mastercard, Eurocard
Any wines for tasting in store? Yes
Comment: Part of the Inter Caves group (*see also* branches in Caen, Calais and Cherbourg), which consists of approximately 90 shops spread throughout France, plus a few additional outlets

in Germany. Although the Caen branch was awarded joint best outlet in that port, they all offer roughly the same range, and have particularly helpful and knowledgeable staff, although the staff at Calais are perhaps a touch happier.

The wines: We were promised a list, but did not receive one, and our representative reported a dozen Champagnes from smaller, lesser known producers, which sound interesting, but the only one submitted was Champagne De Saval, which does not exist as such, but is made by another producer (Baron Albert, we think), and although drinkable was not special. Hopefully we can taste some real small producer Champagnes next time, but submitting a larger number of better selected wines this year has paid off, giving the Inter Caves group a far more impressive entry in this year's *Guide* that it got in the first edition.

RED WINES

BRONZE MEDAL

Domaine le Pian 1992 Vin de Pays du Gard 19FF (£2.35) Soft, silky blackcurrant fruit.

Chatellenie de Lastours NV Corbières 29FF (£3.58) Rich and robust, with a herbal-oak undertone.

GOLD MEDAL

Château de Pech Redon 1991 La Clape 29.50FF (£3.64) Absolutely delightful fruit underpinned by bubble-gum oak, which creates a sort of raspberry ripple flavour. Although it might not sound like it, this is an elegant, classy wine.

Massana 1991 Côtes du Roussillon 29.90FF (£3.69) Could be Rioja if we did not know better.

BRONZE MEDAL

Bourgogne Pinot Noir 1992 Philippe de Marange 35.70FF (£4.41) An elegant Burgundy for the price, with ripe-cherry Pinot Noir fruit.

BRONZE MEDAL

Domaine Duseigneur 1991 Lirac 39.50FF (£4.88) An elegant, fruity Rhône, but we have come across two versions of apparently the same wine: one with a neck-label that has the word 'Lirac' either side of the vintage, and the other with a neck-label that has 'Cru' one side of the vintage and 'Race' the other, and the latter of these seems to have a more smoky-toasty finish.

Juliénas 1992 Domaine de la Bottière 44FF (£5.43) Has some potential for development over the next year or two.

Saumur-Champigny 1992 Domaine du Val Brun 45FF (£5.56) This may lack charm on the nose, but it has good fruit underneath, and should develop more attractive bottle-aromas over the next 18 months or so.

Domaine des Lucques 1990 Graves 47FF (£5.80)
Probably a lot better 18 months ago, but still
makes a decent glass of Bordeaux, even if
prematurely mellow.

WHITE WINES
Baron de Peyrac, Sauvignon 1993 Bordeaux Blanc
17.90FF (£2.21) Although this wine's fresh aroma
shows good typicity, it is too soft to be classic
Sauvignon, although this very softness is what
makes it so easy to drink.

BRONZE MEDAL ***Clos du Zahnacker 1988 Vin d'Alsace*** 60FF (£7.41)
One of the very few classic blends of Alsace, this
wine was probably easier to drink two years ago,
and will undoubtedly find greater harmony in two
years from now, but is currently in a stage of
development where the Riesling is battling
Gewurztraminer.

ROSÉ WINES
***Château la Croix de l'Hosanne 1993 Bordeaux
Clairet*** 22.90FF (£2.83) Highly perfumed, off-dry
rosé with plenty of fruit.
Verdict? 👍👍👍

• 1 BRONZE MEDAL ⑤ **INTERMARCHÉ**
Avenue du Général de Gaulle
CC La Découverte
35400 St-Malo
Tel: (99) 82.51.10
Selling area: 1,450m²

AND

④ **INTERMARCHÉ**
Boulevard Théodore Botrel
35400 St-Malo
Tel: (99) 56.14.70
Selling area: 1,200m² (compare this with the size
of other stores featured in the area, to gauge their
relative size and you will have a rough idea of
how big the range of wines, beers, spirits and
other goods will be).
Opening hours? Mon-Thurs 9am-12.15pm & 2pm-
7.15pm, Fri 9am-12.15pm & 2pm-7.30pm, Sat 9am-
7.15pm
Comment: Most Intermarché on the Channel coast
are relatively small, and although they can be
quite large further inland, this chain is more of the
supermarket ilk than hypermarket. It is also
relatively down-market, with a mostly dull and
uninteresting range of wines, often dominated by

a display of 3-litre wine containers. There are around a dozen different Champagnes, and the fine wines are usually displayed separately (we saw Ducru Beaucaillou 1989 at 85FF, and Pavillon Rouge 1990 at 105FF). We had no success with chairman Marcel Robin, who steadfastly refused to answer our correspondence. It was the same story as last year, with M. Le Goff, Intermarché's drinks buyer.

The wines: We purchased six wines along the same lines as those we bought at Auchan, and when it came to the crunch, Intermarché fared much better, with half of the wines warranting our recommendation, and one even picking up a Bronze medal. And two of those that did not qualify were perfectly drinkable, even if not special enough to qualify for the *Guide*. If only the management of this firm had enough faith in its products to submit a substantial range of its inexpensive wines, they might do well, if this random sampling is anything to go by.

RED WINES
Beaujolais NV Cuvée Joannès 12FF (£1.48) Although not medal potential, you could have knocked us down with a feather when this wine, the second-cheapest Gamay submitted, turned out not only to be drinkable, but expressive of its variety, rather than *macération carbonique*.
Côtes-du-Rhône 1993 Réserve Lescarrat 13FF (£1.60) This soft and fruity wine has a touch more elegance than the other red Rhônes in its price category.

WHITE WINES

BRONZE MEDAL

Reuilly 1993 Cave PD 22.90FF (£2.83) This fresh and assertive Sauvignon is not a wine for wimps. **Verdict?** 👍

• 2 BRONZE MEDALS

③ **LE MOULIN À VINS**
80 boulevard des Talards
35400 St-Malo
Tel: (99) 81.62.80
English spoken? Yes
Opening hours? Mon 3pm-7.30pm, Tues-Sat 9am-12.30pm & 3pm-7.30pm, Sun 9.30am-12noon.
Parking? On street and although no private car park exists as such, if you drive in the rear entrance, via Avenue Roosevelt, it is possible to

park on the left-hand side of the yard.
Shopping trolleys? No
Do they offer to help carry the goods to the car?
Yes
Methods of payment? Sterling, French Francs,
Traveller's cheques, Eurocheques, Visa,
Mastercard
Any wines for tasting in store? Yes
Comment: A well-appointed, double-fronted wine
shop that makes a convenient stop-off en route for
the ferry, Le Moulin à Vins will even deliver the
wines to the terminal for you.
The wines: The owner, Jean Gaillard, searches out
the wines himself, avoiding the *cru classé* and
grand cru wines because he prefers to concentrate
on wines that represent good value in the 50FF
bracket. His list consists of 250 wines, starting at
12FF. Burgundies include Olivier Leflaive. He also
stocks some 50 different malt whiskies. Those
intending to visit the St-Malo area should note
that we believe this outlet may warrant a higher
ranking than that given below, although it
accurately reflects the performance of the wines
submitted, where seven of the 12 wines qualified
for recommendation.

RED WINES
Château la Moulière 1992 Côtes de Duras 24.80FF
(£3.06) Basic Bordeaux with toasty fruit.

BRONZE MEDAL *Domaine de Mazou 1992 Gaillac* 29.50FF (£3.64)
Fresh, *macération carbonique* style, but with more
fruit than most Beaujolais and riper flavours, plus
an intriguing hint of coffee-caramel on the
aftertaste.
Château la Croix de Bayle 1991 Graves de Vayres
31FF (£3.83) A simple Bordeaux, but with young,
gentle fruit that is easy to drink.

WHITE WINES
*Cuvée de Celtes Muscadet de Sèvre et Maine sur
lie 1993 Guilbaud Frères* 24FF (£2.96) The high
acidity in this wine will enable you to serve it with
a wide range of dishes in which acidity plays a
fairly dominant role, either as an ingredient or
part of a dressing.

BRONZE MEDAL *Château la Moulière 1993 Côtes de Duras Sec*
24.80FF (£3.06) Rich with ripe fruit, with firm
structure. Good with food.
Sauvignon Touraine 1993 Domaine du Bouc
34.50FF (£4.26) Good basic Touraine Sauvignon.

ROSÉ WINES
Château Bellevue la Forêt 1992 Côtes du Frontonnais 31FF (£3.83) Young, fresh and very fruity.
Verdict? 🖐🖐

• 1 SILVER MEDAL

② **LES RÉSERVES DU SURCOUF**
4 rue Toulouse
35400 St-Malo
Tel: (99) 40.15.19
English spoken? Not revealed
Opening hours? 9am-1pm & 2.30pm-8pm seven days a week in June through August, closed Tuesday other months
Parking? Only on street
Shopping trolleys? No
Do they offer to help carry the goods to the car? Yes
Methods of payment? French Francs, Traveller's cheques, Eurocheques, Visa, Access, Mastercard
Any wines for tasting in store? Only for special clients!
Comment: The bottles are still standing upright! This is, nevertheless, a rather characterful shop, immensely worth a visit. You should certainly see the cellar, which was once used as a women's prison, and if you have the time, M. Morand the owner will probably tell you a few D-Day stories.
The wines: Again no list, which makes it difficult to assess the range, particularly as M. Morand submitted just three wines. Just one wine passed the test, but he keeps his ranking for this year on the basis of our representative's overall impression.

SILVER MEDAL

RED WINES
Château Cabannieux 1991 Graves Cru Exceptionnel 48FF (£5.93) Scores well for structure. Classic food wine.
Verdict? 🖐🖐

★ *BEST DRINKS OUTLET*
IN ST-MALO
• 1 GOLD MEDAL
• 2 BRONZE MEDALS

① **LE TASTEVIN**
9 rue Val
35400 St-Malo
Tel: (99) 82.46.56 Fax: 99 81 09 69
English spoken? Yes
Opening hours? Tues-Sat 8.30am-12.30pm & 2pm-7.30pm, Sun 9.30am-12.30pm, closed Mon
Parking? Only on street
Shopping trolleys? No

Do they offer to help carry the goods to the car?
Yes
Methods of payment? Sterling, French Francs,
Traveller's cheques, Visa, Mastercard
Any wines for tasting in store? Yes
Comment: Nice, smart *caviste* just a few minutes
from the Old Town, and near the quay, with easy
parking on the street.
Owners Véronique and Marc Robineau are
obviously very proud of their classy shop, with its
shelves of neatly displayed wines, and old
wooden wine press in the centre of the floor, and
so they should be. This outlet has the right
upmarket image for the British who do their
shopping in St-Malo, and the bulk of Le Tastevin's
UK custom is from those with second homes in
and around the town.
The wines: Our provisional rating of this shop
was based entirely on the excellence of this
outlet's list, yet from the result of our tastings
turned out to be very much on the cautious side.

RED WINES

Châteaux Degas 1991 Bordeaux 28FF (£3.46) A
good *petit château* with an elegant richness of fruit.
BRONZE MEDAL | *Domaine de la Mordorée 1992 Côtes-du-Rhône*
32FF (£3.95) An elegant, medium-bodied red of
true Rhône character.
BRONZE MEDAL | *Domaine Sarda-Malet 1990 Côtes du Roussillon*
40FF (£4.94) Lots of fruit with a peach-like
aftertaste: a joy by itself.

ROSÉ WINES

GOLD MEDAL
BEST-QUALITY ROSÉ
WINE OF THE YEAR | *Reuilly 1993 Chassiot* 43FF (£5.31) The best
quality rosé we tasted and an exceptional wine by
any standards. The gentle richness, delicacy of
fruit and long finish of this delightful wine is a
textbook example of what balance is all about. It's
a privilege to taste such a lovely rosé.
Verdict? 👍👍👍

MID-CHANNEL SHOPPING GUIDE

"What is duty-free?" That is the question we are often asked. If there is no UK duty charged on cross-Channel wines, beers and spirits, it is easy to understand why some people wonder what on earth duty-free mean?

It is, nevertheless, very easy to explain. The wines, beers, and spirits you bring back from across the Channel are not free of duty *per se*, but include the amount of duty that is applicable in the country of purchase. You will have paid this automatically in the shop or supermarket at the time of purchase. In France, for example, the rate of duty is just 2p on a bottle of wine and 7.5p on a litre of beer, compared to £1.06 and 62p respectively in the UK. It is this difference that sparked off the huge market build-up for cross-Channel shopping, when the internal borders of the EC were lifted in January 1993. However, duty-free on board the ferries, for example, literally means no duty whatsoever, thus you do not even pay the 2p on wine or the 7.5p on beer. Duty-free spirits offer the biggest savings, for although French duty on spirits is £2 less than the UK rate of £5.55/ bottle, there is still more than £3 to save when it's duty-free. The only downside to buying duty-free spirits on board is the pitifully small allowance: just one-litre! Since January 1993, however, you can claim this allowance both ways, effectively increasing it to two litres for a return trip. And don't forget that it is per person, so you can double this again for a couple. With the cheap day return prices for vehicles with up to five passengers, it could be worthwhile from a duty-free allowance point of view to give granny and her chums a day out!

BEST-VALUE DUTY-FREE FERRY COMPANY OF THE YEAR: BRITTANY FERRIES ★

This award is based on the number of cheapest (or equal cheapest) prices for the products below, from which we subtract the number of most expensive (or equally the most expensive) prices. We also take into account how much cheaper or more expensive those prices are.

Runners up: North Sea Ferries; P&O European Ferries

Without in any way detracting from the achievement of either Brittany Ferries or North Sea Ferries, the best-value duty-free ferry lines will be academic to most travellers, who will use the route best suited to their own needs, which is why we provide below a guide to most duty-free products available on all the different cross-Channel services. In compiling this guide, we noticed that the duty-free prices of most ferry companies are very much a swings and roundabout affair, with both best-bargains and worst-prices. They operate very much like supermarkets, with some loss-leaders to lull the consumer into thinking that there is a tremendous saving to be had across the entire range, but each range is a minefield with plenty of high-profit lines hidden amongst the star-bargains.

Your Duty-Free Allowance

	EACH WAY ALLOWANCE	RETURN TRIP TOTAL
Wine	2 litres	4 litres
Beer	50 litres	100 litres
AND ANY ONE OF THE FOLLOWING		
Spirits[1]	1 litre	2 litres
OR		
Fortified Wine	2 litres	4 litres
OR		
Sparkling Wine	2 litres	4 litres
OR		
Liqueurs[2]	2 litres	4 litres

NOTES: 1. Spirits are defined as any alcoholic beverage over 22% by volume.
2. Liqueurs over 22% do not qualify, and are treated as spirits.

FERRY PRICE GUIDE

All prices are listed from cheapest to most expensive, and refer to one-litre bottles, unless stated otherwise.

Prices were correct at the time of going to press, and do not take into account any special offers. We have shown UK cross-Channel price checks where readily available.

Unless otherwise stated, all spirits sold duty-free mid-channel are in one-litre bottles whereas all spirits sold on shore either side of the Channel are in 70cl.

NOTES

1. Due to the limited storage capacity of the hovercraft and Seacat, the Hoverspeed lines indicated below have been taken from the range available at Hoverspeed's on-shore shops.
2. The prices indicated for Scandinavian Seaways are those for services out of Newcastle. Prices for its Harwich services were provided in Danish Krona, and were for some reason considerably more expensive, even allowing for the fluctuation in exchange rates from the time they were published.
3. Prices for Irish Ferries were unavailable.
4. FF = French Francs; BF = Belgian Francs

SPIRITS

BLENDED SCOTCH WHISKY

Ballantine's

UK Price Check	Harveys	£14.13 (£20.19/Litre)
Mid-Channel	Brittany	£9.70
	Scandinavian	£9.90
	North Sea	£10.50
	Sally	£10.60
Cross-Channel	Auchan	79.80FF/£9.85 (£14.07/Litre)
	Carrefour	83.50FF/£10.31 (£14.73/Litre)
	Wijnhuis Douchy	595.00BF/£12.66 (£18.09/Litre)

Bell's

UK Price Check	Tesco	£14.99/Litre
Mid-Channel	Hoverspeed	£10.50
	North Sea	£10.50
	P&O	£10.50
	Stena	£10.50
	Brittany	£10.60
	Sally	£11.25
Cross-Channel	Continent	79.95FF/£9.87 (£14.10/Litre)
	Champion	81.85FF/£10.10 (£14.43/Litre)
	Monoprix	81.90FF/£10.11 (£14.44/Litre)
	Carrefour	85.00FF/£10.49 (£14.99/Litre)

Bell's Islander

Mid-Channel	P&O	£11.50
	Brittany	£13.50

Claymore

Mid-Channel	Brittany	£8.20
	North Sea	£8.75
	P&O	£8.75

Cutty Sark

UK Price Check	Berry Bros	£18.80/Litre
Mid-Channel	P&O	£9.50

Famous Grouse

UK Price Check	Tesco	£15.99/Litre
Mid-Channel	Brittany	£10.80
	North Sea	£10.95
	P&O	£10.95
	Hoverspeed	£11.00
	Sally	£11.25
	Scandinavian	£11.80
Cross-Channel	Super U	84.95FF/£10.49 (£14.99/Litre)
	Continent	86.00FF/£10.62 (£15.17/Litre)
	Match	92.50FF/£11.42 (£16.31/Litre)
	Shopi	95.80FF/£11.84 (£16.91/Litre)

Grant's

UK Price Check	Tesco	£14.99/Litre
Mid-Channel	North Sea	£9.75
	P&O	£9.75
	Scandinavian	£9.90
	Hoverspeed	£10.00
	Sally	£10.40
Cross-Channel	Auchan	64.95FF/£8.02 (£11.46/Litre)
	Match	69.90FF/£8.63 (£12.33/Litre)

J&B Rare

UK Price Check	Tesco	£14.99 (£21.41/Litre)
Mid-Channel	Brittany	£10.60
	Hoverspeed	£11.50
	North Sea	£11.50
	P&O	£11.50
	Stena	£11.50
Cross-Channel	Auchan	86.50FF/£10.68 (£15.26/Litre)
	Wijnhuis Douchy	830.00BF/£17.66/Litre

Johnnie Walker Red Label

Mid-Channel	Brittany	£9.70
	Scandinavian	£9.90
	Stena	£9.99
	Hoverspeed	£10.50
	North Sea	£10.50
	P&O	£10.50
	Sally	£10.99
Cross-Channel	Delhaize	525.00BF/£11.17 (£15.96/Litre)
	Wijnhuis Douchy	895.00BF/£19.04/Litre

Teachers Highland Cream

UK Price Check	Tesco	£14.99/Litre
Mid-Channel	Hoverspeed	£10.00
	North Sea	£10.25
	P&O	£10.25
	Stena	£10.50
	Sally	£10.60
Cross-Channel	Sainsbury's	79.50FF/£9.81 (£14.01/Litre)

White Horse

Mid-Channel	Sally	£9.20
	Stena	£9.50

Whyte & Mackay

UK Price Check	Tesco	£14.99/Litre
Mid-Channel	North Sea	£9.75
	P&O	£9.75
	Stena	£9.99
	Hoverspeed	£10.00
	Sally	£10.50
	Brittany	£10.60

Vat 69

Mid-Channel	North Sea	£9.90
	Scandinavian	£9.90

DELUXE SCOTCH WHISKY

Ballantine's Gold Seal 12YO

Mid-Channel	Brittany	£16.95
	Stena	£17.50

Bell's 12YO

Mid-Channel	Brittany	£15.95

Chivas Regal 12YO

UK Price Check	Averys	£27.13 (£38.76/Litre)
Mid-Channel	Sally	£16.50
	Brittany	£16.95
	North Sea	£16.95
	P&O	£16.95
	Hoverspeed	£17.00
	Stena	£17.50
	Scandinavian	£21.20

Cross-Channel	Wijnhuis Douchy	1060.00BF/£22.55/Litre

Grant's 12YO

Mid-Channel	Brittany	£12.95
	Hoverspeed	£13.50
	Sally	£13.50
	Stena	£14.50

Haig Dimple

UK Price Check	Averys	£25.02 (£35.74/Litre)
Mid-Channel	Hoverspeed	£16.50
	North Sea	£16.95
	Brittany	£18.40

Johnnie Walker Black Label 12YO

UK Price Check	Tesco	£17.99 (£25.70/Litre)
Mid-Channel	Hoverspeed	£15.50
	North Sea	£15.50
	P&O	£15.50
	Sally	£15.50
	Brittany	£15.95
	Scandinavian	£18.40
Cross-Channel	Wijnhuis Douchy	1295.00BF/£27.55/Litre

Teachers 12YO

Mid-Channel	Brittany	£15.50
	Sally	£15.50

PURE MALT SCOTCH WHISKY

Aberlour 12YO

UK Price Check	Oddbins	£17.99 (£25.70/Litre)
Mid-Channel	Brittany	£14.50
	North Sea	£16.25
	Hoverspeed	£16.50

Balvenie

UK Price Check	Oddbins	£19.99 (£28.56/Litre)
Mid-Channel	Hoverspeed	£17.00
	North Sea	£17.95
	Sally	£17.99

Balvenie Doublewood 12YO

UK Price Check	Victoria Wine	£24.99 (£35.70/Litre)
Mid-Channel	Brittany	£21.95

Bowmore

Mid-Channel	North Sea	£17.50
	Sally	£17.50

Bowmore 12YO

Mid-Channel	P&O	£17.50
	Stena	£17.99
	Hoverspeed	£18.00

Bunnahobhain 12YO

UK Price Check	Oddbins	£20.99 (£29.99/Litre)
Mid-Channel	Hoverspeed	£19.00

Cardhu 12YO

UK Price Check	Victoria Wine	£21.69 (£30.99/Litre)
Mid-Channel	Hoverspeed	£17.50
	North Sea	£17.50
	P&O	£17.50
	Brittany	£18.50

Cross-Channel	Wijnhuis Douchy	1045.00BF/£22.23 (£31.76/Litre)

Craganmore

UK Price Check	Oddbins	£20.49 (£29.27/Litre)
Mid-Channel	Brittany	£18.50
	Scandinavian	£18.90
	Hoverspeed	£20.00

Dalmore 12YO

UK Price Check	Victoria Wine	£21.79 (£31.13/Litre)
Mid-Channel	Sally	£16.80
	North Sea	£16.95
	Brittany	£17.50
	Hoverspeed	£17.50

Dalwhinnie 15YO

UK Price Check	Oddbins	£20.49 (£29.27/Litre)
Mid-Channel	North Sea	£18.25
	Scandinavian	£18.90
	Hoverspeed	£21.00

Glenfiddich

UK Price Check	Oddbins	£18.99 (£27.13/Litre)
Mid-Channel	Sally	£15.99
	Hoverspeed	£16.00
	North Sea	£16.25
	P&O	£16.25
	Brittany	£16.90
	Scandinavian	£18.90
Cross-Channel	Auchan	121.20FF/£14.96 (£21.37/Litre)
	Continent	123.00FF/£15.19 (£21.70/Litre)
	Champion	124.90FF/£15.42 (£22.03/Litre)
	Super U	135.10FF/£16.68 (£23.83/Litre)
	Wijnhuis Douchy	960.00BF/£20.43 (£29.19/Litre)

Glenkinchie 10YO

UK Price Check	Oddbins	£20.49 (£29.27/Litre)
Mid-Channel	Brittany	£18.50
	Scandinavian	£18.90
	Hoverspeed	£20.00

Glenlivet 12YO

UK Price Check	Oddbins	£18.49 (£26.41/Litre)
Mid-Channel	Sally	£16.95
	Hoverspeed	£17.00
	North Sea	£17.50
	P&O	£17.50
	Brittany	£18.95
Cross-Channel	Delhaize	899.00BF/£19.13 (£27.33/Litre)
	Nicolas	165.00FF/£20.37 (£29.10/Litre)

Glenmorangie 10YO

UK Price Check	Oddbins	£20.99 (£29.99/Litre)
Mid-Channel	Sally	£17.95
	Hoverspeed	£18.50
	North Sea	£18.50
	P&O	£18.50
Cross-Channel	Continent	159.00FF/£19.63 (£28.04/Litre)

Glenmorangie 18YO

UK Price Check	Victoria Wine	£32.49 (£46.41/Litre)
Mid-Channel	Brittany	£27.80
	Hoverspeed	£29.00

Glen Moray 12YO

UK Price Check	Victoria Wine	£19.99 (£28.56/Litre)
Mid-Channel	Sally	£17.50

Glen Ord 12YO

UK Price Check	Oddbins	£17.99 (£25.70/Litre)
Mid-Channel	Brittany	£15.95
	North Sea	£15.95
	Sally	£15.95

Highland Park

UK Price Check	Tesco	£19.95 (£28.50/Litre)
Mid-Channel	Sally	£17.50
	North Sea	£17.95
	Hoverspeed	£18.00

Highland Park 12YO

UK Price Check	Oddbins	£20.99 (£29.99/Litre)
Mid-Channel	Scandinavian	£18.50
	Brittany	£18.95

Isle Of Jura 10YO

UK Price Check	Oddbins	£18.49 (£26.41/Litre)
Mid-Channel	Brittany	£15.50
	P&O	£15.75

Lagavulin

UK Price Check	Tesco	£22.49 (£32.13/Litre)
Mid-Channel	Sally	£18.50
	Scandinavian	£18.90

Lagavulin 16YO

UK Price Check	Oddbins	£22.49 (£32.13/Litre)
Mid-Channel	North Sea	£19.25
	P&O	£19.25
	Brittany	£19.95
	Hoverspeed	£20.00

Laphroaig 10YO

UK Price Check	Oddbins	£20.99 (£29.99/Litre)
Mid-Channel	North Sea	£17.95
	P&O	£17.95
	Brittany	£18.95
	Stena	£18.99
	Hoverspeed	£20.00
Cross-Channel	Nicolas	235.00FF/£29.01 (£41.44/Litre)

Macallan 12YO

Mid-Channel	North Sea	£18.95
	P&O	£18.95
	Stena	£18.99
	Hoverspeed	£19.00
	Brittany	£19.95
Cross-Channel	Nicolas	235.00FF/£29.01 (£41.44/Litre)

Miltonduff

Mid-Channel	Hoverspeed	£17.00

Oban 14YO

UK Price Check	Oddbins	£20.49 (£29.27/Litre)
Mid-Channel	Scandinavian	£18.90
	Brittany	£18.95
	North Sea	£18.95
	Hoverspeed	£19.00
Cross-Channel	Wijnhuis Douchy	1295.00BF/£27.55 (£39.36/Litre)

Singleton

UK Price Check	Oddbins	£17.99 (£25.70/Litre)
Mid-Channel	Hoverspeed	£16.50
	North Sea	£16.50

Talisker 10YO

UK Price Check	Oddbins	£21.49 (£30.70/Litre)
Mid-Channel	Scandinavian	£18.90
	Brittany	£18.95
	North Sea	£18.95
	Hoverspeed	£19.00

IRISH WHISKEY

Black Bush De Luxe

UK Price Check	Oddbins	£16.49 (£23.56/Litre)
Mid-Channel	P&O	£14.75
	Brittany	£15.50
	Sally	£15.85
	Stena	£16.25

Bushmills 10YO Malt

UK Price Check	Oddbins	£20.49 (£29.27/Litre)
Mid-Channel	Stena	£15.25
	Sally	£16.99
	Hoverspeed	£17.50
	Brittany	£18.50

Bushmills 1608 12YO

Mid-Channel	Hoverspeed	£16.00
	Brittany	£16.95
	North Sea	£17.25

Jameson

UK Price Check	Oddbins	£13.49 (£19.27/Litre)
Mid-Channel	Scandinavian	£9.90
	Brittany	£10.95
	North Sea	£11.25
	P&O	£11.25
	Hoverspeed	£11.50
	Sally	£11.90
Cross-Channel	Wijnhuis Douchy	645.00BF/£13.72 (£19.60/Litre)

Jameson 1780 12YO

Mid-Channel	North Sea	£12.50
	Sally	£16.25
	Hoverspeed	£17.00

John Power

Mid-Channel	Brittany	£10.95

Old Bushmills

Mid-Channel	Brittany	£9.30

Paddy

UK Price Check	Oddbins	£13.99 (£19.99/Litre)
Mid-Channel	Brittany	£10.95

AMERICAN BOURBON & CANADIAN RYE

Canadian Club

UK Price Check	Oddbins	£15.49 (£22.13/Litre)
Mid-Channel	Scandinavian	£9.90
	P&O	£10.95
	Brittany	£11.30
	Sally	£11.80

		Hoverspeed	£12.00

Jack Daniels

UK Price Check	Oddbins	£16.49 (£23.56/Litre)
Mid-Channel	Brittany	£16.30
	Hoverspeed	£16.50
	North Sea	£16.95
	Sally	£17.99
Cross-Channel	Wijnhuis Douchy	855.00BF/£18.19 (£25.99/Litre)

Jim Beam

UK Price Check	Oddbins	£14.99 (£21.41/Litre)
Mid-Channel	Brittany	£12.30
	North Sea	£12.95
	Sally	£12.95
	P&O	£12.95
	Hoverspeed	£13.00
Cross-Channel	Nicolas	125.00FF/£15.43 (£22.04/Litre)
	Wijnhuis Douchy	599.00BF/£12.74 (£18.20/Litre)

Wild Turkey 8YO

UK Price Check	Oddbins	£16.99 (£24.27/Litre)
Mid-Channel	P&O	£14.50
	Hoverspeed	£15.50

COGNAC

Bisquit ★★★

Mid-Channel	Brittany	£13.95
Cross-Channel	Wijnhuis Douchy	735.00BF/£15.64 (£22.34/Litre)

Camus Grand VSOP

Mid-Channel	Scandinavian	£22.00

Courvoisier ★★★

UK Price Check	Tesco	£23.49/Litre
Mid-Channel	North Sea	£14.50
	P&O	£14.50
	Sally	£14.60
	Hoverspeed	£15.00
	Stena	£15.50
Cross-Channel	Super U	110.00FF/£13.58 (£19.40/Litre)
	Delhaize	663.00BF/£14.11 (£20.16/Litre)
	Wijnhuis Douchy	799.00BF/£17.00 (£24.29/Litre)

Courvoisier VSOP

UK Price Check	Victoria Wine	£28.49 (£40.70/Litre)
Mid-Channel	Hoverspeed	£19.50
	North Sea	£19.50
	Sally	£19.50
	Stena	£19.75
	P&O	£19.95

Hennessy ★★★

UK Price Check	Tesco	£16.49 (£23.56/Litre)
Mid-Channel	Sally	£15.50

Hine VSOP

UK Price Check	Averys	£28.01 (£40.01/Litre)
Mid-Channel	Sally	£19.99
	Hoverspeed	£21.00

Louis Royer VS

Mid-Channel	Brittany	£14.95

Louis Royer VSOP

Mid-Channel	Brittany	£19.95

Martell VS

UK Price Check	Oddbins	£16.79 (£23.99/Litre)
Mid-Channel	Sally	£14.50
	North Sea	£15.25
	P&O	£15.25
	Hoverspeed	£15.50
	Stena	£15.50
	Brittany	£15.95
	Scandinavian	£19.50
Cross-Channel	Match	117.90FF/£14.56 (£20.80/Litre)
	Wijnhuis Douchy	779.00BF/£16.57 (£23.67/Litre)

Martell VSOP

UK Price Check	Oddbins	£25.99 (£37.13/Litre)
Mid-Channel	Sally	£18.75
	Brittany	£19.95
	Stena	£19.99
	Hoverspeed	£20.00
	Scandinavian	£24.00

Martell Napoléon

Mid-Channel	Scandinavian	£42.00

Otard VS

Mid-Channel	Brittany	£14.50

Otard VSOP

Mid-Channel	Brittany	£19.95

Rémy Martin VSOP

UK Price Check	Tesco	£24.99 (£35.70/Litre)
Mid-Channel	Scandinavian	£23.50
	Sally	£23.90
	North Sea	£23.95
	P&O	£23.95
	Stena	£24.99
Cross-Channel	Champion	170.00FF/£20.99 (£29.99/Litre)
	Super U	174.00FF/£21.48 (£30.69/Litre)
	Monoprix	185.80FF/£22.94 (£32.77/Litre)

Rémy Martin Fine Champagne

Mid-Channel	Brittany	£22.50

OTHER BRANDIES

Asbach Uralt

UK Price Check	Victoria Wine	£15.49 (£22.13/Litre)
Mid-Channel	Brittany	£12.50
	North Sea	£12.95
	P&O	£12.95
	Sally	£12.99
	Stena	£13.60
	Scandinavian	£14.00
Cross-Channel	Wijnhuis Douchy	630.00BF/£13.40 (£19.14/Litre)

Bardinet Grape Brandy

UK Price Check	Tesco	£9.99 (£14.27/Litre)
Mid-Channel	Brittany	£8.20
	P&O	£9.75
	Sally	£9.99
	Stena	£9.99

Metaxa Amphora

Mid-Channel	North Sea	£12.95

Metaxa 5 Star

Mid-Channel	Brittany	£10.95
Cross-Channel	Wijnhuis Douchy	530.00BF/£11.28 (£16.11/Litre)

Metaxa 7 Star

Mid-Channel	P&O	£12.95
Cross-Channel	Wijnhuis Douchy	685.00BF/£14.57 (£20.81/Litre)

Three Barrels Grape Brandy

UK Price Check	Tesco	£11.29 (£16.13/Litre)
Mid-Channel	Scandinavian	£8.00
	Sally	£9.40
	Brittany	£9.95
	Hoverspeed	£10.00
	P&O	£10.25
	North Sea	£10.25
	Stena	£10.99

GIN

Beefeater

UK Price Check	Tesco	£14.99/Litre
Mid-Channel	North Sea	£9.25
	P&O	£9.25
	Scandinavian	£9.30
	Brittany	£9.40
	Sally	£9.40
	Hoverspeed	£9.50
	Stena	£9.75

Bombay Sapphire

UK Price Check	Averys	£15.49 (£22.13/Litre)
Mid-Channel	North Sea	£9.95
	P&O	£9.95
	Stena	£9.99
	Hoverspeed	£11.00
	Brittany	£11.75

Gilbeys

Mid-Channel	Brittany	£8.95
	P&O	£8.95
	Sally	£8.99
	Hoverspeed	£9.50
Cross-Channel	Super U	58.90FF/£7.27 (£10.39/Litre)
	Match	59.40FF/£7.33 (£10.47/Litre)
	Delhaize	385.00BF/£8.19 (£11.70/Litre)

Gordons

UK Price Check	Tesco	£13.99/Litre
Mid-Channel	Brittany	£9.40
	North Sea	£9.50
	P&O	£9.50
	Stena	£9.75
	Scandinavian	£9.80
	Sally	£9.99
	Hoverspeed	£10.00
Cross-Channel	Carrefour	59.90FF/£7.40 (£10.57/Litre)
	Monoprix	62.50FF/£7.72 (£11.03/Litre)
	Super U	64.50FF/£7.96 (£11.37/Litre)
	Champion	66.90FF/£8.26 (£11.80/Litre)
	Shopi	69.95FF/£8.64 (£12.34/Litre)
	Delhaize	425.00BF/£9.04 (£12.91/Litre)

	Wijnhuis Douchy	735.00BF/£15.64/Litre
Tanquery		
Mid-Channel	Brittany	£10.80
	Hoverspeed	£11.00
	P&O	£11.25
	Stena	£11.25

RUM

Bacardi

UK Price Check	Oddbins	£11.99 (£17.13/Litre)
Mid-Channel	Scandinavian	£10.20
	Sally	£11.30
	Brittany	£11.50
	North Sea	£11.95
	P&O	£11.95
	Stena	£11.99
	Hoverspeed	£12.00
Cross-Channel	Wijnhuis Douchy	685.00BF/£14.57/Litre

Captain Morgan

UK Price Check	Oddbins	£11.89 (£16.99/Litre)
Mid-Channel	Sally	£9.25
	Brittany	£9.50
	P&O	£9.75
	Hoverspeed	£10.00
	Stena	£10.25
	Scandinavian	£11.00

Lambs Navy Rum

UK Price Check	Tesco	£14.99/Litre
Mid-Channel	Sally	£9.25
	Brittany	£9.50
	North Sea	£9.75
	P&O	£9.75
	Stena	£10.25

Lambs White Rum

UK Price Check	Tesco	£11.39 (£16.27/Litre)
Mid-Channel	North Sea	£9.75
	Hoverspeed	£10.00

Woods 100

UK Price Check	Oddbins	£16.49 (£23.56/Litre)
Mid-Channel	Sally	£11.50
	Hoverspeed	£11.50
	P&O	£11.75
	Stena	£11.99

VODKA

Absolut

UK Price Check	Oddbins	£11.99 (£17.13/Litre)
Mid-Channel	Hoverspeed	£10.00
	P&O	£10.50
	Stena	£10.75
Cross-Channel	Continent	72.00FF/£8.89 (£12.70/Litre)

Finlandia

Mid-Channel	Scandinavian	£8.00
	Hoverspeed	£9.50

Smirnoff Blue Label

UK Price Check	Tesco	£13.59 (£19.41/Litre)
Mid-Channel	Scandinavian	£9.40

	P&O	£10.25
	Brittany	£10.50
	Hoverspeed	£10.50
	Stena	£10.50
	Sally	£10.80

Smirnoff Red Label

UK Price Check	Tesco	£14.75/Litre
Mid-Channel	Brittany	£9.30
Cross-Channel	Continent	56.65FF/£6.99 (£19.99/Litre)
	Carrefour	56.70FF/£7.00 (£10.00/Litre)
	Champion	61.90FF/£7.64 (£10.91/Litre)
	Super U	61.90FF/£7.64 (£10.91/Litre)
	Match	65.65FF/£8.10 (£11.57/Litre)
	Monoprix	68.80FF/£8.49 (£12.13/Litre)
	Shopi	71.50FF/£8.83 (£12.61/Litre)
	Wijnhuis Douchy	615.00BF/£13.09/Litre

Vladivar Silver

UK Price Check	Oddbins	£8.79 (£12.56/Litre)
Mid-Channel	Brittany	£7.95
	Sally	£8.90
	P&O	£8.95

Vladivar Imperial

Mid-Channel	Brittany	£9.95
	P&O	£10.25
	Stena	£10.25
	Hoverspeed	£10.50
	Sally	£10.60

APERITIFS & VERMOUTHS

Campari

UK Price Check	Oddbins	£10.69 (£15.27/Litre)
Mid-Channel	Brittany	£9.75
	North Sea	£9.75
	P&O	£9.75
	Sally	£9.80
	Hoverspeed	£10.00
Cross-Channel	Wijnhuis Douchy	569.00BF/£12.11/Litre

Cinzano Bianco

UK Price Check	Waitrose	£7.89/150cl (£5.26/Litre)
Mid-Channel	Sally	£3.95
	Brittany	£3.99
	P&O	£3.99

Dubonnet

UK Price Check	Waitrose	£5.99 (£8.56/Litre)
Mid-Channel	Brittany	£4.30
	P&O	£5.95

Martini Bianco

UK Price Check	Waitrose	£7.89/150cl (£5.26/Litre)
Mid-Channel	Scandinavian	£3.60
	North Sea	£4.15
	P&O	£4.15
	Hoverspeed	£4.50
	Sally	£4.50

Martini Extra Dry

UK Price Check	Waitrose	£7.89/150cl (£5.26/Litre)
Mid-Channel	Scandinavian	£3.60
	Brittany	£4.10

	North Sea	£4.15
	P&O	£4.15
	Hoverspeed	£4.50
	Sally	£4.60
Cross-Channel	Wijnhuis Douchy	195.00BF/£4.15/Litre

Martini Rosso

UK Price Check	Waitrose	£7.89/150cl (£5.26/Litre)
Mid-Channel	Scandinavian	£3.60
	Brittany	£4.10
	North Sea	£4.15
	P&O	£4.15
	Hoverspeed	£4.50
	Sally	£4.60
Cross-Channel	Wijnhuis Douchy	195.00BF/£4.15/Litre

Pernod

UK Price Check	Oddbins	£13.69 (£19.56/Litre)
Mid-Channel	Sally	£8.70
	Brittany	£8.90
	North Sea	£8.95
	P&O	£8.95
	Hoverspeed	£9.00
	Scandinavian	£11.80
Cross-Channel	Wijnhuis Douchy	695.00BF/£14.79/Litre

Pimms No.1

UK Price Check	Tesco	£10.49 (£14.99/Litre)
Mid-Channel	Brittany	£9.20
	Hoverspeed	£9.50
	P&O	£9.50
	Sally	£10.33
Cross-Channel	Wijnhuis Douchy	475.00BF/£10.11 (£14.44/Litre)

Ricard

Mid-Channel	Brittany	£8.30
	P&O	£8.95
	Hoverspeed	£9.00
Cross-Channel	Wijnhuis Douchy	695.00BF/£14.79/Litre

LIQUEURS

Baileys Irish Cream

UK Price Check	Oddbins	£11.89 (£16.99/Litre)
Mid-Channel	North Sea	£11.25
	P&O	£11.25
	Brittany	£11.50
	Hoverspeed	£11.50
	Sally	£12.15
	Scandinavian	£13.50
Cross-Channel	Wijnhuis Douchy	725.00BF/£15.43/Litre

Bols Apricot Brandy 50cl

UK Price Check	Tesco	£10.99 (£7.85/50cl)
Mid-Channel	North Sea	£5.95
	Hoverspeed	£6.00
	Scandinavian	£7.00
Cross-Channel	Wijnhuis Douchy	420.00BF/£8.94 (£12.77/Litre)

Bols Cherry Brandy 50cl

UK Price Check	Tesco	£10.99 (£7.85/50cl)
Mid-Channel	North Sea	£5.95
	Hoverspeed	£6.00
Cross-Channel	Wijnhuis Douchy	420.00BF/£8.94 (£12.77/Litre)

Cadbury's Cream Liqueur

UK Price Check	Tesco	£10.89 (£15.56/Litre)
Mid-Channel	Hoverspeed	£10.50
	P&O	£10.50
	Sally	£11.99

Cointreau

UK Price Check	Oddbins	£15.99 (£22.84/Litre)
Mid-Channel	North Sea	£12.50
	P&O	£12.50
	Brittany	£12.75
	Sally	£12.99
	Hoverspeed	£13.00
Cross-Channel	Wijnhuis Douchy	895.00BF/£19.04/Litre

Drambuie

UK Price Check	Oddbins	£18.99 (£27.13/Litre)
Mid-Channel	Brittany	£15.40
	Hoverspeed	£15.50
	North Sea	£15.50
	P&O	£15.50
Cross-Channel	Wijnhuis Douchy	999.00BF/£21.26/Litre

Glayva

UK Price Check	Oddbins	£13.99 (£27.98/Litre)
Mid-Channel	North Sea	£12.75
	P&O	£12.75

Grand Marnier

UK Price Check	Oddbins	£19.29 (£27.56/Litre)
Mid-Channel	P&O	£15.25
	Hoverspeed	£15.50
Cross-Channel	Wijnhuis Douchy	975.00BF/£20.74/Litre

Malibu

UK Price Check	Oddbins	£10.75 (£15.36/Litre)
Mid-Channel	Brittany	£8.95
	Sally	£8.99
	Hoverspeed	£9.00
	North Sea	£9.25
	P&O	£9.25

Mandarin Napoléon

UK Price Check	Waitrose	£10.99 (£21.98/Litre)
Mid-Channel	Hoverspeed	£11.50
	North Sea	£11.75
	P&O	£11.75
Cross-Channel	Wijnhuis Douchy	610.00BF/£12.98 (£18.54/Litre)

Southern Comfort

UK Price Check	Oddbins	£15.49 (£22.13/Litre)
Mid-Channel	Brittany	£15.50
	North Sea	£15.50
	P&O	£15.95
	Sally	£15.99
	Hoverspeed	£16.00
	Scandinavian	£18.50
Cross-Channel	Wijnhuis Douchy	670.00BF/£14.26 (£20.37/Litre)

Tia Maria

UK Price Check	Oddbins	£13.99 (£19.99/Litre)
Mid-Channel	Sally	£11.99
	North Sea	£12.75
	P&O	£12.75

	Brittany	£12.95
	Hoverspeed	£14.00
Cross-Channel	Wijnhuis Douchy	535.00BF/£11.38 (£16.26/Litre)

Warninks Advocaat

UK Price Check	Tesco	£9.59 (£13.70/Litre)
Mid-Channel	Sally	£7.99
	Hoverspeed	£8.50
	North Sea	£8.75

PORT

Cockburns Fine Ruby

UK Price Check	Victoria Wine	£6.99 (£9.99/Litre)
Mid-Channel	Hoverspeed	£6.50
	P&O	£6.50
	Sally	£6.50

Cockburns LBV

UK Price Check	Victoria Wine	£9.99 (£14.27/Litre)
Mid-Channel	Brittany	£9.95

Cockburns Special Reserve

UK Price Check	Waitrose	£7.99 (£11.41/Litre)
Mid-Channel	Brittany	£8.75
	P&O	£8.75
	Hoverspeed	£9.00

Croft 10YO Tawny

Mid-Channel	Hoverspeed	£12.50

Croft LBV

Mid-Channel	Brittany	£11.20

Dow's LBV

UK Price Check	Waitrose	£8.45 (£12.07/Litre)
Mid-Channel	Scandinavian	£8.80

Dow's Ruby

UK Price Check	Waitrose	£5.99 (£8.56/Litre)
Mid-Channel	Scandinavian	£6.00

Graham's LBV

UK Price Check	Oddbins	£9.99 (£14.27/Litre)
Mid-Channel	P&O	£9.25
	Hoverspeed	£9.50
	Sally	£9.85
	Brittany	£9.95

Taylors LBV

UK Price Check	Waitrose	£10.45 (£14.93/Litre)
Mid-Channel	P&O	£9.50
	Hoverspeed	£10.00
	Brittany	£10.15
	Sally	£10.15

SHERRY

Croft Original

UK Price Check	Oddbins	£5.99 (£8.56/Litre)
Mid-Channel	Sally	£5.99
	Brittany	£6.50
	North Sea	£6.50
	P&O	£6.50

Dry Sack

Mid-Channel	P&O	£5.75

	Sally	£5.99
	Brittany	£6.30
	Hoverspeed	£6.50
	Scandinavian	£8.40
Cross-Channel	Wijnhuis Douchy	299.00BF/£6.36 (£9.09/Litre)

Harveys Bristol Cream

UK Price Check	Oddbins	£6.29 (£8.99/Litre)
Mid-Channel	Sally	£6.25
	Brittany	£6.50
	Hoverspeed	£6.50
	North Sea	£6.50
	P&O	£6.50
	Scandinavian	£7.90
Cross-Channel	Wijnhuis Douchy	295.00BF/£6.28 (£8.97/Litre)

La Ina Fino

UK Price Check	Victoria Wine	£6.99 (£9.99/Litre)
Mid-Channel	Brittany	£5.95
	P&O	£5.95

Tío Pepe

UK Price Check	Oddbins	£6.99 (£9.99/Litre)
Mid-Channel	North Sea	£6.50
	Hoverspeed	£7.50
	Brittany	£7.80
	Scandinavian	£9.10
Cross-Channel	Wijnhuis Douchy	299.00BF/£6.36 (£9.09/Litre)

BEERS

Please note that because the duty-free prices are for multiple packs of 6, 8, 12 or 24 cans, and the capacity sometimes varies, all prices have been adjusted to single bottles or cans and made relevant to the size indicated immediately after the name of the beer for easy comparison.

Boddingtons Draught 44cl

UK Price Check	Oddbins	£1.19 (single can)
Mid-Channel	North Sea	£64p (12x44cl)
	Stena	75p (12x44cl)

Fosters Export 44cl

UK Price Check	Oddbins	£1.09 (single can)
Mid-Channel	Stena	40p (24x50cl)
Mid-Channel	Stena	36p (24x33cl)

Grolsch 44cl

UK Price Check	Oddbins	£1.19 (single)
Mid-Channel	Sally	41p (24x50cl)
	Stena	44p (24x50cl)

Grolsch 33cl

UK Price Check	Oddbins	75p (single can)
Mid-Channel	North Sea	45p (12x33cl)

Guinness Draught 44cl

UK Price Check	Oddbins	£1.27 (single can)
Mid-Channel	Stena	94p (8x44cl)

Heineken Export 44cl

UK Price Check	Tesco	99p (4x44cl)
Mid-Channel	Stena	78p (12x33cl)

Holsten 33cl

UK Price Check	Oddbins	99p (single can)
Mid-Channel	Sally	30p (24x33cl)
	Scandinavian	50p (6x33cl)

John Smiths Bitter 44cl

UK Price Check	Tesco	68p (24x44cl)
Mid-Channel	Stena	42p (24x44cl)

McEwans 44cl

UK Price Check	Tesco	83p (12x44cl)
Mid-Channel	Scandinavian	57p (4x44cl)

Stella Artois 25cl

UK Price Check	Tesco	42p (24x25cl)
Mid-Channel	Sally	27p (24x44cl)
	North Sea	27p (24x44cl)
Cross-Channel	Delhaize	23.48BF/47p (single can)

THE BUYER'S QUICK REFERENCE A-Z TO EUROPE'S WINES, BEERS AND SPIRITS

The following three sections provide a finger-tip reference to virtually every wine, beer and spirit produced in continental Europe. Within each section the products are listed alphabetically, requiring no prior knowledge of the country, region or area of origin of any wine, beer or spirit in order to locate its description.

WINES

The brief generalisations below make a handy guide to what's what. It is possible, of course, to find exciting wines from areas with even the most awful reputation and coming across such exceptions will be very rewarding, particularly in terms of value for money. It is also possible for the most reliable producer in the greatest wine region to make a disappointing wine now and then. The Golden Rule is, therefore, to taste any wine before you buy it, should you get the opportunity. If you do not get the opportunity and there is no specific recommendation for the wines you encounter in the *The Cross-Channel Shopping Guide*, then the following fingertip reference should help you to bust your way through the maze of European wines.

A-Z OF WINES

NOTE: As many varietal wines are produced all over the world, a number of grape varieties are also listed and an indication is given of the sort of style you might expect, although much will depend on exactly where the grape is grown, who makes the wine and last but not least, how much you pay for it. For definitions of technical and tasting terms or abbreviations, consult the GLOSSARY.

ABANILLA Spain, Murcia (VdlT) Country wines that have yet to make their mark.

ABSTATT Germany, Württemberg One of the best villages in Württemberg. Top single-vineyards: Abstatter Burg Wildeck.

ABTEY Germany, Rheinhessen If you see this name following that of a village on a bottle of Rheinhessen, it is only a *Grosslage* wine.

ACHKARREN Germany, Baden One of the best illages in Baden. Top single-vineyards: Achkarrener Schlossberg.

ADELBERG Germany, Rheinhessen If you see this name following that of a village on a bottle of Rheinhessen, it is only a *Grosslage* wine.

AGLIANICO DEI COLLI LUCANI Italy, Basilicata (VT) Robust reds that are not in the class of those grown on the slopes of Mount Vulture and its surrounding hills. Semi-sweet and sparkling reds also exist.

AGLIANICO DEL VULTURE Italy, Basilicata (DOC) This may be Basilicata's only fine wine, but it happens to be the greatest Aglianico produced in Italy. Big but balanced, these red wines are a bit rustic in their youth, but develop complexity and silky finesse with age. Beware: semi-sweet and sparkling reds are also possible under this appellation.

AHR Germany, (QbA) Surprisingly for the most northerly wine region in Germany, two-thirds of the vines planted are black varieties, but the Ahr is a deep valley protected by surrounding hills, with a rocky, slatey soil that accumulates heat, enabling these vines to flourish. The

Ahr's speciality is the ruby-coloured Rotwein and the lighter Weissherbst, both from either the Spätburgunder (Pinot Noir) or the Portugeiser, or a blend of both. The Weissherbst is fresher, softer and more attractive. The Ahr also produces good and improving Riesling.

AHR GROSSLAGEN Germany, Ahr (Grosslagen) Klosterberg is a *Grosslage*, not a single-vineyard and should be very reasonably priced, unless you are being ripped-off or it happens to be an Eiswein, Beerenauslese or Trockenbeerenauslese.

AHRTALER LANDWEIN Germany (DL) One of 15 Deutscher Landwein appellations, its wines should be simple and light-bodied, with a basic flowery aroma, some grapey fruit and a touch of sweetness on the finish.

AJACCIO France, Corsica (AOC) This appellation on the west coast of the island produces predominantly red wines of good bouquet and medium body, but merely average dry whites and dry rosés.

ALBANA DI ROMAGNA Italy, Emilia-Romagna (DOCG) Italy's first white wine to receive DOCG status, but if you taste this basic dry or semi-sweet wine, you will wonder why.

ALBIG Germany, Rheinhessen One of the best villages in the Rheinhessen. Top single-vineyards: Albiger Schloss Hammerstein.

ALCAMO Italy, Sicily (DOC) Dry, slightly fruity wines of little interest.

ALCOBAÇO Portugal, Estremadura (IPR) Clean fruity reds, the best of which have a good

concentration of berry flavours, whereas the best whites are simply crisp with a touch of spritz and are much less interesting.

ALEATICO Italy, Tuscany (VT) Seldom encountered, rich red dessert wines from the Aleatico, a Muscat-related grape.

ALEATICO DI GRADOLI Italy, Latium (DOC) A soft, aromatic red dessert wine made from the Aleatico grape, thought to be a variant of the Moscato or Muscat.

ALEATICO DI PUGLIA Italy, Apulia (DOC) Italy's best Aleatico is a warm, opulent, aromatic red dessert wine of world class yet, ironically, it is seldom encountered outside of Bari, which is its only area of significant production.

ALELLA Spain, Catalonia (DO) Well-coloured, soft fruity reds, light-bodied, delicately flavoured dry whites and dry rosés.

ALENQUER Portugal, Estremadura (IPR) Clean, fruity reds, the best of which have a good concentration of berry flavours, whereas the best whites are simply crisp with a touch of spritz and are much less interesting.

ALENTEJO Portugal (VR) One of only two Vinhos Regiõaos so far established, but what Portugal's embryonic Country Wine category lacks in numbers, it makes up for in size, as the Alentejo district covers one-third of Portugal. There are some outstanding wines already being produced in the Alentejo and exciting new finds popping up all over the place, but it is such a vast area that it will always be horrendously variable in quality and value. If you see an Alentejo wine, however, it at least warrants a taste.

ALEZIO Italy, Apulia (DOC) Interesting if alcoholic reds and soft, flavourful rosés.

ALICANTE Italy, Tuscany (VT) Fat, juicy-rich, spicy red wine.

ALICANTE Spain, Valencia (DO) Mostly old-fashioned reds and rosés that are typically dark, full and robust.

ALIGOTÉ (Grape) Can be almost Chardonnay in style when produced by top growers in Burgundy, especially Bouzeron, but will often be thin and acidic.

ALMANSA Spain, Castilla-La Mancha (DO) Full, rich, smooth reds and accept-able, fruity rosé.

ALMEIRIM Portugal, Ribatejo (IPR) Lots of white wine, most of which is ordinary, but the reds are full, fruity and rapidly improving.

ALOXE-CORTON France, Burgundy (AOC) Village appellation in the Côte de Beaune producing deeply coloured, firm structured reds of excellent value. A little dry white also made, mostly rich and concentrated.

ALOXE-CORTON PREMIER CRU France, Burgundy (AOC) The reds are even more intense than the village wines. Whites theoretically possible.

ALSACE France, Alsace (AOC) Possibly the most consistent appellation in France. Mostly white. See individual varieties and styles: Auxerrois, Chasselas, Crémant d'Alsace, Edelzwicker, Gewurztraminer, Klevener de Heiligenstein, Muscat, Pinot, Pinot Noir, Riesling, Sylvaner, Tokay-Pinot Gris.

ALSACE GRAND CRU France, Alsace (AOC) Supposedly the cream of

Alsace, these wines are restricted to Riesling, Gewurztraminer, Tokay-Pinot Gris and Muscat grown in one of the region's 50 grands crus, but whereas most of the greatest Alsace wines are sold under this appellation, many are not and, ironically, the quality is not as consistent as it is for the basic Alsace AOC.

ALSACE SÉLECTION DE GRAINS NOBLES France, Alsace (AOC) Luscious, botrytis-affected, intensely sweet wines, astonishingly high in both quality and price. White only and also restricted to Riesling, Gewurztraminer, Tokay-Pinot Gris and Muscat.

ALSACE VENDANGE TARDIVE France, Alsace (AOC) Medium-sweet to sweet wines made from late-harvested grapes. White only, restricted to Riesling, Gewurztraminer, Tokay-Pinot Gris and Muscat.

ALSHEIM Germany, Rheinhessen One of the best villages in the Rheinhessen. Top single-vineyards: Alsheimer Frühmesse.

ALTO ADIGE Italy, Trentino-Alto Adige (DOC) Huge appellation covering 19 varietals (six red, ten dry or sweet white and three dry or sweet rosé) and one dry sparkling wine (from Chardonnay and Pinot grapes). These wines are always well made and usually very good value, including Schiava (or Vernatsch), which is the local tavern wine, but the best varietals are the reds from Cabernet and Lagrein grapes.

ALTO JILOCA Spain, Aragón (VC) Struggling to make the grade.

ALTRHEINGAUER LANDWEIN Germany (DL) One of 15 Deutscher Landwein appellations, its wines should be simple and light-bodied, with a basic

flowery aroma, some grapey fruit and a touch of sweetness on the finish.

ALVARINHO (Grape) The best Vinho Verde grape, occasionally seen on the label of varietal examples.

AMPURDÁN-COSTA BRAVA Spain, Catalonia (DO) Crisp, cherry-coloured reds, pale and fruity whites and rosés, usually with a touch of sweetness and often slightly *pétillant*.

ANGHELU RUJU Italy, Sardinia (VT) Interesting, rich, deep-coloured, sweet red dessert wine.

ANJOU France, Loire (AOC) Reds range from severe to succulent and whites from light and dry to heavy and sweet. The medium-sweet rosé is the most consistent wine in this appellation, but unfortunately it is consistently dire.

ANJOU-VILLAGES France, Loire (AOC) Relatively new appellation restricted to red wines from the Cabernet Franc (mostly) or Cabernet Sauvignon grapes. Good value.

ANJOU COTEAUX DE LA LOIRE France, Loire (AOC) Rare, dry to off-dry white-only appellation.

ANJOU GAMAY France, Loire (AOC) Medium-bodied red wine that is seldom of interest.

ANJOU MOUSSEUX France, Loire (AOC) Variable quality sparkling white and rosé wines.

ANJOU PÉTILLANT France, Loire (AOC) Less fizzy version of Anjou Mousseux, sold in ordinary still-wine bottles.

ANOIA Spain, Catalonia (VC) Struggling to make the grade.

APRILIA Italy, Latium (DOC) Uninspiring red and dry white wines.

APULIA Italy, Apulia (VT) Full, robust red that can be interesting, despite being sold simply as generic Apulia.

AQUILEA Italy, Friuli-Venezia Giulia (DOC) Wide-ranging appellation of several varietal and blended red, dry white and dry rosé wines, mostly made in a light, crisply balanced style.

ARBOIS France, Jura (AOC) Rustic reds, boring dry whites (beware any claiming to be made from the Savagnin – they taste oxidised from the moment they are freshly made!) and a firm, distinctive dry rosé.

ARBOIS MOUSSEUX France, Jura (AOC) Fresh, honest white sparkling wine.

ARBOIS PUPILLIN France, Jura (AOC) Red, dry white, dry rosé, vin de paille and vin jaune from one of the better Arbois villages.

ARBOIS VIN DE PAILLE France, Jura (AOC) Very sweet, distinctive dessert wine, which instantly ages due to the presence of an oxidative-prone grape called the Savagnin.

ARBOIS VIN JAUNE France, Jura (AOC) Literally 'yellow wine', Vin Jaune looks, smells and tastes like a sherry and is supposed to last for decades.

ARBOREA Italy, Sardinia (DOC) Sangiovese reds and dry or semi-sweet Trebbiano whites.

ARNAD-MONTJOVAT Italy, Val d'Aosta (DOC) Red, dry white and sparkling wines that are well made, but of modest quality.

ARNEIS DEI ROERI Italy, Piedmont (VT) Wonderfully rich and idiosyncratic dry white wine from the ancient Arneis grape.

ARRABIDA Portugal, Estremadura (IPR) Clean fruity reds, the best of which have a good concentration of berry flavours, whereas the best whites are simply crisp with a touch of spritz and are much less interesting.

ARRUDA Portugal, Estremadura (IPR) Clean fruity reds, the best of which have a good concentration of berry flavours, whereas the best whites are simply crisp with a touch of spritz and are much less interesting.

ARTÉS Spain, Catalonia (VC) Struggling to make the grade.

ASSMANNSHAUSEN Germany, Rheingau One of the best villages in the Rheingau. Top single-vineyards: Assmannshauser Höllenberg.

ASTI Italy, Piedmont (DOCG) Synonymous with Asti Spumante (whereas Spumante is not, as it can refer to any sparkling wine, dry or sweet).

ASTI SPUMANTE Italy, Piedmont (DOCG) Italy's most famous sparkling wine is the greatest, most succulent and wonderfully flavoured sweet fizz in the world.

ATTILAFELSEN Germany, Baden If you see this name following that of a village on a bottle of Baden, it is only a *Grosslage* wine.

AUFLANGEN Germany, Rheinhessen If you see this name following that of a village on a bottle of Rheinhessen, it is only a *Grosslage* wine.

AUGGEN Germany, Baden One of the best villages in Baden. Top single-vineyards: Auggener Schäf.

AUSLESE Germany (QbA) A sweet, botrytis-affected wine that can be sublime, but beware of cheap

versions, as they are seldom the bargains they appear.

AUSTRALIA An excellent source of superb value and high quality wine, Australia has been flavour of the month amongst the hard-core of younger wine consumers for the last six or seven years. Best values: Shiraz and Sémillon-Chardonnay.

AUSTRIA An excellent source of surprisingly good wines, the borders of Austria will soon be open to EC travellers, which will enable you to bring wine direct from Austria free of duty and without having to declare it.

AUXERROIS (Grape) Often confused with Pinot Blanc, its wines are fatter, with a touch of spice, and the best examples come from Alsace.

AUXERROIS France, Alsace (AOC) Dry and off-dry white wines that are fatter, richer and spicier than Pinot Blanc.

AUXEY-DURESSES France, Burgundy (AOC) Village appellation in the Côte de Beaune producing light, soft, attractively priced reds and modest white Meursault look alikes.

AUXEY-DURESSES-CÔTES DE BEAUNE France, Burgundy (AOC) Synonymous with Auxey-Duresses.

AUXEY-DURESSES PREMIER CRU France, Burgundy (AOC) Great value fine wines that are a distinct step up in quality from those bearing the basic village appellation.

AYMAVILLE Italy, Valle d'Aosta (VT) Crisp, fruity white wine.

AZUAGA Spain, Extramadura (VC) Struggling to make the grade.

BACCHUS (Grape) Grown extensively in Germany and to a lesser extent the UK, this grape makes a vivaciously aromatic and fruity wine.

BACHARACH Germany, Mittelrhein One of the best villages in the Mittelrhein. Top single-vineyards: Bacharacher Posten.

BAD DÜRKHEIM Germany, Rheinpfalz One of the best villages in the Rheinpfalz. Top single-vineyards: Dürkheimer Nonnengarten, Dürkheimer Spielberg, Dürckheimer Michelsberg, Dürkheimer Fuchsmantel, Dürkheimer Abtsfronhof.

BAD KREUZNACH Germany, Nahe One of the best villages in the Nahe. Top single-vineyards: Kreuzacher Kahlenberg, Kreuzacher Krötenpfuhl, Kreuzacher Brückes, Kreuzacher Hinkelstein.

BAD MÜNSTER AM STEIN Germany, Nahe One of the best villages in the Nahe. Top single-vineyards: Münster am Steiner Rotenfels.

BADEN Germany, (QbA) The great variation of climate and soil found in the vineyards of Baden, which stretch 250 miles from Franken in the north, past Württemberg and Hessisches Bergstrasse to Bodensee or Lake Constance in the south, is responsible for a wide range of wines from mild Silvaner, through light and spicy Gutedel, to the pink-hued *Weissherbst*, which is a speciality of the region, to sufficient *Rotwein* to make Baden the second-largest producer of red wine in Germany.

BADEN GROSSLAGEN Germany, Baden (Grosslagen) Tauberklinge, Hohenberg, Mannaberg,

Rittersberg, Stiftsberg, Fürsteneck, Schloss Rodeck, Burg Lichteneck, Burg Zähringen, Schutter-Lindenberg, Attilafelsen, Vulkanfelsen, Burg Neuenfels, Lorettoberg, Vogtei Rötteln and Sonnenufer are all *Grosslagen*, not single-vineyard wines, and should be very reasonably priced, unless you are being ripped-off or it happens to be an Eiswein, Beerenauslese or Trockenbeerenauslese.

BADSTUBE Germany, Mosel-Saar-Ruwer If you see this name following that of a village on a bottle of MSR, it is only a *Grosslage* wine.

BAIRRADA Portugal, Bairrada (DOC) Well-structured reds with lots of summer fruit flavours, the whites are cleaner, fresher and better made than they ever used to be, but lack the same interest.

BAJO-EBRO-MONSTIA Spain, Catalonia (VC) Struggling to make the grade.

BAJO ARAGÓN Spain, Aragón (VdlT) Country wines that have yet to make their mark.

BANDOL France, Provence (AOC) The greatest red wine appellation in Provence, the best of which are dark purple in colour, with a deep and dense bouquet and masses of spicy-plummy fruit. The dry whites are fresher than they used to be, but are not special. Also some attractive dry rosés of individual character.

BANYULS France, Languedoc-Roussillon (AOC) The porty fruit in these big, black fortified wines are made a stone's throw from the Spanish border and are the nearest that France gets to the great wines of the Douro,

especially when sold under the Banyuls Grand Cru appellation. White or tawny are versions also made, but far less successful. Beware those labelled 'rancio' unless you are sure that you like the rancid-maderised style.

BARBARESCO Italy, Piedmont (DOCG) Pure Nebbiolo red wine similar to Barolo, but likely to be softer and easier to drink.

BARBAROSSA DI BERTINORO Italy, Emilia-Romagna (VT) One of Emilia-Romagna's better red wines, but don't get too excited.

BARBERA D'ALBA Italy, Piedmont (DOC) Magnificently rich and fruity red wines that are best drunk young.

BARBERA D'ASTI Italy, Piedmont (DOC) Similar to Barbera d'Alba, but softer and simpler.

BARBERA DEL MONFERRATO Italy, Piedmont (DOC) Red wines that are similar to, but not quite as good as, Barbera d'Asti. Be careful, as semi-sweet and semi-sparkling versions also exist.

BARBERA DI LINERO Italy, Liguria (VT) This red wine is one of the least interesting Barbera.

BARDOLINO Italy, Veneto (DOC) Light reds which can be slightly sparkling, and light dry *chiaretto* or rosé, but not special.

BAROLO Italy, Piedmont (DOCG) Big, full-bodied wine that has always been the king of Italian reds.

BAROLO CHINATO Italy, Piedmont (DOC) A strange animal this: Barolo with quinine added!

BARSAC France, Bordeaux (AOC) Luscious, intensely sweet, botrytis wines that are similar to Sauternes in style.

BÂTARD-MONTRACHET France, Burgundy (AOC) This grand cru in the Côte de Beaune produces one of the greatest dry white wines in the world: full-bodied, intensely rich, masses of fruit.

BAYERISCHER BODENSEE LANDWEIN Germany (DL) One of 15 Deutscher Landwein appellations, its wines should be simple and light-bodied, with a basic flowery aroma, some grapey fruit and a touch of sweetness on the finish.

BAYERN Germany (DT) One of four vast Deutscher Tafelwein regions, Bayern is roughly equivalent to the Franken QbA region. These wines should be simple and light-bodied, with a basic flowery aroma, some grapey fruit and a touch of sweetness on the finish.

BÉARN France, Southwest France (AOC) Light, fresh reds, dry aromatic whites and floral-fruity dry rosés.

BEAUJOLAIS France, Burgundy (AOC) Mostly are boring red wines that taste and smell of peardrops, but some fresh and fruity dry rosé and a tiny amount of interesting dry white.

BEAUJOLAIS-VILLAGES France, Burgundy (AOC) Good producers tend to sell distinctly better wines under this appellation, whether simply labelled as Beaujolais-Villages or actually indicating one of the 38 villages permitted.

BEAUJOLAIS NOUVEAU France, Burgundy (AOC) Supposed to be a fun wine, but the merrymaking is wearing a bit thin for these red wines, which smell like nail-varnish and taste of bubble-gum. A quaffing white is sometimes produced and a dry rosé is theoretically possible.

BEAUJOLAIS PRIMEUR
France, Burgundy (AOC)
Synonymous with
Beaujolais Nouveau.

BEAUJOLAIS SUPÉRIEUR
France, Burgundy (AOC)
Nothing noticeably
superior.

BEAUNE France, Burgundy
(AOC) This village
appellation produces soft-
scented reds that have
gentle fruit. The whites are
less successful and
overpriced.

BEAUNE PREMIER CRU
France, Burgundy (AOC)
Not only a good step from
the village appellation for
the reds, but also the
whites, which at this level
are excellent, capable of
ageing and good value.

BECHTHEIM Germany,
Rheinhessen One of the
best villages in the
Rheinhessen. Top single-
vineyards: Bechtheimer
Geyersberg, Bechtheimer
Stein, Bechtheimer
Gotteshilfe.

BEERENAUSLESE
Germany (QbA) A sweet,
luscious botrytis wine that
comes between an Auslese
and Trockenbeerenauslese.

BELCHITE Spain, Aragon
(VC) Struggling to make the
grade.

BELLAVISTA Italy,
Lombardy Excellent, dry
sparkling wines.

BELLET France, Provence
(AOC) Exceptionally
fragrant red wines for such
a southerly area. The dry
whites and dry rosés are
firm, fine and aromatic.

BENAVENTE Spain,
Castilla-León (VC)
Struggling to make the
grade.

BENIARRÉS Spain, Murcia
(VC) Struggling to make the
grade.

BENSHEIM Germany,
Hessische Bergstrasse One

of the best villages in the
Hessische Bergstrasse. Top
single-vineyards:
Bensheimer Streichling.

BENSHEIM-SCHÖNBERG
Germany, Hessische
Bergstrasse One of the best
villages in the Hessische
Bergstrasse. Top single-
vineyards: Bensheimer
Herrnwingert.

BEREICH WINES
Germany Despite being
much larger than Germa-
ny's infamous *Grosslagen*,
the country's *Bereich* have a
much better reputation. All
Bereich wines must be
prefixed with the term
Bereich, making it
impossible to hoodwink the
public, consequently the
wines usually represent
good value and provide an
honest introduction to the
regions of Germany. Most
are basically fruity wines
with a medium or medium-
sweet flavour.
Walporzheim-Athral is
from Ahr and will be one of
the lightest *Bereich*;
**Rheinburgengau,
Bacharach** and
Siebengebirge are from the
Mittelrhein and will be
slightly richer, but still
fairly light-bodied; **Zell,
Bernkastel, Saar-Ruwer,
Obermosel** and **Moseltor**
are from the Mosel-Saar-
Ruwer and should have the
zippy, zingy, racy style this
region is famous for;
Kreuznach and **Schloss
Böckelheim** are from the
Nahe and will be light and
tangy with fine acidity;
Johannisberg is from the
Rheingau, where the
Riesling takes on the
flavour of peach; **Bingen,
Nierstein** and **Wonnegau**
are from the Rheinhessen,
which make the mildest
wines; while **Mittelhaardt
Deutsche Weinstrasse** and
Südliche Weinstrasse are
from the Rheinpfalz, where
the wines can be fat and
somewhat spicy;
Starkenburg and **Umstadt**

are from the Hessische
Bergstrasse, where the
wines are as mild as
Rheinhessen, but a touch
drier, although not as dry as
Franken's **Steigerwald,
Maindreieck** and
Mainviereck or
Württemberg's **Remstal-
Stuttgart, Württembergisch
Unterland, Kocher-Jagst-
Tauber, Oberer Neckar,
Württembergisch
Bodensee** and **Bayerischer
Bodensee**; while Baden's
**Badisches Frankenland,
Badische Bergstrasse-
Kraichgau, Ortenau,
Breisgau, Kaiserstuhl-
Tuniberg, Markgraflerland**
and **Bodensee** can be just as
dry, but are usually richer
and fuller due to the sunny
southern clime.

BERGERAC France,
Southwest France (AOC)
Good value, medium-
bodied Bordeaux look-alike
reds and attractive, light,
dry rosés.

BERGERAC SEC France,
Southwest France (AOC)
Dry Bordeaux style white
wine.

BERGKLOSTER Germany,
Rheinhessen If you see this
name following that of a
village on a bottle of
Rheinhessen, it is only a
Grosslage wine.

BERLUCCHI Italy,
Lombardy Excellent, dry
sparkling wines.

BERNKASTEL Germany,
Mosel-Saar-Ruwer One of
the best villages in the MSR.
Top single-vineyards:
Bernkasteler Doctor,
Bernkasteler Lay,
Bernkasteler Kardinalsberg.

**BIANCHELLO DEL
METAURO** Italy, Marches
(DOC) Delicate but
uninspiring dry white wine.

BIANCO ALCAMO Italy,
Sicily (DOC) Synonymous
with Alcamo.

BIANCO CAPENA Italy,
Latium (DOC) Uninspiring

dry and semi-sweet white wines from northeast of Rome.

BIANCO DEI COLLI MACERATESI Italy, Marches (DOC) Boring dry white wine.

BIANCO DEL MOLISE Italy, Molise (VT) The basic dry white of the region is best left where it is.

BIANCO DELL'EMPOLESE Italy, Tuscany (DOC) Dry white and vino santo of little interest.

BIANCO DELLA VAL DI NIEVOLE Italy, Tuscany (DOC) Dry, slightly fizzy white wine. Also made in vino santo style.

BIANCO DI CUSTOZA Italy, Veneto (DOC) Smooth, scented, dry white and sparkling wines.

BIANCO DI OSTUNI Italy, Apulia (DOC) Synonymous with Ostuni.

BIANCO DI PITIGLIANO Italy, Tuscany (DOC) Delicate dry white of some character.

BIANCO DI SCANDIANO Italy, Emilia-Romagna (DOC) Full-bodied dry and semi-sweet white wines that may also be sparkling or semi-sparkling.

BIANCO PISANO DI SAN TORPÉ Italy, Tuscany (DOC) Dry white wine and dry or sweet vino santo of no special interest.

BIANCO TOARA Italy, Veneto (VT) Dry, scented white wine, but not special.

BIANCO VERGINE DELLA VALDICHIANA Italy, Tuscany (DOC) Slightly sweet white wines with a bitter-sweet finish.

BICKENSOHL Germany, Baden One of the best villages in Baden. Top single-vineyards: Bickensohler Steinfelsen.

BIENVENUES-BÂTARD-MONTRACHET France,

Burgundy (AOC) Lighter-bodied version of Bâtard-Montrachet.

BIERZO Spain, Castilla-León (DO) This is one of Spain's more exciting new appellations, capable of producing aromatic reds of distinctive character. Whites and rosés also show promise.

BIFERNO Italy, Molise (DOC) Slightly tannic red, lightly aromatic, dry white and fruity dry rosé.

BINGEN Germany, Rheinhessen One of the best villages in the Rheinhessen. Top single-vineyards: Binger Kirchberg.

BINGEN-KEMPTEN Germany, Rheinhessen One of the best villages in the Rheinhessen. Top single-vineyards: Binger Kappellenberg, Binger Schlossberg-Schwätzerchen.

BINGEN-RÜDESHEIM Germany, Rheinhessen One of the best villages in the Rheinhessen. Top single-vineyards: Binger Scharlachberg, Binger Bubenstück, Binger Rosengarten.

BIRKWEILER Germany, Rheinpfalz One of the best villages in the Rheinpfalz. Top single-vineyards: Birkweiler Kastanienbusch.

BISCHOFSKREUZ Germany, Rheinpfalz If you see this name following that of a village on a bottle of Rheinpfalz, it is only a *Grosslage* wine.

BLAGNY France, Burgundy (AOC) Underrated red wine from vineyards overlapping the villages of Meursault and Puligny-Montrachet in the Côte de Beaune.

BLAGNY-CÔTE DE BEAUNE France, Burgundy (AOC) Synonymous with Blagny.

BLAGNY PREMIER CRU France, Burgundy (AOC)

Firmer, more intense version of the basic village wine.

BLANC DE COSSAN Italy, Valle d'Aosta (VT) Fresh, tart blanc de noirs.

BLANC FUMÉ DE POUILLY France, Loire (AOC) Synonymous with Pouilly-Fumé.

BLANC FUMÉ DE POUILLY-SUR-LOIRE France, Loire (AOC) Synonymous with Pouilly-Fumé.

BLANQUETTE DE LIMOUX France, Southwest France (AOC) Sparkling dry white wine with a distinctive, fresh-mown grass character.

BLANQUETTE MÉTHODE ANCESTRALE France, Southwest France (AOC) The first recorded sparkling wine produced in France was a rarity even locally, under its previous AOC Vin de Blanquette, but could become commercially available under its new appellation.

BLANSINGEN Germany, Baden One of the best villages in Baden. Top single-vineyards: Blansinger Wolfer.

BLAUFRÄNKISCH Italy, Friuli-Venezia Giulia (VT) Synonymous with Franconia.

BLAYAIS France, Bordeaux (AOC) Synonymous with Blaye.

BLAYE France, Bordeaux (AOC) Large and diverse appellation of variable quality red and dry white wines, but the best are great value.

BOAL Portugal, Madeira (DOC) Also known as Bual, this is the second-sweetest style of Madeira and has a distinctive baked character with a smoky complexity.

BOCA Italy, Piedmont (DOC) Medium to full,

spicy red wine made from the Nebbiolo grape of Barolo fame.

BODENHEIM Germany, Rheinhessen One of the best villages in the Rheinhessen. Top single-vineyards: Bodenheimer Hoch, Bodenheimer Silberberg, Bodenheimer Westrum.

BOLGHERI Italy, Tuscany (DOC) Delicate, dry white wine and slightly scented rosé of no particular interest.

BONNES MARES France, Burgundy (AOC) Rich-flavoured red wine grand cru of fabulous finesse from the village of Chambolle-Musigny in the Côte de Nuits.

BONNEZEAUX France, Loire (AOC) Full, rich, intensely sweet white wines that lean towards Sauternes in style, but have higher acidity.

BOPPARD HAMM Germany, Mittelrhein One of the best villages in the Mittelrhein. Top single-vineyards: Bopparder Hamm Ohlenberg, Bopparder Hamm Fässerlay.

BORBA Portugal, Alentejo (IPR) Lots of white wine, most of which is ordinary, but the reds are full, fruity and rapidly improving.

BORDEAUX France, Bordeaux (AOC) Lowest Bordeaux appellation for red, dry white and rosé. Some can be interesting, but most are simple, light-bodied and cheap.

BORDEAUX-CÔTES-DE-FRANCS France, Bordeaux (AOC) Rustic reds from an almost forgotten corner of Bordeaux, their robust style is usually softened by a high Merlot content.

BORDEAUX-CÔTES-DE-FRANCS LIQUOREUX France, Bordeaux (AOC)

Very little of this sweet, rich and luscious white is made.

BORDEAUX CLAIRET France, Bordeaux (AOC) Betwixt and between red and rosé, mostly inexpensive, but seldom seen. Look out for Quinsac, the best Clairet village, at the bottom of the label.

BORDEAUX HAUT-BENAUGE France, Bordeaux (AOC) Light-bodied white wines made in dry, medium-sweet and sweet style, from an area between the Entre-Deux-Mers and Premières-Côtes-de-Bordeaux.

BORDEAUX MOUSSEUX France, Bordeaux (AOC) Unexciting white and rosé fizz.

BORDEAUX ROSÉ France, Bordeaux (AOC) Good value dry rosé.

BORDEAUX SEC France, Bordeaux (AOC) Good, bad and ugly dry white, often Sauvignon-dominated.

BORDEAUX SUPÉRIEUR France, Bordeaux (AOC) Red and white wines that are superior to basic Bordeaux by half a degree of alcohol.

BORDEAUX SUPÉRIEUR CLAIRET France, Bordeaux (AOC) Seldom seen, medium-dry red-cum-rosé wine, superior to Bordeaux Clairet by half a degree of alcohol.

BORDEAUX SUPÉRIEUR CÔTES-DE-FRANCS France, Bordeaux (AOC) Half a degree more alcohol than the basic Bordeaux-Côtes-de-Francs.

BORDEAUX SUPÉRIEUR ROSÉ France, Bordeaux (AOC) Full, rich, dry and fruity rosé, of which Rosé des Lascombes is the best.

BORGO AMOROSA Italy, Tuscany (VT) One of Italy's very best pure Sangiovese wines.

BOTTICINO Italy, Lombardy (DOC) Full-bodied Barbera-based red wine that can be of interest.

BÖTZINGEN Germany, Baden One of the best villages in Baden. Top single-vineyards: Bötzinger Lasenberg.

BOURG France, Bordeaux (AOC) Synonymous with Côtes de Bourg.

BOURGEAIS France, Bordeaux (AOC) Synonymous with Côtes de Bourg.

BOURGOGNE France, Burgundy (AOC) The basic Burgundy appellation for red, dry white and dry rosé wine can be very good value, especially for the reds, when chosen from a top grower or quality-conscious *négociant*.

BOURGOGNE-ALIGOTÉ France, Burgundy (AOC) Dry, thin white wines with a sharp, acid bite.

BOURGOGNE ALIGOTÉ BOUZERON France, Burgundy (AOC) Only when it is from the village of Bouzeron can Aligoté be a full and rich dry white wine with plenty of spicy fruit.

BOURGOGNE CLAIRET France, Burgundy (AOC) Rarely encountered red-cum-rosé.

BOURGOGNE CLAIRET HAUTES-CÔTES DE BEAUNE France, Burgundy (AOC) Seldom seen red-cum-rosé from an area behind the true Côte de Beaune.

BOURGOGNE CLAIRET HAUTES-CÔTES DE NUITS France, Burgundy (AOC) Seldom seen appellation for basic red-cum-rosé wine restricted to the Hautes-Côtes de Nuits.

BOURGOGNE CÔTE CHALONNAISE France, Burgundy (AOC) Basic red, dry white and dry rosé. Often good value.

BOURGOGNE CÔTE D'AUXERROIS France, Burgundy (AOC) Basic red, dry white and dry rosé wines from the Chablis district.

BOURGOGNE COULANGES-LA-VINEUSE France, Burgundy (AOC) Unpretentious red wine from the Chablis district.

BOURGOGNE EPINEUIL France, Burgundy (AOC) Red, dry white and dry rosé wines of modest quality from the Chablis district.

BOURGOGNE GRAND-ORDINAIRE France, Burgundy (AOC) As its name suggests, these red and white wines are very ordinary in quality.

BOURGOGNE GRAND-ORDINAIRE CLAIRET France, Burgundy (AOC) Very ordinary red-cum-rosé.

BOURGOGNE HAUTES-CÔTES DE BEAUNE France, Burgundy (AOC) Commonly encountered, good value red, dry white and dry rosé wines from an area behind the true Côte de Beaune.

BOURGOGNE HAUTES-CÔTES DE NUITS France, Burgundy (AOC) Good value, medium-bodied red, but somewhat hefty whites.

BOURGOGNE IRANCY France, Burgundy (AOC) Overrated red wine from the Chablis district.

BOURGOGNE MOUSSEUX France, Burgundy (AOC) Sparkling red wine.

BOURGOGNE ORDINAIRE France, Burgundy (AOC) Synonymous with Bourgogne Grand Ordinaire.

BOURGOGNE ORDINAIRE CLAIRET France, Burgundy (AOC) Synonymous with Bourgogne Grand Ordinaire Clairet.

BOURGOGNE PASSETOUTGRAINS France, Burgundy (AOC) A blend of Gamay and Pinot Noir, made in red or rosé, the best of which are interesting to keep for 2-6 years, but few are special.

BOURGUEIL France, Loire (AOC) Depending where the vines are grown, red Bourgueil can vary from delicious, quaffing style wines that are best drunk young to fuller-bodied, more concentrated wines that definitely repay keeping. The big secret here is that Bourgueil produces one of the best dry rosés in France.

BOZNER LEITEN Italy, Trentino-Alto Adige (QbA) Synonymous with Colli di Bolzano.

BRACHETTO Italy, Piedmont (DOC) Beware: sweet, semi-sparkling and fully sparkling versions of this grapey, Muscat-like red wine exist. Brachetto d'Acqui, Brachetto d'Alba and Brachetto d'Asti can be found.

BRAMATERRA Italy, Piedmont (DOC) Full-bodied red wines that can be interesting if cheap.

BRAUBACH Germany, Mittelrhein One of the best villages in the Mittelrhein. Top single-vineyards: Braubacher Marmorberg.

BRAUNEBERG Germany, Mosel-Saar-Ruwer One of the best villages in the MSR. Top single-vineyards: Brauneberger Juffer, Brauneberger Juffer Sonnenuhr.

BREGANZE Italy, Veneto (DOC) Interesting, but not exciting red and white wines, except for the superb Prato di Canzio and a couple of Bordeaux-blends, which rank amongst the best in Italy.

BRENTINO Italy, Veneto (VT) One of Italy's best Cabernet-based blends.

BRETANZOS Spain, Galicia (VC) Struggling to make the grade.

BRICCO DEL DRAGO Italy, Piedmont (VT) Well-made red wine blend of Dolcetto and Nebbiolo.

BRICCO MANZONI Italy, Piedmont (VT) This deep-coloured, full-bodied, richly-flavoured red wine blend of Dolcetto and Nebbiolo has more class than the Drago.

BRINDISI Italy, Apulia (DOC) Smooth reds and light fruity rosés.

BROUILLY France, Burgundy (AOC) Although this is the least exciting of the ten top-quality Beaujolais cru villages, Brouilly is nonetheless capable of full, fruity and supple red wines that are a million miles away from the peardrop and bubble-gum Beaujolais Nouveau.

BRUNELLO DI MONTALCINO Italy, Tuscany (DOCG) One of Italy's most prestigious wines, made from the Brunello, a localised clone of Sangiovese, but only the best deserve their reputation, otherwise you are better off paying much less for a Rosso di Montalcino.

BRUNO DI ROCCA Italy, Tuscany (VT) One of the very best Franco-Italian grape blends.

BUAL Portugal, Madeira (DOC) See Boal.

BUÇACO Portugal, Beiras (IPR) If you want to buy any of this wine, you will have to visit the Palace Hotel at Buáaco near Coimbra. The hotel actually produces these amazing red and white wines and offers an incredible range of vintages to customers of its restaurant. The white is more interesting than enjoyable, but the red makes Buáaco one of Portugal's greatest wines.

BUCELAS Portugal, Bucelas (DOC) Overrated, excruciatingly dry, very acidic, fruitless white wine from an area of immense potential.

BULGARIA A country that has already provided the UK with Bulgarian Cabernet Sauvignon, a best-selling generic red wine sold at next to nothing, since when more individual wines have come onto the market, indicating an exciting future, particularly for reds.

BULLAS Spain, Murcia (VdlT) Variable quality country wines that fluctuate from dismal to good and promising.

BURG Germany, Franken If you see this name following that of a village on a bottle of Franken, it is only a *Grosslage* wine.

BURG HAMMERSTEIN Germany, Mittelrhein If you see this name following that of a village on a bottle of Mittelrhein, it is only a *Grosslage* wine.

BURG LICHTENECK Germany, Baden If you see this name following that of a village on a bottle of Baden, it is only a *Grosslage* wine.

BURG NEUENFELS Germany, Baden If you see this name following that of a village on a bottle of Baden, it is only a *Grosslage* wine.

BURG RHEINFELS Germany, Mittelrhein If you see this name following that of a village on a bottle of Mittelrhein, it is only a *Grosslage* wine.

BURG RODENSTEIN Germany, Rheinhessen If you see this name following that of a village on a bottle of Rheinhessen, it is only a *Grosslage* wine.

BURG ZÄHRINGEN Germany, Baden If you see this name following that of a village on a bottle of

Baden, it is only a *Grosslage* wine.

BURGENGAU Germany (DT) One of eight Deutscher Tafelwein sub-regions, its wines should be simple and light-bodied, with a basic flowery aroma, some grapey fruit and a touch of sweetness on the finish.

BURGWEG Germany, Nahe If you see this name following that of a village on a bottle of Nahe, it is only a *Grosslage* wine.

BURGWEG Germany, Franken If you see this name following that of a village on a bottle of Franken, it is only a *Grosslage* wine.

BURGWEG Germany, Rheingau If you see this name following that of a village on a bottle of Rheingau, it is only a *Grosslage* wine.

BURKHEIM Germany, Baden One of the best villages in Baden. Top single-vineyards: Burkheimer Schlossgarten.

BUZZETTO DI QUILIANO Italy, Liguria (VT) Lacklustre dry white from the Buzzetto, which is the local name for the ubiquitous Trebbiano.

CA'DEL BOSCO Italy, Lombardy Excellent, dry sparkling wines.

CABARDES France, Languedoc-Roussillon (VDQS) Some elegant reds and dry rosés are possible.

CABERNET D'ANJOU France, Loire (AOC) A medium-sweet rosé that is a smidgen better than Rosé d'Anjou, it demands a premium for having the word Cabernet on the label.

CABERNET DE SAUMUR France, Loire (AOC) If you must have a medium-sweet rosé, this is the preferred

appellation, the best wines having a more delicate, more refined character.

CABERNET FRANC (Grape) Compared to Cabernet Sauvignon, the Franc is commonly perceived as having a greener, grassier style with more raspberry, less blackcurrant in the fruit, but this is a typically Loire-based view. The differences are much less marked in Bordeaux and, when grown in the New World, Cabernet Franc can be positively lush.

CABERNET SAUVIGNON (Grape) The noblest variety of Bordeaux, although you will rarely find a Bordeaux wine made purely from Cabernet Sauvignon. This grape has a greater ability than any other variety to transplant its essential characteristics in the wines it produces around the world. Great Cabernet Sauvignon can be made in every New World country, not to mention the great value wines, which stretch much further, with Bulgaria showing us just a glimpse of what the future could hold if winemaking can be modernised throughout central and southeastern Europe.

CABREO PODERE IL BORGO Italy, Tuscany (VT) One of Italy's best Sangiovese-dominated blends.

CABREO VIGNETO LA PIETRA Italy, Tuscany (VT) One of Italy's best pure Chardonnay wines.

CACC'E MMITTE DI LUCERA Italy, Apulia (DOC) This loosely means 'knock it back', which adequately sums up this full-bodied red wine.

CADILLAC France, Bordeaux (AOC) Least-known appellation in the Premières-Côtes-de Bordeaux, Cadillac is a honey-gold wine with attractive floral fruit and may be sweet or semi-sweet in style.

CAGNINA DI ROMAGNA Italy, Emilia-Romagna (DOC) This sweet, fruity red wine has recently been upgraded to DOC.

CAHORS France, Southwest France (AOC) No longer the 'black wine' of legendary fame, but deep-coloured nonetheless, with blackcurrant fruit and a silky-violetty aftertaste.

CALATAYUD Spain, Aragón (DO) New DO, which means the producers should be trying hard, but no guarantees.

CALDARO Italy, Trentino-Alto Adige (DOC) Soft, fruity reds.

CALUSO PASSITO Italy, Piedmont (DOC) Sweet white wine with lots of body, although most have a little elegance.

CAMPIDANO DI TERRALBA Italy, Sardinia (DOC) Soft, full-bodied reds.

CAMPO DE BORJA Spain, Aragón (DO) The name derives from the notorious Borgia family, which used to run things in this part of Spain in the late-fifteenth century. The history is, however, more interesting than the big, alcoholic red and rosé wines that are made here today.

CAMPO DE CARTAGENA Spain, Murcia (VdlT) Country wines that have yet to make their mark.

CAMPO ROMANO Italy, Piedmont (VT) This semi-sparkling red wine has plenty of fruit, but it is something of an acquired taste.

CAÑAMERO Spain, Extremadura (VdlT) Country wines that have yet to make their mark.

CANDIA DEI COLLI APUANI Italy, Tuscany (DOC) Dry and semi-sweet white wines of no special quality.

CANNETO Italy, Lombardy (VT) Various red wines with a bitter aftertaste.

CANNONAU DI SARDEGNA Italy, Sardinia (DOC) These dry, semi-sweet or sweet red, white, rosé and *liquoroso* wines are as variable in quality as they are in character, but you can find some gems.

CANON-FRONSAC France, Bordeaux (AOC) Synonymous with Côtes-Canon-Fronsac.

CAPANELLE ROSSO Italy, Tuscany (VT) One of Italy's very best pure Sangiovese wines.

CAPO DEL MONTE Italy, Veneto (VT) One of the country's best Franco-Italian grape blends.

CAPRI Italy, Campania (DOC) Easy going, medium-bodied red that is mostly consumed on the island.

CAPRIANO DEL COLLE Italy, Lombardy (DOC) Tart white wine and an interesting but rarely encountered red made from the Sangiovese blended with Marzemino, Barbera and Merlot.

CARAMINO Italy, Piedmont (VT) An up and coming red wine of some style and finesse from the Nebbiolo grape.

CARCAVELOS Portugal, Carcavelos (DOC) Some examples can be delicate and nutty, but they are overrated and grossly overpriced.

CAREMA Italy, Piedmont (DOC) Soft, reliable medium-bodied red from the Nebbiolo.

CARIGNANO DEL SULCIS Italy, Sardinia

(DOC) Smooth red and dry rosé of no repute.

CARIÑENA Spain, Aragón (DO) Pungent, fruity, aromatic reds and white, rosé and fortified wines of extremely rustic style.

CARMIGNANO Italy, Tuscany (DOCG) Essentially a Chianti beefed up by Cabernet, the success of this wine not only forced a similar change of grape content to improve Chianti proper, but won Carmignano its precious DOCG status.

CARSO Italy, Friuli-Venezia Giulia (DOC) Full red wine and rich, spicy, dry white.

CARTAXO Portugal, Ribatejo (IPR) Lots of white wine, most of which is ordinary, but the reds are full, fruity and rapidly improving.

CASSIS France, Provence (AOC) The reds are quite good, but overpriced. The dry whites have interesting aromas, but are flabby and quickly tire. The dry rosés are of moderate interest.

CASTEL DEL MONTE Italy, Apulia (DOC) This appellation produces the best red wines of Apulia, particularly when *riserva*, albeit in restricted numbers. The whites are not special, but Italians are rather partial to the rosé.

CASTEL MITRANO Italy, Apulia (VT) Austere, tannic red wines.

CASTEL SAN MICHELE Italy, Trentino-Alto Adige (VT) One of Italy's best Cabernet-based blends.

CASTELL Germany, Franken One of the best villages in Franken. Top single-vineyards: Casteller Schlossberg, Casteller Kugelspiel, Casteller Hohnart, Casteller Kirchberg.

CASTELLER Italy, Trentino-Alto Adige (DOC)

Dry and semi-sweet red and rosé wines for everyday drinking.

CASTELLI ROMANI Italy, Latium (VT) Red, rosé and dry or semi-sweet white wines.

CASTELLO DI MONTORO Italy, Umbria (VT) One of the very best Franco-Italian grape blends.

CASTELLO DI RONCADE Italy, Veneto (VT) One of Italy's best Cabernet-based blends.

CASTELO RODRIGO Portugal, Beiras (IPR) From the Beira Alta, between the Vinho Verde and Dão districts, where every style of wine is produced in varying quality.

CAVA Spain (DO) Light-bodied, mild flavoured white and rosé sparkling wine with a soft finish.

CEBREROS Spain, Castilla-León (VdlT) These country wines are mostly from the Garnacha or Grenache and are destined to achieve full DO status one day.

CECUBO Italy, Latium (VT) Deep-coloured, sturdy reds of rustic charm.

CELLATICA Italy, Lombardy (DOC) Aromatic and flavoursome red wine with a slightly bitter aftertaste.

CEPARELLO Italy, Tuscany (VT) One of Italy's very best pure Sangiovese wines.

CERASUOLO DI SCILLA Italy, Calabria (VT) Dry and semi-sweet, cherry coloured red wine of no particular interest.

CERASUOLO DI VITTORIA Italy, Sicily (DOC) Simple, cherry-coloured red wine.

CÉRONS France, Bordeaux (AOC) Lighter than neighbouring Barsac, but often just as luscious and always less expensive.

CERVETERI Italy, Latium (DOC) Rustic reds, dry and semi-sweet wines of ordinary quality.

CESANESE DEL PIGLIO Italy, Latium (DOC) A complicated range of red wines, including dry, off-dry, medium-dry, semi-sweet and sweet styles of still, slightly fizzy, semi-sparkling and sparkling wine.

CESANESE DI AFFILE Italy, Latium (DOC) As above but from a different area.

CESANESE DI OLEVANO ROMANO Italy, Latium (DOC) As above but from a different area again.

CHABLIS France, Burgundy (AOC) Should be a dry white, with crisp fruit, but you have to search high and low for good wines within the basic Chablis appellation.

CHABLIS GRAND CRU France, Burgundy (AOC) This is the appellation under which all the greatest Chablis is to be found, but many producers rest on their laurels, so you can also get some rubbish.

CHABLIS PREMIER CRU France, Burgundy (AOC) If you taste enough wines, this is the appellation where you can find best value Chablis.

CHAMBAVE Italy, Valle d'Aosta (DOC) Red, dry white and sparkling wines that are well made, but of only modest quality, except for the dry and sweet *passito* styles of Moscato (sometimes labelled Muscat), which can be utterly sublime.

CHAMBERTIN France, Burgundy (AOC) Full-bodied, yet exquisitely balanced red wine grand cru from the village of Gevrey-Chambertin in the Côte de Nuits.

CHAMBERTIN-CLOS DE BÈZE France, Burgundy (AOC) Not quite as full-bodied as Chambertin, though possibly with more finesse, this red grand cru also comes from the village of Gevrey-Chambertin in the Côte de Nuits.

CHAMBOLLE-MUSIGNY France, Burgundy (AOC) Great finesse for a mere village red wine from the Côte de Nuits.

CHAMBOLLE-MUSIGNY PREMIER CRU France, Burgundy (AOC) Seductive and fragrant red wines.

CHAMPAGNE France, Champagne (AOC) Without question the greatest sparkling wine in the world when produced with care, but beware of the cheapest Champagnes sold in French supermarkets – it's mostly rubbish!

CHAMUSCA Portugal, Ribatejo (IPR) Lots of white wine, most of which is ordinary, but the reds are full, fruity and rapidly improving.

CHAPELLE-CHAMBERTIN France, Burgundy (AOC) Relatively light-bodied red wine grand cru of delightful bouquet and flavour from the village of Gevrey-Chambertin in the Côte de Nuits.

CHARDONNAY (Grape) Simply the greatest dry white wine grape in the world, the Chardonnay is the classic white Burgundy grape, capable of outstanding performance in many countries, particularly California, Australia and New Zealand, you pays your money and takes your choice.

CHARLEMAGNE France, Burgundy (AOC) Grand cru producing great dry white from an almost, but not quite, identical vineyard as Corton-Charlemagne in the Côte de Beaune.

CHARMES-CHAMBERTIN France, Burgundy (AOC) Soft and sumptuous red wine grand cru from the village of Gevrey-Chambertin in the Côte de Nuits.

CHASSAGNE-MONTRACHET France, Burgundy (AOC) This village is more famous for its red than white, although both represent affordable introductions to the greater wines of Montrachet.

CHASSAGNE-MONTRACHET-CÔTE DE BEAUNE France, Burgundy (AOC) Synonymous with Chassagne-Montrachet.

CHASSAGNE-MONTRACHET PREMIER CRU France, Burgundy (AOC) Dry, flavoursome whites and excellent reds that have the weight of a Côte de Nuits and the softness of a Côte de Beaune.

CHASSELAS France, Alsace (AOC) A light, fresh, delicate dry white wine that was once considered too common to be bottled in its pure form, but has been making something of a comeback.

CHÂTEAU-CHALON France, Jura (AOC) The best and longest-lived of 'yellow wines' (see **Arbois Vin Jaune**).

CHÂTEAU GRILLET France, Rhône Valley (AOC) A world-famous dry white wine that has great finesse and drinks well up to about eight years of age, yet has not achieved its full potential.

CHÂTEAUMEILLANT France, Loire (VDQS) Light yet firm reds and fresh, grapey rosés grown on volcanic soils.

CHÂTEAUNEUF-DU-PAPE France, Rhône Valley (AOC) Famous wines that ranging from full-bodied reds of truly great quality

that are rich in warm, spicy fruit and mostly come from individual estates, to simple, medium-bodied reds that are neither better nor worse, than a cheap, honest Côtes-du-Rhône. A small number of estates are now producing fine, dry white wines that are much more than mere curiosities, but watch out: many famous estates continue to make overblown, oxidised and flabby dry whites.

CHÂTILLON-EN-DIOIS France, Rhône Valley (AOC) Light, thin reds and fuller, somewhat more characterful dry whites. Rosés possible.

CHAVES Portugal, Trás-os-Montes (IPR) Part of the former appellation of Trás-os-Montes, which has always been famous for it slightly fizzy pink wines, such as Mateus and Trovador.

CHÉNAS France, Burgundy (AOC) Full and seductively rich red wine from one to ten top-quality cru Beaujolais.

CHENIN BLANC (Grape) Traditional grape of the Loire, where it can produce sublime sweet wines, especially in Vouvray, Montlouis and the Coteaux du Layon appellations. It is less adept at dry styles unless it is grown somewhere special, such as Savennières, and is in the hands of a genius like Jean Baumard, otherwise far too much thin, washed-out, rubbishy Chenin Blanc is produced in all styles throughout the Loire. Some New World examples can be brimming with tropical fruit flavour.

CHEVALIER-MONTRACHET France, Burgundy (AOC) Big, rich and dry white wines with more explosive flavour than Bâtard-Montrachet.

CHEVERNY France, Loire (VDQS) A unique appellation that comprises red, white and rosé wines in both still and sparkling styles. Most generally light, lively and tasty.

CHIANTI Italy, Tuscany (DOGC) Most of the most expensive Chianti is great Italian wine, but that's a minuscule fraction of the Chianti produced, most of which is no better than vin ordinaire.

CHILE Once a source of good value reds, particularly Cabernet Sauvignon, now becoming known for white wines, especially Chardonnay and the steadily improving Sauvignon; although there is still a lot of boring wine sold under this grape that has no Sauvignon in it at all – for true Sauvignon, try Montes.

CHINON France, Loire (AOC) Fine quality medium-bodied red wines.

CHIROUBLES France, Burgundy (AOC) Light-bodied, fragrantly fruity red wine from one to ten top-quality cru Beaujolais.

CHOREY-LÈS-BEAUNE France, Burgundy (AOC) Exciting, underrated reds from a village between Beaune and Aloxe-Corton. One per cent of the production is white.

CHOREY-LÈS-BEAUNE CÔTE DE BEAUNE France, Burgundy (AOC) Synonymous with Chorey-lès-Beaune.

CIGALES Spain, Castilla-León (DO) New DO, which means the producers should be trying hard, but no guarantees.

CILENTO Italy, Campania (DOC) Various dry, semi-sweet, still and sparkling red and rosé wines made from the Primitivo or Zinfandel grape that were upgraded to DOC status in 1989.

CILLEROS Spain, Extramadura (VC) Struggling to make the grade.

CINQUE TERRE Italy, Liguria (DOC) Delicate dry white wine.

CINQUE TERRE SCIACCHETRA Italy, Liguria (DOC) Medium-sweet *passito* white wine.

CIRO Italy, Calabria (DOC) Strong, alcoholic red, white and rosé wines that were famous in antiquity when, hopefully, they were better than they are now.

CLAIRETTE DE BELLEGARDE France, Languedoc-Roussillon (AOC) Dry whites that are mostly dull and boring.

CLAIRETTE DE DIE France, Rhône Valley (AOC) Not to be confused with Clairette de Die Tradition, this is a boring, dry sparkling white wine.

CLAIRETTE DE DIE DEMI-SEC France, Rhône Valley (AOC) Synonymous with Clairette de Die Tradition.

CLAIRETTE DE DIE MOUSSEUX France, Rhône Valley (AOC) Synonymous with Clairette de Die.

CLAIRETTE DE DIE TRADITION France, Rhône Valley (AOC) The thinking man's Asti.

CLAIRETTE DU LANGUEDOC France, Languedoc-Roussillon (AOC) Dull dry whites and resinous medium-sweet fortified wines, including the infamous 'rancio' style, can be found under this appellation.

CLEEBRONN Germany, Württemberg One of the best villages in Württemberg. Top single-vineyards: Cleebronner Michaelsberg.

CLEVNER France, Alsace (AOC) Synonymous with Pinot Blanc.

CLOS DE BÈZE France, Burgundy (AOC) Synonymous with Chambertin-Clos de Bèze.

CLOS DE LA ROCHE France, Burgundy (AOC) Red wine grand cru of deep colour, powerful structure and yet silky texture, from the village of Morey-St-Denis in the Côte de Nuits.

CLOS DE TART France, Burgundy (AOC) Red wine grand cru with penetrating Pinot flavour and fine, spicy-vanilla undertones from the village of Morey-St-Denis in the Côte de Nuits.

CLOS DE VOUGEOT France, Burgundy (AOC) From the village of Vosne-Romanée in the Côte de Nuits, Clos de Vougeot is indubitably the most inconsistent grand cru in Burgundy. This is due, however, to its ownership by no less than 85 different growers of varying degrees of competence. When made by the likes of Drouhin-Laroze, Mugneret, Gros, Rebourseau and others, Clos du Vougeot is indisputably one of Burgundy's greatest wines.

CLOS DES LAMBRAYS France, Burgundy (AOC) Red grand cru from the village of Morey-St-Denis; relatively young vines, just beginning to show their class with the 1990 vintage.

CLOS ST-DENIS France, Burgundy (AOC) Red wine grand cru of firm, fine, intense flavours from the village of Morey-St-Denis in the Côte de Nuits.

CLOS VOUGEOT France, Burgundy (AOC) Synonymous with Clos de Vougeot.

COLARES Portugal, Colares (DOC) Austere, long-lived red wines grown in sand dunes.

COLHEITA PORT Portugal, Douro (DOC) These are Fine Old Tawnies, but with a vintage date. Many are excellent value, but beware, some are not the pure vintage they claim to be.

COLLE DEL CALVARIO Italy, Lombardy (VT) Well-structured red wine of excellent longevity and value, the white is refreshingly fresh and fruity.

COLLE PICCHIONI Italy, Latium (VT) Robust and characterful red made from French and Italian grape varieties.

COLLI ALBANI Italy, Latium (DOC) Soft and fruity, dry and semi-sweet white wines that may be still or sparkling.

COLLI ALTOTIBERINI Italy, Umbria (DOC) Interesting dry whites, firm but fruity Sangiovese-Merlot reds and light-bodied rosés.

COLLI AMERINI Italy, Umbria (DOC) Red and rosé from the Sangiovese and dry white from Trebbiano and Vermentino, these wines have yet to make their mark.

COLLI BERICI Italy, Veneto (DOC) Several red and white varietal wines, of which the rich, chunky Cabernet is best; the superb La Rive Rose ranks as one of the best Italian Cabernet-based blends.

COLLI BOLOGNESE Italy, Emilia-Romagna (DOC) Some interesting red and dry white varietal wines.

COLLI DEL TRASIMENO Italy, Umbria (DOC) Dry and off-dry whites of lacklustre quality, the Sangiovese Gamay reds offer more interest.

COLLI DI BOLZANO Italy, Trentino-Alto Adige (DOC) Soft, fruity reds.

COLLI DI LUNI Italy, Liguria (DOC) Well made red and dry white wines.

COLLI DI PARMA Italy, Emilia-Romagna (DOC) Slightly fizzy red wines and two varietal dry whites, Sauvignon and Malvasia.

COLLI EUGANEI Italy, Veneto (DOC) Of the several blended and varietal red and white wines, the basic red blend is best.

COLLI GORIZIANO Italy, Friuli-Venezia Giulia (DOC) Excellent red and dry white varietal wines, plus an interesting, slightly sparkling, blended white.

COLLI LANUVINI Italy, Latium (DOC) Smooth whites that may be dry or semi-sweet, but seldom interesting.

COLLI MARTANI Italy, Umbria (DOC) Relatively new DOC (1989) covering three varietal wines: Grechetto and Trebbiano for dry white and Sangiovese for red.

COLLI MORENICI MANTOVANI DEL GARDA Italy, Lombardy (DOC) Red, dry white and dry rosé of little interest.

COLLI ORIENTALI DEL FRIULI Italy, Friuli-Venezia Giulia (DOC) With the exception of Picolit, which is famous, but overrated and overpriced, these red and white varietal wines are of an even higher quality than those of Collio Goriziano. The Ronco del Gmeniz ranks as one of the best Bordeaux-type blends in the country.

COLLI PERUGINI Italy, Umbria (DOC) Light, dry whites, full-bodied reds and fresh rosés of minimal interest.

COLLI PIACENTINI Italy, Emilia-Romagna (DOC) A wide range of red and white wine styles: dry, semi-sweet and sweet, and still, slightly fizzy, semi-sparkling and

fully sparkling. Variable quality.

COLLI TORTONESI Italy, Piedmont (DOC) Robust, rustic reds and crisp, dry whites that can also be semi-sparkling.

COLLINE DI AMA Italy, Tuscany (VT) One of Italy's best pure Chardonnay wines.

COLLINE LUCCHESI Italy, Tuscany (DOC) Soft, Chianti-like reds and simple dry whites.

COLLIO Italy, Friuli-Venezia Giulia (DOC) Synonymous with Collio Goriziano.

COLLIOURE France, Languedoc-Roussillon (AOC) Obscure but exciting appellation for powerful, but unfortified, red wines made from early-harvested Banyuls grapes.

COLOMBARD (Grape) Once considered fit for nothing more than distillation, the Colombard now makes fresh, tangy white wine in southwest France. Its high acidity also makes it useful for producing fresh, fruity wine in hotter areas of the New World.

COLTASSALA Italy, Tuscany (VT) One of Italy's best Sangiovese-dominated blends.

CONCA DE BARBERA Spain, Catalonia (DO) Little-known wines, mostly light-bodied dry white and rosé wines that have a delicate fruit flavour, the lacklustre reds are even less frequently encountered.

CONCA DE TREMP Spain, Catalonia (VC) Struggling to make the grade.

CONCERTO Italy, Tuscany (VT) One of Italy's best Sangiovese-dominated blends.

CONDRIEU France, Rhône Valley (AOC) Some great,

some disappointing, dry white wines from the Viognier grape. They are all very expensive, but most are much better value than Château Grillet.

COPERTINO Italy, Apulia (DOC) Full, rich red wines and dry, finely scented rosés.

CORBIÈRES France, Languedoc-Roussillon (AOC) Can range from bulk-blended reds found in French supermarkets, which are often barely more than vin ordinaire in quality, to full, rich and creamy wines of stunning quality, when from the best estates. Rosés and dry whites range from plainly simple to simply plain.

CORI Italy, Latium (DOC) Lacklustre dry, semi-sweet and sweet whites, simple, smooth reds.

CORNAS France, Rhône Valley (AOC) Ink-black, full-flavoured reds of tremendous value.

CORTESE DELL'ALTO MONFERRATO Italy, Piedmont (DOC) Crisp dry white wines of ordinary quality in three different styles: still, semi-sparkling and fully sparkling.

CORTESE DI GAVI Italy, Piedmont (DOC) Also called Gavi or Gavi dei Gavi, this is a very fashionable dry white wine that can vary greatly in quality and style, as a number have a slight fizz, while others are distinctly fizzy and some not fizzy at all. The best have a soft-textured appeal and can develop a honeyed richness in bottle, although none improve beyond two or three years of age.

CORTON France, Burgundy (AOC) The deep, dark, brooding grand cru reds mature into the greatest red wines in the Côte de Beaune. Also full, rich dry whites.

CORTON-CHARLE-MAGNE France, Burgundy (AOC) This grand cru produces the most sumptuous of all dry white Burgundies.

CORUCHE Portugal, Ribatejo (IPR) Lots of white wine, most of which is ordinary, but the reds are full, fruity and rapidly improving.

CORVO Italy, Sicily (VT) Brand name for red, white, sparkling and fortified wines of consistent, but not special, quality. However the smooth, fruity red is usually good value for money.

COSTERS DEL SEGRE Spain, Catalonia (DO) Relatively new DO of variable quality red and white wines, except for Raimat, which stands out for its consistently excellent Chardonnay, Cabernet Sauvignon, Tempranillo and Abadia (red blend).

COSTIÈRES DE NIMES France, Languedoc-Roussillon (VDQS) Formerly Costières du Gard, this appellation produces aromatic reds and soft, fruity rosés of more interest than many AOCs, but the whites are less successful.

CÔTE DE BEAUNE France, Burgundy (AOC) Fine, stylish red and dry white wines from a few plots scattered across the hill overlooking Beaune itself.

CÔTE DE BEAUNE-VILLAGES France, Burgundy (AOC) Excellent value, fruity reds from one or more villages in the Côte de Beaune district.

CÔTE DE BROUILLY France, Burgundy (AOC) Full, rich and flavoursome red wine from one of the ten top-quality cru Beaujolais.

CÔTE DE NUITS-VILLAGES France, Burgundy (AOC) Firm, fruity distinctive reds and a minute quantity of dry white.

CÔTE RÔTIE France, Rhône Valley (AOC) Full, warm, spicy red wines, the best of which are equal to the best Hermitage, although not quite as expensive.

COTEAUX CHAMPENOIS France, Champagne (AOC) The still red, dry white and dry rosé wines of Champagne, but what makes Champagne so great for sparkling wine makes it hostile for still wine, and even the most 'interesting' are horrendously over-priced for their quality.

COTEAUX D'AIX-EN-PROVENCE France, Provence (AOC) Good quality reds, the best dry rosés in Provence and moderate, but improving, dry whites.

COTEAUX D'AIX-EN-PROVENCE-LES BAUX France, Provence (AOC) Excellent red, white and rosé wines from the best village in the above appellation.

COTEAUX D'ANCENIS France, Loire (VDQS) Red Gamay and dry white Malvoisie are the wines that excel here. Also a dry, lively rosé.

COTEAUX DE L'AUBANCE France, Loire (AOC) A rich, semi-sweet white wine that is a rare but rewarding find.

COTEAUX DE PIERREVERT France, Rhône Valley (VDQS) Dull reds and uninspiring dry whites, but decent, crisp, dry rosés.

COTEAUX DE SAUMUR France, Loire (AOC) Relatively rare, semi-sweet, richly flavoured white wine.

COTEAUX DU GIENNOIS France, Loire (VDQS) Dry, light-bodied red and white wines of limited interest.

COTEAUX DU GIENNOIS COSNE-SUR-LOIRE France, Loire (VDQS) The best reds and dry whites of Coteaux du Giennois.

COTEAUX DU LANGUEDOC France, Languedoc-Roussillon (AOC) Some excellent red wines, ranging from everyday drinking ilk to more serious stuff. The dry rosés are infinitely preferable to vastly overpriced Provence rosés. Many of the best come from single villages indicated on the label (Cabrières probably has the best potential and La Clape provides the largest number of the most consistent quality, but they are all worthy of seeking out).

COTEAUX DU LAYON France, Loire (AOC) Golden, soft-textured, sweet white wine of full body and exceptional longevity.

COTEAUX DU LAYON-CHAUME France, Loire (AOC) A distinct step up from the albeit excellent basic Coteaux du Layon.

COTEAUX DU LAYON VILLAGES France, Loire (AOC) Succulent, sweet white wines from the best six villages in the Coteaux du Layon.

COTEAUX DU LOIR France, Loire (AOC) Notice this refers to the Loir, not Loire. Light and generally unexciting red, dry white and dry rosé.

COTEAUX DU LYONNAIS France, Burgundy (AOC) Light-bodied red wines from the Gamay grape, grown just south of Beaujolais.

COTEAUX DU TRICASTIN France, Rhône Valley (AOC) Excellent, deep-coloured, intense-flavoured reds made exclusively from the Syrah grape. Tiny amounts also produced of uninspiring dry whites, but fresh, fruity, outstandingly good rosés.

COTEAUX DU VENDÔMOIS France, Loire (VDQS) Neighbouring area to the Coteaux du Loir, producing basically the same styles of wine from the same grape varieties, but better for VDQS than the Coteaux du Loir is for AOC.

COTEAUX VAROIS France, Provence (VDQS) Unpretentious reds and dry rosés from the heart of Provence.

CÔTES-CANON-FRONSAC France, Bordeaux (AOC) The best wines of Fronsac, these full-bodied reds have a deep colour, dense fruit and the more expensive they are, the greater value for money they represent.

CÔTES-DE-BORDEAUX-ST-MACAIRE France, Bordeaux (AOC) Seldom seen, unpretentious and fruity, sweet white wine.

CÔTES-DE-CASTILLON France, Bordeaux (AOC) Firm, full-bodied, fruit-packed reds that are much admired for their quality, consistency and value.

CÔTES-DU-RHÔNE France, Rhône Valley (AOC) One of the best value reds in France and the dry whites are gradually improving, but forget the rosés.

CÔTES-DU-RHÔNE-VILLAGES France, Rhône Valley (AOC) Some 17 villages in the southern Rhône are eligible for this appellation and most wines are a blend of various villages, which can be very good, although the best wines usually bear the name of a single village. Reds are particularly excellent value for money, generally fuller in body, have greater fruit and show

more character than the basic Côtes-du-Rhône. The dry whites are improving and the rosés can be interesting.

CÔTES D'AUVERGNE France, Loire (VDQS) Good value Beaujolais style red, dry white and dry rosé wines.

CÔTES DE BERGERAC France, Southwest France (AOC) These red wines are from the same area as the basic Bergerac appellation, but have an extra degree of alcohol.

CÔTES DE BERGERAC MOELLEUX France, Southwest France (AOC) Soft, sweet and fat white wines with a fruity aftertaste.

CÔTES DE BLAYE France, Bordeaux (AOC) Unlike Blaye plain and simple, Côtes de Blaye is a dry-white-wine-only appellation, although the wines are just as variable in both quality and style.

CÔTES DE BOURG France, Bordeaux (AOC) While the Côtes de Bourg is just one-fifth the size of neighbouring Côtes de Blaye, it actually produces more wine and, more importantly, of a much finer quality: fruity reds and light, dry whites.

CÔTES DE BUZET France, Southwest France (AOC) Superb value, Bordeaux-type reds, but the dry whites are less interesting.

CÔTES DE DURAS France, southwest France (AOC) Light Bordeaux style red and dry white wines of increasing interest.

CÔTES DE FOREZ France, Loire (VDQS) Light-bodied reds and rosés made from the Gamay, grown even further upstream than the Côtes Roannaises, just west of Beaujolais.

CÔTES DE GIEN France, Loire (VDQS) Synonymous with Coteaux du Giennois.

CÔTES DE GIEN COSNE-SUR-LOIRE France, Loire (VDQS) Synonymous with Coteaux du Giennois Cosne-sur-Loire.

CÔTES DE LA MALEPÈRE France, Languedoc-Roussillon (VDQS) Well-coloured reds of medium-to-full body and elegant, spicy southern fruit. The dry rosés are fruity and attractive.

CÔTES DE MONTRAVEL France, Southwest France (AOC) Fat, fruity white wines, usually quite sweet.

CÔTES DE PROVENCE France, Provence (AOC) Lots of exciting reds, but leave the dry whites and dry rosés in Provence, where the sunshine and general ambience somehow elevates our enjoyment of these wines above their intrinsically moderate quality.

CÔTES DE ST-MONT France, Southwest France (VDQS) Full-flavoured red and dry white wines from the Armagnac district.

CÔTES DE TOUL France, Alsace (VDQS) Light-bodied red, dry white and dry rosé from isolated vineyards west of Nancy.

CÔTES DU BRULHOIS France, Southwest France (VDQS) Rustic Bordeaux-type reds and fresh, easy drinking dry rosés.

CÔTES DU CABARDÈS ET DE L'ORBIEL France, Languedoc-Roussillon (VDQS) Synonymous with Cabardès.

CÔTES DU FRONTONNAIS France, Southwest France (AOC) Medium to full bodied reds, with plenty of flavour and a good colour. Overtly fruity rosés. Look out for those mentioning either Fronton or Villaudaric in the appellation.

CÔTES DU JURA France, Jura (AOC) Generic

appellation for light but elegant reds, unpretentious light, dry whites and fragrant dry rosés.

CÔTES DU JURA MOUSSEUX France, Jura (AOC) This fine, light but persistent white sparkling wine is the Jura's best bubbly.

CÔTES DU JURA VIN DE PAILLE France, Jura (AOC) Very sweet, distinctive dessert wine, which instantly ages due to the presence of an oxidative-prone grape called the Savagnin.

CÔTES DU JURA VIN JAUNE France, Jura (AOC) Generic appellation for sherry-like 'yellow wine', encompassing the two more specific appellations of Vin Jaune L'Étoile, Arbois Vin Jaune and Château-Chalon.

CÔTES DU LUBÉRON France, Rhône Valley (AOC) These good quality red, dry white and rosé wines were upgraded from VDQS in 1992, and are still improving.

CÔTES DU MARMANDAIS France, Southwest France (AOC) Highly successful imitation of Bordeaux reds and rosés.

CÔTES DU ROUSSILLON France, Languedoc-Roussillon (AOC) A number of good value, honest reds of some character and interest.

CÔTES DU ROUSSILLON VILLAGES France, Languedoc-Roussillon (AOC) Fantastic value appellation, the best wines of which outclass the majority of Côtes-du-Rhône.

CÔTES DU ROUSSILLON VILLAGES CARAMANY France, Languedoc-Roussillon (AOC) The fullest, richest and longest-living red wine of Roussillon.

CÔTES DU ROUSSILLON VILLAGES LATOUR DE FRANCE France, Languedoc-Roussillon (AOC) Latour de France is a village, the red wines of which are not as full as those from Caramany, but are equally fine.

CÔTES DU VENTOUX France, Rhône Valley (AOC) Fresh, well-made wines that are lighter-bodied than most southern Rhônes due to the limestone soil. Reds and dry rosés are best, the dry whites being of minimal interest.

CÔTES DU VIVARAIS France, Rhône Valley (VDQS) Light, quaffing reds and pretty pinks can be recommended, but the whites are dull and boring.

CÔTES ROANNAISES France, Loire (VDQS) Distinctive Beaujolais-type quaffing reds and fine, dry, fruity rosés, made from the Gamay grape grown in the upper reaches of the Loire, just west of the Mâconnais district of Burgundy.

COVA DE BEIRA Portugal, Beiras (IPR) From the Beira Alta, between the Vinho Verde and Dão districts, where every style of wine is produced in varying quality.

CRÉMANT D'ALSACE France, Alsace (AOC) Good and improving sparkling wines that are on a par with Crémant de Bourgogne.

CRÉMANT DE BOR-DEAUX France, Bordeaux (AOC) Introduced in 1990 to eventually replace Bordeaux Mousseux, this wine has the least potential of all French Crémant appellations.

CRÉMANT DE BOURGOGNE France, Burgundy (AOC) Sparkling white and rosé, often of good quality, and a suitable alternative to Champagne.

CRÉMANT DE LIMOUX France, Southwest France (AOC) Synonymous with Blanquette de Limoux.

CRÉMANT DE LOIRE France, Loire (AOC) Underrated méthode champenoise appellation that often shows greater consistency than other more famous Loire sparkling wines, due to its ability to be blended from Anjou-Saumur and Touraine wines.

CRÉPY France, Savoie (AOC) Well known to the skiing set, this light-bodied, dry white wine has a floral aroma, is slightly *pétillant* and is a joy to drink after a day on the piste.

CRIOTS-BÂTARD-MONTRACHET France, Burgundy (AOC) The smallest of Montrachet's great dry white wine grand crus, Criots has some of the weight of its illustrious neighbours, but is essentially the palest and most fragrant.

CROZES-HERMITAGE France, Rhône Valley (AOC) The reds are even better value than Côtes-du-Rhône reds, but forget the whites and rosés.

CRUSTED or **CRUSTING PORT** Portugal, Douro (DOC) Blend of high quality Port from two or more years, bottled after up to four years in cask. More forward in style than Vintage Port, but capable of further ageing in bottle, where it throws a similar deposit.

D

DALSHEIM Germany, Rheinhessen One of the best villages in the Rheinhessen. Top single-vineyards: Dalsheimer Steig, Dalsheimer Hubacker.

DÃO Portugal, Dão (DOC) Stern reds and lacklustre

whites from a famous region that, as my teacher always used to tell me, could do better.

DAROGA Spain, Aragón (VC) Struggling to make the grade.

DAUBHAUS Germany, Rheingau If you see this name following that of a village on a bottle of Rheingau, it is only a *Grosslage* wine.

DE VITE Italy, Trentino-Alto Adige (VT) Fragrant, dry white.

DEIDESHEIM Germany, Rheinpfalz One of the best villages in the Rheinpfalz. Top single-vineyards: Deidesheimer Nonnenstück, Deidesheimer Hoheburg, Deidesheimer Hohenmorgen, Deidesheimer Leinhöhle, Deidesheimer Grainhübel, Deidesheimer Herrgottsacker.

DETZEM Germany, Mosel-Saar-Ruwer One of the best villages in the MSR. Top single-vineyards: Detzemer Würzgarten.

DEUTELSBERG Germany, Rheingau If you see this name following that of a village on a bottle of Rheingau, it is only a *Grosslage* wine.

DEUTSCHER SEKT Germany Until a few years ago, this was no different than Sekt, its base wines being trucked in from all and sundry, but this made a mockery of the use of Deutscher to qualify the term Sekt and the Germans were pulled into line by the EC. Now only German wines are allowed for its production. Most is made by cuve close (*see* **Sekt**) and a lot is equally dire, but some good Deutscher Sekt do exist, albeit it in an aromatic, medium-sweet, non-Champagne style. Frankly, however, if you can take a little more

sweetness, you might as well go all the way and buy Moscato d'Asti.

DIENHEIM Germany, Rheinhessen One of the best villages in the Rheinhessen. Top single-vineyards: Dienheimer Tafelstein.

DIRMSTEIN Germany, Rheinpfalz One of the best villages in the Rheinpfalz. Top single-vineyards: Dirmsteiner Jesuitenhofgarten.

DOLCEACQUA Italy, Liguria (DOC) Rich red wine capable of lush, spicy fruit, soft texture.

DOLCETTO Italy, Piedmont (VT) Most examples of Piedmont's famous Dolcetto do not qualify for DOC status, but are plump, purple-coloured red wines that have a low acid content and are easy to drink in a cheap and cheerful way.

DOLCETTO Italy, Piedmont (DOC) The best three Dolcetto DOCs are Dolcetto d'Acqui, Dolcetto d'Alba and, particularly, Dolcetto di Diano d'Alba. Although Dolcetto di Ovada is the longest lived (up to 10 years), this grape is not really supposed to be that serious and the wines inevitably lose the cheery style that makes other Dolcetto so accessible. Other Dolcetto DOCs are produced in Asti, Dogliani and Langhe Monregalesi. (*See* basic **Dolcetto** entry.)

DOMBLICK Germany, Rheinhessen If you see this name following that of a village on a bottle of Rheinhessen, it is only a *Grosslage* wine.

DOMHERR Germany, Rheinhessen If you see this name following that of a village on a bottle of Rheinhessen, it is only a *Grosslage* wine.

DONAU Germany (DT) One of eight Deutscher Tafelwein sub-regions, its

wines should be simple and light-bodied, with a basic flowery aroma, some grapey fruit and a touch of sweetness on the finish.

DONNA MARZIA Italy, Apulia (VT) Full-bodied, alcoholic reds of some interest, but uninspiring dry whites.

DONNAS or **DONNAZ** Italy, Valle d'Aosta (DOC) Soft, well-balanced Nebbiolo red wine with a slightly bitter finish.

DONNICI Italy, Calabria (DOC) Dry fruity red and rosé wines best drunk young.

DORSHEIM Germany, Nahe One of the best villages in the Nahe. Top single-vineyards: Dorsheimer Klosterpfad, Dorsheimer Goldloch, Dorsheimer Burgberg.

DOURO Portugal, Douro (DOC) Best known for Port, the Douro Valley has always produced table wine, but it was not until the 1960s, when Ferreira produced the first vintage of Barca Vehla (Portugal's answer to Spain's Vega Sicilia, in price as well as reputation, and from the same river too) that anyone imagined wines of a high quality could be produced. Now at least one other wine, Quinta do Cotto Grande Eschola, is as stunning as Barca Vehla, and in the last few years it has become a source of increasing interest.

DRAGARSK Italy, Friuli-Venezia Giulia (VT) One of Italy's best Cabernet-based blends.

DURBACH Germany, Baden One of the best villages in Baden. Top single-vineyards: Durbacher Schlossberg, Durbacher Schloss Grohl, Durbacher Schloss Staufenberg, Durbacher Plauelrain.

DUTTWEILER Germany, Rheinpfalz One of the best villages in the Rheinpfalz. Top single-vineyards: Duttweilerer Mandelberg.

E

EBERSTADT Germany, Württemberg One of the best villages in Württemberg. Top single-vineyards: Eberstadter Eberfürst.

ECHÉZEAUX France, Burgundy (AOC) Due to its ownership by some 84 different growers of varying degrees of competence, this red wine grand cru from the village of Flagey-Echézeaux in the Côte de Nuits ranges from fine, fragrant and delicate to light and lacking.

EDELZWICKER France, Alsace (AOC) Dry to off-dry white wine blended from more than one grape variety. Edelzwicker literally means 'noble blend', but the term has long been abused and most Edelzwicker today are barely adequate in quality. Producers of the best blended Alsace wine avoid using the term, preferring to sell their wines by a specific name (such as Pierre Sparr's 'Symphonie' or the single-vineyard wines of Clos du Zahnacker from the co-operative at Ribeauvillé and Clos du Val d'Eléon from Marc Kreydenweiss).

EDESHEIM Germany, Rheinpfalz One of the best villages in the Rheinpfalz. Top single-vineyards: Edesheimer Schloss.

EFRINGEN-KIRCHEN Germany, Baden One of the best villages in Baden. Top single-vineyards: Efringen-Kirchener Kirchberg.

EIBELSTADT Germany, Franken One of the best villages in Franken. Top single-vineyards: Eibelstadter Kapellenberg.

EISACKTALER Italy, Trentino-Alto Adige (QbA) Synonymous with Valle Isarco.

EISWEIN Germany (QbA) Wines with a scintillating balance of sweetness and acidity, made from grapes frozen on the vine, either through frost or snow, they are pressed when still frozen and the ice, which represents the bulk of the grape's water content, is discarded, leaving wines of intense concentration. Rare and very expensive.

EITELSBACH Germany, Mosel-Saar-Ruwer One of the best villages in the MSR. Top single-vineyards: Eitelsbacher Karthaüserhofberger Kronenberg, Eitelsbacher Karthaüserhofberger Sang, Eitelsbacher Karthaüserhofberger Burgberg, Eitelsbacher Marienholz.

EL HIERRO Spain, Canaries (VdlT) Country wines that have yet to make their mark.

ELBA Italy, Tuscany (DOC) Island wines produced from Chianti grapes and just as lacklustre.

ELTVILLE Germany, Rheingau One of the best villages in the Rheingau. Top single-vineyards: Eltviller Taubenberg, Eltviller Langenstück, Eltviller Sonnenberg.

ENCOSTAS DA AIRE Portugal, Estremadura (IPR) Clean fruity reds, the best of which have a good concentration of berry flavours, whereas the best whites are simply crisp with a touch of spritz and are much less interesting.

ENCOSTAS DA NAVE Portugal, Beiras (IPR) From the Beira Alta, between the Vinho Verde and Dão districts, where every style of wine is produced in varying quality, the area

has some up-and-coming red and white wines, including Terras do Demo from renowned oenologist Jaime Brojo.

ENFER D'ARVIER Italy, Valle d'Aosta (DOC) Soft, medium-bodied red wine.

ENGLISH WINE It might seem a bit bizarre to buy English wine in France, but if the UK government is intent on burying one of its own industries (two if you include the British wine retail trade) under a ludicrous burden of tax, then we can expect to see more of these wines on sale across the Channel, if only by the UK retailers over there. There are over 350 English vineyards, some of which produce exciting wines, but many do not.

ENTRE-DEUX-MERS France, Bordeaux (AOC) Crisp, dry and fragrant, Sauvignon-dominated white wine.

ENTRE-DEUX-MERS-HAUT-BENAUGE France, Bordeaux (AOC) Similar to Bordeaux Haut-Benauge, but exclusively dry in style.

ENTRE TEJO E SADO Portugal (VR) One of Portugal's two only Vinhos Regioñaos, its wines have yet to make their mark.

EQUIPE Italy, Trentino-Alto Adige Excellent, dry sparkling wines.

ERBACH Germany, Rheingau One of the best villages in the Rheingau. Top single-vineyards: Erbacher Schlossberg, Erbacher Marcobrunn.

ERBALUCE DI CALUSO Italy, Piedmont (DOC) Fresh, light, dry white wine of no special interest. A *passito* version also exists.

ERDEN Germany, Mosel-Saar-Ruwer One of the best villages in the MSR. Top single-vineyards: Erdener Treppchen, Erdener Prälat.

ERNTEBRINGER
Germany, Rheingau If you
see this name following that
of a village on a bottle of
Rheingau, it is only a
Grosslage wine.

ESCHERNDORF Germany,
Franken One of the best
villages in Franken. Top
single-vineyards:
Escherndorfer Lump.

**EST! EST!! EST!!! DI
MONTEFIASCONE** Italy,
Latium (DOC) Say No! No!!
No!!! to these lacklustre dry
and semi-sweet white
wines.

ESTREMADURA Portugal,
Estremadura (IPR) Clean,
fruity reds, the best of
which have a good
concentration of berry
flavours, whereas the best
whites are simply crisp with
a touch of spritz and are
much less interesting.

ETNA Italy, Sicily (DOC)
The wine that Ulysses
intoxicated the Cyclops
with. There are three types:
a full red and a fruity rosé
that can be recommended
and a soft, bland, dry white
that cannot.

ETSCHTALER Italy,
Trentino-Alto Adige (QbA)
Synonymous with
Valdadige.

EVORA Portugal, Alentejo
(IPR) Lots of white wine,
most of which is ordinary,
but the reds are full, fruity
and rapidly improving.

EWIG LEBEN Germany,
Franken If you see this
name following that of a
village on a bottle of
Franken, it is only a
Grosslage wine.

F

**FALERIO DEI COLLI
ASCOLANI** Italy, Marches
(DOC) Uninspiring dry
white wine.

FALERNO DEL MASSICO
Italy, Campania (DOC) The
modern reincarnation of

ancient Falernium, these
robust reds and dry whites
were upgraded to DOC
status in 1989, but one can
only assume that it was for
historical, not qualitative,
reasons.

FARA Italy, Piedmont
(DOC) Underrated fruity
red wine with a spicy
character.

FARO Italy, Sicily (DOC)
Basic, medium-bodied red.

FAUGÈRES France,
Languedoc-Roussillon
(AOC) Deep, full, warm
and spicy reds and
attractively ripe and fruity
dry rosés.

FAVONIO Italy, Apulia
(VT) The Favonio wines of
Simonini are extraordinarily
fine and well balanced,
high-quality freaks from
Italy's deep south. Various
reds and whites, all
recommended.

FAVORITA Italy,
Piedmont (VT) Crisp, dry
white of no special interest.

FERRARI Italy, Trentino-
Alto Adige Excellent, dry
sparkling wines.

FEUERBERG Germany,
Rheinpfalz If you see this
name following that of a
village on a bottle of
Rheinpfalz, it is only a
Grosslage wine.

FIANO DI AVELLINO
Italy, Campania (DOC)
Above average, southern
dry white appellation.

FIEFS VENDÉENS France,
Loire (VDQS) The reds can
be quite grassy, but the
Cabernet Franc excels in
really hot years. Dry whites
and dry rosés can also be
interesting.

FILZEN Germany, Mosel-
Saar-Ruwer One of the best
villages in the MSR. Top
single-vineyards: Filzener
Herrenberg.

FIORANO Italy, Latium
(VT) One of Italy's best
Cabernet-based blends.

FITOU France, Languedoc-
Roussillon (AOC) Excellent
value, well-coloured, full
and fruity red wines.

FIXIN France, Burgundy
(AOC) Rich, red village
wine that is rustic but a true
vin de garde. Also a rare,
concentrated white.

FIXIN PREMIER CRU
France, Burgundy (AOC)
Deep-coloured red, full of
ripe summer fruit flavour.
Tiny amounts of dry white.

**FLACCIANELLO DELLA
PIAVE** Italy, Tuscany (VT)
One of Italy's very best pure
Sangiovese wines.

FLEIN Germany,
Württemberg One of the
best villages in
Württemberg. Top single-
vineyards: Fleiner
Eselsberg.

FLEURIE France, Burgundy
(AOC) Fresh, floral fragrant
red wine from one to ten
top-quality cru Beaujolais.

FLOC DE GASCOGNE
France, Southwestern
France (AOC) Sweet,
cloying aperitif made from
unfermented grape juice
that has been prevented
from fermenting by the
addition of Armagnac. This
is to Armagnac what the
Pineau des Charentes is to
Cognac, and the unclassi-
fied Ratafia is to Cham-
pagne.

FOIANGHE Italy,
Trentino-Alto Adige (VT)
One of Italy's best
Cabernet-based blends.

FONTANELLE Italy,
Tuscany (VT) One of Italy's
best pure C.

FONTANELLE Italy,
Marches (VT) Smooth,
scented, dry white wine of
some delicacy and interest.

**FORST AN DER
WEINSTRASSE** Germany,
Rheinpfalz One of the best
villages in the Rheinpfalz.
Top single-vineyards:
Forster Jesuitengarten,
Forster Kirchenstück,

Forster Ungeheuer, Forster Pechstein.

FRANCIACORTA Italy, Lombardy (DOC) Excellent, well-coloured red wines that are capable of great richness and some finesse, the dry whites are much less special, but some very good sparkling white and sparkling rosé wines can be found.

FRANCONIA Italy, Friuli-Venezia Giulia (VT) Clean but uninteresting, light-bodied red wine.

FRANKEN Germany, (QbA) Classic Franconian Silvaner (*sic*) is distinctly dry with an earthy or smoky aroma and is bottled in the traditional flask-shaped Bocksbeutel, but the Silvaner is unfortunately giving way to Müller-Thurgau and other more commercial varieties.

FRANKEN GROSSLAGEN Germany, Franken (Grosslagen) Burgweg, Herrenberg, Kapellenberg, Schild, Schlossberg, Schlossstück, Burg, Ewig Leben, Hofrat, Honigberg, Kirchberg, Markgraf Babenberg, Oelspiel, Ravensburg, Rosstal, Teufelstor, Heiligenthal and Reuschberg are all *Grosslagen*, not single-vineyard wines and should be very reasonably priced, unless you are being ripped-off or it happens to be an Eiswein, Beerenauslese or Trockenbeerenauslese.

FRANKISCHER LANDWEIN Germany (DL) One of 15 Deutscher Landwein appellations, its wines should be simple and light-bodied, with a basic flowery aroma, some grapey fruit and a touch of sweetness on the finish.

FRASCATI Italy, Latium (DOC) Light, dry white wine, most of which is bland, although a handful of the more expensive

wines have some interest. Some sweet, semi-sweet and sparkling versions are made.

FREINSHEIM Germany, Rheinpfalz One of the best villages in the Rheinpfalz. Top single-vineyards: Freinsheimer Goldberg.

FREISA D'ASTI Italy, Piedmont (DOC) Fruity red wines of some interest, but beware the various styles: dry or semi-sweet and still, semi-sparkling and fully sparkling.

FREISA DI CHIERI Italy, Piedmont (DOC) As above but from the village of Chieri, just outside Turin.

FRONSAC France, Bordeaux (AOC) Rich, chunky reds that lack the concentration and finesse of Côtes-Canon-Fronsac, but are equally great value.

FRONTIGNAN France, Languedoc-Roussillon (AOC) Synonymous with Muscat de Fontignan.

FUENCALIENTE Spain, Canaries (VdlT) Country wines that have yet to make their mark.

FÜRSTENECK Germany, Baden If you see this name following that of a village on a bottle of Baden, it is only a *Grosslage* wine.

G

GABIANO Italy, Piedmont (DOC) Full-bodied red wine of promising quality from the Barbera grape.

GAILLAC France, Southwest France (AOC) Fresh, light Beaujolais style red, dry white and rosé wines from one of the oldest vineyard areas of France.

GAILLAC DOUX France, Southwest France (AOC) Luscious sweet white wines with a rich peachy fruit flavour.

GAILLAC LIQUOREUX France, Southwest France (AOC) Synonymous with Gaillac Doux.

GAILLAC MOELLEUX France, Southwest France (AOC) Synonymous with Gaillac Doux.

GAILLAC MOUSSEUX France, Southwest France (AOC) Naturally sparkling white and rosé wines that are fresh, fragrant and grapey.

GAILLAC PREMIÈRES CÔTES France, Southwest France (AOC) Similar to Gaillac Doux.

GAILLAC SEC PERLÉ France, Southwest France (AOC) Light, dry, aromatic white wines with a slight sparkle.

GAILLAC SEC PRIMEUR France, Southwest France (AOC) Similar to Gaillac Sec Perlé, but released as a vin nouveau.

GALESTRO Italy, Tuscany (VT) Ultra-clean, light-bodied, dry white of no special interest.

GALVEZ Spain, Castilla-León (VdlT) Country wines that have yet to make their mark.

GAMAY (Grape) The idea that the character of Beaujolais is any way connected to the varietal character of Gamay could not be further from the truth, as most Beaujolais is made by *maceration carbonique*, a process that produces ethyl acetate, which gives the wine its typically pear-drop, bubble-gum or nail-varnish aroma. Great cru Beaujolais, however, is not made or is certainly not dominated by *maceration carbonique* and it is the rich, succulent, lush quality of these wines that should tell you what Gamay is all about.

GAMAY BLANC (Grape) *See* **Melon**.

GAMBELLARA Italy, Veneto (DOC) This diverse appellation includes scented, dry white, semisweet white, sparkling and semi-sparkling white, often semi-sweet, and vino santo, but nothing special.

GATTINARA Italy, Piedmont (DOCG) Red wine blended from Nebbiolo and up to a maximum of 10% Bonarda, which is often chunky in its youth, but ages gracefully.

GAU-BICKELHEIM Germany, Rheinhessen One of the best villages in the Rheinhessen. Top single-vineyards: Gau-Bickelheimer Kapelle.

GAVI Italy, Piedmont (DOC) Synonymous with Cortese di Gavi.

GEDEONSECK Germany, Mittelrhein If you see this name following that of a village on a bottle of Mittelrhein, it is only a *Grosslage* wine.

GEISENHEIM Germany, Rheingau One of the best villages in the Rheingau. Top single-vineyards: Geisenheimer Mönchspfad, Geisenheimer Mäuerchen.

GEVREY-CHAMBERTIN France, Burgundy (AOC) Affectionately known as 'Geoffrey' Chambertin, this village appellation in the Côte de Nuits produces silky, well-perfumed reds.

GEVREY-CHAMBERTIN PREMIER CRU France, Burgundy (AOC) A good step up from the village red.

GEWÜRZTRAMINER France, Alsace (AOC) Big, fat and spicy white wines that have relatively low acidity and are often made in an off-dry style, with more than a touch of sweetness to enhance the fruit.

GEWÜRZTRAMINER (Grape) At its most clear-cut and varietally distinctive in Alsace, where this grape is

big, fat and full of wonderful spicy aromas. It should do well in New Zealand and other New World cool-climate areas, but the vinestock is poor and the wines are thin, washed-out and disappointing.

GHEMME Italy, Piedmont (DOC) Although this Nebbiolo wine is similar in colour and body to Gattinara, it is often more attractive and elegant in its youth.

GHIAIE DELLA FURBA Italy, Tuscany (VT) One of Italy's best Cabernet Sauvignon-dominated blends.

GIGONDAS France, Rhône Valley (AOC) These excellent value red wines are deep in colour and have lots of flavour. The dry rosés are also good value.

GIOIA DEL COLLE Italy, Apulia (DOC) Lacklustre red, dry white and dry rosé wines, but two varietals are interesting: a sweet and aromatic dessert wine from the Aleatico grape, and Primitivo, which is the origin of California's Zinfandel.

GIPFEL Germany, Mosel-Saar-Ruwer If you see this name following that of a village on a bottle of MSR, it is only a *Grosslage* wine.

GIRÒ DI CAGLIARI Italy, Sardinia (DOC) Smooth but alcoholic, dry or sweet red wines and dry or sweet fortified red wines of no special interest.

GIVRY France, Burgundy (AOC) Underrated fruity reds, spicy-buttery dry whites of light to medium body.

GOLDBÄUMCHEN Germany, Mosel-Saar-Ruwer If you see this name following that of a village on a bottle of MSR, it is only a *Grosslage* wine.

GOTTESHILFE Germany, Rheinhessen If you see this name following that of a village on a bottle of Rheinhessen, it is only a *Grosslage* wine.

GOTTESTHAL Germany, Rheingau If you see this name following that of a village on a bottle of Rheingau, it is only a *Grosslage* wine.

GRAACH Germany, Mosel-Saar-Ruwer One of the best villages in the MSR. Top single-vineyards: Graacher Himmelreich, Graacher Josephshöfer, Graacher Domprobst.

GRAFENSTÜCK Germany, Rheinpfalz If you see this name following that of a village on a bottle of Rheinpfalz, it is only a *Grosslage* wine.

GRAFSCHAFT Germany, Mosel-Saar-Ruwer If you see this name following that of a village on a bottle of MSR, it is only a *Grosslage* wine.

GRAND ROUSSILLON France, Languedoc-Roussillon (AOC) Lesser quality fortified wines.

GRAND ROUSSILLON 'RANCIO' France, Languedoc-Roussillon (AOC) Lesser quality fortified wines in the famous rancid-maderised style!

GRANDS ECHÉZEAUX France, Burgundy (AOC) Infinitely finer than Echézeaux, this red wine grand cru from the village of Flagey-Echézeaux in the Côte de Nuits shows great aromatic finesse.

GRANJA Portugal, Alentejo (IPR) Lots of white wine, most of which is ordinary, but the reds are full, fruity and rapidly improving.

GRATTAMACCO Italy, Tuscany (VT) Fruity red and white wines that are easy to drink.

GRAVE DEL FRIULI Italy, Friuli-Venezia Giulia (DOC) Large, complicated, multi-varietal appellation for red, white and rosé wines of varying quality and character, but does include some good wines.

GRAVES France, Bordeaux (AOC) Classic, silky reds that are reminiscent of violets and dry white wines that can range from full and oaky to light and wimpish.

GRAVES DE VAYRES France, Bordeaux (AOC) Nothing to do with the famous Graves of Bordeaux, although both appellations share the same etymological origin (gravelly soil). Graves de Vayres produces medium-bodied reds with lots of fresh, juicy-spicy fruit and light, dry whites.

GRAVES SUPÉRIEUR France, Bordeaux (AOC) This white wine can be dry and similar to Graves plain and simple, but most are sweet, botrytis affected and very similar to Barsac in style.

GRAVINA Italy, Apulia (DOC) Dry or semi-sweet white wines that can be quite fresh and sometimes sparkling.

GRECHETTO Italy, Umbria (VT) Dry and sweet white wines that are not special, but have a pleasant floral aroma.

GRECO Italy, Piedmont (VT) Light, crisp, dry white wine of no great interest.

GRECO Italy, Umbria (VT) Synonymous with Grechetto.

GRECO DI BIANCO Italy, Calabria (DOC) Sweet, white *passito* wine.

GRECO DI TUFO Italy, Campania (DOC) Soft, delicate, dry white wines that may also be sparkling.

GRENACHE (Grape) Important grape for the blended wines of Côtes-du-Rhône, Châteauneuf-du-Pape and Gigondas, the Grenache is also one of the up-and-coming varietal wines of the New World.

GRIGNOLINO D'ASTI Italy, Piedmont (DOC) Lightly tannic red wines with a slightly bitter finish.

GRIGNOLINO DEL MONFERRATO CASALESE Italy, Piedmont (DOC) This Grignolino is usually finer and smoother than the one from Asti.

GRIOTTES-CHAMBERTIN France, Burgundy (AOC) The smallest grand cru in Gevrey-Chambertin on the Côte de Nuits produces soft, succulent, fruity reds.

GROPPELLO Italy, Lombardy (VT) Medium-bodied red wine, good and fruity, although often made in the bitter *amarone* style.

GROS PLANT France, Loire (VDQS) Synonymous with Gros Plant du Nantais.

GROS PLANT DU NANTAIS France, Loire (VDQS) Leaner, meaner version of Muscadet – say no more!

GROSSKARLBACH Germany, Rheinpfalz One of the best villages in the Rheinpfalz. Top single-vineyards: Grosskarlbacher Burgweg.

GROSSLAGEN Germany A bottle bearing a *Grosslage* name looks deceptively like its wine has been produced from an exclusive Einzellage or individually named vineyard, but *Grosslagen* are very large areas and the wine sold under any of these names should be relatively inexpensive, unless you are being ripped-off or it happens to be an Eiswein, Beerenauslese or Trockenbeerenauslese.

GROSSO SENESE Italy, Tuscany (VT) One of Italy's very best pure Sangiovese wines.

GRUMELLO Italy, Lombardy (DOC) Sub-appellation of Valtelina.

GRÜNER VELTLINER (Grape) The most important wine grape in Austria, where most wines are bland vin ordinaire, although great Grüner Veltliner is so peppery-spicy it can burn the tongue.

GRÜNSTADT Germany, Rheinpfalz One of the best villages in the Rheinpfalz. Top single-vineyards: Grünstadter Goldberg.

GÜGLINGEN Germany, Württemberg One of the best villages in Württemberg. Top single-vineyards: Güglinger Michaelsberg.

GÜLDENMORGEN Germany, Rheinhessen If you see this name following that of a village on a bottle of Rheinhessen, it is only a *Grosslage* wine.

GULDENTAL Germany, Nahe One of the best villages in the Nahe. Top single-vineyards: Guldentaler Rosenteich.

GUNDELSHEIM Germany, Württemberg One of the best villages in Württemberg. Top single-vineyards: Gundelsheimer Himmelreich.

GUNTERSBLUM Germany, Rheinhessen One of the best villages in the Rheinhessen. Top single-vineyards: Guntersblumer Steinberg, Guntersblumer Authenthal.

GUTEDEL France, Alsace (AOC) Synonymous with Chasselas.

GUTES DOMTAL Germany, Rheinhessen If you see this name following that of a village on a bottle of Rheinhessen, it is only a *Grosslage* wine.

GUTTENBERG Germany, Rheinpfalz If you see this name following that of a village on a bottle of Rheinpfalz, it is only a *Grosslage* wine.

GUTTURNIO DEI COLLI PIACENTINI Italy, Emilia-Romagna (DOC) Solid red wines from grapes grown in the Piacenza hills where Julius Caesar's father-in-law made a wine that was traditionally drunk from a large vessel called a *gutternium*. Semi-sweet, semi-sparkling reds also produced.

H

HALLGARTEN Germany, Rheingau One of the best villages in the Rheingau. Top single-vineyards: Hallgartener Jungfer.

HAMMELBURG Germany, Franken One of the best villages in Franken. Top single-vineyards: Hammelburger Trautlestal.

HAMMERSTEIN Germany, Mittelrhein One of the best villages in the Mittelrhein. Top single-vineyards: Hammersteiner Schlossberg.

HATTENHEIM Germany, Rheingau One of the best villages in the Rheingau. Top single-vineyards: Hattenheimer Steinberg, Hattenheimer Nussbrunnen, Hattenheimer Engelmannsberg, Hattenheimer Wisselbrunnen, Hattenheimer Mannberg, Hattenheimer Hassel, Hattenheimer Pfaffenberg, Hattenheimer Schützenhaus.

HAUT-COMTAT France, Rhône Valley (VDQS) Rarely encountered red and rosé wines made in a Côtes-du-Rhône style.

HAUT-MÉDOC France, Bordeaux (AOC) Firm-structured, full-bodied red

wines that are reliable and represent great value.

HAUT-MONTRAVEL France, Southwest France (AOC) Fat and fruity semi-sweet or sweet white wines.

HAUT-POITOU France, Loire (AOC) Increasingly good quality wines, despite the fact that Haut-Poitou, some 50 miles south of Tours, is better suited to arable farming than viticulture. Varietal reds are the most promising, but good dry white Sauvignon and some vividly coloured rosé. Chardonnay is the least exciting.

HEILBRONN Germany, Württemberg One of the best villages in Württemberg. Top single-vineyards: Heilbronner Stiftsberg.

HEILIGENSTOCK Germany, Rheingau If you see this name following that of a village on a bottle of Rheingau, it is only a *Grosslage* wine.

HEILIGENTHAL Germany, Franken If you see this name following that of a village on a bottle of Franken, it is only a *Grosslage* wine.

HEIMERSHEIM Germany, Ahr One of the best villages in the Ahr. Top single-vineyards: Heimersheimer Landskrone.

HEPPENHEIM Germany, Hessische Bergstrasse One of the best villages in the Hessische Bergstrasse. Top single-vineyards: Heppenheimer Centgericht.

HERMITAGE France, Rhône Valley (AOC) In terms of quality, these deep coloured, silky, violety, blackcurrant wines are the equivalent of cru classé Bordeaux, but the whites are a curiosity at best.

HERMITAGE VIN DE PAILLE France, Rhône Valley (AOC) Extremely

rare, very great, intensely sweet dessert wines.

HERRENBERG Germany, Mittelrhein If you see this name following that of a village on a bottle of Mittelrhein, it is only a *Grosslage* wine.

HERRENBERG Germany, Franken If you see this name following that of a village on a bottle of Franken, it is only a *Grosslage* wine.

HERRLICH Germany, Rheinpfalz If you see this name following that of a village on a bottle of Rheinpfalz, it is only a *Grosslage* wine.

HESSISCHE-BERGSTRASSE Germany, (QbA) This small, relatively unknown region at the northern tip of Baden's vineyards produces fruity wines with a pronounced earthy acidity.

HESSISCHE BERGSTRASSE GROSSLAGEN Germany, Hessische Bergstrasse (Grosslagen) Rott, Schlossberg and Wolfsmagen are all *Grosslagen*, not single-vineyard wines and should be very reasonably priced, unless you are being ripped-off or it happens to be an Eiswein, Beerenauslese or Trockenbeerenauslese.

HEUCHELBERG Germany, Württemberg If you see this name following that of a village on a bottle of Württemberg, it is only a *Grosslage* wine.

HOCHHEIM Germany, Rheingau One of the best villages in the Rheingau. Top single-vineyards: Hochheimer Domdechaney, Hochheimer Kirchenstück, Hochheimeer Hölle.

HOCHMESS Germany, Rheinpfalz If you see this name following that of a village on a bottle of

Rheinpfalz, it is only a *Grosslage* wine.

HOFRAT Germany, Franken If you see this name following that of a village on a bottle of Franken, it is only a *Grosslage* wine.

HOFSTÜCK Germany, Rheinpfalz If you see this name following that of a village on a bottle of Rheinpfalz, it is only a *Grosslage* wine.

HOHENBERG Germany, Baden If you see this name following that of a village on a bottle of Baden, it is only a *Grosslage* wine.

HOHENNEUFFEN Germany, Württemberg If you see this name following that of a village on a bottle of Württemberg, it is only a *Grosslage* wine.

HÖLLENPFAD Germany, Rheinpfalz If you see this name following that of a village on a bottle of Rheinpfalz, it is only a *Grosslage* wine.

HOMBURG Germany, Franken One of the best villages in Franken. Top single-vineyards: Homburger Kallmuth.

HONIGBERG Germany, Rheingau If you see this name following that of a village on a bottle of Rheingau, it is only a *Grosslage* wine.

HONIGBERG Germany, Franken If you see this name following that of a village on a bottle of Franken, it is only a *Grosslage* wine.

HONIGSÄCKEL Germany, Rheinpfalz If you see this name following that of a village on a bottle of Rheinpfalz, it is only a *Grosslage* wine.

HÖRSTEIN Germany, Franken One of the best villages in Franken. Top single-vineyards: Hörsteiner Abtsberg.

HUNGARY Famous for Tokay and capable of exciting red wines, but subject to inconsistency and will continue to be disappointing until its wine industry is updated, which will require investment from the west.

I COLTRI Italy, Tuscany (VT) One of Italy's best Sangiovese -dominated blends.

I GRIFI Italy, Tuscany (VT) One of Italy's best Sangiovese -dominated blends.

I SODI DI SAN NICCOLO Italy, Tuscany (VT) One of Italy's best Sangiovese-dominated blends.

ICOD Spain, Canaries (VC) Struggling to make the grade.

IHRINGEN Germany, Baden One of the best villages in Baden. Top single-vineyards: Ihringer Winklerberg.

IL FALCONE Italy, Apulia (DOC) Apulia's greatest red wine comes from the DOC of Castel del Monte.

INFERNO Italy, Lombardy (DOC) Sub-appellation of Valtelina.

INGELHEIM-WINTERHEIM Germany, Rheinhessen One of the best villages in the Rheinhessen. Top single-vineyards: Ingelheimer Kirchenstück.

IPHOFEN Germany, Franken One of the best villages in Franken. Top single-vineyards: Iphofer Julius-Echter Berg, Iphofer Kronsberg.

IROULÉGUY France, Southwest France (AOC) An interesting Basque appellation producing deep, dark, tannic reds of good,

honest quality, but dull dry whites.

ISCHIA Italy, Campania (DOC) Uninspiring, medium-bodied reds and slightly aromatic dry whites.

ISONZO Italy, Friuli-Venezia Giulia (DOC) Promising red varietal wines from the Cabernet and Merlot grapes, plus eight white varietals of less consistent quality.

JASNIÈRES France, Loire (AOC) The best area of the Coteaux du Loir that, in hot years, is capable of producing dry white wines that are comparable to Savennières in the Anjou-Saumur district.

JOHANNISBERG Germany, Rheingau One of the best villages in the Rheingau. Top single-vineyards: Johannisberger Schloss Johannisberg, Johannisberg Klaus.

JUGENHEIM Germany, Rheinhessen One of the best villages in the Rheinhessen. Top single-vineyards: Jugenheimer Hasensprung.

JULIÉNAS France, Burgundy (AOC) Spicy-rich, chunky-textured red wine from one of the top-quality cru Beaujolais.

JUMILLA Spain, Murcia (DO) Most Jumilla is a lacklustre red, the whites can be fresh and the rosés are acceptable.

JUMILLA MONASTRELL Spain, Murcia (DO) Full, smooth red wines that are invariably better than those with the straight Jumilla DO.

JURANÇON France, Southwest France (AOC) This off-dry, semi-sweet or sweet white wine with its hints of peaches and pineapple on the palate has been famous since the christening of Henri de Navarre in 1553.

JURANÇON SEC France, Southwest France (AOC) Distinctly dry version of the above white wine.

K

KABINETT Germany (QbA) Usually a touch drier than basic QbA, a Kabinett wine from a good producer often represents the best value and most expressive example of its area of origin.

KAISERPFALZ Germany, Rheinhessen If you see this name following that of a village on a bottle of Rheinhessen, it is only a *Grosslage* wine.

KALLSTADT Germany, Rheinpfalz One of the best villages in the Rheinpfalz. Top single-vineyards: Kallstadter Annaberg, Kallstadter Steinacker, Kallstadter Saumagen.

KALTERERSEE Italy, Trentino-Alto Adige (QbA) Synonymous with Caldaro.

KANZEM Germany, Mosel-Saar-Ruwer One of the best villages in the MSR. Top single-vineyards: Kanzemer Altenberg.

KAPELLENBERG Germany, Franken If you see this name following that of a village on a bottle of Franken, it is only a *Grosslage* wine.

KASEL Germany, Mosel-Saar-Ruwer One of the best villages in the MSR. Top single-vineyards: Kaseler Hitzlay, Kaseler Kehrnagel, Kaseler Herrenberg.

KAUB Germany, Mittelrhein One of the best villages in the Mittelrhein. Top single-vineyards: Kauber Backofen, Kauber Rosstein.

KERNER (Grape) Widely grown in Germany, South Africa and England, where it produces somewhat Riesling-like wines, but with higher natural sugar content.

KIEDRICH Germany, Rheingau One of the best villages in the Rheingau. Top single-vineyards: Kiedricher Sandgrub, Kiedricher Wasseros, Kiedricher Gräfenberg.

KIRCHBERG Germany, Franken If you see this name following that of a village on a bottle of Franken, it is only a *Grosslage* wine.

KIRCHENWEINBERG Germany, Württemberg If you see this name following that of a village on a bottle of Württemberg, it is only a *Grosslage* wine.

KLEINBOTTWAR Germany, Württemberg One of the best villages in Württemberg. Top single-vineyards: Kleinbottwarer Süssmund.

KLEVENER DE HEILIGENSTEIN France, Alsace (AOC) Light, dry white wine with a delicate hint of spice.

KLEVNER France, Alsace (AOC) Synonymous with Pinot Blanc.

KLOSTER LIEBFRAUENBERG Germany, Rheinpfalz If you see this name following that of a village on a bottle of Rheinpfalz, it is only a *Grosslage* wine.

KLOSTERBERG Germany, Ahr If you see this name following that of a village on a bottle of Ahr, it is only a *Grosslage* wine.

KOBLENZ-EHRENBREITSTEIN Germany, Mittelrhein One of the best villages in the Mittelrhein. Top single-vineyards: Koblenzer-Ehrenbreitstein Kreuzberg.

KOBNERT Germany, Rheinpfalz If you see this name following that of a village on a bottle of Rheinpfalz, it is only a *Grosslage* wine.

KOCHERBERG Germany, Württemberg If you see this name following that of a village on a bottle of Württemberg, it is only a *Grosslage* wine.

KOLBENHOFER Italy, Trentino-Alto Adige (VT) A more serious version of Caldaro.

KÖNIGSBACH Germany, Rheinpfalz One of the best villages in the Rheinpfalz. Top single-vineyards: Königsbacher Idig.

KÖNIGSBERG Germany, Mosel-Saar-Ruwer If you see this name following that of a village on a bottle of MSR, it is only a *Grosslage* wine.

KÖNIGSGARTEN Germany, Rheinpfalz If you see this name following that of a village on a bottle of Rheinpfalz, it is only a *Grosslage* wine.

KOPF Germany, Württemberg If you see this name following that of a village on a bottle of Württemberg, it is only a *Grosslage* wine.

KRONENBERG Germany, Nahe If you see this name following that of a village on a bottle of Nahe, it is only a *Grosslage* wine.

KRÖTENBRUNNEN Germany, Rheinhessen If you see this name following that of a village on a bottle of Rheinhessen, it is only a *Grosslage* wine.

KURFÜRSTENSTÜCK Germany, Rheinhessen If you see this name following that of a village on a bottle of Rheinhessen, it is only a *Grosslage* wine.

KURFÜRSTLAY Germany, Mosel-Saar-Ruwer If you see this name following that of a village on a bottle of MSR, it is only a *Grosslage* wine.

L

LA COLLINE DE SARRE ET CHESALLET Italy, Valle d'Aosta (VT) Fresh and fruity red wines.

LA CORTE Italy, Tuscany (VT) One of Italy's very best pure Sangiovese wines.

LA GERCA Spain, Canaries (VdlT) Country wines that have yet to make their mark.

LA MANCHA Spain, Castilla-La Mancha (DO) Enormous output of nothing special, but greatly improving red, dry white and rosé wines.

LA PERGOLE TORTE Italy, Tuscany (VT) One of Italy's very best pure Sangiovese wines.

LA RIVE ROSÉ Italy, Veneto (VT) One of Italy's best Cabernet-based blends.

LA SERENA Spain, Extramadura (VC) Struggling to make the grade.

LA SIERRA DE SALA-MANCA Spain, Castilla-León (VC) Struggling to make the grade.

LA TÂCHE France, Burgundy (AOC) This famous and truly fabulous grand cru from the village of Vosne-Romanée in the Côte de Nuits vies with Richebourg as the second-greatest red wine in Burgundy (after Romanée-Conti, that is).

LACRIMA DI MORRO Italy, Marches (DOC) Soft, medium-bodied red wines of no special interest.

LADOIX France, Burgundy (AOC) Village in the Côte de Beaune that produces red and dry white wines not dissimilar to, but more rustic than, those from neighbouring Aloxe-Corton.

LADOIX-CÔTE DE BEAUNE France, Burgundy (AOC) Synonymous with Ladoix.

LADOIX PREMIER CRU France, Burgundy (AOC) The reds have far more finesse than the basic village wines. Dry white is theoretically possible.

LAFOES Portugal, Beiras (IPR) From the Beira Alta, between the Vinho Verde and Dão districts, where every style of wine is produced in varying quality, with Lafoes specialising in acidic red and white wines of no particular interest.

LAGO DI CALDARO Italy, Trentino-Alto Adige (DOC) Synonymous with Caldaro.

LAGOA Portugal Algarve (DOC) The Algarve was considered unworthy of its appellation, so they split it in four and hoped you would not notice. The local co-operative here and at Tavira make slightly more drinkable wines than the rest, but the truth is that the Algarve is better suited to sunbathing and golf than it is to growing good wine grapes.

LAGOS Portugal, Algarve (DOC) The Algarve was considered unworthy of its appellation, so they split it in four and hoped you would not notice. The truth is the Algarve is better suited to sunbathing and golf than it is to growing good wine grapes.

LAHNTAL Germany, Mittelrhein If you see this name following that of a village on a bottle of Mittelrhein, it is only a *Grosslage* wine.

LALANDE-DE-POMEROL France, Bordeaux (AOC) Some good value reds, but even the best are a pale reflection of classic Pomerol.

LAMBRUSCO Italy, Emilia-Romagna (VT) Traditionally, Lambrusco is an off-dry, bright purple, fizzy wine with simple, cherry-flavoured fruit and low alcohol, but it can also be white or rosé and its bubbles may range from barely perceptible to really frothy. Most exported Lambrusco is sweetened up, but whether it is dry or sweet is of little importance for a wine that is possibly less serious than Tizer and certainly less enjoyable. Should you be an avid Lambrusco fan, you have probably realised by now that you have wasted your money buying this book, but to prevent it being a complete loss, look up Picól Ross.

LAMBRUSCO DI SORBARA Italy, Emilia-Romagna (DOC) It's still a few bubbles short of being a real wine, but this has the most body and flavour of any Lambrusco, and is about as serious as it gets.

LAMBRUSCO GRASPAROSSA DI CASTELVETRO Italy, Emilia-Romagna (DOC) Not quite serious, but this is certainly superior to non-DOC Lambrusco.

LAMBRUSCO MANTOVANO Italy, Lombardy (VT) Lambrusco normally comes from Emilia-Romagna, but Lombardy has the dubious honour of making this one.

LAMBRUSCO REGGIANO Italy, Emilia-Romagna (DOC) The lightest DOC Lambrusco.

LAMBRUSCO SALAMINO DI SANTA CROCE Italy, Emilia-Romagna (DOC) This is the most aromatic version of Lambrusco you can find, and the best examples can match the standard of Lambrusco di Sorbara.

LAMEGO Portugal, Beiras

(IPR) From the Beira Alta, between the Vinho Verde and Dão districts, where every style of wine is produced in varying quality.

LAMEZIA Italy, Calabria (DOC) Light-bodied, delicately fruity reds.

LANDWEIN DER MOSEL Germany (DL) One of 15 Deutscher Landwein appellations, its wines should be simple and light-bodied, with a basic flowery aroma, some grapey fruit and a touch of sweetness on the finish.

LANDWEIN DER SAAR Germany (DL) One of 15 Deutscher Landwein appellations, its wines should be simple and light-bodied, with a basic flowery aroma, some grapey fruit and a touch of sweetness on the finish.

LANGENLONSHEIM Germany, Nahe One of the best villages in the Nahe. Top single-vineyards: Langenlonsheimer Steinchen.

LATE-BOTTLED or **LBV PORT** Portugal, Douro (DOC) A pure vintage that usually, but not necessarily, comes from a lesser year. It is bottled later than Vintage Port, after the wine has thrown its deposit in cask and is thus able to remain bright and sediment free for a considerable time in bottle, improving for up to five or six years.

LATISANA Italy, Friuli-Venezia Giulia (DOC) Various red and white varietals of modest interest, but worth a taste.

LATRICIÈRES-CHAMBERTIN France, Burgundy (AOC) Apart from Camus, Drouhin-Laroze, Ponsot and Trapet, this red wine grand cru from Gevrey-Chambertin on the Côte de Nuits is disappointing and overpriced.

LAUFFEN Germany, Württemberg One of the best villages in Württemberg. Top single-vineyards: Lauffener Katzenbeisser.

LAUMERSHEIM Germany, Rheinpfalz One of the best villages in the Rheinpfalz. Top single-vineyards: Laumersheimer Mandelberg.

LEINSWEILER Germany, Rheinpfalz One of the best villages in the Rheinpfalz. Top single-vineyards: Leinsweilerer Sonnenberg.

LESSINI DURELLO Italy, Veneto (DOC) Dry white and sparkling white wine from an area close to Soave, the fizz is supposed to show promise.

LESSONA Italy, Piedmont (DOC) A well-scented red wine with rich fruit and some finesse.

L'ETOILE France, Jura (AOC) Dry white similar to Crépy, but more expressive, with scents of Alpine herbs and bracken.

L'ETOILE MOUSSEUX France, Jura (AOC) Not as good as Côtes du Jura Mousseux, but more potential than Arbois Mousseux.

LETTERE Italy, Campania (VT) Soft, well rounded red wines of good value.

LETWEN Germany, Mosel-Saar-Ruwer One of the best villages in the MSR. Top single-vineyards: Letwener Laurentiuslay.

LEVERANO Italy, Apulia (DOC) Alcoholic reds, soft, dry whites and fresh, fruity rosés.

LIEBFRAUENMORGEN Germany, Rheinhessen If you see this name following that of a village on a bottle of Rheinhessen, it is only a *Grosslage* wine.

LIEBFRAUMILCH Germany (QbA) Cheap, blended German wine that

should be regarded as nothing more than a vin de table, even though it boasts Qualitätswein or Quality Wine status. Should be medium sweet, pleasantly fruity with a grapey aroma, but the point is that if you like Liebfraumilch, you will like 99 out of 100 German wines in the same price bracket, so don't be put off by all those long, confusing German names.

LIMOUX France, Southwest France (AOC) This dull, still wine version of Blanquette de Limoux just goes to prove how much Limoux benefits from bubbles.

LINDAU Germany (DT) One of eight Deutscher Tafelwein sub-regions, its wines should be simple and light-bodied, with a basic flowery aroma, some grapey fruit and a touch of sweetness on the finish.

LINDAUER SEEGARTEN Germany, Württemberg If you see this name following that of a village on a bottle of Württemberg, it is only a *Grosslage* wine.

LINDELBERG Germany, Württemberg If you see this name following that of a village on a bottle of Württemberg, it is only a *Grosslage* wine.

LIRAC France, Rhône Valley (AOC) Once famous for its rosés, it is the reds that are now most successful, particularly in hotter years, when the wines are deep, dark and silky. Surprisingly fragrant dry whites are also produced.

LISON-PRAMAGGIORE Italy, Veneto (DOC) Excellent red wine from the Cabernet, and even better Merlot, but the dry white Tocai is much more modest.

LISTRAC France, Bordeaux (AOC) Up-and-coming red wine that shows the fruit and finesse of St-Julien with the underlying firmness of St-Estèphe.

LLIBER-JAVEA Spain, Murcia (VC) Struggling to make the grade.

LOCOROTONDO Italy, Apulia (DOC) Light, fruity, dry white wines that can sometimes be sparkling.

LORELEYFELSEN Germany, Mittelrhein If you see this name following that of a village on a bottle of Mittelrhein, it is only a *Grosslage* wine.

LORETTOBERG Germany, Baden If you see this name following that of a village on a bottle of Baden, it is only a *Grosslage* wine.

LOS ARRIBES DEL DUERO-FERMOSELLE Spain, Castilla-León (VdlT) Country wines that have yet to make their mark.

LOUPIAC France, Bordeaux (AOC) Sweet to intensely sweet, medium-bodied white wines that are luscious, unctuous and superb value.

LUGANA Italy, Lombardy (DOC) Soft, dry white wine of acceptable quality, produced from vines along the shore of Lake Garda.

LUMASSINA Italy, Liguria (VT) Dull, dry white.

LUSSAC-ST-EMILION France, Bordeaux (AOC) Light but well balanced reds of modest quality.

M

MACABÉO (Grape) Cava grape sometimes used to make dry white table wines, especially in the Penedés region of Spain.

MÂCON France, Burgundy (AOC) When its good, dry white Mâcon is probably the best value, fresh, quaffing Chardonnay in the world. The dry rosé version of Mâcon can be light and

attractive, but forget the reds!

MÂCON-VILLAGES France, Burgundy (AOC) The dry white is usually excellent value, whether simply labelled Mâcon-Villages, or with one of the 42 permitted villages (Mâcon-Clessé, Mâcon-Lugny etc), but only a handful of the reds are worth drinking. Dry rosé is possible.

MÂCON SUPÉRIEUR France, Burgundy (AOC) Red, dry white and dry rosé of no noticeable superiority.

MADEIRA Portugal, Madeira (DOC) Great fortified wines of varying degrees of sweetness that are literally maderised by a heating process, endowing them with the greatest longevity of any known wine (*see* basic styles: **Bual, Malmsey, Sercial** and **Verdelho**).

MADIRAN France, Southwest France (AOC) Deep, dark red wines with rich, powerful flavours and lots of chewy tannins.

MAIKAMMER Germany, Rheinpfalz One of the best villages in the Rheinpfalz. Top single-vineyards: Maikammerer Kirchenstück, Maikammerer Immengarten.

MAIN Germany (DT) One of eight Deutscher Tafelwein sub-regions, its wines should be simple and light-bodied, with a basic flowery aroma, some grapey fruit and a touch of sweetness on the finish.

MALBEC (Grape) Traditionally used to add colour to Bordeaux blends, the Malbec was also responsible for creating the reputation of the 'black wine of Cahors', although its role in this wine today is very minor. Up-and-coming varietal in the New World, particularly Australia.

MALMSEY Portugal, Madeira (DOC) The richest, sweetest style of Madeira, great examples of which are luscious, honeyed and show great finesse.

MALVASIA DELLE LIPARI Italy, Sicily (DOC) Sweet, aromatic *passito* white wine.

MALVASIA DI BOSA Italy, Sardinia (DOC) Some interesting finds amongst these rich sweet or dry, full-bodied whites, and sweet or dry fortified whites.

MALVASIA DI CAGLIARI Italy, Sardinia (DOC) Uninteresting dry and sweet alcoholic whites, and dry and sweet fortified whites.

MALVASIA DI CASORZO D'ASTI Italy, Piedmont (DOC) Slightly aromatic sweet red and rosé wine, which can be still or sparkling.

MALVASIA DI CASTELNUOVO DON BOSCO Italy, Piedmont (DOC) Similar to the above.

MALVASIA DI PLANARGIA Italy, Sardinia (VT) Unfettered by DOC regulations, E & G Arru manage to make a sort of superior Malvasia di Bosa with this wine.

MALVOISIE DE COSSAN Italy, Valle d'Aosta (VT) Smooth, semi-sweet white wine with a slightly bitter finish.

MANCHUELA Spain, Castilla-León (VdlT) Variable quality country wines that fluctuate from dismal to good and promising.

MANDELHÖHE Germany, Rheinpfalz If you see this name following that of a village on a bottle of Rheinpfalz, it is only a *Grosslage* wine.

MANDROLISAI Italy, Sardinia (DOC) Well-scented reds and dry rosés.

MANNABERG Germany, Baden If you see this name following that of a village on a bottle of Baden, it is only a *Grosslage* wine.

MARANGES France, Burgundy (AOC) Elegant light red and dry white wines from three villages in the south of the Côte de Beaune.

MARANGES CÔTE DE BEAUNE France, Burgundy (AOC) Synonymous with Maranges.

MARANGES PREMIER CRU France, Burgundy (AOC) Red and dry white wines that are firmer and more concentrated than those with the basic village appellation.

MAREMMA Italy, Tuscany (VT) Light but well-made and fruity red, dry white and rosé wines.

MARGAUX France, Bordeaux (AOC) Exquisitely balanced, full-bodied red wines that can have deep colour, yet great elegance.

MARIENGARTEN Germany, Rheinpfalz If you see this name following that of a village on a bottle of Rheinpfalz, it is only a *Grosslage* wine.

MARINO Italy, Latium (DOC) Light, dry, uninteresting white wine.

MARKGRAF BABENBERG Germany, Franken If you see this name following that of a village on a bottle of Franken, it is only a *Grosslage* wine.

MARKSBURG Germany, Mittelrhein If you see this name following that of a village on a bottle of Mittelrhein, it is only a *Grosslage* wine.

MARQUÉS DE GRIÑON Spain, Castilla-León In addition to its fresh elegant white wines, which claim the Rueda DO, this

producer also makes a Cabernet-Merlot, which is not even classified as a VC, yet is one of Spain's most stunning red wines.

MARSALA Italy, Sicily (DOC) Complicated range of idiosyncratic fortified wines, which can be classified by their colour, sweetness and age. The various colours are *oro* or golden, *ambra* or amber and *rubino* or ruby-red. Classification of sweetness are *secco* or dry (although it can contain up to 40 grams per litre of sugar, which would make it *demi-sec* in a sparkling wine), *semisecco* or semi-dry (but will contain between 40 and 100 grams per litre of sugar and is really semi-sweet) and *dolce* or sweet. The different ages are Marsala Fine for at least one year (or only four months if aromatised or flavoured), Marsala Superiore for at least two years, Marsala Riserva or Superiore Riserva for at least four years, Marsala Vergine or Solera for at least five years and Marsala Stravecchio or Solera Riserva or Vergine Riserva or Vergine Stavecchio or Solera Stravecchio for at least 10 years. SOM (Superior Old Marsala), LP (London Particular) and GD (Gariboldi Dolce) are all officially classified as Marsala Superiore. Vergine is the lightest style.

MARSANNAY France, Burgundy (AOC) Famous for orange-tinged, ripe, fruity rosé, this village in the Côte de Nuits has been trying since 1987 to establish a reputation for its less successful, somewhat ungenerous and light-weight, red and white wines.

MARSANNAY-LA-CÔTE France, Burgundy (AOC) Synonymous with Marsannay.

MARSANNE (Grape) A Rhône grape also grown in

Australia, where it makes Chardonnay type wines that are often quite oaky.

MARTINA Italy, Apulia (DOC) Firm but uninspiring dry white wines that may be sparkling, from the village of Martina Franca.

MARTINA FRANCA Italy, Apulia (DOC) Synonymous with Martina.

MASIANCO Italy, Veneto (VT) Dry, fruity white wine, but not special.

MASO LODRON Italy, Trentino-Alto Adige (VT) One of Italy's best Cabernet-based blends.

MATANEGRA Spain, Extramadura (VdlT) Country wines that have yet to make their mark.

MATINO Italy, Apulia (DOC) Robust reds and sturdy rosé.

MAULBRONN Germany, Württemberg One of the best villages in Württemberg. Top single-vineyards: Maulbronner Eilfingerberg.

MAURIZIO ZANELLA Italy, Lombardy (VT) Named after the owner of Ca'del Bosco, this full, rich and unctuous red wine is considered to be one of Italy's finest Bordeaux-style blends.

MAURY France, Languedoc-Roussillon (AOC) Fortified wines with numerous different possibilities of styles, although most are pale-coloured, with a curious combination of toasty, tangy, berry flavours, made entirely from the Grenache grape.

MAURY 'RANCIO' France, Languedoc-Roussillon (AOC) As above, but spoilt by the rancid-maderised effect of the 'rancio' process.

MAXIMIN GRÜNHAUS Germany, Mosel-Saar-Ruwer One of the best villages in the MSR. Top single-vineyards: Maximin Grünhauser Abtsberg, Maximin Grünhauser Bruderberg, Maximin Grünhauser Herrenberg.

MAZIS-CHAMBERTIN France, Burgundy (AOC) A red wine grand cru of great potential complexity from the village of Chambolle-Musigny in the Côte de Nuits.

MAZOYÈRES-CHAMBERTIN France, Burgundy (AOC) Synonymous with Charmes-Chambertin.

MEDDERSHEIM Germany, Nahe One of the best villages in the Nahe. Top single-vineyards: Meddersheimer Rheingrafenberg.

MÉDOC France, Bordeaux (AOC) All these red wines aspire to the Haut-Médoc style, but have less concentration.

MEERSPINNE Germany, Rheinpfalz If you see this name following that of a village on a bottle of Rheinpfalz, it is only a *Grosslage* wine.

MEHRHÖLZCHEN Germany, Rheingau If you see this name following that of a village on a bottle of Rheingau, it is only a *Grosslage* wine.

MELISSA Italy, Calabria (DOC) Full-bodied reds and crisp, dry whites.

MELMSHEIM Germany, Württemberg One of the best villages in Württemberg. Top single-vineyards: Melmsheimer Katzenörhrle.

MELON (Grape) A synonym of the Muscadet grape currently gaining favour in various North American wine areas, although many consumers there think the wine is actually made from melons! It would cause far less confusion if producers used

its better known synonym, which is the Gamay Blanc.

MENETOU-SALON France, Loire (AOC) Underrated crisp, dry Sauvignon Blanc wines that are at least as good as Sancerre.

MÉNTRIDA Spain, Castilla-La Mancha (DO) Cheap, basic red and rosé, consumed locally.

MERANER HÜGEL Italy, Trentino-Alto Adige (QbA) Synonymous with Meranese di Collina.

MERANESE DI COLLINA Italy, Trentino-Alto Adige (DOC) Light-bodied, delicately scented reds.

MERCUREY France, Burgundy (AOC) Exceptional quality fruity reds and spicy-buttery dry whites of light to medium body.

MERCUREY PREMIER CRU France, Burgundy (AOC) Fine red and dry white Burgundies at reasonable prices.

MERLOT (Grape) Great Bordeaux grape capable of luscious, velvety red wine, the Merlot is currently very fashionable in the States.

MERXHEIM Germany, Nahe One of the best villages in the Nahe. Top single-vineyards: Merxheimer Römerberg.

MESENICH Germany, Mosel-Saar-Ruwer One of the best villages in the MSR. Top single-vineyards: Mesenicher Abteiberg, Mesenicher Deuslay.

MEURSAULT France, Burgundy (AOC) Famous for its nutty-buttery dry white wines from the Côte de Beaune, but the quality is not always what it should be. Fine reds also produced.

MEURSAULT-BLAGNY France, Burgundy (AOC) Alternative appellation for Blagny.

MEURSAULT-CÔTE DE BEAUNE France, Burgundy (AOC) Synonymous with Meursault.

MEURSAULT-SANTENOTS France, Burgundy (AOC) Confusing appellation for dry white wines of premier cru status produced from the Santenots vineyard in Volnay!

MEURSAULT PREMIER CRU France, Burgundy (AOC) The chances of finding great red and white Meursault are much improved under this appellation.

MICHELFELD Germany, Baden One of the best villages in Baden. Top single-vineyards: Michelfelder Himmelberg.

MICHELSBERG Germany, Mosel-Saar-Ruwer If you see this name following that of a village on a bottle of MSR, it is only a *Grosslage* wine.

MINERVOIS France, Languedoc-Roussillon (AOC) Rough and ready reds, good value dry rosés and rarely-encountered dry whites.

MIRALDUOLO Italy, Umbria (VT) One of Italy's best pure Cabernet Sauvignon wines.

MITTELRHEIN Germany, (QbA) A patchwork of primarily Riesling vineyards perched on precarous slopes, the Mittelrhein produces wines of high quality, well worth seeking out.

MITTELRHEIN GROSSLAGEN Germany, Mittelrhein (Grosslagen) Schloss Reichenstein, Schloss Stahleck, Burg Hammerstein, Burg Rheinfels, Gedeonseck, Herrenberg, Lahntal, Loreleyfelsen, Marksburg, Schloss Schönburg and Petersberg are all *Grosslagen*, not single-vineyard wines and should be very reasonably priced, unless you are being ripped-off or it happens to be an Eiswein, Beerenauslese or Trockenbeerenauslese.

MONBAZILLAC France, Southwest France (AOC) Excellent value Sauternes-style sweet white wine.

MONICA DI CAGLIARI Italy, Sardinia (DOC) Delicately scented reds that can be sweet or dry. Fortified versions also exist.

MONICA DI SARDEGNA Italy, Sardinia (DOC) Medium-bodied reds of some fragrance.

MONTAGNE-ST-EMILION France, Bordeaux (AOC) Full, rich reds from one of the two best St-Emilion satellite appellations, the other being St-Georges-St-Emilion.

MONTAGNY France, Burgundy (AOC) A good value dry white wine, somewhat fuller and fatter than a Mâcon.

MONTAGNY PREMIER CRU France, Burgundy (AOC) Delicious dry white wine with a buttery-rich flavour that is more reminiscent of a Côte de Beaune than a Mâcon.

MONTANCHEZ Spain, Extramadura (VdlT) Country wines that have yet to make their mark.

MONTE ANTICO Italy, Tuscany (VT) Various red and white Chianti-like wines.

MONTECARLO Italy, Tuscany (DOC) Some interesting dry white wines of some character and elegance.

MONTECOMPATRI-COLONNA Italy, Latium (DOC) Lacklustre dry and semi-sweet white wines.

MONTEFALCO Italy, Umbria (DOC) Red wines

that are not special, except for Sagrantino, a varietal wine of deep colour and luscious fruit. A red Sagrantino *passito* also exists.

MONTELLO E COLLI ASOLANI Italy, Veneto (DOC) Various red and white varietal wines, including Cabernet and Merlot, but not special.

MONTEPULCIANO CERASUOLO DEL MOLISE Italy, Molise (VT) Simple, fresh, cherry-coloured wines that are best drunk young.

MONTEPULCIANO D'ABRUZZO Italy, Abruzzi (DOC) Red wines that can be either soft and plump or rich and tannic, but virtually all examples are really good stuff. The Abruzzi's finest wine.

MONTEPULCIANO DELLE MARCHE Italy, Marches (VT) Rustic reds that are not in the same class as the Montepulciano d'Abruzzo, but some can be rich, fruity and good value.

MONTEPULCIANO DEL MOLISE Italy, Molise (VT) Not in the same class as the Montepulciano d'Abruzzo, but this well-coloured, full-bodied red wine is smooth, fruity and distinctly more reliable than the Montepulciano delle Marche.

MONTEPULCIANO DI BASILICATA Italy, Basilicata (VT) Full-bodied, scented reds of some interest.

MONTESCUDAIO Italy, Tuscany (DOC) Light, soft red, white and vino santo wines of little interest.

MONTHÉLIE France, Burgundy (AOC) Vividly coloured, silky red wine and a little dry white from the most underrated village in Burgundy. Côte de Beaune.

MONTHÉLIE-CÔTE DE BEAUNE France, Burgundy (AOC) Synonymous with Monthélie.

MONTHÉLIE PREMIER CRU France, Burgundy (AOC) Exquisite red Burgundy at relatively inexpensive prices. Dry white is theoretically possible.

MONTLOUIS France, Loire (AOC) Forget the dry and semi-sweet styles of this white wine, it is the intensely sweet versions described as *moelleux* on the label that are nothing less than sensational.

MONTLOUIS MOUSSEUX France, Loire (AOC) Good quality sparkling white wines made in dry to sweet styles.

MONTLOUIS PÉTILLANT France, Loire Delicately rich and fruity, slightly sparkling white wines.

MONTRACHET France, Burgundy (AOC) Many consider this to be the greatest dry white wine in the world, and when fully mature it truly does have the most glorious and expressive character of all white Burgundies.

MONTRAVEL France, Southwest France (AOC) Crisp, dry, aromatic white wines.

MONTSCLAPADE Italy, Friuli-Venezia Giulia (VT) One of Italy's best Cabernet-based blends.

MONTUNI DEL RENO Italy, Emilia-Romagna (DOC) Lacklustre dry, semi-sweet and semi-sparkling white wines.

MONZINGEN Germany, Nahe One of the best villages in the Nahe. Top single-vineyards: Monzinger Rosenberg, Monzinger Frühlingsplätzchen.

MORELLINO DI SCANSANO Italy, Tuscany

(DOC) Good Brunello-type red wines.

MOREY-ST-DENIS France, Burgundy (AOC) This village appellation in the Côte de Nuits produces vividly coloured, lively and expressive reds and rich, dry, full-bodied whites.

MOREY-ST-DENIS PREMIER CRU France, Burgundy (AOC) A definite step up from the albeit excellent village wines.

MORGEX ET LA SALLE Italy, Val d'Aosta (DOC) Light, fragrant, dry white wines from some of the highest mountain vineyards in Europe.

MORGON France, Burgundy (AOC) The best rank with Moulin-à-Vent as the most sturdy and longlived of the ten top-quality cru Beaujolais.

MORI VECIO Italy, Trentino-Alto Adige (VT) One of Italy's best Cabernet-based blends.

MORIO-MUSKAT (Grape) This very aromatic grape is, strangely, a cross between two very neutral varieties, Sylvaner and Pinot Blanc.

MORMORETO Italy, Tuscany (VT) One of Italy's best Cabernet Sauvignon-dominated blends.

MOSCADELLO DI MONTALCINO Italy, Tuscany (DOC) Wonderfully aromatic, dry and sweet, still, sparkling and fortified white wines.

MOSCATO D'ASTI Italy, Piedmont (DOCG) Similar to Asti Spumante, but with a minimum pressure (strength of mousse) of three atmospheres, as opposed to five. Still or slightly fizzy Asti should, in theory, carry the Moscato Naturale d'Asti appellation, but in practice 'Naturale' is often missing from the name on the label, so it is impossible to know how

much fizz, if any, this wine will have.

MOSCATO D'ASTI SPUMANTE Italy, Piedmont (DOCG) Synonymous with Moscato d'Asti. Moscato Spumante without the Asti or any other village can, however, refer to any blended sparkling Moscato wine and most of the blend will probably come from the south of Italy.

MOSCATO DEL VULTURE Italy, Basilicata (VT) Sweet white dessert wines, usually sparkling.

MOSCATO DI NOTO Italy, Sicily (DOC) Sweet, aromatic, white wines that may be natural, sparkling or fortified.

MOSCATO DI PANTELLERIA Italy, Sicily (DOC) Sicily's best Moscato. As for Moscato di Noto.

MOSCATO DI SCANZO Italy, Lombardy (VT) Great Moscato.

MOSCATO DI SIRACUSA Italy, Sicily (DOC) Rich, sweet, smooth white wines of some interest.

MOSCATO DI SORSO-SENNORI Italy, Sardinia (DOC) Full, luscious, sweet, aromatic white wines that can be found in natural and *liquoroso* styles.

MOSCATO DI STREVI Italy, Piedmont (VT) Not so famous, but usually just as good as Moscato d'Asti.

MOSCATO DI TRANI Italy, Apulia (DOC) Smooth sweet, aromatic white wine, the *liquoroso* version of which will be fortified.

MOSCATO NATURALE D'ASTI Italy, Piedmont (DOC) As the name suggests, these wines are occasionally still, but they often show the barest hint of a prickle and can sometimes be slightly sparkling or even semi-sparkling. They are always, however, succulently rich and sweet.

MOSCATO SPUMANTE Italy Not the real thing from Asti, but can be almost as good, if well selected.

MOSEL Germany (DT) One of eight Deutscher Tafelwein sub-regions, its wines should be simple and light-bodied, with a basic flowery aroma, some grapey fruit and a touch of sweetness on the finish.

MOSEL-SAAR-RUWER Germany, (QbA) If you stick to Rieslings, you will find the best MSR wines have supreme elegance and a tantalizing piquancy that sets them apart from those of every other German wine region, especially when from warmer vintages.

MOSEL-SAAR-RUWER GROSSLAGEN Germany, Mosel-Saar-Ruwer (Grosslagen) Goldbäumchen, Grafschaft, Rosenhang, Schwarze Katz, Weinhex, Badstube, Vom Heissen Stein, Kurfürstlay, Michelsberg, Münzlay, Nacktarsch, Probstberg, Schwarzlay, St-Michael, Römerlay, Schwarzberg, Königsberg, Gipfel and Schloss Bübinger are all *Grosslagen*, not single-vineyard wines and should be very reasonably priced, unless you are being ripped-off or it happens to be an Eiswein, Beerenauslese or Trockenbeerenauslese.

MOULIN-À-VENT France, Burgundy (AOC) The deep colour, intense fruit and tannic structure of Moulin-à-Vent make it the most sturdy, compact and long-lived of the ten top-quality cru Beaujolais.

MOULIS France, Bordeaux (AOC) Tremendous value red wines that have more power than those from neighbouring Margaux, but lack the finesse.

MOULIS-EN-MÉDOC France, Bordeaux (AOC) Synonymous with Moulis.

MOURA Portugal, Alentejo (IPR) Lots of white wine, most of which is ordinary, but the reds are full, fruity and rapidly improving.

MOURVÈDRE (Grape) An underrated Rhône variety that is widely cultivated throughout southern France and in Spain, where it is known as the Mataro. It should be used to make more varietal wines in the New World, particularly Australia, where it is the fifth most important black grape variety.

MÜLLER-THURGAU (Grape) Grown extensively in Germany and England, the Müller-Thurgau is sometimes referred to as Riesling-Sylvaner or Rivaner (but not Rieslaner, which is a different cross) and produces a typically flowery-fruity wine. If you have tasted any Liebfraumilch or inexpensive Niersteiner, you have tasted Müller-Thurgau.

MÜLLER THURGAU DI ZIANO Italy, Emilia-Romagna (VT) This dry, crisp white wine is a serious match to English Müller-Thurgau!

MUNDELSHEIM Germany, Württemberg One of the best villages in Württemberg. Top single-vineyards: Mundelsheimer Käsberg.

MUNIESA Spain, Aragón (VC) Struggling to make the grade.

MÜNSTER-SARMSHEIM Germany, Nahe One of the best villages in the Nahe. Top single-vineyards: Münster Dautenflanzer.

MÜNZLAY Germany, Mosel-Saar-Ruwer If you see this name following that of a village on a bottle of MSR, it is only a *Grosslage* wine.

MUSCADELLE (Grape) A singular variety that has nothing to do with either the Muscat or Muscadet grapes, although its musky flavour is somewhat reminiscent of the former.

MUSCADET (Grape) *(See Melon entry.)*

MUSCADET France, Loire (AOC) The bone-dry wines sold under the basic appellation seldom rise above the level of mouth-puckering.

MUSCADET DE SÈVRE-ET-MAINE France, Loire (AOC) From a vast number of properties, it is possible to select several good Muscadet, which should be lean, but never mean.

MUSCADET DES COTEAUX DE LA LOIRE France, Loire (AOC) This is the best Muscadet appellation in the really big, hot sunny years.

MUSCAT France, Alsace (AOC) Fine, fragrant, dry white wine with floral aroma and very little acidity.

MUSCAT (Grape) There are numerous related varieties, sub-varieties and localised clones that come under this generic name, but they all have that wonderful heady aroma and rich, musky flavour, which comes through whether the wine is Muscat d'Alsace, Muscat de Beaumes-de-Venise, Rivesaltes, Frontignan (*et al*), Moscato d'Asti, Muscat of Samos or whatever. If you have ever bitten into a crunchy grape, either white or black, and tasted what can only be described as perfume, you have eaten a Muscat.

MUSCAT DE BEAUMES-DE-VENISE France, Rhône Valley (AOC) Wonderfully clean and pure, fortified Muscat that is best drunk young.

MUSCAT DE FRONTIGNAN France, Languedoc-Roussillon (AOC) Raisiny rich, fortified Muscat, made in a sweet style with a fat, honeyed aftertaste. Historically more famous than Muscat de Beaumes-de-Venise.

MUSCAT DE LUNEL France, Languedoc-Roussillon (AOC) Less weight than the Frontignan, but just as sweet and more fragrant.

MUSCAT DE MIREVAL France, Languedoc-Roussillon (AOC) Less concentrated than the Frontignan, but equally sweet, it often has a finer balance of acidity.

MUSCAT DE RIVESALTES France, Languedoc-Roussillon (AOC) This excellent, sweet fortified wine should not be confused with Rivesaltes plain and simple, which are not pure Muscat.

MUSCAT DE ST-JEAN-DE-MINERVOIS France, Languedoc-Roussillon (AOC) Superb, sweet, fleshy, fortified wines with a fresh, grapey, apricoty flavour from a corner of Minervois, which is better known for its relatively inferior dry red wines.

MUSIGNY France, Burgundy (AOC) Smooth, stylish and seductive red grand cru wines from the village of Chambolle-Musigny in the Côte de Nuits.

MUSSBACH Germany, Rheinpfalz One of the best villages in the Rheinpfalz. Top single-vineyards: Mussbacher Eselshaut.

NACKTARSCH Germany, Mosel-Saar-Ruwer If you see this name following that of a village on a bottle of MSR, it is only a *Grosslage* wine.

NAHE Germany, (QbA) The sunny microclimate and varied soils of the Nahe combine to produce wines that have the elegance of a Rheingau, the body of a light Rheinhessen and the acidity of a Mosel, but with a perfumed aroma that is unique to the Rieslings of this region.

NAHE GROSSLAGEN Germany, Nahe (Grosslagen) Kronenberg, Pfarrgarten, Schlosskapelle, Sonnenborn, Burgweg, Paradiesgarten and Rosengarten are all *Grosslagen*, not single-vineyard wines and should be very reasonably priced, unless you are being ripped-off or it happens to be an Eiswein, Beerenauslese or Trockenbeerenauslese.

NAHEGAUER LANDWEIN Germany (DL) One of 15 Deutscher Landwein appellations, its wines should be simple and light-bodied, with a basic flowery aroma, some grapey fruit and a touch of sweetness on the finish.

NARDO Italy, Apulia (DOC) Robust, alcoholic reds.

NASCO DI CAGLIARI Italy, Sardinia (DOC) Finely scented, delicate white wines that can be dry or sweet, natural or fortified.

NAVARRA Spain, Basque Country (DO) A sort of rustic Rioja, with typically oaky reds, crisp dry whites and fresh, fruity rosés.

NÉAC France, Bordeaux (AOC) Theoretically possible to find, although this appellation has not been used since the growers have been allowed to use the Lalande-de-Pomerol.

NEBBIOLO D'ALBA Italy, Piedmont (DOC) Pure Nebbiolo red wines from an area between Barolo and Barbaresco, but beware the

sweet and sparkling versions that also exist.

NEBBIOLO DEL PIEMONTE Italy, Piedmont (VT) Most are simple red wines, but exceptionally fine examples are made in great years by the best Barolo and Barbaresco producers.

NECKAR Germany (DT) One of four vast Deutscher Tafelwein regions, Neckar is roughly equivalent to the Württemberg QbA region. These wines should be simple and light-bodied, with a basic flowery aroma, some grapey fruit and a touch of sweetness on the finish.

NEEF Germany, Mosel-Saar-Ruwer One of the best villages in the MSR. Top single-vineyards: Neefer Frauenberg.

NEIPPBERG Germany, Württemberg One of the best villages in Württemberg. Top single-vineyards: Neippberger Schlossberg.

NEUENAHR Germany, Ahr One of the best villages in the Ahr. Top single-vineyards: Neuenahr Sonnenberg.

NEUSTADT-GIMMELDINGEN Germany, Rheinpfalz One of the best villages in the Rheinpfalz. Top single-vineyards: Neustadt-Gimmeldinger Kapellenberg.

NEUWEIER Germany, Baden One of the best villages in Baden. Top single-vineyards: Neuweierer Heiligenstein.

NIEDERFLÖRSHEIM Germany, Rheinhessen One of the best villages in the Rheinhessen. Top single-vineyards: Niederflörsheimer Frauenberg.

NIERSTEIN Germany, Rheinhessen One of the

best villages in the Rheinhessen. Top single-vineyards: Niersteiner Heiligenbaum, Niersteiner Kranzberg, Niersteiner Orbel, Niersteiner Oelberg, Niersteiner Hipping, Niersteiner Pettenthal, Niersteiner Brudersberg, Niersteiner Hölle, Niersteiner Brückchen, Niersteiner Paterberg.

NORDHEIM Germany, Franken One of the best villages in Franken. Top single-vineyards: Nordheimer Vögelein.

NORHEIM Germany, Nahe One of the best villages in the Nahe. Top single-vineyards: Norheimer Dellchen.

NUITS France, Burgundy (AOC) Seldom seen appellation synonymous with Nuits-St-Georges.

NUITS-ST-GEORGES France, Burgundy (AOC) Village appellation that produces firm, full-bodied reds that sometimes lack character and finesse. Dry white is possible.

NUITS-ST-GEORGES PREMIER CRU France, Burgundy (AOC) These wines have all the body and structure of those under the village appellation, plus plenty of character and finesse. Also produces a dry, powerful, fat and spicy white.

NUITS PREMIER CRU France, Burgundy (AOC) Seldom seen appellation synonymous with Nuits-St-Georges Premier Cru.

NURAGUS DI CAGLIARI Italy, Sardinia (DOC) Dry and semi-sweet semi-sparkling wines of little interest.

NUS Italy, Piedmont (DOC) Fragrant red wines and both dry and sweet *passito* styles of white wine from the Malvoisie or Pinot Grigio grape.

NUSSDORF Germany, Rheinpfalz One of the best villages in the Rheinpfalz. Top single-vineyards: Nussdorfer Herrenberg.

O BOLO Spain, Galicia (VC) Struggling to make the grade.

OBERBERGEN Germany, Baden One of the best villages in Baden. Top single-vineyards: Oberberger Bassgeige.

OBERMOSCHEL Germany, Nahe One of the best villages in the Nahe. Top single-vineyards: Obermoscheler Geissenkopf.

OBERRHEIN Germany (DT) One of four vast Deutscher Tafelwein regions, Oberrhein is roughly equivalent to the Baden QbA region. These wines should be simple and light-bodied, with a basic flowery aroma, some grapey fruit and a touch of sweetness on the finish.

OBERROTWEIL Germany, Baden One of the best villages in Baden. Top single-vineyards: Oberrotweiler Eichberg, Oberrotweiler Henkenberg.

OBERWESEL Germany, Mittelrhein One of the best villages in the Mittelrhein. Top single-vineyards: Oberweseler St-Martinsberg, Oberweseler Römerkrug.

OBIDOS Portugal, Estremadura (IPR) Clean fruity reds, the best of which have a good concentration of berry flavours, whereas the best whites are simply crisp with a touch of spritz, and are much less interesting.

OCKFEN Germany, Mosel-Saar-Ruwer One of the best villages in the MSR. Top single-vineyards: Ockfener Bockstein.

OELSPIEL Germany, Franken If you see this name following that of a village on a bottle of Franken, it is only a *Grosslage* wine.

OESTRICH Germany, Rheingau One of the best villages in the Rheingau. Top single-vineyards: Oestricher Lenchen.

OLTREPÒ PAVESE Italy, Lombardy (DOC) An all-encompassing appellation for too many different styles and qualities to make any sensible recommendation, but they are certainly worth tasting.

OPPENHEIM Germany, Rheinhessen One of the best villages in the Rheinhessen. Top single-vineyards: Oppenheimer Herrenberg, Oppenheimer Kreuz, Oppenheimer Daubhaus, Oppenheimer Sackträger.

ORDENSGUT Germany, Rheinpfalz If you see this name following that of a village on a bottle of Rheinpfalz, it is only a *Grosslage* wine.

ORTA VOVA Italy, Apulia (DOC) Full-bodied vinous reds and dry rosés.

ORTENBERG Germany, Baden One of the best villages in Baden. Top single-vineyards: Ortenberger Schlossberg.

ORVIETO Italy, Umbria (DOC) Although these dry and semi-sweet white wines are hugely overrated, a few producers do make outstanding examples.

OSTHOFEN Germany, Rheinhessen One of the best villages in the Rheinhessen. Top single-vineyards: Osthofer Liebenberg.

OSTUNI Italy, Apulia (DOC) Delicate, dry white wines.

OSTUNI OTTAVIANELLO Italy, Apulia (DOC) Uninspiring light red wine from Ostuni.

P

PACHERENC DU VIC-BILH France, Southwest France (AOC) This dry white wine comes from Madiran and has soft, floral aromas, fruit-salad flavours and an off-dry, medium-sweet or sweet finish.

PAGADEBIT DI ROMAGNA Italy, Emilia-Romagna (VT) Dry and semi-sweet white wines that can have some delicacy.

PALAZZO ALTESI Italy, Tuscany (VT) One of Italy's very best pure Sangiovese wines.

PALETTE France, Provence (AOC) High quality red wines of some finesse, but the whites and rosés are not exciting.

PALMELA Portugal, Setúbal (IPR) An area made famous by João Pires Palmela, an early-picked Muscat with a touch of residual sugar highlights the flowery-peachy character of this ravishingly fresh and vital white wine.

PARADIESGARTEN Germany, Nahe If you see this name following that of a village on a bottle of Nahe, it is only a *Grosslage* wine.

PARELLADA (Grape) Cava grape sometimes used to make dry white wines, especially in the Penedés region of Spain.

PARRINA Italy, Tuscany (DOC) Soft, Sangiovese-based red wines with attractively delicate fruit from Tuscany's most southerly DOC, but the whites are not so interesting.

PARSAC-ST-EMILION France, Bordeaux (AOC)

These wines are usually sold under the Montagne-St-Emilion appellation.

PATRIMONIO France, Corsica (AOC) Some fine red wines, but the dry whites and dry rosés are not special, although quite fragrant and well made.

PAUILLAC France, Bordeaux (AOC) Pauillac includes the famous châteaux of Latour, Lafite and Mouton and vies with Margaux as the greatest red wine appellation of Bordeaux.

PÉCHARMANT France, Southwest France (AOC) The finest red wines of Bergerac.

PENEDÉS Spain, Catalonia (DO) Primarily white wines of average quality, but includes some exceptional red wines. Some rosés and fortified wines are also produced.

PENTRO Italy, Molise (DOC) Slightly tannic reds of no special interest.

PENTRO DI ISERNIA Italy, Molise (DOC) Synonymous with Pentro.

PERL Germany, Mosel-Saar-Ruwer One of the best villages in the MSR. Top single-vineyards: Perler Hasenberg.

PERNAND-VERGELESSES France, Burgundy (AOC) The most northerly Côte de Beaune village can produce fine red and dry white wines, but too many sold under the village appellation are rustic, overrated and overpriced.

PERNAND-VERGELESSES-CÔTE DE BEAUNE France, Burgundy (AOC) Synonymous with Pernand-Vergelesses.

PERNAND-VERGELESSES PREMIER CRU France, Burgundy (AOC) These elegant reds and mellow whites have the class that the basic village wines lack.

PESSAC-LÉOGNAN France, Bordeaux (AOC) Most of the finest red and white wines of Graves have been sold under this appellation since (the harvest of) 1987.

PETERSBERG Germany, Rheinhessen If you see this name following that of a village on a bottle of Rheinhessen, it is only a *Grosslage* wine.

PETERSBURG Germany, Mittelrhein If you see this name following that of a village on a bottle of Mittelrhein, it is only a *Grosslage* wine.

PETIT CHABLIS France, Burgundy (AOC) These dry white wines are mostly lean, mean and meagre.

PFAFFENGRUND Germany, Rheinpfalz If you see this name following that of a village on a bottle of Rheinpfalz, it is only a *Grosslage* wine.

PFÄLZER LANDWEIN Germany (DL) One of 15 Deutscher Landwein appellations, its wines should be simple and light-bodied, with a basic flowery aroma, some grapey fruit and a touch of sweetness on the finish.

PFARRGARTEN Germany, Nahe If you see this name following that of a village on a bottle of Nahe, it is only a *Grosslage* wine.

PIAVE Italy, Veneto (DOC) A large area producing eight varietals, of which the red Cabernet and Raboso wines can be very good.

PICCONE Italy, Piedmont (VT) Robust reds from Gattinara-like blend.

PICOL ROSS Italy, Emilia-Romagna (VT) This dry, aromatic, fruity, semi-sparkling red wine is the best non-DOC Lambrusco available. Lambrusco lovers

should also look up Scorza Amara.

PIESPORT Germany, Mosel-Saar-Ruwer One of the best villages in the MSR. Top single-vineyards: Piesporter Goldtröpfchen.

PILGERPFAD Germany, Rheinhessen If you see this name following that of a village on a bottle of Rheinhessen, it is only a *Grosslage* wine.

PINEAU CHARENTAIS France, Cognac (AOC) Synonymous with Pineau des Charentes. (*See* **Pineau des Charentes** entry.)

PINEAU DES CHARENTES France, Cognac (AOC) Sweet, cloying aperitif made from unfermented grape juice that has been prevented from fermenting by the addition of Cognac. This is to Cognac what the Floc de Gascogne is to Armagnac, and the unclassified Ratafia is to Champagne.

PINHEL Portugal, Beiras (IPR) From the Beira Alta, between the Vinho Verde and Dão districts, where every style of wine is produced in varying quality, although Pinhel specialises in a dry, full, earthy white and makes the only rosé in the area.

PINOT France, Alsace (AOC) Synonymous with Pinot Blanc.

PINOT BLANC France, Alsace (AOC) Fresh, deliciously fruity, dry white wine.

PINOT BLANC (Grape) Apart from Alsace, this grape can be successful to one degree or another in Burgundy, Germany, Italy and elsewhere.

PINOT CHARDONNAY-MÂCON France, Burgundy (AOC) Alternative appellation for dry white Mâcon.

PINOT GRIS (Grape) Another grape that is at its

absolute best in Alsace where it has a rich, succulent, spicy character not found in Pinot Gris wines made elsewhere.

PINOT GRIS France, Alsace (AOC) Synonymous with Tokay-Pinot Gris.

PINOT NOIR France, Alsace (AOC) Not great quality, but good and improving red wine that is well perfumed, with elegant fruit and a very pure varietal character.

PINOT NOIR (Grape) The world's most elusive classic red wine grape, more Pinot Noirs disappoint than excite, even in Burgundy, but it is capable of producing a red wine of incomparable finesse and grace. With good but patchy results in New Zealand and Oregon, the two areas most people thought best suited to the Pinot Noir, it has been a great surprise to everyone that Santa Barbara in Southern California should be the most consistent producer of fine Pinot Noir outside of Burgundy.

PINOTAGE (Grape) An unfashionable grape variety developed in South Africa, its quality has probably been underrated due to high-cropping and the commercial level of its vinification. Also planted in New Zealand, California and various other areas, but has yet to establish its true quality.

PLANALTO-MIRANDES Portugal, Trás-os-Montes (IPR) The extreme eastern section of the former appellation of Trás-os-Montes, in the hinterland of the Upper Douro, an area made famous by Sogrape's Planalto, a rich white wine with the flavour of honeyed fruit.

POLLINO Italy, Calabria (DOC) Full, fruity, *chiaretto* wines.

POMEROL France, Bordeaux (AOC) Merlot-dominated wines of surprisingly deep colour, the finest Pomerol have velvety-rich, succulent fruit that is capable of aging gracefully.

POMINO Italy, Tuscany (DOC) Fine red wines, very successful dry whites and semi-sweet, red and white vino santo.

POMMARD France, Burgundy (AOC) Once infamous for its dark, alcoholic and soupy red wines, Pommard was reborn some 10 years ago and the best growers now produce very exciting wines indeed.

POMMARD PREMIER CRU France, Burgundy (AOC) Currently producing some of the most exciting red Burgundies, especially those from various specific vineyards in the premiers crus of Les Rugiens, which makes deep and voluptuous wines, and Les Épenots, which is softer and more fragrant.

PORT Portugal, Douro (DOC) The world's greatest fortified red wine, although a little white Port is also produced (*see* basic styles: **Colheita Port, Crusted** or **Crusting Port, Late-Bottled Port, Ruby Port, Single Quinta Port, Tawny Port, Vintage Character Port, Vintage Port** and **White Port**).

PORTALEGRE Portugal, Alentejo (IPR) Lots of white wine, most of which is ordinary, but the reds are full, fruity and rapidly improving.

PORTIMÃO Portugal, Algarve (DOC) The Algarve was considered unworthy of its appellation, so they split it in four and hoped you would not notice. The truth is that the Algarve is better suited to sunbathing and golf than it is to growing good wine grapes.

PORTULANO Italy, Apulia (VT) Ample red of full body, rich flavour and excellent longevity.

POUILLY-FUISSÉ France, Burgundy (AOC) Apart from a handful of truly exceptional wines, you might as well save your money and buy St-Véran or Mâcon Blanc.

POUILLY-LOCHÉ France, Burgundy (AOC) Mâcon-style dry white.

POUILLY-SUR-LOIRE France, Loire (AOC) Beware! This dull and boring wine is not Pouilly-Fumé. It is not even Sauvignon Blanc.

POUILLY-VINZELLES France, Burgundy (AOC) More Mâcon-style dry white.

POUILLY BLANC FUMÉ France, Loire (AOC) Synonymous with Pouilly-Fumé.

POUILLY FUMÉ France, Loire (AOC) The best Sauvignon Blanc produced in the Loire.

POZOHONDO Spain, Castilla-León (VdlT) Variable quality country wines that fluctuate from dismal to good and promising.

PREMIERES-CÔTES-DE-BORDEAUX France, Bordeaux (AOC) A rapidly rising Bordeaux red wine star in the value-for-money stakes, but the semi-sweet white wines are generally unexciting.

PREMIERES CÔTES DE BLAYE France, Bordeaux (AOC) Some serious reds and dry, grapey whites are produced in this appellation, which is on a par with the best Côtes de Bourg.

PRIMITIVO DI MANDURIA Italy, Apulia (DOC) Dry to semi-sweet, full-bodied red wine that may be fortified, from the original Zinfandel grape.

PRIORATO Spain, Catalonia (DO) Rare, but mostly oxidised, wines. Red, white and rosé wines, both still and fortified are produced, even the table wines contain 14-18% alcohol!

PROBSTBERG Germany, Mosel-Saar-Ruwer If you see this name following that of a village on a bottle of MSR, it is only a *Grosslage* wine.

PROSECCO DI CONEGLIANO-VALDOBBIADENE Italy, Veneto (DOC) Dry and semi-sweet fizzy wines that have large bubbles and a dull flavour. Still whites are equally lacklustre.

PUISSEGUIN-ST-EMILION France, Bordeaux (AOC) These red wines are as rich as Montagne-St-Emilion, but more rustic and lack the finesse.

PULIGNY-MONTRACHET France, Burgundy (AOC) One of the two Montrachet villages in the Côte de Beaune that are responsible for producing some of the world's greatest dry white wines is also capable of very high quality at basic village level. The reds, however, demand a premium more for their scarcity than their quality, although it, too, can be quite good.

PULIGNY-MONTRACHET-CÔTE DE BEAUNE France, Burgundy (AOC) Synonymous with Puligny-Montrachet.

PULIGNY-MONTRACHET PRE-MIER CRU France, Burgundy (AOC) For anyone who has not tasted any of the grands crus of Montrachet, the best premiers crus will leave you

wondering what on earth could be better. These are great wines and you will have to pay great prices. Reds are theoretically possible.

Q

QUARTS-DE-CHAUME France, Loire (AOC) Slightly lighter than Bonnezeaux and usually a touch less sweet, Quarts-de-Chaume can, however, have more finesse. In great vintages they are indisputably the finest dessert wines in the entire Anjou-Saumur district.

QUERCIAGRANDE Italy, Tuscany (VT) One of Italy's very best pure Sangiovese wines.

QUINCY France, Loire (AOC) Crisp wine capable of rich gooseberry fruit in warm years.

QUINTA DA BACALHOA Portugal, Setúbal American-owned, Australian-made, Portugese-marketed red wine of stunning quality made from Cabernet and Merlot grapes.

R

RABOSO Italy, Veneto (DOC) Excellent value red wine full of sunny fruit and capable of ageing.

RAMITELLO Italy, Molise (VT) Good full-bodied red from the Sangiovese and Montepulciano grapes, but the white and the sparkling versions of red and white wines are not special.

RANDERSACKER Germany, Franken One of the best villages in Franken. Top single-vineyards: Randersackerer Sonnenstuhl, Randersackerer Pfülben, Randersackerer Teufelskeller, Randersackerer Dabug.

RASTEAU France, Rhône Valley (AOC) Coarse, pithy wines, made from predominantly Grenache grapes and fortified.

RASTEAU 'RANCIO' France, Rhône Valley (AOC) As for Rasteau, but allowed to deteriorate by leaving in casks exposed to the sunlight for two years, hence its rancid smell and taste.

RATAFIA DE CHAM-PAGNE France, Champagne Sweet, cloying aperitif made from unfermented grape juice that has been prevented from fermenting by the addition of Cognac. Although not classified as an AOC, this is to Champagne what the Floc de Gascogne is to Armagnac, and Pineau des Charentes is to Cognac.

RAUENTHAL Germany, Rheingau One of the best villages in the Rheingau. Top single-vineyards: Rauenthaler Baiken, Rauenthaler Wülfen.

RAVELLO Italy, Campania (VT) Full-bodied red wine of some regard, made from Aglianico, Merlot and various other grapes. Dry white and rosé of less interest.

RAVENSBURG Germany, Franken If you see this name following that of a village on a bottle of Franken, it is only a *Grosslage* wine.

REBSTÖCKEL Germany, Rheinpfalz If you see this name following that of a village on a bottle of Rheinpfalz, it is only a *Grosslage* wine.

RECIOTO DELLA VALPOLICELLA Italy, Veneto (DOC) Deep-coloured, dry, semi-sweet and sweet red wines made from *passito* grapes.

RECIOTO DI SOAVE Italy, Veneto (DOC) Of the awful, oxidised sweet and semi-sweet wines that dominate this appellation, Anselmi's glorious, lush and complex Recioto di Soave dei Capitelli is in a completely different league.

REDONDO Portugal, Alentejo (IPR) Lots of white wine, most of which is ordinary, but the reds are full, fruity and rapidly improving.

REGALEALI Italy, Sicily (VT) Rich, full-bodied, soft, red wines and crisp, dry rosés and whites of some interest.

REGENSBURGER LANDWEIN Germany (DL) One of 15 Deutscher Landwein appellations, its wines should be simple and light-bodied, with a basic flowery aroma, some grapey fruit and a touch of sweetness on the finish.

RÉGNIÉ France, Burgundy (AOC) This medium-bodied, elegant red wine is the newest of the ten top-quality cru Beaujolais, and should therefore be trying to justify its elite status.

REGUENGOS Portugal, Alentejo (IPR) Lots of white wines, most of which are ordinary, but the reds are full, fruity and rapidly improving.

REHBACH Germany, Rheinhessen If you see this name following that of a village on a bottle of Rheinhessen, it is only a *Grosslage* wine.

REICHENSTEINER (Grape) Grown widely in Germany and England, the Reichensteiner produces mild-flavoured, slightly aromatic wines.

REMSHALDEN-GRUNBACH Germany, Württemberg One of the best villages in Württemberg. Top single-vineyards: Remshalden-Grunbacher Klingle.

RETZBACH Germany, Franken One of the best

villages in Franken. Top single-vineyards: Retzbacher Benediktusberg.

REUILLY France, Loire (AOC) Fine, grassy Sancerre-type whites and surprisingly good reds and rosés, full of raspberry fruit.

REUSCHBERG Germany, Franken If you see this name following that of a village on a bottle of Franken, it is only a *Grosslage* wine.

RHEIN Germany (DT) One of eight Deutscher Tafelwein sub-regions, its wines should be simple and light-bodied, with a basic flowery aroma, some grapey fruit and a touch of sweetness on the finish.

RHEIN-MOSEL Germany (DT) One of four vast Deutscher Tafelwein regions, Rhein-Mosel is roughly equivalent to all but the Saar in the Mosel-Saar-Ruwer QbA region. These wines should be simple and light-bodied, with a basic flowery aroma, some grapey fruit and a touch of sweetness on the finish.

RHEINBLICK Germany, Rheinhessen If you see this name following that of a village on a bottle of Rheinhessen, it is only a *Grosslage* wine.

RHEINBURGEN LANDWEIN Germany (DL) One of 15 Deutscher Landwein appellations, its wines should be simple and light-bodied, with a basic flowery aroma, some grapey fruit and a touch of sweetness on the finish.

RHEINGAU Germany, (QbA) The Riesling luxuriates on the Rheingau's single, sun-blessed slope, producing lush, elegant, peach-flavoured wines of inimitable style and quality.

RHEINGAU GROSSLAGEN Germany,

Rheingau (Grosslagen) Burgweg, Daubhaus, Deutelsberg, Erntebringer, Gottesthal, Heiligenstock, Honigberg, Mehrhölzchen, Steil and Steinmächer are all *Grosslagen*, not single-vineyard wines and should be very reasonably priced, unless you are being ripped-off or it happens to be an Eiswein, Beerenauslese or Trockenbeerenauslese.

RHEINGRAFENSTEIN Germany, Rheinhessen If you see this name following that of a village on a bottle of Rheinhessen, it is only a *Grosslage* wine.

RHEINHESSEN Germany, (QbA) Some 50% of all Liebfraumilch comes from the Rheinhessen. The diversity of soils and microclimates produces a plethora of styles from numerous grape varieties, and wines from the so-called Rhine Terrace and are held in great esteem.

RHEINHESSEN GROSSLAGEN Germany, Rheinhessen (Grosslagen) Abtey, Adelberg, Kaiserpfalz, Kurfürstenstück, Rheingrafenstein, Sankt Rochuskapelle, Auflangen, Domherr, Güldenmorgen, Gutes Domtal, Krötenbrunnen, Petersberg, Rehbach, Rheinblick, Sankt Alban, Spiegelberg, Vogelsgarten, Bergkloster, Burg Rodenstein, Domblick, Gotteshilfe, Liebfrauenmorgen, Pilgerpfad and Sybillenstein are all *Grosslagen*, not single-vineyard wines and should be very reasonably priced, unless you are being ripped-off or it happens to be an Eiswein, Beerenauslese or Trockenbeerenauslese.

RHEINISCHER LANDWEIN Germany (DL) One of 15 Deutscher Landwein appellations, its wines should be simple and light-bodied, with a basic flowery aroma, some grapey fruit and a touch of sweetness on the finish.

RHEINPFALZ Germany, (QbA) The wines of the Rheinpfalz are generally fatter and more spicy than those of the Rheinhessen.

RHEINPFALZ GROSSLAGEN Germany, Rheinpfalz (Grosslagen) Feuerberg, Grafenstück, Hochmess, Hofstück, Höllenpfad, Honigsäckel, Kobnert, Mariengarten, Meerspinne, Pfaffengrund, Rebstöckel, Rosenbühl, Schenkenböhl, Schnepfenflug an der Weinstrasse, Schnepfenflug vom Zellertal, Schwarzerde, Bischofskreuz, Guttenberg, Herrlich, Kloster Liebfrauenberg, Königsgarten, Mandelhöhe, Ordensgut, Schloss Ludwigshöhe and Trappenberg are all *Grosslagen*, not single-vineyard wines and should be very reasonably priced, unless you are being ripped-off or it happens to be an Eiswein, Beerenauslese or Trockenbeerenauslese.

RIAS BAIXAS Spain, Galicia (DO) Various red, white and rosé wines, the best known and most enjoyable of which are the soft, perfumed white wines made from Albariño grapes, which are a bit like the very best of Portugal's Vinhos Verdes.

RIBATEJO Portugal, Ribatejo (IPR) Lots of white wine, most of which is ordinary, but the reds are full, fruity and rapidly improving.

RIBEIRA DO ULLA Spain, Galicia (VC) Struggling to make the grade.

RIBEIRA SACRA Spain, Galicia (VdlT) Country wines that have yet to make their mark.

RIBEIRO Spain, Galicia (DO) Well-coloured reds with crisp fruit, high acidity and, sometimes, even a touch of *pétillance*.

RIBERA ALTA DEL GUADIANA Spain, Extremadura (VdlT) Country wines that have yet to make their mark.

RIBERA BAJA DEL GUADIANA Spain, Extremadura (VdlT) Country wines that have yet to make their mark.

RIBERA DEL ARLANZA Spain, Castilla-León (VC) Struggling to make the grade.

RIBERA DEL DUERO Spain, Castilla-León (DO) This is the appellation from which Vega Sicilia, Spain's most expensive red wine, comes. Also Pesquera, which American wine guru Robert Parker dubbed the Pétrus of Spain. There are other very good, if not quite so lofty, wines produced here, but there are a lot of very ordinary wines too, hence Ribera del Duero has not been elevated to DOC status with Rioja, although one day it surely will be.

RICHEBOURG France, Burgundy (AOC) Gloriously rich, grand cru red with a heavenly bouquet and voluptuous fruit, from the village of Vosne-Romanée in the Côte de Nuits.

RIESLANER (Grape) Not to be confused with the Rivaner (Müller-Thurgau), this is in fact a Sylvaner and Riesling cross and its relatively rich, somewhat mild wines should therefore be called Sylving, if anything.

RIESLING (Grape) Classic German variety that has no peers when it comes to high sugar-acidity levels, the Riesling has a relatively low potential alcohol and an intense yet delicate flavour.

It can be extremely long lived and, with some bottle-age, great Rieslings can develop a vivid, zesty bouquet often referred to as 'petrolly'. Although this description is misleading, it is also a fact that many casual drinkers simply do not like a 'petrolly' Riesling and it does not matter a fig to them if others think it is one of the world's greatest wines.

RIESLING France, Alsace (AOC) Crisp and racy dry white wines, the best of which require ageing.

RIOJA Spain, Basque Country (DOC) The only DOC (superior to DO) belongs to Spain's greatest red wine appellation, which is consistent and good value at all price levels. Additionally, there are two basic styles of dry white and dry rosé, one oaky, the other fresh, and both have good fruit. Beware the less interesting medium sweet white and rosé.

RITTERSBERG Germany, Baden If you see this name following that of a village on a bottle of Baden, it is only a *Grosslage* wine.

RIVESALTES France, Languedoc-Roussillon (AOC) Sweet, blended, fortified wine of no special interest.

RIVESALTES 'RANCIO' France, Languedoc-Roussillon (AOC) As above, but spoilt further by the rancid-maderised effect of the 'rancio' process.

RIVIERA DEL GARDA BRESCIANO Italy, Lombardy (DOC) Light reds with a slightly bitter aftertaste and soft, fruity rosés.

RIVIERA LIGURE DI PONENTE Italy, Liguria (DOC) Four former *vini da tavola* were grouped together to form this DOC: Ormeasco and Pigato, which are bright coloured, juicy-fruity red wines and Rossese and Vermentino, which are fuller and more spicy.

RÖDELSEE Germany, Franken One of the best villages in Franken. Top single-vineyards: Rödelseer Küchenmeister, Rödelseer Schwanleite.

ROERO Italy, Piedmont (DOC) An interesting blend of the ancient Arneis grape with the classic Nebbiolo produces a dry white wine of some character.

ROMANÉE, LA France, Burgundy (AOC) This grand cru is in the same class as Richebourg (also from the village of Vosne-Romanée in the Côte de Nuits), but is less accessible and not as immediately voluptuous.

ROMANÉE-CONTI France, Burgundy (AOC) This grand cru makes a red wine of a stunning quality, which yields an array of incredibly complex flavours that continuously unfold, layer after layer, resulting in a wine of unparalleled depth and concentration. Well, it is the most expensive Burgundy in the world!

ROMANÉE-ST-VIVANT France, Burgundy (AOC) A relatively light-bodied red wine grand cru from the village of Vosne-Romanée in the Côte de Nuits, but not at all lacking in length and finesse.

ROMANIA An underrated country capable of producing some excellent red wines.

RÖMERLAY Germany, Mosel-Saar-Ruwer If you see this name following that of a village on a bottle of MSR, it is only a *Grosslage* wine.

RÖMERTOR Germany (DT) One of eight Deutscher Tafelwein sub-regions, its

wines should be simple and light-bodied, with a basic flowery aroma, some grapey fruit and a touch of sweetness on the finish.

ROMORANTIN (Grape) An up-and-coming if obscure variety confined to the Loire, where its wines can be delicate and flowery if the vine is not overcropped.

RONCO CASONE Italy, Emilia-Romagna (VT) An austere, deep-coloured, *barrique*-aged Sangiovese that needs time to soften.

RONCO DEI CILIEGI Italy, Emilia-Romagna (VT) Top-class Sangiovese red wine, with silky fruit, a touch of *barrique* character and masses of finesse.

RONCO DEI ROSETI Italy, Friuli-Venezia Giulia (VT) From Abbazia di Rosazzo, this is one of Italy's best Franco-Italian grape blends.

RONCO DEL GMENIZ Italy, Friuli-Venezia Giulia (DOC) Part of the Colli Orientali appellation and one of Italy's best Cabernet-based blends.

RONCO DELLE ACACIE Italy, Friuli-Venezia Giulia (VT) Brilliant *barrique*-aged dry white wine, with oodles of mouthwatering fruit.

RONCO DELLE GINESTRE Italy, Emilia-Romagna (VT) Light, quick developing, but fine red wine made from Sangiovese.

RONCO DI MOMPIANO Italy, Lombardy (VT) Smooth, aromatic reds from a blend that includes Merlot.

ROSA DEL GOLFO Italy, Apulia (VT) One of Italy's finest rosés.

ROSA DI ALBENGA Italy, Liguria (VT) Vividly coloured dry rosé of some character.

ROSATO DEL MOLISE Italy, Molise (VT) Simple, everyday dry rosé.

ROSATO DEL MOLISE-FIORE Italy, Molise (VT) Slightly more characterful than the basic Rosato del Molise.

ROSATO DELLA LEGA Italy, Tuscany (VT) Simple, dry rosé from Chianti.

ROSATO DELLE MARCHE Italy, Marches (VT) Decent, dry rosé made from a blend of Sangiovese and Montepulciano.

ROSATO DI MONTANELLO Italy, Marches (VT) Light, dry, fruity rosé of some individual character.

ROSÉ D'ANJOU France, Loire (AOC) (*See* **Anjou** entry.)

ROSÉ D'ANJOU PÉTILLANT France, Loire (AOC) (*See* **Anjou Pétillant** entry.)

ROSÉ DE LOIRE France, Loire (AOC) A dry rosé that is all too often dull and boring.

ROSÉ DES RICEYS France, Champagne (AOC) One-off appellation for a dry rosé still wine made in the south of Champagne, the special character of which emerges exclusively in good vintages at low yields, which is why you will seldom encounter Rosé des Riceys and, when you do, only one in six will be worth buying.

ROSENBÜHL Germany, Rheinpfalz If you see this name following that of a village on a bottle of Rheinpfalz, it is only a *Grosslage* wine.

ROSENGARTEN Germany, Nahe If you see this name following that of a village on a bottle of Nahe, it is only a *Grosslage* wine.

ROSENHANG Germany, Mosel-Saar-Ruwer If you

see this name following that of a village on a bottle of MSR, it is only a *Grosslage* wine.

ROSETTE France, Southwest France (AOC) Sweet white wines, the best of which can be soft and delicate.

ROSPEIRA Portugal, Beiras Premium quality sparkling wine of modest quality made by Seagram.

ROSSESE DI DOLCEACQUA Italy, Liguria (DOC) Synonymous with Dolceacqua.

ROSSO ARMENTANO Italy, Emilia-Romagna (VT) Successful red wine blend of Italian and French grapes.

ROSSO BARLETTA Italy, Apulia (DOC) Medium-bodied, ruby-coloured red wine of everyday quality, normally consumed locally.

ROSSO CANOSA Italy, Apulia (DOC) Firm, slightly tannic red wines.

ROSSO CONERO Italy, Marches (DOC) Fine, rich, full-bodied red wines from the Montepulciano grape.

ROSSO D'ARQUATA Italy, Umbria (VT) One of the very best Franco-Italian grape blends.

ROSSO DEL MOLISE Italy, Molise (VT) Unexciting, basic red wine of the Molise region.

ROSSO DELLA BISSERA Italy, Emilia-Romagna (VT) A deep-coloured, rustic red with rich fruity taste and the capacity to age.

ROSSO DELLA LEGA Italy, Tuscany (VT) Everyday red wines from Chianti.

ROSSO DI CERIGNOLA Italy, Apulia (DOC) Interesting, rustic red of full body and flavour.

ROSSO DI CORINALDO Italy, Marches (VT)

Consistently well made red wines of medium body and exuberant, spicy fruit.

ROSSO DI MONTALCINO Italy, Tuscany (DOC) Always better value than its more famous elder brother Brunello di Montalcino, and sometimes better quality too.

ROSSO DI MONTEPULCIANO Italy, Tuscany (DOC) Supposedly the lesser and/or younger wines of Vino Nobile di Montepulciano, these red wines are often more accessible and easier to enjoy.

ROSSO PICENO Italy, Marches (DOC) Fine, firm red wines with juicy fruit, from the Sangiovese and Montepulciano grapes.

ROSSTAL Germany, Franken If you see this name following that of a village on a bottle of Franken, it is only a *Grosslage* wine.

ROTT Germany, Hessische Bergstrasse (Gross) If you see this name following that of a village on a bottle of Hessische Bergstrasse, it is only a **Grosslage** wine (*see* basic **Grosslagen** entry.)

ROUSSETTE DE SAVOIE France, Savoie (AOC) Drier than Roussette de Bugey.

ROUSSETTE DU BUGEY France, Savoie (VDQS) Light, fresh, unpretentious dry white.

ROXHEIM Germany, Nahe One of the best villages in the Nahe. Top single-vineyards: Roxheimer Höllenpfad.

RUBINO COLLE DEL SOLE-POLIDORI Italy, Umbria (VT) One of the very best Franco-Italian grape blends.

RUBINO DI CANTAVENNA Italy, Piedmont (DOC) Full-bodied red wine blend of

mostly Barbera, Grignolino and sometimes a little Freisa.

RUBY PORT Portugal, Douro (DOC) The cheapest Ruby Ports are, with White Ports, barely one year old and the least likely to provide enjoyment. Fine Old Ruby, however, is well worth consideration, being similar to a Late-Bottled Port, except that it is blended from two or more vintages.

RUCHÉ DI CASTAGNOLE MONFERRATO Italy, Piedmont (DOC) Fashion-able new red wine from the Ruché, an ancient grape of obscure origin.

RUCHOTTES-CHAMBERTIN France, Burgundy (AOC) This red wine grand cru from the village of Gevrey-Chambertin in the Côte de Nuits is usually the lightest and most disappointing of the Chambertin lookalikes, although top growers such as Roumier and Rousseau produce splendidly rich wines of an altogether different class.

RÜDESHEIM Germany, Nahe One of the best villages in the Nahe. Top single-vineyards: Rüdersheimer Goldgrube.

RÜDESHEIM Germany, Rheingau One of the best villages in the Rheingau. Top single-vineyards: Rüdesheimer Bischofsberg, Rüdesheimer Drachenstein, Rüdesheimer Kirchenpfad, Rüdesheimer Berg Rottland, Rüdesheimer Berg Roseneck, Rüdesheimer Berg Schlossberg, Rüdesheimer Klosterlay.

RUEDA Spain, Castilla-León (DO) Fresh, elegant whites and dull, flabby fortified wines.

RULLY France, Burgundy (AOC) Excellent value red and dry white Burgundies.

RULLY PREMIER CRU
France, Burgundy (AOC)
Côte de Beaune quality at a
more affordable price.

RUPPERTSBERG
Germany, Rheinpfalz One
of the best villages in the
Rheinpfalz. Top single-
vineyards: Ruppertsberger
Reiterpfad.

S

SAALECK Germany,
Franken One of the best
villages in Franken. Top
single-vineyards: Saalecker
Schlossberg.

SAAR Germany (DT) One
of eight Deutscher
Tafelwein sub-regions, its
wines should be simple and
light-bodied, with a basic
flowery aroma, some
grapey fruit and a touch of
sweetness on the finish.

SAARBURG Germany,
Mosel-Saar-Ruwer One of
the best villages in the MSR.
Top single-vineyards:
Saarburger Rausch.

SACEDON-MONDÉJAR
Spain, Castilla-León (VdlT)
Country wines that have yet
to make their mark.

**SAGRANTINO DI
MONTEFALCO** Italy,
Umbria (DOCG) Recently
promoted to DOCG, this
wine used to be part of the
Montefalco DOC (which is
essentially a Sagrantino-
influenced blend), but the
pure version of this unusual
native grape variety is
much the superior wine and
a DOCG has apparently
been in the offing for some
time. The wine is red, dry
and distinctive, although a
little sweet is occasionally
made in the *passito* style.

SALICE SALENTINO
Italy, Apulia (DOC) Rich,
alcoholic, full-bodied reds
and smooth, alcoholic rosés.

SALZBERG Germany,
Württemberg If you see
this name following that of

a village on a bottle of
Württemberg, it is only a
Grosslage wine.

SAMMARCO Italy,
Tuscany (VT) One of Italy's
best Cabernet Sauvignon-
dominated blends.

SAN COLOMBANO Italy,
Lombardy (DOC) Robust
red from the province of
Milan.

**SAN COLOMBANO AL
LAMBRO** Italy, Lombardy
(DOC) Synonymous with
San Colombano.

SAN GIORGIO Italy,
Umbria (VT) One of the
very best Franco-Italian
grape blends.

SAN LEONARDO Italy,
Trentino-Alto Adige (VT)
One of Italy's best
Cabernet-based blends.

SAN MATEO Spain,
Murcia (VC) Struggling to
make the grade.

SAN SEVERO Italy, Apulia
(DOC) Red, dry white and
dry rosé of little interest.

SAN ZENO Italy, Trentino-
Alto Adige (VT) One of
Italy's best Cabernet-based
blends.

SANCERRE France, Loire
(AOC) Interesting, light-
bodied, floral reds and
rosés from the Pinot Noir
and full, grassy whites.

SANG DES SALASSES
Italy, Valle d'Aosta (VT)
Light, fresh and fruity red
wines with a slightly bitter
finish.

SANGIOVESE (Grape) The
principal grape variety of
Chianti can lack fruit and
charm in its pure form,
although a number of
fabulous 100% Sangiovese
new-wave wines (such as
Ceparello from Isole e
Olena) have shown that it is
only a matter of careful
yields, selection and
vinification.

**SANGIOVESE DEI COLLI
PESARESI** Italy, Marches
(DOC) Be sure to taste first,

but some of these red wines
can be fine indeed.

**SANGIOVESE DELLE
MARCHE** Italy, Marches
(VT) Simple Chianti-like vin
ordinaire consumed locally.

**SANGIOVESE DI
ROMAGNA** Italy, Emilia-
Romagna (DOC) Solid red
wines that seldom excite,
unless from exceptional
vineyards such as Fattoria
Paradiso's Vigneti delle
Lepri.

**SANGIOVETO DI
COLTIBUONO** Italy,
Tuscany (VT) One of Italy's
very best pure Sangiovese
wines.

SANKT ALBAN Germany,
Rheinhessen If you see this
name following that of a
village on a bottle of
Rheinhessen, it is only a
Grosslage wine.

SANKT MAGDALENER
Italy, Trentino-Alto Adige
(QbA) Synonymous with
Santa Maddalena.

**SANKT
ROCHUSKAPELLE**
Germany, Rheinhessen If
you see this name following
that of a village on a bottle
of Rheinhessen, it is only a
Grosslage wine.

**SANT'ANNA DI ISOLA
CAPO RIZZUTO** Italy,
Calabria (DOC) Strong reds
and firm rosés of no
particular interest.

SANTA MADDALENA
Italy, Trentino-Alto Adige
(DOC) Smooth, full-bodied
red that is eminently
drinkable, but does not live
up to Mussolini's assertion
that this is one of Italy's
greatest wines.

SANTAREM Portugal,
Ribatejo (IPR) Lots of white
wines, most of which are
ordinary, but the reds are
full, fruity and rapidly
improving.

SANTENAY France,
Burgundy (AOC) This
village in the Côte de
Beaune produces fresh,

frank and firm reds. Just 2% of the wine is white.

SANTENAY-CÔTE DE BEAUNE France, Burgundy (AOC) Synonymous with Santenay.

SANTENAY PREMIER CRU France, Burgundy (AOC) The reds are more expressive than the village wines. White is seldom encountered.

SASSELLA Italy, Lombardy (DOC) The best sub-appellation of Valtelina.

SASSICAIA Italy, Tuscany (VT) One of Italy's very best pure Cabernet Sauvignon wines.

SAUMUR France, Loire (AOC) The whites are made in dry, sweet and semi-sweet styles and can be likened to a leaner version of Vouvray; the reds range from light and feeble to full and rich.

SAUMUR-CHAMPIGNY France, Loire (AOC) Without doubt one of the Loire Valley's greatest red wines.

SAUMUR MOUSSEUX France, Loire (AOC) Sparkling white and rosé wines that are distinctly superior to Anjou Mousseux.

SAUMUR PÉTILLANT France, Loire (AOC) Rarely-encountered semi-sparkling wine not dissimilar to Montlouis Pétillant.

SAUSSIGNAC France, Southwest France (AOC) Full, fat, semi-sweet white wines with rich, alcoholic finish.

SAUTERNES France, Bordeaux (AOC) Considered by many to be the greatest dessert wine in the world.

SAUVIGNON (Grape) Fresh, zesty grape that is appreciated for its grassy character, but can be taken to extremes, when it may

have the 'cat's pee' aroma, which is not as bad as it sounds and is certainly okay in the New World, where the grapes ripen. This excessive aroma can, however, be excruciatingly unpleasant in the Loire, where overcropped vineyards seldom ripen grapes in an average to poor year.

SAUVIGNON DE ST-BRIS France, Burgundy (VDQS) A pure Sauvignon Blanc wine grown in the Chablis district.

SAVAGNIN (Grape) Not to be confused with the Sauvignon, this variety comes from the Jura, where it is responsible for the Sherry-like vin jaune, the most famous of which is Château-Chalon. The Sherry aroma is not simply a product of vin jaune, however, it is also intrinsic to the grape, so beware table wines bearing the name of this grape.

SAVENNIÈRES France, Loire (AOC) In the hands of Jean Baumard, certain vineyards such as Clos du Pappillon are capable of producing the world's greatest dry Chenin Blanc wines.

SAVIGNY France, Burgundy (AOC) Synonymous with Savigny-lès-Beaune.

SAVIGNY-CÔTE DE BEAUNE France, Burgundy (AOC) Synonymous with Savigny-lès-Beaune for red wines only.

SAVIGNY-LÈS-BEAUNE France, Burgundy (AOC) Delicious, easy to drink reds and fine, well-flavoured, dry whites.

SAVIGNY-LÈS-BEAUNE-CÔTE DE BEAUNE France, Burgundy (AOC) Synonymous with Savigny-lès-Beaune for red wines only.

SAVIGNY-LES-BEAUNE PREMIER CRU France,

Burgundy (AOC) Synonymous with Savigny-lès-Beaune.

SAVIGNY PREMIER CRU France, Burgundy (AOC) Splendid reds and whites of a distinctly higher quality than the albeit excellent village wines.

SAVUTO Italy, Calabria (DOC) Light but appealing red, white and rosé wines.

SCHALKSTEIN Germany, Württemberg If you see this name following that of a village on a bottle of Württemberg, it is only a *Grosslage* wine.

SCHENKENBÖHL Germany, Rheinpfalz If you see this name following that of a village on a bottle of Rheinpfalz, it is only a *Grosslage* wine.

SCHEUREBE (Grape) If harvested early, Scheurebe may be as unpleasant as an overcropped Loire Sauvignon from a poor year, but when late-harvested, this grape can produce beautifully aromatic and fruity wine.

SCHILD Germany, Franken If you see this name following that of a village on a bottle of Franken, it is only a *Grosslage* wine.

SCHIOPPETTINO Italy, Friuli-Venezia Giulia (VT) Ripe, round, spicy red wine made from the Schioppettino, an ancient Friulian grape variety that was nearly extinct until this wine suddenly became fashionable in the 1980s.

SCHLOSS BÜBINGER Germany, Mosel-Saar-Ruwer If you see this name following that of a village on a bottle of MSR, it is only a *Grosslage* wine.

SCHLOSS LUDWIGSHÖHE Germany, Rheinpfalz If you see this name following that of a village on a bottle of Rheinpfalz, it is only a *Grosslage* wine.

SCHLOSS REICHENSTEIN Germany, Mittelrhein If you see this name following that of a village on a bottle of Mittelrhein, it is only a *Grosslage* wine.

SCHLOSS RODECK Germany, Baden If you see this name following that of a village on a bottle of Baden, it is only a *Grosslage* wine.

SCHLOSS SCHÖNBURG Germany, Mittelrhein If you see this name following that of a village on a bottle of Mittelrhein, it is only a *Grosslage* wine.

SCHLOSS STAHLECK Germany, Mittelrhein If you see this name following that of a village on a bottle of Mittelrhein, it is only a *Grosslage* wine.

SCHLOSSBERG Germany, Franken If you see this name following that of a village on a bottle of Franken, it is only a *Grosslage* wine.

SCHLOSSBERG Germany, Hessische Bergstrasse If you see this name following that of a village on a bottle of Hessische Bergstrasse, it is only a *Grosslage* wine.

SCHLOSSBÖCKELHEIM Germany, Nahe One of the best villages in the Nahe. Top single-vineyards: Schlossböckelheimer Kupfergrube, Schlossböckelheimer Königsfels, Schlossböckelheimer Felsenberg, Schlossböckelheimer Hermannshöhle, Schlossböckelheimer Hermannsberg, Schlossböckelheimer Steinberg.

SCHLOSSKAPELLE Germany, Nahe If you see this name following that of a village on a bottle of Nahe, it is only a *Grosslage* wine.

SCHLOSSSTÜCK Germany, Franken If you see this name following that of a village on a bottle of Franken, it is only a *Grosslage* wine.

SCHNEPFENFLUG AN DER WEINSTRASSE Germany, Rheinpfalz If you see this name following that of a village on a bottle of Rheinpfalz, it is only a *Grosslage* wine.

SCHNEPFENFLUG VOM ZELLERTAL Germany, Rheinpfalz If you see this name following that of a village on a bottle of Rheinpfalz, it is only a *Grosslage* wine.

SCHÖNBERGER (Grape) Can be a good, aromatic variety in Germany, where it is widely planted, but it is sometimes too catty in English wines.

SCHOZACHTAL Germany, Württemberg If you see this name following that of a village on a bottle of Württemberg, it is only a *Grosslage* wine.

SCHUTTER-LINDENBERG Germany, Baden If you see this name following that of a village on a bottle of Baden, it is only a *Grosslage* wine.

SCHWARZBERG Germany, Mosel-Saar-Ruwer If you see this name following that of a village on a bottle of MSR, it is only a *Grosslage* wine.

SCHWARZE KATZ Germany, Mosel-Saar-Ruwer If you see this name following that of a village on a bottle of MSR, it is only a *Grosslage* wine.

SCHWARZERDE Germany, Rheinpfalz If you see this name following that of a village on a bottle of Rheinpfalz, it is only a *Grosslage* wine.

SCHWARZLAY Germany, Mosel-Saar-Ruwer If you see this name following that of a village on a bottle of MSR, it is only a *Grosslage* wine.

SCHWEIGEN-RECHTENBACH Germany, Rheinpfalz One of the best villages in the Rheinpfalz. Top single-vineyards: Schweiger Sonnenberg.

SCORZA AMARA Italy, Emilia-Romagna (VT) Scorza Amara is a local variant of the Lambrusco grape. It is produced in a very similar semi-sparkling style, but with slightly fuller fruit.

SEHNDORF Germany, Mosel-Saar-Ruwer One of the best villages in the MSR. Top single-vineyards: Sehndorfer Klosterberg.

SEKT 'Germany' A cheap and anonymous sparkling wine made in, but not necessarily from, Germany by the so-called *cuve close* method, where the wine undergoes its second fermentation (which creates the fizz) not in bottles, which is how Champagne is made, but inside large tanks, after which it is filtered and bottled. Much of the base wines used for Sekt is trucked in from low quality areas of Italy and France. The amount of Sekt produced is enormous (between two and three times the amount of Champagne produced), but it is just bland and fizzy, so traditionally virtually no Sekt is exported. (*See also* **Deutscher Sekt** entry.)

SÉMILLON (Grape) Capable of producing fat, waxy fruit, sometimes a touch spicy, Sémillon is at its finest (either in its pure form or blended with Sauvignon) in Sauternes. It is developing as a dry white wine varietal in the new world, especially in Australia where they sensibly ignored Bordeaux traditions and cleverly blended it with

Chardonnay to make Burgundy type wines cheaper and more accessible. In New Zealand, it is often cropped early to add grassy 'Sauvignon' character to the Sauvignon.

SERCIAL Portugal, Madeira (DOC) The lightest and driest style of Madeira, the Sercial grape was once thought to be the Riesling grape, but this has now been disproved.

SERRIG Germany, Mosel-Saar-Ruwer One of the best villages in the MSR. Top single-vineyards: Serriger Herrenberg, Serriger Schloss Saarfelser.

SETÚBAL Portugal, Setúbal (DOC) Once famous for its now rather passé fortified Moscatel, this area has been reborn in the hands of Peter Bright, an Australian wine-wizard who was responsible for such exciting modern wines as Quinta da Bacalhôa.

SEYSSEL France, Savoie (AOC) Deliciously fruity *après-ski* dry white.

SEYSSEL MOUSSEUX France, Savoie (AOC) Dry sparkling wine with a full yeasty nose and fine, persistent bubbles.

SEYVAL BLANC (Grape) Hybrid that is at its best in England, where the wines can be somewhat Sauvignon in style.

SHIRAZ (Grape) *(See* **Syrah** entry.)

SINGLE QUINTA PORT Portugal, Douro (DOC) A wine from a single-vineyard (or should be), usually produced in lesser years, but often just as good as Vintage Port because the *quinta* in question is usually one of the finest vineyards belonging to the Port house in question. As such, these *quintas* normally form the heart of the relevant Vintage Ports in best years and on their own can

provide sensational Ports in even disappointing years.

SIZZANO Italy, Piedmont (DOC) Good quality, full-bodied red wine produced from a Gattinara-like blend from just south of Ghemme.

SOAVE Italy, Veneto (DOC) Most are overpriced, even if they are the cheapest wines in the shop, but Soave Classico is worth tasting as a handful are quite good.

SOLAIA Italy, Tuscany (VT) One of Italy's best Cabernet Sauvignon-dominated blends.

SOLATIO BASILICA Italy, Tuscany (VT) One of Italy's best Sangiovese-dominated blends.

SOLICCHIATO BIANCO DI VILLA FONTANE Italy, Sicily (VT) Characterful, semi-sweet dessert wine made from sun-dried grapes.

SOLOPACA Italy, Campania (DOC) Smooth reds and soft, dry whites that sometimes excel.

SOMMERACH Germany, Franken One of the best villages in Franken. Top single-vineyards: Sommeracher Katzenkopf.

SOMMERHAUSEN Germany, Franken One of the best villages in Franken. Top single-vineyards: Sommerhauser Steinbach.

SOMONTANO Spain, Aragón (DO) Light to medium bodied wines, the whites of which are lacklustre, but the reds and rosés can have attractive, fragrant fruit.

SONNENBORN Germany, Nahe If you see this name following that of a village on a bottle of Nahe, it is only a *Grosslage* wine.

SONNENBÜHL Germany, Württemberg If you see this name following that of a village on a bottle of

Württemberg, it is only a *Grosslage* wine.

SONNENUFER Germany, Baden If you see this name following that of a village on a bottle of Baden, it is only a *Grosslage* wine.

SORNI Italy, Trentino-Alto Adige (DOC) Interesting, soft red wines and light, delicately dry whites.

SPANNA Italy, Piedmont (VT) Spanna is the local name for the Nebbiolo grape and wines under this name are often regarded as little more than the most basic of their type. In the hands of a specialist producer, however, Spanna can rival all but the best Barolo and Barbaresco.

SPÄTLESE Germany (QbA) Semi-sweet to sweet wine made from late-harvest grapes.

SPIEGELBERG Germany, Rheinhessen If you see this name following that of a village on a bottle of Rheinhessen, it is only a *Grosslage* wine.

SQUINZANO Italy, Apulia (DOC) Full, robust reds and slightly scented dry rosés.

ST-AMOUR France, Burgundy (AOC) Fine coloured red wine with a seductive bouquet and soft, appealing fruit from one of the ten top-quality cru Beaujolais.

ST-AUBIN France, Burgundy (AOC) This underrated village in the Côte de Beaune is an excellent source for super-value Burgundies: delicious, ripe, fragrant reds and rich, often scintillating, whites.

ST-AUBIN-CÔTE DE BEAUNE France, Burgundy (AOC) Synonymous with St-Aubin.

ST-AUBIN PREMIER CRU France, Burgundy (AOC) The best dry white premiers crus of St-Aubin are often a match for the village wines of Puligny and are always less expensive, while the reds can be compared to those of Chassagne-Montrachet.

ST-CHINIAN France, Languedoc-Roussillon (AOC) These fine, fragrant red wines are as near to Bordeaux as can be found in the Languedoc-Roussillon area of southern France. Also delightfully dry and delicate rosés.

ST-ÉMILION France, Bordeaux (AOC) The best of these relatively light-bodied reds have a silky elegance and great length, but there are more than 1,000 different wines made within a six-mile radius of the village of St-Emilion, thus there is an extreme variance in quality.

ST-ESTÈPHE France, Bordeaux (AOC) These big, spicy reds have plenty of fruit and no longer conform to the austere and ungenerous style of their past.

ST-GEORGES-ST-EMILION France, Bordeaux (AOC) These deep-coloured, plummy wines are second only to Montagne-St-Emilion in terms of the St-Emilion satellite appellations.

ST-GOARSHAUSEN Germany, Mittelrhein One of the best villages in the Mittelrhein. Top single-vineyards: St-Goarshausener Hesserb.

ST-JOSEPH France, Rhône Valley (AOC) Apart from a handful of exceptional producers, these are mostly dull and lacklustre red and dry white wines.

ST-JULIEN France, Bordeaux (AOC) The classic claret, St-Julien cannot be rivalled for its elegance and purity.

ST-MICHAEL Germany, Mosel-Saar-Ruwer If you see this name following that of a village on a bottle of MSR, it is only a *Grosslage* wine.

ST-NICOLAS-DE-BOURGUEIL France, Loire (AOC) Red wines of some finesse that age well despite their relatively light style.

ST-PÉRAY France, Rhône Valley (AOC) Firm, fruity dry white.

ST-PÉRAY MOUSSEUX France, Rhône Valley (AOC) Boring white sparkling wines.

ST-POURÇAIN France, Loire (VDQS) Reds that range from Beaujolais-type to Passetoutgrains lookalikes, fragrant dry rosés and some interesting dry whites blended from the Tresallier, Chardonnay and Sauvignon grapes.

ST-ROMAIN France, Burgundy (AOC) Good value, rustic reds and fresh, dry, lively whites from the Côte de Beaune.

ST-ROMAIN-CÔTE DE BEAUNE France, Burgundy (AOC) Synonymous with St-Romain.

ST-VÉRAN France, Burgundy (AOC) Excellent value Mâcon-style dry white wine from an area that overlaps Mâcon and Beaujolais.

STARKBURGER LANDWEIN Germany (DL) One of 15 Deutscher Landwein appellations, its wines should be simple and light-bodied, with a basic flowery aroma, some grapey fruit and a touch of sweetness on the finish.

STAUFENBERG Germany, Württemberg If you see this name following that of a village on a bottle of Württemberg, it is only a *Grosslage* wine.

STE-CROIX-DU-MONT France, Bordeaux (AOC) Fine, viscous, value-for-money sweet wines almost up to the quality of those made in neighbouring Loupiac.

STE-FOY-BORDEAUX France, Bordeaux (AOC) Soft, easy-drinking reds and attractive, crisp and fruity dry whites, but the semi-sweet white wines are uninspiring.

STEIL Germany, Rheingau If you see this name following that of a village on a bottle of Rheingau, it is only a *Grosslage* wine.

STEINMÄCHER Germany, Rheingau If you see this name following that of a village on a bottle of Rheingau, it is only a *Grosslage* wine.

STERI Italy, Sicily (VT) The deep-coloured, full-bodied, rich-flavoured reds are worth buying, but the crisp whites are merely passable.

STETTEN Germany, Württemberg One of the best villages in Württemberg. Top single-vineyards: Stettener Brotwasser, Stettener Lindhälder.

STIFTSBERG Germany, Baden If you see this name following that of a village on a bottle of Baden, it is only a *Grosslage* wine.

STOCKHEIM Germany, Württemberg One of the best villages in Württemberg. Top single-vineyards: Stockheimer Altenberg.

STROMBERG Germany, Württemberg If you see this name following that of a village on a bottle of Württemberg, it is only a *Grosslage* wine.

SÜDBADISCHER LANDWEIN Germany (DL) One of 15 Deutscher Landwein appellations, its wines should be simple and light-bodied, with a basic flowery aroma, some grapey fruit and a touch of sweetness on the finish.

SÜDTIROLER Italy, Trentino-Alto Adige (QbA) Synonymous with Alto Adige.

SULZFELD Germany, Baden One of the best villages in Baden. Top single-vineyards: Sulzfelder Burg Ravensburger.

SULZFELD Germany, Franken One of the best villages in Franken. Top single-vineyards: Sulzfelder Maustal, Sulzfelder Cyriakusberg.

SWÄBISCHER LANDWEIN Germany (DL) One of 15 Deutscher Landwein appellations, its wines should be simple and light-bodied, with a basic flowery aroma, some grapey fruit and a touch of sweetness on the finish.

SYBILLENSTEIN Germany, Rheinhessen If you see this name following that of a village on a bottle of Rheinhessen, it is only a *Grosslage* wine.

SYLVANER (Grape) A prolific variety that usually makes light-bodied, early drinking wine of ordinary quality, although a handful of producers in Alsace may sometimes produce a stunning Sylvaner. German wine enthusiasts consider Franken's Sylvaner, with its smoky aroma and distinctive earthy fruit, to be of note.

SYLVANER France, Alsace (AOC) Should be dry and fresh, with sappy uncompli- cated fruit, but often tart and disappointing.

SYRAH (Grape) The great red wine grape of Hermitage and Côte-Rôti, not to mention the superb value appellations of Crozes-Hermitage and Cornas. Syrah is grown in many other countries, but outside France it definitely fares best in Australia, although the style is very different. Neither better, nor

worse, but somehow much warmer and spicier.

TACELENGHE Italy, Friuli-Venezia Giulia (VT) This red wine takes its name from the local dialect for *tazzalingua*, which means a sharpness on the tongue and this reflects the wine's tannic character, although it softens with age.

TACORONTE-ACENTEJO Spain, Canaries (DO) Uneven, but rapidly improving quality, despite struggling against the greater, quicker profits from banana crops. Some reds are quite serious.

TARRAGONA Spain, Catalonia (DO) Robust reds that lack finesse, dry whites that can be aromatic, but tend to lack freshness, and surprisingly good and fruity rosés. Fortified wines also produced.

TAUBERBERG Germany, Württemberg If you see this name following that of a village on a bottle of Württemberg, it is only a *Grosslage* wine.

TAUBERKLINGE Germany, Baden If you see this name following that of a village on a bottle of Baden, it is only a *Grosslage* wine.

TAURASI Italy, Campania (DOCG) This full, robust red is a true vin de garde of surprising class, consider- ing its humble area of origin.

TAVEL France, Rhône Valley (AOC) Overrated dry rosé.

TAVERNELLE Italy, Tuscany (VT) One of Italy's very best pure Cabernet Sauvignon wines.

TAVIRA Portugal, Algarve (DOC) The Algarve was considered unworthy of its appellation, so they split it in four and hoped you

would not notice. The local co-operative here and at Lagoa make slightly more drinkable wines than the rest, but the truth is the Algarve is better suited to sunbathing and golf than it is that to growing good wine grapes.

TAVIRA Portugal, Beiras (IPR) From the Beira Alta, between the Vinho Verde and Dão districts, where every style of wine is produced in varying quality.

TAWNY PORT Portugal, Douro (DOC) The cheapest Tawnies will be a blend of red and white wines, but because of the use of old reserves, some can be surprisingly good. Fine Old Tawny is, however, the Real Thing, full of rich, caramel, coffee flavour. It is a far more accessible wine than Vintage Port (especially for the uninitiated), it is also more consistent and you are less likely to make an expensive mistake buying on spec. The 10 Year Old is sensational value, 20 Year Old the ultimate choice for quality and 30 Year Old, although of great quality and fascinating to sip, has a style that is closer to a liqueur than a Tawny Port. (*See also* **Colheita Port** entry.)

TAZZELENGHE Italy, Friuli-Venezia Giulia (VT) Synonymous with Tacelenghe.

TEMPRANILLO (Grape) The most important Rioja variety, the Tempranillo is generally underrated throughout the rest of the wine world, although it could make a very interesting varietal in California and elsewhere.

TERLANER Italy, Trentino- Alto Adige (QbA) Synonymous with Terlano.

TERLANO Italy, Trentino- Alto Adige (DOC) Soft, dry blended whites and five varietal, all similar in quality and consistency to those of Alto Adige.

TEROLDEGO ROTALIANO Italy, Trentino-Alto Adige (DOC) Interesting, full-bodied reds, especially the *Superiore* version.

TERRA ALTA Spain, Catalonia (DO) Red, white, rosé and fortified wines of no special interest.

TERRALBA Italy, Sardinia (DOC) Synonymous with Campidano di Terralba.

TERRE ROSSE CHARDONNAY Italy, Emilia-Romagna (VT) This fine Chardonnay is made in authentic Latin style and is a thousand times better than Emilia-Romagna's Albana di Romagna, Italy's first white wine to receive DOCG status.

TEUFELSTOR Germany, Franken If you see this name following that of a village on a bottle of Franken, it is only a *Grosslage* wine.

THÜNGERSHEIM Germany, Franken One of the best villages in Franken. Top single-vineyards: Thüngersheimer Johannisberg, Thüngersheimer Scharlachberg.

TIERRA BAJA DE ARAGÓN Spain, Aragón (VdlT) Country wines that have yet to make their mark.

TIERRA DE BARROS Spain, Extramadura (VdlT) Variable quality country wines that fluctuate from dismal to good and promising.

TIERRA DEL VINO DE ZAMORA Spain, Castilla-León (VdlT) Country wines yet to make their mark.

TIGNANELLO Italy, Tuscany (VT) One of Italy's best Sangiovese-dominated blends.

TOCAI DI SAN MARTINO DELLA

BATTAGLIA Italy, Lombardy (DOC) Flowery but full-flavoured dry white wine.

TOKAY-PINOT GRIS France, Alsace (AOC) Rich and creamy dry white wine with fine acidity and fat-spicy complexity.

TOKAY D'ALSACE France, Alsace (AOC) Synonymous with Tokay-Pinot Gris.

TOMAR Portugal, Ribatejo (IPR) Lots of white wine, most of which is ordinary, but the reds are full, fruity and rapidly improving.

TORBATO DI ALGHERO Italy, Sardinia (VT) Crisp, dry whites with a fine, fruity balance.

TORCOLATO Italy, Veneto (VT) Forget the pathetic Picolit and infamous vino santo, this is Italy's greatest dessert wine.

TORGIANO Italy, Umbria (DOC) This DOC was built on the reputation of Lungarotti's excellent Rubesco Torgiano, particularly the Vigna Monticchio and white Torgiano may now be produced.

TORO Spain, Castilla-León (DO) If you avoid the local co-operative, you can find some excellent reds, which are often oak-aged. The whites and rosés are also promising.

TORRE ALEMANNA Italy, Apulia (VT) Interesting deep-coloured, full-bodied red blended from several grapes including Malbec.

TORRE ERCOLANA Italy, Latium (VT) One of the very best Franco-Italian grape blends.

TORRE QUARTO Italy, Apulia (VT) Fine full-bodied, fruity red wine of appeal, plus less interesting dry white and dry rosé.

TORRES Portugal, Estremadura (IPR) Clean

fruity reds, the best of which have a good concentration of berry flavours, whereas the best whites are simply crisp with a touch of spritz and are much less interesting.

TORRETTE Italy, Valle d'Aosta (DOC) Red wines that are surprisingly deep in colour and body for their Alpine provenance.

TOURAINE France, Loire (AOC) All manner and quality of wines are sold under this appellation: from sparkling red, white and rosé made in dry through to sweet styles (of which the brut white and rosé are best), to still red and white varietal wines: the Gamay is particularly fresh and a good Touraine Sauvignon is better than an average, but expensive, Sancerre. The rosés are drier and a shade more subtle than those from Anjou.

TOURAINE-AMBOISE France, Loire (AOC) Some interesting reds, uninspiring whites, but the rosés can be mouthwatering.

TOURAINE-MESLAND France, Loire (AOC) Some delicious reds and rosés that rank with Bourgueil, but the whites tend to be acidic in all except the hottest years.

TOURAINE AZAY-LE-RIDEAU France, Loire (AOC) Delicate, light-bodied whites, most of which are dry, although some may be *demi-sec*.

TOURAINE MOUSSEUX France, Loire (AOC) Good value red, white and rosé fizz.

TOURAINE PÉTILLANT France, Loire (AOC) Slightly sparkling red, white and rosé wines with attractive, refreshing fruit.

TRAPPENBERG Germany, Rheinpfalz If you see this name following that of a village on a bottle of

Rheinpfalz, it is only a *Grosslage* wine.

TREBBIANO (Grape) *See* **Ugni Blanc** entry.

TREBBIANO Italy, Lacklustre white wine grape.

TREBBIANO D'ABRUZZO Italy, Abruzzi (DOC) Usually neutral dry white wines, although occasional examples can be delicately scented.

TREBBIANO DI ROMAGNA Italy, Emilia-Romagna (DOC) Dry, neutral whites and equally boring dry, semi-sweet and sweet sparkling wines.

TRENTINO Italy, Trentino-Alto Adige (DOC) Similar to Alto Adige for quality, consistency and the different varietals available, but the style is usually softer and less racy.

TRISTO DI MONTESECCO Italy, Marches (VT) Unusual but delightful blended dry white wine with soft, creamy fruit.

TRITTENHEIM Germany, Mosel-Saar-Ruwer One of the best villages in the MSR. Top single-vineyards: Trittenheimer Apotheke, Trittenheimer Altärchen.

TROCKENBEERENAUSLESE Germany (QbA) Great German botrytis wine that is as sweet and concentrated as Sauternes, but much higher acidity makes it more tangy and less of a food wine. Very rare and very expensive.

TURSAN France, Southwest France (VDQS) Similar reds to Madiran, the best Tursans are finer in quality, but not quite as concentrated. Also full, rich, somewhat rustic dry whites.

TXAKOLI Spain, Basque Country (DO) New DO, which means that the producers should be trying hard, but no guarantees.

UERZIG Germany, Mosel-Saar-Ruwer One of the best villages in the MSR. Top single-vineyards: Uerziger Würzgarten.

UGNI BLANC (Grape) The Ugni Blanc makes a more drinkable everyday dry white wine in France than it does as the Trebbiano in Italy.

UNGSTEIN Germany, Rheinpfalz One of the best villages in the Rheinpfalz. Top single-vineyards: Ungsteiner Herrenberg.

UNTERBADISCHER LANDWEIN Germany (DL) One of 15 Deutscher Landwein appellations, its wines should be simple and light-bodied, with a basic flowery aroma, some grapey fruit and a touch of sweetness on the finish.

UTIEL-REQUENA Spain, Valencia (DO) Surprisingly fine red and rosé wines.

VAL D'AOSTA Italy, Val d'Aosta(DOC) New region-wide appellation encompassing virtually every style of wine imaginable, most of which are better enjoyed in the Val d'Aosta's magnificent surroundings than they are when brought home. Most wines are blended, although some varietals are allowed, but the better wines all have more specific sub-appellations: Arnad-Montjovat, Chambave, Donnas or Donnaz, Morgex et la Salle, Nus and Torrette.

VAL D'ARBIA Italy, Tuscany (DOC) Dry fruity whites and dry or sweet vino santo.

VAL DI CORINA Italy, Tuscany (DOC) Red Sangiovese and dry white Trebbiano wines that have yet to make their mark.

VALCALEPIO Italy, Lombardy (DOC) Interesting Cabernet-Merlot reds and light, dry and delicate whites.

VALDADIGE Italy, Trentino-Alto Adige (DOC) Crisp dry whites and semi-sweet wines both white and red.

VALDEORRAS Spain, Galicia (DO) A variable appellation, but a couple of good producers (the Co-operativa O Barco and Bodega Jesus Nazareno) make attractive, aromatic red wines and clean fruity rosés.

VALDEPEÑAS Spain, Castilla-La Mancha (DO) La Mancha's solitary fine wine district, Valdepeñas can produce surprisingly well-balanced red, dry white (less interesting) and rosé wines, despite its torrid heat.

VALENÇAY France, Loire (VDQS) Well-made, fragrant reds, simple dry whites and soft, creamy off-dry rosés.

VALENCIA Spain, Valencia (DO) Some high-tech wineries are producing fine-flavoured, fruity reds, light-bodied dry whites and gentle, fruity rosés, as well as the excellent value fortified Moscatel for which Valencia is best known.

VALGELLA Italy, Lombardy (DOC) Most productive, least interesting sub-appellation of Valtelina.

VALLE DE MONTERREY Spain, Galicia (VdlT) Country wines that have yet to make their mark.

VALLE DEL MIÑO-OURENSE Spain, Galicia (VdlT) Country wines that have yet to make their mark.

VALLE ISARCO Italy, Trentino-Alto Adige (DOC)

Various white wine varietal of reliable quality.

VALLÉ D'AOSTA Italy, Val d'Aosta (DOC) Synonymous with Val d'Aosta.

VALPANTENA Italy, Veneto (DOC) Single-village Valpolicella.

VALPAÇOS Portugal, Trás-os-Montes (IPR) Part of the former appellation of Trás-os-Montes, which has always been famous for its slightly fizzy pink wines such as Mateus and Trovador, although Valpaços has always produced far better, assertively fruity red wines.

VALPOLICELLA Italy, Veneto (DOC) Apart from the excellent full and juicy red wine produced by a handful of quality-conscious growers, Valpolicella should not be touched, even with a barge-pole.

VALPOLICELLA RIPASSO Italy, Veneto (VT) Interesting if idiosyncratic red wine made by fermenting Valpolicella on the expended lees of Valpolicella Recioto.

VALTELLINA Italy, Lombardy (DOC) Light-scented, medium-bodied reds of simple but pleasing character.

VALTELLINA SUPERIORE Italy, Lombardy (DOC) Red wines of considerable colour, richness and elegance.

VALTIENDAS Spain, Castilla-León (VC) Struggling to make the grade.

VALWIG Germany, Mosel-Saar-Ruwer One of the best villages in the MSR. Top single-vineyards: Valwiger Herrenberg.

VAROSA Portugal, Beiras (IPR) From the Beira Alta, between the Vinho Verde and Dão districts, where every style of wine is produced in varying quality.

VEGA SICILIA Spain, Castilla-León (DO) Spain's most expensive red wine is a huge, meaty red that sometimes justifies its price, although the quality of its vintages varies far more than the weather does.

VELLETRI Italy, Latium (DOC) Uninspiring dry and semi-sweet white wines and equally lacklustre reds.

VENEGAZZU DELLA CASA Italy, Veneto (VT) One of Italy's best Cabernet-based blends.

VERDELHO Portugal, Madeira (DOC) This tangy, medium-sweet Madeira lacks the mouth-filling weight of Bual, but has somewhat more body than Sercial and can age very gracefully.

VERDICCHIO DEI CASTELLI DI JESI Italy, Marches (DOC) Popular dry white wines of very basic and declining quality, also in sparkling and semi-sparkling styles.

VERDICCHIO DI MATELICA Italy, Marches (DOC) If you want the best Verdicchio, this is it, as it comes from the hilly zone in the centre of the Verdicchio area. Make sure you taste before you buy.

VERMENTINO DI GALLURA Italy, Sardinia (DOC) Dry, light-bodied whites that are soft to flabby, but always clean.

VERNACCIA DI ORISTANO Italy, Sardinia (DOC) Dry, slightly bitter white wines, Sherry-like in style, plus dry or sweet fortified versions.

VERNACCIA DI SAN GIMIGNANO Italy, Tuscany (DOC) Some of these dry white wines can be deliciously crisp and full of vibrant fruit.

VERNACCIA DI SERRAPETRONA Italy, Marches (DOC) Dry and sweet sparkling red wines.

VERRENBERG Germany, Württemberg One of the best villages in Württemberg. Top single-vineyards: Verrenberger Verrenberg.

VESUVIO Italy, Campania (DOC) Lacklustre red, dry white, rosé, sparkling and sweet fortified wines are made from vines growing on the volcanic slopes of the still active Mount Vesuvius.

VETRICE Portugal, Douro Premium sparkling wine of modest quality made by Schramsberg of California.

VIDIGUEIRA Portugal, Alentejo (IPR) Lots of white wine, most of which is ordinary, but the reds are full, fruity and rapidly improving.

VIGNETO FRATTA Italy, Veneto (VT) One of Italy's best Cabernet-based blends.

VIGORELLO Italy, Tuscany (VT) One of Italy's best Sangiovese-dominated blends.

VILLA BANFI Italy, Trentino-Alto Adige Excellent, dry sparkling wines.

VILLA DI CAPEZZANA Italy, Tuscany (VT) One of Italy's best pure Chardonnay wines.

VIN D'ALSACE France, Alsace (AOC) Synonymous with Alsace AOC.

VIN DE CORSE France, Corsica (AOC) Generic appellation for red, dry white and dry rosé wines of rustic character, which can be enjoyed on holiday, but lose their charm if taken home. Wines with the more specific appellations of Calvi, Coteaux du Cap Corse, Figari, Porto Vecchio and Sartène can prove to be more individual in character.

VIN DE FRONTIGNAN
France, Languedoc-Roussillon (AOC) Synonymous with Muscat de Frontignan.

VIN DE MOSELLE France, Alsace (VDQS) Light, dry and insubstantial red and dry white wines from the upper reaches of the Moselle (which becomes the Mosel as it flows into Germany).

VIN DE PAILLE D'ARBOIS France, Jura (AOC) Deep, rich, very sweet white wine with a distinctively crisp finish.

VIN DE PAILLE DE L'ÉTOILE France, Jura (AOC) Very sweet, distinctive dessert wine, which instantly ages due to the presence of an oxidative-prone grape called the Savagnin.

VIN DE PAYS France (VdP) An unpretentious group of red, white and rosé wines, vins de pays are intended to be simple quaffing wines that display the rudimentary characteristics of their geographical areas of origin. In theory, every French departement has the right to this appellation, but many do not possess commercial vineyards, while others have not bothered due to the greater profitability of selling their wines under more famous AOC names. Some, such as Bas-Rhin and Haut-Rhin in Alsace and Côte-d'Or in Burgundy, have only recently begun to do so on a very limited scale. There are three multi-departmental appellations called regional vins de pays, but it is the vast number of small zonal vins de pays that offer the greatest chance of finding interesting little wines of more individual character.

VIN DE PAYS CATALAN
France, Languedoc-Roussillon (VdP) A zonal vin de pays of very successful, well-coloured, fruity red wine (70%) made from the Grenache, Carignan and Cinsault grapes, dry rosé (20%) and dry white (10%), with vins primeurs a speciality, account for the output of this prolific zone.

VIN DE PAYS CHARENTAIS France, Cognac (VdP) A zonal vin de pays of crisp, tangy dry white wines that are really good. Some red and rosé is also made.

VIN DE PAYS D'AGENAIS France, Southwest (VdP) A zonal vin de pays of mostly rustic red blends of Fer and Abouriou. Some crisp dry white and a little dry rosé are also produced.

VIN DE PAYS D'ALLOBROGIE France, Savoie (VdP) A zonal vin de pays of white wine, dominated by the Jacquère grape, accounting for 95% of the total output. Reds are mostly Gamay and/or Mondeuse-based. The wines are in a sort of rustic Savoie style.

VIN DE PAYS D'ARGENS France, Provence (VdP) A zonal vin de pays of red, white and rosé wines in a rustic Provence style.

VIN DE PAYS D'OC France, Languedoc-Roussillon (VdP) A regional vin de pays of red (75%), white (5%) and rosé (20%) wines of variable, but usually acceptable, quality. The 'Oc' of this regional vin de pays is southern dialect for 'yes', it being 'Oui' elsewhere in France, thus Languedoc, the 'tongue of Oc'.

VIN DE PAYS D'URFÉ France, Loire (VdP) A zonal vin de pays of red wine for the most part, produced in

modest quantities, although white and rosé may also be produced.

VIN DE PAYS D'UZEGE France, Languedoc-Roussillon (VdP) A zonal vin de pays of red (70%), white (10%) and rosé (20%) wines, of good Languedoc style.

VIN DE PAYS DE BESSAN France, Languedoc-Roussillon (VdP) A zonal vin de pays. Dry, aromatic rosé wines are the best known, but dry white (40%) and a little red is also produced.

VIN DE PAYS DE BIGORRE France, Southwest (VdP) A zonal vin de pays of mostly full, rich, Madiran-type red wine, plus a little good crisp, dry white. Rosé may also be produced.

VIN DE PAYS DE CASSAN France, Languedoc-Roussillon (VdP) A zonal vin de pays of two-thirds red wine, one-third rosé, produced in only modest quantities.

VIN DE PAYS DE CAUX France, Languedoc-Roussillon (VdP) A zonal vin de pays of good, typical, dry and fruity rosé in a Languedoc style. Red (40%) and a little white is also made.

VIN DE PAYS DE CESSENON France, Languedoc-Roussillon (VdP) A zonal vin de pays of red wines of a rustic St-Chinian style, plus a little rosé.

VIN DE PAYS DE CUCUGNAN France, Languedoc-Roussillon (VdP) A zonal vin de pays of essentially red wines, although rosé may be produced.

VIN DE PAYS DE FRANCHE COMTÉ France, Jura & Northeast (VdP) A zonal vin de pays of red, white and rosé wines. The white is of particular note.

VIN DE PAYS DE L'ARDAILHOU France, Languedoc-Roussillon (VdP) A zonal vin de pays of fruity red wine and a little dry rosé, from an area on the Hérault coast.

VIN DE PAYS DE L'ARDECHE France, Rhône (VdP) A departmental vin de pays of red and white wines from a range of Rhône and Bordelais grapes, produced on a limited scale.

VIN DE PAYS DE L'AUDE France, Languedoc-Roussillon (VdP) A departmental vin de pays of fresh and fruity wine, roughly 75% red and 25% rosé, plus a little white.

VIN DE PAYS DE L'AVEYRON France, Southwest (VdP) A departmental vin de pays of primarily fresh, light, red wines. Some aromatic dry white rosé wines also produced.

VIN DE PAYS DE L'HAUTERIVE EN PAYS D'AUDE France, Languedoc-Roussillon (VdP) A zonal vin de pays of red wine made from a range of typical Languedoc and southwestern grape varieties. A little vin primeur is made, and small amounts of white and rosé are also produced.

VIN DE PAYS DE L'HÉRAULT France, Languedoc-Roussillon (VdP) A departmental vin de pays of red (75%), rosé (20%) and white (5%) wines. This vin de pays departement yields a staggering nine million cases (810,000 hectolitres) from what was once the heart of Midi mediocrity. Improved viti-vinicultural techniques have transformed its production into far better wines.

VIN DE PAYS DE L'ILE DE BEAUTÉ France, Corsica (VdP) A zonal vin de pays of red and rosé wines accounting for 95%, white the other 5%, of the vast production of Corsica.

VIN DE PAYS DE L'INDRE-ET-LOIRE France, Loire (VdP) A departmental vin de pays of red, white and rosé wines from traditional Loire grape varieties.

VIN DE PAYS DE L'YONNE France, Burgundy (VdP) A departmental vin de pays of white wines only, produced in small quantities.

VIN DE PAYS DE LA BÉNOVIE France, Languedoc-Roussillon (VdP) A zonal vin de pays of red (75%), white (20%) and rosé (5%) wines, in a Coteaux du Languedoc style.

VIN DE PAYS DE LA CITÉ DE CARCASSONNE France, Languedoc-Roussillon (VdP) A zonal vin de pays of red (approximately 75%) and rosé (approximately 25%) from 11 communes around the spectacular walled city of Carcassonne, produced from a wide range of grapes. White wine may also be produced.

VIN DE PAYS DE LA CÔTE-D'OR France, Burgundy (VdP) A departmental vin de pays of rarely encountered rustic Burgundy wines, mostly white.

VIN DE PAYS DE LA CÔTE VERMEILLE France, Languedoc-Roussillon (VdP) A zonal vin de pays of red, white and rosé wines from the Collioure area of Roussillon. The actual vin de pays region was created in 1987.

VIN DE PAYS DE LA DORDOGNE France, Southwest (VdP) A departmental vin de pays of rustic Bergerac style for both red and white wine.

VIN DE PAYS DE LA DROME France, Rhône (VdP) A departmental vin de pays of red, white and rosé wines, from typical Rhône grape varieties, similar in style to Coteaux du Tricastin AOC.

VIN DE PAYS DE LA GIRONDE France, Bordeaux (VdP) A departmental vin de pays of red and white wines from isolated areas not classified for the production of Bordeaux.

VIN DE PAYS DE LA HAUTE-VALLÉE DE L'AUDE France, Languedoc-Roussillon (VdP) A zonal vin de pays of red wines made from Bordelais grape varieties for the most part, although dry white and rosé wines are also made.

VIN DE PAYS DE LA HAUTE-VALLÉE DE L'ORB France, Languedoc-Roussillon (VdP) A zonal vin de pays of mostly red, but also rosé wines, with very limited production.

VIN DE PAYS DE LA HAUTE GARONNE France, Southwest (VdP) A departmental vin de pays of red and rosé wines made from the Négrette grape in the Fronton area, and from the Merlot, Cabernets, Syrah and Jurançon noir in scattered patches elsewhere. Overall production is very small.

VIN DE PAYS DE LA LOIRE-ATLANTIQUE France, Loire (VdP) A departmental vin de pays of red and rosé wines, including a pale vin gris, are made from the Gamay and Groslot grapes, white Folle blanche and Melon de Bourgogne are used for white, with some interesting developments using Chardonnay.

VIN DE PAYS DE LA MEUSE France, Lorraine

(VdP) A departmental vin de pays of red and rosé wines, including a pale vin gris, made from Pinot noir and Gamay grapes, and white wine from Chardonnay, Aligoté and Auxerrois.

VIN DE PAYS DE LA NIÈVRE France, Loire (VdP) A departmental vin de pays of red, white and rosé wines, production of which is mostly confined to the areas of Charité-sur-Loire, La Celle-sur-Nièvre and Tannay.

VIN DE PAYS DE LA PETITE CRAU France, Provence (VdP) A zonal vin de pays of red (70%), white (15%) and rosé (15%) wines, in a style that bridges Rhône and Provence.

VIN DE PAYS DE LA PRINCIPAUTÉ D'ORANGE France, Provence (VdP) A zonal vin de pays. A full red wine, made predominantly from Rhône grape varieties. Rosé may also be produced.

VIN DE PAYS DE LA SARTHE France, Loire (VdP) A departmental vin de pays of red, white and rosé wines may be made, although production of this vin de pays departement is minuscule and, as far as I am aware, limited to just one grower in Maráon.

VIN DE PAYS DE LA VALLÉE DU PARADIS France, Languedoc-Roussillon (VdP) A zonal vin de pays of red wine produced in large quantities. A little wine is made as vin primeur.

VIN DE PAYS DE LA VAUNAGE France, Languedoc-Roussillon (VdP) A zonal vin de pays of light red wine that is in typical Languedoc style.

VIN DE PAYS DE LA VENDÉE France, Loire (VdP) A departmental vin de pays of red, white and

rosé wines, produced in small quantities, in a similar style to Fiefs Vendéens (which was a vin de pays until it was promoted to VDQS status in December 1984).

VIN DE PAYS DE LA VICOMTÉ D'AUMELAS France, Languedoc-Roussillon (VdP) A zonal vin de pays of red (80%) and rosé (20%), plus a tiny amount of white wine. The grapes used are tradition-ally southwestern varieties.

VIN DE PAYS DE LA VIENNE France, Loire (VdP) A departmental vin de pays of red, white and rosé wines produced in and around the Haut-Poitou district.

VIN DE PAYS DE LA VISTRENQUE France, Languedoc-Roussillon (VdP) A zonal vin de pays of red and rosé wines produced in very small quantities. White wine may also be produced.

VIN DE PAYS DE PÉZENAS France, Languedoc-Roussillon (VdP) A zonal vin de pays of roughly 70% red wine and 30% rosé, along with a tiny amount of white and vins primeurs.

VIN DE PAYS DE RETZ France, Loire (VdP) A zonal vin de pays of predomi-nantly rosé wine made from the Groslot grape, although a little Cabernet franc-based red, and a very tiny amount of white is produced.

VIN DE PAYS DE ST-SARDOS France, Southwest (VdP) A zonal vin de pays of red, white and rosé wines from a typically southwestern hotchpotch of grape varieties.

VIN DE PAYS DE THÉZAC-PERRICARD France, Southwest (VdP) A zonal vin de pays on the far eastern edge of and

producing fuller wines than the Lot-et-Garonne vin de pays.

VIN DE PAYS DES ALPES-MARITIMES France, Provence (VdP) A departmental vin de pays of some 70% red and 30% rosé made from Carignan, Cinsault, Grenache, Ugni blanc and Rolle grapes, mostly from the communes of Carros, Mandelieu and Mougins. White wines may also be produced.

VIN DE PAYS DES ALPES DE HAUTE-PROVENCE France, Provence (VdP) A departmental vin de pays of roughly two-thirds red and one-third dry white wine, mainly from the southeast of the departement. Rosé may also be produced.

VIN DE PAYS DES BALMES DAUPHINOISES France, Savoie (VdP) A zonal vin de pays of dry white (60%), made from the Jacquère and Chardonnay grapes, and red (40%) made from Gamay and Pinot noir. Rosé may also be produced.

VIN DE PAYS DES BOUCHES-DU-RHONE France, Provence (VdP) A departmental vin de pays of predominantly warm, spicy red wine made in the Provence style. Most of the rest is dry rosé, with just a tiny amount of rather dull, dry white.

VIN DE PAYS DES COLLINES DE LA MOURE France, Languedoc-Roussillon (VdP) A zonal vin de pays of red (65%), dry rosé (30%) and dry white (5%) wines. The red and rosé are a blend of local grape varieties with those of the southwest; the white wine is basically made from the Ugni blanc.

VIN DE PAYS DES COLLINES RHODANIENNES France, Rhône (VdP) A zonal vin de pays of red wine (95%) from a base of Gamay and Syrah, and Marsanne-dominated dry white wine (5%). Rosé may also be produced, and a little vin primeur is made.

VIN DE PAYS DES COMTÉS DE RHONDANIENS France, Rhône-Savoie (VdP) A regional vin de pays created as recently as 1989, Comtés de Rhodaniens encompasses eight departements and eight zonal vins de pays. Strangely, the wines must be accepted as one of the eight zonal vins de pays before they can apply for this contradictory regional appellation.

VIN DE PAYS DES COTEAUX CÉVENOLS France, Languedoc-Roussillon (VdP) A zonal vin de pays of red (60%) and dry rosé (40%) wines, both in honest, fruity Languedoc style. Dry white wines may also be produced.

VIN DE PAYS DES COTEAUX CHARITOIS France, Loire (VdP) A zonal vin de pays of white wines from the Loire Valley.

VIN DE PAYS DES COTEAUX D'ENSERUNE France, Languedoc-Roussillon (VdP) A zonal vin de pays of two-thirds red wine and one-third rosé, from primarily Languedoc grapes augmented by the Syrah and some traditional varieties from the southwest.

VIN DE PAYS DES COTEAUX DE BESSILLES France, Languedoc-Roussillon (VdP) A zonal vin de pays of red, white and rosé wines from the Hérault departement of Languedoc-Roussillon. The actual vin de pays region was created in 1987.

VIN DE PAYS DES COTEAUX DE CEZE France, Languedoc-

Roussillon (VdP) A zonal vin de pays of approximately two-thirds red and one-third rosé wine, plus a little dry white in basic Côtes-du-Rhône style.

VIN DE PAYS DES COTEAUX DE COIFFY France, Northeast (VdP) A zonal vin de pays of little seen, mostly Gamay red wines.

VIN DE PAYS DES COTEAUX DE FONTCAUDE France, Languedoc-Roussillon (VdP) A zonal vin de pays of red (80%) in a light and fresh style, and dry rosé (20%) wines.

VIN DE PAYS DES COTEAUX DE GLANES France, Southwest (VdP) A zonal vin de pays of mainly red, Gamay-and Merlot-dominated wines, plus a little rosé.

VIN DE PAYS DES COTEAUX DE L'ARDECHE France, Rhône (VdP) A zonal vin de pays of particularly successful spicy red wine (90%), rosé (7%) and white (3%), made from grapes of Bordelais and Rhône origin. The area has a huge annual production, in excess of two million cases (180,000 hectolitres).

VIN DE PAYS DES COTEAUX DE LA CABRERISSE France, Languedoc-Roussillon (VdP) A zonal vin de pays of red (80%) and rosé (20%) wines, with some vins primeurs.

VIN DE PAYS DES COTEAUX DE LAURENS France, Languedoc-Roussillon (VdP) A zonal vin de pays of red, barely any white, but some rosé, made from local traditional grape varieties, augmented by the Syrah.

VIN DE PAYS DES COTEAUX DE MIRAMONT France,

Languedoc-Roussillon (VdP) A zonal vin de pays of predominantly red wines, made from traditional local grape varieties, plus the Syrah. A little rosé and some vins primeurs produced.

VIN DE PAYS DES COTEAUX DE MURVIEL France, Languedoc-Roussillon (VdP) A zonal vin de pays of red (80%) and rosé (20%) wines of typical Languedoc light fruitiness.

VIN DE PAYS DES COTEAUX DE NARBONNE France, Languedoc-Roussillon (VdP) A zonal vin de pays of red, white and rosé wines from the coastal edge of Corbières.

VIN DE PAYS DES COTEAUX DE PEYRIAC France, Languedoc-Roussillon (VdP) A zonal vin de pays of full and rustic red wines (85%), made from local grape varieties augmented by the Syrah. The remainder is rosé, plus a little white.

VIN DE PAYS DES COTEAUX DES BARONNIES France, Rhône (VdP) A zonal vin de pays of red (95%) and rosé (5%) wines, made from traditional Rhône grapes to which Bordelais varieties may be added. A little white is also made.

VIN DE PAYS DES COTEAUX DES FENOUILLEDES France, Languedoc-Roussillon (VdP) A zonal vin de pays of red (90%), white (2%) and rosé (8%) wines, in a full, rich Roussillon style.

VIN DE PAYS DES COTEAUX DU CHER ET DE L'ARNON France, Loire (VdP) A zonal vin de pays of reds and vin gris rosé made from the Gamay, and dry white wine from the Sauvignon blanc.

VIN DE PAYS DES COTEAUX DU GRÉSIVAUDAN France, Savoie (VdP) A zonal vin de pays of red and rosé Savoie-style wines made from Gamay, Pinot and Etraire de la dui (a local grape variety), and Jacquère-based dry white wines.

VIN DE PAYS DES COTEAUX DU LIBRON France, Languedoc-Roussillon (VdP) A zonal vin de pays of red (80%) and rosé (20%) made from the traditional grapes of southwest France.

VIN DE PAYS DES COTEAUX DU LITTORAL AUDOIS France, Languedoc-Roussillon (VdP) A zonal vin de pays of red (up to 85%) and rosé (15%) wines. A little white wine is produced from Grenache blanc and Macabéo grape varieties.

VIN DE PAYS DES COTEAUX DU PONT DU GARD France, Languedoc-Roussillon (VdP) A zonal vin de pays of typical Languedoc-style red and rosé wines. Dry white is also made, and vins primeurs are a local speciality.

VIN DE PAYS DES COTEAUX DU QUERCY France, Southwest (VdP) A zonal vin de pays of richly coloured, full-bodied, but precocious Gamay and Merlot-dominated red wines.

VIN DE PAYS DES COTEAUX DU SALAGOU France, Languedoc-Roussillon (VdP) A zonal vin de pays of red (80%) and rosé (20%) wines, made from typical Languedoc grape varieties.

VIN DE PAYS DES COTEAUX DU SALAVES France, Languedoc-Roussillon (VdP) A zonal vin de pays of red (80%) and rosé (20%) wines from a large range of Languedoc,

southwest and Bordelais grapes. Very small quantities of white vin primeur are also produced.

VIN DE PAYS DES COTEAUX DU TERMÉNES France, Languedoc-Roussillon (VdP) A zonal vin de pays of red, white, rosé and vins primeurs, produced irregularly, from vines in the centre of Hautes-Corbières.

VIN DE PAYS DES COTEAUX ET TERRASSES DE MONTAUBAN France, Southwest (VdP) A zonal vin de pays of red and rosé wines from the Pays de la Garonne.

VIN DE PAYS DES COTEAUX FLAVIENS France, Languedoc-Roussillon (VdP) A zonal vin de pays of red (60%), rosé (30%) and white (10%) wines, from typically Languedoc grape varieties. The vin de pays is named after the Roman Emperor Flavius.

VIN DE PAYS DES CÔTES CATALANES France, Languedoc-Roussillon (VdP) A zonal vin de pays of red and rosé wines made from the Cabernets, Gamay, Syrah, Tannat and Jurançon noir grape varieties. White wine may also be made.

VIN DE PAYS DES CÔTES DE GASCOGNE France, Southwest (VdP) A zonal vin de pays of tangy, dry white wines that are the non-distilled produce of Armagnac. Wines made from the Colombard grape are the lightest, those from the Ugni blanc are fatter and more interesting, and the Manseng and Sauvignon blanc are also used. Red and rosé wines are also made.

VIN DE PAYS DES CÔTES DE LASTOURS France, Languedoc-

Roussillon (VdP) A zonal vin de pays of mainly red (80%) and rosé (20%) wines. White wines may also be produced and vins primeurs are a local speciality.

VIN DE PAYS DES CÔTES DE LÉZIGNAN France, Languedoc-Roussillon (VdP) A zonal vin de pays of red wine (80%), made from typical Languedoc grapes, dry rosé (20%), and a token amount of white.

VIN DE PAYS DES CÔTES DE LIBAC France, Languedoc-Roussillon (VdP) A zonal vin de pays on the northern extremity of Languedoc, producing light reds and soft whites.

VIN DE PAYS DES CÔTES DE MONTESTRUC France, Southwest (VdP) A zonal vin de pays of red wines made from the Alicanté Bouschet, Cabernets, Malbec, Merlot and Jurançon noir grape varieties, and white wines made from the Colombard, Mauzac and Ugni blanc.

VIN DE PAYS DES CÔTES DE PÉRIGNAN France, Languedoc-Roussillon (VdP) A zonal vin de pays of mostly red and rosé wines, from the lesser sites of La Clape. White wine may also be produced, and some vin primeur.

VIN DE PAYS DES CÔTES DE PROUILLE France, Languedoc-Roussillon (VdP) A zonal vin de pays of red, white and rosé wines, from the Aude departement.

VIN DE PAYS DES CÔTES DE THAU France, Languedoc-Roussillon (VdP) A zonal vin de pays of red (60%), rosé (35%) and white (5%) wines.

VIN DE PAYS DES CÔTES DE THONGUE

France, Languedoc-Roussillon (VdP) A zonal vin de pays of red (70%) and rosé (25%) wines made from local grape varieties. The 5% of white wine is essentially Ugni blanc-based. The vins primeurs of Merlot, Syrah and Carignan are a speciality.

VIN DE PAYS DES CÔTES DU BRIAN France, Languedoc-Roussillon (VdP) A zonal vin de pays of red and rosé wines made from a range of Languedoc grapes in which the Carignan dominates and to which the Syrah may be added.

VIN DE PAYS DES CÔTES DU CÉRESSOU France, Languedoc-Roussillon (VdP) A zonal vin de pays of typically light and fruity Languedoc wine produced in fairly large amounts. 60% is red, 15% white and 25% rosé.

VIN DE PAYS DES CÔTES DU CONDOMOIS France, Southwest (VdP) A zonal vin de pays of red wines (60%), dominated by the Tannat grape, and white (40%), made from the Colombard or Ugni blanc. A little rosé is also produced.

VIN DE PAYS DES CÔTES DU TARN France, Southwest (VdP) A zonal vin de pays of red, white and rosé wines made from Bordelais and southwestern grape varieties, plus, uniquely for France, the Portugais Bleu.

VIN DE PAYS DES CÔTES DU VIDOURLE France, Languedoc-Roussillon (VdP) A zonal vin de pays of two-thirds red and one-third rosé wines.

VIN DE PAYS DES DEUX-SEVRES France, Loire (VdP) A departmental vin de pays of simple wines of a frank nature, from the vineyards with the richest soil (and thus the poorest as far as wine production is concerned) in the Nantais.

VIN DE PAYS DES GORGES DE L'HÉRAULT France, Languedoc-Roussillon (VdP) A zonal vin de pays of red (70%) and rosé (30%) in typical Languedoc style. White wine may also be produced.

VIN DE PAYS DES GORGES ET CÔTES DE MILLAU France, Southwest (VdP) A zonal vin de pays of red wines from the Gamay, Syrah, Cabernets, Malbec and Fer accounting for nearly all production. Vin primeur is a speciality, and a minute amount of white is made. Rosé may also be produced.

VIN DE PAYS DES HAUTES-ALPES France, Rhône-Provence (VdP) A departmental vin de pays of mostly red wines produced from essentially Rhône grapes, but in a somewhat rustic Provençal style.

VIN DE PAYS DES HAUTS DE BADENS France, Languedoc-Roussillon (VdP) A zonal vin de pays of red and rosé wines in a rustic Minervois style.

VIN DE PAYS DES LANDES France, Southwest (VdP) A departmental vin de pays of red, white and rosé wines. Approximately 80% is red, and the grapes used are traditional southwestern varieties.

VIN DE PAYS DES MARCHES DE BRETAGNE France, Loire (VdP) A zonal vin de pays of predominantly Gamay and Cabernet franc red and rosé wines.

VIN DE PAYS DES MAURES France, Provence (VdP) A zonal vin de pays of approximately two-thirds red wine and one-third rosé, plus a tiny amount of white, account for this area's Provençal-style wines.

VIN DE PAYS DES MONTS DE LA GRAGE France, Languedoc-Roussillon (VdP) A zonal vin de pays of red and rosé wines in a basic Languedoc style, often beefed-up with Syrah grapes.

VIN DE PAYS DES PYRÉNÉES-ATLANTIQUES France, Southwest (VdP) A departmental vin de pays of two-thirds red and one-third white wine, produced from traditional southwestern grape varieties.

VIN DE PAYS DES PYRÉNÉES-ORIENTALES France, Languedoc-Roussillon (VdP) A departmental vin de pays of full and fruity red, white and rosé wines, produced in large quantities.

VIN DE PAYS DES SABLES DU GOLFE DU LION France, Provence (VdP) A zonal vin de pays of two-thirds red wine, one-third rosé, including a large proportion in pale vin gris style, plus a small amount of white wine. The vines belonging to this zonal vin de pays are ungrafted and grown on an amazing sand-bar with seawater on both sides.

VIN DE PAYS DES TERROIRS LANDAIS France, Southwest (VdP) A zonal vin de pays in Aquitaine and Charentes, created in 1987.

VIN DE PAYS DES VALS D'AGLY France, Languedoc-Roussillon (VdP) A zonal vin de pays of red (95%), white (1%) and rosé (4%) wines, along with a little vin primeur.

VIN DE PAYS DU BAS-RHIN France, Alsace (VdP) A departmental vin de pays of insignificant quantity from Alsace varieties.

VIN DE PAYS DU BÉRANGE France, Languedoc-Roussillon (VdP) A zonal vin de pays of red and rosé wine from traditional local grapes augmented by the Syrah. White wine may also be produced.

VIN DE PAYS DU BOURBONNAIS France, Loire (VdP) A zonal vin de pays of rare wine from a white-only area in the Loire Valley.

VIN DE PAYS DU CHER France, Loire (VdP) A departmental vin de pays of mostly Touraine-like, Gamay-based red wine, plus a small amount of dry rosé in a light vin gris style. A little dry white Sauvignon blanc is also produced that can be compared to a sort of rustic Sancerre or Menetou-Salon.

VIN DE PAYS DU COMTÉ DE GRIGNAN France, Rhône (VdP) A zonal vin de pays of Grenache-dominated red wines for the most part, but some rosé and dry white wines may also be produced, the latter from Ugni blanc and a string of Rhône varieties.

VIN DE PAYS DU COMTÉ TOLOSAN France, Southwest (VdP) A regional vin de pays of red, white and rosé wines, produced in modest quantities.

VIN DE PAYS DU GARD France, Languedoc-Roussillon (VdP) A departmental vin de pays of two-thirds red wine and one-third white and rosé. These wines have undergone much improvement since the days of the infamous Midi.

VIN DE PAYS DU GERS France, Southwest (VdP) A departmental vin de pays of light-bodied, rustic red, dry white and dry rosé wines from in the Armagnac area.

VIN DE PAYS DU HAUT-RHIN France, Alsace (VdP)

A departmental vin de pays of insignificant quantity from Alsace varieties.

VIN DE PAYS DU JARDIN DE LA FRANCE France, Loire (VdP) This huge regional vin de pays encompasses 13 departements, embracing the entire Loire Valley. Some 65% of the production consist of varietal wines, with simple red Gamay and crisp, dry white Sauvignon wines the most important.

VIN DE PAYS DU LOIR-ET-CHER France, Loire (VdP) A departmental vin de pays of red, white and rosé wines, including a pale vin gris, made from traditional Loire grape varieties.

VIN DE PAYS DU LOIRET France, Loire (VdP) A departmental vin de pays of red and rosé, including a pale vin gris style, made from the Gamay grape, plus Sauvignon blanc white account for the small output of this area.

VIN DE PAYS DU LOT France, Southwest (VdP) A departmental vin de pays of mostly red wines from an area that overlaps the northern perimeter of Cahors, although the wines can seldom be compared.

VIN DE PAYS DU LOT-ET-GARONNE France, Southwest (VdP) A departmental vin de pays of primarily red wine that is similar to, but not as good as, Côtes du Marmandais.

VIN DE PAYS DU MAINE-ET-LOIRE France, Loire (VdP) A departmental vin de pays of red, white and rosé wines made in substantial quantities from traditional Loire grape varieties.

VIN DE PAYS DU MONT-BAUDILE France, Languedoc-Roussillon (VdP) A zonal vin de pays of approximately two-thirds

red and one-third rosé, plus a little white wine.

VIN DE PAYS DU MONT-BOUQUET France, Languedoc-Roussillon (VdP) A zonal vin de pays of two-thirds red wine and one-third rosé, produced in a rather full Languedoc style.

VIN DE PAYS DU MONT-CAUME France, Provence (VdP) A zonal vin de pays of red (55%), rosé (40%) and white (5%) wines, produced mostly from traditional Rhône valley grape varieties, although Cabernet sauvignon is used to great effect for some red wines.

VIN DE PAYS DU PUY-DE-DOME France, Loire (VdP) A departmental vin de pays of red, white and rosé wines of simple, rustic quality.

VIN DE PAYS DU TARN-ET-GARONNE France, Southwest (VdP) A departmental vin de pays of mostly red wine, though some rosé is also made.

VIN DE PAYS DU TORGAN France, Languedoc-Roussillon (VdP) A zonal vin de pays of red, white and rosé wines, from the Aude departement. The vin de pays used to be known as Coteaux Cathares.

VIN DE PAYS DU VAL-DE-CESSE France, Languedoc-Roussillon (VdP) A zonal vin de pays of red, white and rosé wines from the Aude departement.

VIN DE PAYS DU VAL-DE-DAGNE France, Languedoc-Roussillon (VdP) A zonal vin de pays of red, white and rosé wines, produced in substantial quantities.

VIN DE PAYS DU VAL D'ORBIEU France, Languedoc-Roussillon (VdP) A zonal vin de pays of two-thirds red and one-third rosé wines, produced from traditional Rhône grape varieties. White wine may also be produced and vin primeur is made.

VIN DE PAYS DU VAL DE MONTFERRAND France, Languedoc-Roussillon (VdP) A zonal vin de pays of red (70%), white (10%) and rosé (20%) wines, with vin primeur and *vin d'une nuit* local specialities, produced in large quantities.

VIN DE PAYS DU VAR France, Provence (VdP) A departmental vin de pays of red (65%), white (5%) and rosé (30%) wines, produced in a spicy Provençal style.

VIN DE PAYS DU VAUCLUSE France, Rhone-Provence (VdP) A departmental vin de pays of red (70%), white (15%) and rosé (15%) wine, in typically southern Rhône style, produced in very large quantities.

VIN DE SAVOIE France, Savoie (AOC) Light, fresh, attractively fruity wines with a fragrant character in red, dry white and dry rosé style. Look out for individual villages, especially Abymes, Aprémont and Chignin for white. Lots of good producers.

VIN DE SAVOIE AYZE MOUSSEUX Savoie (AOC) Wispy, light, dry white fizz of interesting quality from a single village.

VIN DE SAVOIE AYZE PÉTILLANT Savoie (AOC) Semi-sparkling version of above.

VIN DE SAVOIE MOUSSEUX France, Savoie (AOC) Consistent but underrated sparkling white wine.

VIN DE SAVOIE PÉTILLANT France, Savoie (AOC) Semi-sparkling version of previous entry.

VIN DU BUGEY France, Savoie (VDQS) Light, dry, refreshing red, white and rosé, often sold as pure varietals. Best wines often indicate a village name.

VIN DU BUGEY CERDON MOUSSEUX France, Savoie (VDQS) Dry, sparkling white wine from the best village in the Bugey district.

VIN DU BUGEY CERDON PÉTILLANT France, Savoie (VDQS) Dry, slightly sparkling white wine from the best village in the Bugey district.

VIN DU BUGEY MOUSSEUX France, Savoie (VDQS) Generic white fizz.

VIN DU BUGEY PÉTILLANT France, Savoie (VDQS) Easy drinking, off-dry, semi-sparkling white wine.

VIN JAUNE D'ARBOIS France, Jura (AOC) The 'yellow wine' of Arbois looks, smells and tastes like a sherry and is supposed to last for decades.

VIN JAUNE DE L'ETOILE France, Jura (AOC) Same as Arbois, but from a smaller area.

VIN SANTO Italy, Tuscany (VT) A red or white *passito* wine that may be sweet, semi-sweet or dry, vino santo is usually very expensive, seldom excites and will probably be oxidised.

VIN SANTO Italy, Umbria (VT) Umbria's ubiquitous *passito* wine is similar to the Tuscan examples.

VIN SEC DE BORDEAUX France, Bordeaux (AOC) Synonymous with Bordeaux Sec.

VINATTIERI ROSSO Italy, Tuscany (VT) One of Italy's very best pure Sangiovese wines.

VINHO VERDE Portugal, Minho (DOC) Should be fresh and lively, but most

lack fruit and have a strangely metallic taste, although you might not notice this until you bring a case home. Beware: most Vinho Verde in Portugal is red and even the white is different to the sweetened, fizzed-up stuff they export. After the warning, you may be surprised to learn that there are some very good single-quinta Vinhos Verdes: but taste first.

VINI DEL PIAVE Italy, Veneto (DOC) Synonymous with Piave.

VINO DELLA SIGNORA Italy, Tuscany (VT) Aromatic dry white wine of no particular interest.

VINO NOBILE DI MONTEPULCIANO Italy, Tuscany (DOCG) The finest wines resemble the best Chianti Riserva, but can be more generous in style.

VINO NOVELLO DI ERBUSCO Italy, Lombardy (VT) Fruity red wine best drunk within a few months of the harvest.

VINOS DE MADRID Spain, Madrid (DO) New DO, which means the producers should be trying hard, but no guarantees.

VINS D'ENTRAYGUES ET DU FEL France, Southwest France (VDQS) Light rustic reds and light, crisp-dry whites and rosés.

VINS D'ESTAING France, Southwest France (VDQS) Light-bodied fruity reds, simple dry whites and rosés.

VINS DE L'ORÉANAIS France, Loire (VDQS) Light, delicate reds, surprisingly smooth whites and fresh, crisp, attractive dry rosés.

VINS DE LAVILLEDIEU France, Southwest France (VDQS) Medium-coloured, medium-bodied red with fresh and fruity flavour.

VINS DE MARCILLAC France, Southwest France

(AOC) Rough and rustic when young, these reds can soften after a few years in bottle. Ripe, robust dry whites.

VINS DU THOUARSAIS France, Loire (VDQS) Light, fragrant red and white wines from the south of the Anjou-Saumur district.

VINTAGE CHARACTER PORT Portugal, Douro (DOC) An ambiguous category that can provide good buys, but the suggestion that these wines have a Vintage Port character is definitely misleading, as they are nothing more (or less) than Fine Old Ruby Ports in all but name.

VINTAGE PORT Portugal, Douro (DOC) The greatest of all Ports, consequently the most expensive, but not all Vintage Port is great Port and buying on spec can be a very expensive mistake (unless you buy Taylors because you can always sell it for a profit). There is a huge difference between great Tawny Port and great Vintage Port. Fine Old Tawny is aged in cask and therefore ready to drink, with a rich, silky texture and lush, caramel, cream and coffee flavours. It is a wine that will beguile first time drinkers, whereas the uninitiated can be alarmed by a great Vintage Port, especially as most are drunk far too young. Even so, a Vintage Port is a totally different animal, having been bottled after just 18 months in cask. It is bottle-matured wine with a fruitiness not evident in Fine Old Tawnies, and it has a personality that is split between the grape and the spirit used to fortify it. Given time in cask, this becomes the wonderful, smooth character of a Fine Old Tawny, but the effect in bottle is different and takes longer, requiring at least another 15 years – often 25

or 30 – to reach an appropriate balance. Then, if it is a great Vintage Port, it will be totally integrated, with a heady bouquet and sultry, spicy flavours. And even at 25 years of age it will retain a grapey fruitiness, yet have the greatest potential for complexity of any known wine.

VINTAGE TUNINA Italy, Friuli-Venezia Giulia (VT) Expensive, but this fabulous, super-fruity, dry white wine is worth every penny.

VIOGNIER (Grape) Very special grape responsible for Condrieu and Château Grillet in the Rhône, where the best examples are highly perfumed with delicate, peachy fruit. Recently developed a cult-following in various parts of the New World, notably California, but the wines, although sometimes quite good, lack the special character of true Viognier.

VOGELSGARTEN Germany, Rheinhessen If you see this name following that of a village on a bottle of Rheinhessen, it is only a *Grosslage* wine.

VOGTEI RÖTTEL Germany, Baden If you see this name following that of a village on a bottle of Baden, it is only a *Grosslage* wine.

VOLNAY France, Burgundy (AOC) This village appellation in the Côte de Beaune produces soft, silky red wines that are equal in quality to those of Gevrey-Chambertin and Chambolle-Musigny in the Côte de Nuits.

VOLNAY-SANTENOTS France, Burgundy (AOC) Fine quality red wines from Les Santenots, a vineyard that is, confusingly, in Meursault, not Volnay! The whites must be sold as Meursault Premier Cru or Meursault-Santenots.

VOLNAY PREMIER CRU France, Burgundy (AOC) Markedly superior to the albeit excellent village appellation.

VOM HEISSEN STEIN Germany, Mosel-Saar-Ruwer If you see this name following that of a village on a bottle of MSR, it is only a *Grosslage* wine.

VOSNE-ROMANÉE France, Burgundy (AOC) Village appellation in the Côte de Nuits that consistently produces sleek, stylish reds of very fine quality.

VOSNE-ROMANÉE PREMIER CRU France, Burgundy (AOC) Finer, more aromatic version of the village wine.

VOUGEOT France, Burgundy (AOC) Some fine flavoured well-balanced reds, but can be variable. Whites are theoretically possible.

VOUGEOT PREMIER CRU France, Burgundy (AOC) Overpriced reds and whites of variable quality.

VOUVRAY France, Loire (AOC) Forget the dry and semi-sweet styles of this white wine, it is the intensely sweet versions described as *moelleux* on the label that are nothing less than sensational.

VOUVRAY MOUSSEUX France, Loire (AOC) These sparkling white wines are softer and fuller than Saumur.

VOUVRAY PÉTILLANT France, Loire (AOC) Attractive, fragrant, semi-sparkling wines that are soft, smooth and easy to drink.

VULKANFELSEN Germany, Baden If you see this name following that of a village on a bottle of Baden, it is only a *Grosslage* wine.

W

WACHENHEIM Germany, Rheinpfalz One of the best villages in the Rheinpfalz. Top single-vineyards: Wachenheimer Gerümpel, Wachenheimer Goldbächel, Wachenheimer Fuchsmantel.

WALLHAUSEN Germany, Nahe One of the best villages in the Nahe. Top single-vineyards: Wallhauser Sonnenweg, Wallhauser Felseneck.

WALLUF Germany, Rheingau One of the best villages in the Rheingau. Top single-vineyards: Wallufer Walkenberg.

WALPORZHEIM Germany, Ahr One of the best villages in the Ahr. Top single-vineyards: Walporzheimer Gärkammer, Walporzheimer Himmelchen, Walporzheimer Pfaffenberg.

WALSHEIM Germany, Rheinpfalz One of the best villages in the Rheinpfalz. Top single-vineyards: Walsheimer Silberberg.

WARTBÜHL Germany, Württemberg If you see this name following that of a village on a bottle of Württemberg, it is only a *Grosslage* wine.

WAWERN Germany, Mosel-Saar-Ruwer One of the best villages in the MSR. Top single-vineyards: Wawerner Herrenberg.

WEHLEN Germany, Mosel-Saar-Ruwer One of the best villages in the MSR. Top single-vineyards: Wehlener Sonnenuhr.

WEIKERSHEIM Germany, Württemberg One of the best villages in Württemberg. Top single-vineyards: Weikersheimer Schmecker.

WEINHEX Germany, Mosel-Saar-Ruwer If you see this name following that of a village on a bottle of MSR, it is only a *Grosslage* wine.

WEINSBERG Germany, Württemberg One of the best villages in Württemberg. Top single-vineyards: Weinsberger Schemelsberg.

WEINSTEIGE Germany, Württemberg If you see this name following that of a village on a bottle of Württemberg, it is only a *Grosslage* wine.

WEISENHEIM Germany, Rheinpfalz One of the best villages in the Rheinpfalz. Top single-vineyards: Weisenheimer Mandelgarten.

WERLAU Germany, Mittelrhein One of the best villages in the Mittelrhein. Top single-vineyards: Welauer Ameisenberg.

WHITE PORT Portugal, Douro (DOC) Except for Ferreira's smooth and deliciously fruity Superior White, most White Ports taste and smell like flabby, oxidised sherry.

WILTINGEN Germany, Mosel-Saar-Ruwer One of the best villages in the MSR. Top single-vineyards: Wiltinger Scharzhofberger, Wiltinger Braune Kupp, Wiltinger Kupp, Wiltinger Braunfels.

WINDESHEIM Germany, Nahe One of the best villages in the Nahe. Top single-vineyards: Windesheimer Sonnenmorgen.

WINKEL Germany, Rheingau One of the best villages in the Rheingau. Top single-vineyards: Winkeler Schloss Vollrads, Winkeler Jesuitengarten, Winkeler Hasensprung.

WOLFSMAGEN Germany, Hessische Bergstrasse If you see this name following that of a village on a bottle of Hessische Bergstrasse, it is only a *Grosslage* wine.

WUNNENSTEIN Germany, Württemberg If you see this name following that of a village on a bottle of Württemberg, it is only a *Grosslage* wine.

WÜRTTEMBERG Germany, (QbA) Württemberg is not very well known because there is very little demand outside the region itself for the light-bodied red and rosé *Schillerwein* it produces

WÜRTTEMBERG GROSSLAGEN Germany, Württemberg (Grosslagen) Hohenneuffen, Kopf, Sonnenbühl, Wartbühl, Weinsteige, Heuchelberg, Kirchenweinberg, Lindelberg, Salzberg, Schalkstein, Schozachtal, Staufenberg, Stromberg, Wunnenstein, Kocherberg, Tauberberg and Lindauer Seegarten are all *Grosslagen*, not single-vineyard wines, and should be very reasonably priced, unless you are being ripped-off or it happens to be an Eiswein, Beerenauslese or Trockenbeerenauslese.

WÜRZBURG Germany, Franken One of the best villages in Franken. Top single-vineyards: Würzburger Stein, Würzburger Innere Leiste.

X

XAREL-LO (Grape) Cava grape sometimes used to make dry white table wines, especially in the Penedés region of Spain.

Y

YECLA Spain, Murcia (DO) Best for reds, which are either ink-black and heavy or cherry-coloured with better balance and good fruit. Also attractive dry rosés, but the whites are clean at best.

ZAGAROLO Italy, Latium (DOC) Lacklustre dry and semi-sweet white wines from east of Frascati.

ZELL Germany, Baden One of the best villages in Baden. Top single-vineyards: Zeller Abtsberg.

ZELL Germany, Mosel-Saar-Ruwer One of the best villages in the MSR. Top single-vineyards: Zeller Domherrenberg, Zeller Petersborn-Kabertchen.

ZELTINGEN Germany, Mosel-Saar-Ruwer One of the best villages in the MSR. Top single-vineyards: Zeltinger Himmelreich, Zeltinger Sonnenuhr.

BEERS

Understanding beer can be as pleasurable and as stimulating as understanding wine, although coming to terms with the different products is not quite as bewildering. There is not the vast number of grape varieties to comprehend, no intricate infrastructure of regions, districts, areas and properties within each country to grapple with, and no vintages to confuse the issue. Furthermore, there are just 3,000 brewers worldwide to contend with, instead of well over 50,000 wine producers.

You may be able to tell the difference between a glass of bitter, mild, stout or lager just by looking at the stuff, but as they are all essentially fermented from malted barley with a handful of hops, have you ever wondered what is it that makes each type of beer so different? As the simplest overview, it is worth grasping two basic categories of beer: so-called 'top-fermented' and 'bottom-fermented', terms that might more accurately be renamed open-fermented and closed-fermented.

Keeping to the customary terms, however, we can lump all traditional British beers, from bitter to stout, plus wheat beers and German Altbier and Kölsch, into the 'top-fermented' category, whereas every lager style and all American malt liquors are classified as 'bottom-fermented'. You will find an explanation of these and other generic beers in the entries below, together with a brief description of continental Europe's most famous brands, plus a number of slightly more obscure beers, including some draught and seasonal brews.

A-Z OF BEER

NOTES If any of the following descriptions refer to a type or style of beer you are unfamiliar with, you should refer to the separate entry for that beer. For definitions of technical and tasting terms or abbreviations, consult the GLOSSARY. To avoid confusion and keep consistency with wine and spirit entries, no reference is made to a beer's OG or Original Gravity. The OG is not, in any case, an indication of a beer's strength, merely its potential strength prior to fermentation; the actual alcoholic strength will depend on how much sugar is left in the product after fermentation. All beer strengths given below are actual, not potential, thus expressed as a percentage ABV (Alcohol By Volume). Please bear in mind that the ABV stated for generic styles will be a guide only, the actual strength varying from brew to brew.

3 MONTS Brasserie St-Sylvestre, France Amber-coloured, 'top-fermented' ale brewed from Pilsener malt to produce a delicately rich flavour, with some creamy-malty fruitiness and bitter coffee finish.

33 EXPORT Pelforth Brewery, France Ubiquitous, light, bland, export-style, lager-type with a soft fizz.

ABBAYE, ABBEY or ABDIJ BEER (Generic) Belgium/Holland A commercial product that imitates the Trappist style (see Trappist entry) or is brewed under licence from Trappist monks, but is not necessarily made in an abbey or by monks. Belgian producers are most numerous and include Brasserie St-Sylvestre (lush, fruity Abbey-type beer with a deep, smooth, creamy finish, called Bière des Templiers), Brasserie Union (a deep, dark beer with a heady finish, Cuvée de l'Ermitage is appreciated by many strong-beer lovers), De Kluis (Benedict is an excellent abbey-style beer from a top-performing brewery), Moortgat (Sloeber is the darkest of this brewery's off-dry, abbey-style beers, while Deugniet, Hapkin, Lucifer and Maredsous are all lightish and off-dry to one degree or another), Van Eecke (very well hopped Poperings Hommelbier), while good Dutch examples come from Raaf (a fine Dubbel and big and blustery Trippel with a smooth, malty flavour and a touch of sourness on the finish). The French brewery of Rimaux produces an abbey-type beer near the Belgian border, but it is not exceptional.

ADELSCOTT BIÈRE AU MALT A WHISKY Grande Brasserie Alsacienne d'Adelshoffen, France Nothing to do with Malt Whisky *per se*, this beer get its name because it is brewed in part from the whisky malt, which gives this rich but delicately malty beer its slightly smoky character.

ADELSHOFFEN EXPORT Grande Brasserie Alsacienne d'Adelshoffen, France A light, lager-type beer that is conditioned for 6-8 weeks, which might not be long for a 'bottom-fermented' beer, but is more than most French lagers receive.

ADLERBRÄU Aguila Brewery, Spain Copper-coloured 'bottom-fermented' beer with a light, fruity-malty character and some hoppiness on the finish.

AECHT SCHLENKERLA RAUCHBIER MÄRZEN Heller Brewery, Germany The most famous of all *Rauchbieren* or smoked beers is produced as a *Märzenbier* style for the Schlenkerla tavern in Bamberg, Franconia.

AERTS 1900 Palm Brewery, Belgium Golden-coloured 'top-fermented' bottle-conditioned ale with a dry, fruity flavour and well-hopped finish.

AFFLIGEM Affligem Brewery, Belgium Abbey type beer.

AGUILA PILSENER Aguila Brewery, Spain This bitter-sweet, malty, so-called Pilsener is not made from Pilsener malt.

AGUILA RESERVA EXTRA Aguila Brewery, Spain A premium lager style with delicate aromas and a smooth, bitter-sweet taste.

ALE The common term for any English-style, 'top-fermented' beer, an ale is always a beer, but not all beers are necessarily ales.

ALFA BEER Alfa Brewery, Holland Light, bland, lager type.

ALT or **ALTBIER** (Generic) Germany Literally means 'old beer' but actually refers to a generally overrated 'top-fermented' beer, usually brewed in Düsseldorf, typically copper in colour and cold-conditioned in the manner of a 'bottom-fermented' beer. Producers of this style include Arcen (light, dry and rather restrained Dutch attempt), Dinkelacker (uninspiring Stamm Alt), Dortmunder Actien (lacklustre), Dortmunder Kronen (all froth and no flavour), König (nothing special) and Lindener Gilde (fine quality Broyan Alt). Confusingly, the use of *Alt* sometimes conforms to its literal sense, denoting a beer that has well-aged or has undergone a long conditioning period, often a *Dunkel* or a *Weissbier*.

ALT DUNKEL (Generic) Germany A well-aged or long-conditioned dark lager, producers of which include Ayinger (the Altbairisch Dunkel is the most distinctive beer within this style), Euler (Alt Wetzlar), Paulaner (the Alt-Münchner Dunkel is the very best *Alt Dunkel*) and Tucher (Alt Franken Export Dunkel).

ALT-MÜNCHNER DUNKEL Paulaner Brewery, Germany This full, dark coloured beer with its smooth, well-aged, malty taste and dry finish is the best *Alt* (aged) *Dunkel* style available.

ALT WEISSBIER (Generic) Germany A well-aged or long-conditioned wheat beer, the best known producer of which is Pinkus Müller. Its *Alt Weissbier* is rich, ripe and well-honed, with a soft, malty flavour.

ALTBAIRISCH DUNKEL Ayinger Brewery, Germany This deep, dark, rich, *Dunkel* or lager-style beer is the most distinctive of its type, although its big, sweet, fruity-malty flavour, which is vaguely reminiscent of fine old tawny port, is something of an acquired taste.

ALTBAYERISCHE WEISSBIER Paulaner Brewery, Germany A wheat beer that has undergone a lengthy conditioning and is appreciated for its suppleness and fruity aftertaste.

ALTFORSTER ALTBIER Arcen Brewery, Holland Light, dry and rather restrained for an *Altbier* style.

ANGELUS BIÈRE DE FROMENT Brasserie d'Annoeullin Not a wheat beer as such and certainly not of the cloudy ilk, Angelus is, however, produced from a significant percentage of wheat (about 30%) and has some of the spicy fruit associated with that style.

ANIMATOR Hacker-Pschorr Brewery, Germany A decent *Doppelbock* of no special character.

ARABIER De Dolle Brewery, Belgium The De Dolle Brouwers or 'The Mad Brewers' are two Belgians, Joe and Kris Herteleer, who caught the beer-bug in the UK when they purchased a home brew kit from Boots! Arabier is a pale-coloured, 'top-fermented' beer with a fine fruity flavour and well-hopped finish.

ARCENER GRAND PRESTIGE Arcen Brewery, Holland A deep, dark and very strong, bottle-conditioned beer that claims to be a barley wine.

ARCENER STOOM BIER Arcen Brewery, Holland Nicely hopped 'bottom-fermented' ale with a crisp finish and a welcome touch of bitterness.

ARCENER STOUT Arcen Brewery, Holland Dark coloured 'top-fermented' beer with typical bottled stout coarseness, but the flavour has nice chocolatey-malty overtones and a pleasingly dry, bitter finish.

ARCENER TARWE Arcen Brewery, Holland Cidery Dutch attempt at a lightly-hopped Bavarian wheat beer.

ASTRA PILSENER Bavaria St-Pauli Brewery, Germany Typically hoppy, soft-spritzy Pilsener-style.

ASTRA URTYP Bavaria St-Pauli Brewery, Germany Simple, bland, lager-type.

AUGUSTINER HELL Augustiner Brewery, Germany This delicately rich, soft and malty beer is about as good as *Hell* gets!

AVENTINUS Schneider Brewery, Germany The best product from this small wheat beer specialist brewery.

B

BACCHUS St-Louis Brewery, Belgium A 'top-fermented', claret-coloured beer, with sweet-and-sour fruit flavour and a sharp, bitter-sweet finish.

BAFFO D'ORO Moretti Brewery, Italy A premium beer brewed in honour of the gentleman with a *baffo d'oro* or 'golden moustache' who appears on the label of all Moretti beers.

BAJUVATOR Tucher Brewery, Germany A decent but not outstanding *Doppelbock*.

BARLEY WINE A misnomer for high-strength beer traditionally sold in small bottles called nips, barley wine is a true ale, although almost too fruity for most people's concept of beer and yet too malty to be mistaken for wine. Usually has an alcoholic content of at least 6% ABV, sometimes closer to 11%.

BAVARIA Bavaria Brewery, Holland Cheap, light, malty tasting beer.

BECK'S BIER Beck's Brewery, Germany Basic, light, bland, lager-type.

BELLE-VUE Belle-Vue Brewery, Belgium Lacklustre *Lambic*.

BENEDICT De Kluis Brewery, Belgium An abbey-style beer from a top-performing brewery. *(See* also **Hoegaarden** entry.)

BERLINER WEISSE (Generic) Germany This classic, cloudy Berlin wheat beer is significantly different to other German white or wheat beers (*see* **Wheat Beer** entry), being lower in alcohol (closer to 3% ABV) and very fizzy. Producers of this style include Schultheiss (its Berliner Weiss is considered to be the finest of its type), VEB (Berliner Kindle Weisse is classic, with a spicy, stewed apple flavour and sour cream aftertaste, but while its basic Berliner Weisse is good, it does lack a certain concentration).

BERNKASTELER PILS Bürger Brewery, Germany Light, Pils-style beer of average quality made from non-Pilsener malt.

BIER TRAPPISTE (Generic) Belgium/Holland *(See* **Trappist** entry.)

BIÈRE BLANCHE (Generic) Belgium A white or wheat beer, often comparable to a German *Weissebier*. (*See* **Wheat beer** entry.)

BIÈRE DE GARDE (Generic) France Literally a beer for laying down, a *Bière de Garde* originally referred to a 'top-fermented', copper-coloured, bottle-conditioned brew of high strength, but the term has been so abused that it will probably be a filtered commercial product, 'bottom-fermented', and any strength from 4.5-7.55% ABV. These beers are sometimes sold in one of three different styles: *blonde* or pale, *ambrée* or gold and *brune* or brown. Producers of this style include Brasserie d'Annoeullin (Pastor Ale is light, yet rich and assertive), Brasserie La Choulette (several fine, bottle-conditioned beers: rich and warm Bière des Sans Culottes; smooth, golden Brassin Robespierre; and a soft, strong and fruity La Choulette), Yves Castelain (three different styles, all filtered, but not pasteurised, under the Ch'Ti label: simple, malty *Blonde*; the fuller and more complex *Ambrée* and the much richer, porty *Brune*; very pale, organically produced Jade; and the full, fruity St-Arnoldus, the brewery's only unfiltered *Bière de Garde*), Brasserie Duyck (intensely fruity Jenlain), Monceau St-Waast (rather unusual *Bière de Garde* with a malty palate and a sharp, assertive fruity finish, called Vieille Garde), St-Arnold (light and clinically clean Réserve du Brasseur), St-Léonard (popular, moderate) and Terken (soft, floral, export lager-type called Septane 5).

BIÈRE DE LUXE France Sometimes synonymous with *Bière de Garde*. (*See* **Bière de Garde** entry.)

BIÈRE DES SANS CULOTTES Brasserie La Choulette, France Described on the label as a 'Bière Deluxe sur lie' this is, in fact, one of the best *Bières de Garde* and one of the few still sold as a bottle-conditioned beer. Bière des Sans Culottes has an amber colour, a full, warm nose dominated by fruity, bottle-aromas and a rich palate packed with malty flavour, followed by a fine fruity finish.

BIÈRE DES TEMPLIERS Brasserie St-Sylvestre, France Lush, fruity Abbey-type beer with a deep, smooth, creamy finish.

BIÈRE DU NORD France Literally means beer of the north, but commonly used to describe a *Bière de Garde.* (*See* **Bière de Garde** entry.)

BIRRA FRIULANA Moretti Brewery, Italy Clean, easy drinking, spritzy 'bottom-fermented' beer with a soft, lightly-hopped, creamy-malty finish, supposedly in the Pilsner-style, but contains no Pilsner malt.

BITBURGER PILS Bitburger Brewery, Germany A delicate, dry, well-aged lager made from non-Pilsener malt.

BITTER An English term for a well-hopped draught ale that is typically copper-coloured with ruddy glints and a slight but distinctive bitter taste that is unspoilt by the fizziness of CO_2. It is unrealistic to expect the so-called bitter that is sold in a can to have any semblance of true draught beer character. Most bitter is 3.75-4% ABV, although Best or Special will be 4-4.75%, and some go as high as 5.5%.

BLANCHE DE BRUGES or **BRUGS TARWEBIER** Gouden Boom brewery, Belgium Typically fizzy wheat beer, quite spicy with a sour finish.

BOCK (Generic) Germany A strong 'bottom-fermented' beer in excess of 6.25% ABV and usually of a lager type, although the colour can range from pale blond, through copper-hued to dark (especially non-German versions). Producers include Dortmunder Kronen (crisp, dry, dark Steinbock), Einbecker Brauhaus (excellent, strong Ur-Bock Dunkel), Einbecker Brauhaus (strong, light-coloured and less characterful than the Ur-Bock Dunkel), EKU (decent, pale-coloured Edelbock), Forschungs (big, lusty St-Jacobus Blonder Bock), Heller (Classic Ur-Bock), Spaten (everday-drinking, pale-coloured Franziskus Heller Bock), Spezial (classic). Lindeboom in Holland produces a Dutch version, while Faxe produce an unpastuerised Bock-style in Denmark. (*See* also **Bock Dunkel, Doppelbock, Eisbock, Maibock** and **Weizenbock** entries.)

BOCK DUNKEL (Generic) Germany A strong, dark lager of greater potential than a simple dark *Bock*, its producers include Dinkelacker (uninspiring Cluss Bock Dunkel), Einbecker Brauhaus (excellent Ur-Bock Dunkel of real depth and quality), Kaltenberg (unpasteurised, very malty with a coffee-like aftertaste) and Kulmbacher (soft, fine-flavoured Klosterbock Dunkel). (*See* also **Bock** and **Dunkel** entries.)

BOFFERDING Brasserie Nationale, Luxembourg Delicate lager with some hop character on the finish.

BOSKEUN De Dolle Brewery, Belgium The De Dolle Brouwers or 'The Mad Brewers' are two Belgians, Joe and Kris Herteleer, who caught the beer-bug in the UK when they purchased a home brew kit from Boots! Boskeun is a 'top-fermented', mid-amber coloured beer sold during Easter.

BOTTLE-CONDITIONED A beer that is either unfiltered or has been bottled with a small yeast and sugar solution. In both instances, the fermentation process continues in the bottle, adding a touch of fizziness through the natural CO_2 produced, on top of which it brings a certain plumpness and fruitiness to the beer, but also creates some sediment, which is why a bottle-conditioned beer must be poured with extreme care if you are to avoid the dregs and keep the ale starbright.

BRAND IMPERATOR Brand Brewery, Holland A copper-coloured Bock-type beer with a creamy-malty flavour and a slightly sweet finish.

BRAND PILS Brand Brewery, Holland Mild, but well-hopped Pilsener-style lager made from non-Pilsener malt.

BRAND UP Brand Brewery, Holland Immeasurably better Pilsener-style than the Brand Pils, although made from similar non-Pilsener malt. This beer has a longer flavour and a more assertive, bitter finish.

BRASSIN ROBESPIERRE Brasserie La Choulette, France This bottle-conditioned *Bière de Garde* is a golden-coloured nectar of surprising strength, smoothness and finesse.

BRÄU WEISSE Ayinger Brewery, Germany Frothy-white wheat beer with a tart, spicy aftertaste, Brau Weiss is bottle-conditioned with sediment from the previous brew.

BREMER WEISSE Haake-Beck Brewery, Germany A fresh, zesty wheat beer with a sharp, fruity finish.

BRIGAND St-Louis Brewery, Belgium Strong, amber-coloured, 'top-fermented' bottle-conditioned ale in a corked bottle.

BRILJANT De Kroom Brewery, Holland Light in body, full in flavour, with a dry, malty finish.

BRINCKHOFF'S NO.1 Dortmunder Union Brewery, Germany Despite its title, Brinckhoff's No.1 is disappointing for a supposedly super-premium beer, and certainly not the number one beer at DUB, an accolade that must go to the brewery's excellent DUB Export.

BROWN ALE This is the bottled version of draught mild, thus the opposite number to pale ale (the bottled version of bitter), which is why a 'brown and light' is the equivalent to a 'mild and bitter' for the bottled beer drinker. Brown ale is dark brown in colour, slightly sweet to very sweet in flavour and often a touch stronger than its pale ale cousin. Despite its fame, Newcastle Brown is not a true brown ale, being much lighter in colour, less sweet and significantly stronger in alcohol (4-4.5% ABV compared to 3-3.5%).

BROYAN ALT Lindener Gilde Brewery, Germany A fine *Altbier*.

BRUGS TARWEBIER or **BLANCHE DE BRUGES** Gouden Boom Brewery, Belgium Typically fizzy wheat beer, quite spicy with a sour finish.

BRUGSE TRIPEL Gouden Boom Brewery, Belgium This is not a Trappist beer, the 'Tripel' (not *Trippel*) is merely used in a similar sense to denote a very strong beer. Brugse Tripel is a brown ale with a powerful, peppery-hop aroma, lush, creamy flavour and a tangy, bitter-hop finish.

BRUNA Moretti Brewery, Italy Decent, dark lager type of some depth and character.

BUDELS ALT Budels Brewery, Holland An unpasteurised premium-style, lager-type of some interest.

BUDWEISER BUDVAR Czech Republic Although the Budvar Brewery opened 20 years after Anheuser-Busch started brewing Budweiser in the States, the name itself derives from a type of beer that has been brewed in the Czech village of Budweis since the 13th century. Unlike the American version, it is an all-malt beer that has traditionally been somewhat sweeter and fuller than Pilsener, with a fine, flowery hop aroma and good bitterness.

BUDWEISER USA The American-brewed version is not even similar to the Czech product (*see* previous entry), having less alcohol, a lighter body, less hoppy character, a different taste due to the inclusion of other ingredients (mostly rice) and a much softer, less bitter finish.

BURKARDUS Würzburger Hofbräu Brewery, Germany An uninspiring, deepish-coloured Bavarian beer.

BUSH BEER Dubuisson Brewery, Belgium Very strong, copper-coloured, 'top-fermented' beer with a big malty taste and a well-hopped finish.

C

CAPUCIJN Budels Brewery, Holland Fairly strong Dutch attempt at a *Rauchbier* with an assertive, smoky character.

CARLSBERG LAGER Carlsberg Brewery, Denmark Nothing to get excited about, although the authentic Danish brew does have a distinct edge over the fizzy, bland, blond stuff brewed under Carlsberg's licence throughout the world. (For more interesting Carlsberg beers *see* **Carlsberg Special Strong, Carlsberg Påske Bryg 1847** and **Elephant** entries.)

CARLSBERG PÅSKE BRYG 1847 Carlsberg Brewery, Denmark Darkish, sweet, malty bottom-fermented beer, not dissimilar to a barley wine.

CARLSBERG SPECIAL STRONG LAGER Carlsberg Brewery, Denmark A fairly distinctive, lightly-hopped beer that is immeasurably better than Carlsberg's basic lager, but not quite in the class of Carlsberg's Elephant brew (*see* **Elephant** entry), although obviously stronger.

CD-PILS Dinkelacker Brewery, Germany More of a novelty than a Pils.

CELEBRATOR Ayinger Brewery, Germany Classic *Doppelbock* with a rich, mellow flavour and dry finish.

CERES PILSNER Ceres Brewery, Denmark A light, lacklustre, so-called Pilsener-style.

CH'TI Yves Castelain Brewery, France The Ch'Ti label encompasses three different styles of *Bière de Garde*, all of which are filtered, but not pasteurised: simple, malty *Blonde*; the fuller and more complex *Ambrée* and the much richer, porty *Brune*.

CHIMAY BLUE Chimay Brewery, Belgium The strongest and best of Chimay's three intensely fruity, colour-graded Trappist beers, the blue label/cap is also the most fruity, with intense berry flavours that can improve a year or two in bottle.

CHIMAY GRANDE RÉSERVE Chimay Brewery, Belgium The same beer as Chimay's blue label, the Grande Réserve is sold in a full wine-bottle size (75cl) with a proper cork, and ages longer and better.

CHIMAY RED Chimay Brewery, Belgium The red label/cap may be the lowest in strength of Chimay's three Trappist beers, but this copper-coloured ale has a delightful, sweet-coconutty aroma, with soft, creamy fruit on the palate and a gentle hopped finish.

CHIMAY WHITE Chimay Brewery, Belgium Chimay's middle-strength Trappist beer, the white label/cap has the leanest aroma, a more peppery, relatively less fruity palate and spicy, dried-fruit, resinous finish.

CHOUFFE, LA Achouffe Brewery, Belgium Strong, amber-gold, 'top-fermented', unpasteurised, bottle-conditioned beer brewed from spring water in the Ardennes La Chouffe has a big, sleepy-hop aroma, nicely hopped palate and a true bitter finish.(See also **McChouffe** entry.)

CHOULETTE, LA Brasserie La Choulette, France Described on the label as a *'Bière Deluxe sur lie'* this is, in fact, one of the best *Bières de Garde* and as its *'sur lie'* suggests, one of few still sold as a bottle-conditioned beer.

CHRISTIAN HENNINGER PILSENER Henninger Brewery, Germany Quite why the same Brewery should sell both Pilsener and Pilsner (Kaiser Pilsner) is a bit of a mystery, particularly as neither are worth putting on a party for!

CHRISTMAS BEERS International Whatever the national terminology (French use both *Bière de Noèl* and the somewhat

Franglais *Bière Christmas*), Christmas beers usually indicate a stronger, darker version of the principal brew.

CHRISTOFFEL BIER St-Christoffel Brewery, Holland Not a strong beer in the conventional sense, the Christoffel Bier weighs in at a handsome but not awesome 5.1% ABV. It is, however, a hefty-flavoured beer with a huge, hoppy character and a truly dry finish with a massive, bitter aftertaste.

CLUB-WEISSE Spaten Brewery, Germany A decent but not special wheat beer (see, however, **Franziskaner Hefe-Weissbier** entry).

CLUSS BOCK DUNKEL Dinkelacker Brewery, Germany Uninspiring dark, malty, lager-style.

CRISTAL ALKEN Cristal Alken Brewery, Belgium Well-hopped, pale Pilsener-style beer.

CUVÉE DE L'ERMITAGE Brasserie Union, Belgium Deep, dark abbey-style beer with a heady finish, Cuvée de l'Ermitage is well appreciated by many strong-beer lovers.

D

D'AFFLIGEM Affligem Brewery, Belgium Abbey type beer.

DAB ALTBIER Dortmunder Actien Brewery, Germany Uninspiring quality.

DAB EXPORT Dortmunder Actien Brewery, Germany Not special.

DAB MAIBOCK Dortmunder Actien Brewery, Germany Lacklustre.

DAB MEISTER PILS Dortmunder Actien Brewery, Germany Boring.

DAB ORIGINAL Dortmunder Actien Brewery, Germany Pale 'bottom-fermented' beer with a bitter-malty taste and some hoppy character.

DAB TREMANATOR DOPPELBOCK Dortmunder Actien Brewery, Germany Sounds quite terrifying for such a docile brew.

DAS FEINE HOFMARK Hofmark Brewery, Germany Two Pilsener-type beers, both made from the same spring that feeds Pilsen in the Czech Republic. The Würzig Herb is delicate and classy, with fine hoppy aroma and a long, dry finish, and the Würzig Mild, which is sweeter and smoother, but not classic, nor does it have the finesse and balance of the Herb.

DE KONINCK De Koninck Brewery, Belgium A stylish, copper-coloured 'top-fermented' ale with a fruity, well-hopped flavour.

DE NEVE LAMBIC De Neve Brewery, Belgium Although owned by Belle-Vue, which makes uninspiring *Lambic* beers, De Neve is an excellent example of this unusual type of beer.

DE TROCH De Troch Brewery, Belgium Darker than normal, full-flavoured, but rather fizzy *Lambic* beer.

DELICATOR Hofbräuhaus Brewery, Germany A classic, deep, dark and full-flavoured *Doppelbock*.

DEUGNIET Moortgat Brewery, Belgium A lightish, off-dry, abbey-style beer.

DIÄT PILS (Generic) Germany A diabetic, not diet-conscious, version of Pils or Pilsener, low in carbohydrates, but fairly high in alcohol (and, therefore, full of calories!). Holsten's Diät Pils is the original Diät Pils and one of Holsten's better beers. *(See* **Pils** entry.)

DOM PILSENER Euler Brewery, Germany Rather mild and slightly sweet for a Pilsener.

DOMINATOR DOMMELSCH SPECIAAL Dommels Brewery, Holland An excellent, strong beer, with soft fruity flavour and a fine, malty finish.

DOPPELBOCK (Generic) Germany Literally 'double-bock', Doppelbock is an extra-strong version of Bock, at least 7.5% ABV, but usually more. Producers include Augustiner (an expressive, dark and malty brew called Maximator), Ayinger (rich and mellow with a dry finish, called Celebrator), Bavaria St-Pauli (an Urbock that is actually a *Doppelbock*, though of little note), EKU (at 13.5% ABV, Kulminator is the world's second-strongest beer), Elbschloss (a rich and malty brew called Ratsherrn, under-stated as *Bock* on the label), Herforder (very dark and malty) and Dortmunder Actien Brewery (docile DAB Tremanator), Hofbräuhaus (a classic called Delicator), Paulaner (the Salvator was the very first *Doppelbock* produced, and is one of the best today). *(See* **Bock, Bock Dunkel, Maibock** and **Weizenbock** entries.)

DORT or **DORTMUNDER** (Generic) Germany A pale-coloured, export-type lager brewed in Dortmund, it has a distinctive, malty character and is drier than a Munich beer. Most of the beers produced by the Dortmunder breweries (DAB, DUB, Dortmunder Hansa, Dortmunder Kronen, Dortmunder Ritter, Dortmunder Thier etc) are indicative of this style, unless otherwise described. Furthermore, the Gulpener Brewery makes a reason-ably successful Dutch Dort, while Alfa, also in Holland, brews a much sweeter and stronger Super-Dort.

DRAUGHT BEER A generic term for any beer served on tap, the word draught means to draw, indicating that draught beers were originally drawn by gravity (straight from the cask) or by a beer engine, a mechanical device that manually pumps the beer up from the cellar. Although there would be about as much natural CO_2 in such beers as found in an average still wine, the head or froth consists of nothing but pure air. This is not so, however, for so-called draught beers are served from little flick-taps and push-buttons; these are mass-market fizzy beers which should really be called keg beers, not draught.

DRAUGHTFLOW™ SYSTEM A system developed by Guinness, which employs a plastic device at the bottom of a can to force minuscule bubbles of nitrogen into the beer, to replicate the creamy, non-CO_2 head of a draught stout. This has since been used by Murphy's and Beamish, and is now employed on bitter beers (Guinness, Boddington's, Flowers and others). Such a creamy head on a bitter is unusual, but no further away from the real draught product than regular canned bitters, which are fizzed up with CO_2. A Draughtflow bitter is no replacement for a good pint, but is preferable as a compromise for those who do not like fizzy beers.

DUB BRINCKHOFF'S NO.1 Dortmunder Union Brewery, Germany A disappointing super-premium beer that is not a patch on this brewery's DUB Export.

DUB EXPORT Dortmunder Union Brewery, Germany Typically fine malty-style, smooth-tasting, golden beer.

DUB SIEGEL PILS Dortmunder Union Brewery, Germany A light, malty so-called Pils-style beer made from non-Pilsener malt, Siegel Pils is a pleasant enough brew with a very light hoppiness, but not special.

DUBBEL (Generic) Belgium/Holland One of three styles of Trappist beer, the *Dubbel* falls between the basic strength and a *Trippel*. Producers of this style include Abdij der Trappisten Westmalle (dark brown colour with a ripe, malty flavour and a fairly dry, fruity finish), Maes (sold under the Grimbergen label, the *Dubbel* has a dark brown colour with a ripe, chocolate-malty flavour and sweetish finish that sets it apart from the *Dubbel*) and Westvleteren Trappist (with no so-called single version commercialised by the order of St-Sixtus, this is the most basic style of Trappist beer sold by the Westvleteren monastery). *(See* **Trappist** entry.)

DUIVEL Vanderlinden Brewery, Belgium An idiosyncratic blend of *Lambic* beer and traditional 'top-fermented' ale.

DUNKEL (Generic) Germany A *Dunkel* is simply a dark, malty lager of no special quality, usually dry, but sometimes sweet to one degree or another, and occasionally prefixed with *Alt*. Although *Alt* normally refers to a 'top-fermented' beer *(see* **Alt** or **Altbier** earlier), here it would be used in its literal sense to refer to a well-aged or long conditioned *Dunkel*, which is, of course, 'bottom-fermented'. Producers include Augustiner (a so-called Dunkel Export, which is not very impressive, and a Dunkel Volbier, which is), Ayinger (rich and sweet with fruity-malty aftertaste reminiscent of fine old tawny port), Dinkelacker (dark and malty, but uninspiring), Hofbräuhaus (a Dunkel-Weizen that is not a *Dunkel* as such, but a splendid dark wheat beer), Kaltenberg (unpasteurised, very malty and coffee-like König Ludwig Dunkel), Kulmbacher Münchshof (a strong but soft and fine-flavoured Klosterbock Dunkel), Paulaner (full and dark Alt-Münchner with a smooth, malty taste), Spaten (this brewery's Export Dunkel is, with Augustiner's Dunkel Volbier, one of the best of its ilk) and Tucher (smooth and mature Franken Export Dunkel). *(See* also **Bock Dunkel** entry.)

DUVEL Moortgat Brewery, Belgium Duvel means 'devil' and the head on this pale-coloured fizzy beer can be such a devil to contain that the brewery had to invent a specially-shaped bottle to contain it.

E

EDELBOCK EKU Brewery, Germany A decent, pale-coloured Bock.

EDEL-EXPORT Lindener Gilde Brewery, Germany Uninspiring lager-type.

EDEL-HELL Haake-Beck Brewery, Germany Pale-coloured, basic lager-type of no interest.

EDELHELL EXPORT Hacker-Pschorr Brewery, Germany The pale, premium version of Hacker-Pschorr's everyday Münchner Hell, Edelhell Export is richer, drier and slightly more bitter.

EDELSTOFF Augustiner Brewery, Germany An

Export-style beer with a typically pale colour and generous, smooth flavour.

EDEL WEIZEN Hofbräuhaus Brewery, Germany Fine wheat beer with lots of sharp-fruity flavour.

EGELANTIER De Kroom Brewery, Holland Full-bodied, tawny-coloured 'bottom-fermented' beer.

EISBOCK (Generic) Germany The Eiswein of the beer world, this is a Doppelbock that has gone through an 'ice-machine', which freezes out a significant proportion of the beer's water content, thereby increasing its alcoholic strength and concentrating the flavour. The most famous producer of this style is Kulmbacher Reichelbräu, whose Bayrisch G'froms is big and blowsy, with an intense aftertaste. *(See* also **Bock, Bock Dunkel, Doppelbock, Maibock** and **Weizenbock** entries.)

ELEPHANT Carlsberg Brewery, Denmark A characterful, strong lager with a lightly hopped, tangy flavour.

ERDINGER HEFE-WEISSBIER Erdinger Brewery, Germany This cloudy-white, bottle-conditioned wheat beer is fizzy with a fluffy head, an apple fruitiness on the palate and a spicy, bitter-sweet finish.

ERDINGER PINKANTUS WEIZENBOCK Erdinger Brewery, Germany A strong, amber-coloured, *Bock*-style wheat beer, with a tart, bitter-sweet finish.

EULER HELL Euler Brewery, Germany Typical pale-coloured *Hell* beer of little interest.

EULER LANDPILS Euler Brewery, Germany Better

than Euler's Dom Pilsener, but lacks the finesse of a true Pils-style.

EXCLUSIV Bavaria St-Pauli Brewery, Germany An uninspiring export-style lager, little different in quality than the Astra Urtyp.

EXPORT (Generic) Germany In Germany, the term Export has a very specific meaning, indicating a light-coloured, lager-style beer that is fuller than a Pilsener, but not quite as dry. Producers of this style are legion, but include Augustiner (fine, pale and generous beer called Edelstoff), Binding (called Export Privat, but not special), Dortmunder Actien (slightly malty), Dortmunder Hansa (soft and malty), Dortmunder Kronen (extraordinarily lusty for this style, but its super-smooth texture, sultry malty character, beautiful balance and delicately dry finish make it the finest Export style available), Dortmunder Ritter (firm and fruity with a good dry finish), Dortmunder Thier (can sometimes rival Dortmunder Kronen Export), Dortmunder Union Brewery (typically fine malty premium style), Herforder (simple malty flavour), Hofbräuhaus (crisp style, almost like a fuller-bodied Pilsener) and Holsten (boring).

EXPORT International Can apply to any beer, indicating a premium brew. It implies that it will be stronger than the domestic version of the same beer because export beers were originally beefed-up to enable them to survive long voyages through extremes of heat, but there is no guarantee that they will be. In Germany, Export has a more specific meaning.

FARO (Generic) Belgium A very sweet generic version of *Lambic* beer, its producers include Lindemans and Mort Subite. *(See also* **Lambic** entry.)

FAXE FAD Faxe Brewery, Denmark An unpasteurised, but unimpressive so-called draught-style beer.

FEST BOCK Faxe Brewery, Denmark Unpastuerised Bock-style beer.

FESTIVAL SUPERGUEUZE Eylenbosch Brewery, Belgium Known affectionately as 'Superglue', this is a very full and smooth *Lambic* beer with an incredible three years conditioning prior to bottling.

FORST PILS Forst Brewery, Italy Premium-style lager made from non-Pilsener malt.

FORTUNATOR Ayinger Brewery, Germany Synonymous with Celebrator *(see* **Celebrator** entry).

FRAMBOISE, FRAMBOSEN, FRAMBOZEN or **FRAMBOZENBIER** (Generic) Belgium A raspberry-macerated version of *Lambic* beer, its producers include Liefmans (whose idiosyncratic, brown-ale-based *Frambozenbier*, with its huge raspberry flavour, well-hopped character and sweet and sour finish is one of the best), Lindemans, Chantillon (for the very best, *see* **Rosé de Gambrinus** entry), St-Louis and Vanderlinden (very good and fruity). *(See also* **Lambic** entry.)

FRANZISKANER HEFE-WEISSBIER Spaten Brewery, Germany This is a full, spicy-apple flavoured wheat beer with a voluminous head and dry finish.

FÜRSTENBERG PILSENER Fürstenberg Brewery, Germany Nicely hopped, delicately rich and satisfying Pilsener of style and quality.

G

GAMLE CARLSBERG SPECIAL DARK LAGER Carlsberg Brewery, Denmark This brewery's dark lager is in the Münchner-style, and although it is a decent, characterful brew, which is much better than the basic Carlsberg Lager, it is not quite as good as the Carlsberg Special Strong Lager.

GAMMEL PORTER or **IMPERIAL STOUT** Carlsberg Brewery, Denmark Not at all bad for a 'bottom-fermented' Stout-style.

GAULOISE Du Bocq Brewery, Belgium Strong ale of good aroma and full character on the palate.

GEORGE KILLAIN'S BIÈRE ROUSSE Pelforth Brewery, France Full-bodied, rich, 'top-fermented' malty-flavoured brew, also known as Irish Red.

GEREONS Sion Brewery, Germany This standard quality *Kölsch* has much less finesse than the straight Sion Kölsch

GILDE PILSENER Lindener Gilde Brewery, Germany A Pilsener-style of some finesse, but not special.

GILDENBIER Haacht Brewery, Belgium Hugely rich and sweet, 'top-fermented' dark brown ale.

GIRAF Albani Brewery, Denmark Bland light-lager style.

GOLDEN BUSCH PILS Busch Brewery, Germany The sort of beer that bridges the gap between so-called Pils and commercial lager.

GOUDEN CAROLUS Gouden Carolus Brewery, Belgium Deep-flavoured, smooth, 'bottom-fermented' beer with a smooth, sultry finish.

GOUDENBAND Liefmans Brewery, Belgium Top of the range brown ale from top-performing brown ale brewer, Goudenband has distinctive chocolatey-fruit on the palate and a fairly dry finish. It receives up to 12 months' conditioning and will improve for a further two years.

GOUVERNEUR Lindeboom Brewery, Holland A tawny-coloured, lager-type of some interest.

GRAND CRU (Generic) Belgium An indistinct and misleading term widely used in Belgium for its greatest beers, its producers include Cantillon (a smooth, distinctive, vintage-dated *Lambic* beer), De Kluis (this Grand Cru is a paler, stronger version of the brewery's basic Hoegaarden, a wheat beer flavoured with coriander and curaçao, which honeys well with age), Rodenbach (a selected bottling of the two year old beer used in the basic Rodenbach brew, which is a blend of old and new ales) and Slaghmuylder (called Stropken Grand Cru, a smooth, malty, 'top-fermented' beer, although apparently not the spicy brew it used to be).

GREAT DANE, THE Faxe Brewery, Denmark An interesting, unpasteurised, export-type canned lager from a small, independent brewery.

GRENZQUELL Bavaria St-Pauli Brewery, Germany

Light, dry, but uninspiring Pilsener-style.

GRIMBERGEN DUBBEL Maes Brewery, Belgium Dark brown Trappist-style beer with a ripe, chocolate-malty flavour and sweetish finish.

GRIMBERGEN TRIPPEL Maes Brewery, Belgium Paler than the *Dubbel*, this Trappist-style beer is stronger, with a fruitier-malty character and a dryish finish.

GROLSCH AMBER Grolsch Brewery, Holland Copper-coloured lager-type of some interest and character.

GROLSCH PREMIUM LAGER Grolsch Brewery, Holland Fine, hoppy aromas and fresh, delicate fruit are the hallmark of this excellent lager brewed from Pilsener malt.

GROLSCH Grolsch Brewery, Holland Best-selling Dutch Pilsener-type beer.

GUEUZE (Generic) Belgium A blend of old and young *lambic* beer, the yeast in the younger ale provoking another fermentation, resulting in a fizzy *lambic* that is usually sweet to one degree or another. Producers of this style include Eylenbosch (the Festival Supergueuze has an astonishing three years' conditioning prior to bottling), Lindemans, Mort Subite (variable), St-Louis (particularly sweet), Timmermans (the best, unless you include Eylenbosch's splendidly quirky Festival Supergueuze) and Vanderlinden (excellent Vieux Foudre Gueuze). (*See* **Lambic** entry.)

GULPENER DORT Gulpener Brewery, Holland Successful Dutch attempt at the pale-coloured *Dort* or

---

Fermenting the Facts

The earliest ales were all 'top-fermented' in open vessels, but this term did not creep into our 'beerspeak' vocabulary until after the Germans had developed the first so-called 'bottom-fermented' beer *circa* 1420 (the first documented mention of 'bottom-fermented' beer). It was the brewers in the Bavarian Alps who discovered that beer lost its natural cloudy appearance when stored in mountain caves. They were unaware of the reason, that the ice-cold temperature caused the yeast and other sediments to fall to the bottom of the vessel. In fact, they did not even know about the existence of yeast in beer or its role in the fermentation process. They did, however, know that when beer was being made they could see the frothy effect of fermentation on the top of the liquid, which bubbled away ferociously, but at colder temperatures this activity was much less noticeable, produced a starbright beer (not necessarily pale, as some lagers are quite dark in colour) and when the beer was removed, they discovered a residue of fermentation matter collected at the bottom of the vessel, from which they concluded it was 'bottom-fermented'.

When scientists began to understand the behaviour of yeast in the 19th century, brewers started to develop various different strains of yeast specifically for either 'top-fermented' or 'bottom-fermented' beers and over the years traditional practices have evolved so that we can new roughly define the following:

'Top-fermented' Beers are fermented at warmer temperatures (commonly 20°C/68°F) with air-contact and stored preferably for no more than a couple of days or, at most, a couple of weeks (there is no benefit derived from the maturation process), but at a normal temperature, not chilled.

'Bottom-fermented' Beers are fermented at colder temperatures (commonly 8°C/46°F) with as little air-contact as possible and cold-stored for as long as possible. Six months was once considered the minimum period, and some brands of limited production still maintain this standard or higher, but most large-volume commercial brands are aged for less than six weeks.

The ideal drinking temperature for a beer is directly related to its temperature of fermentation, thus a 'bottom-fermented' beer such as a lager should be chilled, while a 'top-fermented' beer like bitter should not (on the other hand, it should not be warm, just a good cellar temperature and a warm cellar is not a good cellar).

Dortmunder style of lager, Gulpener is a strong export-type beer with the rich malty character of an authentic German brew.

HAPKIN Moortgat Brewery, Belgium A lightish, off-dry, abbey-style beer.

HEFE (Generic) Germany Literally means yeast, thus prefixing the name of a beer, usually a wheat beer, with this word indicates a bottle-conditioned ale with a suspended yeast sediment. (*See* **Wheat Beer** entry.)

HEINEKEN LAGER BEER Heineken Brewery, Holland Light, fresh, international best-seller.

HELL or **HELLES** (Generic) Germany A pale-coloured, lager-type beer of no great distinction, its producers include Augustiner (the best, and so good that it actually does have distinction), Einbecker Brauhaus (strong, light-coloured Ur-Bock Hell), Haake-Beck (Edel-Hell) and Euler (typical of style). (*See* also **Münchener Hell** entry.)

HENRI FUNCK STRONG LAGER Mousel & Clausen Brewery, Luxembourg A richer, smoother, much more malty, but far less hoppy version of Mousel Premium Pils. (*See* **Mousel Premium Pils** entry.)

HERFORDER PILS Herford Brewery, Germany One of the few Pils that is actually brewed from genuine Pilsener malt, this beer has a very long and delicate flavour with true Pilsener bitterness on the finish.

HERREN PILS Stuttgarter Hofbräu Brewery, Germany Delicate and refined, but somewhat sweet style of Pils.

HERRENHÄUSER PILSNER Herrenhäusen Brewery, Germany A typical, smooth Pilsner-style of no real interest.

HOEGAARDEN GRAND CRU De Kluis Brewery, Belgium Paler and stronger version of this brewery's basic Hoegaarden.

HOEGAARDEN or **WITTE VAN HOEGAARDEN** De Kluis Brewery, Belgium Hoegaarden was once the most famous wheat beer village in Belgium, with over 30 breweries, but as this style of beer gave way to modern beers, all the breweries gradually went out of business. De Kluis was a brave revival of an abandoned brewery in 1965, but has required investment

from the Stella Artois group to survive. Hoegaarden is a well-hopped, cloudy yellow-white wheat beer, considered by some to be the finest of its type. Interestingly it is spiced with coriander and curaçao, an ancient but seldom practised custom producing a typically tangy beer with a bitter fruit flavour that honeys with age.

HOLSTEN-EDEL Holsten Brewery, Germany Holsten's most basic brew.

HOLSTEN DIÄT PILS Holsten Brewery, Germany The original Diät Pils and one of Holsten's better beers. (*See* **Diät Pils** entry.)

INDIA PALE ALE When the canal linking the Trent river to the port of Hull was built, this gave the Bass brewery at Burton-on-Trent quick and easy access to the export trade. At the height of colonial trade with the British East Indies, the export brew of Burton Pale Ale became known as India Pale Ale and the name has stuck. Worthington's bottle-conditioned White Shield is considered by many to be the classic pale ale.

IRLE EDEL-PILS Irle Brewery, Germany Light, crisp and well-aged Pils-style.

JADE Yves Castelain Brewery, France A very pale, filtered, but unpasteurised and organically produced *Bière de Garde*.

JAHRHUNDERTBIER Ayinger Brewery, Germany Hop-dominated, light-golden, 'bottom-fermented', export-style beer with a smooth, malty taste and bitter, hoppy-resinous finish.

JENLAIN Brasserie Duyck, France Unpasteurised, but not bottle-conditioned, this beer has an amber-gold colour and a ripe fruitiness that is so intense it is reminiscent of liquorice.

JEVER EXPORT Jever Brewery, Germany An export-style lager that is firmer and more characterful than Exclusiv, which is produced by Jever's parent company Astra.

JEVER PILS Jever Brewery, Germany One of the finest Pils available, despite the absence of Pilsener malt in the brew.

JUBILEEUW De Leeuw Brewery, Holland Pale-coloured, premium-style beer with a smooth, malty flavour.

JULIUS De Kluis Brewery, Belgium An extraordinarily strong beer for a pale ale. (*See* also **Hoegaarden** entry.)

JUPILER Jupiler Brewery, Belgium Jupiler utilises rice in its brew, Belgium's best-selling Pilsener-style. A typically commercial, pale-coloured, fizzy product that would be greatly improved if conditioned for six months instead of six weeks.

K

KAISER PILSNER Henninger Brewery, Germany Quite why the same brewery should sell both Pilsner and Pilsener (Christian Henninger Pilsener) is a bit of a mystery, particularly as neither are worth putting on a party for!

KAISERDOM RAUCHBIER Bürgerbräu Brewery, Germany A copper-coloured ale with the distinctive smoky aroma of a *Rauchbier*.

KEG BEER An inferior form of draught beer (although keg beer is often sold as draught), this mass-market fizzy stuff is full of CO_2 and served via electronic pumps. Real draught ale, on the other hand, is served through a mechanical pump, or direct from the barrel, and its head or froth consists of nothing but pure air.

KELLERBIER (Generic) Germany An unfiltered, well-hopped lager of lower than normal fizz.

KILLAIN'S BIÈRE ROUSSE Pelforth Brewery, France Full-bodied, rich, 'top-fermented' malty-flavoured brew, also known as Irish Red.

KLOSTER BIER or **KLOSTERBIER** (Generic) Germany Literally a 'cloister beer', this is similar to an abbey beer in that it refers to a commercial product that no longer has to be brewed by the monastery that first originated the beer. In this sense, it is an honest version of those abbey beers that are also not brewed by their religious creators. Producers of the *Klosterbier* style include Euler (more of an over-processed version of Euler Hell than an abbey-type beer), Kulmbacher Mönchshof (a Kloster Schwarz-bier or 'black' beer, which is ultra-smooth and malty) and Kulmbacher Mönchshof (a strong but soft and fine-flavoured Klosterbock Dunkel).

KÖLSCH (Generic) Germany A soft, somewhat fruity, pale-golden, lager-style beer (4.5% ABV) associated with Cologne. Producers of these include Küppers (the basic Kölsch is rather sweet and boring, but Küppers Weiss, which is not a *Weissbier*, merely an unfiltered version of Küppers Kölsch, which gives the beer a certain

fruitiness, is a far superior product), Malzmühl (the Mühlen has more delicacy and aroma than most *Kölsch*) and Sion (this brewery's fresh, flowery and aromatic basic *Kölsch* has a degree of finesse that not only puts it above Sion's more upmarket Gereons, but makes it the best quality *Kölsch* available).

KÖNIG-ALT König Brewery, Germany Not this brewery's best beer.

KÖNIG LUDWIG DUNKEL Kaltenberg Brewery, Germany An unpasteurised malty *Dunkel* with a malty-coffee aftertaste, this beer is named after the brewer's great grandfather, mad King Ludwig, who ruled Bavaria at the time when all lagers were brewed as dark as this.

KÖNIG PILSENER König Brewery, Germany Rather full and rich for a Pilsener-style, but has great character and a long, heady finish.

KÖNIGSBACHER PILS Königsbacher Brewery, Germany Not as full as the König Pilsener, but every bit as rich, with a finer balance, a nice hoppy aroma and more bitterness on the finish.

KRÄUSENBIER (Generic) Germany A fizzy, unfiltered beer. Although any style of beer can be *Kräusen*, Haake-Beck's Kräusen Pils is perhaps the most classic example.

KREIK (Generic) Belgium A cherry-macerated version of *Lambic* beer, its producers include Lindemans (one of the best), Mort Subite (variable), St-Louis and Timmermans (one of the best), Liefmans (this idiosyncratic brown-ale-based cherry-flavoured Kriekbier, with its piquant fruit, well-hopped character and sweet and sour finish is

the very best *Kreik* available) and Vanderlinden (fresh, aromatic View Foudre Kriek). (*See* **Lambic** entry.)

KROMBACHER PILS Krombacher Brewery, Germany A delicate Pilsener-style beer made from non-Pilsener malt, Krombacher Pils has a well-hopped finish.

KRONEN CLASSIC Dortmunder Kronen Brewery, Germany Premium lager-style beer with a typically smooth, malty taste.

KRONEN EXPORT Dortmunder Kronen Brewery, Germany This deliciously dry, pale-coloured, distinctive, export-type beer is wonderfully lusty and smooth in flavour, yet beautifully balanced, with a delicately dry finish.

KRONEN PILS Dortmunder Kronen Brewery, Germany Light, Pilsener-style beer made from non-Pilsener malt, Kronen Pils has enough bitterness to offset its sweetish finish.

KRUIDENBIER (Generic) Belgium Flemish for 'spiced beer'.

KULMBACHER SCHWEIZERHOF-BRÄU Kulmbacher Schweizerhof Brewery, Germany Well-respected Pilsener-style with a long dry finish.

KULMINATOR 28 EKU Brewery, Germany At 13.5%, this fine if heady, full-flavoured *Doppelbock* claims to be the world's strongest beer.

KÜPPERS KÖLSCH Küppers Brewery, Germany Rather sweet and boring for a *Kölsch*.

KÜPPERS WIESS Küppers Brewery, Germany Not a *Weissbier*, this is merely an unfiltered version of

Küppers Kölsch, which gives the beer a certain fruitiness, making it a far superior product.

KWAK PAUWEL Kwak Pauwel Brewery, Belgium Very strong, claret-coloured, 'top-fermented' ale with an intense malty flavour and a full, warming finish.

L

LA BIÈRE DE DÉMON Enfants de Gayant Brewery, France So-called because of its strength (12% ABV), which makes it the world's strongest lager.

LA ROSSA Moretti Brewery, Italy Strong, ruddy-copper-coloured 'bottom-fermented' beer with lots of malty character and a clean, well-hopped finish.

LAGER The name is derived from the German *Lager* or storehouse, as this 'top-fermented' beer is traditionally aged for up to six months (although most commercial brews will be less than six weeks old when sold) at a very cold temperature, which precipitates the finest suspended matter, rendering the beverage starbright, although not necessarily pale (*Münchener*, *Dunkel* and certain *Bock* for example, are all, types of dark lager).

LAGER Spezial Brewery, Germany Not so much a lager as a *Rauchbier*, this beer has a light, smooth malty flavour with a rich, caramelised, smoky aftertaste.

LAMBIC (Generic) Belgium A rustic wheat beer of ancient origin and true individual character. The wheat, which represents up to 40% of the mash, is not malted, the beer is produced by a naturally

occurring, wild yeast ferment and has a distinctive sour flavour (4.5-5.5% ABV). Producers who specialise in this style include Belle-Vue (lacklustre), Boon (numerous blended *Lambic* beers of varying age and style are sold under the Marriage Parfait label and rank with the Cantillon Grand Cru as the very best that *Lambic* beers can offer), Cantillon (smooth and distinctive, vintage-dated *Lambic* called Grand Cru is, with Boon's Marriage Parfait, probably the very best of its type), Girardin (can approach the quality of Boon's Marriage Parfait and Cantillon's Grand Cru), De Neve (owned by Belle-Vue, but far superior to the *Lambic* sold under that label), De Troch (darker than normal, full-flavoured, rather fizzy) and Timmermans (lovely sharp finish) and Vanderlinden (while the Duvel is a strange brew, combining a *Lambic* beer with a traditional 'top-fermented' ale) and Vandervelden (the Oude Beersel is very dry with an acquired resinous taste, which many beer specialists consider to be the finest of all *Lambic* beers). (*See* also **Faro, Gueuze, Kreik** and **Frambosen** entries.)

LE FRUIT DEFENDU or **DE VERBODEN FRUCHT** De Kluis Brewery, Belgium The label of this rich, claret-coloured, coriander-spiced, strong ale depicts Adam tempting Eve not with an apple, but with a glass of what we are led to believe is beer, although cider would surely be more appropriate in the situation.

LIEFMANS Liefmans Brewery, Belgium Classic brown ale from one of the greatest brown ale brewers in the world, Liefmans bottom of the range brown ale (*see* also **Goudenband**

entry) is conditioned for six weeks and back-blended with a small amount of a previous brew that has been aged for up to 10 months.

LIGHT ALE The bottled form of bitter, but lighter in colour and body. The term light ale is often used synonymously with pale ale, although the latter has a more specific connotation. (*See* also **Pale Ale** entry.)

LIMBURGER EXPORT Busch Brewery, Germany Lightly aromatic with the fizzy and typically overly clean palate of an Export style beer.

LOBURG Artois Brewery, Belgium Danish-style premium lager.

LÖWENBRÄU PILS Löwenbräu Brewery, Germany Although a predictably light-flavoured Pils in style, this beer does have a well-hopped aroma.

LÖWENBRÄU SPECIAL EXPORT Löwenbräu Brewery, Germany A typical, smooth palate, premium lager that is commonly produced under licence.

LUCIFER Moortgat Brewery, Belgium A lightish, off-dry, abbey-style beer from the producers of that other satanic brew, Duvel, meaning 'Devil'.

LUTÈCE BIÈRE DE PARIS Brasserie Nouvelle de Lutèce, France Rich, malty, 'bottom-fermented' brown ale-type brew that was once popular in Paris.

M

MAES PILS Maes Brewery, Belgium A light, flowery Pilsener-style beer with a soft, delicate, malty-fruity palate.

MAIBOCK or **MAI-BOCK** (Generic) Germany Literally a 'spring-bock', this is a pale-coloured Bock brewed in the springtime and sold at a premium price. Producers of this style include Ayinger (more fruit than most), Jever (firm and fuller than usual), Dortmunder Actien Brewery (not special), Einbecker Brauhaus (full and malty with a nicely hopped finish), Herforder (rather standard), Hofbräuhaus (its deeper colour is more *Bock* than *Maibock*, but its huge, complex flavour puts it at the very top of the *Maibock* league), Holsten (fruity-malty) and Würzburger Hofbräu (simple). (*See* also **Bock, Bock Dunkel, Doppelbock, Eisbock** and **Weizenbock** entries.)

MAINGOLD Kulmbacher Mönchshof Brewery, Germany Simple, light, malty export-style.

MAISEL'S DAMPFBIER Maisel Brewery, Germany A strange, 'top-fermented' brew that is pale copper in colour, very fruity to taste but with a creamy-spicy aftertaste

MALTEZER De Ridder Brewery, Holland A pale-coloured lager with a predictably malty taste.

MAREDSOUS Moortgat Brewery, Belgium A lightish, off-dry, abbey-style beer.

MARIAGE PARFAIT Boon Brewery, Belgium The perfect marriage refers to the blended *Lambic* beers of varying age and style that are sold under this label.

MÄRZEN or **MÄRZENBIER** (Generic) Germany Literally means 'March beer', which might come as a bit of a surprise, as this malty, bronze or copper-coloured beer is only available in October! It is, however, brewed in March and stored until Munich Oktoberfest. Usually 5.5% ABV or more.

Producers of this style include Ayinger (lighter in colour than most, but has a fine malty aroma and smooth flavour), Hacker-Pschorr (the Oktoberfest is a soft, malty, amber-coloured beer with a more hoppy character than most *Märzenbier*), Kulmbacher Mönchshof (typical malty character) and Spaten (many believe this brewery's Ur-Märzen to be the finest available). Some *Märzen* that are made in a typical, smoky *Rauchbier* style (*see* **Rauchbier** entry) are Heller (the Aecht Schlenkerla is the most famous *Rauchbieren* and is produced as a *Märzenbier* for the Schlenkerla tavern in Bamberg, Franconia) and Spezial (very smoky, approaches the quality of Schlenkerla).

MAXIMATOR DOPPELBOCK Augustiner Brewery, Germany Expressive, dark and malty.

McCHOUFFE Achouffe Brewery, Belgium A much darker, stronger and fruitier version of La Chouffe. (*See* also **La Chouffe** entry.)

McFARLAND Dreher Brewery, Italy Malty, amber-red brew designed to attract lovers of so-called *Scotch Ale*.

MEISTER PILS Dortmunder Actien Brewery, Germany Boring.

MEISTER PILS Schwaben Bräu Brewery, Germany Fine Pils of some delicacy and a long, dry finish.

MESTREECHS AAJT Gulpener Brewery, Holland The sour taste in this unusual brew is reminiscent of a *Lambic* beer, only it is Dutch not Belgian, made from barley, not wheat, and looks more like a brown ale.

METEOR PILS Brasserie Meteor, France A Pilsener-type brewed from non-Pilsener malt, Meteor has

interesting toasty aromas and a delicately rich, well-hopped, bitter finish.

MILD ALE Lighter examples do exist, but most mild is dark brown and soft-tasting with a sweetness that devotees enjoy for its lingering quality whereas bitter drinkers find it cloying. Like most things, it's a matter of taste, although the cynic's answer to that is you either have taste or you don't!

MÖNCHSHOF-PILSENER Kulmbacher Mönchshof Brewery, Germany Dry Bavarian Pilsener of fleeting interest.

MORAVIA PILS Holsten Brewery, Germany This light but well-hopped beer with its delicate aroma is the best that Holsten brews.

MORETTI Moretti Brewery, Italy Fizzy, light-lager style.

MOUSEL PREMIUM PILS Mousel & Clausen Brewery, Luxembourg A light, Pils-style made without Pilsener malt, with a delicately rich, malty style and a well-hopped finish.

MÜHLEN KÖLSCH Malzmühl Brewery, Germany A *Kölsch* of more delicacy and aroma than most.

MÜNCHENER (Generic) Germany A dark lager with 5% ABV, brewed in Munich, it is somewhat sweeter than a Dortmund beer.

MÜNCHENER HELL (Generic) Germany A pale lager of no great distinction, a touch of sweetness and less than 4% ABV, brewed in Munich. Producers include Hacker-Pschorr (light and rustic with a well-hoped, bitter-sweet finish) Spaten (finer and more delicate than some so-called Pilsener beers).

MÜTZIG Mutzig Brewery, France Large volume,

typical Alsatian light-lager style.

NASTRO AZZURO Peroni Brewery, Italy This lager is biggest selling beer produced by Italy's largest Brewery.

OERBIER De Dolle Brewery, Belgium The De Dolle Brouwers or 'The Mad Brewers' are two Belgians, Joe and Kris Herteleer, who caught the beer-bug in the UK when they purchased a home brew kit from Boots! *Oerbier*, or 'original bier', is a dark, ruddy-brown, 'top-fermented' beer with a sweet, peppery-hop aroma, an intense fruit flavour, aniseed undertones and big, bitter finish.

OKTOBERFEST MÄRZEN Hacker-Pschorr Brewery, Germany This soft, malty, amber-coloured seasonal beer has more hoppy character than most *Märzenbier*.

OKTOBERFEST Würzburger Hofbräu Brewery, Germany Darkish brew of little interest.

ORANJEBOOM Oranjeboom Brewery, Holland Popular, light, bland lager-style beer.

ORIGINAL MÜNCHNER HELL Paulaner Brewery, Germany A well above average, pale-coloured *Heller* beer with a fairly full, dryish flavour and crisp finish.

ORVAL Brasserie d'Orval, Belgium A strange, orange-coloured Trappist beer that is initially 'top-fermented', but undergoes a 'bottom-fermented' bottle-conditioning, albeit at a warmer temperature more

suited for 'top-fermented' yeast. Not the strongest of Trappist beers, Orval is considered by many to be the finest. Its unusual brewing methods, barely touched on here, produce a unique ale of intensely powerful aroma and flavour, full of thirst-making, rather than thirst-quenching, fruit and a massive, dry, bitter-hop finish.

OUD BEERSEL Vandervelden Brewery, Belgium A very dry *Lambic* with an acquired resinous taste, although many beer specialists consider it to be the finest of all *Lambic* beers.

PALE ALE A name applied to a particular bottled-version of draught bitter, pale ale was first brewed in London in the mid-18th century, but did not gain fame until Bass produced this style of beer at its Burton-on-Trent brewery, since when Burton has become synonymous with pale ale. This is because the Burton water contains gypsum, which precipitates the most ultra fine sediments suspended in a beer, providing a much paler shade of ale: hence Pale Ale, thus Burton Pale Ale. (*See* also **India Pale Ale** entry.)

PAREL Budels Brewery, Holland Fine quality, fairly strong 'top-fermented' beer with a delicately rich aftertaste.

PASTOR ALE Brasserie d'Annoeullin, France A filtered but unpasteurised *Bière de Garde* that is light in body, yet rich in flavour, with assertive fruit softening to a lush, full finish.

PELFORTH BRUNE Pelforth Brewery, France Dark, full-bodied, malty beer with a smooth finish.

PELFORTH PALE Pelforth Brewery, France The light-bodied pale Pelforth does not have the quality or character of the *Brune*.

PILS, PILSENER or **PILSNER** Much abused designations that now encompass lager-type beers of any strength, quality or age, these terms were originally restricted to lagers brewed in the Czech village of Pilsen. As Pilsener caught on, the Czech village name was coined for any top-quality, well-hopped lager of at least 5% ABV, which was brewed from Pilsener malt to give the very long and delicate, almost floral flavour for which this beer was justifiably famous. Real Pilsener or Pilsner Urquell from the Czech Republic is best enjoyed in a Prague bar, as the genuine article found elsewhere in the world is not quite as fresh and snappy. So-called Pilsener (or Pils or Pilsner) is now brewed all over the world, and the best imitations are usually German, although the use of Pilsener malt is rapidly diminishing in all but the finest examples. Producers include Ceres (light, lacklustre), Dortmunder Actien (dull DAB Meister Pils), Dortmunder Hansa (light, wishy-washy Pils), Dortmunder Kronen (fresh and hoppy Pilskrone), Dortmunder Ritter (too much clumsy malt, not enough flowery finesse for a true Pils), Dortmunder Thier (a Pils that has some hoppy character, but is not special), EKU (a Pils that is too full to be classic), Forschungs (called Pilsissimus, it defies pronunciation should you have one too many), Gulpen (amusingly named X-Pert, this Dutch super-premium style beer has a touch too much colour for a classic Pilsener, but is beautifully bottle-conditioned, adding a smooth, refined quality to its nicely hopped palate and finish), Haake-Beck (light, basic, but a delightfully fresh and aromatic, if somewhat fluffy-headed bottle-conditioned Kräusen Pils), Hacker-Pschorr (bog-standard Pils), Holsten (soft, easy, unexciting Pilsener), Kulmbacher Mönchshof (dry, simple Pilsener), Kulmbacher (well-respected Schweizerhof-bräu, with a classic, long, dry finish), Kulmbacher Löwenbräu (light but hoppy Pils), Lindeboom (decent Dutch Pilsener), Tucher (off-dry, simple Pilsener) and Würzburger Hofbräu (simple, malty Pils).

PILSISSIMUS Forschungs Brewery, Germany An interesting malty-styled Pils, but don't try to pronounce it if you have had a few too many.

PILSKRONE Dortmunder Kronen Brewery, Germany A fresh Pils-style with a pleasantly hoppy character, but lacks the class and concentration of Kronen's Export and Classic beers.

PILSNER URQUELL Czech Republic *See* **Pils** entry.

PINKUS ALT Pinkus Müller Brewery, Germany Although this 'top-fermented', pale-coloured beer utilises 60% Pilsener malt and 40% wheat malt, it is neither a Pilsener nor a wheat beer as such. Pinkus Alt is an interesting oddity with a rich, ripe, malty flavour that reflects its four months' conditioning.

PINKUS HEFE WEIZEN Pinkus Müller Brewery, Germany A delicate, spritzy white or wheat beer with an easy-drinking, mild finish.

PINKUS PILS Pinkus Müller Brewery, Germany Lightly-hopped Pilsener of reasonable quality.

PINKUS SPECIAL Pinkus Müller Brewery, Germany A 100% organic beer made in true Pilsener-style, with fine, long, delicate flavour and a well-hopped finish.

PINSEBRYG Neptun Brewery, Denmark A strong, smooth, but rather bland beer with a repulsive green colour, deliberately induced to herald the beginning of spring!

PIPAIX (Generic) Belgium A type of *Saison* beer, usually in a large corked bottle and may be aged for up to 12 months. (*See* **Saison** entry.)

POPERINGS HOMMELBIER Van Eecke Brewery, Belgium A well hopped abbey-style beer.

PORTER Albani Brewery, Denmark Sweet, malty and appreciated by some.

PRINZREGENT LUITPOLD WEISSBIER Kaltenberg Brewery, Germany This is a crisp, unpasteurised wheat beer with a typically tart taste, reminiscent of stewed apple on the finish.

PSCHORR-BRÄU WEISSE Hacker-Pschorr Brewery, Germany Fluffy-headed wheat beer with a sour-biscuity flavour, finishing with a fine, spiced-apple tang.

R

RAAF DUBBEL Raaf Brewery, Holland A fine, smooth and strong abbey beer.

RAAF TRIPPEL Raaf Brewery, Holland Big and blustery abbey beer with a smooth, malty flavour and a touch of sourness on the finish.

RAFFO Peroni Brewery, Italy Typically lightweight, bland Italian lager-style.

RATSHERRN BOCK Elbschloss Brewery,

Germany Rich, malty *Doppelbock* style, despite its understated name.

RATSHERRN PILS Elbschloss Brewery, Germany Nicely dry Pilsener-style.

RATSKELLER EDEL-PILS Lindener Gilde Brewery, Germany A Pilsener-style of some finesse, better than the straight Gilde Pilsener, but not special.

RAUCHBIER (Generic) Germany A copper-coloured 'bottom-fermented' beer with a distinctive smoky-biscuity taste, which comes from malt grains that are put through a special smoking process. Producers of this style include Bürgerbräu (distinctive, copper-coloured Kaiserdom) and Spezial (confusingly named Lager, this beer has a light, smooth malty flavour with the rich, caramelised, typically smoky aftertaste of a *Rauchbier*). Some *Rauchbier* are made as Märzenbier (*see* **Märzenbier** entry), including Heller (whose Aecht Schlenkerla is the most famous *Rauchbier* and produced as a *Märzenbier*, albeit for the restricted availability of the Schlenkerla tavern in Bamberg, Franconia) and Spezial (very smoky, approaches the quality of Schlenkerla). Budels in Holland makes Dutch *Rauchbier* called Capucijn (fairly strong with an assertive, smoky finish), while Poretti does the same in Italy with its Splügen Fumée (ruddy copper-coloured brew with a smoky character on the finish).

RAUCHENFELS STEINBIERE Rauchenfels Brewery, Germany This brewery revived the concept of 'stone-beer', which harked from times prior to the development of metal kettles, when huge, baking hot stones were heated and dropped in to heat up the wort which, in its wooden vessel could not be boiled by direct heat. The result (in the version brewed by Rauchenfels today, anyway) is a smooth, rich-tasting beer with a curious, smoky-caramelised aftertaste. A 'stone-beer' has an acquired taste, which the cult-following of Rauchenfels has obviously acquired.

RAUCHENFELS STEINWEIZEN Rauchenfels Brewery, Germany The wheat beer version of 'stone-beer', Steinweisen is a predictably sharper taste, and is preferred by Rauchenfels cult-following.

RED ERIC Ceres Brewery, Denmark A dry, lager-type of little interest but for the fact that it used to be rosé-coloured until an EC ban.

RÉSERVE DU BRASSEUR St-Arnold Brewery, France A light, clinically clean, filtered *Bière de Garde*.

RÉSERVE ST-LANDELIN Rimaux Brewery, France An unexceptional *abbey*-type beer.

ROCHEFORT Rochefort Brewery, Belgium Trappist beer: typical, malty Trappist beer.

RODENBACH GRAND CRU Rodenbach Brewery, Belgium An exclusive bottling of the two year old beer that is used to fortify and mellow the basic Rodenbach blend, the Grand Cru is fuller and smoother, with a more pronounced sour note on the finish.

RODENBACH Rodenbach Brewery, Belgium A 'top-fermented', red-coloured beer blended from young and old ales, full of sour fruit and a sharp, bitter finish.

ROLAND (Generic) Belgium A type of *Saison* beer, usually in a large corked bottle, and may be aged for up to 12 months. (*See* **Saison** entry.)

ROSÉ DE GAMBRINUS Cantillon Brewery, Belgium A smooth, Frambozen *Lambic* with a sharply fruity finish.

ROYAL DUTCH POST HORN Breda Brewery, Holland Light, lager-type.

RUBIN EKU Brewery, Germany Deep, dark export-style *Dunkel* of decent quality.

SAISON (Generic) Belgium A regional style of 'top-fermented' beer, a *Saison* is usually amber or light copper in colour, with a fluffy head, a certain sweet-cum-sour yeasty-fruitiness on the palate and a soft but nicely hopped finish and probably bottle-conditioned. Its producers include Du Bocq (fairly basic stuff, sold as Saison Régal), Saison Dupont and Saison Silly. *Pipaix, Roland* and *Voisin* are different types of *Saison* beer which come in large, corked bottles and may improve for up to 12 months after purchase.

SALVATOR Paulaner Brewery, Germany Supposedly the very first *Doppelbock* produced, Salvator's full and rich flavour enables it to keep up with the best of the imitators it has spawned.

SAN MIGUEL PREMIUM LAGER San Miguel Brewery, Spain Soft, malty-style lager with some hoppiness on the finish.

SANS SOUCI Moretti Brewery, Italy Finer version of the basic Moretti lager style, the pale colour, delicacy of flavour and

well-hopped character make it a fine Pilsener-type.

SANWALD HEFE WEISS Dinkelacker Brewery, Germany Run-of-the-mill wheat beer.

SCHÄFF-FEUERFEST Schäffbräu Brewery, Germany A dark and very strong *Doppelbock* which is conditioned for at least 12 months, has a big burst of fruit on the palate and thankfully little fizz.

SCHIERLINGER ROGGEN Schierlinger Brewery, Germany An unusual, 'top-fermented' rye beer, Roggen is deep bronze in colour, packs a fruity punch and has a distinctive, spicy-bitter finish.

SCHNEIDER-WEISSE Schneider Brewery, Germany A classic wheat beer.

SCHULTHEISS BER-LINER WEISSE Schultheiss Brewery, Germany The greatest of all *Berliner Weisse*.

SCOTCH ALE Scotland Dark, strong (up to 10% ABV), malty ale with ripe, fruity overtones. Much copied elsewhere.

SELECTA XV San Miguel Brewery, Spain Smoother, richer, more malty and much fruitier version of the Premium Lager.(*See* **San Miguel Premium Lager.**)

SEPTANE 5 Terken Brewery, France A soft, floral *Bière de Garde* that is filtered and reminiscent of an export lager.

SEZOENS PILS Martens Brewery, Belgium Reasonable replica of the Pilsener-style.

SEZOENS Martens Brewery, Belgium Pale, hoppy-fruity brew that falls somewhere between a *Saison* and a Pilsener.

SIEGEL PILS Dortmunder Union Brewery, Germany

A light, malty so-called Pils-style made from non-Pilsener malt, Siegel Pils is a pleasant enough brew with a very light hoppiness, but not special.

SION KÖLSCH Sion Brewery, Germany Fresh, flowery, aromatic *Kölsch* of some finesse.

SKOL Breda Brewery, Holland Light, tasteless lager-type.

SLOEBER Moortgat Brewery, Belgium The darkest of this brewery's off-dry, abbey-style beers.

SPATEN PILS Spaten Brewery, Germany Good Pils-style, but really no better than this brewery's *Münchner Hell*.

SPÉCIALE ENGHIEN Saison Silly Brewery, Belgium This *Saison* beer is a stronger version of the Doublette Engheim. (*See* **Saison** entry.)

SPÉCIALE PALM Palm Brewery, Belgium Golden-coloured 'top-fermented' ale with a dry, citrussy flavour and an assertive, well-hopped finish.

SPLÜGEN FUMÉE Poretti Brewery, Italy Ruddy copper-coloured brew with the smoky character of a *Rauchbier*.

ST-ARNOLDUS Yves Castelain Brewery, France A full, fruity and unfiltered *Bière de Garde*.

ST-JACOBUS BLONDER BOCK Forschungs Brewery, Germany Big, lusty brew with lots of sweet, malty flavour.

ST-LANDELIN RESERVE Rimaux Brewery, France An unexceptional abbey-type beer.

ST-LÉONARD St-Léonard Brewery, France A popular

Bière de Garde of moderate quality.

STAMM ALT Dinkelacker Brewery, Germany Uninspiring *Altbier*.

STAROPRAMEN Staropramen Brewery, Czech Republic Soft, malty export type beer that lacks the hoppy finesse of the best Czech beers.

STAUDER PILS Stauder Brewery, Germany Basic Pils-style of no special interest.

STEINBOCK Dortmunder Kronen Brewery, Germany A crisp, dry, dark *Bock*.

STELLA ARTOIS Artois Brewery, Belgium Pale-coloured, light-bodied, typically fizzy Pilsener-style.

STILLE NACHT De Dolle Brewery, Belgium The De Dolle Brouwers or 'The Mad Brewers' are two Belgians, Joe and Kris Herteleer, who caught the beer-bug in the UK when they purchased a home brew kit from Boots! Still Nacht is a 'top-fermented', deep-coloured, seasonal beer sold at Christmas.

STOUT There are two basic types of stout: bitter stout and sweet (or milk) stout. The sweet stuff, as epitomised by Mackeson and many other regional brews, is not dissimilar to a gassier, richer, darker version of mild. Classic stout is, however, bitter stout and Guinness, Murphy's and Beamish are all first-rate. They are also all Irish, of course, although stout is a derivative of porter, an entirely English creation that has fallen by the wayside. Perversely, no such similar products are made by a British brewery, let alone an English one, although Mackeson is, as indicated earlier, just one of many British sweet stouts

produced. Draught stout is about is 4-4.5% ABV and bottled 4.5-5%, although bottled versions, exported to the tropics can be as high as 8%. The startling difference between bottled and draught bitter stout, whether Guinness, Murphy's or Beamish, is one of gas. The bottled version, like all bottled beers, contains CO_2, which is coarse on the tongue and accentuates the extreme bitter character of a stout, whereas a head on the draught version is principally nitrogen, an inert gas that is smooth on the tongue and the creamy effect this provides subdues the bitter elements. Draught Guinness in the all-black can, not the gold one, was the first stout to utilise the Draughtflow™ System, which employs nitrogen to produce a very similar creamy effect in a can, since when Beamish and Murphy's have followed suit. The same technology has been applied to Guinness Draught Bitter in a can, a move that has been followed by Boddington, Flowers and others. (*see* **Draughtflow™ System**.)

STROPKEN GRAND CRU Slaghmuylder Brewery, Belgium A smooth, sophisticated 'top-fermented' beer with fine malty flavour, but its not the spicy brew it once used to be.

SUPER-DORT Alfa Brewery, Holland Sweet and strong.

SUPER LEEUW De Leeuw Brewery, Holland Pale lager style of some interest.

SWINKELS Bavaria Brewery, Holland Cheap, light, malty-tasting beer.

SYLVESTER Brand Brewery, Holland A 'top-fermented' beer that is dark-tawny in colour, full in body, with a dry, concentrated, fruity flavour.

SYMPATOR Würzburger Hofbräu Brewery, Germany A *Doppelbock* of little note.

THE GREAT DANE Faxe Brewery, Denmark An interesting, unpasteurised, export-type canned lager from a small, independent Brewery.

TRAPPIST, TRAPPISTE or **TRAPPISTENBIER** Belgium/Holland Copper-coloured, 'top-fermented' ale of significant strength (6-9% ABV), which is always bottle-conditioned, a Trappist beer is a robust product, but should always be ripe, round and fruity (not unlike how you would imagine a bottle-conditioned barley wine might taste) and comes in three styles of increasing strengths: the basic Trappist beer, which is often referred to as a Single, *Dubbel* and *Trippel*. Only five breweries run by monks belonging to the Trappist Order are allowed, by law, to make and sell Trappist beer: Chimay, Westmalle, Westvleteren, Orval and Rochefort in Belgium and Schaapskooi in Holland. The monks of the Notre Dame abbey at Scourmont were the first to perfect and market the Trappist style of beer under the Chimay label. (*See* **Dubbel** and **Trippel** entries.)

TREMANATOR DOPPELBOCK Dortmunder Actien Brewery, Germany Sounds so terrifying for such a docile brew.

TRIPPEL (Generic) Belgium/Holland The strongest of the three styles of Trappist beer, its producers include Abdij der Trappisten Westmalle (very pale-coloured, Westmalle's *Trippel* is more citrussy and assertive than its *Dubbel*), Maes (sold under the

Grimbergen label, the *Trippel* is stronger and paler than the *Dubbel*, with a fruitier-malty character and a dryish finish), and Schaapskooi (strong, spicy beer from Holland's only Trappist Brewery). (*See* **Trappist** entry.)

TUBORG Tuborg Brewery, Denmark Various lightly-hopped lagers are produced under the internationally well-known Tuborg label.

UR-BOCK DUNKEL Einbecker Brauhaus, Germany Strong, dark lager of excellent depth and quality.

UR-BOCK HELL Einbecker Brauhaus, Germany Strong, light-coloured lager of far less character than the *Dunkel*.

UR-BOCK Heller Brewery, Germany Classic *Bock*

UR-MÄRZEN Spaten Brewery, Germany Many believe this to be the finest *Märzenbier* currently in production.

UR- or **URQUELL** Literally means 'source of', but it's so misused it means nothing most of the time.

UR-WEIZEN Höll Brewery, Germany Copper-coloured wheat beer, full of rich, fruity, bottle aromas.

URBOCK Bavaria St-Pauli Brewery, Germany Not a *Bock* as such, but a *Doppelbock*, although this beer's mediocre quality makes it rather a moot point.

UREICH PILS Eichbaum Brewery, Germany A well-brewed, delicate rendition of the Pils-style made from non-Pilsener malt, Ureich Pils has a nice hoppy-malt feel in the mouth.

URSTOFF Kulmbacher Mönchshof Brewery,

Germany A deep, dark *Doppelbock* of some note.

URTYP 1634 Paulaner Brewery, Germany A well-coloured export-style Dunkel, but not as good as the firm's basic Alt-Münchner.

VAN VOLLENHOVEN STOUT Heineken Brewery, Holland A Dutch attempt at the stout style using 'bottom-fermentation' techniques; it is strange, but not unpleasant.

VELTINS PILSENER Veltins Brewery, Germany Rather sweet, but well-balanced Pilsener-style beer produced in small quantities.

VIEILLE GARDE Monceau St-Waast Brewery, France A rather unusual *Bière de Garde* with a malty palate and a sharp, assertive fruity finish.

VIEUX FOUDRE GUEUZE Vanderlinden Brewery, Belgium This deep coloured blend of old and young *Lambic* beers is very lively, with a full, fluffy head and a fine, assertive finish.

VIEW FOUDRE KRIEK Vanderlinden Brewery, Belgium Splendidly fresh and aromatic, if you like sweet cherry-flavoured beer.

VLAAMSE BOURGOGNE Bois Brewery, Belgium Fairly sweet, 'top-fermented' burgundy-coloured beer, full of sour fruit flavours and a sharp, bitter-sweet finish.

VOISIN (Generic) Belgium A type of *Saison* beer, usually in a large corked bottle, and may be aged for up to 12 months. (*See* **Saison** entry.)

W

WARSTEINER PILSENER
Warsteiner Brewery, Germany Typical premium-type Pilsener-style beer with a delicate aroma and overly clean palate.

WARSTEINER PREMIUM VERUM
Warsteiner Brewery, Germany A light, premium beer made in the Pilsener style, but without Pilsener malt.

WEISSE or WEISSEBIER
(Generic) Germany Generic terms for white beer, which is synonymous with wheat beer. (*See* **Wheat Beer** entry.)

WEIZENBIER
(Generic) Germany A term for wheat beer, which can be either pale (*see* **Wheat Beer** entry) or dark. (*See* **Dunkel Weizen.**)

WEIZENBOCK
(Generic) Germany A dark version of wheat beer, which is 'top-fermented' as a *Weizenbier* should be, rather than 'bottom-fermented' as a *Bock* is. Producers of this style include Erdinger (strong, amber-coloured, with a tart, bitter-sweet finish called Pinkantus), Höll (tart and spicy, with stewed apple fruit taste) and Maisel (big-bodied, intense flavour).

WESTMALLE TRAPPISTENBIER DUBBEL
Abdij der Trappisten Westmalle Brewery, Belgium Dark brown Trappist beer with a ripe, malty flavour and a fairly dry, fruity finish.

WESTMALLE TRAPPISTENBIER TRIPPEL
Abdij der Trappisten Westmalle Brewery, Belgium Very pale-coloured Trappist beer, more citrussy and assertive than the *Dubbel*.

WESTVLETEREN ABBOT
Westvleteren Trappist Brewery, Belgium The Abbot (recognised by its yellow crown-cap) is the strongest beer produced by the monastery.

WESTVLETEREN DUBBEL
Westvleteren Trappist Brewery, Belgium As no single version is commercialised by the order of St-Sixtus, this double (recognised by its green crown-cap) is the most basic style of Trappist beer sold by the monastery.

WESTVLETEREN EXTRA
Westvleteren Trappist Brewery, Belgium The Extra (recognised by its blue crown-cap) is fruity and sharp, coming between the Special and Abbot in terms of strength.

WESTVLETEREN SPECIAL
Westvleteren Trappist Brewery, Belgium The Special (recognised by its red crown-cap) is creamier, spicier and stronger than the *Dubbel*, but has less strength than the Extra.

WESTVLETEREN ST-SIXTUS
(Generic) Belgium Any Westvleteren beer that has a label or includes the name St-Sixtus will not be the authentic Trappist beer, which carries no label, but it will be a very good, authorised replica which has been brewed by a nearby commercial Brewery, under licence from the monastery.

WESTVLETEREN St-Sixtus
Brewery, Belgium Although the authentic Westvleteren Trappist beer is brewed by the monks and at the monastery of the Trappist order of St-Sixtus in Westvleteren, it has no label, no mention of St-Sixtus and can only be identified by the name of Westvleteren on the crown-cap or the Westvleteren name embossed on the bottle. Any beer that has a label or includes the name St-Sixtus, will be brewed by a nearby commercial Brewery, under licence from the monastery.

WHEAT BEER
A 'top-fermented' beer fermented from a mix of wheat malt (usually a minimum 50%) and barley malt, which usually produces a very pale beer with an alcoholic strength of just over 5% ABV, a sour, fruity-biscuity flavour (distinctive brews often have a spiced-apple character) and a substantial sediment (those prefixed with *Hefe* labour this point). Unlike most bottle-conditioned ales, the sediment in a wheat beer is supposed to be poured into the glass to produce the desired cloudy effect. It gives the beer its special fruity roundness and, of course, makes the beer fizzy to one degree or another, and when poured often throws such a vast, fluffy, voluminous head that it requires the use of a special glass to contain it. Most wheat beers are German, but Belgium also has a certain renown, particularly for its rustic *Lambic* beers. Producers of this style include Arcen (Arcener Tarwe is a lightly-hopped, cidery Dutch attempt at this style), Ayinger (Bräu Weisse is a frothy-white, tart, spicy beer that has been conditioned with sediment from the previous brew), De Kluis (the Hoegaarden or Witte Van Hoegaarden is a well-hopped, cloudy yellow-white beer, spiced in the old style with coriander and curaçao, typically tangy to taste, with a bitter fruit flavour that honeys with age), Dinkelacker (Weizen Krone and a *Hefe* called Sanwald, both run-of-the-mill), EKU (run-of-the-mill Weizen), Erdinger (fizzy *Hefe* with a fluffy head, apple fruitiness on the palate and a spicy, bitter-sweet finish), Gouden Boom (typically fizzy, quite spicy,

with a sour finish, called Blanche de Bruges or Brugs Tarwebier), Haake-Beck (fresh, zesty Bremer Weisse, with a sharp, fruity finish), Hacker-Pschorr (Pschorr-Bräu Weisse has a fluffy-head and a sour-biscuity flavour with a fine spiced-apple tang), Hofbräuhaus (an Edel Weizen with lots of sharp-fruity flavour), Höll (a copper-coloured Ur-Weizen, full of rich, fruity, bottle-aromas), Hofbräuhaus (Dunkel-Weizen is not a *Dunkel*, as such, but a splendid dark wheat beer), Kaltenberg (the crisp, unpasteurised Prinzregent Luitpold Weissbier has a typically tart taste, which is reminiscent of stewed apple on the finish), Löwenbräu (cidery *Hefe*), Maisel (a Weizen Kristall-Klar that is effervescent, predictably crystal-clear and well appreciated by some, plus a tawny-coloured *Hefe* with a sour-apple taste), Paulaner (the Altbayerische Weissbier undergoes a lengthy conditioning and is appreciated for its supple fruitiness), Pinkus Müller (its Alt Weissbier is rich, ripe and well-honed, with a soft, mature, malty flavour, while the *Hefe* is delicate and spritzy, with an easy, mild finish), Raaf (a bitter-sweet Witbier that incorporates Pilsener malt, giving the beer its long, delicate citrus flavour), Rauchenfels (Steinweisen is the wheat beer version of a 'stone-beer' -*see* **Rauchbier** entry -which is predictably sharper to taste and the preferred beer of Rauchenfels healthy cult-following), Schneider (the straight Schneider Weiss is a classic, although the Aventinus is even better), Schulteiss (its Berliner Weiss is considered to be the finest of its type), Spaten (decent but not special basic wheat beer, but a full, spicy-apple flavoured *Hefe* called

Franziskaner), Tucher (lacklustre Weizen and Hefe), VEB (Berliner Kindle Weisse is classic, with a spicy, stewed apple flavour and sour cream aftertaste, but while its basic Berliner Weisse is good, it does lack a certain concentration) and Würzburger Hofbräu (crisp and fruity *Hefe*). (*See* also **Alt Weissbier, Berliner Weiss, Bière Blanche, Dunkel Weizen, Hefe, Lambic, Weissebier, Weizenbier, Weizenbock** and **Whitbier** entries.)

WHITBIER (Generic) Belgium A white or wheat beer, often comparable to a German Weissebier.

WHITE BEER Synonymous with pale-coloured wheat beer. (*See* **Weissebier** entry.)

WICKÜLER PILSENER Wicküler Brewery, Germany The light aroma and overly clean palate of this beer is typical of the Premium-type Pilsener-style.

WITBIER Raaf Brewery, Holland A bitter-sweet wheat beer that incorporates Pilsener malt and has long, delicate citrus flavour.

WITTE VAN HOEGAARDEN or **HOEGAARDEN** De Kluis Brewery, Belgium Hoegaarden was once the most famous wheat beer village in Belgium, with over 30 breweries, but as this style of beer gave way to modern beers, all the breweries gradually went out of business. De Kluis was a brave revival of an abandoned brewery in 1965, but has required investment from the Stella Artois group to survive. Hoegaarden White is a well-hopped, cloudy yellow-white wheat beer, considered by some to be the finest of its type. Interestingly, it is spiced with coriander and curaçao, an ancient but seldom practised custom that

produces a typically tangy beer with a bitter fruit flavour that honeys with age.

WÜRZIG HERB Hofmark Brewery, Germany (*See* **Das Feine Hofmark** entry.)

WÜRZIG MILD Hofmark Brewery, Germany (*See* **Das Feine Hofmark** entry.)

X-PERT Gulpen Brewery, Holland A so-called super-premium style, this Dutch beer has a touch too much colour for a classic Pilsener, but is beautifully bottle-conditioned, adding a smooth, refined quality to its nicely hopped palate and finish.

ZWICKELBIER (Generic) Germany An unfiltered beer, of no great distinction.

SPIRITS

Although some appellation-based spirits such as Cognac, Armagnac and Calvados do exist, the concept of origin is rarely applied by the spirits industry. Perhaps the biggest problem is the proliferation of foreign-distilled look alike spirits. The most and worst of these are distilled legally (if amorally, from a European perspective) in the Far East and Third World countries, but are not allowed to be sold within the confines of the EC. There is, however, nothing to prevent the owner of an international brand of non-appellation spirits (gin, vodka etc) from licensing its production in any country, including those of the EC, although these inevitably turn out to be inferior to the original product. A brand's recipe will often be altered to cater for local tastes, posing a significant problem in Greece and Portugal, where the trend is for sweeter spirits; generic styles seem to fly out of the window. Beware: it is one thing to make a good saving on your favourite brand, but if the spirit has not been distilled in the same country, it could be a waste of money, so always check the small print on the label to see where it was distilled.

Distilling the Facts

A spirit is the distilled product of a crude alcoholic base called a 'wash' which, depending on the spirit in question, may be fermented from grain, fruit or vegetables. The wash is then heated until it vaporises, which is captured in the cap of the boiling pot and piped-off through a tank of cold water, where the vapour condenses, reverting to its liquid state. As alcohol vaporises at a lower temperature than water, it can easily be extracted by controlling the temperature at which the wash is heated. The liquid that drips out of the end of a distillation pipe is not, however, pure alcohol, as it contains some water and a tiny but significant amount of flavour and aroma compounds from the initial crude base; the exact proportions will depend on the temperature and duration of the distillation, the number of times it is distilled and various other factors. The more times a product is distilled, the more refined it becomes, but it also reduces the amount and type of aroma/flavour compounds. Spirits are generally distilled to a much higher alcohol level than required, then diluted

with rain or distilled water. In the case of spirits that are aged in cask (Scotch, Irish Whiskey, Cognac, Armagnac), where some of the alcohol has been lost through evaporation over many years, the amount of water added will be proportionally lower.

Colourful Story

Immediately after distillation, all spirits are as clear and colourless as gin and vodka. Any that are not will be the result of deliberate colouring, usually with caramel. The classic case to explain how and why this practice evolved is Jamaican Rum, which used to be shipped to this country in old sherry butts. The butts had arrived in the West Indies on an earlier ship, which had been transporting sherry, and in those days most sherry was dark and sweet. They were then refilled with the colourless rum and shipped back to Great Britain. When it arrived, the Jamaican rum had acquired a deep colour, but occasionally it was shipped back in casks not used for sweet sherry and the rum would have very little colour. Customers complained to the innkeeper. They wanted the rum they were used to, which was dark, of course. The inn-keeper complained to the shippers, who then began adding caramel to any pale looking rum, to keep a consistent colour and everyone was happy.

From Strength to Strength

Readers who remember that most spirits used to be 70° proof might wonder about today's products, which are generally registered at 40% alcohol by volume. They are, however, exactly the same strength, using two totally different systems. In

the good old days, which is to say before the Common Market, we used the Sykes system, rather than the percentage by volume of alcohol found in a product. Sykes was a wonder -fully empiric system, whereby someone soaked gunpowder with a spirit, then set a match to it! If it exploded, this was taken as proof of the spirit's potency, hence the use of the term 'proof' for alcoholic strength. If it did not explode, then the spirit was not 100° proof. Gunpowder-exploding strength was thus deemed to be 100° while water was, naturally, 0°, and with the invention of the hydrometer, every alcoholic beverage could be graded on this scale of 0-100. This might seem nice and metric but, of course, it was not. When it became possible to measure pure alcohol, this turned out to be 175° on the Sykes scale and 100° proof was merely 57.14286°, which hardly trips off the tongue. All things considered, it was lucky that 70° proof converted neatly to 40% ABV.

Still Here

The distillation of a spirit is greatly affected by the type of still used and the number of distillations employed. There are two basic types of still: the simple type known a pot-still and the more complex continuous still (sometimes called the Coffey-still or patent-still). The pot-still is used for Cognac, Armagnac, malt whisky and some types of rum, while the continuous still is used for grain whisky, vodka and other spirits. Some gins and rums are produced by a combination of both types of still. The pot-still could not be simpler, merely consisting of a giant pot which is filled with the crude alcoholic beverage, and heated. The pot has a tall cone-shaped head that narrows to form the pipe along which the vapour from the heated alcoholic beverage flows, the pipe coiling through a large tank of cold water called a condenser. Many pot-still spirits are distilled twice, in which case two pot-stills are usually set up in tandem, the initial spirit dripping out of the condenser of the first into the pot of the second. Although the workings of a continuous still are too intricate to describe adequately in a book such as this, suffice to say that as its name implies the vapour from the heated alcoholic beverage is continuously re-circulated until a distillate of the desired strength is achieved. A **warning** for anyone daft enough to distil his or her own spirit: in theory distillation is simple, but in practice it requires considerable skill and knowledge to separate the good 'heart' (ethyl alcohol) of the vapour from the poisonous 'heads' (methyl alcohol) and 'tails' (amyl alcohol), which are called 'foreshots' and 'feints' in Scotland, so don't do it!

A-Z OF SPIRITS

NOTE Although the A-Z Quick References do not include British or Irish products because they are supposed to assist readers in understanding unfamiliar continental European drinks, Scotch whisky is included in the entries below because it features so prominently in cross-Channel shopping and, frankly, a guide to spirits that omits Scotch would appear somewhat odd. As the exception has been made for Scotch, it would seem unfair not to include

its Irish counter -part. For definitions of technical and tasting terms or abbreviations, consult the GLOSSARY.

★★★ France The lowest Cognac designation, three star Cognacs have a legal minimum age of just two years, although in the UK and Ireland local laws demand a minimum of at least three years, and many are nearer to five. (*See* **Cognac** entry.)

A

AGUARDENTE DE BAGACERIRA or BAGACERIRA Portugal The Portuguese equivalent of *Marc* should be avoided at all costs. (*See* **Marc** entry.)

AGUARDENTE or AGUARDENTE DE VINHO Portugal (*See* **Portuguese Brandy** entry.)

AKVAVIT Denmark A neutral spirit distilled from either potatoes or grain, then re-distilled with caraway or dill in much the same way as, but not tasting like, gin. The best-known brand is Aalborg.

ALISIER or ALIZIERGEIST France A fine Alsatian *alcool blanc* or white spirit distilled from, but not flavoured by, the fermented juice of rowan berries, which makes a mild but distinctive *eau-de-vie*.

ARMAGNAC France The oldest of all brandies, Armagnac is produced in Gascony, south of Bordeaux, from the Ugni Blanc, Folle Blanche, Colombard, Jurançon and Baco grapes. The Folle Blanche used to be traditional to Armagnac, accounting for virtually its entire production, whereas for Cognac it has always been the Ugni Blanc. The varietal difference can best be discerned by comparing older brandies from the two

regions. The Ugni Blanc now dominates both the Charente (98%) and Gascony (80%). Differences today between Armagnac and Cognac include location (Cognac being north of Bordeaux), soil (sand is considered best in Armagnac, while it is chalk in Cognac), distillation (Armagnac being single continuous-distilled to 63% ABV maximum, although 53-58% is more common, whereas Cognac is double-distilled to 70% ABV by pot-still), maturation (Armagnac in the 'black' oak of Monzelun, Cognac in Limousin or Tronçais oak), dilution (as Armagnac is distilled to a much lower strength, it requires far less dilution by rain or distilled water), production (20 million cases of Armagnac, compared to 130 million of Cognac) and type of producer (Armagnac is made by a large number of family distillers, whereas the Cognac industry is dominated by a small number of comparatively huge concerns). The average Armagnac is, therefore, a more individual product, but rustic and generally less consistent than the average Cognac. Armagnac is not cheap, but the cheaper Armagnacs are a far better buy than cheaper Cognacs. The best Armagnacs do not have the finesse or elegance of a great Cognac, but that does not mean that they actually lack finesse or elegance, just that these qualities are less significant and the single distillation gives qualities that are an essential part of Armagnac's charms. But perhaps the most conspicuous difference between these two great brandies is the smaller proportion of water required to bring down Armagnac's strength to the desired level. This not only provides Armagnac with a greater concentration of original spirit flavour, but for a Cognac and an Armagnac of similar maturation time in cask, it also preserves a more oaky flavour for the Armagnac. Overall, Armagnac is fuller, fatter, richer and riper than Cognac, exhibiting a degree of vanilla-oak character that is found only in genuinely old, deluxe Cognacs. The quality of Armagnac can vary according to its area of production (see in order of excellence **Bas Armagnac**, **Haut Armagnac** and **Ténarèze** entries) or age (see in order of excellence **Vintage Armagnac, Hors d'Age, XO, Napoléon** and **VSOP** entries). Producers include Castarède (strong on natural-strength, vintage Armagnac), Château de Cassaigne (immaculately conceived Armagnac distilled in a château that was once the property of the Bishops of Condom), Château de Labaude (fine XO and superb range of vintages), Château de Tariquet (stylish), Croix des Salles (classic old Armagnacs), Dupeyron (pure Folle Blanche Armagnacs), Faget (great individual character), Domaine de Gaycross (Armagnac from the creator of Floc de Gascogne), Gelas (classic *Hors d'Age*), Janeau (lovely Réserve, which is older than either Janeau's XO or Napoléon, both of which are also excellent), J. de Malliac (beautiful Grand Bas Folle Blanche and numerous superb old vintages), Marquis de Montesquiou (wide range of classic Armagnacs), Samalens (brilliantly expressive 100 year old Relique du Siècle) and Sempe (young Napoléon, but good old vintages).

ASBACH Germany Classic German brandy, Asbach leans more towards Cognac than Armagnac, although it uses wines from both regions. (See **German Brandy** entry.)

B

BAS ARMAGNAC France The top-rated of Armagnac's three districts, Bas Armagnac brandy has the most finesse, with a bouquet that is often reminiscent of violets or, if pure Folle Blanche, prunes. Bas Armagnac has its own appellation, products of which are usually well worth seeking out. (See **Armagnac, Haut Armagnac** and **Ténarèze** entries.)

BIRNENGEIST, BIRNGEIST or **BIRNENWASSER** Germany The German equivalent of *Poire William*. (See **Poire William** entry.)

BOIS COMMUNS France Gradations of quality within the six districts that comprise the Cognac region are based on the amount of chalk found in the soil, by which system Bois Communs is ranked sixth. Cognacs produced entirely from the Bois Communs district are so disappointing in quality that they do not warrant their own Cognac appellation. (See **Cognac** entry.)

BONS BOIS France Gradations of quality within the six districts that comprise the Cognac region are based on the amount of chalk found in the soil, by which system Bons Bois is ranked fifth. Cognacs produced entirely from the Bons Bois district are very modest in quality, but have their own Bons Bois Cognac appellation. They have a certain *goût de terroir*, which gives the brandy its rustic character. Some Cognacais say they are extremely useful for blending purposes, while others confess after a few glasses of XO that the blending theory is just nonsense,

claiming that Bons Bois can only dilute the quality of a brandy, dull its finesse and increase its profit. (See **Cognac** entry.)

BORDERIES France Gradations of quality within the six districts that comprise the Cognac region are based on the amount of chalk found in the soil, by which system Borderies is ranked third, although its brandy is so sought after that the price is almost the same as that for the more prestigious Petite Champagne district. Precociousness and mellowness are the Borderies two desirable qualities, as the Cognac produced ages at just three quarters the rate of a Petite Champagne Cognac, yet retains almost as much finesse, thus a judicious amount in a blend enables it to be brought on to the market earlier, making a significant saving in terms of maturation costs. Cognacs produced entirely from the Borderies district have the right to their own Borderies Cognac appellation, although nobody bothers to age even the best Borderies beyond 15 or 20 years. (See **Cognac** entry.)

BRAIE DE HOUX France Synonymous with Houx. (See **Houx** entry.)

BRAIE DE SORBE France Synonymous with Sorbier. (See **Sorbier** entry.)

BRAIE DE SUREAU France Synonymous with Sureau. (See **Sureau** entry.)

BRANDY DE JEREZ Spain A curious thing about Spanish brandy is that it is either unfairly dismissed by Cognac snobs or ludicrously overrated by peninsular plebs. There are several types of Spanish brandy, but Brandy de Jerez accounts for over 90% of the total production and is the only official Spanish brandy appellation. Most standard quality Spanish brandies, including Brandy de Jerez, are bland, while most deluxe brandies are too rich, too full and very clumsy with a sweet, cloying sort of vanilla-oak pervading every aspect of aroma and flavour. Somewhere in the middle ground, however, there are some fine Spanish brandies that represent excellent value for money. The best producers include Blazquez (soft and generous Felipe II, one of the better cheap brandies), Bobadilla (lush, dry Gran Capitan), Caballero (Decano is the best of Spain's cheaper, standard brandies), Croft (very classy Brandy Croft, yet even classier Solera Privado), Domecq (the Fundador is fine, dry and firm, despite being one of Spain's best-selling cheaper brandies, although the Carlos I and Marqués de Domecq are well worth the premium these deluxe brandies command), Garvey (the Gran Garvey has rare finesse, but is not in the same class as this firm's Renacimiento, which some think to be the finest brandy produced in Spain), Gonzalez Byass (stylish Byass 96, beautifully structured Lepanto), Lustau (the Señor is rich and oaky, but has the structure and class to take it) Osborne (the Conde de Osborne has great class and finesse, if you can put up with the decidedly weird bottle that was designed by Salvador Dali) and Terry (excellent, fruity Centenario, even finer 1900).

BRANDY International A generic term for any grape-based spirit, the word derives from the Dutch *Brantjwyn* or 'burnt wine', alluding to the fact that wine is boiled down by burning over a fire. The word brandy is also used in a looser context, to encompass any fruit-based spirit, and is thus synonymous with the French term of *eau-de-vie*. Armagnac and Cognac may both be called brandy, but the reverse does not apply. (*See* **Armagnac** and **Cognac**, also **French Brandy, German Brandy, Greek Brandy, Italian Brandy, Portuguese Brandy** and **Spanish Brandy** entries.)

BRANTWEIN Germany The lowest classification of German *Asbach*. (*See* **German Brandy** entry.)

BRIMBELLE France A fine Alsatian *alcool blanc* or white spirit distilled from, but not flavoured by, the fermented juice of brambles, the fruit character of which comes through on the aftertaste as just the merest nuance.

C

CALVADOS DU PAYS D'AUGE France The best and most distinctive Calvados comes from the lush orchards of the Auge valley.

CALVADOS France Often described as the world's greatest apple brandy, Normandy's Calvados can in fact be made from either cider or *poiré* (fermented pear juice). Usually it is both, even if the emphasis is decidedly apple-based, as the inclusion of pears in the ferment is said to add elegance and finesse. Calvados is double-distilled in a pot-still, receives considerable ageing in oak casks, and the rich and substantive brandy produced is indeed worthy of its worldwide acclaim.

CAMPBLETOWN MALTS Scotland Single malt whiskies from distilleries which are located in one of the four classic whisky regions of Scotland, an area near Campbletown in the Mull of Kintyre. Few distilleries exist, but the full-bodied, intensely flavoured and beautifully matured, smoky malts of Campbletown are now enjoying something of a mini-revival, thanks to the quality and perseverance of the Springbank Distillery.

COGNAC France The most famous of all brandies, Cognac is produced in Charente, north of Bordeaux, from the Ugni Blanc, Folle Blanche, Colombard, Jurançon, Blanc-ramé, Montils and Sémillon grapes. The Ugni Blanc represents 98% of Cognac's total production. This used to be one of the glaring differences between Cognac and Armagnac, as the latter was once almost entirely Folle Blanche, but only old vintage Armagnacs can illustrate this varietal contrast today. Other significant differences applicable to current production include location (Armagnac being south of Bordeaux), soil (chalk is considered best in Cognac, while it is sand in Armagnac), distillation (Cognac being double-distilled to 70% ABV by pot-still, whereas 63% is the maximum allowed for single continuous-distilled Armagnac and 53-58% is common), maturation (Cognac in Limousin or Tronçais oak, Armagnac in the 'black' oak of Monzelun), dilution (as Cognac is distilled to a much higher strength, it requires a far greater dilution by rain or distilled water), production (130 million cases of Cognac, compared to 20 million of Armagnac) and type of producer (Cognac is dominated by a small number of comparatively huge concerns, Armagnac by a large number of family distillers). The average Cognac is, therefore, a more consistent, albeit more anonymous, product and, due to the double-distillation, the best Cognacs possess more finesse and elegance. An interesting admission was made when I told the deputy head of one of Cognacs greatest and most famous houses that I preferred Armagnac because it was less diluted and more authentic than all but the very best Cognacs. He agreed! 'Personally' he confessed, 'I wouldn't touch anything less than an XO or a Napoléon.' So there you have it, right from the horse's mouth. Sceptics might think that he is only trying to push everyone into drinking expensive Cognacs, but there is so little XO and the like that it would be commercial madness. Three star represents 50% of all Cognac sold and even the pretentious VSOP claims a whacking great 40% of the market. Cognac firms depend on sales of these cheaper brandies (although the VSOP is overpriced) and the person in question will not thank me for revealing his true opinion. I have purposely not named him or his firm because the rest of Cognac would probably lynch him, but it is a true story and it is also surely no coincidence that André Simon once said something very similar, when he declared that 'Good Armagnac can be very good and much better than ordinary Cognac, but the best Armagnac cannot hope to approach, let alone rival, the best Cognac.' Armagnac devotees might not agree entirely with his sentiments, but most drinkers of both brandies should be honest enough to concede that his statement contains a lot of truth. The quality of Cognac can vary according to its area of production (*see* in order of excellence **Grande Champagne, Grand Fine Champagne, Petite**

Champagne, Borderies, Fins Bois, Bon Bois and **Bois Communs** entries) or age (*see* in order of excellence **XO, Napoléon, VSOP** and **★★★** entries).

Producers include Biscuit (50-year-old Extra Vieille and an incredible 100-year-old Privilège d'Alexandre Biscuit), Camus (generally overrated, but a good Napoléon nevertheless), Courvoisier (one of the truly great Cognac house, excellent Napoléon and XO), Croizet (lovely old Cognac), Delamain (classic Cognacs, especially the Très Vieux and the Réserve de la Famille), Dor (really old Cognacs of classic quality), Pierre Ferrand (excellent family-owned, single-vineyard Cognacs, especially the 45-year-old Abel and 70-year-old Ancestrale), Frappin (stick to the superb, single-vineyard, pure Grande Champagne Cognacs under the Domain Frappin label), Gautier (superb XO), Paul Giraud (a silky-soft Vieille Réserve of great delicacy and finesse), Henessy (the largest Cognac producer sells one of the fullest and most complex XO brandies on the market), Hine (most Hine Cognacs are light and elegant in style, with an XO that is unrivalled for finesse), Lhéraud (fine, organically produced, single-vineyard, pure Petite Champagne), Martell (best-known for Cordon Bleu, which is in fact older than its Napoléon Cognac, although the Cordon d'Argent is XO quality and far superior to both, while the recently launched Classique is a very special blend of 40 and 50-year-old Cognacs and undoubtedly the best Martell blend to date), Menard (a 50-year-old blend called Ancestrale), Otard (good XO), Prince Hubert de Polignac (co-operative-

produced Cognac), Paulet (some extraordinarily good Cognacs, especially its outstanding Château Paulet XO Fine Champagne), Peyrot (superb Très Vieille and a fine single-vineyard Grande Champagne), Prunier (well-respected, family-owned Cognac house), Rémy-Martin (while the cheaper blends are disappointing, even within their own modest category, Rémy-Martin's more expensive blends are truly superior Cognacs, especially the 50-year-old Louis XIII, which is sold in a crystal Baccarat replica of the Cognac flask found at the 16th century site of the Battle of Jarnac), Renault (producer of some of the sweetest, fattest Cognacs), Roullet (superb Très Rare) and Louis Royer (good XO Réserve from Japanese-owned firm).

COING France A popular Alsatian *alcool blanc* or white spirit distilled from, but not flavoured by, the fermented juice of the quince, which makes a mildly aromatic *eau-de-vie*.

CORENWIJN Holland A highly rated spirit, Corenwijn literally means 'corn wine', although it is, of course, a distillate of corn wine (barley, maize and rye). Like gin, it is thrice-distilled, but unlike that other Dutch classic, Corenwijn is then aged in wooden casks for several.

CUMIN France A fine Alsatian *alcool blanc* or white spirit distilled from cumin, the full spicy character of which comes through on the aftertaste. A bit like gripe water for grown ups.

DELUXE WHISKEY or **WHISKY** International A deluxe Scotch whisky should contain more than

40% malt whisky, which is the average for a blended Scotch, although there is no legal requirement for it to do so. In general, though, a deluxe Scotch will be smoother, richer and more mature than the basic blended product from the same distillery and this applies in relative terms to deluxe whiskies produced outside of Scotland.

E

EAU-DE-VIE DE ALISIER France Synonymous with Alisier. (*See* **Alisier** entry.)

EAU-DE-VIE DE BRAIE DE HOUX France Synonymous with Houx. (*See* **Houx** entry.)

EAU-DE-VIE DE BRAIE DE SORBE France Synonymous with Sorbier. (*See* **Sorbier** entry.)

EAU-DE-VIE DE BRAIE DE SUREAU France Synonymous with Sureau. (*See* **Sureau** entry.)

EAU-DE-VIE DE BRIMBELLE France Synonymous with Brimbelle. (*See* **Brimbelle** entry.)

EAU-DE-VIE DE COGNAC France Synonymous with Cognac. (*See* **Cognac** entry.)

EAU-DE-VIE DE COING France Synonymous with Coing. (*See* **Coing** entry.)

EAU-DE-VIE DE CUMIN France Synonymous with Cumin. (*See* **Cumin** entry.)

EAU-DE-VIE DE FRAISE DE BOIS France Synonymous with Fraise de Bois. (*See* **Fraise de Bois** entry.)

EAU-DE-VIE DE FRAISE France Synonymous with Fraise. (*See* **Fraise** entry.)

EAU-DE-VIE DE FRAMBOISE France Synonymous with Framboise. (*See* **Framboise** entry.)

EAU-DE-VIE DE HOUX France Synonymous with Houx. (*See* **Houx** entry.)

EAU-DE-VIE DE KIRSCH France Synonymous with Kirsch. (*See* **Kirsch** entry.)

EAU-DE-VIE DE MARC DE SAVOIE France Synonymous with Marc de Savoie. (*See* **Marc de Savoie** entry.)

EAU-DE-VIE DE MARC DU CENTRE-EST France Typically rough and ready marc produced from the dregs of grapes grown in a vast swathe of vineyards extending from Champagne in the north to Beaujolais in the south. (*See* **Marc** entry.)

EAU-DE-VIE DE MIRABELLE France Synonymous with Mirabelle. (*See* **Mirabelle** entry.)

EAU-DE-VIE DE MURE SAUVAGE France Synonymous with Mure Sauvage. (*See* **Mure Sauvage** entry.)

EAU-DE-VIE DE MURE France Synonymous with Mure. (*See* **Mure** entry.)

EAU-DE-VIE DE MYRTILLE France Synonymous with Myrtille. (*See* **Myrtille** entry.)

EAU-DE-VIE DE POIRE WILLAMINE France Synonymous with Poire William. (*See* **Poire William** entry.)

EAU-DE-VIE DE POMME France Synonymous with Pomme. (*See* **Pomme** entry.)

EAU-DE-VIE DE PRUNELLE SAUVAGE France Synonymous with Prunelle de Sauvage. (*See* **Prunelle de Sauvage** entry.)

EAU-DE-VIE DE PRUNELLE France Synonymous with Prunelle. (*See* **Prunelle** entry.)

EAU-DE-VIE DE QUETSCH France Synonymous with Quetsch. (*See* **Quetsch** entry.)

EAU-DE-VIE DE REINE CLAUDE France Synonymous with Reine Claude. (*See* **Reine Claude** entry.)

EAU-DE-VIE DE SORBIER France Synonymous with Sorbier. (*See* **Sorbier** entry.)

EAU-DE-VIE DE SUREAU France Synonymous with Sureau. (*See* **Sureau** entry.)

EAU-DE-VIE DE VIN DE SAVOIE France Rarely encountered brandy, unless you're on the *piste* in Savoie.

EAU-DE-VIE DE VIN ORIGINAIRE DU CENTRE-EST France This brandy can be made from grapes grown in a vast swathe of vineyards extending from Champagne in the north to Beaujolais in the south.

EAU-DE-VIE DES CHARENTES France Synonymous with Cognac. (*See* **Cognac** entry.)

EAUX-DE-VIE DE CIDRE DE BRETAGNE France A purely cider-based brandy from an area to the southwest of Calvados region, this *eau-de-vie* does not, however, have the quality or character of the more famous product. (*See* **Calvados** entry.)

EAUX-DE-VIE DE CIDRE DE NORMANDIE France A purely cider-based brandy produced in an area that overlaps much of the Calvados region, this *eau-de-vie* does not, however, have the quality or character of the more famous product. (*See* **Calvados** entry.)

EAUX-DE-VIE DE CIDRE DU MAINE France A purely cider-based brandy produced in an area that overlaps the south of the Calvados region, this *eau-de-vie* does not, however, have the quality or character of the more famous product. (*See* **Calvados** entry.)

EAUX-DE-VIE DE FAUGÈRES France

Synonymous with Faugères. (*See* **Faugères** entry.)

EAUX-DE-VIE DE MARC DE BOURGOGNE France Strong, coarse and aggressive marc produced in the Burgundy region. (*See* **Marc** entry.)

EAUX-DE-VIE DE MARC DE CHAMPAGNE France Synonymous with Marc de Champagne. (*See* **Marc de Champagne** entry.)

EAUX-DE-VIE DE MARC DES CÔTES-DU-RHONE France Typically rough and ready marc, although the marcs of pure Viognier produced in Condrieu and Château Grillet are rare, aromatic exceptions. (*See* **Marc** entry.)

EAUX-DE-VIE DE MARC ORIGINAIRE D'AQUITAINE France The coarser version of the Eaux-de-Vie de Vin Originaire d'Aquitaine. (*See* **Marc** entry.)

EAUX-DE-VIE DE MARC ORIGINAIRES DE FRANCHE-COMTÉ France Typically rough and ready marc produced to the east of Burgundy's Côte d'Or. (*See* **Marc** entry.)

EAUX-DE-VIE DE MARC ORIGINAIRES DE PROVENCE France Typically rough and ready marc produced in the Provence region. (*See* **Marc** entry.)

EAUX-DE-VIE DE MARC ORIGINAIRES DES COTEAUX DE LA LOIRE France Produced in an area encompassing much of the Loire Valley and its hinterland, this is not as rough as some marcs, but what it lacks in aggressiveness, it also lacks in character. (*See* **Marc** entry.)

EAUX-DE-VIE DE MARC ORIGINAIRES DU BUGEY France Synonymous with Marc du Bugey. (*See* **Marc du Bugey** entry.)

EAUX-DE-VIE DE MARC ORIGINAIRES DU LANGUEDOC France Typically rough and ready marc produced in the Midi region of France. (*See* **Marc** entry.)

EAUX-DE-VIE DE POIRÉ DE BRETAGNE France A purely *poiré*-based brandy from an area to the southwest of Calvados region, this *eau-de-vie* does not, however, have the quality or character of the more famous product. (*See* **Calvados** entry.)

EAUX-DE-VIE DE POIRÉ DE NORMANDIE France A purely *poiré*-based brandy produced in an area that overlaps much of the Calvados region, this *eau-de-vie* does not, however, have the quality or character of the more famous product. (*See* **Calvados** entry.)

EAUX-DE-VIE DE POIRÉ DU MAINE France A purely *poiré*-based brandy produced in an area that overlaps the south of the Calvados region, this *eau-de-vie* does not, however, have the quality or character of the more famous product. (*See* **Calvados** entry.)

EAUX-DE-VIE DE VIN DE BOURGOGNE France Synonymous with Fine de Bourgogne. (*See* **Fine de Bourgogne** entry.)

EAUX-DE-VIE DE VIN DE LA MARNE France Synonymous with Fine de la Champagne. (*See* **Fine de la Champagne** entry.)

EAUX-DE-VIE DE VIN DES CÔTES-DU-RHONE France Not quite the value of its vinous cousin.

EAUX-DE-VIE DE VIN ORIGINAIRE D'AQUITAINE France Basic brandy from the southwest of France, including (theoretically at least) both Cognac and Armagnac, not to mention Bordeaux, which has its own appellation. In practice, however, the brandy sold under this designation will be from vineyards outside the more classic areas.

EAUX-DE-VIE DE VIN ORIGINAIRES DE FRANCHE-COMTÉ France A rather ordinary brandy produced to the east of Burgundy's Côte d'Or, but having none of the richness and character of Fine de Bourgogne.

EAUX-DE-VIE DE VIN ORIGINAIRES DE PROVENCE France Seldom encountered brandies of ordinary quality, except for some extraordinary oddities from Bandol.

EAUX-DE-VIE DE VIN ORIGINAIRES DES COTEAUX DE LA LOIRE France Produced in an area encompassing much of the Loire Valley and its hinterland, this fresh and vibrant *eau-de-vie* is well worth searching for.

EAUX-DE-VIE DE VIN ORIGINAIRES DU BUGEY France Rarely encountered brandy, unless you're on the *piste* in Savoie.

EAUX-DE-VIE DE VIN ORIGINAIRES DU LANGUEDOC France Bland brandy from the Midi region of France.

ENZIAN Germany The German equivalent of Gentian. (*See* **Gentian** entry.)

ERDLBEERGEIST Germany The German equivalent of Fraise. (*See* **Fraise** entry.)

EXTRA OLD France This Cognac designation is usually indicated on a bottle as XO. (*See* **Cognac** and **XO** entries.)

F

FAUGÈRES France Some distinctive, underrated, but rapidly rising Faugères wines are made, but the spirit has not been encountered. Readers comments are welcome.

FINE BORDEAUX France Relatively new appellation of fairly expensive brandies that have yet to prove their worth, despite coming from a region that is squeezed between Cognac and Armagnac.

FINE CHAMPAGNE France A Cognac designation for a blend of Grande Champagne and Petite Champagne, a Fine Champagne must contain at least 50% Grande Champagne. (*See* **Cognac, Grande Champagne** and **Petite Champagne** entries.)

FINE DE BOURGOGNE France Some rich and distinctive brandies lurk beneath this Burgundian appellation.

FINE DE LA CHAMPAGNE France Nothing like Armagnac in character and not quite the class of a decent Cognac, Champagne's *eau-de-vie* does, however, have more finesse and greater consistency than most other regional brandies. The finesse comes from the wine used for distillation, which is low in alcohol and high in acidity, whereas the consistency is due to a far less esoteric reason because, despite the multiplicity of brands, there is just one distiller and that is Goyard. This does have a drawback in terms of variety and *real* choice, although some Champagne houses claim *their* Fine Champagne is produced only from *their* grapes.

FINS BOIS France Gradations of quality within the six districts that comprise the Cognac region are based on the amount of chalk found in the soil, by which system Fins Bois is ranked fourth. Cognacs produced entirely from the Fins Bois district mature quicker than those of the Borderies and have infinitely less finesse, but they do have the right to their own Fins Bois Cognac appellation. (*See* **Cognac** entry.)

FRAISE DE BOIS France The wild fruit version of Fraise, this *eau-de-vie* is distilled from the fermented juice of tiny, succulent forest strawberries, which are costly to collect, but make an even more delectable spirit.

FRAISE France A fine Alsatian *alcool blanc* or white spirit distilled from, but not flavoured by, the fermented juice of strawberries, although the fruit character pours through on the nose, palate and aftertaste of this *eau-de-vie*.

FRAMBOISE France A top quality Alsatian *alcool blanc* or white spirit distilled from, but not flavoured by, the fermented juice of raspberries, the fruit character of which comes through on the aftertaste as just the merest nuance. Framboise is expensive but exquisite, and many believe it to be the finest of all Alsace *eau-de-vie*.

FRENCH BRANDY France French grape brandies other than those sold under a specific appellation, especially Armagnac and Cognac, are usually cheap and bland. The use of the term Napoléon is of no significance whatsoever.

G

GENEVER Holland Nothing to do with the Swiss city, which ends with an 'a', not 'er' (although sometimes spelt Geneva, not to mention Jenever and, synonymous with this are Holland's and Schiedam), *genever* is in fact the Dutch for juniper, which is the principal ingredient of gin and has thus given name to a particular style of gin with a highly refined, but distinctive, juniper berry flavour. (*See* **Gin** entry.)

GENTIAN France An Alsatian *alcool blanc* or white spirit distilled from, but not flavoured by, the root of the gentian plant, which gives a dry tasting spirit with a muddy, herbal aftertaste.

GERMAN BRANDY Germany Traditionally made not from German wines, but imported wines, mainly from Italy and France, often from Armagnac or Cognac, and the wines are fortified before being transported to Germany. Aficionados of German brandy admire its clean, crisp style, while its detractors find them anonymous and over-processed. The best producers are Asbach (classic, as far as German brandies go) and Pabst & Richarz (the Pfälzer Weinbrand is 100% pure German according to Nicholas Faith, author of *Cognac & Other Brandies*).

GIN International Although an international product, gin is truly the speciality of Holland, the UK and, outside the remit of this guide, the USA. The name stems from *ginepro*, the Italian for juniper, which is found in Tuscany and forms the principal ingredient of gin. Most gin is triple continuous-distilled and grain-based, but sugar beet and potatoes are also commonly used, particularly on the continent. A raw, neutral, white spirit is first distilled and then it is re-distilled to produce a more refined spirit, which is then mixed with the flavourings that give gin its distinctive flavour and distilled once again. The actual mix is kept a secret by producers of each brand, but it is generally understood that they include juniper berries, coriander seeds, angelica root, cardamom seed, orris root, orange peel and various other, more obscure ingredients. Gin is so highly distilled and rectified that it contains practically no higher alcohols, the impurities which trigger the classic hangover, which is why for centuries it has been dubbed 'the purest of all spirits'. Even the water used to dilute gin to the desired strength is de-mineralised. (*See* **Genever, London Dry Gin, Plymouth Gin** and **Steinhäger** entries.)

GRAIN WHISKEY or **WHISKY** International The mash used in the production of grain whisky is composed of a mixture of malted and non-malted cereals, mostly maize, and undergoes one continuous still distillation, which contrasts with pure malt whisky, which is made exclusively from 100% malted barley and double distilled in a pot-still.

GRANDE CHAMPAGNE France No connection whatsoever with the district of Champagne, which is much further north, this Cognac designation merely derives from the type of soil (*Campanian* chalk) that is found in the best areas of Cognac. Gradations of quality within the six districts that comprise the Cognac region are in fact based on the amount of chalk found in the soil. Grande Champagne, for example, has as much as 90% chalk, well above the second ranked district of Petite Champagne, which has just 25-35% chalk.

GRANDE FINE CHAMPAGNE France Synonymous with Grande Champagne. (*See* **Grande Champagne** and **Cognac** entries.)

GRAPE BRANDY International A generic term for any grape-based spirit, the word brandy derives from the Dutch *Brantjwyn* or 'burnt wine', alluding to the fact that wine is boiled down by burning over a fire. Grape brandy is more precise than brandy plain and simple, and although both Armagnac and Cognac may be called brandy, the reverse does not apply. (*See* **Armagnac** and **Cognac**, also **French Brandy, German Brandy, Greek Brandy, Italian Brandy, Portuguese Brandy** and **Spanish Brandy** entries.)

GRAPPA Italy The Italian equivalent of marc. (*See* **Marc** entry.)

GREEK BRANDY Greece Possibly the best of Greek spirits, although many would not touch it with a barge-pole. If you are game, you could do worse than try Metaxa or Botrys.

H

HAUT ARMAGNAC France The largest of Armagnac's three districts, it has the lowest rating and is the least planted, contributing just 4% of the total Armagnac produced, yet still has the right to its own Haut Armagnac appellation, which is shamelessly used to give the false impression of an *haut* or 'High' Armagnac. (*See* **Armagnac, Bas Armagnac** and **Ténarèze** entries.)

HIGHLAND MALTS Scotland Single malts from distilleries located in the greatest of Scotland's four classic whisky regions, the

Highlands. The area comprises the Grampians, the Western and Eastern Highlands, Speyside and Northern Highlands. Of all these internal districts, the Speyside is usually singled out as the best, and within Speyside itself, many regard the tiny sub-district around the glen of the Livet river as producing the crème de la crème of Scotland's greatest malts. All Highland malts are said, however, to have an unrivalled delicacy of body, flavour and smokiness. Classic examples include Aberlour Glenlivet, Balvenie, Clynelish, Cragganmore, Dalmore, Dufftown Glenlivet, Glenallachie, Glenburgie, Glendronach, Glendullan, Glen Elgin, Glenfarclass, Glenfiddich, Glen Grant, Glen Keith, Glenlossie, Glenmorangie, Glen Moray, Glenordie, Glenturret, Linkwood, Lochnagar, Longmorn, Macallan, Macduff, Millburn, Mill Burn, Miltori Duff, Mortlach, Oban, Singleton, Strathisla, The Glenlivet, Tormore Glenlivet, Tamdhu, Tamnavulin-Glenlivet, Tomatin and Tomintoul. Two other Highland malts that are excellent despite their seemingly non-serious names, are Inchgower from Bells and Knockando.

HIMMEERGEIST Germany The German equivalent of Framboise. (*See* **Framboise** entry.)

HOLLAND'S Holland Synonymous with Genever. (*See* **Genever** entry.)

HORS D'AGE France The equivalent designation to XO, Hors d'Age is traditionally an Armagnac term, but also occasionally used in Cognac. (*See* **XO** entry.)

HOUX France An Alsatian speciality *alcool blanc* or

white spirit that is distilled from the crushed and macerated holly berries.

IRISH WHISKEY Ireland Always spelt with an 'e', Irish whiskey was probably produced before Scotch whisky. Most Irish whiskey is predominantly grain and almost invariably blended, although Bushmills Malt is a famous exception. Irish blends are generally fuller and slightly darker than Scotch, with a more flowery aroma. Classic examples of this style include Bushmills, of course, Jameson, Middleton, Paddy, Powers, while excellent whiskies of a lighter style are produced by Colleraine, Dunphy's, Hewitts, Murphy's and Tullamore. (*See* **Whisky** or **Whiskey** entry.)

ISLAY MALTS Scotland Single malt whiskies from distilleries located on the Isle of Islay, one of the four classic whisky regions of Scotland. While other whisky producing islands in Scotland have just one or two distilleries, Islay is littered with them. Islay malts are very distinctive and full-bodied, with a rich, deep, firm and penetrating flavour, a certain smokiness, and very little peatiness. Laphroaig is the most famous of Islay malts, but other classics include Ardbeg, Bowmore, Bruichladdich, Glen Ila, Lagavulin and Pride of Islay.

ITALIAN BRANDY Italy Italian brandy is rarely fit for drinking, primarily because it is mostly grappa, which is the Latin equivalent of marc. Of the real grape brandies that are produced, the best come from Stock (especially the XO and vintage-dated VSOP).

JENEVER Holland Synonymous with Genever. (*See* **Genever** entry.)

KIRSCH France The most ubiquitous of Alsatian *alcool blanc* or white spirit, Kirsch is distilled from, but not flavoured by, the fermented juice of black Morello cherries, mashed and distilled with their own stones. The cherry character comes through on the aftertaste as just the merest nuance. If the price seems ludicrously cheap, check the alcoholic strength, as a diluted version for cooking is sold at only 15% ABV or thereabouts. (*See* also **Lapoutroie Kirsch** entry.)

KORN Germany A rustic German version of Holland's Corenwijn. (*See* **Corenwijn** entry.)

LAPOUTROIE KIRSCH France A fine Alsatian *alcool blanc* or white spirit distilled from, but not flavoured by, the fermented juice of Merises, a cultivated 'wild' black cherry, the fruit character of which comes through on the aftertaste as just the merest nuance. (*See* also **Kirsch** entry.)

LONDON DRY GIN International Although originally an English product, London Dry Gin is now produced throughout the world with varying degrees of success. What distinguishes the renditions of London Dry Gin from other styles is its extreme dryness and the emphasis it places on certain ingredients, namely angelica,

orange peel, lemon peel and cinnamon. (*See* **Gin** entry.)

LOWLAND MALTS Scotland Single malt whiskies from distilleries located in one of the four classic whisky regions of Scotland, the Lowlands is an area south of an imaginary line drawn from Dundee to Greenock. Lowland malts are light and soft with a delicate aroma and an elegant, slightly sweet finish. Classic Lowland malts include Auchentoshan, Littlemill, Glenkinchie and Rosebank.

MALT WHISKY International Should be made from 100% pure malted barley. (*See* **Pure Malt Scotch** and **Single Malt Scotch** entries.)

MARC D'ALSACE GEWÜRZTRAMINER France The most traditional of all Alsace *eaux-de-vie* and the only one to have its own official appellation, although the region produces various *marcs* and a large range of fruit *eaux-de-vie*. As might be expected, Marc d'Alsace Gewurztraminer is one of the most aromatic brandies made, but like most marc it is fairly aggressive. (*See* **Marc d'Alsace, Marc de Muscat, Marc de Riesling** and **Marc de Tokay** entries.)

MARC D'ALSACE France Although most marc produced in Alsace is of a varietal nature, in common with its range of varietal wines, this blended version is also fairly widely encountered in the region but, unlike Marc d'Alsace Gewurztraminer, it has no official appellation. (*See* **Marc** and **Marc d'Alsace Gewurztraminer** entries.)

MARC D'AUVERGNE
France Typically rough and ready marc produced in the upper reaches of the Loire Valley. (*See* **Marc** entry.)

MARC DE BOURGOGNE
France Strong, coarse and aggressive marc produced in the Burgundy region. (*See* **Marc** entry.)

MARC DE CHAMPAGNE
France Rough and leathery brandy with a fiery taste, made from the residue of AOC grapes. (*See* **Marc** entry.)

MARC DE LORRAINE
France A protected appellation, even though it is obviously more obscure than the seldom encountered wines of Lorraine. (*See* **Marc** entry.)

MARC DE MUSCAT
France In common with the region's range of varietal wines, most marc produced in Alsace is of the same varietal nature. Unlike Marc d'Alsace Gewurztraminer, however, the Muscat version has no official appellation, although many consider it to be the finest of all Alsace marc. (*See* **Marc** and **Marc d'Alsace Gewurztraminer** entries.)

MARC DE RIESLING
France In common with the region's range of varietal wines, most marc produced in Alsace is of the same varietal nature. Unlike Marc d'Alsace Gewurztraminer, however, the Marc de Riesling version has no official appellation. (*See* **Marc** and **Marc d'Alsace Gewurztraminer** entries.)

MARC DE SAVOIE France Rarely encountered marc, unless you're on the *piste* in Savoie. Even then it's not worth the bother. (*See* **Marc** entry.)

MARC DE TOKAY France In common with the region's range of varietal wines, most marc produced in Alsace is of the same

varietal nature. Unlike Marc d'Alsace Gewurztraminer, however, the Marc Tokay (Pinot Gris) version has no official appellation. (*See* **Marc** and **Marc d'Alsace Gewurztraminer** entries.)

MARC DU BUGEY France Rarely encountered marc, unless you're on the *piste* in Savoie. Even then, it's not worth the bother. (*See* **Marc** entries.)

MARC France Remove all the romance and rustic charms that mysteriously surround marc and you are left with a crude and aggressive brandy made from the residue of skins and pips that is left over after pressing – literally the dregs of winemaking. These dregs are mixed with water to form a dirty-brown slurry, which is fermented into a foul-tasting brew. No amount of distillation can convert this disgusting base into anything other than the roughest, toughest, meanest brandy in the world. It is literally an essence of dregs.

MIRABELLE DE LOR-RAINE France The Lorraine version is just as delicious as the more commonly encountered Mirabelle from Alsace.

MIRABELLE France A fine Alsatian *alcool blanc* or white spirit distilled from, but not flavoured by, the fermented juice of the golden Mirabelle plum, the fruit character of which comes through on the aftertaste as just the merest nuance. The perfume of the Mirabelle plum is, however, quite powerful on the aroma of this spirit, which is a particularly soft and succulent *eau-de-vie*.

MURE SAUVAGE France The wild fruit version of the above blackberry spirit from Alsace.

MURE France A rich Alsatian *alcool blanc* or white spirit distilled from,

but not flavoured by, the fermented juice of blackberries, the fruit character of which comes through on the aftertaste as just the merest nuance.

MYRTILLE France A fine Alsatian *alcool blanc* or white spirit distilled from, but not flavoured by, the fermented juice of blueberry or huckleberry, the fruit character of which comes through on the aftertaste as just the merest nuance. You certainly get your money's worth with this *eau-de-vie*, according to the locals, who claim that it not only cures all manner of intestinal disorders, but gives you 'the eyes of a cat'!

NAPOLÉON Armagnac/ Cognac, France Traditional Cognacais term more recently adopted for Armagnac, Napoléon brandy is legally the equivalent to an XO. Most firms tend to make the XO the more superior, older brandy, which in practice places this designation between that of VSOP and XO. However, it is far closer to the latter than the former, most Napoléon Armagnac and Cognac having a minimum age of 7-15 years, while the best will be 35 years old, with a good dash of 50-year-old reserves. (*See* **Cognac** and **XO** entries.)

O

ORKNEY Scotland The malts from this island wilderness are rich and full-bodied with a sweetish, smoky palate that hints of an almost wild, bracken, herbal-peatiness. Prime examples include Highland Park, Old Orkney and Pride of Orkney.

P

PETITE CHAMPAGNE
France No connection
whatsoever with the district
of Champagne, which is
much further north, this
Cognac designation merely
derives from the type of soil
(*Campanian* chalk) that is
found in the best areas of
Cognac. Gradations of
quality within the six
districts that comprise the
Cognac region are, in fact,
based on the amount of
chalk found in the soil.
Petite Champagne, for
example, has 25-35% of
chalk, which ranks it
second. (*See* **Cognac** entry.)

**PETITE FINE CHAM-
PAGNE** France Synony-
mous with Petite
Champagne. (*See* **Petite
Champagne** and **Cognac**
entries.)

PLYMOUTH GIN
International So-called
because Dutch gin, the
original product, was
always shipped through
this port. In theory,
Plymouth Gin should be
fuller, richer and not quite
as dry as London Dry Gin,
but in practice this is not
always so clear, and it
certainly is a less distinctive
spirit. Traditionally used for
pink gins, and a favourite
with the Royal Navy.

POIRE WILLAMINE
France Synonymous with
Poire William. (*See* **Poire
William** entry.)

POIRE WILLIAM France
An easy-drinking Alsatian
alcool blanc or white spirit
distilled from, but not
flavoured by, the fermented
juice of William pears, the
fruit character of which
comes through on the
aftertaste as just the merest
nuance.

POMME France A fine
Alsatian *alcool blanc* or
white spirit distilled from,
but not flavoured by,
fermented apple juice.
Pomme is nothing like

Calvados, being much
lighter, some would say
more elegant, and certainly
underrated.

PORTUGUESE BRANDY
Portugal A country of great
potential for brandy,
although it consistently and
persistently fails to live up
to it. The best exceptions are
Caves Alianáa (good,
straight Antiqua), Aveleda
(good and improving
Adega Velha) and Palacio
de Brejeira (Aguardente
Velha).

PRUNELLE SAUVAGE
France A fine Alsatian
alcool blanc or white spirit
distilled from, but not
flavoured by, the fermented
juice of sloe berries, this *eau-
de-vie* was the after-dinner
tipple of Georges Simenon's
famous Maigret character.

PRUNELLE France A fine
Alsatian *alcool blanc* or
white spirit distilled from,
but not flavoured by, the
fermented juice of ★★★,
the fruit character of which
comes through on the
aftertaste as just the merest
nuance.

PURE MALT SCOTCH
Scotland Pure malt Scotch
is made from 100% malted
barley that has been
distilled in a pot-still twice.
It can be a single malt or
blended. (*See* **Single Malt
Scotch** entry.)

Q

QUETSCH France A fine
Alsatian *alcool blanc* or
white spirit distilled from,
but not flavoured by, the
fermented juice of the
Quetsch, a highly aromatic
purple plum, the fruit
character of which comes
through on the aftertaste as
just the merest nuance.

R

REINE CLAUDE France
A fine Alsatian *alcool blanc*

or white spirit distilled
from, but not flavoured by,
the fermented juice of
greengage, the fruit
character of which comes
through on the aftertaste as
just the merest nuance.

RESERVE France This
Cognac designation has the
same legal connotation as
XO. (*See* **Cognac** and **XO**
entrie.)

ROSEBANK Scotland
Classic single Lowland
malt. (*See* **Lowland Malts**
entry.)

S

SCHIEDAM Holland
Synonymous with Genever.
(*See* **Genever** entry.)

SCHNAPPS, SCHNAPS or
SNAPS Holland/Germany
A vague, generic term
encompassing any strong,
dry, white spirit.

SCOTCH or **SCOTCH
WHISKY** Scotland Unless
clearly labelled a Malt
Whisky or Pure Malt
Whisky, most Scotch
encountered will be a blend
of roughly 65% plain grain
whisky and 35% malt
whisky, with so-called
deluxe blends containing a
relatively higher proportion
of malt. Grain whisky is
distilled once using a
continuous still, malt
whisky is distilled twice
using a pot-still. The legal
definition of Scotch is not
that the raw material (ie, the
grain, be it maize or barley)
should come from Scotland,
but that the whisky is
distilled and matured in the
country. Scotch must also
be aged in cask for a
minimum of three years.
(*See* **Deluxe Whiskey** or
Whisky, Grain Whiskey or
Whisky, Pure Malt Scotch
and **Single Malt Scotch**
entries.)

SINGLE MALT SCOTCH
Scotland Pure malt Scotch
from a single distillery, the

basic style of which conforms to their areas of origin, of which there are four classic ones: Lowlands, Highlands, Campbletown and Islay. Other areas include the Isle of Jura, Tobermory on the Isle of Mull, the Isle of Skye and the Orkney Islands. Not all single malts are great whiskies, of course, but many are and as a group they represent most of the great Scotch whiskies. (*See* **Pure Malt Scotch** and **Highland Malts, Lowland Malts, Campbletown Malts** and **Islay Malts** entries.)

SORBIER France A fine and unusual Alsatian *alcool blanc* or white spirit distilled from, but not flavoured by, the fermented juice of the sorb or service apple, a firm, white, cherry-like fruit, rather than a wild apple as such.

SPANISH BRANDY Spain A curious thing about Spanish brandy is that it is either unfairly dismissed by Cognac snobs or ludicrously overrated by peninsular plebs. There are several types of Spanish brandy, but Brandy de Jerez accounts for over 90% of the total production and is the only official Spanish brandy appellation (*see* **Brandy de Jerez** entry). Outside of Jerez, tiny amounts of brandy are produced in almost every corner of Spain, but of these Catalonia is the most important area of production. Most standard quality Spanish brandies are bland, while most deluxe brandies are too rich, too full and very clumsy with a sweet, cloying sort of vanilla-oak pervading every aspect of aroma and flavour. Somewhere in the middle ground, however, there are some fine Spanish brandies that represent excellent value for money.

The two best Catalonian producers are Mascaro (really classy Don Narciso, but there is another Narciso, so look out for the 'Don') and Torres (especially the Imperial and Honorable brandies).

STEINHÄGER Germany A smooth, subtle yet distinctive gin produced in an unorthodox manner that involves no flavouring other than juniper berries. (*See* **Gin** entry.)

SUREAU France A fine Alsatian *alcool blanc* or white spirit distilled from, but not flavoured by, the fermented juice of elderberries, which makes one of the richest and fullest of *eaux-de-vie*.

TÉNARÈZE France Of all Armagnac districts, Ténarèze produces brandies that have the greatest potential longevity. Ténarèze has its own appellation, products of which are usually well worth seeking out. (*See* **Armagnac, Bas Armagnac** and **Haut Armagnac** entries.)

V

VIEILLE RÉSERVE France This Cognac designation has the same legal connotation as XO. (*See* **Cognac** and **XO** entries.)

VIEUX France This Cognac designation has the same legal connotation as XO. (*See* **Cognac** and **XO** entry.)

VINTAGE ARMAGNAC France Rare and expensive, but if well made and very old, it can be worth every penny. Unlike wine, however, spirits do not alter, let alone improve, once they have been bottled, so there is little point in buying an old

vintage that was bottled a long time ago. It is the time in cask that is all important, as this reduces alcoholic strength by natural evaporation and both converts and marries the so-called impurities, which make a youthful, rustic and fiery Armagnac into the wonderfully complex bouquet of a great old Armagnac. (*See* **Armagnac** entry.)

VODKA International Vodka originated in the vast Slavic area of eastern Europe, where the word itself is a diminutive for water, which is apt for a spirit that, like gin, is so pure and highly rectified that it is brilliantly crystal-clear. It is traditionally produced from potatoes, but large, commercial brands also employ grain, sugar beet and grapes. The Slavs conjured up vodka for two specific reasons: one, to create a neutral spirit that could be used as a base for mixed drinks, and two, to produce a spirit so strong that it would not freeze in the bitterly cold winter conditions the Slavs have to endure. Although most commercial vodka today will be of normal spirit strength (40% ABV), this last criterion determined the intensive rectification process, which in turn resulted in the super-strength vodkas of Poland and Russia. Such strong spirits were never intended to be consumed in their pure, undiluted form.

VO France This Cognac stands for Very Old and has the same legal definition as for VSOP. (*See* **Cognac** and **VSOP** entries.)

VS France This designation stands for Very Special Cognac, although the brandy sold under it cannot be at all special, the definition being exactly the same legal as that for a ★★★ (three-star) brandy.

This is the lowest category of Cognac, with a minimum age of just two years, although in the UK and Ireland local laws demand a minimum of three years, and many are nearer to five. (*See* **Cognac** and ★★★ entries.)

VSOP France A designation for both Armagnac and Cognac, the youngest brandy in a VSOP or Very Superior Old Pale Cognac blend must be at least four years old, although many have a minimum age of 5-10 years. Do not think that this is the first rung of high quality Cognacs. It is not. Or it is no longer. It arguably was when three star used to represent 65% of all Cognac sold and VSOP commonly contained 20 year old brandies, limiting its sales to just 25%, but now that three star has shrunk to 50% and VSOP has grown to more than 40%, it can only be viewed as the second rung of Cognac's most basic brandies. This is why the deputy of a famous Cognac house once told me that he would not touch a Cognac beneath Napoléon or XO standard. A VSOP is a less traditional, but less abused designation in Armagnac. (*See* **Cognac** entry.)

WACHOLDER Holland Synonymous with Steinhäger. (*See* **Steinhäger** entry.)

WEINBRAND Germany The highest classification of German Asbach. (*See* **German Brandy** entry.)

WHISKY or **WHISKEY** International An amber-coloured, grain-based spirit produced all over the world, although Scotch is the best-known and most highly rated. Whiskey with an 'e' is seldom, if ever, seen on a bottle of Scotch, although the legal definition of this spirit allows for the use of both 'whisky' and 'whiskey'. The longer spelling is, however, traditionally used for Irish whiskies, Canadian Rye and American Bourbon. It is common to see both or either spelling in all other countries, where the quality is equally inconsistent. (*See* **Deluxe Whiskey** or **Whisky, Grain Whiskey** or **Whisky, Irish Whiskey, Pure Malt Scotch, Scotch Whisky** and **Single Malt Scotch** entries.)

XO Armagnac/Cognac, France This designation, which stands for Extra Old, has the highest legal connotation of all Cognacs and Armagnacs, requiring that the youngest brandy in the blend must be at least six years old, although most probably have a minimum age of 20 years, with the best blends containing a good dash of brandies up to 50 years of age.

Z

ZWETSCHENWASSER Germany The German equivalent of Quetsch. (*See* **Quetsch** entry.)

GLOSSARY

ABV (beer, wine & spirits) The abbreviation for Alcohol By Volume, which is expressed as a percentage and is commonly used for wines and beers. Although the strength of a beer is usually expressed as Original Gravity, ABV is used for beers throughout this book to maintain consistency with wine and beer references. The OG is not, in any case, an indication of a beer's strength, merely its potential strength prior to fermentation. *See* **OG**.

AOC (wine) *Appellation d'Origine Contrôlée* is the top rung in the French wine quality system, although in practice it includes everything from the greatest French wines to the absolute pits.

Appellation (wine) Usually refers to an official geographically-based designation for a wine.

Bereich (wine) A wine district in Germany that contains smaller *Grosslagen* and is itself part of a larger *Anbaugebiete*.

Blanc de Blancs (wine) Literally 'white of whites', a white wine made from white grapes, a terms that is often, but not exclusively, used for sparkling wines.

Blanc de Noirs (wine) Literally 'white of blacks', a white wine made from black grapes, a term that is often, but not exclusively, used for sparkling wines. In the New World, the wines usually have a tinge of pink, often no different than a fully-fledged rosé, but a classic *blanc de noirs* should be as white as possible without using artificial means.

Botrytis (wine) Literally rot, which is usually an unwanted disorder of the vine, but botrytis cinerea, or noble rot, is necessary for the production of the finest quality of sweet wines and, perhaps confusingly, it is commonly contracted to botrytis or botrytised grapes, when discussing such wines.

Botrytis cinerea (wine) The technically correct name for noble rot, the only rot that is not simply welcome by winemakers, but quite emphatically longed for in the sweet wine areas.

Botrytised grapes (wine) Literally 'rotten grapes', but commonly used for grapes that have been affected by botrytis cinerea.

Brut (wine) Normally reserved for sparkling wines, *Brut* literally means raw or bone dry, but in practice there is always some sweetness, and so it can at the most only be termed dry. It is the necessarily high acidity of sparkling wines (to carry the flavour through the bubbles on to the palate) that demands that a *Brut* wine be sweetened with up to 15 grams per litre of sugar. Only a sparkling wine described as Extra Brut will contain no added sugar, but most Crémant d'Alsace wines are in the *Brut* style.

Carbon dioxide (wine) This is naturally produced in the fermentation process, when the sugar is converted into almost equal parts of alcohol and carbon dioxide or CO_2. The CO_2 is normally allowed to escape as a gas, although a tiny amount will always be present in its dissolved form (H_2CO_3) in any wine, even a still one, otherwise it would taste dull, flat and lifeless. If the gas is prevented from escaping, the wine becomes sparkling.

CO_2 (wine) *See* **Carbon dioxide**.

Cold-conditioned (beer) The cold maturation period of a beer, usually one that has been 'bottom-fermented', which may last as long as six months.

Demi-sec (wine) Literally semi-dry, but actually quite sweet, this term is usually reserved for sparkling wines. It is also used in areas such as Vouvray, where *Moelleux* (sweet) wines are made in the greatest vintages, *Sec* (dry) wines are made in much less ripe years and *demi-sec* wines are made in good to middling years.

DL (wine) Germany's *Deutscher Landwein* is theoretically the equivalent of the French *Vin de Pays*. *See* **VdP**.

DOC (wine) Italy's *Denominazione di Origine Controllata* is theoretically the equivalent of the French AOC. *See* **AOC**.

DOC (wine) Portugal's *Denominaçao de Origem Controlada* is theoretically the equivalent of the French AOC. *See* **AOC**.

DOC (wine) Spain's *Denominacion de Origen Calificada* is theoretically the equivalent of the Italian DOCG. *See* **DOCG**.

DOCG (wine) Italy's *Denominazione di Origine Controllata e Garantita* is theoretically one step above the French AOC. Ideally it should be similar to, say, a *Premier* or *Grand Cru* in Burgundy or a *Cru Classé* in Bordeaux, but in reality, it is almost as big a sop as Italy's DOC itself.

DT (wine) Germany's *Deutscher Tafelwein* is theoretically the equivalent of the French *Vin de Table*. See **VdT**.

Eau-de-vie or (plural) **Eaux-de-vie** (spirit) Ubiquitous French term that is synonymous with brandy, *eau-de-vie* literally means 'water of life', as does the Gaelic *uisgebeatha* (which is the etymological origin of the word 'whisky') and the Latin *aqua vitae* (origin of 'Aquavit').

Fat (wine) A wine full in body and extract.

Grande Marque (wine) Literally a great or famous brand, in the world of wine the term *grande marque* is specific to Champagne and applies to members of the Syndicat de Grandes Marques.

Grist (beer & spirits) After the malting process, the malt is dried, sieved and milled into what is known as the grist. In the brewing of beer, the malt may be roasted prior to milling, if a dark beer is to be produced.

Hops (beer) The flower of the hop, either dried or in the form of a concentrate, is widely used to flavour or, to be more precise, season a beer during the brewing process.

HT (retail) This stands for *Hors Tax* or 'excluding tax', the tax in question being TVA or VAT (18.6% in France), so be prepared for this to be added to your bill.

IGT (wine) Italy's *Indicazione Geografica Tipica* is theoretically the equivalent of the French *Vin de Pays*. See **VdP**.

IPR (wine) Portugal's *Indicaçao de Proviencia Regulamentada* is theoretically the equivalent of the French *Vin de Pays*. See **VdP**.

Liquorous or **Liquoroso** (wine) Literally liqueur-like, this term is often applied to dessert wines of an unctuous and viscous quality.

Malt and **Malting** (beer & spirits) Malt is the biscuity-smelling germinated grain of cereal (usually barley) and malting is application of warmth and moisture that germinates the grain.

Maltose (beer & spirits) Maltose is the fermentable sugar extracted from malt during the mash.

Mash and **Mashing** (beer & spirits) A mash is the combination of malt grist (usually barley) and hot water, which forms a porridge-like mixture; this takes place in a large vessel called a mash-tun. The mashing process converts the malt into a fermentable sugar called maltose.

Méthode Champenoise (wine) Process whereby an effervescence is produced through secondary fermentation in bottle, used for Champagne and other good quality sparkling wines.

Moelleux (wine) An intensely sweet wine, usually indicating a *botrytis* character.

MSR (wine) An abbreviation for Mosel-Saar-Ruwer.

Mutage, mute or **muting** (wine) To stop a fermentation from starting or continuing by the addition of alcohol, which overwhelms the yeast.

Oenologist (wine) A trained chemist specialising in wine.

OG or **Original Gravity** (beer) In beerspeak, the strength of a beer is often referred to by the brew's Original Gravity, but this is not strictly true. The OG refers to the potential strength of beer before its fermentation, whereas the actual alcoholic strength depends on how much sugar is left after fermentation, and that is subject to how sweet or dry the product is supposed to be.

Passito (wine) The Italian equivalent of a *vin de paille* or straw wine, where the grapes are either left on the vine after the leaves have dropped and are thus cut off from the plant's metabolic system as its sap withdraws into its roots, or stored for a few weeks on straw mats, or hanging over straw in a warm room. This dehydrates the grapes, concentrating the wine, which is usually made into a sweet or intensely sweet style.

Peaty (spirits) The peaty character in some Scotch, particularly certain single malts, comes from the peat that has traditionally been used to fire the kilns which dry the malted barley, overlaying it with an inherently peaty smokiness.

Pétillant (wine) A wine with enough residual carbonic gas to create a light sparkle.

QbA (wine) Germany's *Qualitätswein bestimmter Anbaugebiete* is theoretically the equivalent of the French AOC. See **AOC**.

Rectify (spirits) Rectifying a spirit by constant re-distillation in a continuous still produces the purest of spirits, free of higher alcohols and other impurities. The more rectified, the more pure the spirit and the more pure the spirit, the more neutral in character it gets.

Seasonal beer (beer) Beers that are produced at certain times of the year, such as

Maibock, which is brewed in spring and sold at a premium. Some seasonal beers are specifically brewed to celebrate festive occasions, such as *Märzenbier*, which is made in March and aged for several months so that it is at its peak for drinking during the *Oktoberfest*.

Sleepy-hop aroma (beer) The powerful, resinous aroma reminiscent of hop-pillows.

SO_2 (wine) Sulphur dioxide is a preservative and anti-oxidant, which is essential to prevent oxidation from contact with the air. Most winemakers and certainly all fine-winemakers use only a small amount, but the highest dose applied by the most heavy-handed winemaker is insignificant compared to the amount of SO_2 we consume in food every day.

Sommelier (wine) The French term for a wine waiter, sommeliers are usually extremely knowledgeable and in good restaurants they delight in recommending a specific wine to go with the food you order; it will seldom be the most expensive.

Soupy or **Souped-up** (wine) Implies a wine has been blended with something richer or more robust. A wine may well be legitimately souped-up, or it could mean that the wine has been played around with. The wine might not be correct, but it could still be very enjoyable.

Spicy (wine) A varietal characteristic of certain grapes such as Gewürz-traminer. The Tokay-Pinot Gris and Auxerrois definitely also have some spiciness.

Spritz, or **spritzig** Synonymous with *pétillant*.

TTC (retail) Stands for *tout taxes comprises* or all taxes included.

TVA (retail) Stands for *taxe à la valeur ajoutée* or Value Added Tax – VAT in other words (or should that be in other letters or in the same letters, just a different order?).

VC (wine) Spain's *Vino Comarcal*, which is itself an abbreviated form in the singular of *Otras Comarcas con Derecho a la Utilización de Mención Geográfica en Vinos de Mesa*, an appellation midway between DO and VdlT, which is theoretically the equivalent of the French VDQS. *See* **VDQS**.

VDLT (wine) Spain's *Vino de la Tierra* is theoretically the equivalent of the French *Vin de Pays*. *See* **VdP**.

VdP (wine) In France, *vin de pays* is literally a country wine or legally a *Vin de Table* from a geographic area, which is a category of splendid value in the UK, where the wines are selected with care, but it is more of a minefield in France, particularly in supermarkets and hypermarkets.

VDQS (wine) In France, *Vin Delimité de Qualité Supérieur* is an appellation midway between an AOC and a *Vin de Pays*. *See* **VdP**.

VdT (wine) In France, *Vin de Table* is the lowest rung in the French wine quality system, a blended *vin ordinaire* that must not state any grape variety or area of production.

Vieille or **Vieux** (wine & spirits) For wines, the use of these terms usually refer to the age of the vines (eg., *vieilles vignes*) which, if older, normally yield a relatively richer wine. For spirits these terms invariably suggest an

exceptionally long ageing of the product (eg., *vieux marc*), but buyers should be warned that there is no legal definition controlling use.

Vin de garde (wine) A wine capable of real improvement if allowed to age.

Vin de pays (wine) *See* VdP.

Vin de table (wine) *See* VdT.

Vin ordinaire (wine) Literally an ordinary wine, this term is synonymous with the derogatory meaning of table wine.

Vin Santo or **Vino Santo** (wine) Literally means 'holy wine', this is an oxidised sweet wine similar in style to a *passito* wine. It is a speciality of Tuscany, and there are numerous different methods of production.

Vino da tavola (wine) *See* VT.

VM (wine) Portugal's *Vinho de Mesa* is theoreti-cally the equivalent of the French *Vin de Table*. *See* VdT.

VM (wine) Spain's *Vino de Mesa* is theoretically the equivalent of the French *Vin de Table*. *See* **VdT**.

VR (wine) Portugal's *Vinho Regionão* is theoretically the equivalent of the French *Vin de Pays*. *See* **VdP**.

VT (wine) Italy's *Vino da Tavola* is theoretically the equivalent of the French *Vin de Table*, but due to inherent inadequacies of the Italian wine régime, this category includes some of Italy's greatest wines, whereas the DOC encompasses much of the country's worst plonk.

Wort (beer & spirits) A clarified, maltose-rich liquid that results from the

mashing process, the wort
is drained of the spent
grains and fed into a brew-
kettle, where it is boiled for
an hour or two. This is, in
fact, the brewing process
and in the brewing of beer,
it is at this juncture that the
hops or hop-extract will be
added. After brewing, the
cooled wort is ready for the
yeast and the fermentation
process.

GETTING ACROSS
THE CHANNEL

Use the following guide to decide the nearest, quickest, best or cheapest method to cross the Channel. This chapter contains information and prices of the Channel Tunnel shuttle service and every sea route by ferry, Seacat, jetfoil or hovercraft from the UK and Ireland to the ports of any other country in the EC that we could ascertain currently exist (we would be pleased to hear from you about any others). The entries are in alphabetical order of the port of departure, and certain details may be repeated in order to make the information about each route self-sufficient. For all-year-round special reductions, *see* also **Don't Kick the Bucket Shop!** (page 356.)

NOTES
Vehicle length: Unless otherwise specified, all prices are based on a vehicle (car or van) up to 6 metres in length.
Minimum: The lowest, off-season, cheap-time return price (standard, not offers).
Maximum: The highest, peak-season, peak-time return price (open-ended return).
Child: Defined as under 14 years of age.
Disclaimer: Although every care has been taken to ensure the accuracy of the following prices and other information in the following entries, we cannot accept any responsibility and recommend you check precise details of your intended crossing before making a booking by ringing the numbers indicated under **Operators** in each entry.

BILBAO
See **Portsmouth to Bilbao**

BOULOGNE
See **Folkestone to Boulogne**

CAEN
See **Portsmouth to Caen**

CALAIS
See **Dover to Calais**

CHERBOURG
See **Cork to Cherbourg**
    Poole to Cherbourg
    Portsmouth to Cherbourg
    Rosslare to Cherbourg
    Southampton to Cherbourg

CORK TO CHERBOURG
Cherbourg is ideal for Normandy and Brittany.
Operators: Irish Ferries (*tel:* 00 353 1 6610511)
Frequency: 1 sailing each way per week
Duration: 18 hours 30 minutes

Return Fare Tariff

Irish Ferries	Minimum	Maximum
Vehicle + 1 adult	IR£160	IR£365
Vehicle + 2 adults	IR£210	IR£475
Vehicle + 2 adults + 3 children	IR£255	IR£550
Adult foot passenger or extra car passenger	IR£ 55	IR£110
Child foot passenger or extra car passenger	IR£ 15	IR£ 25

Important Note: *Prices are in Irish Punts.*

CORK TO LE HAVRE
The best aspect of Le Havre is from the rear-view mirror, as you leave
this port for almost anywhere else in Normandy.
Operators: Irish Ferries (*tel:* 00 353 1 6610511)
Frequency: 1 sailing each way per week
Duration: 21 hours 30 minutes

Return Fare Tariff

Irish Ferries	Minimum	Maximum
Vehicle + 1 adult	IR£160	IR£365
Vehicle + 2 adults	IR£210	IR£475
Vehicle + 2 adults + 3 children	IR£255	IR£550
Adult foot passenger or extra car passenger	IR£ 55	IR£110
Child foot passenger or extra car passenger	IR£ 15	IR£ 25

Important Note: *Prices are in Irish Punts.*

CORK TO ROSCOFF
Roscoff is almost as convenient as St-Malo for the Dordogne,
Bordeaux, Cognac, Armagnac and Spain, and the coastal route to
these destination is wonderfully scenic.
Operators: Brittany Ferries (*tel:* 01705 8227701 or 01752 221321)
Frequency: Up to 2 sailings each way per week
Duration: 13 hours 30 minutes

Return Fare Tariff

Brittany Ferries	Minimum	Maximum
Vehicle + 1 adult	IR£135	IR£392
Vehicle + 2 adults	IR£185	IR£529
Vehicle + 2 adults + 3 children	IR£201	IR£663
Adult foot passenger or extra car passenger	IR£ 18	IR£ 50
Child foot passenger or extra car passenger	IR£ 45	IR£137

Important Note: *Prices are in Irish Punts.*

CORK TO ST-MALO

St-Malo offers the shortest drive from a French Channel port to the Dordogne, Bordeaux, Cognac, Armagnac and Spain.

Operators: Brittany Ferries (*tel:* 01705 8227701 or 01752 221321)
Frequency: 1 sailing each way per week
Duration: 18 hours 30 minutes

Return Fare Tariff

Brittany Ferries	Minimum	Maximum
Vehicle + 1 adult	IR£135	IR£392
Vehicle + 2 adults	IR£185	IR£529
Vehicle + 2 adults + 3 children	IR£201	IR£663
Adult foot passenger or extra car passenger	IR£ 18	IR£ 50
Child foot passenger or extra car passenger	IR£ 45	IR£137

Important Note: *Prices are in Irish Punts.*

DIEPPE
See **Newhaven to Dieppe**

DOVER TO CALAIS

Without doubt the most important and, therefore, lucrative cross-Channel route, with up to 120 crossings per day, each way, in the high season. Much depends on when and how you travel, but it is certainly true that the Dover-Calais run is at least as expensive as the much longer routes to and from the Brittany coast, and there are many instances when it costs much more. The reason why is quite simple: demand. Whenever there is sufficient demand, the operators will charge as much as they think the market can bear. This is what happens in a free market economy, and if you don't like it, then the answer is equally as simple: don't travel at peak times – go in the middle of the night during the low season.

Operators: Hoverspeed (*tel:* 01304 240241), P&0 European Ferries (*tel:* 01304 203388), Stena Sealink (*tel:* 01233 647047)
Frequency: Up to 50 sailings, 14 hovercraft flights, and a predicted

(promises, promises!) 60 Channel Tunnel Shuttles (4 per hour at peak times) each way per day
Duration: 35 minutes (hovercraft), 75 minutes (P&O), 90 minutes (Stena Sealink)

Tunnel Vision II

As for Le Shuttle, the question is not so much when it will open, but if. What with the constant postponements, optimists believe the most likely opening date now will March 1995, which will be almost one year since President Mitterand and the Queen cut the ribbon, well behind its scheduled 1993 opening, and £5 billion over budget, not to mention £11 billion in debt. Coincidentally, March is the date that Tesco intends opening its Cité Europe branch, but we do not believe in such coincidences. After all, why would a street-wise operator like Tesco plan to miss the first 12 months of trading? In our humble opinion, Le Shuttle will be a flop. The tunnel will survive, but Eurotunnel will not. How can it? Eurotunnel must earn £11 billion in excess of its operating costs before it can make 50p profit. With heavy investments from over 200 banks, the European Investment Bank, the European Coal and Steel Consortium, and thousands of private shareholders, there is widespread belief that Eurotunnel will not be allowed to go bust, but will blunder on like some massive third world loan that can never be repaid. We disagree. Eurotunnel cannot possibly earn that 50p profit. It seems inevitable that Eurotunnel will go bust, and when it does 200 banks will have to write off their loans, the European Investment Bank will end up with egg on its face, and private investors will wish they had sold their shares when they were worth as much as 50% of the price paid. Without such a burden of debt, the tunnel could be profitable, just as Concorde became after writing off the cost of its construction. However any new operator is likely to derive most of its income from Eurostar and commercial freight, allowing Le Shuttle to tick over on a far less grandiose scale than the 60 shuttles each way it is promising now.

Return Fare Tariff

Hoverspeed	Minimum	Maximum
Vehicle + 1 adult	£102	£299
Vehicle + 2 adults	£127	£324
Vehicle + 2 adults + 3 children	£138	£334
Extra adult car passenger	£ 25	£ 25
Adult foot passenger	£ 50	£ 50
Child foot passenger or extra car passenger	£ 25	£ 25
P&O European Ferries	**Minimum**	**Maximum**
Vehicle + 1 adult	£ 57	£275
Vehicle + 2 adults	£ 76	£320
Vehicle + 2 adults + 3 children	£ 77	£340
Adult foot passenger or extra car passenger	£ 25	£ 59
Child foot passenger or extra car passenger	£ 15	£ 26

Important Note: *The above fares apply to a standard car size, which on all P&O routes is 6.5m.*

Le Shuttle	Minimum	Maximum
Vehicle + 1 adult	£130	£310
Vehicle + 2 adults	£130	£310
Vehicle + 2 adults + 3 children	£130	£310
Adult foot passenger or extra car passenger	£ -	£ -
Child foot passenger or extra car passenger	£ -	£ -

Important Notes: *(1) The Channel Tunnel terminal is not actually at Dover, but situated just outside Folkestone although, for all pricing intents and purposes, the Shuttle competes with above-water means of travel on the Dover to Calais route. (2) The price is for vehicles **up to 6.5m** and includes all occupants, thus there is no charge for extra passengers. (3) The Shuttle is a service that will be operated under the Eurostar name by British, French and Belgian railways. It does not accept foot passengers, although one wonders how many spivs will be selling lifts. (4) A special introductory fare of £125 (normally £280) for a two-day return Sundays to Thursdays, was offered to anyone who travelledi between 5 June and 21 July 1994, but that was when the Shuttle was due to commence operations in May of that year. When it was once again postponed, this time to October 1994, we were advised that this special price may no longer be available. Now that the opening has been offically postponed until November, and unofficially not likely before the New Year, nobody has any idea what special intorductory prices will be offered, if any. See Tunnel Vision at the end of this chapter.*

Stena Sealink	Minimum	Maximum
Vehicle + 1 adult	£ 50	£274
Vehicle + 2 adults	£ 50	£302
Vehicle + 2 adults + 3 children	£ 50	£374
Adult foot passenger or extra car passenger	£ 8	£ 28
Child foot passenger or extra car passenger	£ 6	£ 24

DUNKERQUE
See **Ramsgate to Dunkerque**

ESBJERG
See **Harwich to Esbjerg**
Newcastle to Esbjerg

EUROPOORT (Rotterdam)
See **Harwich to Europoort**
Hull to Europoort

FELIXSTOWE TO ZEEBRUGGE

Zeebrugge is a straight drive from Lille, Antwerp, Brussels and beyond, making it one of the best Channel port gateways to Europe.

Operators: P&O European Ferries (*tel:* 01303 203388)

Frequency: 2 sailings each way per day

Duration: 5 hours 45 minutes (daytime), 8 hours (nighttime)

Return Fare Tariff

P&O European Ferries	Minimum	Maximum
Vehicle + 1 adult	£ 49	£260
Vehicle + 2 adult	£ 61	£285
Vehicle + 2 adults + 3 children	£ 64	£299
Adult foot passenger or extra car passenger	£ 20	£ 48
Child foot passenger or extra car passenger	£ 10	£ 25
OAPs	£ 15	£ 40

Important Note: *The above fares apply to a standard car size, which on all P&O routes is 6.5m.*

FOLKESTONE TO BOULOGNE

Boulogne is within 20 minutes of the pan-European motorway network, and is the most convenient port for the more local attractions of Le Touquet, Agincourt and Montreuil (a defunct but charming port, with an old walled town with cobbled streets, which managed to escape the ravages of the Second World War). Hoverspeed's Seacat is not just the only service between the UK and Boulogne, but it also guarantees to be 10% cheaper than any Dover to Calais fare offered by either P&O or Stena Sealink during the same period of the day.

Operators: Seacat (*tel:* 01304 240241)

Frequency: up to 6 sailings each way per day

Duration: 55 minutes

Return Fare Tariff

Seacat	Minimum	Maximum
Vehicle + 1 adult	£ 92	£238
Vehicle + 2 adults	£115	£256
Vehicle + 2 adults + 3 children	£125	£288
Adult foot passenger or extra car passenger	£ 44	£ 44
Child foot passenger or extra car passenger	£ 23	£ 23

HAMBURG

See **Harwich to Hamburg**
Newcastle to Hamburg

HARWICH TO ESBJERG

This overnight journey typically departs Harwich at 5pm, arrives Esbjerg at 1.45pm the next day. Although there is just one operator, Scandinavian Seaways, it is the AA's favourite. The AA have awarded Scandinavian Seaways vessels, which are more like cruise ships than car ferries, a greater number of Five Stars for their facilities than any other line.

Operators: Scandinavian Seaways (*tel:* 01244 240240)
Frequency: Up to 1 sailing each way per day (349 passages a year)
Duration: 19 hours 45 minutes

Return Fare Tariff

Scandinavian Seaways	Minimum	Maximum
Vehicle + 1 adult	£282	£418
Vehicle + 2 adults	£423	£503
Vehicle + 2 adults + 3 children	£643	£958
Adult foot passenger or extra car passenger	£216	£306
Child foot passenger or extra car passenger	£108	£153

Important Note: <u>All</u> the above prices **include cabins**, but not meals, which are at the traveller's own expense.

HARWICH TO EUROPOORT (Rotterdam)

Both day and night sailings available, typically departing Harwich at 11.30 in the morning or evening, the overnight passage arriving at Europoort (the Hook of Holland port for the city of Rotterdam) at 7am while, of course, the daytime trip arrives at 7pm.

Operators: Stena Sealink (*tel:* 01233 647047)
Frequency: Up to 2 sailings each way per day
Duration: 7 hours 30 minutes

Return Fare Tariff

	Minimum	Maximum
Vehicle + 1 adult	£ 86	£240
Vehicle + 2 adults	£ 86	£302
Vehicle + 2 adults + 3 children	£ 86	£404
Adult foot passenger or extra car passenger	£ 32	£ 62
Child foot passenger or extra car passenger	£ 19	£ 34

HARWICH TO HAMBURG

This overnight journey typically departs Harwich at 3.30pm, arrives Hamburg at 1pm the next day. Although there is just one operator, Scandinavian Seaways, it is the AA's favourite. The AA have awarded Scandinavian Seaways vessels, which are more like cruise ships than car ferries, a greater number of Five Stars for their facilities than any other line.

Operators: Scandinavian Seaways (*tel:* 01255 240240)
Frequency: Up to 1 sailing each way per day (344 passages a year)
Duration: 20 hours 30 minutes

Return Fare Tariff

Scandinavian Seaways	Minimum	Maximum
Vehicle + 1 adult	£265	£360
Vehicle + 2 adults	£387	£532
Vehicle + 2 adults + 3 children	£606	£826
Adult foot passenger or extra car passenger	£198	£248
Child foot passenger or extra car passenger	£ 99	£124

Important Note: <u>All</u> *the above prices* **include cabins,** *but not meals, which are at the traveller's own expense.*

HAVRE, LE
See **Cork to Le Havre**
   Portsmouth to Le Havre
   Rosslare to Le Havre

HULL TO EUROPOORT (Rotterdam)

An overnight journey, departing Hull at 6.30pm, arriving Europoort (the Hook of Holland port for the city of Rotterdam) at 8am the next day. North Sea Ferries won the Best All Round Ferry Service Award from *The Daily Telegraph* in 1993, which is no surprise, as the dinner and breakfast that is included in the price must make this route, and the one to Zeebrugge, the greatest bargain Channel crossing. In addition to all the facilities expected on the latest super-ferries, North Sea Ferries have a cinema that shows the latest releases, live entertainment from Latin American to piano classics, a discothèque, casino and, of course, cabins galore. Furthermore, everyone who takes his car on a North Sea Ferry receives a discount card that can save you up to 50% off the cost of accommodation in Ibis, Arcade, Novotel, Mercure and Sofitel hotels in France, Belgium, Germany, Italy, Holland, Switzerland and Austria. It's enough to make southerners drive to Hull just to cross the Channel.
Operators: North Sea Ferries (*tel:* 01482 77177)
Frequency: 1 sailing each way per day
Duration: 13 hours 30 minutes

Return Fare Tariff

North Sea Ferries	Minimum	Maximum
Vehicle + 1 adult	£120	£248
Vehicle + 2 adults	£175	£358
Vehicle + 2 adults + 3 children	£258	£538
Adult foot passenger or extra car passenger	£ 55	£110

Child foot passenger or extra car passenger   £ 33   £ 67

Important Note: <u>All</u> *the above prices include a five course evening meal and full English breakfast.*

HULL TO ZEEBRUGGE

An overnight journey, departing Hull at 6.15pm, arriving Zeebrugge at 8.30am the next day. North Sea Ferries won the Best All Round Ferry Service Award from *The Daily Telegraph* in 1993, which is no surprise as the dinner and breakfast that is included in the price must make this route, and the one to Rotterdam, the greatest bargain Channel crossing. In addition to all the facilities expected on the latest super-ferries, North Sea Ferries have a cinema that shows the latest releases, live entertainment from Latin American to piano classics, a discothèque, casino and, of course, cabins galore. Furthermore, everyone who takes his car on a North Sea Ferry receives a discount card that can save you up to 50% off the cost of accommodation in Ibis, Arcade, Novotel, Mercure and Sofitel hotels in France, Belgium, Germany, Italy, Holland, Switzerland and Austria. It's enough to make southerners drive all the way to Hull just to cross the channel.

Operators: North Sea Ferries (*tel:* 01482 77177)
Frequency: 1 sailing each way per day
Duration: 14 hours 15 minutes

Return Fare Tariff

North Sea Ferries	Minimum	Maximum
Vehicle + 1 adult	£120	£248
Vehicle + 2 adults	£175	£358
Vehicle + 2 adults + 3 children	£258	£538
Adult foot passenger or extra car passenger	£ 55	£110
Child foot passenger or extra car passenger	£ 33	£ 67

Important Note: <u>All</u> *the above prices include a five course evening meal and full English breakfast.*

LE HAVRE

See **Cork to Le Havre**
   Portsmouth to Le Havre
   Rosslare to Le Havre

NEWCASTLE TO ESBJERG

This overnight journey typically departs Newcastle 5.30pm, arrives Esbjerg at 1.30pm the next day. Although there is just one operator, Scandinavian Seaways, it is the AA's favourite. The AA have awarded Scandinavian Seaways vessels, which are more like cruise ships than car ferries, a greater number of Five Stars for their facilities than any other line.

Operators: Scandinavian Seaways (*tel:* 01255 240240)
Frequency: Up to 1 sailing each way per day (349 passages a year)
Duration: 19 hours

Return Fare Tariff

Scandinavian Seaways	Minimum	Maximum
Vehicle + 1 adult	£232	£368
Vehicle + 2 adults	£516	£744
Vehicle + 2 adults + 3 children	£622	£988
Adult foot passenger or extra car passenger	£156	£248
Child foot passenger or extra car passenger	£ 78	£124

Important Note: *All the above prices include cabins, but not meals, which are at the traveller's own expense.*

NEWCASTLE TO HAMBURG

This overnight journey typically departs Newcastle at 1pm, arrives Hamburg at 1.30pm the next day. Although there is just one operator, Scandinavian Seaways, it is the AA's favourite. The AA have awarded Scandinavian Seaways vessels, which are more like cruise ships than car ferries, a greater number of Five Stars for their facilities than any other line.
Operators: Scandinavian Seaways (*tel:* 01255 240240)
Frequency: Up to 2 sailings each way per week
Duration: 23 hours 30 minutes

Return Fare Tariff

Scandinavian Seaways	Minimum	Maximum
Vehicle + 1 adult	£212	£324
Vehicle + 2 adults	£476	£656
Vehicle + 2 adults + 3 children	£552	£834
Adult foot passenger or extra car passenger	£136	£204
Child foot passenger or extra car passenger	£ 68	£102

Important Note: *All the above prices include cabins, but not meals, which are at the traveller's own expense.*

NEWHAVEN TO DIEPPE

Dieppe is the ideal choice for motoring along the Alabaster Coast, which stretches 96km (60 miles) from this port to Étretat, and provides some of the most dramatically beautiful cliff-top views in France.
Operators: Stena Sealink (*tel:* 01233 647047)
Frequency: Up to 4 sailings each way per day
Duration: 4 hours

Return Fare Tariff

Stena Sealink	Minimum	Maximum
Vehicle + 1 adult	£ 50	£252

Vehicle + 2 adults	£ 50	£304
Vehicle + 2 adults + 3 children	£ 50	£388
Adult foot passenger or extra car passenger	£ 8	£ 52
Child foot passenger or extra car passenger	£ 6	£ 28

OOSTENDE
See **Ramsgate to Oostende**

OUISTREHAM (for Caen)
See **Portsmouth to Caen**

PLYMOUTH TO ROSCOFF
Roscoff is almost as convenient as St-Malo for the Dordogne, Bordeaux, Cognac, Armagnac and Spain, and the coastal route to these destinations is even more scenic.
Operators: Brittany Ferries (*tel:* 01705 8227701 or 01752 221321)
Frequency: Up to 3 sailings each way per day
Duration: 6 hours

Return Fare Tariff

Brittany Ferries	Minimum	Maximum
Vehicle + 1 adult	£ 59	£257
Vehicle + 2 adults	£ 74	£318
Vehicle + 2 adults + 3 children	£ 86	£376
Adult foot passenger or extra car passenger	£ 15	£ 72
Child foot passenger or extra car passenger	£ 8	£ 36

PLYMOUTH TO SANTANDER
Brittany Ferries sail from Plymouth to Santander most of the year, but transfer this operation to Portsmouth during the winter months (prices are identical from each port).
Operators: Brittany Ferries (*tel:* 01705 8227701 or 01752 221321)
Frequency: Up to 2 sailings each way per week
Duration: 23-24 hours (from Plymouth), 30-31 hours (from Portsmouth)

Return Fare Tariff

Brittany Ferries	Minimum	Maximum
Vehicle + 1 adult	£126	£426
Vehicle + 2 adults	£164	£548
Vehicle + 2 adults + 3 children	£202	£624
Adult foot passenger or extra car passenger	£ 38	£128
Child foot passenger or extra car passenger	£ 19	£ 64

POOLE TO CHERBOURG

This is the shortest route across the western Channel and ideal for Normandy and Brittany. If you have not travelled to Cherbourg from Poole, don't be alarmed at the sight of '*Truckline Ferries*' on the side of your ship. It is not a rough-and-ready transporter specifically for trucks, but quite a nice car ferry with all the usual amenities.

Operators: Brittany Ferries (*tel:* 01705 8227701 or 01752 221321)
Frequency: Up to 2 sailings each way per day
Duration: 4 hours 15 minutes

Return Fare Tariff

Brittany Ferries	Minimum	Maximum
Vehicle + 1 adult	£ 51	£222
Vehicle + 2 adults	£ 63	£266
Vehicle + 2 adults + 3 children	£ 75	£297
Adult foot passenger or extra car passenger	£ 12	£ 59
Child foot passenger or extra car passenger	£ 6	£ 30

POOLE TO ST-MALO

St-Malo offers the shortest drive from a French Channel port to the Dordogne, Bordeaux, Cognac, Armagnac and Spain.

Operators: Brittany Ferries (*tel:* 01705 8227701 or 01752 221321)
Frequency: Up to 4 sailings each way per week
Duration: 8 hours

Return Fare Tariff

Brittany Ferries	Minimum	Maximum
Vehicle + 1 adult	£ 81	£259
Vehicle + 2 adults	£100	£322
Vehicle + 2 adults + 3 children	£116	£385
Adult foot passenger or extra car passenger	£ 19	£ 74
Child foot passenger or extra car passenger	£ 10	£ 37

PORTSMOUTH TO BILBAO

The ferry actually docks at Santurtzi, 13km (8 miles) northwest of Bilbao itself.

Operators: P&O European Ferries (*tel:* 01304 240077)
Frequency: Up to 2 sailings each way per week
Duration: 33-34 hours (to Bilbao) and 30 hours (from Bilbao), the difference being due to the direction of the currents

Return Fare Tariff

P&O European Ferries	Minimum	Maximum
Vehicle + 1 adult	£156	£508
Vehicle + 2 adults	£213	£680

Vehicle + 2 adults + 3 children	£273	£817
Adult foot passenger or extra car passenger	£ 57	£172
Child foot passenger or extra car passenger	£ 30	£ 73

Important Note: *The above fares apply to a standard car size, which on all P&O routes is 6.5m. Price* **includes standard inside cabin.**

PORTSMOUTH TO CAEN

The ferries do not actually dock at Caen, but at Ouistreham, which is 14km (9 miles) inland from the city itself. Caen is an ideal Channel port for Normandy, Brittany and Paris.
Operators: Brittany Ferries (*tel:* 01705 8227701 or 01752 221321)
Frequency: Up to 3 sailings each way per day
Duration: 6 hours

Return Fare Tariff

Brittany Ferries	Minimum	Maximum
Vehicle + 1 adult	£ 55	£243
Vehicle + 2 adults	£ 69	£296
Vehicle + 2 adults + 3 children	£ 82	£341
Adult foot passenger or extra car passenger	£ 14	£ 66
Child foot passenger or extra car passenger	£ 7	£ 33

PORTSMOUTH TO CHERBOURG

Cherbourg is ideal for Normandy and Brittany.
Operators: P&O European Ferries (*tel:* 01304 203388)
Frequency: Up to 3 sailings each way per day
Duration: 4 hours 45 minutes (daytime), 8 hours 45 minutes to 9 hours 45 minutes (night-time)

Return Fare Tariff

P&O European Ferries	Minimum	Maximum
Vehicle + 1 adult	£ 51	£236
Vehicle + 2 adults	£ 63	£292
Vehicle + 2 adults + 3 children	£ 75	£340
Adult foot passenger or extra car passenger	£ 18	£ 59
Child foot passenger or extra car passenger	£ 9	£ 30

Important Note: *The above fares apply to a standard car size, which on all P&O routes is 6.5m.*

PORTSMOUTH TO LE HAVRE

The best aspect of Le Havre is from the rear-view mirror, as you leave this port for almost anywhere else in Normandy.
Operators: P&O European Ferries (*tel:* 01304 203388)
Frequency: Up to 3 sailings each way per day
Duration: 5 hours 45 minutes (daytime), 7-9 hours (night-time)

Return Fare Tariff

P&O European Ferries	Minimum	Maximum
Vehicle + 1 adult	£ 55	£249
Vehicle + 2 adults	£ 69	£311
Vehicle + 2 adults + 3 children	£ 82	£371
Adult foot passenger or extra car passenger	£ 20	£ 66
Child foot passenger or extra car passenger	£ 10	£ 33

Important Note: *The above fares apply to a standard car size, which on all P&O routes is 6.5m.*

PORTSMOUTH TO SANTANDER

The Brittany Ferries route to Santander operates from Plymouth most of the year, but transfers to Portsmouth during the winter months. The prices are identical from each port, although the journey is 6-7 hours longer from Portsmouth. *See* **Plymouth to Santander**

PORTSMOUTH TO ST-MALO

St-Malo offers the shortest drive from a French Channel port to the Dordogne, Bordeaux, Cognac, Armagnac and Spain.
Operators: Brittany Ferries (*tel:* 01705 8227701 or 01752 221321)
Frequency: Up to 1 sailing each way per day
Duration: 8 hours 30 minutes

Return Fare Tariff

Brittany Ferries	Minimum	Maximum
Vehicle + 1 adult	£ 59	£259
Vehicle + 2 adults	£ 74	£322
Vehicle + 2 adults + 3 children	£ 88	£385
Adult foot passenger or extra car passenger	£ 15	£ 74
Child foot passenger or extra car passenger	£ 8	£ 37

RAMSGATE TO DUNKERQUE

The attraction of Dunkerque now is that with the recent construction of the A16, which takes you to Lille via the A25, it is convenient to the network of motorways that link most major European cities.
Operators: Sally Line (*tel:* 01843 5955222)
Frequency: 5 sailings each way per day
Duration: 2 hours 30 minutes

Return Fare Tariff

Sally Line	Minimum	Maximum
Vehicle + 1 adult	£ 44	£227
Vehicle + 2 adults	£ 58	£252
Vehicle + 2 adults + 3 children	£ 58	£252
Extra adult car passenger	£ 14	£ 25

Adult foot passenger	£ 22	£ 44
Extra child car passenger	£ 10	£ 15
Child foot passenger	£ 11	£ 22

RAMSGATE TO OOSTENDE

You have the choice of taking a lazy ferry ride or the dash and splash of a jetfoil. Oostende is close to Lille, Brussels and Antwerp, thus a doorway to Holland, Luxembourg, Germany and beyond.

Operators: Oostende Line (operated in partnership with Sally Line) (*tel:* 01843 5955222)

Frequency: 5 sailings each way per day

Duration: 4 hours (ferry), 105 minutes (jetfoil)

Return Fare Tariff

Oostende Line	Minimum	Maximum
Vehicle + 1 adult	£ 44	£227
Vehicle + 2 adults	£ 58	£252
Vehicle + 2 adults + 3 children	£ 58	£252
Extra adult car passenger	£ 14	£ 25
Adult foot passenger	£ 22	£ 44
Extra child car passenger	£ 10	£ 15
Child foot passenger	£ 11	£ 22

ROSCOFF

See **Cork to Roscoff**
  Plymouth to Roscoff

ROSSLARE TO CHERBOURG

Cherbourg is ideal for Normandy and Brittany.

Operators: Irish Ferries (*tel:* 00 353 1 6610511 or, in the Republic of Ireland, 01 6610511)

Frequency: 2 sailings each way per day

Duration: 19 hours

Return Fare Tariff

Irish Ferries	Minimum	Maximum
Vehicle + 1 adult	IR£160	IR£365
Vehicle + 2 adults	IR£210	IR£475
Vehicle + 2 adults + 3 children	IR£255	IR£550
Adult foot passenger or extra car passenger	IR£ 55	IR£110
Child foot passenger or extra car passenger	IR£ 15	IR£ 25
Important Note: *Prices are in Irish Punts.*		

ROSSLARE TO LE HAVRE

The best aspect of Le Havre is from the rear-view mirror, as you leave this port for almost anywhere else in Normandy.

Operators: Irish Ferries (*tel:* 00 353 1 6610511 or, in the Republic of Ireland, 01 6610511)

Frequency: 3 sailings each way per day

Duration: 21 hours 30 minutes

Return Fare Tariff

Irish Ferries	Minimum	Maximum
Vehicle + 1 adult	IR£160	IR£365
Vehicle + 2 adults	IR£210	IR£475
Vehicle + 2 adults + 3 children	IR£255	IR£550
Adult foot passenger or extra car passenger	IR£ 55	IR£110
Child foot passenger or extra car passenger	IR£ 15	IR£ 25

Important Note: *Prices are in Irish Punts.*

ST-MALO

See **Cork to St-Malo**
Pool to St-Malo
Portsmouth to St-Malo

SANTANDER

See **Plymouth to Santander**
Portsmouth to Caen

SOUTHAMPTON TO CHERBOURG

Cherbourg is ideal for Normandy and Brittany.

Operators: Stena Sealink (*tel:* 0233 647047)

Frequency: Up to 2 sailings each way per day

Duration: 4-5 hours

Return Fare Tariff

Stena Sealink	Minimum	Maximum
Vehicle + 1 adult	£ 59	£236
Vehicle + 2 adults	£ 59	£290
Vehicle + 2 adults + 3 children	£ 59	£362
Adult foot passenger or extra car passenger	£ 16	£ 54
Child foot passenger or extra car passenger	£ 8	£ 24

ZEEBRUGGE

See **Felixstowe to Zeebrugge**
Hull to Zeebrugge

DON'T KICK THE BUCKET SHOP!

The difference between using bucket shops for airlines and ferries is that the choice of when you can go is so much greater when sailing. When you fly with bucket shop prices you are also dumped in baggage class without any chance of upgrading. With bucket-shop sailing, however, you can buy a Club Class upgrade on board for just £4-£6 in the daytime or £8.50-£10 at night. The best deals we could find are offered by The Travel Market of Dover, which runs the 'Ferry Travel Club'. Membership costs £6 per year or £25 for 5 years, and this entitles you to take advantage of offers in a regular newsletter. For full and up-to-date details, contact The Travel Market Limited, PO Box 105, Dover, Kent CT17 9TP (tel: 01304 213533). Another bucket shop we have encountered recently is Ferry Plus, which is not a club as such, thus no membership fee is involved, but it does claim to beat any cheaper price you are offered from any ferry club. This sort of cheapest price guarantee is becoming quite widespread, but what we would like to know is what happens if two different firms pledge to be the cheapest for the same route? Still, it's worth checking out, For full and up-to-date details of Ferry Plus, call its Hotline on 0181 680 4400 between 9am and 5.30pm Monday to Saturday.

INDEX OF RETAIL OUTLETS

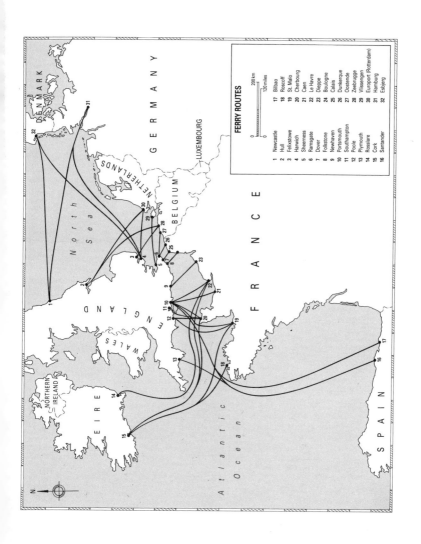

FERRY ROUTES

0	200 km	17	Bilbao
0	120 miles	18	Roscoff
		19	St. Malo
1	Newcastle	20	Cherbourg
2	Hull	21	Caen
3	Felixstowe	22	Le Havre
4	Harwich	23	Dieppe
5	Sheerness	24	Boulogne
6	Ramsgate	25	Calais
7	Dover	26	Dunkerque
8	Folkstone	27	Oostende
9	Newhaven	28	Zeebrugge
10	Portsmouth	29	Vlissingen
11	Southampton	30	Europoort (Rotterdam)
12	Poole	31	Hamburg
13	Plymouth	32	Esbjerg
14	Rosslare		
15	Cork		
16	Santander		